A Natural History of the Hawaiian Islands

Selected Readings

A Natural History of the Hawaiian Islands

Selected Readings

Edited by E. Alison Kay

University of Hawaii

Distributed by The University Press of Hawaii

Honolulu

First printing 1972
Second printing 1976

For Edwin H. Bryan, Jr., who, for fifty years, has studied, taught, and sought to preserve the natural history of Hawaii Nei

CONTENTS

PREFACE

"How oddly what ought to be readily accessible facts
have got themselves tucked into near oblivion," rumi-
nated one novelist in an introduction curiously appropriate to a discussion of a volume on Hawaiian natural
history. The Hawaiian Islands are scientifically
renowned for volcanoes and coral reefs, and for a biota
even richer and more intriguing to the evolutionist
than that of the Galápagos, but much of the information
is widely dispersed, tucked into monographs and journals
available only in reference libraries and special collections, and, for practical purposes, inaccessible to
the casual student, teacher, and visitor interested in
the natural phenomena of the Hawaiian Islands. The
classic summary works of Bryan (1915) and Zimmerman
(1948) are out of print; the more recent works of
Carlquist (1965, 1970) deal only with the terrestrial
aspects of Hawaiian natural history. The purpose of
this book is, therefore, to make accessible some primary
source materials on Hawaiian natural history.

In compiling the selections I tried to work without bias. One bias became apparent early in the selection process, however, and the result is a volume
clearly evolutionary in its overtones. With evolution
as the underlying theme, the selections were made with
three criteria in mind. (1) I was concerned with the
relevance of the article to a generalized phenomenon
illustrating some aspect of the natural history of the
Islands. Many illuminating and elegant articles were
excluded because they were so encyclopedic as to preclude seeing "the wood for the trees." On the other
hand, the selections were not limited to those concerned
only with the Hawaiian Islands, and in several instances

I went beyond the bounds of purely Hawaiian natural
history to include articles which are relevant to the
trend of geological and biological phenomena in the
Islands. (2) The papers were chosen for their breadth
of scope and information. As a consequence, there is
some repetition of facts and dates -- climatic conditions, temperatures, and so forth. To have eliminated
the facts in any one paper would have detracted from
the thrust of the paper, and I do not apologize for
the repetition. (3) I tried to choose papers by scientists who have worked in the field, either in Hawaii
or in the tropics. It is only to be regretted that
space limitations preclude the inclusion of a host of
papers by many eminent scientists who have devoted their
lives to work on the Hawaiian environment.

This book was prompted not only by the many expressions of interest in Hawaiian natural history from
students, teachers, and visitors to Hawaii, but especially by the efforts of professors William A. Gosline and
Charles Lamoureux of the University of Hawaii. For the
past five years they have taught a course in the natural
history of the Hawaiian Islands. They not only encouraged me in the preparation of the book, but guided the
selection of articles. I am deeply grateful to them
for their help, as I am to the several authors who wrote
articles especially for the book and to the many who
permitted us to reprint their works.

REFERENCES

Bryan, W. A.   1915. *Natural history of Hawaii.*
    Honolulu, Hawaii.

Carlquist, S. 1965. *Island life.* Doubleday, Garden
    City, New York.

————————   1970. *Hawaii: a natural history.*
    Doubleday, Garden City, New York.

Zimmerman, E. C. 1948. *Insects of Hawaii,* vol. 1.
    Introduction. University of Hawaii Press, Honolulu,
    Hawaii.

Section 1

The Pacific Basin and Hawaii: History and Process

INTRODUCTION

> Among the groups of Polynesia, the Hawaiian ex-
> ceeds all others in geological interest. The
> agency of both fire and water in the formation
> of rocks, is exemplified not only by results,
> but also by processes now in action; and the
> student of nature may watch the steps through
> the successive changes. He may descend to the
> boiling pit and witness the operations in the
> vast laboratory, with the same deliberation as
> he would examine the crucible in a chemist's
> furnace. Thus the manner in which mountains
> are made, and islands built up, becomes a
> matter of observation.
>
> J. D. Dana, 1849, *United States Exploring
> Expedition*, vol. 10, *Geology*

A knowledge of geological history and process are indis-
pensable for an appreciation and understanding of the
natural history of the Hawaiian Islands. As self-
evident as this statement may seem, it bears repeating,
for the physical features and biota of Hawaii today are
intimately tied to both the geological evolution of the
Pacific basin and to that of the islands themselves.
Stretching in a 2,000-mile arc from 22° N to 19° N, the
Hawaiian Islands originated by volcanic action in the
sea some 10 million years ago and today comprise a
panorama of land forms reflecting a history of volcanic
action and reef building from northwest to southeast.
The volcanic characteristics of Kure, Midway, and
others of the Leeward Islands in the northwestern part
of the island chain lie beneath thick caps of coral
reef; the island of Hawaii to the south is largely
Pliocene, its volcanoes still spewing forth masses of
hot, molten lava. Between the coral atolls of the
north and the still-active volcanoes on Hawaii are
islands which are variously dissected volcanic domes,
their coastlines fringed by coral reefs, solution
benches, and calcareous sand beaches.

The paper by Menard and Hamilton sets the stage for
a discussion of the evolution of the Hawaiian Islands
within the Pacific basin; that of Ladd, Tracey, and Gross
recounts the history of one of the islands as interpreted
from drill cores made through the reef cap; and the
papers of Eaton and Murata on volcanoes, Ladd on reef
building, Wentworth on bench-forming processes, and
Moberly, Baver, and Morrison on the source and variation
of littoral sand describe the processes which sculptured
the land forms and which continue today to change the
form of the islands.

PALEOGEOGRAPHY OF THE TROPICAL PACIFIC

H. W. MENARD AND EDWIN L. HAMILTON

Scripps Institution of Oceanography, San Diego
U. S. Navy Electronics Laboratory, San Diego
California

RESEARCH into the paleogeography of the tropical Pacific has been of considerable interest and importance to several scientific disciplines, especially to geology, botany, zoology, and geography. Many conflicting speculations concerning the ancient geography of this vast area have found their way into print. The earlier speculations were those of biologists who were attempting to explain animal and plant dispersions. Thus we have various speculations concerning sunken continents, isthmian links, and sunken islands. An outstanding example of fine work in this category is that of Zimmerman (1948), whose *Introduction* (Vol. I), *Insects of Hawaii* is a landmark in the field of paleogeography; his summary of the geology of the central Pacific is an excellent piece of work, which, unfortunately, has not been widely known among marine geologists.

Since World War II, and especially during the past decade, many expeditions have fielded in the central Pacific. This work has major implications for paleogeography. Definite parameters have been placed on speculations concerning the ancient geography of the area. For example, we now know that there is no possibility that sunken continents could have been in the area since the Middle Mesozoic and are highly improbable before that time. Enough age datings are available to indicate the probable ages of the present atoll and island structures, and we can estimate what the paleogeography of the area might have been since the Cretaceous.

This paper will summarize the existing data from the field of marine geology which bear on paleogeographic problems of the tropical Pacific; it is intended to be a background for discussions of the biogeography of the area.

TOPOGRAPHY AND STRUCTURE

Although the attention of this symposium is directed primarily toward the tropical Pacific, it is difficult to apply any divisions based on climate to considerations of the basic structure of the basin. For this reason, the basin as a whole will be treated as a unit and discussed in order of decreasing size of relief.

The most fundamental divisions of the basin are the broad deep "normal" basin of the north and western Pacific and the East Pacific Rise, and related broad, shallow "abnormal" structures of the east and south Pacific. The normal basin has a depth ranging between 5–6 kilometers except for local

Reprinted from J. L. Gressitt, ed., *Pacific Basin Biogeography: A Symposium* (Honolulu: Bishop Museum Press, 1963), p. 193–217, by permission of H. W. Menard and the Bishop Museum. Presented at the Tenth Pacific Science Congress, Hawaii, 1961.

relief. Almost everywhere the small-scale relief consists of an endless expanse of abyssal hills with a relief of less than 1 kilometer and a diameter of 5–10 kilometers. The origin of these hills is by no means established, but an analysis of echograms suggests that the dominant form is a dome and that many abyssal hills are produced by laccolithic intrusions and other volcanic phenomena (Menard, 1959). Rising above the hills are several thousand volcanoes with a relief between 1–5 kilometers (Fig. 1). Usually they are arrayed along lines and, in general, resemble island groups of volcanoes such as the Samoan Islands in all respects except size. Geophysically the "normality" of the basin can be defined in terms of the remarkable consistency of various types of measurements. As determined by ship-borne seismic stations, the normal oceanic crust consists of a layer of unconsolidated sediment a few hundred meters thick, a "second layer" of consolidated sediment and volcanic rock which is more variable but, roughly, 1 kilometer thick, and a third layer about 5 kilometers thick which is separated from the mantle by the Mohorovicic discontinuity (Raitt, 1956; Hamilton, 1959). Through this crust flows heat generated by the decay of radioactive material. A score of measurements give a very consistent value of about 1×10^{-6} cal/cm^2 sec, which is about the same as the average of continental measurements (Bullard, Maxwell, and Revelle, 1956; Von Herzen, 1959). Finally, the normality of the basin is indicated by a uniform absence of earthquakes.

Compared to the normal of the basin, the great East Pacific Rise is abnormal in almost every respect (Menard, 1960). Essentially it is a bulge of the sea floor 2–3 kilometers high, 2,000–4,000 kilometers wide and more than 10,000 kilometers long, extending from the south central Pacific to the Gulf of Alaska. The topographic bulge is produced by a very similar bulge of the underlying mantle. The crest of the rise is seismically active and in most places is broken by faulting into ridges and troughs parallel to the general trend of the rise. Heat flow is two to eight times normal, and the third crustal layer averages only 3.8 kilometers thick, or about three-fourths of normal. On the broad flanks of the rise, the crustal thickness is normal, but the heat flow averages far less than normal. The flanks have been torn into crustal blocks by transverse wrench faults. Topographically, the wrench faults are marked by fracture zones which are bands of very irregular topography with a relief of a few kilometers, a width of a few hundred kilometers, and a length of a few thousand kilometers. Vertical faulting of very large areas is indicated by regional differences in depth on opposite sides of the fracture zones. Wrench faulting along the fracture zones can be measured because of the offset of magnetic anomalies which form a distinctive pattern below the sea floor. The offsets measured off California on three different faults range between 150 and 1,200 kilometers and are the largest known on earth (Menard, 1955b; Vacquier, Raff, and Warren, 1961).

The central and western Pacific regions have various characteristics which indicate that they are intermediate in character between the normal basin and the oceanic rise. The regions are not active seismically, heat flow is normal, and, except directly adjacent to island groups, so is the crustal section. The chief criterion of abnormality is topographic. The region is dotted

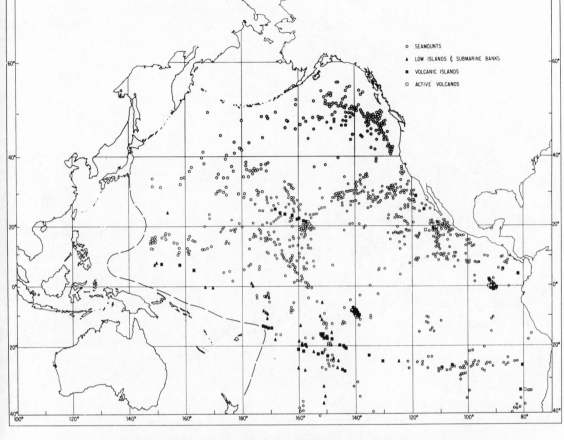

FIGURE 1.—Seamounts and islands of the Pacific Basin.

with large submarine volcanoes, which formerly were islands, but now have subsided ½ kilometer or more below sea level. The former volcanic islands now capped with coral are atolls, but many others lack coral and are guyots—flat-topped seamounts identifiable as former islands by their form and the shallow-water fossils dredged from them (Fig. 2). Along the center line of the whole Pacific are three great groups of atolls and guyots—the Tuamotu and Line Islands and the Mid-Pacific Mountains. These groups, in general, consist of rather small volcanoes rising above great steep-sided ridges. This center line in the Pacific is the only center of an ocean basin which does not have a broad oceanic ridge or rise under it. If a rise did exist under the central Pacific in the past, the ridges and drowned islands would be the remnants of the ridge and trough topography of its crest.

Several other island and seamount chains and groups are of interest in our study: the Marshall Islands with their many atolls and seamounts; the flat-topped seamounts of the Emperor Range in the northwest Pacific; the Mariana Islands, related to the Mariana Trench, which, southwest of Guam, contains the deepest waters in any sea (approximately 10,600 meters); and

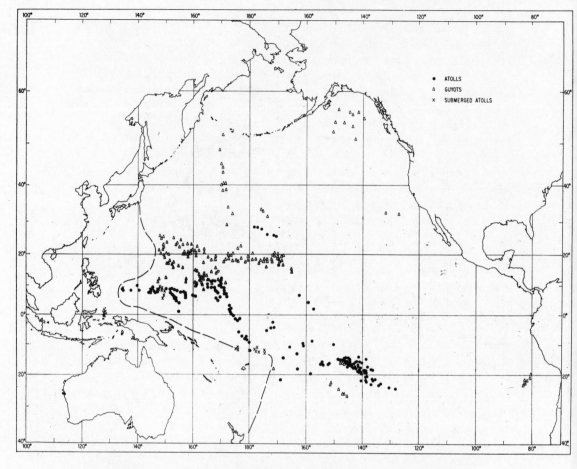

FIGURE 2.—Atolls and guyots (flat-topped seamounts) of the Pacific Basin.

the Marcus–Necker Rise, which trends east–west, includes the Mid-Pacific Mountains, and intersects the Hawaiian Ridge at Necker Island.

MARINE SEDIMENTS OF THE TROPICAL PACIFIC

The first sediment distribution charts of the oceans were published by Murray and Renard (1891) as a result of the sediments collected on the Challenger Expedition of 1872–1876. Since that time our knowledge of deep oceanic sedimentation has slowly increased; during the past two decades the rate of the acquisition of knowledge has been considerably accelerated. All expeditions involved in studies of the geology of the sea floor now take sediment samples. The principal method is by coring, wherein a "pipe" is plugged into the sea floor and a vertical section of sediments is recovered. Typical core lengths are 1 to 3 meters; core lengths to 7 meters are common, and the record is approximately 30 meters. Sediments and rocks are also recovered by dredging and snapper sampling.

In the shallow waters (less than 50 meters) of the continental shelves, atolls, and islands, sediments are frequently collected by diving with self-contained underwater breathing apparatus. Two other recent developments hold promise for the future: deep submersibles (for example, the bathyscaphe *Trieste*) will selectively sample at all depths, and a free-corer will allow sampling in all depths without winch or wire.

Several recent papers have summarized, and brought up to date, our knowledge of the general sediment distributions of the Pacific Basin (Arrhenius, 1961; Bezrukov, 1959, 1960; Griffin and Goldberg, in press; Revelle and others, 1955). A very brief summary will provide background.

The sources of deep-sea sediments are biological remains of planktonic organisms, echinoid spines, fish and mammal bone and teeth, sponge spicules, benthic organisms, minerals formed in place on the sea floor, volcanic materials eroded from subaerial land masses and ejected into the atmosphere or coming from underwater eruptions or flows, and materials from the continental land masses which are brought to the deep sea by winds, water currents, or turbidity currents formed by sediment-laden water masses.

Dredge hauls and photographs of the sea floor have shown that there is widespread collection of manganese–iron oxide around hard objects such as volcanic materials, sharks' teeth, bones, and even hardened bits of calcareous ooze (Mero, 1959; Shipek, 1960). Phosphatization of calcareous material is fairly common; silicification, although present, is less common.

There are two main types of sediments on the deep-sea floor; these are "red" clay and calcareous ooze. In general, calcareous ooze collects on the sea floor in waters shallower than about 4,600 meters, while red clay is the sediment type normally found in deeper waters. Calcareous material apparently is dissolved while settling through the water column, and after it arrives at the bottom; the latter process is thought the more important.

Around volcanic islands the dominant sediment constituents are volcanic materials ejected or eroded from the adjacent land mass; around coral atolls there is much coral and coralline algal debris.

Calcareous ooze is sometimes defined as fine-grained, pelagic sediments having more than 30 percent $CaCO_3$. This calcareous material is formed dominantly from the shells, or tests, of planktonic Foraminifera living in the upper waters of the euphotic zone, and from the minute skeletal plates of coccolithophorids, which are flagellated Protista. In rather restricted areas the siliceous tests of Radiolaria and diatoms may collect in significant amounts.

Where the sediment constituents are not masked by planktonic materials, turbidity-current deposits, or debris from volcanic islands or coral atolls (and this occurs in waters deeper than about 4,600 meters), the sediment type is a fine-grained plastic clay (red clay, as noted above).

Persons interested in detailed discussions of the sources, constituents, and geochemistry of pelagic sediments are referred to recent excellent summaries by Arrhenius (1961), Goldberg and Arrhenius (1958), Ericson and others (1961), and Goldberg (1961).

Paleontological and radioactive dating methods (see references in paragraph above) have determined that the rates of deposition in the deep Pacific Basin are of the order of 0.4 to 1.3 centimeters per 1,000 years for calcareous ooze and 0.04 to 0.5 centimeters per 1,000 years for clay for the pre-Recent. Most investigators agree that the present rate is three or four times that of the Tertiary.

The transportation of sediment constituents to the site of deposition, and the processes acting on them on the bottom, are of importance in our present study of paleogeography. The topographic control of sedimentation and the movement of sediments by turbidity currents will be discussed in a later section. The winnowing and erosion of bottom sediments by water currents and the slumping of sediments have had important consequences for our study, in that they have caused variations of accumulation and exposure of older sediments. Therefore, these sediments allow some conclusions as to paleoclimatology and geologic history; these subjects will be discussed further in the section on age dating.

Recent studies by Rex and Goldberg (1958) and Griffin and Goldberg (in press) have brought out the importance of wind transport of mineral particles from land areas. These studies show that there is a marked latitudinal dependence in the quartz content of pelagic clays which is best explained by correlations with wind directions of the upper atmosphere. This type of study can be of importance in determining the variations of wind directions during geologic history, and thus furnish important evidence on paleoclimatology and, possibly, information on one method of animal dispersion in ancient times.

Oxygen-isotope studies of the biological constituents (Foraminifera) of Pacific sediments have led to the important conclusion that Pacific bottom waters have cooled by about 10° C. during the Tertiary (Emiliani, 1954); these studies have far-reaching implications in paleoclimatology and paleontology which will be discussed in the section on paleoclimatology.

Prior to the seismic refraction surveys of the past decade, Kuenen (1950, pp. 386–399) estimated the volumes of sediments which should be present in oceanic basins using five different approaches based on rates of sedimentation, relative amounts of various kinds of sediments, volcanism, the sodium content of the oceans, and geochemical studies. Seismic refraction surveys in the Pacific Basin during the past decade have defined two layers overlying the "basalt" or gabbro of the earth's outer crust. The upper layer, averaging about 300 meters in thickness, is undoubtedly sediment not yet lithified. The material of the second layer is in doubt; some scientists believe it may be volcanic, others think it more likely to be the lithified equivalent of overlying sediment in areas away from volcanic islands and seamounts. Near centers of volcanism, the second layer is apt to be combinations of lava flows, dikes, sills, ash layers, and lithified sediments. The Mohole Project, now under way, should result in critically important information on the thicknesses of sediments and their ages and environmental conditions, which will, in turn, have important bearings on paleogeography. As of now, however, we must be content with the few meters of upper sediments which we can core.

Surrounding the large groups of islands and drowned, ancient islands of the central and western Pacific, are associated annular belts of volcanic rocks and sediment derived from volcanic sources, called archipelagic aprons

(Menard, 1955a). A few seismic stations show that the second crustal layer has an abnormal thickness of several kilometers (Gaskell, 1954). Although in most places the nature of the second layer is questionable, in the aprons there is no possible source except submarine lava flows and pyroclastics. This follows from the fact that the only possible significant source of nonsubmarine volcanic materials is the islands surrounded by the aprons and from the further fact that the volume of an individual apron is several orders of magnitude larger than the adjacent islands.

Although the main volume of the aprons is derived from submarine fissure flows, the surface appears to be composed of the deposits of turbidity currents spreading out from the islands. This conclusion is based on the nature of the sediments and also on the remarkable smoothness of the surface. For example, turbidity current deposits with a source in the Mid-Pacific Mountains have been identified on the adjacent smooth apron. Although turbidity currents have smoothed aprons in the past, they are not necessarily important contributors of sediment to all the aprons at present. In the vicinity of the Society and Tuamotu Islands, the aprons are more or less paved with manganese nodules. Inasmuch as the nodules accrete at rates of only a fraction of a millimeter per 1,000 years, it is apparent that the deposition of sediment must be even slower, or the aprons would be buried.

FOSSIL AND RADIOACTIVE EVIDENCE FOR AGE DATING

The faunal sequences through geologic time are fairly well established for fossils commonly found on land. These sequences have been keyed into the Geologic Time Scale and there are enough radioactive age dates also keyed into this scale so that we know, approximately, the amount of actual time involved. Paleontological dating of fossils found on and in the sea floor must be related to the fossil sequences determined from land areas; this will be true until continuous sediment and rock samples to a considerable depth in the sea floor can be obtained and studied. The only present hope of such samples lies in the drilling now planned under the Mohole Project.

Allan (1953), in his report to the Eighth Pacific Science Congress on "Datum-Planes in the Geological History of the Pacific Region," discussed at some length the fossil animals most apt to form datum planes and listed a considerable bibliography. He concluded that our best hope for usable fossils for interregional correlations lay with those animal groups which were planktonic or which were planktonic during some part of their life. We agree with this concept.

For the various animal groups which have been of utility in dating, we refer the reader to Allan's report (1953). Since that study, there have been a number of discoveries which emphasize the importance of several fossil groups. The Radiolaria, chiefly through the work of Riedel (for example, 1957), have been shown to be important, especially in deep-sea clays where the Foraminifera are not usually found. The diatoms have also received more study and can be of utility for the same reason. The larger Foraminifera have been found at several places in the Pacific Basin, and furnish interesting examples of animal dispersion. Bramlette (1958) has shown that the minute, calcareous, skeletal plates of coccolithophorids (flagellated Protista, sometimes classed as algae) are exceedingly abundant in deep-sea calcareous sediments, especially in Early Tertiary deposits in which they may be more important than the Foraminifera. Other important fossil groups will be noted in Table 1 and in subsequent discussions.

In general, the radioactive and fossil dating of deep-sea sediments has taken us back no further in time than the Early Tertiary. The fact that we can go back that far is remarkable, in view of the continuous, if slow, sedimentation on the sea floor, and the shallowness of the sediment depths that we can core. These determinations have shown that many areas of the deep-sea floor have Tertiary sediments exposed at the surface of the sediment or buried just beneath the surface. The findings have shown that there is much sediment movement, because of slumps, slides, or lack of accumulation because of deep currents.

In reconstructing the paleogeography of the tropical Pacific it is impor-

TABLE 1

EARLIEST PALEONTOLOGICAL AGE-DATINGS IN THE TROPICAL PACIFIC

LOCATION	FOSSILS	GEOLOGIC AGE*	REFERENCE	REMARKS
Viti Levu, Fiji	Foram.	LEo	Cole, 1961	Surface sample
Hawaiian Is.	——	T–Ple	Stearns, 1946	Geomorphic evidence
Caroline Is. Yap	Foram.	EO	Cole, Todd, and Johnson, 1960	Surface sample
Mariana Is. Guam	Foram.	LEo	Cole, Todd, and Johnson, 1960	Surface sample
Saipan	Foram.	EEo	Cloud, Schmidt, and Burke, 1956	Surface sample
Tuamotu Ridge	Foram.	LEo	Cole, 1959	Dredge haul
Marshall Is. Eniwetok	Foram.	LEo	Cole, 1957; Todd and Low, 1960	Drill hole
Sylvania	Foram.	EEo	Hamilton and Rex, 1959	Dredge haul
Mid-Pac. Mts. Cape Johnson	(Reef coral– rudistids)	MC	Hamilton, 1956	Dredge haul
Hess	(Reef coral– rudistids)	MC	Hamilton, 1956	Dredge haul
Tonga	Foram.	LEo	Cole, 1961	Surface sample
Palau Is.	Foram.	LEo	Cole, 1950	Surface sample
Erben Guyot	Foram.	Mi	Carsola and Dietz, 1952	Dredge haul
Fractured Zones	——	LMe–ET	Menard, 1955	Geomorphic evidence
Great Trenches	——	LC–ET	Hess, 1948; Menard and Dietz, 1951	Geomorphic evidence

* Earliest geologic-age datings indicated by letters as follows: E = Early, M = Middle, L = Late, and:

Mesozoic–Me
Cretaceous–C
Tertiary–T
Paleocene–P
Eocene–Eo
Oligocene–O

Miocene–Mi
Pliocene–Pl
Quaternary–Q
Pleistocene–Ple
Recent–R

Example: LEo = late Eocene.

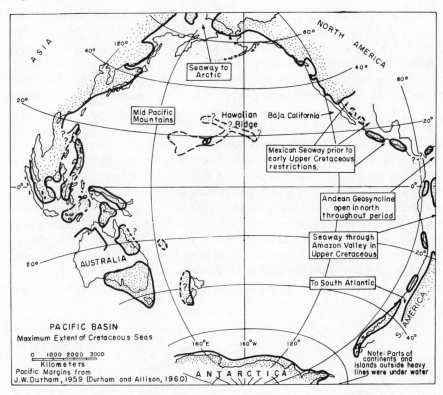

FIGURE 3.—The Pacific Basin during Cretaceous time.

tant to determine the oldest dates for various islands, ridges, and seamounts, and the evidence for important events thereafter. Table 1 lists these fossil occurrences, and excludes the determinations made in deep-sea sediments. Figures 3 and 4 show the locations of these age datings.

In discussing Table 1, the evidence on age dating will be summarized without repeating references given in the table. Only the earliest known datings will be mentioned; later events are dated on many of the structures.

The oldest fossil faunas of the Pacific Basin were found in 1950 by dredge hauls taken by the Scripps Institution–Navy Electronics Laboratory Expedition on peaks of the main ridge of the Mid-Pacific Mountains, about 1,600 kilometers west of the Hawaiian Islands (Fig. 3). These peaks now appear as flat-topped seamounts and are submerged to depths of 1,300 to 1,700 meters. In addition to the fossils, the dredges contained sand grains, cobbles, and boulders derived from an olivine basalt source. On the tops of two of these features, dredge hauls brought up an integrated Cretaceous (Aptian to Cenomanian) fauna of reef coral, rudistids (a Cretaceous mollusk) and other pelecypods, stromatoporoids (an extinct group thought to have been coelenterates), gastropods, and an echinoid. In one core, taken near the base of a flat-topped seamount, the basaltic gravel layers contained Late Cretaceous planktonic Foraminifera (Hamilton, 1956). Paleocene and Eocene Foraminifera occurred on four of the seamounts.

The evidence indicates that in Cretaceous time the flat-topped seamounts were a chain of basaltic islands; these islands were eroded to relatively flat banks on which a reef coral–rudistic fauna found lodgment and grew into reefs on and among the erosional debris. They never became fully developed atolls. The flat-topped seamounts were apparently submerged during the Cretaceous to below the zone of reef-coral growth; finally they sank to present depths.

After the Cretaceous (except for the Paleocene sediments noted above), the next age datings are from the Early Eocene (Table 1; Fig. 4). In the Marshall Islands, drill holes have been bored into the reef structure of Bikini and through the Eniwetok structure. In the latter atoll, the material just above the olivine basalt core of the atoll was late Eocene. On Sylvania Guyot, a flat-topped seamount at a depth of 1,300 meters, adjacent to, and connected with the foundations of Bikini, early Eocene planktonic Foraminifera were found inside a dredged sample of volcanic tuff-breccia. It appears that these datings indicate that the Marshall Islands were at or near the surface of the sea during the early to late Eocene. The foundations of Eniwetok are about 1,400 meters below present sea level; the flat top of Sylvania is now at a depth of approximately 1,250 meters. It appears that the northern Marshall Islands area has

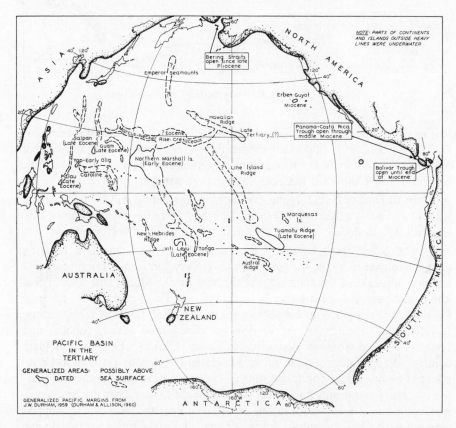

FIGURE 4.—The Pacific Basin during the Tertiary. Those areas enclosed by dashed lines have no dates, but are possibilities for ridges and/or peaks which could have been above water.

subsided well over 1,200 meters since the Eocene, relative to the surface of
the sea.

The only other early Eocene dating is from surface samples taken on
Saipan in the Mariana Islands.

In the late Eocene we have datings from Viti Levu, Fiji Islands, Guam,
Mariana Islands, rock from a dredge haul on the Tuamotu Ridge, Eniwetok
bore-holes (as previously described), Tonga, and the Palau Islands.

Earliest datings younger than Eocene are known from Yap, Caroline
Islands (early Oligocene), and Erben Guyot, a flat-topped seamount between
Hawaii and the west coast of the United States (Miocene).

The great fractured zones of the northeast Pacific and the great trenches
around the Pacific Basin are thought to have been formed during the Late
Mesozoic or Early Tertiary. The islands of Hawaii are still thought, by geomorphic and other evidence (but not definite age datings), to have been above
water during the Tertiary—probably Late Tertiary—and Pleistocene.

FOSSIL EVIDENCE FOR FAUNAL MIGRATION

Zimmerman (1948) provides a brilliant summary, not only of biological
matters, but of the known geology of the Pacific Basin. His ideas on faunal
migrations stressed the possibility of ancient islands now sunk beneath the sea
or present as the core, or base, of atolls. This idea, first suggested by Wallace
(1881) and subsequently by many others, appears, in the light of the explorations of the past decade, to be a real possibility.

Ladd (1960) gives an excellent summary of modern evidence on marine
faunas, faunal relations, means of dispersal, and modern evidence from marine
geological exploration of the Pacific Basin and on the islands of the tropical
Pacific.

It has always been presumed that ancient planktonic faunas would be
widespread in the Pacific. This is now known to be true: planktonic fossils
from the Late Cretaceous to Recent are now known (as previously discussed)
from widely separated locations in the Pacific Basin. The presence of shallow-
water fossil reef corals, pelecypods, gastropods, echinoids, and larger Foraminifera, all of which are not planktonic (although some have planktonic or
nearly planktonic larvae), however, now demonstrates to us that animal migrations took place across deep waters from Cretaceous to Recent times, just as
they are presumed to be doing today. There is no chance that these fossils
migrated across land bridges or across the sunken continents so popular in
yesteryear; they appeared in the middle of the Pacific on the tops of volcanic
peaks, built up from the sea floor.

In short, the fact of animal migrations is proved; it remains to prove
exactly how they migrated. The findings from exploration of the sea floor have
shown that the Pacific Ocean has existed in about its present form and depth
since the Cretaceous; these findings have also shown, as Ladd (1960) stated,
that "The Pacific island area may have been, in effect, a giant archipelago in
Cretaceous and Tertiary times." Thus, the ideas summarized by Zimmerman

(1948) concerning the possibilities of island steppingstones appear to be more and more valid as exploration continues. The other means of dispersal have been summarized by Zimmerman (1948) and Ladd (1960), and will be discussed at this symposium. It should be noted, however, that recent conclusions concerning the distribution of quartz in deep-sea sediments have stressed the importance of wind as a means of sediment transport from adjacent continents, and have furnished some patterns of these ancient winds. Further study may yield information of value in tracing animal dispersions which might have been the result of winds.

The affinities of the present marine faunas of the tropical Pacific now appear to be with the faunas of the Indo-Pacific, to the southwest. The only other affinity shown is that of the Cretaceous, shallow-water faunas of the Mid-Pacific Mountains. During the Cretaceous and Early Tertiary, the southern Mexico–Central American area was an open seaway (Durham and Allison, 1960). This area was part of the world-encircling Tethys Sea, which also lay across the Caribbean Sea, the Mediterranean, Asia Minor, parts of India, and Southeast Asia. The currents in this sea probably ran east to west; therefore it should be expected that faunas might migrate in that direction. This appears to be true: The reef coral–rudistid faunas of the Mid-Pacific Mountains are typical of the marine faunas of the same period in other parts of the Tethys Sea, especially Mexico and the Caribbean. Inasmuch as the Tethys Sea covered southern Mexico and Central America during much of the Early Tertiary, it would not be surprising to find ancient faunal affinities of the modern Pacific Basin marine faunas to be with those of the same period from the Caribbean, Mexican, and Central American areas. It would be hard to prove which way the animals migrated, because the Tethys Sea also lay across parts of the Indo-Pacific and contained a common fauna; but, owing to the probable east-to-west direction of currents, migration was probably also east to west.

GEOLOGIC HISTORY OF THE CENTRAL PACIFIC

Our discussion of the geologic history of the central Pacific sea floor will be confined to events after the Cretaceous. As discussed above, the Cretaceous is the oldest dating for the whole basin; prior to that time we have no age-dated facts on which to base speculation. Certain computations based on total thicknesses of sediments, assuming the second layer in the deep basins to be the lithified equivalent of the overlying types of sediments, indicate great age (Paleozoic to Pre-Paleozoic: Hamilton, 1960). Beloussov (1960) believed the oceans to be no older than Mesozoic. For a fact, we know that the Pacific Basin was a deep-sea area in the Middle Cretaceous, with a depth in the Mid-Pacific Mountains area of at least 3,200 meters (the relief between the sea floor and the adjacent flat-topped seamounts from which reef-coral was dredged).

The problem of seamount subsidence, and its associated question of oceanic deepening, is at the present time not entirely solved. We know from gravimetric and morphologic studies that a small seamount is entirely supported by the earth's crust without isostatic compensation, but at the base of larger seamounts there is almost perfect compensation (Worzel, Talwani, and Landisman, 1960). Larger seamounts in the Pacific Basin frequently have annular moats around them, indicating depression of the earth's crust. The great weight of the Hawaiian Ridge has apparently caused an elastic down-bowing of the earth's crust so that this ridge is in the center of a depression (the Hawaiian Deep) outside of which there is an arch; the whole ridge appears to be isostatically compensated (Hamilton, 1957). We can, therefore, expect great seamounts, and especially ridges large enough to support islands, to subside, somewhat, owing to their great weight; this would explain local and regional sinking.

Another mechanism for general subsidence of a ridge or large area of the sea floor would be in the creation of a great rise, such as the East Pacific Rise, possibly caused by serpentinization of mantle material (Hess, 1954), or by convection currents in the earth's mantle followed by evolution through faulting and fracturing of a line of volcanic seamounts and islands on the crest of the rise, and finally, subsidence of the rise owing to cessation of the convection current or by deserpentinization of mantle material.

A third type of general explanation for large-scale sea-floor subsidences has been put forward by Beloussov (1960), Rubey (1951), and others. These explanations concern the general deepening of the oceans in connection with world-wide tectonics.

Regardless of the motivating force, we know that sea-floor subsidence or increases in ocean volume have taken place on a grand scale. The flat tops of seamounts in the Mid-Pacific Mountains are now drowned by approximately 1,500 meters of water; in the northern Marshall Islands a similar relative subsidence has been shown.

STRUCTURAL EVOLUTION

At present earthquakes are almost absent in the Pacific Basin except along the East Pacific Rise. There are active volcanoes, but they are not particularly abundant. Consequently the basin appears to be one of the most stable regions on earth. The existence of thousands of inactive submarine volcanoes and of enormous submarine wrench faults raises the question of whether the present is abnormally quiet or whether geological time is adequate to produce the volcanoes and faults in a relatively stable basin. The answer depends on the amount of time available.

Large submarine volcanoes and islands may be considered to be grouped in clusters of perhaps 20, and the life of a group estimated as of the order of 10^6–10^7 years. The total number of volcanoes in the basin has been estimated at 10^4 (Menard, 1959), which gives 500 clusters. If the volcanoes have been forming in the basin for a period comparable to the age of the earth, say 3×10^9 years, the average rate of formation of clusters is only one in 6×10^6 years. Only one cluster need be active at a time, and the present rate of volcanism with four island groups active would be much higher than normal. However, from direct fossil evidence, there is no indication that any of the volcanoes are older than 10^8 years. If this is the total time available, the rate of formation of clusters averages one in 2×10^5 years. For an average life of 10^6 years, the rate of volcanism would be about the same as at present; but for a life of 10^7 years, it would be ten times the present rate. Within the accuracy of the estimates, it appears quite possible that all the volcanoes in the basin could have been produced at a uniform rate during the last 10^8 years.

Seismicity is another matter. The Pacific floor is cut by numerous faults which are not now the locus of earthquakes. At some time they must have been active, and large crustal blocks were moved both vertically and horizontally. The evidence for vertical movement, although not necessarily along faults, is extremely widespread in the basin. Scores of guyots and atolls demonstrate subsidence of 1–2 kilometers and large crustal blocks have been displaced vertically as much as 1 kilometer.

The development of volcanic islands and vertical movements of the sea floor have clearly influenced the biogeography of the Pacific Basin. However, more speculative, but far greater geological phenomena may have had a much more important effect. By all considerations, the most important geological phenomenon observable in the Pacific Basin at present is the East Pacific Rise, produced by a bulge in the underlying mantle. The origin and age of the bulge are not known, but a very large region of the sea floor has been elevated. Likewise it is not certain whether the bulge is permanent, but it appears that it may have had a relatively short life compared to that of the earth. The argument is as follows: All ocean basins have a rise or ridge in the middle except the Pacific. The Pacific has a median line of great ridges capped with atolls and guyots which would be the topography expected if a broad rise formerly existed and had since collapsed, and therefore the ridges may be the remnant of such a rise. Several former islands along this median line were at the surface roughly 10^8 years ago, and this gives the order of magnitude of life of a rise. If vast bulges of the sea floor have existed at various times and places in the ocean basins, their influence on biogeography must have been profound. According to the convection-current hypothesis of the origin of oceanic rises (Menard, 1960), continents may be torn asunder if they lie over the crests of rises, and both continental and oceanic crustal blocks may be transported across distances as great as 1,000 kilometers by convection currents. Melanesia may be a region being deformed in just this way at present. Moreover, when a bulge develops in the sea floor, any large seamounts become islands, and very long lines of island steppingstones become available for faunal migration.

In summation, geophysical measurements have demonstrated the complete difference between the continental and oceanic crust; it appears highly unlikely that one can be changed into the other, as supposed by pioneer biogeographers.

On the other hand, a growing body of information shows that vertical movements of the oceanic crust have been widespread and common, and that island steppingstones have been available in the past where none now exist. Moreover, oceanic rises may be temporary features and, if so, extensive shallow regions may have existed in the open Pacific Basin. It appears possible that isthmian links may not require a continental crust at all.

CORAL ATOLLS

Many important advances have been made in the past 20 years in studies of the characteristics and probable formation of coral atolls; most of these advances have been made in the central Pacific.

The mapping and drilling at Bikini and Eniwetok (Emery, Tracey, and Ladd, 1954), dredge hauls, coring, and mapping in the northern Marshall Islands and Mid-Pacific Mountains (Hamilton, 1956), and other studies of coral reefs and volcanic structures have solved the problem of coral-reef genesis in the central Pacific. These great coral and algal structures are caps on the tops of volcanic seamounts which were either individual peaks or peaks on submarine ridges; many of them were apparently planed more or less flat at the sea surface where the coral began to grow (Fig. 5). Later the seamount (or island) subsided slowly enough for the growth of algae and coral to keep pace with the sinking to form the modern atolls. The flat-topped seamounts of the Mid-Pacific Mountains furnish an example of coral lodgment on a flat platform. If submergence in the area had been slower, the Cretaceous coral would have kept pace with the sinking, would have remained at or near the sea surface, and would probably have formed an atoll. The eventual results might well have been similar to the atolls at Bikini and Eniwetok, the latter structure having apparently been formed on two such flat-topped seamounts.

The dating of fossil material discussed elsewhere in this paper indicates that the atolls of the central Pacific began to grow at the surface in the Late Cretaceous and Early Tertiary.

An important problem in connection with the formation of atolls is whether the sea floor sank or the ocean level went up. Most marine geologists today think that the sea floor has subsided on a local or regional basis, as in the Hawaiian area (Hamilton, 1957), but there is a small minority who think that perhaps the ocean volume increased enough to explain most of the relative sinking of the seamounts. If the latter idea is correct, something on the order of a 30 percent increase in the volume of the oceans must have occurred during the last 100 million years.

It can be seen from the foregoing that, of all the coral atoll theories, Darwin's emerges as the most valid for oceanic atolls, when altered by some aspects of Daly's Glacial Control Theory. This is especially true when one realizes that Darwin postulated the growth of atolls from submerged banks, with and without submergence of the foundation and without going through the intermediate stages of a fringing or barrier reef.

PALEOCLIMATOLOGY

At the present time there are scores of papers on the climates of past ages. These papers cover the whole of the Geologic Time Scale. Fortunately for our present study the most valid data are for Cretaceous to present-day climates, and coincide with the period of established age-datings in the Pacific Basin. Durham (1959) has an excellent recent summary of these data,

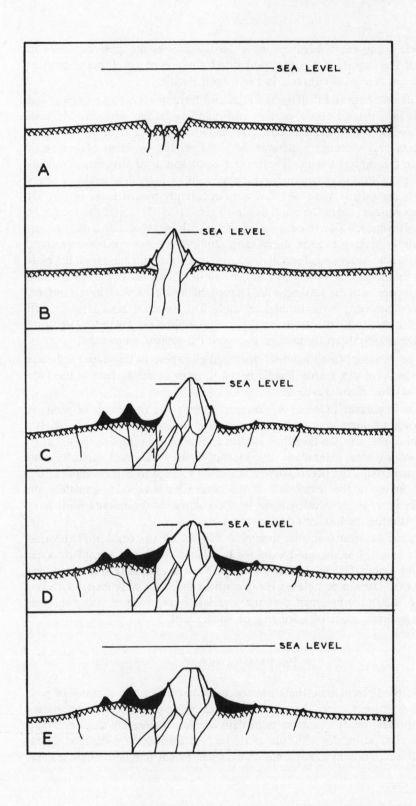

wherein he discusses the evidence from continental flora and fauna and the evidence from the marine faunas. Dorf (1960) summarizes the evidence, particularly for the flora. Bandy (1960) summarizes the evidence from studies of planktonic Foraminifera bearing on paleoclimates. Durham's and Bandy's papers are especially applicable to our studies in the Pacific.

Durham (1959) discusses the bases for paleoclimatological conclusions. The most important of these is the "Principle of Uniformitarianism"—that the principles and processes operating in the past are the same, or closely similar, to those of today. The reader is referred to Durham (1959) for discussion of detailed and critical factors involved in these interpretations of past climates, and to his references for an introduction to the literature on the subject.

The summary presented below is supported (Durham, 1959; Bandy, 1960; Dorf, 1960) by the studies of past climates on the continental flora and fauna, and by studies of the marine faunas—for example, reef corals, mollusks, gastropods, echinoids, and Foraminifera.

In the Late Cretaceous, there was a world-encircling tropical and semitropical climatic zone surrounding the Tethys Sea; the 18° C. isotherm in the Pacific extended to about 53° N. Lat., according to Durham (1959); Bandy (1960), on the basis of Foraminifera, places the 20° C. isotherm at closer to 60° N. Lat. Bandy notes in his data a cooling of later Cretaceous waters which is not apparent from other studies. The evidence from the Mid-Pacific Mountains is entirely in accord with Durham's findings in that this locality extends the tropical to semitropical Tethyan climates into the middle Pacific.

The Early Tertiary was also a time of wide extension of tropical and semitropical climates. During the Eocene the 20° C. isotherm was still north of 50° N. Lat. (Durham, 1959). From Early Tertiary to the Pliocene there was a gradual cooling of surface waters and restriction of warm climatic zones toward the equator, so that by Pliocene time the climatic zones were virtually where they are today. There were, apparently, fluctuations of climate in late Pliocene time, followed by the well-known fluctuations during the Pleistocene.

Recent findings from geological explorations in the central Pacific indicate that the conclusions outlined above are valid. Presumed tropical and semitropical Paleocene and Eocene foraminiferal faunas have been collected from the Mid-Pacific Mountains area and from other localities in the central Pacific. Emiliani (1954) in his studies of oxygen isotopes notes a progressive cooling of Pacific bottom waters of approximately 10° C. from the Early Tertiary to the present time. Arrhenius (1951) also records in his eastern equatorial Pacific cores restriction of tropical and semitropical zones toward the equator. The recent drillings on Bikini and Eniwetok have proved a continuous sequence of warm-water faunas in the central Pacific from the Eocene to the present time (Emery, Tracey, and Ladd, 1954).

FIGURE 5.—Evolution of some sea-floor features: (a) linear fractured zone (example: Great Fracture Zones of the northeast Pacific); (b) a new volcano which is supported by the earth's crust (example: many seamounts along fractured zones); (c) the line of seamounts, or ridge, builds up until it causes a downbowing of the earth's crust, thus creating marginal depressions with some filling (example: the southern Hawaiian Ridge); (d) erosion continues, the depressions are filled by submarine volcanic extrusions and erosional material (example: Marquesas Islands); (e) if eroded to a flat bank and relatively sunk below the surface, the island, or seamount, becomes a guyot (flat-topped seamount)—if coral was present at the surface and kept pace with the sinking, an atoll would form.

It is known that the areal extent of warm-water, calcareous, deep-sea deposits was much wider during the Tertiary than it is today. Arrhenius (1961) estimates that such deposits may have extended as far north as 45° N. Lat. in the Early Tertiary. In many areas, Tertiary sediments containing microfossils indicating warmer waters are found just beneath the present-day clays, which affirms this conclusion. Furthermore, the study of microfossils from cores, and other studies, have shown that the warmer climatic zones were merely shifted toward the equator and that these warm-water organisms lived throughout the climatic fluctuations of the Pleistocene; these data are in accord with the findings of Vaughan and Wells (1943) in relation to reef corals.

Although there was a considerable restriction of warm climates toward the equator, at no time during the Pleistocene was the central Pacific so cold as to kill off the tropical faunas (such as reef coral and Foraminifera), which was one of the postulates of Daly in his Glacial Control Theory.

In summary, we can say that the area of our immediate interests—the present tropical Pacific—has been tropical to semitropical from the Late Cretaceous to the present time, including the ice ages of the Pleistocene, and that there was a gradual cooling of surface waters and a restriction of the warmer zones toward the equator during these times, but this would only affect the areas beyond our immediate interests.

An interesting and significant corollary to the above climatic conclusions is their impact on evidences of polar wandering and their correlation with the findings of paleomagnetism.

Gutenberg (1951, Fig. 12, p. 202) summarized the older evidence on polar wandering. In general these data would place the North Pole during the Cretaceous in the northeast Pacific at about 45° N. Lat., 150° W. Long. Durham (1952, 1959) critically examined the paleontological data, both floral and faunal, and concluded that no such pole position was possible because the faunal and floral evidence placed the North Pole in about the same position from the Cretaceous to the Recent as it is now. His findings were based on the fact that the warm climatic zones form a belt around the earth, the plane of which is normal to the axis of the poles, and, furthermore, these belts during the times in question, although wider, were in the same general positions in which they are found today.

Recent summaries of the paleomagnetic data have concluded that the position of the North Pole during the Jurassic was about 80° N. Lat. (Collinson and Runcorn, 1960); that during the Cretaceous the pole was about 18° from the present position; and that later, in the Tertiary, it virtually coincided with today's position (Cox and Doell, 1960). The evidence from paleontology and paleomagnetism is thus brought closer into line and, in fact, is not critically divergent. Another pertinent fact concerning polar wanderings is that the Cretaceous warm-water faunas of the Mid-Pacific Mountains (about 17° N. Lat., 174° W. Long.) form an immovable peg, not involved in continental drift, around which the tropical and semitropical paleolatitudes cannot be shifted. In other words, the central Pacific data fall within the Cretaceous belt shown by Durham and make it of world-encircling extent. The virtual coincidence of the Cretaceous–Recent paleontologic and paleomagnetic conclusions regarding the pole positions casts serious doubt on large-scale "drift," with the exception of east-west drift, of the continents during this time.

LITERATURE CITED

ALLAN, R. S.
1953. "Report of Chairman of the Standing Committee on Datum-Planes in the Geological History of the Pacific Region." *Proc. Eighth Pacific Sci. Cong.* (Quezon City) **2**:325-423.

ARRHENIUS, G.
1951. *Sediment Cores from the East Pacific.* Swedish Deep-Sea Expedition, Vol. 5. Göteborg.
1961. "Pelagic Sediments." Preprint from M. N. HILL (editor), *The Sea: Ideas and Observations.*

BANDY, O. L.
1960. "Planktonic Foraminiferal Criteria for Paleoclimate Zonation." *Science Rep. Tohoku Univ.* 2nd ser. (Geology). Spec. Vol. 4, pp. 1-8.

BELOUSSOV, V. V.
1960. "Development of the Earth and Tectogenesis." *J. Geographic Res.* **65**: 4127-4146.

BEZRUKOV, P. L.
1959. "Some Zonation Problems of Sedimentation in the World Ocean." *Internat. Oceanographic Cong.* (New York). (Abstract.)
1960 "Sedimentation in the North-Western Part of the Pacific Ocean." *Twenty-first Internat. Geological Cong.* (Abstract.)

BRAMLETTE, M. N.
1958. "Significance of Coccolithophorids in Calcium Carbonate Deposition." *Bull. Geological Soc. America* **69**:121-126.

BULLARD, E. C., A. A. MAXWELL, and R. REVELLE
1956. "Heat Flow through the Deep-Sea Floor." *Advances in Geophysics* **3**: 153-181.

CARSOLA, A. J., and R. S. DIETZ
1952. "Submarine Geology of Two Flat-topped Northeast Pacific Seamounts." *American J. Science* **250**:481-497.

CLOUD, P. E., JR., R. G. SCHMIDT, and H. W. BURKE
1956. *Geology of Saipan, Mariana Islands: Pt. 1. Geology.* U. S. Geological Survey Prof. Pap. 280-A. Washington, D.C.

COLE, W. S.
1950. *Larger Foraminifera from the Palau Islands.* U. S. Geological Survey Prof. Pap. 221-B. Washington, D.C.
1957. *Larger Foraminifera from Eniwetok Atoll Drill Holes.* U. S. Geological Survey Prof. Pap. 260-V. Washington, D.C.
1959. *"Asterocyclina* from a Pacific Seamount." *Contrib. Cushman Foundation Foram. Res.* **10**:10-14.
1961. *Upper Eocene and Oligocene Larger Foraminifera from Viti Levu, Fiji.* U. S. Geological Survey Prof. Pap. 374-A. Washington, D.C.

COLE, W. S., R. TODD, and C. G. JOHNSON
1960. "Conflicting Age Determinations Suggested by Foraminifera on Yap, Caroline Islands." *Bull. American Paleontology* **41**(186):77-112.

COLLINSON, D. W., and S. K. RUNCORN
1960. "Paleomagnetic Observations in the United States: New Evidence for Polar Wandering and Continental Drift." *Bull. Geological Soc. America* **71**:915-958.

COX, A., and R. R. DOELL
1960. "Review of Paleomagnetism." *Bull. Geological Soc. America* **71**:645-768.

DORF, E.
>   1960. "Climatic Changes of the Past and Present." *American Scientist* **48**: 341-364.

DURHAM, J. W.
>   1952. "Early Tertiary Marine Faunas and Continental Drift." *American J. Science* **250**:321-343.
>   1959. "Paleoclimates." In *Physics and Chemistry of the Earth,* Vol. 3, pp. 1-16.

DURHAM, J. W., and E. C. ALLISON
>   1960. "The Geologic History of Baja California and Its Marine Faunas." *Systematic Zoology* **9**:47-91.

EMERY, K. O., J. I. TRACEY, JR., and H. S. LADD
>   1954. *Geology of Bikini and Nearby Atolls: Pt. 1, Geology.* U. S. Geological Survey Prof. Pap. 260-A. Washington, D.C.

EMILIANI, C.
>   1954. "Temperatures of Pacific Bottom Waters and Polar Superficial Waters during the Tertiary." *Science* **119**:853-855.

ERICSON, D. B., M. EWING, G. WOLLIN, and B. C. HEEZEN
>   1961. "Atlantic Deep-Sea Sediments." *Bull. Geological Soc. America* **72**:193-286.

GASKELL, T. F.
>   1954. "Seismic Refraction Work by H. M. S. *Challenger* in the Deep Oceans." *Proc. Royal Soc., London,* Ser. A, **222**:356-361.

GOLDBERG, E. D.
>   1961. "Chemical and Mineralogical Aspects of Deep-Sea Sediments." In *Physics and Chemistry of the Earth,* Vol. 4, pp. 281-302.

GOLDBERG, E. D., and G. ARRHENIUS
>   1958. "Chemistry of Pacific Pelagic Sediments." *Geoch. et Cosmoch. Acta* **13**: 153-212.

GRIFFIN, J., and E. D. GOLDBERG
>   In press. "Clay Mineral Distributions in Oceanic Areas." In M. L. HILL (editor), *The Sea: Ideas and Observations.*

GUTENBERG, B. (Editor)
>   1951. *Internal Constitution of the Earth.* (2nd ed.) New York: Dover.

HAMILTON, E. L.
>   1956. *Sunken Islands of the Mid-Pacific Mountains.* Geological Soc. America Mem. 64.
>   1957. "Marine Geology of the Southern Hawaiian Ridge." *Bull. Geological Soc. America* **68**:1011-1026.
>   1959. "Thickness and Consolidation of Deep-Sea Sediments." *Bull. Geological Soc. America* **70**:1399-1424.
>   1960. "Ocean Basin Ages and Amounts of Original Sediments." *J. Sedimentary Petrology* **30**:370-379.

HAMILTON, E. L., and R. W. REX
>   1959. *Lower Eocene Phosphatized* Globigerina *Ooze from Sylvania Guyot.* U. S. Geological Survey Prof. Pap. 260-W. Washington, D.C.

HESS, H. H.
>   1948. "Major Structural Features of the Western North Pacific." *Bull. Geological Soc. America* **59**:417-446.
>   1954. "Geological Hypotheses and the Earth's Crust under the Oceans." *Proc. Royal Soc., London* **222**:341-348.
>   1955. "The Oceanic Crust." *J. Marine Res.* **14**:423-439.

KUENEN, P. H.
>   1950. *Marine Geology.* New York: Wiley.

LADD, H. S.
  1960. "Origin of the Pacific Island Molluscan Fauna." *American J. Science* **258**-A:137-150.

LADD, H. S., and S. O. SCHLANGER
  1960. *Drilling Operations on Eniwetok Atoll.* U. S. Geological Survey Prof. Pap. 260-Y. Washington, D.C.

MENARD, H. W.
  1955a. "Archipelagic Aprons." *Bull. American Assoc. Petroleum Geologists* **40**:2195-2210.
  1955b. "Deformation of the Northeast Pacific Basin and the West Coast of North America." *Bull. Geological Soc. America* **66**:1149-1198.
  1959. "Geology of the Pacific Sea Floor." *Experientia* **15**:205-213.
  1960. "The East Pacific Rise." *Science* **132**:1737-1746.

MENARD, H. W., and R. S. DIETZ
  1951. "Submarine Geology of the Gulf of Alaska." *Bull. Geological Soc. America* **62**:1263-1286.

MERO, J. L.
  1959. *Economics of Mining and Processing of Deep-Sea Manganese Nodules.* Inst. Marine Resources, Univ. California, Preliminary Rep.

MURRAY, J., and A. F. RENARD
  1891. *Report on the Deep-Sea Deposits Based on the Specimens Collected during the Voyage of HMS* Challenger *in the Years 1872 to 1876.* London: Longmans.

RAITT, R. W.
  1956. "Seismic Refraction Studies of the Pacific Basin: Pt. 1." *Bull. Geological Soc. America* **67**:1623-1640.

REVELLE, R.
  1944. *Marine Bottom Samples Collected in the Pacific by the* Carnegie *on Its Seventh Cruise.* Carnegie Institution Pub. 556. Washington, D. C.

REVELLE, R., M. N. BRAMLETTE, G. ARRHENIUS, and E. D. GOLDBERG
  1955. *Pelagic Sediments of the Pacific.* Geological Soc. America Spec. Pap. 62, pp. 221-236.

REX, R. W., and E. D. GOLDBERG
  1958. "Quartz Contents of Pelagic Sediments of the Pacific Ocean." *Tellus* **10**: 153-159.

RIEDEL, W. R.
  1957. "Radiolaria: A Preliminary Stratigraphy." *Rep. Swedish Deep-Sea Exped.* Vol. 6, *Sediment Cores from the West Pacific,* No. 3, pp. 61-96.

RUBEY, W. W.
  1951. "Geologic History of Sea Water: An Attempt to State the Problem." *Bull. Geological Soc. America* **62**:1111-1148.

SHIPEK, C. J.
  1960. "Photographic Study of Some Deep-Sea Floor Environments in the Eastern Pacific." *Bull. Geological Soc. America* **71**:1067-1074.

STEARNS, H. T.
  1946. *Geology of the Hawaiian Islands.* Div. of Hydrography, Hawaii. Bull. 8.

TODD, R., and D. LOW
  1960. *Smaller Foraminifera from Eniwetok Drill Holes.* U. S. Geological Survey Prof. Pap. 260-X. Washington, D.C.

VACQUIER, V., A. D. RAFF, and R. E. WARREN
  1961. "Horizontal Displacements in the Floor of the Pacific Ocean." *Bull. Geological Soc. America* **72**:1251-1258.

VAUGHAN, T. W., and J. W. WELLS
1943. *Revision of the Suborders, Families, and Genera of the Scleractinia.* Geological Soc. America Spec. Pap. 44.

VON HERZEN, R.
1959. "Heat-Flow Values from the Southeastern Pacific." *Nature* **183**:882-883.
1960. "Pacific Ocean-Floor Heat Flow Measurements during the IGY." Assoc. Seism. Phys. Interior Earth. Abstract 190. Helsinki.

WALLACE, A. R.
1881. *Island Life.* New York: Harper.

WORZEL, J. L., M. TALWANI, and M. LANDISMAN
1960. "Gravity Anomalies in Sea Mounts." Assoc. Seism. Phys. Interior Earth. Abstract 50. Helsinki.

ZIMMERMAN, E. C.
1948. *Insects of Hawaii.* Vol. 1, *Introduction.* Honolulu: Univ. Hawaii Press.

Drilling on Midway Atoll, Hawaii

Harry S. Ladd

Joshua I. Tracey, Jr.

M. Grant Gross

Abstract. *Two holes drilled through reef sediments into basalt have established a geologic section through the Miocene. Midway was built above the sea by flows that were weathered and partially truncated in pre-Miocene time. After submergence, volcanic clays were reworked and covered by limestones. Overall submergence was interrupted at least twice by emergence. The limestones have been leached, recrystallized, and partially dolomitized.*

Midway atoll and its neighbor Kure, at the northwest end of the Hawaiian chain that stretches for 1600 miles (2550 km) across the central Pacific (Figs. 1 and 2), have long been regarded by geologists as the oldest members of this island group. Field evidence suggests that volcanism was initiated on the northwest, progressing southeastward to the Island of Hawaii, where volcanic activity still persists (*1*). As lavas were piled upon the sea floor to form the first islands, the load depressed the crust and the islands slowly subsided. This apparently was a slow process; coral reefs capping some of the former islands were able to maintain their tops near sea level by growing upward. Thus the islands at the northwest end of the chain are now atolls; the younger islands to the southeast are composed of volcanic mountains fringed with coral reefs. If such, in brief, has been the history of the Hawaiian Islands, there should be a geologic section beneath the reef islands recording much of Hawaii's history. To test this postulated history, Ladd proposed in 1960 that a deep hole be drilled on Midway, this atoll being selected over its neighbor Kure for logistical reasons.

Before the expensive process of drilling was attempted, seismic and magnetic surveys were carried out to determine the approximate thickness of the postulated cap of reef rock. Two brief seismic surveys were made by George Shor and his associates of the Scripps Institution of Oceanography. The first, strictly a land survey along the south side of Sand Island, was made in 1963 (*2*); the second survey was made in the lagoon, in December 1964, specifically to determine the thickness of coral beneath the northern part of the lagoon (*3*), where a magnetic low had been reported by the Naval Oceanographic Office (Project Magnet) (*4*). The geophysical surveys indicated the presence of a significant section of sediments beneath the islands on the south, with a progressive thickening northward under the lagoon.

Two holes were drilled during the summer of 1965 (Fig. 1). The first, on Sand Island, entered basalt at 516 feet (1550 m) and was continued to 568 feet. The second, the Reef hole, was drilled from a barge resting on the northern edge of the lagoon floor. It entered basalt at 1261 feet and was continued to 1654 feet. In each hole some 400 feet of post-Miocene limestones were penetrated, below which was a thin zone of upper Miocene (Tertiary *g*) sediments. In the Reef hole the upper Miocene sediments were underlain by approximately 500 feet of lower Miocene limestones (Tertiary *e*), and these, by about 170 feet of reworked volcanic clays, some lignitic, also of early Miocene age.

The drill was a truck-mounted Failing Model 2500 with reinforced tower (5). Cuttings and cores to a depth of 70 feet were taken with rock bit and conventional diamond core barrel. At depths greater than 70 feet a rubber-sleeve core barrel, yielding a 3-inch (7½-cm) core, was used almost exclusively. In the deeper of the two holes, three 1-inch oriented cores were taken (6). The size and amount of casing used and the amounts of core recovered are shown in Table 1. Sea water was used as drilling fluid with salt-water mud.

The first hole was drilled on Sand Island without difficulty. The geophysical surveys had indicated a thickening of the section to the north under the lagoon; consequently the site for the second hole was a flat sandy area just inside the reef on the north side of the lagoon, where the depth of water at high tide was 8 feet. This site was cleared of minor coral growth, and a course through the coral-studded lagoonal terrace was mapped by divers and marked with buoys.

The drill and all equipment, weighing 120 tons, were loaded aboard a steel barge measuring 120 by 30 feet. The barge, furnished by the U.S. Navy, was then towed to the drill site by a Navy LCM. After being jockeyed into position at the drill site, the barge was pumped full of sea water so that it settled to rest firmly on the sand bottom (Fig. 3). The drill tower, when raised, was guyed to nearby massive coral heads and steel piling.

The sediment sections cored on Midway are calcareous except in zones near the contact with the underlying basalts. The upper 200 feet in each hole is composed of unlithified material consisting mostly of aragonite and magnesian-calcite ($MgCo_3$, 12 to 16 percent, molar). Below 200 feet, calcite dominates, and much of the limestone is hardened by recrystallization. In the Reef core, parts of the limestone section are dolomitized. Below the calcareous section in both holes are zones of reworked volcanic clays, some of them calcareous, along with a few thin seams of lignitic clay and beds of basalt conglomerate. These relations are shown in Fig. 4 (7) and are briefly described in Table 2.

In the Reef core, dolomite and dolomitic limestone occurred at intervals between 426 and 930 feet; the 64-foot section from 426 to 490 feet is almost solid dolomite. Calcium-rich dolomite occurs as isolated crystals and in orange-colored crusts of crystals from 560 feet to 811 feet. We found no evidence that dolomite is forming on Midway today (8).

Preliminary determinations of the ages of the sediments in the cores are based primarily on the occurrence of diagnostic Foraminifera. Cole is studying the larger forms; Ruth Todd and Doris Low, the smaller ones. Their findings to date are summarized below.

Cole states (9):

Five species of larger Foraminifera were recovered. In the lower part of the Reef hole two zones of larger Foraminifera were encountered. The upper zone had abundant specimens of *Miogypsinoides dehaartii* (van der Vlerk), and *Austrotrillina*

Table 1. Summary of depths, casing, and core recovery.

Hole	Depth (feet)	Casing (feet)	Footage cored (rubber sleeve) (feet)	Core recovery (feet)	Core recovery (%)
Sand Island	568	122*	481.5	346.85	72
Reef	1654	190† 800‡	1358.5	1254.8	92

* Casing diameter, 12¾ inches.   † Casing diameter, 16 inches.   ‡ Casing diameter, 12 inches.

Fig. 1 (above). Location of Midway and of the holes drilled.

Fig. 2 (above right). Bathymetric chart of Midway area; depths are given in fathoms. [U.S. Naval Oceanographic Office]

Fig. 3 (right). Drill rig on steel barge resting on lagoon floor in 8 feet of water near the northern edge of Midway's lagoon. The lighter areas around the barge are sand; the darker areas are living corals and algae. The dark-bordered irregular areas (upper left) are eroded remnants of an older reef now several feet above sea level. Beyond the old reef lies a narrow reef platform on which the waves of the open sea are breaking. [Photograph by Commander N. R. Wooden, U.S.N.]

striata Todd and Post, and was followed by a zone of *Spiroclypeus margaritatus* (Schlumberger). These three species are known markers for upper Tertiary *e* (early Miocene) in the western Pacific. This lower section is correlated with sections in the Kita-Daitō-Jima (North Borodino Island), the Bikini and Eniwetok holes, and with surface outcrops of Saipan, Guam, and Borneo.

In the upper part of the drill holes *Heterostegina suborbicularis* d'Orbigny, *Marginopora vertebralis* Quoy and Gaimard, and *Sorites orbiculus* (Forskål) were recovered. These species with a known, relatively long stratigraphic range in the Indo-Pacific region are not especially diagnostic, except to suggest that the sediments in which they occur are Tertiary *e* (early Miocene) or younger.

Ruth Todd and Doris Low recognize several assemblages of smaller Foraminifera. They report (*10*):

The reworked clays that underlie the limestones in the Reef hole contain a fauna fairly rich in specimens but poor in species (total 19). The age appears to be early Miocene (Tertiary *e*). The assemblage is dominated by bolivinids and buliminids, is definitely marine and was probably deposited in shallow, relatively calm water, near shore or within a lagoon. . . .

In the lower part of the deeper hole we find *Austrotrillina*, a genus believed to have become extinct in the early Miocene (Tertiary *e*). Its presence at Midway is noteworthy because it is unknown in North or South America and thus far has been reported only from the Tethys basin, from Spain through the Near East, and into Australia and the western Pacific (Saipan, Eniwetok, Bikini). . . .

Near 450 feet in both cores, the presence of *Valvulammina marshallana* Todd and Post and other forms suggests a correlation with beds assigned to the late Miocene (Tertiary *g*) at Bikini and Eniwetok. . . .

Rich and varied assemblages of smaller Foraminifera occur in the post-Miocene sediments at both sites.

Hazel (*11*) reports that many cores from both sites have yielded large numbers of ostracods, particularly hemicytherids, bairdiids, and loxoconchids. These are not of immediate value in determining the age of the deposits, as no information is available on the fossil ostracods of the islands of the open Pacific. Five assemblages are recognized, their generic composition suggesting early Miocene to Quaternary ages. All assemblages are normal marine assemblages except those from certain beds in the middle part (137 to 260 feet) of the Sand Island core, where the brackish-water ostracod *Cyprideis* occurs in abundance. The limestones containing this fauna were probably deposited in a mesohaline lagoon.

The corals that are an important constituent of the existing reefs were at least equally important in earlier periods of Midway's history. Wells, who is studying both the living reef corals and the fossils from the cores, states (*12*) that the Recent reef coral fauna of Midway is slightly attenuated, as would be expected from its latitude (28°14′N) and its position as an outpost of the Hawaiian fauna. Of the 15 coral genera known to live in more southerly parts of Hawaii, nine occur at Midway. Most of the genera are widely distributed in the Indo-Pacific, to the outer limits of the tropical zone. The six Recent genera from Hawaii that have not been found at Midway are exceedingly rare in the Hawaiian Islands. The Miocene coral fauna, according to Wells, was more diversified than later assemblages, suggesting a more favorable regime.

Reef-building coralline algae, like the reef corals, appear to have been at least as important in the early history of Midway as they are today. Other less abundant groups of fossils—brachiopods, echinoids, bryozoans, and crustacea—are all represented in the cores and are being studied. It is hoped that much may be learned about the vegetation of Midway during Miocene and later times from an examination of the several lignitic zones.

In the upper 200 feet of the post-Miocene section, the mollusks are well preserved, many retaining traces of their original color pattern. They rep-

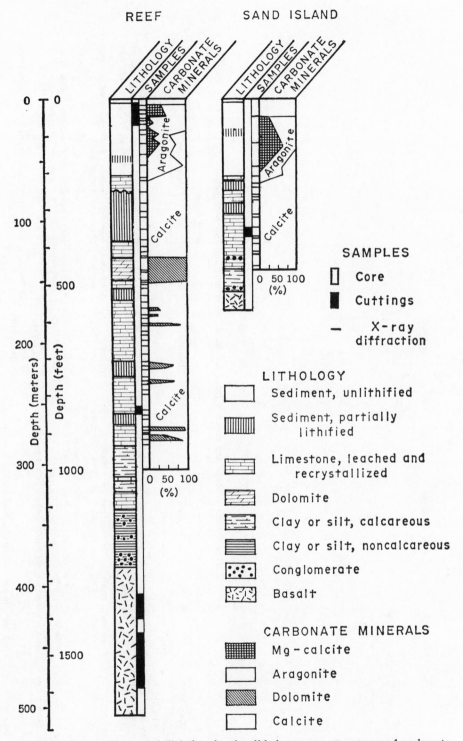

Fig. 4. Preliminary logs of drill holes showing lithology, core recovery, and carbonate-mineral composition (7).

Table 2. Description of cores and cuttings from the Sand Island hole and the Reef hole.

Sand Island hole		Reef hole	
Depth*	Description	Depth†	Description
9–36 (0–6.0)	Fill, coral-algal sand, and gravel	16–210 (1.7–60.8)	Sediment, unlithified, and coral-algal limestone; minor lithification at 150 feet; possible soil zone at 77 feet; land snail shell (*Ptychodon*) at 116 to 130 feet
36–208 (6.0–58.4)	Sediment, unlithified, with coral-algal fragments and soft calcareous mud; land snail shells at 116 to 130 feet; brackish water ostracods at 137 to 208 feet; *Pisulina* sp. at 175 to 180 feet	210–296 (60.8–87.0)	Limestone, partially leached and recrystallized and partially lithified calcareous sand
208–337 (58.4–97.7)	Limestone, partially leached and recrystallized, and partially lithified calcareous sand and mud; aragonitic shells at 238, 243, and 258 feet may be derived from younger deposits above; brackish-water ostracods *Cyprideis* at 208 to 260 feet, very abundant at 242 to 259 feet	296–386 (87.0–114.4)	Partially lithified calcareous mud and sand; some solution features
337–443 (97.7–130.0)	Limestone, leached and recrystallized and partially lithified calcareous sand; basalt pebbles at 428 to 443 feet	386–426 (114.4–126.6)	Limestone, friable, algal-foraminiferal
443–460 (130.0–135.2)	Limestone, brown, recrystallized irregularly lithified calcareous sand near base; Foraminifera: *Valvulammina marshallana* at 445 to 446 feet	426–489 (126.6–145.8)	Dolomite, algal-foraminiferal, leached and recrystallized
460–502 (135.2–148.0)	Volcanic marl; oyster shells in green clay at 483 to 484 feet	489–563 (145.8–168.5)	Limestone, dolomitic, leached and recrystallized and partially lithified sand; porcellanous dolomite at 489 to 505 feet; Foraminifera: *Valvulammina marshallana*, *Asterigerina tentoria*, and *Cribrogoesella parvula* at 495 to 500 feet

Depth	Description
502–516 (148.0–152.2)	Sandy basalt conglomerate; green clay and many mollusk impressions, probable base of marine section at 502.4 feet
516–568 (152.2–168.1)	Basalt, dark gray, palagonite and calcite in vesicles
563 (168.5)	Carbonaceous clay
563–711 (168.5–213.5)	Dolomitic limestone, leached and recrystallized; brown sparry calcite abundant; dolomite occurs as rhombs. Foraminifera: *Miogypsinoides dehaartii* at 590 to 600 feet
711–751 (213.5–225.7)	Partially lithified dolomitic sand; dolomite occurs as rhombs
751–845 (225.7–254.3)	Limestone, leached and recrystallized; dolomite rhombs in cavities
845–885 (254.3–266.5)	Partially lithified calcareous sand and mud
885–934 (266.5–281.5)	Dolomitic limestone; orange dolomite rhombs; clay layer, reddish brown at 914 feet; partially lithified dolomitic sand, argillaceous at 925 to 930 feet; Foraminifera: *Miogypsinoides dehaartii* at 901 to 906 and 926 to 927 feet, *Austrotrillina striata* at 901 to 927 feet
934 (281.5)	Gray-to-black carbonaceous clay
934–995 (281.5–300.1)	Tuffaceous limestone leached and recrystallized; Foraminifera: *Miogypsinoides dehaartii* at 946 and 956 feet, *Spiroclypeus margaritatus* at 960 to 961 feet
995–1121 (300.1–338.5)	Reworked volcanic clays; some carbonaceous silt and clay layers; Foraminifera: abundant *Amphistegina* at 1045 feet, *Spiroclypeus margaritatus* at 1029 to 1091 feet, *Austrotrillina* sand at 1117 feet
1121–1261 (338.5–381.4)	Volcanic clay, variable color; basalt conglomerate layers abundant; brown clay with small Foraminifera and ostracods at 1165 feet; lignitic clay layers at 1242 and 1255 feet
1261–1654 (381.4–500.9)	Basalt, dark gray, vesicular

* Depths of top and bottom of core, in feet below drilling platform, which was 16.5 feet (5.0 m) above mean lower low water; figures in parentheses are depths in meters below mean lower low water. † Depth in feet below drilling platform, which was 10.5 feet (3.2 m) above mean lower low water; figures in parentheses are depths in meters below mean lower low water. Water depth at drilling site was approximately 5.5 feet below mean lower low water.

resent reef and lagoon assemblages that are somewhat restricted in number and variety, as is the fauna found on the atoll today. Included, however, are some interesting occurrences. In the Sand Island hole at depths of 175 to 180 feet, for example, three shells of a species of *Pisulina* were recovered. This neritid is known only from a few species living today in India and Ceylon and from one fossil species recovered from beds of late Miocene (Tertiary *g*) age in a drill hole on Bikini Atoll (*13*).

Also in the Sand Island hole, at depths of 137 to 165 feet, eight specimens of a minute land shell, *Ptychodon*, were found, and a single specimen of a larger and distinctly different species of the same genus was recovered from the Reef hole at a depth of 116 to 130 feet. Land snails of this type do not live on existing atolls but they are widely distributed on high volcanic islands and on limestone islands rising 200 feet or more above the sea (*14*).

In the recrystallized and partly dolomitized limestones below 200 feet, larger mollusks are fairly abundant, but most of them are poorly preserved as molds or calcite casts. Like the younger mollusks they represent assemblages of reef and lagoon genera. The clays and tuffaceous beds below the limestones contain a few layers literally covered with fragile mollusk impressions, and other beds of heavy oyster shells record brackish conditions.

The sediments drilled on Midway rest on a series of weathered basalt flows. Depths to the basalt are greater on the north side of the atoll than on the south. Probably Midway's volcanic foundation was partially truncated by wave action on the northeast or windward side before the mound was completely submerged and covered by sediments. This northward thickening of the sediment section, indicated by preliminary seismic and magnetic surveys, was confirmed by drilling. The sediment thicknesses drilled were only

about half the thickness predicted by geophysical means (*15*).

The bathymetric chart (Fig. 2) indicates that volcanic material was erupted from a number of vents in the vicinity of Midway and Kure. If the resulting seamounts ever reached the surface or were capped by reefs, they have since been truncated by wave action. One prominent seamount, comparable in size to Midway, lies to the northeast; others lie to the southwest.

All flows reached by the drill under Midway appear to have issued from vents on land or in very shallow water. Vesicular zones are well developed, and no pillow structures have been recognized. Macdonald, who has made a preliminary examination of all volcanic cores, states (*16*) that in gross petrographic features the Midway basalts closely resemble subaerial flows exposed on the island of Oahu.

In an attempt to determine the age of the basalts, samples from three of the freshest-looking cores from the Reef hole were submitted to Marvin A. Lanphere of the U.S. Geological Survey for potassium-argon age determinations. Two of these samples looked promising, as they contained no devitrified glass or alteration minerals in the groundmass. The age of one sample from a depth of 1594 feet (333 feet below the top of the basalt) is 15.7 ± 0.9 million years. That of the second sample, from a depth of 1600 feet (330 feet below the top of the basalt) is 16.6 ± 0.9 million years. There is no reason to believe that the dated basalts analyzed represent younger material injected into the basalt sequence as dikes or sills. The basalts above and below the samples tested do show evidence of weathering, and apparently the samples selected had also lost argon during weathering.

Midway is the fifth open-sea atoll to be studied by deep drilling and the second atoll whose limestone cap has been completely penetrated. Certain stratigraphic features of the sedimen-

Table 3. Deep drilling on atolls in the open Pacific Ocean.

Place and date	Latitude	Total sedi-ments	Ages	Stratigraphic intervals			Amount of lithifi-cation	Dolomiti-zation	Faunal sequen-ces*	Solution uncon-formities†
				Post-Miocene section	Tertiary f	Tertiary e				
Ellice Islands:										
Funafuti, 1896–98	8°30′S	1114+	Pleistocene to Recent	1114+			Extensive	Extensive	Absent	Present
Kita-Daito-Jimō, 1936	26°N	1416+	Tertiary e to Recent	340	Absent	1076+	Moderate	Extensive	Present	Not rec-ognized
Marshall Islands:										
Bikini, 1947	11°30′N	2556+	Tertiary e to Recent	700	186	1390+	Slight	None	Present	Present
Eniwetok, 1951–52	11°35′N	4610	Tertiary b to Recent	615	220	1700	Moderate	Slight	Present	Present
Midway, 1965	28°N	1261	Tertiary e to Recent	462	Absent	501, limestone; 110, clay	Extensive	Moderate	Present	Present

*See 18.   †See 19.

tary sections drilled are listed in Table 3 and represented graphically in Fig. 5.

The post-Miocene limestones at Midway and at Kita-Daitō-Jima are thinner than those in the Ellice and Marshall Island areas. This is of interest in that both Midway and Kita-Daitō-Jima lie outside the tropics in what may be called the marginal zones of present reef growth. Funafuti, which lies closest to the equator, has by far the thickest section of post-Miocene rocks. These differences suggest that the varied reef assemblages of the tropics lead to a more rapid rate of reef growth, but the controlling factors probably are rates of subsidence and duration of periods of emergence. Neither the Midway nor the Kita-Daitō-Jima sections contain any sediments formed during Tertiary f. Both atolls may have been above the sea and undergoing erosion during this part of the early Miocene.

The limestone sections drilled on Midway (Fig. 5) resemble those in the two deepest holes (E-1 and F-1) drilled on Eniwetok in that they contain appreciable thicknesses of hard and firm recrystallized reef rock, but they differ from those sections in that they contain no intervals of aragonitic sediments below the recrystallized limestones. The partially dolomitized carbonate section in the Reef core from Midway is intermediate between the extensively dolo-

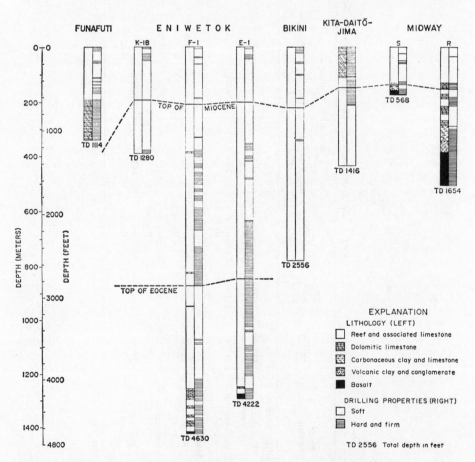

Fig. 5. Summary of results of deep drilling on atolls in the open Pacific Ocean. [After H. S. Ladd and S. O. Schlanger, *U.S. Geol. Survey Profess. Paper 260-Y* (1960), fig. 287]

mitized sections at Funafuti and Kita-Daitō-Jima and the slightly dolomitized section at Eniwetok. Dolomite was not detected in the carbonate section at Bikini.

The Midway sections contain beds of volcanic clay and conglomerate. The 170-foot section of bedded volcanic and lignitic clays found below the limestones in the Reef core on Midway have no counterpart in the other atoll sections.

At Midway, basaltic lavas were poured out to build a mound rising nearly 3 miles above the ocean floor. The exact date at which the mound reached the surface is not known, but the subaerial or shallow-water lava flows that cap it were weathered and at least partially truncated by wave action prior to the Miocene.

In the early Miocene (Tertiary e) the northern part of the eroded mound was covered by swamps. The mound subsided, and the swamps were covered by shallow marine waters in which ostracods and smaller foraminifera lived on a muddy bottom. Altogether, 170 feet of lignitic beds and clays were accumulated.

As the waters cleared, reef corals and calcareous algae became established on the reworked volcanic clays, moving in, probably, from a more northerly site to windward. As subsidence continued, 500 feet of reef limestone were accumulated, apparently under lagoonal conditions. Water circulation may at times have been restricted, permitting the formation of dolomitizing solutions (8).

At or near the end of Tertiary e, the reef emerged, and the entire limestone section stood above water during Tertiary f. The limestones were thoroughly leached and recrystallized. Resubmergence followed in the late Miocene (Tertiary g), and more than 100 feet of shallow-water lagoonal limestones were deposited. These deposits covered the altered limestones on the north side of the atoll and the higher area to the south. This interval of limestone deposition appears to have continued into the Pleistocene.

Altogether, about 250 feet of post-Miocene beds were accumulated before there was another major interruption. This change—like the one that interrupted the early Miocene sequence—was caused by emergence of the atoll. In this instance the withdrawal may have been due to the eustatic lowering of the sea caused by Pleistocene glaciation. It may be possible to tie the 200-foot solution unconformity of Midway to the extensive submarine platform lying 180 feet below sea level off the island of Molokai and elsewhere in Hawaii (17). During this period of emergence the newly formed limestones were leached and recrystallized.

When subsidence recommenced, the altered limestones were covered by about 200 feet of reef and lagoonal sediments. These beds have not been emergent for long periods and exhibit no evidence of leaching or extensive recrystallization.

The last recorded event was the growth of a now-emergent reef, remnants of which are found on most of Midway's rim (Fig. 3). This reef apparently flourished when the sea stood several feet higher than it does now. The earliest date obtained in several carbon-14 determinations made on the exposed reef rock by Meyer Rubin of the Geological Survey was 2400 years ago. The old reef is now eroded and no part now rises more than 3 feet above high-tide level, but it probably represents the Recent negative shift in sea level of 5 to 6 feet, evidence for which, from many parts of the Pacific, has been described.

HARRY S. LADD
JOSHUA I. TRACEY, JR.
U.S. Geological Survey,
Washington, D.C.

M. GRANT GROSS
Smithsonian Institution,
Washington, D.C.

References and Notes

1. J. D. Dana, *U.S. Exploratory Expedition 1838–42* (1849), vol. 10, pp. 279–84, 414–17.
2. G. Shor, *Scripps Inst. Oceanog. Tech. Mem. 136* (1963); *Nature* **201**, 1207 (1964).
3. ——, R. Phillips, H. Kirk, *Marine Phys. Lab. SIO Ref. 64–14* (1964).
4. "U.S. Naval Oceanographic Office, Midway Islands, Total Magnetic Intensity Chart, Aeromagnetic Survey" (1963); "U.S. Naval Brochure No. 3" (1966), p. II-A-5.
5. The drilling equipment and a seven-man crew were furnished by Layne International, Inc.; all the drilling was done under the supervision of William Craddick. The drill was operated continuously in 12-hour shifts. A geologist or geological assistant was on duty at all times. In this work we were assisted by Theodore K. Chamberlain, W. Storrs Cole, William Ebersole, and Ted Murphy.
6. The oriented cores were taken under the direction of Charles E. Ward of Christensen Diamond Products Company.
7. X-ray diffraction analysis was used to identify and to estimate the abundance of the carbonate minerals in finely ground samples, 69 from the Reef core, 21 from the Sand Island core. The results of six to ten analyses of each sample were averaged. The $MgCO_3$ content of the magnesian calcites was estimated from the data of J. R. Goldsmith *et al.* [*Geochim. Cosmochim. Acta* **7**, 212 (1955)]. The dolomites were shown, from the data of J. R. Goldsmith and D. L. Graf [*J. Geol.* **66**, 678 (1958)], to be rich in calcium.
8. N. D. Newell *et al.*, *The Permian Reef Complex of the Guadalupe Mountains Region, Texas and New Mexico—A Study in Paleoecology* (Freeman, San Francisco, 1953); J. E. Adams and M. L. Rhodes, *Bull. Amer. Assoc. Petrol. Geologists* **44**, 1912 (1960); K. S. Deffeyes, F. J. Lucia, P. K. Weyl, *Science* **143**, 678 (1964); R. A. Berner, *ibid.* **147**, 1297 (1965); S. O. Schlanger, *Sci. Rep. Tohoku Univ., Second Ser.* **37**, 15 (1965).
9. W. S. Cole, unpublished manuscript.
10. R. Todd and D. Low, unpublished manuscript. R. Todd and R. Post, *U.S. Geol. Survey Profess. Paper 260-N* (1954); R. Todd and D. Low, *U.S. Geol. Survey Profess. Paper 260-X* (1960).
11. J. E. Hazel, written communication.
12. J. W. Wells, written communication.
13. H. Ladd, *U.S. Geol. Survey Profess. Paper 531* (1966), p. 59.
14. ——, *J. Paleontol.* **32**, 183 (1958).
15. Preliminary seismic surveys suggested a thickness of sediment beneath Sand Island of 0.26 to 0.29 km (853 to 951 feet) (see 2), but basalt was found at 516 feet. Under the north half of the Midway lagoon, volcanic rock was predicted between 0.63 and 0.71 km (2067 and 2329 feet), but the drill entered basalt at 1261 feet. George Shor, who was in charge of the preliminary seismic surveys and who made additional observations at Midway after the drilling was completed, is preparing a further report on this matter.
16. G. A. Macdonald, oral communication.
17. H. T. Stearns, *Z. Geomorphol. Supp.* **3**, 9 (1961).
18. These are primarily zones of diagnostic larger Foraminifera that match the sequences established in Indonesia.
19. S. O. Schlanger, *U.S. Geol. Surv. Profess. Paper 260-BB* (1963), p. 994.
20. The project discussed here was carried out under the auspices of the Hawaii Institute of Geophysics, University of Hawaii, with financial support (grant No. GP4728) from the National Science Foundation. Other agencies collaborating included the U.S. Geological Survey and the Office of Naval Research. In planning the work, Ladd was assisted by George P. Woollard and Gordon A. Macdonald, co-investigators in the project. In connection with planning, thanks are also due to Dr. William E. Benson of the National Science Foundation, V. C. Mickle of the George E. Failing Company, and Rear Admiral Charles W. Thomas (Ret.) of the University of Hawaii. During our stay at Midway, Captain F. D. Milner, Commanding Officer, and his associates cooperated fully. The cores and cuttings obtained during the drilling have been placed on permanent deposit at the Hawaii Institute of Geophysics, University of Hawaii. Publication of this report is authorized by the Director of the U.S. Geological Survey and by the Secretary of the Smithsonian Institution.

How Volcanoes Grow

Geology, geochemistry, and geophysics disclose the constitution and eruption mechanism of Hawaiian volcanoes.

J. P. Eaton and K. J. Murata

Summarizing the state of volcanological knowledge in 1952, Howel Williams (1) observed: "Much has been learned about the distribution, internal structure, and products of volcanoes, but pitifully little about the causes and mechanism of eruption." To remedy this deficiency he called for more intensive, continuous observations of well-chosen active volcanoes, with geophysics and geochemistry supplementing the traditional tools of geology. Current investigations of the U.S. Geological Survey's Hawaiian Volcano Observatory are much like those envisaged by Williams, and they are yielding an exciting new insight into the internal workings of volcanoes.

No volcano has influenced our conception of the vital processes of active volcanism more than Kilauea. Geologists drawn to Hawaii by travelers' accounts of fantastic activity at this volcano were so impressed by what they saw that they framed whole theories of volcanic action around it. Even though its prime attraction, the renowned lava lake that circulated almost continuously within its great summit caldera for at least a century, was destroyed in 1924, Kilauea and its giant neighbor, Mauna Loa, have remained very active, one or the other having erupted about once in two years since that date. The comparative simplicity, the large size, and the frequent,

voluminous, nonviolent eruptions of Hawaiian volcanoes make them ideally suited to illustrate the fundamental processes of volcanism. Here these processes can be studied safely and conveniently, in isolation from the great complications of structure and contaminating rocks that render most volcanoes so baffling.

In 1823 William Ellis (2) found within Kilauea caldera "an immense gulf, in the form of a crescent, upwards of two miles in length, about a mile across, and apparently 800 feet deep. The bottom was filled with lava, and the southwest and northern parts of it were one vast flood of liquid fire in a state of terrific ebullition. . . ." Through the century that followed, visitors to Kilauea recorded successive infillings and collapses of Ellis' "gulf," as lava poured up through conduits beneath its floor and accumulated, crusted over, and partially congealed within it, later to be withdrawn into the depths or poured out through great fissures in the flank of the volcano.

Continuous observation of the lava lake began with the establishment of the Hawaiian Volcano Observatory on the rim of Kilauea caldera in 1912 (3). Detailed measurements of the height, size, and shape of the liquid surface of the lake (Fig. 1) as well as occasional measurements of its temperature and chemical analyses of the gases escaping from it were made from 1912 until the lake was destroyed by the eruption of 1924. The usefulness

The authors are members of the staff of the U.S. Geological Survey's Hawaiian Volcano Observatory, Hawaii National Park, Hawaii.

Fig. 1. Lava lake in Halemaumau, 23 January 1918. Floating islands of congealed lava are surrounded by molten lava. In the foreground, an overflow from the lake has chilled to pahoehoe lava. In the background can be seen the wall of Kilauea caldera and the gentle slopes of the southwest rift zone of Mauna Loa.

of seismograph and tiltmeter observations for deciphering unseen subterranean changes in the volcano was also demonstrated during these years when Jaggar (4) and his collaborators were collecting a wealth of data on Kilauea's baffling lava lake.

Setting and Geology

The geologic mapping of the Hawaiian Islands, carried out jointly by the U.S. Geological Survey and the Hawaii Division of Hydrography during the 1930's and 1940's, opened new dimensions in the study of Hawaiian volcanoes (5). A thorough investigation of volcanic processes necessarily awaited an adequate geological description of the volcanoes. By mapping structures visible at the surface, by examining the shallow interior of the volcanoes in the sections exposed by faulting and erosion, and by studying very carefully the nature, variation,

and distribution of the lavas composing the great Hawaiian shields, geologists have sketched the framework of the volcanoes' structure and history.

Mauna Loa and Kilauea form the southern part of the island of Hawaii at the southeastern end of the Hawaiian Ridge, a great range of volcanic mountains rising from the floor of the Pacific Ocean and stretching 1600 miles northwestward from Hawaii to Kure Island (Fig. 2, inset). Volcanism appears to have progressed from the northwest toward the southeast along the ridge. Wave-wrecked volcanoes of the northwestern half of the ridge approach the surface as shoals or support low-lying coral atolls. Farther southeastward, remnants of volcanic rock rising in small islands still withstand the vanquishing sea. Only along the southeastern quarter of the ridge do the great volcanoes stand high above the sea, where they form the large inhabited islands of the Hawaiian group. Even here the evidence for migration of activity southeastward is strong, for volcanoes in the northwestern part of this group are deeply dissected, while Mauna Loa and Kilauea, still in vigorous activity at the southeastern end, are hardly marred by erosion.

From its great length and narrow width it is apparent that the Hawaiian Ridge marks the course of a major fracture in the earth's crust through which lava has poured at different centers and different times to build the volcanoes that form it. The ridge rises from the axis of a broad swell on the ocean floor and is flanked, near its southeastern end, by an ocean deep that runs down its northeast side and hooks around the south end of the island of Hawaii (6).

Volcanoes of the ridge are built upon the simplest known section of the earth's crust (the Pacific basin is floored only by approximately 5 kilometers of basalt, covered by about 1 kilometer of sediments and resting directly upon the earth's mantle), and they are separated from other tectonically active regions by at least 2000 miles of seismically quiet ocean floor. Thus, in magnificent isolation, volcanic processes originating in the mantle raise the giant Hawaiian mountains to heights approaching 6 miles (10 kilometers) above the ocean floor.

Hawaiian volcanoes bear little resemblance to steep-sided, central-type composite volcanoes like Fujiyama, in Japan. Rather, they are shaped like a warrior's shield, with a broad domical summit and gently sloping sides, and they attain enormous size. Mauna Loa rises more than 30,000 feet above its base on the ocean floor and has a volume of about 10,000 cubic miles. Even at sea level, about 16,000 feet above its base, it is more than 70 miles long. The volcanoes are built almost entirely of thin flows of fluid basaltic lava, poured out chiefly from long fissures concentrated in relatively narrow rift zones.

On surface evidence, rift zones appear to determine the location and shape of the volcanoes. Most commonly, each volcano has two principal rift zones meeting in the summit region at angles of 130° to 180°. The vertex of this angle usually points away from the unbuttressed flank of the Hawaiian ridge adjacent to the volcano. Rift zones are predominantly either almost parallel or more or less perpendicular to the axis of the ridge, but just how these zones are related to the fundamental fracture beneath the ridge is not clear.

The summits of several volcanoes are indented by calderas formed by collapse of the surface rocks when support was withdrawn from below. Kilauea caldera, subcircular in plan and eccentrically set in the summit of the volcano, is 2½ miles long and 2 miles wide. Its floor, a low dome of lava flows that slope outward from Halemaumau, site of the old lava lake and principal vent of Kilauea, is almost 500 feet below the caldera rim on the northwest but level with the rim on the south. The present floor is about 600 feet higher than that depicted in a sketch by Malden (7) in 1825.

Along some rift zones, especially near their upper ends, are found other prominent collapse craters. The variation in size as well as the nature of pit craters, as these features are called, is well demonstrated by the "Chain of Craters" along the upper section of Kilauea's east rift zone. Here, pit craters range from the "Devils Throat," formed by a single collapse that left a pit 50 feet across and 250 feet deep with an overhanging lip, to the giant Makaopuhi (Fig. 3), the result of at least two episodes of collapse and two of flooding by lava that formed a gulf almost a mile across and 900 feet deep.

Prominent lateral faults, some of them submarine, flank several of the volcanoes. Notable among these are

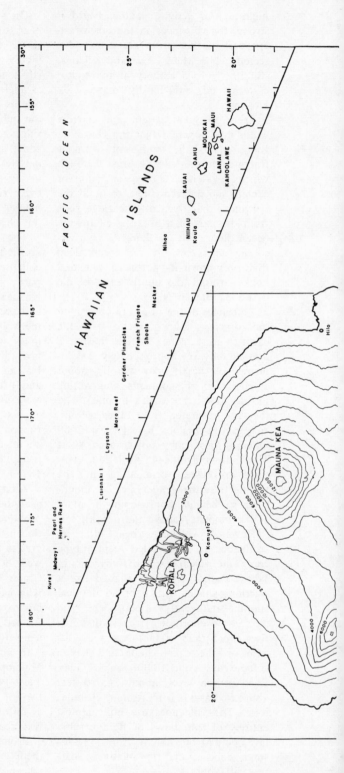

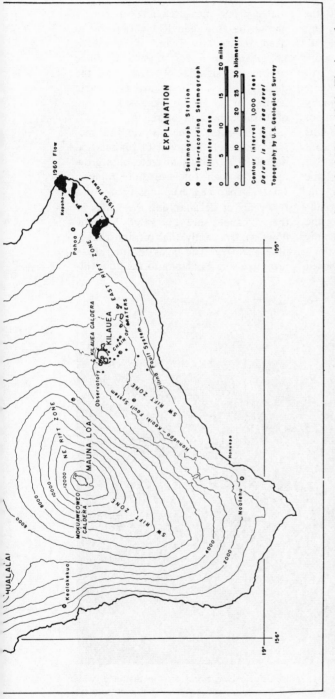

Fig. 2. Map of Hawaii showing seismograph stations, tiltmeter bases, and the Kilauea lava flows of 1955 and 1960. The inset shows the entire chain, stretching 1600 miles northwestward from Hawaii to Kure Island.

the Honuapo-Kaoiki fault system, which separates Kilauea from Mauna Loa and extends from just north of Kilauea caldera southwestward to the sea near Honuapo, and the Hilina fault system (Fig. 4), which drops a 30-mile-long segment of Kilauea's south flank abruptly toward the sea. Although the absolute movement on these faults cannot be specified, it is distinctly possible that the wholesale uplift of the Hawaiian Ridge along such faults has been responsible for a significant fraction of its height.

Hawaiian lava flows, both the smooth, glassy-skinned pahoehoe and the indescribably rough, clinkery-surfaced aa, are intricately broken by the processes that form them. The volcanic edifices built of these shattered flows are mammoth piles of rubble, shored up beneath the rift zones by thousands of thin, nearly vertical dikes of strong, dense basalt. Their bulk density, estimated from measurements of gravity across the Hawaiian Ridge (8) and in deep wells on the island of Hawaii, is no greater than 2.3 grams per cubic centimeter, significantly less than the density, about 2.8 grams per cubic centimeter, of an unvesiculated column of basaltic magma at depth.

To judge from the historic and geologically recent behavior of Mauna Loa and Kilauea, Hawaiian volcanoes grow almost to their full size quite rapidly. Intervals between eruptions are only a few years or decades, and the flanks of the volcanoes are blanketed by new flows so frequently that erosion makes little headway. The lavas forming these primitive shields belong to the "tholeiit-

Fig. 3. Makaopuhi viewed from the west. A prehistoric lava pond, in the distance, was exposed by a later collapse in the foreground. The small pond of lava at the bottom of the deeper pit, 900 feet below the present rim, was poured into Makaopuhi in 1922. [R. T. Haugen, National Park Service]

Fig. 4. Hilina Pali fault scarp. This scarp, 1500 feet high, has been almost completely mantled by recent prehistoric lava flows. View is toward the southwest.

ic" basalt series and differ primarily only in their content of olivine crystals. Although surging fountains of gas-inflated lava are often propelled hundreds of feet into the air by gas released from the lava as it approaches the surface within the vent fissure, these eruptions show little real explosivity and build only small cinder cones, spatter cones, and spatter ramparts around their vents.

After the volcanoes reach maturity the interval between eruptions increases, perhaps to a century or more, erosion begins to predominate over growth, and subtle changes appear in the chemistry and mineralogy of the lavas, which pass over into the alkalic basalt series. Eruptions become more explosive, building larger cinder cones around the vents.

Even after Hawaiian volcanoes are overcome by old age and are transfigured by profound erosion, occasional renewals of volcanism pour out additional lavas of the alkalic basalt series or even more highly differentiated lavas such as the felspathoid-bearing flows of Oahu and Kauai.

The outstanding questions of the origin of magma, the mechanism of eruption, and the differentiation of magma are strongly interdependent, and any answer proposed for one must be compatible with data for the others. The mechanism of eruption plays a central role. It must account for how and by what path magma is brought to the surface, why the volcanoes erupt intermittently, and how volcanic structures such as rift zones, pit craters, and calderas are produced, and it must provide the intratelluric environment necessary for the differentiation observed in the lavas.

Current Investigations

To extend the physical description of the volcanoes to depth and to obtain information on the active proc-

esses within them, the methods of geology must be supplemented by those of geophysics and geochemistry. During the last few years the staff of the U.S. Geological Survey Volcano Observatory in Hawaii has been augmented, and its facilities have been expanded and modernized to equip it for the necessary multidiscipline attack on the problems of Hawaiian volcanism.

A modernized seismograph network is giving us a better understanding of the internal structure of the volcanoes and is revealing some surprising evidence on processes within them. New instruments for measuring slight deformations of the earth's surface are providing information on the underground movement and accumulation of magma. Work at the Survey's recently constructed Geochemical Laboratory is helping to unravel the mysteries of origin, underground history, and petrographic variations of Hawaiian lavas through a systematic, detailed study of the chemistry and petrology of the lavas and of the chemistry of the gases given off by the volcanoes during and between eruptions.

Evidence from Geophysics

A variety of events within the volcanoes set up characteristic disturbances which are transmitted as elastic vibrations to the surface of the earth through the rocks composing the volcanoes and the crust and mantle of the earth beneath. These fleeting seismic pulsations carry vital information not only on the time, location, intensity, and nature of the events from which they spring, but also on the geologic structure and physical properties of the rocks through which they pass en route to the surface.

To capture these important data, a network of very sensitive seismographs is being developed in the Hawaiian Islands (Fig. 2). At the heart of the system four vertical-component seismometers, located in critical positions within a 15-kilometer radius of the observatory at the summit of Kilauea, transmit signals over telephone wires to the observatory, where four pens trace visible records of the motion of the ground at the seismometers. Seismographs in five other stations on the perimeter of the island of Hawaii provide critical additional data needed to locate earthquakes originating in and beneath the volcanoes, and seismographs in one station on Maui and one on Oahu extend the network to the distances required to permit the delineation of the structure of the crust under the Hawaiian Ridge.

Hawaii has earthquakes because it has volcanoes. In terms of numbers, practically all the earthquakes in the Hawaiian area occur in or beneath the active volcanoes and are intimately associated with eruptions. A significant few, however, including most of Hawaii's largest, originate on lateral faults at some distance from the calderas and rift zones that give rise to so many quakes during eruptions. Although some earthquakes along the lateral faults originate at depths as great as 30 kilometers, most of them are relatively shallow. They appear to mark gross readjustments in the rocky basement in response to the slow growth of the volcanoes and to the internal forces that build them.

Findings on the relation between travel time and distance for the strong seismic waves generated by large earthquakes on Hawaii and transmitted through the Hawaiian Ridge or refracted through the crust and mantle below to the most distant seismographs of the network are the data from which we can compute the "structure" of the earth beneath the volcanoes. Conventional interpretation of the travel-time curves indicates that there is a layered structure which represents a broad approximation of conditions along the Hawaiian Ridge. The implication of flat-lying, smooth contacts between discrete rock units should not be taken literally, especially for the portion of the structure lying above the level of the ocean floor surrounding the islands.

The near-surface speed of the longitudinal wave, P, is surprisingly low, only about 3 km/sec, and testifies to the loose, rubbly nature of the flows composing the shields. From a moderate depth below the surface (here taken as about sea level) to a depth of several kilometers below sea level, the speed of P is about 4 km/sec. Below a depth of 3 kilometers the speed of P jumps abruptly to about 5.25 km/sec. The travel-time curves suggest that the speed of P increases still more, perhaps by a slow transition rather than an abrupt increase, to about 6.8 km/sec in the crust above the mantle. At a depth of about 14 kilometers the speed of P jumps to 8.25 km/sec, marking the top of the earth's mantle at the Mohorovičić discontinuity. These data are plotted in Fig. 5 with those obtained by Raitt (9) from a seaborne seismic profile off the coast of Hawaii. Of special interest is the close correspondence in the depth to the Mohorovičić discontinuity beneath the ocean and beneath the Hawaiian Ridge. It appears that the crust under Hawaii has been only slightly depressed by the enormous volcanoes built upon it.

An accurate knowledge of just where earthquakes originate within the volcanoes is very important to our understanding of internal structure. Earthquakes do not occur at random but are concentrated in zones or along structures undergoing strain. Thus, from the earthquakes that occur beneath the Honuapo-Kaoiki fault system, which separates the southwest flank of Kilauea from Mauna Loa, we know that the system extends to a depth of at least 15 kilometers and

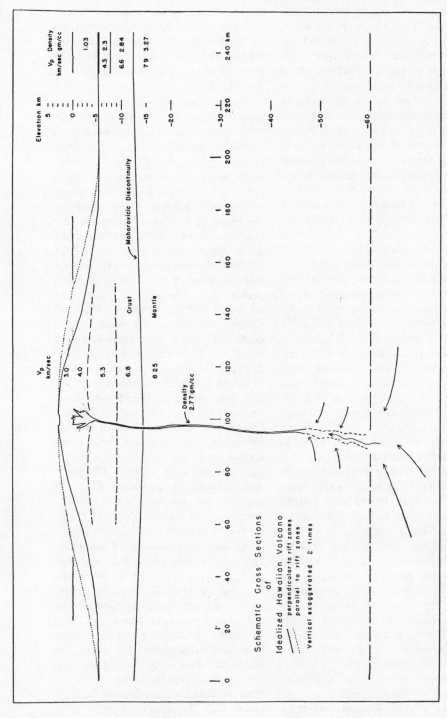

Fig. 5. Schematic cross sections of an idealized Hawaiian volcano. Magma from a source about 60 kilometers deep streams up through permanently open conduits and collects in a shallow reservoir beneath the caldera. Occasional discharge of lava from the shallow reservoir through dikes that split to the surface constitute eruptions. Note the elongation of the volcano along the rift zones and the relatively slight depression of the Mohorovičić discontinuity beneath the volcano. Data for the oceanic cross section on the right are from Raitt (9) and Worzel and Shurbet (13).

that it is still very active. Likewise, earthquakes originate from near the surface to depths as great as 30 kilometers along the Hilina fault system just south of Kilauea caldera, but farther east along this fault system earthquakes originating from depths greater than 10 kilometers are rare. Since about 1955, when a seismograph network capable of making reasonably accurate focal-point determinations was developed, the deepest earthquakes in the Hawaiian area have been recorded from a zone approaching a depth of 60 kilometers beneath the summit of Kilauea. In addition, thousands of quakes originate at shallow depths in the vicinity of Kilauea caldera when the volcano is swelling or shrinking in response to the movement of magma below. During the last two major eruptive cycles the east rift zone of Kilauea has produced only very shallow earthquakes, except very close to the caldera, and probably does not extend to a depth lower than the ocean floor.

Insight into processes at work in the volcanoes can also be gained from the nature, sequence, or association of disturbances recorded on the seismographs. Some of these disturbances are quite unearthquake-like and are apparently generated only by active volcanoes. When lava is pouring out at the surface during an eruption the entire region around the vent rocks gently to and fro as long as the vent is active. From seismographic evidence we know that this disturbance, called harmonic tremor from the sinusoidal nature of its seismic record, is generated near the earth's surface, probably by the rapid flow of magma through the feeding conduits. Because harmonic tremor rarely occurs when no eruption is in progress, its occurrence is excellent evidence that lava is streaming through conduits underground.

Great swarms of small earthquakes accompany several different processes in the volcano. Unlike a large tectonic earthquake and its aftershocks, where one large quake is followed by many smaller ones, the earthquakes in these swarms are uniformly small. The swarm usually begins slowly, rises to a maximum (in both average size and frequency of earthquakes), and then dies off slowly or abruptly, according to the nature of the process generating the earthquakes. Moderate swarms of tiny, sharp, highly localized earthquakes accompany the extension of dikes toward the surface before eruptions. Such swarms cease abruptly when lava pours out at the surface. More impressive swarms of larger, shallow quakes scattered through the summit of Kilauea attend the rapid subsidence of the caldera and its environs when lava drains out through the rift zone of the volcano during flank eruptions. These swarms begin and end gradually.

Occasionally great swarms of tiny-to-moderate, sharp earthquakes, totaling several thousand during the few days they last, emanate from depths between 45 and 60 kilometers beneath the summit of Kilauea. These are the deepest quakes that occur in Hawaii, and they bear no immediate, obvious relation to events closer to the surface. Usually they are accompanied by many hours of continuous, somewhat irregular tremor (spasmodic tremor) of weak-to-moderate intensity. The zone from which these disturbances stem is deep within the earth's mantle, three to four times deeper than the Mohorovičić discontinuity under Kilauea. Such activity appears to mark the zone from which magma is collected and fed into the system of conduits leading to the heart of Kilauea. If the magma rises from greater depths, this is at least the deepest zone in which its upward migration is marked by detectable seismic disturbances.

Whether Mauna Loa has a separate source of such activity beneath its summit we cannot yet say. No such source has been detected in the last five years, since sensitive seismographs have been in operation on Hawaii, but neither has Mauna Loa shown any sign of unrest during this interval.

Although seismic disturbances disclose what is happening within the volcano and when and where these changes are occurring, they tell us very little about the likelihood that a particular disturbance will culminate in an eruption. Geophysical measurements of another sort, the measurement of tilting of the ground surface around the summit of the volcano, provide more direct evidence on the readiness of the volcano to erupt. As lava wells up within the volcano the surface of the ground above bulges upward and the flanks of the bulge tilt outward, and when an eruption pours the lava out at the summit or on the flank of the volcano, the ground above the emptying reservoir subsides.

Before an eruption these changes are subtle and slow, and extreme care is required to detect them. Conventional tiltmeters are sufficiently sensitive, but they are so strongly influenced by accidental local vagaries of earth structure and weather that their records are unreliable. To provide high reliability as well as high sensitivity and to make it possible to set up many low-cost tilt-measuring stations, an unconventional tiltmeter employing permanent tilt bases and an ultrasensitive, portable, water-tube leveling system has been developed. Successive relevelings at a tilt base, which consists of three permanent piers set in the ground at the vertices of an equilateral triangle 50 meters on a side, can detect tilting of the earth's surface as slight as 1 millimeter in 5 kilometers (10).

Case History: Kilauea Eruption, 1959–60

Even while the water-tube leveling system was being refined and tested

between November 1957 and August 1958, preliminary readings on an experimental tilt base at Uwekahuna showed that the ground surface was tilting steadily outward from the caldera. By October 1958, measurements at additional tilt bases newly installed in a ring around the caldera revealed that the entire caldera rim was tilting outward. Analysis of tilting around the summit of Kilauea detected by the expanding network of tilt bases between October 1958 and February 1959 indicated that the entire summit region was swelling as magma slowly welled up from the depths and accumulated a few kilometers beneath the south rim of the caldera.

After the occurrence of several moderate earthquakes just southeast of the caldera on 19 February, the swelling stopped, and from May until August the summit of the volcano subsided slowly. Then a great swarm of deep earthquakes and associated tremor from a source about 55 kilometers deep and a few kilometers northeast of the Kilauea caldera kept Hawaiian seismographs in almost constant agitation between the 14th and 19th of August (Fig. 6). Magma moving into conduits beneath Kilauea during this episode made itself felt at the surface shortly, for rapid swelling of the volcano resumed between August and October (Fig. 7, inset A).

In its early stages, swelling of Kilauea took place with little or no seismic accompaniment. Lava rose from the depths and streamed slowly toward the shallow reservoir. At most, occasional intervals of weak harmonic tremor, originating perhaps 5 to 15 kilometers beneath the surface and lasting about half an hour, marked the lava's upward migration.

In the months preceding the 1959 outbreak of Kilauea there was no general increase in seismic activity, as there had been before the 1954 eruption. The first suspicious sign appeared during September 1959, when a series of very shallow, tiny earthquakes began recording on the North Pit seismograph on the northeast rim of Halemaumau. By the first of November, quakes of this swarm exceeded 1000 per day, but they were so small they barely were recorded on other seismographs only one mile away. A hurried remeasurement of tilting at bases around the caldera during the second week of November revealed that dramatic changes were in progress: the summit of Kilauea was swelling at least three times faster than during previous months (Fig. 7, inset *A*). In mid-afternoon on 14 November earthquakes emanating from the caldera suddenly increased about tenfold in number and intensity. At frequent intervals during the next 5 hours the entire summit region shuddered as earthquakes marked the rending of the crust by the eruptive fissure splitting toward the surface. Then, at 8:08 P.M., the lava broke through in a half-mile-

long fissure about half-way up the south wall of Kilauea Iki crater, just east of Kilauea caldera. Abruptly the swarm of earthquakes stopped, and seismographs around the caldera began to record the strong harmonic tremor characteristic of lava outpouring from Hawaiian volcanoes (Fig. 8).

During the next 24 hours the erupting fissure gradually shortened until only one fountain remained active. But then the rate of lava outpouring, which had decreased as the erupting fissure shortened, began to increase again, and it continued to increase steadily until the fountain died out suddenly on 21 November. The 40 million cubic yards of lava poured into Kilauea Iki crater filled it to a depth of 335 feet, slightly above the level of the vent.

Seismographs and tiltmeters warned that the eruption was not over. Feeble harmonic tremor that persisted after

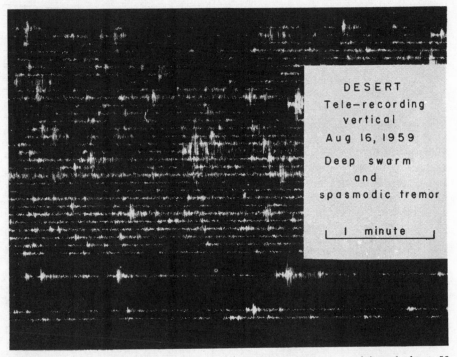

Fig. 6. A swarm of deep earthquakes and spasmodic tremor that originated about 55 kilometers beneath Kilauea caldera on 16 August 1959. Such activity appears to mark the movement of lava into the conduits beneath Kilauea. This seismogram was recorded on smoked paper at the observatory, 14 kilometers from the desert seismometer that detected these disturbances.

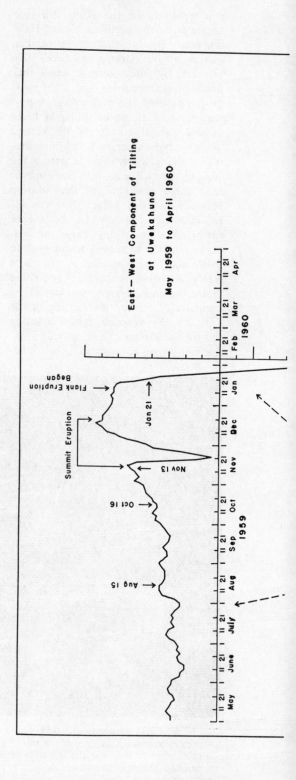

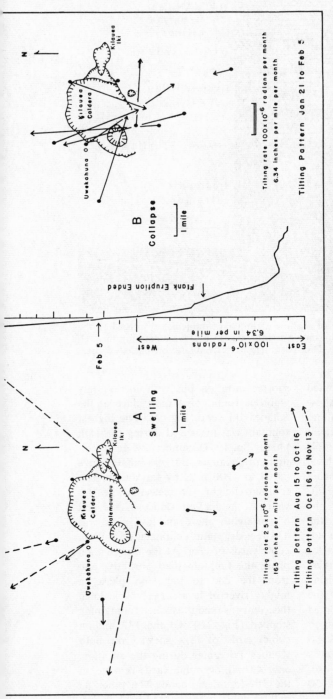

Fig. 7. Ground tilting at stations around Kilauea caldera associated with the 1959–1960 eruption. The east-west component of tilting at Uwekahuna shows the swelling and collapse of the summit of Kilauea as a function of time. Westward tilting (up) corresponds to swelling, and eastward tilting (down), to collapse. Inset *A* illustrates the pattern of tilting around the caldera during two periods of swelling. Inset *B* illustrates the pattern during collapse. Note the 40-fold difference in scale between *A* and *B*.

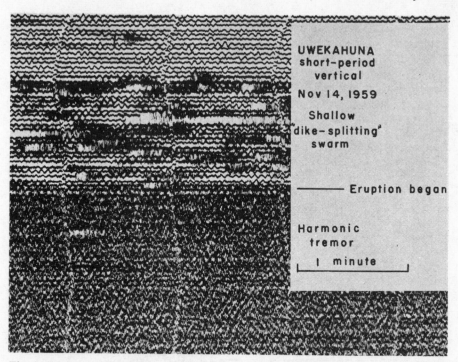

Fig. 8. Seismogram showing a swarm of shallow earthquakes immediately preceding the eruption in Kilauea Iki, followed by harmonic tremor caused by lava streaming through the erupting fissure near the surface. This seismogram is from a short-period vertical seismograph at Uwekahuna.

the fountain died was soon augmented by a growing swarm of tiny, shallow quakes such as preceded the eruption; and tiltmeters, which recorded a rapid deflation of the shallow lava reservoir while the fountain poured out its lava, revealed that the volcano was being inflated rapidly once more (Fig. 7). At 1:00 A.M. on 26 November the main vent of the first phase of the eruption revived. By 4:35 P.M. an additional 4.7 million cubic yards of lava had poured into the pond, increasing its depth to 350 feet and raising its surface high above the level of the original vent. Again the fountain died abruptly, and this time lava began to pour back down the vent. By 12:30 P.M. the next day 6 million cubic yards of lava had disappeared from the lake, leaving a black ring of frozen lava 30 feet above its receding surface.

During the following three weeks 14 more eruptive phases of shorter and shorter duration but with increasingly vigorous fountaining took place at the Kilauea Iki vent (Fig. 9). The highest fountain was measured during the 15th phase, on 19 December, when a column of incandescent, gas-inflated lava jetted to 1900 feet, by far the greatest fountain height yet measured in Hawaii. At its highest stand, at the end of the eighth phase, the lava pond was 414 feet deep and contained 58 million cubic yards of lava. At the end of each phase the fountain died abruptly, and from the 2nd to the 16th phase, a mighty river of lava surged back down the vent as soon as the fountaining stopped (Fig. 10). Of the 133 million cubic yards of lava spewed out into Kilauea Iki crater during the eruption, only 48 million cubic yards remains in the 367-foot-deep pond. The other 85 million cubic yards poured back underground almost as soon as it collected in the Kilauea Iki lava pond, where its volume could be so conveniently measured.

Tiltmeters around Kilauea caldera showed that the volcano was swelling rapidly as phase after phase of the eruption delivered its lava to the surface and then swallowed it up again. When surface activity ceased at Kilauea Iki on 21 December, far more lava was stored in the shallow reservoir beneath the caldera than when the eruption began (Fig. 7). It appeared that Kilauea was in an unstable state and that further activity was very likely.

During the last week of December a swarm of small earthquakes began to record on the seismograph at Pahoa. By means of a sensitive portable seismograph the source of these earthquakes was soon traced to the east rift zone of Kilauea, about 25 miles east of the caldera, near the site of the first outbreak of the 1955 eruption

(Fig. 2). The magma that inflated the summit region most probably exerted pressure on the plastic core of the rift zone, and earthquakes revealed where the rift zone yielded and where dikes began to extend toward the surface.

Early in January the frequency and size of earthquakes from the east rift zone increased, and the region from which they emanated moved on toward the sea. On 13 January the village of Kapoho was rocked by frequent, very shallow earthquakes, and by nightfall a graben 0.5 mile wide and 2 miles long that contained about half of the town had subsided several feet. At 7:30 P.M. the earthquake swarm gave way to harmonic tremor, and the flank eruption broke out along a fissure 0.75 mile long near the center of the subsiding graben, a few hundred yards north of Kapoho and nearly 30 miles east of the summit of Kilauea.

During the next five weeks nearly

Fig. 9. Five-hundred-foot lava fountain in Kilauea Iki crater at 7:00 A.M. on 5 December, 1959. Note the new cinder cone at left of the fountain and the lake of fresh lava 400 feet deep in the foreground. The west wall of Kilauea caldera and the southeast flank of Mauna Loa are in the background of the picture, which was taken with the camera facing west.

160 million cubic yards of lava poured out of the vent north of Kapoho and reshaped the topography of the eastern tip of Hawaii (Fig. 2). As the flow from the vent to the sea 2 miles away gradually built higher and higher, lava crowded out of the natural channel that initially confined it. Sluggish flows spread laterally from the main channel, destroying almost all of Kapoho, south of the vent, and most of the village of Koae, north of the vent. Dikes 15 to 20 feet high, built in a futile attempt to confine or divert flows that threatened a residential community along the seashore 2 miles southeast of Kapoho, were completely overwhelmed, and the lava moved on to destroy a portion of that community.

On 17 January, only four days after the flank eruption began, the summit of Kilauea began to subside precipitously as lava began to drain from beneath the caldera and to move through the rift zone toward the Kapoho vent (Fig. 7, inset *B*). By the end of January a

Fig. 10. A river of lava pouring back into the Kilauea Iki vent at 7:30 A.M. on 19 December 1959. The top of the cone is 400 feet higher than the vent. The picture was taken with the camera facing south.

UWEKAHUNA
short–period
vertical

Mar II, 1960

Shallow
summit collapse
swarm

⊢ I minute ⊣

Fig. 11. Seismogram showing a swarm of shallow earthquakes caused by rapid subsidence and deformation of the summit of Kilauea. This swarm lasted for several weeks. The seismogram was recorded on a short-period vertical seismograph at Uwekahuna.

strong swarm of shallow earthquakes was in progress at Kilauea caldera, where the brittle surface rocks were failing under the rapid and severe deformation caused by continuing subsidence (Fig. 11). On 7 February an unseen fissure broke through into the still liquid core of the 300-foot-deep pond of lava erupted into Halemaumau in 1952, and the floor of Halemaumau settled about 150 feet as the liquid beneath it drained away. A smaller area in the center of the floor dropped an additional 200 feet, but it was partially refilled by sluggish flows of viscous lava draining from under the subsiding crust of the pond around it.

By the first of April, when rapid subsidence and the swarm of earthquakes it caused had ceased, tiltmeters around the summit indicated that the ground surface above the shallow reservoir that was deflated during the flank eruption had sunk about 5 feet. The total volume of collapse at the

summit (the volume swept out by the surface of the volcano as its summit subsided), estimated from tiltmeter data, is close to the total volume of lava erupted at the surface.

Comparisons of temperatures and silica content of the lava erupted at Kilauea Iki and at Kapoho provide additional data on the underground history of Hawaiian lava. Temperatures measured in the core of the fountain at Kilauea Iki were consistently above 1120°C (measured with a hot-wire optical pyrometer and uncorrected for departure from black-body radiation). During a single phase of the eruption the temperature of the lava usually increased from about 1120°C near the beginning of the phase to about 1150°C near the end. The maximum temperature was measured during the fourth phase, when 1190°C was recorded. During early phases the silica content of the lava varied between 46.3 and 49.5 percent, but after the fourth phase it stabilized at about 46.8 percent. Petrographically the lava is a tholeiitic picrite basalt, consisting of olivine phenocrysts set in a fine-grained groundmass of plagioclase feldspar, pyroxene, and glass.

The lava erupted during the first two weeks of the flank eruption closely resembled the lava erupted in the same region in 1955. These lavas are tholeiitic basalts, poor in olivine but containing abundant phenocrysts of plagioclase feldspar and pyroxene. The silica content was about 50 percent, and the temperature was only 1050° to 1060°C, fully 100°C cooler than the lava at Kilauea Iki. After the second week the lava emerging from the Kapoho vent began to change; the silica content dropped, and the temperature increased. During the last week of voluminous lava eruption in February the temperature reached a maximum of 1130°C and the composition approached that of the lava erupted at Kilauea Iki.

It seems quite probable that the lava poured out during the first two weeks of the flank eruption had remained stored in the rift zone since at least 1955, if not since 1924, when lava drained from the summit into the east rift zone but failed to reach the surface. The chemical composition and mineralogy of this lava reveal a degree of differentiation that is unusual for Kilauea. The last lava erupted at Kapoho petrographically resembles Kilauea Iki lava, and it is entirely possible that magma moved from the summit reservoir, down through the rift zone, to the Kapoho vent during the course of the flank eruption.

Origin of the Magma

Although the geophysical evidence presented above permits us to trace the movement of magma through the volcano, it does not suggest why nor how magma enters the volcano at depth and rises through it to heights approaching 10 kilometers above the ocean floor to pour out at the surface. The "ascensive force of the lava," as it was called by Dana (*11*), was attributed by Daly (*12*) to the lower average density of the column of lava as compared to that of the crust of the earth above the zone in which the lava begins its journey to the surface. New information on the structure of the earth's crust beneath the Pacific basin requires that we revise the details of the model presented by Daly. We suggest that the crust here is much thinner than he believed it to be, and few geologists would now subscribe to the view that there is an eruptible basaltic glassy substratum underlying a crystalline crust. In principle, however, no better explanation of the ascensive force has been offered than that proposed by Daly.

If we assign densities to the molten lava column and to the various earth layers reported by Raitt for the Pacific basin in the Hawaiian region, we can compute the minimum depth at which lava can enter the volcanic system and be forced to the summits of the volcanoes. The densities given in Fig. 5 for the layers in Raitt's oceanic crust are those of the standard oceanic crustal gravity section adopted by Worzel and Shurbet (*13*). For the average density of the basaltic lava column we shall adopt Daly's estimate of 2.77 grams per cubic centimeter. Balancing the densities of the lava column and the crust, we find that to raise the lava z kilometers above sea level the lava column must extend at least to a depth x below sea level, where $x = 32.34 + 5.54\ z$ kilometers. Thus, to raise lava to the summit of Kilauea (1.2 kilometers), the lava column must extend to a depth of at least 39 kilometers below sea level; and to raise lava to the summit of Mauna Loa (4.2 kilometers), it must extend to a depth of at least 57 kilometers. These figures are in good agreement with the depth at which, according to the evidence of swarms of deep earthquakes and tremor, lava is fed into the Kilauea system.

Data from still another quarter, the study of surface waves of large earthquakes, throw additional light on the origin of Hawaiian lavas. Recent analyses of the dispersion of Rayleigh waves crossing the Pacific basin reveal that the rigidity of the mantle decreases somewhat at a depth of 60 kilometers (14). In view of the two other lines of evidence suggesting that Hawaiian magma originates at about this depth, it seems reasonable to conclude that the softening of the mantle at 60 kilometers is caused by partial melting of a peridotite mantle to yield an eruptible basaltic fraction. Perhaps, to go back to glassy substratum like that postulated by Daly but of higher density, the cooling and the consequent partial crystallization of a noneruptible, dense, glassy mantle drives off a lighter basaltic fraction that can be erupted to the surface.

Mechanism, Composition, and Kinetics of Eruption of the Lavas

Let us recapitulate the evidence on the mechanism of eruption presented above and examine, by following the magma on its course through the volcano, how that mechanism explains surface geologic features. When magma enters the deep conduit beneath Kilauea (a portion of the fundamental fracture beneath the Hawaiian Ridge that is currently active) it begins a slow ascent through the heated depths toward the cooler crust and volcanic pile above. The movement of magma into the conduit at depth is relatively slow and steady, being governed, perhaps, by the rate at which the magma can be separated from the mantle and funneled into the open conduit. After leaving the upper portion of the mantle and traversing the basaltic layer that floored the ancient ocean, the magma emerges into the lighter, weaker rocks composing the

volcanic pile and collects in a reservoir only a few kilometers beneath the surface. Upwelling of lava and consequent inflation of the high-level reservoir are slow processes that continue for months or even years prior to an eruption. Mounting pressure within the expanding reservoir finally drives the magma into dikes that split the frozen crust above the reservoir. When one of these dikes breaks through to the surface, an eruption ensues; the reservoir shrinks, and the pressure within it decreases as lava is discharged.

Basalt occupies a key position in modern theories of petrogenesis, and most, if not all, other kinds of igneous rocks are considered to have their ultimate origins in basaltic magmas. Thus, the chemical differentiation of basaltic magmas is a fundamental geochemical problem that has occupied the attention of many investigators throughout the world. Study of this differentiation in basaltic areas on the continents is complicated by the ever-present possibility that basaltic magmas may become contaminated by the diverse rocks that make up the crust of the continents. In the Hawaiian province, with its simple basaltic substratum, the possibility of such contamination is minimal, so magmatic differentiation may be investigated here with confidence.

Occasionally magma from the main reservoir is driven laterally into the mobile core of a rift zone, and failure of the confining rocks at some point along the rift results in a flank eruption, sometimes miles from the summit of the volcano. Discharge of lava at a low elevation along a rift zone can cause a much greater drop in reservoir pressure than can result from a summit eruption. The volume of flank eruptions and the consequent reservoir deflation and ground-surface subsidence are much larger than for summit eruptions.

Rift zones, like the central reservoir, appear to be relatively shallow structures. They are zones split by countless dikes seeking to discharge lava at a low elevation through a long channel that cuts the cold crust in competition with other dikes that provide shorter channels through the cold crust to higher elevations near the summit. Concentration of these dikes in a zone and the ultimate generation of a molten rift-zone core result from the tendency for each dike to heat the rocks around it and lessen the freezing effect of the cold crust on later dikes that follow nearby paths.

Rapid, severe deflation of the central reservoir or of its lateral protrusions into the rift-zone cores can lead to the collapse of the ground surface by withdrawal of support from below. This process, which is especially severe for flank eruptions far down the slopes of the volcano, seems to be responsible for the formation of pit craters and calderas.

The work of Cross (15), Washington (16), Macdonald (17), Wentworth and Winchell (18), and Powers (19), among others, has disclosed a wide range in chemical composition among Hawaiian basaltic lavas and has established the broad outline of genetic relationships among rocks of different composition. Analyses of typical examples of the different types of Hawaiian rocks are given in Table 1.

The division of basaltic rocks into a tholeiitic series and an alkalic series, first made for the basaltic rocks of Scotland by Bailey and others (20), is also useful in the study of the Hawaiian rocks, as was recently shown by Tilley (21). As emphasized by Macdonald (17), the fundamental primitive magma of Hawaii is tholeiitic olivine basalt (Table 1, sample A). Sample A closely approximates the average composition of tholeiitic lavas from the currently active mature volcanoes Kilauea and Mauna Loa, and this general type of lava makes up the great bulk of each of the Hawaiian Islands. Rocks of the alkalic basalt series are produced in

Table 1. Chemical composition of typical Hawaiian rocks (these compositions are plotted on Fig. 12).

Compound	Tholeiitic basalt series*				Alkalic basalt series[†]		
	A	B	C	D	E	F	G
SiO_2	50.94	50.08	46.59	62.23	50.09	62.19	43.28
Al_2O_3	12.97	13.73	6.69	12.03	19.49	17.43	14.43
Fe_2O_3	1.95	1.32	2.20	5.55	0.73	1.65	0.70
FeO	8.96	9.79	10.46	4.76	8.47	2.64	10.92
MgO	10.68	7.89	21.79	2.05	4.33	0.40	11.68
CaO	9.88	11.50	7.41	4.25	6.92	0.86	11.22
Na_2O	1.99	2.18	1.33	3.20	4.82	8.28	2.49
K_2O	0.37	0.56	0.28	1.36	1.93	5.03	0.83
H_2O^+	0.12	0.02	0.37	0.33	.32	0.39	0.05
H_2O^-	0.04	0.00	0.04	0.52	.08	0.14	0.03
TiO_2	1.78	2.60	1.83	2.18	2.47	0.37	4.12
P_2O_5	0.21	0.26	0.11	0.01	0.78	0.14	0.31
MnO	0.17	0.17	0.18	0 43	0.15	0.32	0.13
CO_2	0.04	0.01				0.02	
Cr_2O_3			0.13			tr.	0.10
NiO			0.12				
SO_3			0.00			0.00	0.20
Total	100.10	100.11	100.53	99.21[‡]	100.58	99.93[§]	100.54[‖]

*(A) Tholeiitic olivine basalt, Mauna Loa, at highway at south boundary of Waiakea Forest Reserve, 2.65 km northwest of the Olaa sugar mill, island of Hawaii. Analyst, L. N. Tarrant (31). (B) Tholeiitic basalt, Kilauea, splash from lava lake, 1917, island of Hawaii. Analyst, L. N. Tarrant. Reanalysis of a previously described sample. New analyses published with permission of H. A. Powers (19). (C) Mafitic gabbro porphyry, Kilauea, Uwekahuna laccolith in the wall of the caldera, island of Hawaii. Analyst, G. Steiger (32). (D) Granophyre, Koolau Volcano, quartz dolerite dike at Palolo quarry in the southeastern part of Honolulu, island of Oahu. Analyst, K. Nagashima (33). †(E) Hawaiite (andesine andesite), Mauna Kea, elevation 2700 feet, on northwest flank near Nohonaohae, island of Hawaii. Analyst, H. S. Washington (16). (F) Trachyte obsidian, Hualalai, Puu Waawaa, island of Hawaii. Analyst, W. F. Hillebrand (15). (G) Picritic alkalic basalt, Haleakala Volcano, lava flow of 1750(?) on the southwest slope near Makena, island of Maui. Analyst, M. G. Keyes (34). ‡Includes 0.31 SrO. §Includes 0.03 BaO and 0.04 ZrO₂. ‖Includes 0.05 BaO.

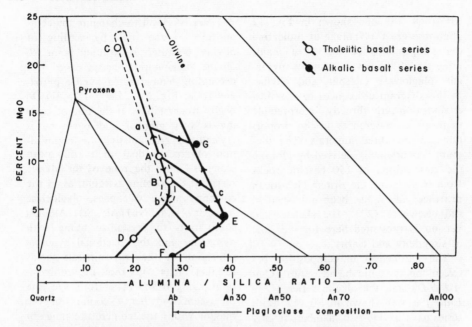

Fig. 12. Diagram showing interrelationships among typical Hawaiian volcanic rocks as manifested by their composition with respect to magnesia and alumina-silica ratio. Open circles, rocks of the tholeiitic basalt series listed in Table 1; solid circles, rocks of the alkalic basalt series. Tholeiitic olivine basalt (point A) is the primary magma of Hawaii; all other rock types are derived from it by fractional crystallization. The fractional crystallization of the different minerals and the resulting changes in the composition of tholeiitic and alkalic magmas are as follows: Olivine loss; A-B and c-E; olivine gain; A-C and c-G; pyroxene plus plagioclase loss; B-b-D and E-d-F; pyroxene loss; a-G, A-c, B-E, and b-d. The zone enclosed by a dashed line marks the range in composition found in tholeiitic lavas of the currently active volcanoes Kilauea and Mauna Loa.

lesser quantities in the declining stages of volcanic activity and, on the island of Hawaii, characteristically occur as mantles over the tholeiitic shields of the extinct or late-stage volcanoes Mauna Kea, Kohala, and Hualalai.

The analyses in Table 1 pose the fundamental geochemical problem of explaining the differentiation of primitive tholeiitic magma to produce the other types of rocks with such greatly different composition. An adequate theory must not only satisfy the chemical criteria but must also correlate existing information on the relative amounts of the different types of rocks, their sequence of eruption, the melting and reaction relationships among the constituent minerals, and the kinetics of ascent and cooling of molten magmas.

All investigators of Hawaiian basalts

since Cross (*15*) have emphasized the role of kinetics of eruption in controlling the extent and nature of differentiation of basaltic magma, but they have not agreed on the precise mechanism of control. Particularly, the mechanism of transition from tholeiitic to alkalic magmas during the life cycle of a volcano, has remained in doubt. Our studies suggest that the transition is mainly the result of progressively more favorable conditions becoming established for extensive fractional crystallization of pyroxene during the later stages of a volcano, when magmas rise and cool very slowly and eruptions become very infrequent. This dynamical-chemical relationship is here discussed briefly with the aid of Fig. 12.

Of the many different ways in which analyses of basaltic lavas may be plotted for study, the one shown in Fig. 12 offers the great advantage of indicating the compositions of the three major minerals of the lavas—namely, pyroxene, plagioclase feldspar, and olivine. In this diagram differences in chemical composition are directly interpretable in terms of differences in the proportions of the three minerals. The diagram was originally derived by plotting the composition of 150 basaltic rocks from Hawaii and the British Hebridean province, and it has been published in full elsewhere (22). The skeletonized version is presented here for the sake of simplicity and clarity.

The parallelism in composition between the tholeiitic basalt series (C-a-A-B-b-D) and the alkalic series (G-c-E-d-F) is well shown in Fig. 12. Both series have olivine-rich members (C-a-A and G-c) and a group of closely related differentiates with progressively increasing content of silica (B-b-D and E-d-F). In the tholeiitic series, this group includes rocks, such as granophyre (D), that are rich in quartz, whereas in the alkalic series even the most siliceous member (trachyte F) is free of quartz but is rich in alkalic feldspar.

Molten tholeiitic magma of composition A, rising toward the surface, cools and first precipitates olivine [(Mg, Fe)$_2$SiO$_4$] crystals, which grow rapidly in size to a diameter of several millimeters (23). Olivine, having a greater specific gravity, tends to sink in the molten magma. This simple act of separating the crystal from the melt in which it formed changes the composition of the melt along the line A to B, and the composition of the underlying magma that receives the settling olivines, along the line A to C. Thus originate two complementary types of lavas, tholeiitic basalt (B) which is poorer in olivine, and picritic basalt (C) which is richer in olivine, than the parent magma. It should be noted that a shift in composition anywhere in the diagram involves such a fractional crystallization of one or more minerals.

There is a limit to changing the composition of the melt by settling of olivine because, at around point B, olivine precipitation ceases, and with decreasing temperatures augitic pyroxene [(Ca, Mg, Fe^{2+}, Fe^{3+}) (Si, Al)$_2$O$_6$] begins to crystallize. If the rate of cooling is very gradual and pyroxene is crystallized fractionally, the composition of the residual melt will move along B-E into the zone of the alkalic series. If the cooling is rapid, as in the currently active volcanoes, plagioclase feldspar [(Ca, Na)(Al, Si) AlSi$_2$O$_8$] soon starts to crystallize along with pyroxene, and the fractional syncrystallization of the two minerals yields residual melts with tholeiitic compositions along B-b-D. Therefore, the rate of ascent and hence cooling of the magma within the temperature range of the initial crystallization of pyroxene is of utmost importance in the differentiation of basaltic magma.

The spectacular eruptions of Kilauea and Mauna Loa permit us to observe tholeiitic lavas in the making. As indicated in Fig. 12, however, only a part of the tholeiitic series is represented among the lavas of these two volcanoes. Compositions between b-D apparently require a somewhat slower regimen of cooling than that experienced by materials that reach the surface, and rocks with such compositions may be crystallizing at depth within the two volcanoes. In the deeply dissected Koolau Volcano on Oahu and in Tertiary volcanoes of the British Hebrides, such rocks are found characteristically as dikes, sills, and other intrusive bodies. The entire tholeiitic series of rocks, therefore, appears to be a product of conditions that prevail in basaltic volcanoes that erupt vigorously and frequently.

Kilauea and Mauna Loa erupt on the average every few years. The reduced vigor of volcanoes that have reached the stage of producing alkalic lavas is illustrated by Hualalai on the island of Hawaii and Haleakala on the island of

Maui. One hundred and sixty and about 210 years, respectively, have passed since these volcanoes last erupted (24). The more sluggish and halting ascent of the magma in such volcanoes allows the very slow cooling that is necessary for fractional crystallization of pyroxene.

The general derivation of alkalic magmas through fractional crystallization of pyroxene is shown in Fig. 12, starting from four illustrative points (a, A, B, and b) in the tholeiitic series. There are differences in the details of the fractional crystallization process along the four paths, but discussion of these differences will be deferred to a subsequent article. Within the alkalic series itself, the same fractional crystallization of olivine and of pyroxene and feldspar takes place as in the tholeiitic series and accounts for the parallelism in composition between the two series. In general, the olivine and pyroxene that are fractionally crystallized from the cooler alkalic magmas are richer in ferrous iron.

The world-wide problem of the origin of tholeiitic and alkalic basalts is being actively investigated by many petrologists, some of whom favor a separate derivation of the two compositional series from different depths in the mantle of the earth. Our studies suggest, rather, that the composition of basaltic rocks is primarily a function of the rate of ascent and cooling of a single fundamental magma. With the geological, geophysical, and geochemical techniques now available at the observatory located on an active volcano, it should be possible to obtain experimental verification of this interesting relationship between kinetics of eruption and composition of erupted lavas, at least within the tholeiitic basalt series.

Volcanic Gases

In Hawaii, volcanic gases are manifested most spectacularly during an eruption in the effervescing fire fountains, which squirt a pulsating stream of molten lava up to heights of a thousand feet and more. In other volcanic regions, such as Indonesia (25), they give rise to more explosive and deadly phenomena like *nuée ardente* eruptions. A typical composition (in volume percent) of Hawaiian magmatic gases, as established through the work of Shepherd (26), Jaggar (27), and Naughton and Terada (28), is as follows: H_2O, 79.31; CO_2, 11.61; SO_2, 6.48; N_2, 1.29; H_2, 0.58; CO, 0.37; S_2, 0.24; Cl_2, 0.05; A, 0.04. The proportions of the constituents vary over a certain range, and Ellis (29) has shown that the variations are largely accountable in terms of shifts in gas equilibria with changing temperature. The role of gases in controlling the state of oxidation of the magma requires thorough investigation (30).

Volcanic gases, in whole or in part, represent primordial materials reaching the surface of the earth for the first time. Thus, over the span of geological time the accumulation of such gases from innumerable eruptions determined the evolutionary course of our atmosphere and hydrosphere. The new Geochemical Laboratory is equipped with a mass spectrometer for rapid analysis of gases, and a program of systematically analyzing all volcanic exhalations has been started.

Summary

Hawaiian volcanoes offer an unmatched opportunity for studying the mechanism of eruptions and the differentiation of primitive tholeiitic basaltic magma. They are located near the center of the Pacific basin, more than 2000 miles from the nearest region of active tectonism, and the story of their origin and continuing activity is one of pure volcanism. Because their lavas experience a minimal exposure to contamination by heterogeneous crustal rocks as they rise to the surface, fractional crystallization plays the dominant role in producing changes in the chemical composition of the lavas extruded at different stages in the life cycle of the volcanoes.

The enormous size, relatively simple structure, and frequent voluminous eruptions of Hawaiian volcanoes all permit the effective use of seismographs and tiltmeters in delineating their internal structure and in detecting the movement and accumulation of magma within them. Other more general geophysical investigations of the Pacific crust and the mantle below provide additional evidence on where Hawaiian magma originates and how it is driven to the surface.

The ultimate cause of volcanism is the fundamental instability of the crust and upper mantle of the earth. About 60 kilometers beneath the Pacific the rocks of the mantle yield a fluid fraction with the composition of tholeiitic basalt. The density of this basaltic magma fraction is less than the average density of the 50 kilometers of mantle (peridotite?), 5 kilometers of basaltic crust, and 5 kilometers of water that lie above it, and if the opportunity arises it can be squeezed to the surface by the weight of the material above. The fundamental fracture beneath the Hawaiian Ridge has tapped this source of magma and provides the avenue through which it can escape to the surface.

Lava rising through the fundamental fracture beneath Kilauea accumulates slowly in a shallow reservoir only a few kilometers beneath the caldera. At irregular intervals dikes project upward from the expanding reservoir, and if the expansion and consequent pressure within the reservoir are great enough, the dikes break through to the surface and discharge the accumulated lava in an eruption.

Geochemical studies show that while the volcanoes are vigorously active, the most striking variation in their lavas is the content of olivine. Rapid delivery of magma to the surface permits only slight cooling underground, and the only mineral that iš fractionally crystallized in significant amounts is olivine, which is depleted from some flows and concentrated in others. When activity declines and magma wells up from depth much less rapidly, it remains in the shallow reservoirs for increasingly longer periods of time. Here the magma cools so slowly through the temperature range in which pyroxene crystallizes that this mineral, as well as the early-formed olivine, settles out of the melt and is immobilized on the floor of the reservoir. Such separation of pyroxene "desilicates" the tholeiitic parent magma and changes its composition to that of alkalic basalt, the predominant lava of the declining stage of Hawaiian volcanism. The temperature, composition, and rate of ascent of the basaltic magma to the surface, therefore, are closely interrelated, and the study of the complex interrelationships of these geophysical and geochemical factors constitutes the fascinating work of observing how volcanoes grow.

References and Notes

1. H. Williams, *Quart. J. Geol. Soc. London* **109**, 311 (1954).
2. W. Ellis, *Journal of William Ellis, A Narrative of a Tour Through Hawaii in 1823* (Hawaiian Gazette Co., Honolulu, new ed., 1917).
3. Founded, and initially financed, jointly by the Massachusetts Institute of Technology and The Hawaiian Volcano Research Association, the Hawaiian Volcano Observatory was transferred to the U.S. Government in 1917. Since 1948 it has been operated by The U.S. Geological Survey with the encouragement and support of The National Park Service. Publication of this article is authorized by the director of The U.S. Geological Survey.
4. T. A. Jaggar, *Bull. Seismol. Soc. Am.* **10**, 155 (1920).
5. H. T. Stearns and G. A. Macdonald, *Hawaii Div. Hydrog. Bull. 9* (1946).
6. E. L. Hamilton, *Bull. Geol. Soc. Am.* **68**, 1011 (1957).
7. W. T. Brigham, *B. P. Bishop Museum Mem.* **2**, No. 4, 379 (1909).
8. G. P. Woollard, *Trans. Am. Geophys. Union* **32**, 358 (1951).
9. R. W. Raitt, *Bull. Geol. Soc. Am.* **67**, 1623 (1956).
10. J. P. Eaton, *Bull. Seismol. Soc. Am.* **49**, 301 (1959).
11. J. D. Dana, *Characteristics of Volcanoes* (Dodd, Mead, New York, 1890).

12. R. A. Daly, *Igneous Rocks and the Depths of the Earth* (McGraw-Hill, New York, 1933).
13. J. W. Worzel and G. L. Shurbet, "Gravity Interpretations from Standard Oceanic and Continental Crustal Sections," *Geol. Soc. Am. Spec. Papers No. 62* (1955), pp. 87–100.
14. J. Dorman, M. Ewing, J. Oliver, *Bull. Seismol. Soc. Am.* **50**, 87 (1960).
15. W. Cross, "Lavas of Hawaii and their Relations," *U.S. Geol. Survey Profess. Papers No. 88* (1915).
16. H. S. Washington, *Am. J. Sci.* **6**, 339 (1923).
17. G. A. Macdonald, "Petrography of the Island of Hawaii," *U.S. Geol. Survey Profess. Papers No. 214D* (1949).
18. C. K. Wentworth and H. Winchell, *Bull. Geol. Soc. Am.* **58**, 49 (1947).
19. H. A. Powers, *Geochim. et Cosmochim. Acta* **7**, 77 (1955).
20. E. B. Bailey *et al.*, "Tertiary and Post-Tertiary Geology of Mull, Loch Aline, and Oban," *Mem. Geol. Survey, Scotland* (1924).
21. C. E. Tilley, *Quart. J. Geol. Soc. London* **106**, 37 (1950).
22. K. J. Murata, *Am. J. Sci.* **258-A**, 247 (1960).
23. H. I. Drever and R. Johnston, *Trans. Roy. Soc. Edinburgh* **63**, 289 (1957).
24. G. A. Macdonald, *Catalogue of the Active Volcanoes of the World Including Solfatara Fields*: pt. 3, *Hawaiian Islands* (International Volcanological Association, Naples, 1955).
25. R. W. Van Bemmelen, *The Geology of Indonesia*: vol. 1A, *General Geology* (Government Printing Office, The Hague, Netherlands, 1949).
26. E. S. Shepherd, *Am. J. Sci.* **35-A**, 311 (1938).
27. T. A. Jaggar, *ibid.* **238**, 313 (1940).
28. J. J. Naughton and K. Terada, *Science* **120**, 580 (1954).
29. A. J. Ellis, *Am. J. Sci.* **255**, 416 (1957).
30. F. E. Osborn, *ibid.* **257**, 609 (1959).
31. G. A. Macdonald and J. P. Eaton, *U.S. Geol. Survey Bull. No. 1021-D* (1955), p. 127.
32. R. A. Daly, *J. Geol.* **19**, 289 (1911).
33. H. Kuno, K. Yamasaki, C. Iida, K. Nagashima, *Japan. J. Geol. and Geography, Trans.* **28**, 179 (1957).
34. H. S. Washington and M. G. Keyes, *Am. J. Sci.* **15**, 199 (1928).

Reef Building

The growth of living breakwaters has kept pace with subsidence and wave erosion for fifty million years.

Harry S. Ladd

Whether one first sees a reef from the sea or from the air, one cannot but be impressed, not so much by the beauty of the curious structure as by its ability to withstand the force of the waves that ceaselessly break upon its seaward edge. It has been estimated that normal waves dissipate 500,000 horsepower—one-fourth the power generated at Boulder Dam—against the windward side of an open sea atoll (*1*). How can lowly plants and animals build a structure to withstand such forces? Actually, the forces of storm waves are many times as great, and though the reefs are damaged by storms, they do survive. Furthermore, as has been demonstrated, some of them have survived for as long as 50 million years. These structures are truly worthy of an engineer's respect.

Since the earliest days of navigation, mariners have known reefs at first hand and have feared their power to break up ships. The venturesome Lieutenant (later Captain) James Cook was wrecked on the Great Barrier Reef in 1770 and had to careen the *Endeavour* for extensive repairs before continuing his first globe-encircling voyage (*2*). Captain Henry Wilson, whose ship the *Antelope* was wrecked on a reef in Palau in 1783, was less fortunate. He and his crew had to build a new ship before proceeding homeward (*3*). Another famous explorer, La Pérouse, like his contemporary Captain Cook, was making a scientific expedition around the world when both of his frigates, the *Astrolabe* and the *Boussole*, were lost, in 1788, on the dangerous outer reefs of Vanikoro in the Santa Cruz Islands (*4*).

The Christian missionaries, who closely followed these early Pacific explorers, also had their difficulties in navigating under sail. The missionary ship *Duff*, in the midst of a lengthy voyage among the islands of the southwest Pacific, struck a reef in the little-known waters of eastern Fiji. She struck at night but managed to back off, leaving nothing to the reef but her name (*5*). The mission schooner *Harrier* was not so fortunate on the Great Barrier Reef (Fig. 1).

In 1890 there was a disastrous wreck on a reef in Torres Strait, near Thursday Island. The British India liner *Quetta*, of 3484 tons, bound from Brisbane to London with 293 persons aboard, was passing through Adolphus Channel, a reef area believed to have been adequately charted. Steaming through calm waters on a bright moonlight night she struck a flourishing coral pinnacle rising from 13 fathoms and sank within three minutes, with a loss of 133 lives. Sixteen years later divers blasted a porthole from the sunken ship's side, which had been thickly overgrown with coral. The charts available to the *Quetta* in 1890 were based on surveys made between 1802 and 1860, and it is possible, although not probable, that the pinnacle that ripped open two-thirds of the ship's bottom had

The author is affiliated with the U.S. Geological Survey, Washington, D.C., in the Branch of Paleontology and Stratigraphy

Reprinted from *Science* 134(3481): 703–715 (15 September 1961), by permission of the author and *Science*. Copyright 1961 by the American Association for the Advancement of Science.

Fig. 1. Wreck of the New Guinea mission schooner *Harrier* on the Great Barrier Reef of Australia. [Courtesy W. H. Allen and Co., Ltd.]

grown sufficiently in the years that followed the surveys to become a menace to navigation after the charts were made (6). Atlantic reefs also have taken their toll (Fig. 2).

Storms, inadequate charting, poor night visibility, and faulty navigation have all played parts in driving ships onto reefs, but one large modern tanker lies rusting on a Pacific atoll for a different reason. During World War II she entered the deep narrow pass leading to a lagoon where much of the U.S. Fleet was stationed. The tanker was loaded with fuel for the fleet but had not been given proper identification signals, and those in charge of security were loath to clear her. She was ordered to turn back, even though this was obviously impossible in the narrow reef pass. To this day the reef organisms near the site of the wreck have not fully recovered from the oil bath that followed.

Reefs, however, are constructive as well as destructive. Some of the finest tropical harbors are protected by natural breakwaters in the form of reefs (Fig. 3). In Ceylon attempts are now being made to stimulate and control coral growth in binding artificial breakwaters (7).

Reef lagoons and atoll islands were used as stepping-stones and way stations by early Polynesian voyagers, who eventually sailed their outrigger canoes all the way from Indonesia to the high volcanic islands of Hawaii. Trading vessels of all sorts found safe anchorage in lagoons in the years that followed. During the Pacific campaign of World War II, protective reefs played a most important role in island defense.

Appearance of a Reef

What does a reef look like? At high tide nothing may be visible but a line of white breakers, possibly with a band of green water behind it. At low tide, in areas where tides have a range of several feet, the broad reef flat may be awash or actually out of water, revealed as a brown band. Part of the surface may be a smooth sand flat on which one

Fig. 2. Wreck on Andros Island reef, in the Bahamas. [Fritz Goro, *Life*]

Fig. 3. The reef-protected harbor of Suva, Fiji. The entrance is through Levu passage, which breaks the barrier on the left. [Rob Wright, Fiji official photograph]

could ride a bicycle, and I have seen planed rock pavements so smooth that one could—though I have never tried! —go about on roller skates. More often, tide pools, microatolls, and areas of short-branched or knobby coral heads make up parts of the surface. Water-filled pools help give a deceptive appearance of levelness.

The Builders

All wave-breaking reefs in the tropical seas are commonly called coral reefs, though both biologists and geologists have known for more than 50 years that on many reefs the calcareous algae are the essential, and in some places the most abundant, contributors. The corals exhibit greater variation in form and color than do the lime-secreting algae, and this diversity is doubtless responsible for the ease with which they won first place in the eyes of early observers (Fig. 4). The tips of many graceful staghorn corals are brilliant blue or violet; other palmate corals are bright pink or claret, yellow, green, or brown; most massive hemispherical colonies are more drab, but in some each corallite of the honeycomb surface contains a central "eye" of fluorescent green. When the colonies are intermingled in a pool or are cemented at various angles on the wall of a reef channel the effect is striking, to say the least.

Algae, on the other hand, are mostly shades of brown, yellow, or purple, and a single type of uniform shape and color will dominate a given area of a reef. Along the seaward edge the buttresses between channels may be covered almost entirely by pink or purplish globular colonies, and the result, though colorful, is unvaried; the encrusting type of algae may form a flattish pavement uniformly brown or yellowish-brown in color.

These two groups—the corals and the algae—are the important reef builders. The corals add bulk, the algae function as cementing agents. Among numerous minor contributors are the Foraminifera, both encrusting and benthonic types. The latter, though small individually, live in such abundance on reef flats that their shells, carried shoreward by the waves, form the bulk of the sands of the beaches that fringe reef-encircled islands.

Occurring widely, but in lesser abundance, are many other invertebrates —echinoids (sea urchins), mollusks, and tube-secreting worms. These minor groups may also function as agents of reef destruction. Locally, certain types of boring echinoids occur in tremendous numbers and may literally riddle a rock pavement solidly built by corals and algae. Several types of worms and clams bore into coral heads, both living and dead. When broken open, many corals are seen to be pierced by holes and to resemble a Swiss cheese. Other destructive borers include algae, sponges, and barnacles.

Wave-Resisting Features

The amounts of calcium carbonate taken from sea water to build a reef are impressive. At Eniwetok Atoll, for example, the limestone mass (reef complex) that caps the volcanic foundation contains more than 250 cubic miles of limestone; practically all the limestone was secreted by shallow-water organisms. The most noteworthy feature, however, is not the volume but the fact that parts of the mass of skeletal material are so constructed or so cemented that the reef can grow upward to low-tide level and maintain itself against wave attack. How is this accomplished?

Three distinct elements or processes are involved: (i) the growth forms of the builders, which enable them to construct an efficient baffle that, in addition to bringing a constant supply of refreshing sea water to all parts of the organisms, robs the incoming waves of much of their force by spreading the water in all directions; (ii) cementation by the organisms to the foundation on which they grow and to each other; (iii) lithification of sediments, probably an inorganic process, which takes place beneath reef flats and at intertidal levels on shore. The first two processes are well understood, the third is not.

Growth forms. The algae and corals that flourish along the margin of a reef exhibit two dominant growth forms. Some grow as thin veneers that do not break the force of the waves but do function efficiently as cementing agents. Others build spongelike structures that are so porous or intricately branched that the force of the oncoming wave is diverted and spread widely in many directions. The surface densely covered by such colonies acts like blotting paper.

The baffle effect, efficiently performed by the individual colonies along the margin, is repeated on a larger scale by major reef structures developed in the same area. The grooves and buttresses of the "toothed edge" (Fig. 5) concentrate the power of the oncoming waves

into trenches, some of which lead through the marginal zone as surge channels below the reef surface (8). The lower part of each wave attempts to enter caverns below the reef surface. The resistance encountered in these already filled chambers absorbs some of the waves' power; another part is absorbed by spouting, geyserlike blow holes and by thousands of tiny holes in the pavement behind the marginal ridge. With each incoming wave water oozes upward through this sievelike pavement. The caverns beneath the reef margin have not been studied in detail, but enough is known to justify comparison with the well-known "room-and-pillar" caverns of mining operations.

Organic cementation. Encrusting calcareous algae (*Porolithon* and other lithothamnia) function effectively as enveloping lamellar growths that bind loose fragments to the growing reef edge, and they may even smother colonies of living coral. These organisms flourish in a constant supply of moving water, and they form a fairly solid pavement on the back slope of the marginal

Fig. 4. Rich growth of corals exposed at low tide on Crescent Reef, Great Barrier, Australia. [W. Saville Kent, courtesy W. H. Allen and Co., Ltd.]

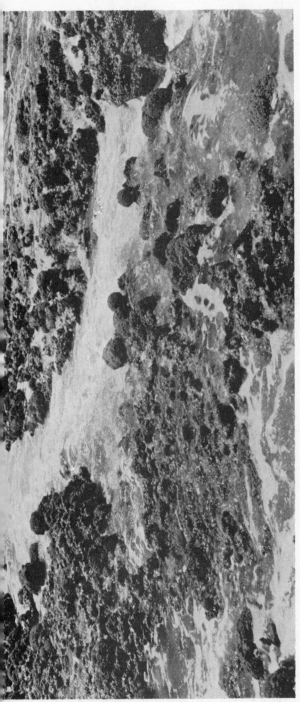

Fig. 5. Measuring depth in the surge channel through the algal ridge of the Bikini reef. [Fritz Goro, *Life*]

ridge, where weakened surges pass landward and where other water wells upward through the porous reef structure. Many of the corals along the reef edge also adopt the veneering habit, forming a living calcareous blanket that, when opportunity permits, may extend itself over areas of living algae. I have measured single colonies of veneering coral that extend for 30 feet along the reef margin.

Lithification. From the standpoint of reef stability and the development of wave-resisting qualities the reef margin is the crucial area. In this area organic binding seems to be the important process, but in other parts of the reef—on the wide flats behind the margin and even on the beaches—other processes of cementation occur. These bind the sediments of the flat and the sands of the beaches into fairly hard rock. The processes are probably chemical, in large part.

Current Problems

Much of the present-day interest in reefs began shortly after Pearl Harbor, when we lost Guam, Wake, and the Philippines. We planned to recapture these reef-encircled islands and to occupy many others captured or long held by the Japanese. This planning, and our early attacks such as that at Tarawa, revealed how little we knew about reefs and the waters surging over them. Special reports summarizing all available information, hastily prepared for the Armed Services, were of some assistance, but it was not until after the war that intensive field investigations of reefs and reef islands were undertaken as part of military terrain studies. These studies, supported by the Army and carried out by U.S. Geological Survey personnel, coupled with the intensive reef studies made at Bikini and nearby atolls in the Marshall Islands, supported by the Armed Forces and the U.S. Atomic Energy Commission, have given us the sort of reef information that we lacked during the Pacific campaign of World War II.

Somewhat earlier—in the late 'twenties and 'thirties—oil was discovered in large quantities in certain ancient reefs. These discoveries continued after the war (9) and greatly stimulated reef work in general. A third factor that dates from the war years is the increase in activity in the fields of oceanography and marine geology.

Seaward Margin of the Reef

The most vital part of a reef is the marginal zone along the windward side. This is the zone where living organisms are concentrated, and it is the site of the most persistent wave attack. The remainder of the reef is largely dependent upon this zone, which is the place where building must take place if the reef is to flourish and expand. An understanding of growth processes in the windward marginal zone is an essential part of the story of reef building. Ironically, this is the zone least accessible to direct observation. Problems and questions still remain to be solved and answered.

The zone of marginal growth, as here defined, consists of three distinct parts. The first is a ridge of living algae that rises above the reef flat and may be widely exposed at times of low tide. It is cut at fairly regular intervals by surge channels (Fig. 5). The next is a zone below low tide on the seaward slope, which consists of deep grooves separated by wide buttresses. This is the "toothed edge" so clearly visible from the air (Fig. 6). The lower part, at least, is a zone of rich coral growth, possibly the richest of all, that extends downward to the ends of the longest grooves at about 50 feet below sea level. This zone is so inaccessible that it has been dubbed the *mare incognitum.* A third zone, in the moderately illuminated waters below normal wave base, at depths of 50 to 150 feet, is a zone where corals of a somewhat different type grow in abundance, but it has been only superficially explored by dredging (*10*).

The submarine "toothed edges" of most windward reefs have been described from many areas. The patterns, so sharply marked on air photographs, have been observed somewhat more closely by swimmers. As yet, however, because of hazardous sea conditions, no one has succeeded in making a detailed examination at close range. Most workers, I among them, have regarded the groove-and-buttress system as primarily constructional, the buttresses being due to organic growth. Others believe that

the grooves have been excavated by erosion and that growth is a relatively unimportant factor (*11*). The work being done by Thomas Goreau on the reefs of Jamaica supports the belief that the buttresses are constructional and is impressively documented (Fig. 7) (*12*). Newell *et al.* (*13*) described and illustrated closely spaced furrows or grooves from the Bahamas. As these are cut in oölitic country rock they certainly were *not* formed by growth. They may be due to erosion, as Newell and his associates suggest, but conceivably they could have been formed by solution when the sea stood lower. In any event, they do not closely resemble the typical

Fig. 6. Buttresses and grooves of the toothed edge of a windward reef, Bikini Atoll. The buttresses rise from a submarine terrace about 20 feet below the surface. [R. Dana Russell, air photograph from about 500 feet]

Fig. 7. Diver inspecting the under side of a flow-sheet of the coral *Monastrea annularis*, growing on the forward edge of the buttress on a reef near Boscobel, Jamaica. Depth, about 30 feet; the buttress terminates at 60 feet. [Thomas Goreau]

grooves found off existing reefs in the Pacific. Cloud noted what appeared to be similar grooves in the face of a basalt-floored bench in Hawaii (14) but stated that he had not studied them. If the typical grooves are primarily erosional it is remarkable that they are well-nigh universal off windward reefs yet rare in other types of rock. It seems to me quite possible that improved diving techniques will eventually settle this most interesting problem.

SCUBA diving by reef students may also permit a closer examination of the growth zone immediately below the *"mare incognitum."*

Rate of Growth and Other Problems

Direct examination of exposed sections of elevated reefs and examination of samples obtained by drilling have shown that corals and other builders have persisted for long periods of time, long even when reckoned geologically. The calcareous skeletons left by one generation are superimposed on the skeletons of earlier generations, eventually accumulating thick deposits of limestone. The rate at which this rock-building takes place is of prime interest, and numerous attempts to measure it have been, and are being, made. The bulky skeletons of sessile corals lend themselves to measurement, though, as Vaughan pointed out, they are not ideal subjects (15). Vaughan made thousands of measurements of growth on 25 species, both naturally growing and artificially cemented to terra cotta or concrete disks fixed to iron stakes driven into the sea bottom. Mayor (16) measured the growth of corals in Samoa; Edmondson (17) did so in Hawaii. The late T. A. Stephenson and his wife Anne carried out well-organized and exceedingly valuable growth studies of several sorts on the Great Barrier Reef (18). One of the corals measured by the Stephensons is shown in Fig. 8. A number of fine

studies of coral growth have also been made by the Japanese (19).

In 1960 J. Edward Hoffmeister began a long-term study of the Florida reef tract. His project includes growth experiments on reef corals similar to those mentioned above. Hoffmeister planted his first corals on the edge of the reef near Key Largo, an area lying between Dry Tortugas and the Bahamas where Vaughan made earlier studies. In addition to measuring growth rates on corals in their chosen environment Hoffmeister is transferring colonies from one environment to another to determine the effects of such changes.

The growth rate of individual colonies of coral is, of course, only an in-

Fig. 8. Growth of coral planted on the Great Barrier Reef. This specimen (*Acropora quelchi*) increased 57 and 78 percent, respectively, on the greater and lesser diameters in a period of 187 days. White squares represent square centimeters. [T. A. Stephenson, courtesy Anne Stephenson and the British Museum (Natural History)]

direct measure of the growth rate of the reef surface. Estimates of the percentage of the reef surface covered by various species have to be made, and several types of losses have to be estimated and deducted. An over-all figure for reef growth, based on coral measurement, is probably less than 14 millimeters per year. This figure is comparable to estimates based on the measurements of organic productivity by Sargent and Austin (20) and by H. T. Odum and E. P. Odum (21).

The plant and animal communities that live on reef surfaces have long excited the interest of marine biologists, as attested by a voluminous literature. Several thousand organisms that live on reefs have been named and described, and much attention has been given to the life habits of the builders and of the organisms whose activities destroy reef rock. These studies have been carried on, and are being carried on, at biological laboratories established in reef areas and by special expeditions sent out to study reef problems. Examples are the comprehensive work done by (i) the British on the Great Barrier Reef of Australia, particularly the work of the expedition of 1928–29 under the leadership of C. M. Yonge (22); (ii) the laboratory maintained by the Japanese in Palau for 10 years; (iii) the laboratories of the University of Hawaii; and (iv) the Carnegie Laboratory that operated for many years at Dry Tortugas and in nearby areas (activities in these areas have now been taken over by the University of Miami in Florida and the Lerner Laboratory at Bimini in the Bahamas). Institutions such as the Bishop Museum of Honolulu have supported many expeditions studying reefs in various parts of the Pacific, and the Pacific Science Board has sponsored many special atoll studies.

Studies of organic productivity, mentioned in connection with reef growth, have led to interesting conclusions about reef builders. Sargent and Austin (20) found the rate of productivity to be higher on areas of the reef than in the surrounding waters of the open sea, and concluded that reefs are self-maintaining structures. The Odums discovered that the average coral colony contained three times as much plant as animal tissue, most of the plant material being filamentous green algae in the coral skeleton. They concluded that the reef they studied represented a true ecological climax or open steady-state system (21). Hedgpeth expressed skepticism, suggesting that the experiments be repeated several times at different seasons to test some of the assumptions on which measurements were made (23).

Among many other biological problems directly connected with reef builders are those involving the production of skeletal calcium carbonate by the corals with the aid of symbiotic algae (zooxanthellae) (24).

Reef Blocks

On the surface of many reef flats, blocks of reef rock occur near the seaward margin. They range in size from coral boulders a foot or more across to massive blocks 20 or 30 feet long. The largest block noted during the Marshall Islands investigations was estimated at 200 tons. The block shown in Fig. 9 was estimated at 150 tons. Some earlier workers interpreted large reef blocks as outliers or remnants of former reefs or islands. Indeed, it is difficult to determine the origin of some large blocks because the actual contact with the reef surface may be obscured by solution pits or overgrown by encrusting organisms. Some of the largest blocks may be remnants of an older reef, but there is now general agreement that most reef blocks are plucked from the reef edge or from the reef flat by storm waves.

The mechanics involved in moving the largest blocks are hard to understand, but the winds and waves that accompany hurricanes, typhoons, and tsunamis could move enormous masses if they were to strike an overhanging reef edge partially exposed at low tide (25). On 14 September 1953 there was a severe earthquake in Fiji. According to reports, the barrier reef on the eastern side of Suva harbor was raised about one foot, and large blocks of rock were thrown upon the reef by the tidal wave that followed the quake (26). In some areas reef blocks seem to follow a definite pattern, but the reasons for this are not clearly understood (27), and additional surveys would be welcome.

Landslides

In considering problems connected with the surfaces of reefs, the slopes below the sea, which control the outline of the reef at the surface, raise some interesting questions. Atolls tend to be circular, but many of the larger ones depart widely from this plan. They may show broad bights that are concave relative to the sea. Such indentations

in the reef margin are well developed at Bikini Atoll, and submarine surveys there show that they continue to great depths. Fairbridge has suggested (28) that these are landslide scars, but those who charted the atoll (27) believe it more likely that the spurs and intervening bights reflect the original irregular shape of the flat-topped seamount on which the atoll was built. Drilling has shown that much of the reef complex of Bikini is unconsolidated, but there is believed to be a marginal wall of consolidated rock that would prevent large-scale slides. This question may eventually be resolved by additional drilling to more firmly establish the existence of the postulated marginal wall.

Passes

Most atoll and barrier reefs are broken by passes, some deep, others shallow. These have not received as much study as the more accessible reefs that border them, but enough has been done on passes through atolls to indi-

Fig. 9. Reef block on a reef off Enirik Island, Bikini Atoll. [J. I. Tracey, Jr., U.S. Geological Survey]

cate that they probably record important steps in the Pleistocene history of reef building.

Each of the several large atolls studied in the northern Marshall Islands is cut by a single deep pass that is approximately as deep as the deeper parts of the lagoon behind it. Shallower passes through the reef are only as deep as the terrace that is well developed in the lagoon and on the seaward side of the reef. The deeper parts of the lagoon floor and the deep passes are thought to have been developed during the Pleistocene when, periodically, sea level stood several hundred feet lower than it does now. During the warmer interglacial stages of the Pleistocene, reefs developed on the prepared surface, growing upward more rapidly around the margins than elsewhere. This reef is thought to have flourished over the wide area now covered by the shallow terraces inside and outside the lagoon. The present reef is thought to have grown up during the postglacial rise of sea level, the shallow passes representing areas where for various reasons, possibly largely ecologic, the new reef did not flourish. This explanation, involving ideas suggested by Daly (29) and Kuenen (30), was given strong support by the detailed surveys of lagoons and passes made in the Marshall Islands (27). Its soundness should be tested by similar detailed surveys in other areas.

The lagoons of barrier reefs and the passes that connect them with the open sea are much less well known than comparable structures of atolls. The depths of some passes through barrier reefs exceed 100 fathoms. This is a promising field for future studies.

Beach Rock

Hard layers of calcareous sandstone and conglomerate occur on parts of many beaches behind fringing and offshore reefs. The layers, in most places, dip toward the sea or lagoon at angles of 8 to 10 degrees. The rock is especially well indurated on exposed surfaces, becoming more crumbly below. Beach rock is characteristically an intertidal deposit and, at best, the layers are but a few feet thick. Drilling on atoll islands shows that the layers are almost invariably present at intertidal levels (31). The beach-rock layers are wave-resistant and on many reef islands form the nearest approach to a persistent layer of hard rock.

The process of cementation, in many areas, seems definitely to be occurring at the present time. In the Marshall Islands, for example, a piece of a Japanese glass fishing float was discovered by J. I. Tracey firmly cemented in beach rock (27). Many explanations for the formation of beach rock have been suggested. They involve evaporation of interstitial water and cementation by certain types of algae, by bacteria, and so on, but none is satisfactory as a general explanation. Emery and Cox (32) thought that detailed mapping of the occurrences might show significant relationships to the abundance and composition of ground water or to other factors of shore environment. They mapped widely scattered occurrences in Hawaii but were unable to give a satisfactory explanation. Richard Russell and his associates have recently completed an extended investigation of occurrences in the Caribbean area, with results as inconclusive as those of Emery and Cox in Hawaii (33).

Intertidal Erosion

The layers of beach rock that occur on many of the beaches behind reefs are subject to chemical erosion. Contiguous pits and basins are developed on exposed bedding surfaces, being especially numerous in the seaward half of the beach-rock belt. They are highly irregular, being often separated from each other only by knife-edge ridges. These depressions obviously are formed by solution, as are the deep nips that are invariably present on all limestone shores in the tropics at about high-tide level. This type of solution is limited to intertidal levels where marked diurnal changes take place, yet the process is difficult to understand because normal surface sea water is known to be supersaturated with calcium carbonate. Revelle and Emery have suggested a hypothesis involving slow complexing or slow hydration and dehydration (34).

All reef investigators agree that some solution takes place at intertidal levels in reef areas, but since the process is not well understood, there is considerable disagreement as to its effectiveness. Revelle and Emery stated that the very existence of the broad and dead reef flat just below low-tide level indicated the efficacy of such solution, and they pointed out that it is as effective in sheltered lagoons as on exposed shores.

Much evidence indicating widespread reef planation—by solution, or waves, or a combination of the two—has been reported from the Pacific islands. For example; on the reef flats of Okinawa, MacNeil (35) found blocks of an older limestone (late Tertiary or early Pleistocene), weighing many tons, perched on pedestals of reef limestone 5 to 6 feet high at appreciable distances from the shore. The limestone blocks, broken from shore cliffs, appeared to have crept, slid, or rolled over underlying clays until they came to rest on a reef flat that stood 5 to 6 feet higher than it does now. Since that time they have been isolated by erosion that has planed 5 to 6 feet from the rest of the reef flat.

Recently, Norman Newell has questioned interpretations such as those given above. His investigations in the western Atlantic led him to believe that sea level is now at its highest position since the close of the Pleistocene and that intertidal erosion at this level has been negligible. He suggested that the elevated terraces in the Pacific may be of Pleistocene age (36). His conclusions involve a number of assumptions, and it can hardly be said that they invalidate the evidence for rapid intertidal erosion in the Pacific. Additional determinations of ages obtained from radiocarbon and other measurements from widely scattered areas may eventually resolve some of the differences of interpretation.

Origin of Reef Islands

The small low islands of sand and coarser debris that are found on many reefs, particularly on atolls, may be related to the postulated recent negative shift in the strand line of about 6 feet. Such a eustatic shift would stimulate erosion of any reefs that had grown to a higher level, resulting in masses of reef debris above the new (lower) sea level. Wave action is now shifting these masses slowly across the reef flat, and many are being reduced in size by wave activity. Evidence for this is seen in lines of truncated beach rock beyond the limits of the existing islands.

The Reef Complex

In 1950 Henson suggested the term *reef complex* for the aggregate of reef limestones and calcareous rocks associated with them (37). It is a useful term that includes the surface reefs, all outer reef structures, and the deposits that underlie the flat and the lagoon. The sediments making up the complex may be several thousand feet thick, with bulk ten times that of the controlling reef frame.

Charles Darwin was the first to think seriously about the thickness of reefs. His brilliant deductive theorizing on the nature of reef building was done before he had had an opportunity to see a true reef. He was, however, familiar with the effects of elevation of the land and with denudation and the deposition of sediment. Mentally substituting subsidence for elevation, and coral growth in shallow water for sediment deposition, he reasoned that the three main types of reef—the fringing reef along the shore, the barrier separated from the shore by a lagoon, and the atoll without a central island—might be genetically related and controlled by slow subsidence. Thus, with upward and outward growth on a sinking island, a fringing reef could become a barrier, and the barrier, in turn, an atoll. He recognized, however, that an atoll could be developed directly from a shallow-water bank without passing through the intermediate barrier stage (38).

It is difficult to generalize on the relative importance of vertical as compared with horizontal growth. In the Pacific, where atolls abound, it appears that many have grown upward on truncated platforms without ever being fringing reefs or barriers. Vertical growth in some areas amounts to several thousands of feet. If the submarine buttresses that fringe many atolls are growth forms, they are growing laterally as well as vertically, and in turn, the marginal zone of the surface reef is growing laterally over the buttress area.

Charles Darwin was the first of several students of coral formations to refer to them picturesquely as monuments or tombstones over subsiding land. W. M. Davis, who saw reefs only as physiographic features, referred to the low-lying atolls as "inscrutable." The core drill established the aptness of Darwin's simile and the ineptness of Davis's adjective. Along with its cores and cuttings, however, the drill brought up problems not envisaged by either Darwin or Davis. Some of these still await a satisfactory solution.

The drill holes put down by the British on Funafuti Atoll in the Ellice Islands penetrated 1114 feet of Quaternary reef limestone, and below about 750 feet the rock was heavily dolomitized (39). The hole drilled by the Japanese on Kita-daito-shima ended in Miocene ["Oligocene"] beds at 1416 feet, the upper levels being dolomitized (40). The deepest hole on Bikini (Fig. 10) went 2556 feet into Miocene, with no trace of dolomite. On Eniwetok the drills went beyond 4000 feet to a basaltic foundation below upper Eocene limestones. One hole showed a little dolomite in the Eocene rocks, the other showed much more, also in the Eocene; there was a trace of dolomite in the Miocene rocks but none in the younger beds (31). S. O. Schlanger, of the U.S. Geological Survey (41), concluded that the island dolomites were formed in several ways. Others who are studying the Pacific island dolomites include Donald Graf of the Illinois Geological Survey, Julian Goldsmith of the University of Chicago, R. G. C. Bathurst of Liverpool, England, and a group from the Shell Development Company of Houston, headed by F. J. Lucia. When all these workers have reported, we shall, no doubt, know much more about the origin of dolomite. At the present time the problem of atoll dolomites is far from complete solution. The situation has not been simplified by the discovery of dolomite in Miocene ooze below 11,700 feet of water off the coast of Mexico in the preliminary Mohole drilling project.

Drilling of the "inscrutable atolls" has brought forth other interesting complications. The over-all history, as postulated by Darwin, has been one of submergence. In parts of the Pacific the submergence started at least as far back as the Eocene, and during the intervening 50 million years there have been several subintervals of considerable length when the tops of the atolls stood hundreds of feet above the sea. Eniwetok Atoll was a high island and bore a high-island fauna and flora— not once but several times. Drill samples from Eniwetok Atoll have yielded land shells of a type that lives on high islands rather than on atolls. There also are rich concentrations of spores and pollens that record the existence on the

Fig. 10. Deep drilling on the lagoon shore of Bikini Island. [U.S. Navy]

emerged atoll of a tropical deciduous forest (*42*). This paleontological evidence is supported by petrologic evidence. J. I. Tracey of the U.S. Geological Survey, who made a detailed petrologic study of the Bikini cores and cuttings, recognized a · recrystallized (calcite) zone in the Miocene at a depth of more than 1000 feet, overlain by beds containing unaltered (aragonitic) shells and skeletons (*27*). As the upper layers of ocean waters are saturated with calcium carbonate, Tracey con-

cluded that the leaching and recrystallization took place during a period of emergence. Schlanger, who studied the petrology of Eniwetok samples, found zones of leaching and recrystallization similar to those of Bikini. He has called them "solution unconformities" (*41*).

Reef Foundations

With the drilling of one reef (Eniwetok) to its volcanic foundation (Fig.

11) we have obtained a fairly good picture of how that particular reef was started, and we know the length of its life. Its base was laid in late Eocene time on the tops of truncated volcanoes two miles above the floor of the deep ocean. We are probably justified in extending the Eniwetok findings to other atolls in the Marshall Islands and, perhaps, to other atolls in the Pacific Basin proper. When, however, we consider atolls outside the basin we are less sure of our ground. When, for example, we cross the andesite line that separates the Pacific Basin from Melanesia, we enter a province where uplift, rather than subsidence, appears to have been the dominant geologic process in post-Tertiary times.

There are many barrier reefs and some atolls in Melanesia, and along with them are elevated Tertiary and younger reefs as much as 1000 feet above sea level. The Mbukatatanoa (Argo) reefs in eastern Fiji, for example,

form an atoll comparable in size to the larger atolls of the Pacific Basin, though somewhat more irregular in outline. The nature of the foundation upon which it grows and the thickness of the reef are not known, as neither drilling nor seismic investigations have ever been made there. The numerous barrier reefs in the same area have been examined in a few places. They lie off islands on which Tertiary and younger limestones are exposed above volcanics, but we have no definite idea of the nature of the foundation of the existing reefs or of the thickness of the structures.

Several submerged banks that may represent "drowned" reefs have been examined. One of these, Alexa Bank, in Fiji, measures 5 by 10 miles and has a raised rim and other features which suggest that it may once have been an atoll. A seismic survey indicated a depth of calcareous material of several thousand feet, comparable to that found

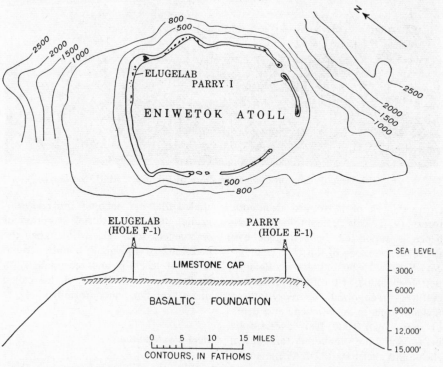

Fig. 11. Generalized chart and section of Eniwetok Atoll. [Contours from a chart prepared by K. O. Emery, 1954; after Ladd and Schlanger, 1960]

at Bikini and Eniwetok atolls. The bank is assumed to have a volcanic foundation (*43*).

In the Indian Ocean, where atolls also occur, we know practically nothing about the nature of the reef foundations.

Links to Other Sciences

The building of reefs is primarily a biological process, but geological processes such as erosion and sedimentation enter as soon as the first reef organism is damaged by wave attack. Thereafter, reef building is a combination of organic and inorganic growth. Ultimately the effects spread to many other scientific fields.

Oceanography. Oceanography is concerned primarily with the chemistry of ocean waters and with their movements. In a broader sense it includes studies of bottom topography and many aspects of marine biology. On this latter basis, reef building is not only *linked* to oceanography—it is an integral part of it. I shall not attempt to discuss this broader relationship but shall cite a specific example in which the growth of reefs has, in an important way, directly affected strictly oceanographic processes.

The 50 atolls and small coral islands that form the Marshall and Gilbert island chain are spread across some 800 miles of ocean. The chain stands athwart the Equatorial Current system, and small and insignificant as the reefs are at the surface, they cause large-scale eddies in the North Equatorial Current, the Equatorial Countercurrent, and, possibly, the South Equatorial Current (*44*). Acting with surprising effectiveness as a topographic barrier, the scattered atolls affect the circulation, the temperature, and the salinity of an enormous area of deep ocean.

Geomorphology. Existing reefs and reefs of the past are specialized land forms and have always had a strong appeal for the physiographer or geomorphologist. Recently emerged reefs, whether fringing, barrier, or atoll, retain their characteristic form for appreciable lengths of time, and a close study of the limestones of which they are composed will, in many instances, support the reef interpretation. Limestone masses of other types that have been elevated for long periods of time may, through the vagaries of atmospheric solution, assume a reeflike shape that may lead to the erroneous interpretation that they are reefs. All elevated limestone masses in the tropics tend eventually to assume a basin shape that strongly suggests that of an atoll, yet the mass may be composed of bedded limestones that accumulated below wave base. It is not safe, therefore, to assume, as some physiographers have done, that all basin-shaped islands were once atolls. Submerged banks and terraces may also represent old reefs, but none of these have been examined with sufficient thoroughness to establish their origin beyond question.

In the tropics all limestone masses that rise above the sea bear a nip or notch, whose center lies at about high-tide level. On most limestone islands there are remnants of what appears to be an older nip, whose center lies about 6 feet above present high-tide level. The prevalence of such an older nip in widely separated parts of the Pacific has led many workers to conclude that it records a time when the sea stood 6 feet higher than it does now. Attempts to date the beginning of the 6-foot fall by radiocarbon analyses have been, and are being, made. Cloud, after reviewing all types of evidence, suggested that the shift began 3000 (± 1500) years ago (*45*).

It should be pointed out that in the Pacific there is at least one area without an older 6-foot nip. Every one of the numerous limestone islands of Palau in the western Pacific shows a well-developed nip at existing high-tide level, but no trace of an older, elevated nip has been found. Wave erosion is known to be a factor in nip formation, but the controlling factor seems to be intertidal solution. In Palau, where rainfall is heavy and vegetation is dense—to yield necessary carbonic acid—it may be that solution proceeds faster than it does elsewhere. Conceivably, it may have proceeded so rapidly that all traces of an earlier nip have been destroyed.

Elevated and submerged reefs preserve evidence that points clearly to shifts in the strand line. In many instances this evidence seems to be tied to local elevation or submergence of the island or continental coast near which the features appear. Islands separated by several hundreds of miles may exhibit elevated strand-line features or buried zones of leached limestone that can be correlated, suggesting that the changes in land and sea were essentially uniform throughout an entire island group. Attempts have been made to extend correlations of this sort beyond single groups; indeed, such correlations have been stretched one-third of the way around the world—from the southwest Pacific through Hawaii to the eastern shores of North America (46). Those who support such interpretations postulate eustatic (worldwide) changes of sea level. The changes, however, imply a stability of the lands that is hard to accept because in many areas, including many island areas, there have been uplifts and submergences in fairly recent geologic time. In parts of the southwest Pacific, islands separated by only a few miles preserve old strand lines at different levels, and in other places the lines on opposite sides of a single island cannot be correlated, as the island has been tilted during elevation.

Attempts to correlate emerged and submerged strand lines over wide areas will doubtless continue, for they offer fascinating fields for speculation. As isotopic methods for dating limestones are improved it may be possible to establish some correlations more accurately

and, perhaps, to come to some measure of agreement about eustatic shifts of sea level in late geologic time.

Petroleum geology. Structures having many of the characteristics of existing reefs have long been recognized in our older fossiliferous rocks, including those of the Paleozoic. Some geologists and biologists were loath to make direct comparisons between ancient and existing reefs because present-day reef builders did not exist in Paleozoic time. As early as 1911, however, Vaughan summarized available evidence and concluded that Paleozoic reefs were formed under conditions (depth, temperature, water circulation, type of bottom, composition, and specific gravity of oceanic waters) essentially similar to those of today (47). This interpretation took on great practical significance when rich deposits of oil were found by drilling ancient reefs.

As early as 1927 it was recognized that the Permian Capitan limestone of west Texas and southeast New Mexico had many of the characteristics of a reef (48), and in 1929 it was so described (49). This interpretation has since been documented by intensive studies (50). This ancient reef, which became a leading producer in the "Reef fields," compares favorably in size with the largest of existing reefs, as it is several miles wide, hundreds of miles long, and thousands of feet thick.

Similar discoveries in other widely scattered areas have demonstrated that ancient reefs form excellent reservoir rocks. In 1947, for example, the first wells were drilled into a Devonian dolomitized reef in Alberta, Canada. This became the highly productive Leduc field (Fig. 12) (51). With the help of the drill, geologists have learned more about ancient reef builders, about the regional relations of buried reef masses, and about the diagenetic changes (consolidation, cementation, dolomitization, and so on) that have taken place in the original reef rock. Needless to say, both geologists and geochemists have been

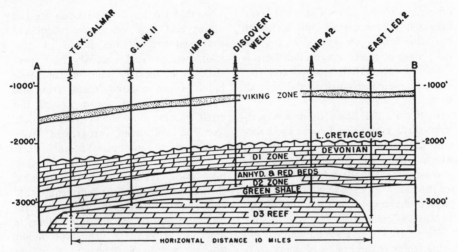

Fig. 12. Northeast-southwest section across the Leduc field. The vertical scale is exaggerated 20 times. [After Waring and Layer, 1950]

aided in their investigations by studies of existing reefs.

Sedimentation. Reefs and their associated lagoons form nearly ideal sites for the study of many sedimentary processes. The lagoon of an atoll may be regarded as a large but fairly well controlled laboratory specializing in locally derived calcareous sediments. No foreign material enters the circuit except for minute pelagic organisms that come in over the windward reef, accompanied, on rare occasions, by pieces of pumice that have floated in from an up-wind volcano. The encircling reef effectively controls the waves and swells of the open sea, though a typhoon or hurricane may, on occasion, interrupt the established routine. Most reef lagoons lie in the trade-wind belt, and for nine months each year the winds blow fairly steadily from one direction. This may lead to the establishment of a primary circulation (overturning wind-driven circulation) and a secondary circulation (rotary circulation composed of two counter-rotating compartments) (*52*). Waters from the open sea feed this system over the windward reefs, and a comparable amount of water escapes through leeward passes and over the leeward reef.

The absence of terrigenous sediment on an atoll reduces the operation of many sedimentary processes to their simplest terms. There are no clay minerals, and much of the clay-size carbonate, apparently, is carried out of the lagoon. Most of the material accumulated in the lagoon is coarse clastic sediment. All deposition is in fairly shallow waters, and definite patterns can be recognized and mapped (see *27* and *53*).

Structural geology and geophysics. As mentioned in the section on geomorphology, both elevated and submerged reefs preserve evidence that points clearly to shifts in the strand line. In areas where the shift appears to have been regional, the reef evidence may give valuable support to theories involving major earth structures. In the western Pacific, for example, beyond the andesite line that separates the Pacific Basin proper from the continental area, many of the numerous islands are arranged in arcs that are convex with respect to the basin. Most of these arcs have deep trenches along their convex fronts, and there is much evidence from the study of seismology, volcanology, and earth gravity to indicate that these are active areas of orogenic deformation. There are considerable differences of opinion as to how the forces are acting and about the timing of major events, but there is agreement on certain aspects, and reef studies have contributed to the over-all study.

In the Pacific Basin there are scattered surface atolls and submerged flat-topped seamounts (guyots), both of which indicate submergence. The guyots now lie several thousand feet below the sea surface, yet dredging on them has yielded shallow-water organisms as old as Middle Cretaceous (54).

Biogeography. As already noted, existing reefs are the homes of many sorts of plant and animal communities. No other environment in the sea supports such a variety and abundance of life. Scattered as they are over an area of more than 50 million square miles, reefs offer unrivaled opportunities for the study of geographic distribution and the relations of organisms to each other. The faunas and floras of ancient reefs are as yet comparatively little known, but the field holds much promise, and studies of older reefs should add greatly to our understanding of present geographic patterns.

As an example, I should like to cite a proposal for which definite plans are now being considered. The plan calls for the drilling and sampling of a deep hole on Midway Island in the Hawaiian Islands—a hole that would penetrate the sediments beneath the existing reef and reach the basaltic foundation. The importance of Midway becomes clear if we briefly review the known and the assumed history of the Hawaiian Islands.

The surface geology of the Hawaiian Islands—located in the center of the world's largest ocean—has been worked out in considerable detail (55). The chain stretches for 1600 miles from northwest to southeast. The exposed rocks are almost entirely volcanic, the oldest probably being late Tertiary in age. Geologists have long favored the

view that the northwest islands are the oldest and that volcanism progressed southeastward to the island of Hawaii, where such activity still persists. It is thought that the outpouring of lavas to build islands from the floor of the deep sea depressed the crust, causing slow submergence which, like the volcanism, progressed from northwest to southeast. Islands, such as Midway, on the northwest, are now coral reefs, and a considerable thickness of calcareous sediments probably lies beneath them. If several thousand feet of fossiliferous sediments underlie Midway, a drill hole might disclose a history dating back to the Cretaceous or even earlier. Before attempting the expensive process of drilling it would be well to check the thickness of the sedimentary cap with a seismic refraction survey. Plans for such a survey are being formulated, and it is hoped that drilling will follow.

If such a drill hole can demonstrate and document an appreciably longer geological history for Hawaii than is indicated by its youthful surface rocks, it would offer a reasonable solution for one long-standing biogeographical problem and might throw considerable light on another.

1) If it can be shown that the Hawaiian Islands date back as far as the Cretaceous, and if it is assumed that they were built up slowly—flow by flow—as they are being enlarged today, it will appear that there may have been some land in existence during all post-Cretaceous time. In that case, the land plants and the land invertebrates (land shells), which show a high percentage of endemism and have long been recognized as ancient stocks, would always have had a home of sorts. There would be no conflict between biological and geological evidence.

2) If the marine invertebrates obtained from such a drill hole are comparable in diversity and abundance with the faunas obtained from similar drill holes in the Marshall Islands, this

would lend support to the suggestion that many elements of the Indo-Pacific fauna (now widely thought to have migrated *from* Indonesia) actually originated in the mid-Pacific and migrated, with the help of favorable winds and currents, *toward* Indonesia (*56, 57*).

References and Notes

1. W. Munk and M. Sargent, *U.S. Geol. Survey Profess. Papers No. 260-C* (1954).
2. J. Gwyther, *Captain Cook and the South Pacific* (Houghton Mifflin, Boston, 1954).
3. G. Keats, *An Account of the Pelew Islands* (Luke White, Dublin, 1793).
4. R. Discombe and P. Anthonioz, *Pacific Discovery* 3, No. 1 (1960).
5. J. Wilson, *A Missionary Voyage . . . in the Ship Duff* (Chapman, London, 1799).
6. W. Saville Kent, *Proc. Roy. Soc. Queensland* 42 (1891); *The Great Barrier Reef of Australia* (Allen, London, 1893).
7. J. W. Wells, written communication (1961).
8. Munk and Sargent (*1*) estimated that 95 percent of the incoming wave was dissipated by friction, largely within the surge channels; the other 5 percent was converted to potential energy to maintain a water level at the outer edge of the reef.
9. T. Link, *Bull. Geol. Soc. Am.* 60, 381 (1949).
10. J. Wells, *Geol. Soc. Am. Mem. No. 67* (1957), vol. 1.
11. P. E. Cloud, Jr., after studying the reef off Saipan and in other parts of the Pacific, favored erosion as the more important factor but admitted that in some areas growth might be a controlling factor [*U.S. Geol. Survey Profess. Papers No. 280-K* (1959)].
12. T. Goreau, *Ecology* 50, No. 1 (1959).
13. N. D. Newell, J. K. Rigby, A. J. Whiteman, J. S. Bradley, *Bull. Am. Museum Nat. Hist.* 97 (1951).
14. P. E. Cloud, Jr., *Atoll Research Bull. No. 12* (1952), p. 43.
15. "The proportion of living tissues to the stony skeleton is relatively small, and as the skeleton after very young stages usually is not entirely covered by the living soft parts, other organisms may attach themselves to the previously formed skeleton, and increase its weight, or boring organisms may enter the skeleton, begin its destruction, and decrease its weight. As many boring organisms have calcareous tests, they destroy a part of the original skeleton and add the weight of their own. Minute algae . . . bore into the skeleton and ramify through it almost or quite to the boundary of the living soft parts" [T. W. Vaughan, *Carnegie Inst. Wash. Yearbook, 1915* (1916)].
16. A. G. Mayor, *Carnegie Inst. Wash. Publ., Dept. Marine Biol. No. 19* (1924), pp. 51–72.
17. C. H. Edmondson, *Bishop Museum Bull. No. 58* (1929).
18. T. A. Stephenson and A. Stephenson, *Sci. Repts. Great Barrier Reef Expedition* (1933), vol. 3, No. 7.
19. T. Tamura and Y. Hada, *Sci. Rept. Tôhoku Imperial Univ.* (1932), vol. 7, No. 4, pp. 433–455; S. Motada, *Palao Trop. Biol. Studies* 2, 1 (1940); S. Kawaguti, *ibid.* 2, 309 (1941).
20. M. Sargent and T. Austin, *U.S. Geol. Survey Profess. Papers No. 260-E* (1954).
21. H. T. Odum and E. P. Odum, *Ecol. Monographs* 25, 291 (1955).
22. C. M. Yonge, *A Year on the Great Barrier Reef* (Putnam, London, 1930).
23. J. Hedgpeth, *Geol. Soc. Am. Mem. No. 67* (1957), pp. 39–40.
24. T. Goreau summarized some of the problems of growth and calcium carbonate deposition in reef corals in an article beautifully illustrated in color. Goreau described an isotope-tracer technique in which radioactive calcium-45 is used. He found that corals are unable to distinguish between stable and radioactive varieties of calcium. His method proved so sensitive that growth could be measured in specimens exposed to calcium-45 for only a few hours [*Endeavour* 20, 32 (1961)].
25. Examples of the ability of storm waves to damage the reef edge were observed along the southern side of Bikini atoll. In this area, in addition to reef blocks on the surface, there are sharp re-entrants in the overhanging reef margin. The largest of these is more than 500 feet wide and extends into the reef as much as 200 feet. The collapsed sections now rest on a shallow terrace, and their outlines match the re-entrants above.
26. *Pacific Islands Monthly* 24, No. 3, 31 (1953). John W. Wells examined these blocks when he visited the site in 1954.
27. K. O. Emery, J. I. Tracey, Jr., H. S. Ladd, *U.S. Geol. Survey Profess. Papers No. 260-A* (1954).
28. R. W. Fairbridge, *Geograph. J.* 115, 84 (1950).
29. R. A. Daly, *Am. J. Sci.* 30, 297 (1910).
30. P. H. Kuenen, *Marine Geology* (Wiley, New York, 1950).
31. H. Ladd and S. Schlanger, *U.S. Geol. Survey Profess. Papers No. 260-Y* (1960).
32. K. O. Emery and D. C. Cox, *Pacific Sci.* 10, 382 (1956).
33. R. Russell, "Prelim. notes on Caribbean beach rock," *Louisiana State Univ. Coastal Studies Institute Publ.* (1958).
34. R. Revelle and K. O. Emery, *U.S. Geol. Survey Profess. Papers No. 260-T* (1957).
35. F. S. MacNeil, *Bull. Geol. Soc. Am.* 61, 1307 (1950).
36. N. D. Newell, *Science* 132, 144 (1960).
37. F. Henson, *Bull. Am. Assoc. Petrol. Geologists* 34, No. 2, 215 (1950).
38. C. Darwin, *On the Structure and Distribution of Coral Reefs* (Scott, London), p. 185.
39. G. Hinde *et al.*, "The Atoll of Funafuti," *Proc. Roy. Soc. (London)* (1904).
40. S. Hanzawa, *Jubilee Publ., Prof. H. Yabe's 60th Birthday* (1940), vol. 2, p. 755.
41. S. O. Schlanger, written communication.
42. E. B. Leopold, written communication.
43. "Shipboard Report of Capricorn Expedition," *Scripps Inst. Oceanog. Rept. No. 53–15* (1953), p. 4. The bank is more fully described by R. W. Fairbridge and H. B. Stewart, Jr., *Deep-Sea Research* 7 (1959), 100 (1960). The seismic survey was conducted by Russell Raitt.
44. M. Robinson, *U.S. Geol. Survey Profess. Papers No. 260-D* (1954).
45. P. E. Cloud, Jr., *Sci. Monthly* 79, 195 (1954).
46. H. T. Stearns, *Bull. Geol. Soc. Am.* 46, 1071 (1945).
47. T. W. Vaughan, *ibid.* 22, 238 (1911).
48. P. B. King and R. E. King, *Univ. Texas Bull. No. 2801* (1928), pp. 109–145.
49. E. R. Lloyd, *Bull. Am. Assoc. Petroleum Geologists* 13, 645 (1929).

50. P. B. King *U.S. Geol. Survey Profess. Papers No. 215* (1948); N. D. Newell, J. K. Rigby, A. G. Fischer, A. J. Whiteman, J. E. Hickox, J. S. Bradley, *The Permian Reef Complex of the Guadalupe Mountains Region, Texas and New Mexico* (Freeman, San Francisco, 1953).

51. W. Waring and D. Layer, *Bull. Am. Assoc. Petroleum Geologists* **34**, 295 (1950).

52. W. von Arx, *U.S. Geol. Survey Profess. Papers No. 260-B* (1954).

53. E. McKee, J. Chronic, E. Leopold, *Bull. Am. Assoc. Petroleum Geologists* **43**, 501 (1959); J. I. Tracey, Jr., D. Abbott, T. Arnow, *Bishop Museum Bull. No. 222* (1961).

54. In a comprehensive report on the sunken islands of the mid-Pacific Mountains [*Geol. Soc. Am. Mem. No. 64* (1956)], Edwin Hamilton reported that shallow-water fossils of Middle Cretaceous age had been dredged from flat-topped seamounts lying less than 800 miles from Hawaii.

55. The general geology of the larger islands of Hawaii has been described and mapped under a long-term cooperative project between the Division of Hydrography in Hawaii and the U.S. Geological Survey. The work was done under the leadership of Harold T. Stearns and Gordon A. Macdonald. The last volume in the impressive series of reports, one dealing with Kauai, appeared in 1960 (G. Macdonald, D. Davis, D. Cox).

56. H. S. Ladd, *Am. J. Sci.* **258**, 137 (1960).

57. Publication of this article was authorized by the director of the U.S. Geological Survey. I am indebted to Joshua I. Tracey, Jr., and F. C. Whitmore, Jr., of the Geological Survey, and to John W. Wells of Cornell University, who read the manuscript critically and offered valuable suggestions.

Marine Bench-forming Processes: Water-Level Weathering

CHESTER K. WENTWORTH

Board of Water Supply, Honolulu, Hawaii

INTRODUCTION

Purpose of Study: Differences of interpretation as to amount of emergence of emerged benches by different students in the same regions and by various students in widely separated regions suggest a generally inadequate knowledge of marine bench-forming processes and the exact relation to sea level in which various benches are formed.[1] Preliminary observations on modern bench-forming processes on Oahu, Hawaii, in relation to the local conditions and shore rocks have indicated that several distinct processes are active and are producing various characteristic bench attitudes and forms. Textbooks generally, beyond a few generalizations as to wave attack on jointed rocks and use of rock debris as tools, have practically nothing to say about the distinctive physical and chemical processes by which various coastal rocks are attacked, each according to its structure and peculiar composition.[2] Because of the variety of its coastal rocks, the comparatively low tidal range, the ready accessibility of most parts of its coast, and the convenience of geologic observation at all seasons, the island of Oahu has been especially favorable for desultory holiday studies, carried on in an effort to describe in detail the types of benches and to work out a rational explanation of each.

1. R. A. Daly, various papers 1915 to date.
   C. K. Wentworth and H. S. Palmer, "Eustatic Bench of the North Pacific," Bull. Geol. Soc. Amer., Vol. 36, pp. 521-544, 1925.
   Douglas Johnson, "Supposed Two-Metre Eustatic Bench of the Pacific Shores," Comptes Rendus du Congrès Internat. de Géographie, Tome II, Travaux de la Section II, pp. 1-6, 1931.
   W. A. Johnson, "Lack of Evidence . . . for Recent Sinking of Ocean Level," Am. Jour. Sci., 5th Series, Vol. 12, pp. 249-253, 1926.
   H. T. Stearns, "Shore Benches on the Island of Oahu, Hawaii," Bull. Geol. Soc. Amer., Vol. 46, pp. 1467-1482, 1935.
2. T. C. Chamberlin and R. D. Salisbury, *Geology,* Vol. 1, pp. 342-354, 1909.
   R. S. Tarr and L. Martin, *College Physiography,* pp. 351-380, 1921. (This is one of the best treatments, with some suggestive references to kind of rock and organic factors, but little specific description.)
   D. W. Johnson, *Shore Processes and Shoreline Development,* pp. 55-83, 1919.
   E. De Martonne, *Traité de géographie physique,* Vol. 2, pp. 971-978, 1926.

Reprinted from the *Journal of Geomorphology* 1:6–32 (1938), by permission of Mrs. Juliette Wentworth and Columbia University Press.

The intent of the study is to provide a critical analysis and genetic interpretation of the microgeomorphic details to be seen on the Oahu coast. Both the logic of general method and many of the specific situations encountered in bench studies have been suggestively outlined by Douglas Johnson in his paper on the "Role of Analysis in Scientific Research."[3] It is not intended in the present investigation to support or to repudiate any particular interpretation of Oahu's benches; though a re-examination of earlier interpretations of emergence or submergence is an appropriate sequel.

Method and Scope: The entire shoreline of the island of Oahu was traversed on foot during the period 1934 to 1936 and various critical places have been visited many times under different conditions of tide and weather. Several of the localities have been known intimately by the writer since his earlier studies of pyroclastic rocks in 1923-1924. In a few instances two or three days at a stretch were devoted to the work but much of it has consisted of single days, or half days, devoted to detailed note-taking, and the making of sketches and photographs. Close attention has been paid to heights of tide and the determination of mean sea level, in critical places using portable tide-gages of the types described elsewhere.[4]

A few preliminary attempts have been made to carry out experimental studies, planned in an effort to verify, or to evaluate the potency of postulated bench-forming processes, but it has not yet proved practicable to devote sufficient time to these to achieve significant results. It is hoped that work of this sort may be accomplished later.

The essential method has been to describe and interpret the features seen, in relation to the modern or to an earlier position of the sea, and to recognize the several simple, pure types of benches conditioned by a peculiar interaction between the sea and the rock. When these types had been identified, it became possible to recognize various complex or hybrid coastal benches, where one process succeeds another laterally along the coast, with the two merging their products along a transition stretch, or where two maintain a certain balance or alternation of effective action.

Description of Oahu Shoreline: The island of Oahu has a roughly trapezoidal form with a maximum diagonal length of about 45 miles. Its

3. Douglas Johnson, "Role of Analysis in Scientific Research," Bull. Geol. Soc. America, Vol. 44, pp. 461-494, 1933.
4. Chester K. Wentworth, "Simple Portable Tide Gages," Jour. Wash. Acad. Sciences, Vol. 26, pp. 347-352, 1936.

area is 604 square miles. Its length of coastline, disregarding embay-
ments less than one mile across, is about 169 miles, and disregarding
only indentations less than one-tenth mile across, the total length is
about 233 miles.[5] In making these measurements the line was carried
either on the outer, or inner side of walled and partly land-locked salt
water fishponds, by whichever route was the shortest and most in line
with the adjacent shore pattern. The shoreline of a circular island

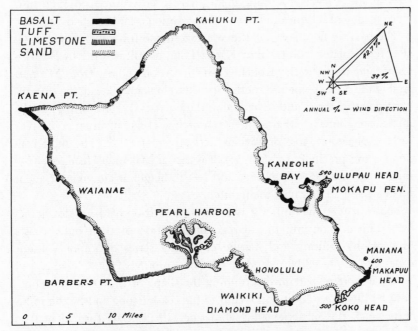

FIGURE 1: Map of island of Oahu, showing generalized distribution of
shore rocks. The symbols show the character of the rock at the waterline; in some places mapped as sand or limestone, basalt cliffs lie a few
yards inland. Small stretches of shoreline developed on alluvial materials
are included with the sand. The wind rose shows the classification of
wind directions from 1905 to 1930.

of 604 square miles has a length of 87 miles, hence the coastal index of
the Oahu shore, using the more generalized and shorter coastal length, is
1.94.

The accompanying map, Figure 1, shows the distribution of rock types

5. H. S. Palmer, in a series of measurements of shorelines of several islands, reported
   185 miles for Oahu, including Pearl Harbor. Exact agreement among different
   observers, even with identical conventions, is difficult of practical attainment.

around the Oahu shore. Heights in feet of precipitous cliffs at a few points are indicated by figures and arrows. The horizontal patterns of the Oahu shoreline and to some extent the vertical profiles, are a product of complex land-forming processes, more so than on any other island of the Hawaiian group. The fundamental trapezium is due to the sub-parallelism of the northeast and southwest coasts with the main rift line of the Hawaiian volcanic chain. Along these lines outer parts of the Koolau and Waianae volcanic domes have been removed, though how much by downfaulting and how much by erosion is still an open question.

The basaltic flow lavas of the Waianae dome form the present coast at a few isolated points from Kaena Point southeastward to Brown's Camp and those of the Koolau dome at various points from Waimea around the north point and southeastward to Makapuu Head, the easternmost point of the island. Even along these coasts the greater part of the immediate shore is either sand beach or low cliffs cut in emerged reef rock, terrigenous fans, or various derivatives of these. The most continuous and precipitous cliff in basalt is that at Makapuu Head, over $1\frac{1}{2}$ miles long and ranging to over 500 feet in height at an angle of about 60 degrees at a point near the lighthouse.

Subsequent to the building and mature dissection of the major domes by stream erosion and the marked modification of their outer coasts probably by faulting and marine erosion, a series of minor volcanic cones was produced by secondary volcanic eruptions. These have played a very important part in determining the shape of the Oahu shoreline, both by the direct addition of land to the coastal zone and by the influence which the subaerial and submarine salients thus formed had on the movement of waves and currents and on the growth of reef and accumulation of land-derived sediments which form the coastal plain. The coastal plain on which Honolulu is built is largely due to the influence of the pyroclastic craters of the Salt Lake district, Punchbowl, and the Diamond Head-Kaimuki prominence. The oblique Koko peninsula is formed chiefly of basaltic tuff of the Koko Crater, Koko Head and Hanauma Bay craters. Ulupau Head, a tuff cone, and Puu Hawaiiloa, a basalt and cinder cone, form the two projecting points of Mokapu peninsula, between which is the sweeping curve of Mokapu beach, and inland from which is the low coral flat of the peninsula, emerged in geologically recent time to a few feet above sea level. Manana Island, perhaps because of deeper water or stronger wave action, has remained an island, nearly a mile offshore.

During Pleistocene time, fluctuations of sea level due most probably to glacial control, have caused a shifting of the Oahu shoreline from 250 above to 300 feet below the present level.[6] Fringing reefs have grown at various levels and shore benches and alluvial flats formed at corresponding positions. Forms produced during one stand of the sea have been subject to reinforcement, or more commonly to destruction during another stand, with the result that at any level within the limits mentioned a complex pattern of rocks forms a potential shore. The composition of the present shore is as follows: basalt, 16.4 miles, or 9.7%; tuff, 9 miles, or 5.3%; reef rock and calcareous sandstone, 52 miles, or 31%; sand beach, 91 miles, or 54%. This subdivision refers to the terrane at the actual water line and was measured in relation to the 169 mile total. With a rise of sea level of 25 feet the percentage of basalt and tuff would be increased, calcareous rocks also probably, and beach diminished, though the action of waves would bring about an equilibrium perhaps not much different from the present.

The Regimen of Marine Action: No continuous measurements or quantitative records of the force, direction, and type of wave attack are available for various times and places on Oahu. Nor are such known to the writer for any other coast in the world, though some measurements of exceptional conditions are reported by Johnson.[7] The chief emphasis has been on the demonstration of the impressive power of waves, rather than on an analysis of the whole effect of the sea on the land.

It is unfortunate that there are no data to indicate the complete pattern of water movement around the coast since one of the results of the present study is the demonstration that on some coasts the most distinctive features are not the product of direct or violent wave attack.

Prime force in the movement of sea water in Hawaii lies in the trade winds. These blow from northeast and east about 80% of the time, with an average velocity of about 9 miles per hour. During a few days each year, chiefly during the winter period, there are reversals of prevailing winds during which the so-called kona (meaning leeward, or reverse of tradewind) wind blows from the southwest.

The prevailing ocean currents in this section of the north Pacific move southwestward with a velocity of between 1 and 2 miles per hour. The

6. H. T. Stearns, "Pleistocene Shore Lines on the Islands of Oahu and Maui, Hawaii," Bull. Geol. Soc. Amer., Vol. 46, p. 1955, 1935.
7. D. W. Johnson, *Shore Processes and Shoreline Development,* pp. 62-72, New York, 1919.

extreme tidal range is under three feet. No detailed determination or compilation of relative times of tide, or of co-tidal lines for the island has been made, but the extreme difference is of the order of two hours. It is difficult to form an adequate picture of the coastal conditions of waves and surf from the data given above. These are everywhere related in an intimate and complex manner to the configuration of the shore and the offshore bottom and the direction from which the wind and waves are coming. As on nearly all coasts there is commonly a marked freshening of wind and increase of wave vigor after sunrise and during the day, so that the sea is usually calmer during early morning hours and rougher in the afternoon and evening. This factor is usually of greater importance in determining safe access to reefs on foot or to rocky coasts by boat than is the exact stage of tide, though the suitable conjunction of the two is most favorable.

Wave action around the coast of Oahu is variable in diurnal and tidal cycles, and in longer periods of several days to several weeks. At times the various benches standing 2 to 10 feet above sea level are dry and scarcely reached by spray. More commonly an occasional wave breaks over the seaward margin of the bench and spray is thrown over even the wider benches. Less frequently, storm conditions prevail and large waves wash over all benches and shore features to 12 or 15 feet above sea level. One or more fishermen annually are drowned by being carried off benches or shore rocks by especially strong waves and in many places constant vigilance is required to avoid being soaked by spray.

At various places on the Koko coast there is evidence that spray is at times thrown more than 100 feet above sea level in quantities to do considerable geologic work. At one point at an elevation of about 40 feet a block of tuff 8 x 8 x 2 feet, and estimated to weigh 7 tons, has been twisted out of its natural position and moved several feet. The site is practically at the edge of a nearly vertical sea cliff and there is no doubt that the movement of the block was accomplished by storm waves, or by torrents of returning spray. In the same area are water-leveled patches which will be mentioned below.

On the Waianae coast south of Brown's Camp where the shore is composed of sandstone, the higher part of the exposed sandstone is surmounted, at about 15 feet above sea level, by a rampart of tumbled blocks quarried from the seaward slopes. These range up to eight or ten tons in weight and indicate that powerful wave action reaches well above sea level during exceptional storms. Back of this rampart the sandstone ledge is lower and farther back is a beach ridge, whose crest reaches in places to 20 or 25 feet above sea level. This ridge is commonly somewhat covered by vegetation and has been raised in places by eolian action, but appears to have been built chiefly by waves of the present sea.

It appears that whereas moderately strong wave action is more persistent on the northeastern shores of Oahu, the wave attack is at certain times fully as strong from the southwesterly and westerly direction as ever from the other side. No records made by comparable methods are available to show the actual relative wave action conditions on shores exposed in various directions and with varying degrees of protection by offshore reefs. Certain shores, such as that of Kaneohe Bay on the northeast side, are flanked by broad areas of living coral reef and exhibit features indicating a relatively feeble wave attack.

Classification of Benches: There are four chief processes forming or modifying benches on Oahu shores. These have been designated as (1) Water-level weathering, (2) Solution benching, (3) Ramp abrasion, (4) Wave quarrying. (See Figures 2, 3 and 4.) Each of these has its most perfect development in situations where the shore rock and the marine conditions are favorable to it and unfavorable to any of the others. Some of the processes are aided by sand, gravel or blocks in the shore zone, others are hindered or their products destroyed by these tools, some processes are aided by certain rock structures or constitutions, others are hindered by the same conditions. In a later section it is proposed to discuss the interaction between the typical processes and the various factors of the sea, the rock, the shore zone and the land back of the shore, that tend to produce mixed or hybrid shore benches. Attention will first be given to the pure types, commencing with water-level weathering and benches affected by this process.

WATER-LEVEL WEATHERING

Regional Distribution: Water-level weathering affects chiefly two types of rocky shores, those cut in palagonite tuff, and those cut in much-weathered basalt in which relatively resistant dikes occur. The chief localities are the tuff shores of Diamond Head, the Koko region from Koko Head northeastward past Koko Crater, Manana Island, and Ulupau Head. No water-leveled benches of consequence occur along the low, tidal flat shores off the Salt Lake craters. The chief examples of water-level weathering in weathered basalt occur in the Lanikai-Kaneohe

FIGURE 2: Water-leveled bench on seaward shore of Manana Island, a mile offshore from the Waimanalo coast of Oahu. The rock is palagonite tuff. This bench area is remarkable for its size, 440 feet long and 200 to 250 feet wide inland from the shore, due in part to the fact that it is cut across the central vent of one of the craters of the island. The edges of inward dipping beds, as seen from overlooking cliffs, form a striking concentric pattern. The main area shows variations of level of less than 6 inches. A number of rampart remnants, as seen at the left, mark the seaward margin and rise 5 to 10 feet above the bench level. The elevation ranges from 11.80 to 12.10 feet above mean sea level.

FIGURE 3: Solution bench cut in reef limestone east of Waimea Bay, Oahu. This bench is here about 3 feet above mean sea level and landward from it is a rather broad area of pitted limestone, not yet completely reduced to the level at which solution stops.

FIGURE 4: Abrasion ramp bench at Mokapu Landing, Oahu. This ramp type (foreground) is cut here in limestone containing masses of tuff, the whole being reduced to a rather smooth sloping surface by the movement of detritus across it. At the left and seaward of the ramp is a fringe of imperfect solution bench, and in the distance is pure solution bench with an undercut nip and pitted reef limestone inshore from it. The higher ground is part of Ulupau tuff crater.

region where the rock of the Kailua basalt formation forms a few shore points, and notably on the two Mokulua Islands off the Lanikai coast.

Examples of water leveling on the Diamond Head coast are somewhat meager and imperfect. Most of this coast is fringed by reef a short distance offshore which not only breaks the force of waves and probably has favored the development of parent bench at a low level, but also yields considerable detritus and helps to maintain a veneer of beach material on the bench. The Diamond Head bench is therefore more largely of the abrasion ramp type and only locally shows well-marked water-leveling features. A few very small remnants of such bench are found on the Black Point shore.

A wealth of bench features is shown in the Koko region commencing with the first exposures of tuff on the eastern shore of Maunalua Bay (Figure 5). Inside the reef line where waves break, the bench is very low, only one or two feet above sea level, and inclines to the abrasion ramp type, conditioned by the presence of beach detritus derived from low cliffs and brought down the rill channels to the coast. Farther south, outside the reef where offshore depths are greater and wave action is stronger, two types of coastal profile are found. There are a few water-leveled bench areas here, but much of the Koko Head Coast to the entrance to Hanauma Bay is marked by steep, wave-quarried profiles. Hanauma Bay, except for the beach at its head, and much of the coast eastward past Koko Crater are marked by fine examples of bench due to water-level weathering, with wave-quarried portions on the more exposed points and abrasion ramps adjacent to small bay-head beaches. This is unquestionably the best-known and most conspicuous and complete assemblage of water-leveled features.

On part of the seaward coast of Manana Island (more colloquially known as Rabbit Island) wave-quarried profiles are prominent and around both sides of the island with considerable variation due to the structure of the tuff there is a rude transition to water-leveled bench and abrasion ramps as the beach on the leeward side is approached. This beach is formed at the point of interference of waves passing around the two sides of the island. However, in addition to the benches described for Manana Island, there is found on the windward side, in the area in-

FIGURE 5: View of benched shore extending eastward from Hanauma Bay. The rock is tuff and the distinctive features of the bench are due to water-level weathering, though quarrying has had much to do in the carving of the parent notch against the land slope.

cluding the structural center of one of the cones of the island, a water-leveled bench 250 feet wide and 440 feet long, which will be described in detail below.

Benches of this type on the Ulupau Head coast are somewhat limited in extent and are mingled with various hybrid benches. Besides the various combinations with solution bench, and abrasion ramp on the west side toward Mokapu Landing, there is a long stretch of bench cut in a reef formation which contains enormous talus blocks of Ulupau tuff, fallen down during an earlier stand of the sea. The features produced by coastal attack on this giant breccia will be described in a subsequent paper.

Water-leveled benches on the Lanikai-Kaneohe rocky points and on the shores of the Mokulua Islands are somewhat more irregular than those on the tuff and occur at varying levels, separated by the nearly vertical and more resistant dikes. They are associated with various wave-quarried profiles in which rock structure has played a prominent part.

As elsewhere stated, it is intended in this paper not to discuss the problem of shifting sea level and historical significance of various benches, but rather to deal with these questions in a paper to be published after the several bench-forming processes have been described in detail. However, descriptive accuracy demands reference, in the case of the conspicuous, seaward bench of Manana Island, to certain previous estimates of its size and elevation.

In regard to this locality Stearns says,

Palmer and Wentworth described the bench on Manana Island as eustatic and estimated it to be 5 to 15 feet above mean sea level, but the United States Geological Survey topographic map shows that it lies below the 10-foot contour. Actually, most of the bench is only 1 to 3 feet above mean sea level except on the windward side, where it reaches 5 to 7 feet in height. As shown in plate 133, the bench is awash in a calm sea, and the notch at the base of the cliff at its inland edge is being actively cut.[8]

That much of the shore bench on Manana Island is less than 10 feet above sea level is freely granted, as also that the principal bench level declines markedly from the windward to the leeward side. Moreover, it is clear that much of the bench does not directly indicate the eustatic shift which Stearns is disposed to repudiate, but which the present writer believes is still well supported by other evidence. With these con-

8. H. T. Stearns, "Shore Benches on the Island of Oahu, Hawaii," Bull. Geol. Soc. Amer., Vol. 46, p. 1475, 1935.

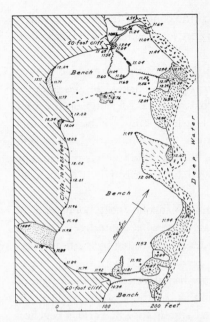

FIGURE 6: Map of great Manana Island bench, showing outlines and elevations of points around margin. The cross-hatched area is chiefly bare tuff, rising in slopes from 25 to 40 degrees, inland from the cliffs which line the bench. Several small abrasion ramps, with a slight accumulation of beach debris, are stippled. Along the shore are rugged rampart remnants, with culminating elevations as shown, and the seaward face of the cliff is pitted by sea urchin borings. Mapped by plane table and stadia rod at 50 feet to the inch. Elevations based on datum established by portable tide gage. (See text.)

cessions aside, there remain other parts of the quoted statement which it is quite impossible to accept. A recent plane table and stadia survey shows that the great windward unit is 440 feet long by 200 to 250 feet wide, and that an area of about 1¾ acres maintains elevations of 11.80 to 12.10 feet above mean sea level (Figure 6). These elevations are referred to a datum determined by portable tide gage by methods described elsewhere.[9] In this instance, 35 measurements were made over a period of nearly six hours, on both rising and falling tide, and gave an average having a probable error (of instrumental determination), when corrected for tidal phase, of 0.066 feet. The short period of measurements and other factors not readily evaluated may introduce an error in the datum of as much as 0.2 or 0.3 feet, an amount which is unimportant in the matter at issue. It is evident that for the most conspicuous unit of the windward bench the quoted estimate of elevation (5 to 7 feet) is much too low, as is also Stearns' estimate of size (150 by 210 feet) contained in the caption of his Plate 133.

The writer finds no justification for reference to the U. S. G. S. topographic map as indicative of elevations wholly below 10 feet, since the

9. C. K. Wentworth, "Simple Portable Tide Gages," Jour. Wash. Acad. Sciences, Vol. 26, pp. 347-352, 1936. In connection with the mapping and the securing of tide gage readings under conditions complicated by spray and the necessary height of the instrument, the writer was assisted by H. W. Beardin, M. Kirschman, and R. Lee.

only known map carrying 10-foot contours (Koko Head quadrangle, Island of Oahu, Scale 1/20,000, Advance Sheet, Photolithographic) shows 10-foot contours only on the leeward fourth of the island. Around the remainder, the lowest contour line indicates 50 feet, clearly outlining the area of the great seaward bench, but of course giving no significant indication of its height.

Exception must also be taken to the statement that the seaward bench is "awash in a calm sea." That this statement refers to the bench unit shown in Figures 2 and 6 is clear, since reference is made to Plate 133, in which its outlines are unmistakable.

The present writer, having spent parts of eight days in the past four years on Manana Island, much of this time in critical observations on this bench unit, recognizes that in average weather successive waves send greater or smaller amounts of water flooding over the bench from the slightly broken portion of the frontal cliff, and it is probable that during storms an occasional high wave may truly wash over the bench. Such wash reaches the nip at the inner margin which shows combined effects of such wave work and water-level weathering.

Even granting that the surface of the bench in moderate, or even calm weather, standing 12 feet above sea level, is invaded quite regularly by sea water thrown onto its seaward edge by waves and spray, the writer does not by any means consider this equivalent to being "awash in a calm sea." On many parts of the Koko coast tons of sea water in moderate weather are flung onto benches or slopes, 10 or even 20 feet above sea level, but these would hardly be considered awash. Nor does he agree that the nip at the rear is being "actively cut" by direct sea wave attack. Both these statements convey an erroneous impression, consistent perhaps with the concept of bench units only slightly above sea level, but definitely misleading in reference to the actual elevation of the bench as recently measured.

Returning to the description of the bench surface, emphasis is placed on the remarkable uniformity of level of the resistant edges of dipping tuff beds. When the bench is continually overrun by sea water in rippling floods a few inches deep, only those resistant layers show which are higher by one or two inches, or which form margins of slight terraces. However, in especially calm weather, when little or no sea water is being added to bench pools, these are separated by an intricate network of dry-topped ridges which strikingly indicate the concentric, indipping structure of the tuff around the old vent. Change of level of the water pools by two inches, as the water drains off, produces a striking increase in the extent and complexity of the pattern of emerged resistant layers. At the time of low water one can reach practically the whole area dry-shod.

Chief exception is found in a few pits or enlarged joints which have been cut to not over 2 or 3 feet below the general level, in areas mostly not over 3 or 4 feet across. On both sides of the great bench, laterally along the shore, are re-entrants where lesser bench units are arranged in terraces to form outlets. Still farther, in both directions are shore stretches of bench and cliff produced probably by wave quarrying and on which are some fairly large, water-leveled units which rise well above the level of the great bench, at least to 15 or 16 feet above sea level, though no detailed measurements were made. Whatever conclusion may finally be reached in the question of the emerged, eustatic bench, or in the genetic allocation of various surfaces now found conspicuously marked by water-leveling, it does not appear valid, in view of their elevations and the other evidences revealed by detailed and repeated

FIGURE 7: View of water-level bench along east shore of Hanauma Bay. This bench was evidently for a long time well protected by the seaward rampart, of which a fragment is shown in the middle distance, but is now being invaded through the action of water leveling at lower levels which has destroyed much of the rampart.

study, to consider the higher kerfs on the seaward side of Manana Island as originally formed in relation to the present sea.

SYSTEMATIC DESCRIPTION

Range in Elevation: Water-leveled benches are developed and widened at whatever elevation water can accumulate and be retained in initial basins produced by the erosional work of some other agent. The process is active to some extent in depressions on inland rock surfaces which do not concern us here, having been observed by the writer on granite surfaces in Missouri and other rocks elsewhere. In general the water-leveling is effective between 2 and 20 feet above sea level. Locally the height of most effective weathering depends on the prevailing vigor of wave action. The bench, to be most effectively leveled, must be low enough to have water from waves or spray thrown on it fairly frequently to maintain the pool, yet not so low as to suffer continuous washing in ordinary weather (Figure 7). Pools must be maintained or replaced, but must be prevailingly quiet pools surrounded by prevailingly dry rock, since the water-level weathering appears to go on most rapidly in the narrow zone which is wetted and dried most frequently, or perhaps where a capillary fringe is continuously maintained.

On coasts where spray reaches 50 feet or more above sea level, owing to strong waves and special configuration, one occasionally finds small pits or alcoves with clear marks of water leveling at such levels, but these become much more abundant and clear below the 20 or 15 foot level, and the widest and best developed high benches on exposed coasts are at 10 or 12 feet above sea level. On the other hand, in sheltered places such as the head of Hanauma Bay, the chief bench is at not over two to three feet above sea level. The prevalence of initial benches capable of being dressed by water-level weathering at low elevations in sheltered places and at high elevations in exposed situations is not at all accidental, since it is thought that a similar principle of most rapid wastage of the wetted and dried zone operates with wave quarrying by which the initial benches were probably developed on exposed and sheltered coasts at correspondingly suitable elevations.

The arrangement of bench elevations is well shown at the headland marked by the well-known Koko blowhole. (See Figures 8 and 9.) The blowhole rises from a sea cave to form a hole about 4 feet in diameter in the surface of a bench 12.5 feet above sea level, which is about 30 feet

FIGURE 8: Detail of multiple bench at Koko blowhole. The bench unit in the foreground and at the left is 4.5 feet above sea level, those visible above it are at elevations of 9.0, 11.5 and 12 feet. *(See Figure 9)*

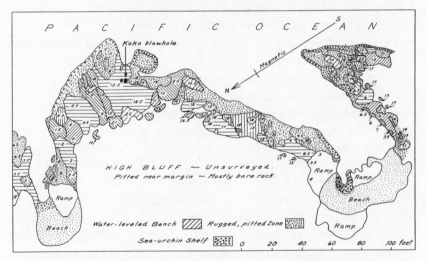

FIGURE 9: Map of shore area in vicinity of Koko blowhole, Oahu, showing generalized classification of surface features. Numerals show the elevation above the mean sea level of benches and of summits of ramparts. The chief bench units are shown, but the rampart zone is much generalized and a complete map would show additional bench patches in the rampart areas.

wide and long. On the east side, around the shore of a small inlet, the bench declines by a series of sharply marked steps (Figure 8) to 2 feet above sea level. On the western side is a similar lowering of the bench, but here more of the low area is included in the rampart zone. Inland are higher bench remnants as shown on the map of Figure 9. Such headlands practically everywhere show higher bench levels at the point and lower levels each way toward the bay heads.

Inspection of the map, where numerous bench levels are recorded in detail for the blowhole locality, will indicate the difficulty encountered by anyone who attempts to correlate benches as upper and lower, or as modern and emerged. Candor forces one to the conclusion that whereas there probably are benches largely wrought in relation to a higher sea level, as indicated more clearly by other types of bench features, the detailed levels of the water-level bench probably can not be used to determine the amount of emergence, unless by some cumulative, statistical procedure not yet successfully applied.

Width and Length: Width and length of benches as a whole depend somewhat on the continuity and width of wave quarrying and continuity of rock structure, but the extent of individual pool levels is determined by the nature of the process. Each pool is at first as large as the depression on which water can stand. If the bottom is not level it tends to become leveled off by the greater attack on high points left emerged as the water level falls by evaporation. Similarly the margins and the outlet lip tend to be extended and lowered. The width of the bench is ultimately limited by the width of the cut scarf on the coast, but proximately by the interference with other benches at slightly different levels. The limit, laterally along the coast, is fixed in similar fashion. Cutting of the bench level by weathering alone becomes slow as soon as the nip of the cliff proper is reached, though this is commonly dressed to a much more acute angle than that which would be developed by wave quarrying. Extension of the individual bench level toward the sea is limited by the necessity for retention of the water in a pool by a rampart along the water's edge (Figure 10). As soon as this pitted rampart is removed along any considerable length of the seaward margin of the bench, so that the water is free to run off the bench at various points this edge is broken down and the destruction of the larger bench commences, commonly resulting in formation of lesser benches at lower levels where the structure is favorable (Figure 7).

Common dimensions of component parts of the bench are of the order of 10 feet wide and 20 to 30 feet long. Many small areas less than five feet square can be found wherever the process is conspicuous. In a few places bench areas varying but a few inches from uniform levelness of 50 by 100 feet can be found, and the most remarkable example of all is that on the seaward side of Manana Island, where only one or two steps of an inch or two in height break the surface of a water-leveled

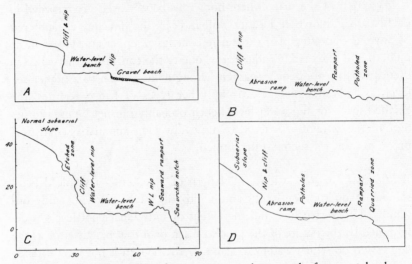

FIGURE 10: Shore profiles drawn to approximate scale from notebook sketches.
A. West shore of Hanauma Bay.   B. Leeward shore, Manana Island
C. Hanauma Bay.   D. West shore, Koko Head
Profile C is perhaps the normal, pure type; the combinations with beaches or abrasion features are due to interference by detritus capable of doing abrasive work.

bench 250 feet wide by nearly 500 feet long, developed at a twelve foot elevation on the concentric structure of mostly in-dipping beds around the filled vent of one of the cones of that island. Two rampart remnants rise about ten feet higher than the bench surface on its seaward margin, to show its kinship with other typical benches of this type (Figure 2).

Offshore depths vary greatly, adjacent to the benches. Some of the benches are inshore from reefs where depths do not exceed three or four feet, but others are in places exposed to more violent wave action where depths are at least 20 or 30 feet close inshore. Offshore sea bottom configuration is not well known in detail applicable to this study.

Relation to Structure: The most striking water-leveled benches are developed on beds of tuff which dip at a considerable angle, 15 or more degrees. Strata which are nearly horizontal tend to be quarried or stripped off in a somewhat irregular or wavy fashion, which interferes with the best pool weathering. Because of the relation of the coast to the structures of existing tuff cones, the beds dip nearly seaward more commonly than the opposite, but in many places dip laterally along the coastline. Here the seaward and landward edges of the water-leveled areas are often cut in clear lines across the strike of the strata, in other places these lines may coincide more or less closely with the strike. On the surfaces of the leveled areas, the harder strata often rise one to several inches above the surfaces of softer strata, so that the structure is indicated in marked relief, commonly accentuated when the harder ridges rise very slightly above the water of a drying pool (Figures 11 and 12). It is not uncommon for the edge of a more resistant stratum to form the margin separating two parts of the bench at slightly different levels, the variation being usually from a few inches to a foot or two at the most.

Seaward Ramparts: The most typical bench areas are separated from the cliff at the water's edge by a zone of slightly higher rock that we here call a rampart or rampart zone. The rampart has a rugged, irregular surface, in which the bedded structure of the tuff and the incorporated blocks and bombs of harder material are brought out by deep etching. Minor areas of water-level weathering occur on the rampart, but it is in the main a distinct zone, the controlling points of which rise from a few inches to several feet above the bench level. The inner edge of the rampart is dressed by the invading bench cutting and a part of the height of the rampart may be due to slow reduction of the bench back of it, but according to the general interpretation here put forth, there must in all cases have been some rim to initiate the process.

The outer surface of the rampart in places forms a vertical cliff, dropping into water several feet deep, and in others slopes at lesser angles down to 40 or 30 degrees with subordinate benching due to minor wave quarrying, water leveling, or to the work of sea urchins. In various places the surface of this outer face is literally riddled by the characteristic rounded, elongated, and merged pits several inches deep, occupied by sea urchins. That these animals do actually, in course of time, bore these holes there is no doubt, and the fragile form of the rock

FIGURE 11: Bench on west shore of Hanauma Bay on which a central belt is being cut somewhat lower than the remainder, due to lowering of the outlet. *(See Figure 12)*

FIGURE 12: Detail of eastern end of bench shown in Figure 11, showing controlling outlet and higher areas, parts of the rampart. Note the distinct nip around parts of the margin of pool area.

surface left when their borings have been generally developed in the zone up to three or four feet above sea level must aid destruction at this level. Details of the sea-urchin work will be presented elsewhere.

In the typical relation of the rampart to the water-level bench, the top and outer face of the bench by its position must be generally wetted by sea water at times when the water in the bench pool is being replenished by spray. On the other hand, in very quiet weather all of its surface except a few pits must dry out, while the water is still retained in the pool. Whether it be the frequency of change between a wet and a dry condition, or the maintenance of a capillary condition in the rock just at and above the water level in the pools, it is clear that rock so situated is subject to softening and removal, while rock more generally dry or wet, or subject to longer cycle alternation, is more stable. This appears to explain the relative preservation of the rampart, in its exposed position. That its surface shows a slow destruction by differential weathering, with no indication of removal of its fragile features by abrasion or wave quarrying, is strongly confirmatory of the view that the present water-level bench is being enlarged without effective interference from abrasion, quarrying, or any destructive mechanical effect of wave movement. It is unthinkable that the level bench has been shaped by mechanical action of waves first moving over the high rampart.

Form of Nip: Two chief forms of nip occur, with numerous transition examples. The first is a small radius notch, cut farthest into the rock horizontally at an inch or two above the level of the bench pool. This type of notch often cuts into, or across, a steep or vertical surface developed by other processes. The radius of curvature of these nips is commonly three or four inches.

The second type is apparently developed in places where pool water slops more freely above the pool level. This starts above water level as a ramp-like surface rising inland at 15 or 20 degrees but usually steepening to become nearly or quite vertical at two or three feet inland and the same in height above the pool. This form suggests abrasive action near the bottom, though the necessary detritus is rarely present, but may be due to a graded position of the alternately wet and dry rock. Whatever the immediate process, the form is apparently due to the successive washing up the cliff slope of the water in the larger pools, since this type occurs more commonly on inner margins subject to notable secondary wave wash across the bench. The first type of nip is apparently due to direct sapping at the water level of a predominantly quiet pool.

Bench Details: The typical bench is one on which the margins are definite and on which the water stands as a unit pool. Few benches show perfect adherence to these conditions. As stated above, the tendency to irregular stripping tends to destroy any bench cut on nearly horizontal strata and the best benches are developed on strata with a marked dip. Here the traces of resistant and less resistant strata are indicated by ridges and intervening elongate pits (Figure 11). The tops of many of the ridges are remarkably level and conform to the elevation of the full pool when successive waves send sea water rippling across the pool and over the outlet. The bottoms of the pits may be more irregular, and in places the pits are a foot deep. More commonly bench units some tens of feet in extent show only a few inches' variation in level from ridge tops to deepest pit bottoms.

Evaporation of the water in pools during quiet weather leads to emergence of the ridges and separation into subordinate pools, in which slightly different levels may develop. Rippling of water in the drying pools by wind tends to maintain a slight spilling from one pool into the next. This has two consequences; first, the lowest parts of the ridge crests tend to be persistently wetted, even after the ridge is generally emerged, with the result that it is lowered by weathering, and second, the slopping over from one pool to another, through wind action, probably tends to equalize the levels of adjacent remnant pools separated by a narrow ridge, and thus prevents any great difference being developed by differential evaporation. Sub-surface seepage probably works to the same end. Thus, while the lowering of water in the remnants of a unit pool by evaporation tends to develop a characteristic etched texture in which the structure is clearly shown, the nature of the process sets a limit to the relief so developed, usually 2 to 6 inches, and only the accident of a definite difference in level of outlet brings about the marked reduction of one component of a bench below another, when they have once been merged.

The outlets of water-level pools are commonly at one end or one corner rather than directly on the main seaward front. It is presumable that an outlet in a prominent frontal position would tend to permit access of ocean water so freely as to somewhat defeat the more quiet action of pool water and that such an outlet would also tend to be more quickly modified. A fairly continuous rampart zone seems pre-requisite to initial development of the most typical benches. The outlets of individual bench units can be easily identified and invariably correspond with the level at which widening of the bench is active.

Successive terraces are developed by water-leveling in several ways. The commonest is found where a relativly high bench area is developed on a headland, like that at the Koko blowhole (see Figures 8 and 9), and lower bench units are developed successively on either side toward more sheltered shores. The exact levels are due to chance effects of structure, though the gradual decline of the level of most marked recession of the cliff is thought to be due to quarrying at the zone of alternate wetting and drying.

Another very frequent arrangement of terraces is developed where a bench of fairly great extent along the coast is invaded by a widening outlet bay started by a break in the rampart zone. On either side the original accordant bench levels may still be preserved, but where the break has occurred it is usual for a series of benches in terraced relationship to lead down to the common outlet. This process is most apt to occur where the strike of the rock strata is transverse to the coastline

Successive benches, one behind another, facing the coast are occasionally found but are less typical. Both the limited width of the eroded zone and the attitude, directly facing the coast, seem less favorable to the development of benches terraced parallel than to the development of those roughly transverse to the coastline.

Probable Nature of Process: A few preliminary attempts to artificially induce rock decomposition or disintegration at the zone of wetting have been unsuccessful. It is believed, however, that the attack on the rock is a physical process, akin to slacking of shales when exposed to water and with rock pressure released, which proceeds so much more rapidly with repeated submergence and emergence than with continuous immersion. Obviously, the tuff on which the benches are typically developed yields enormously more slowly than many shales, such as the Pierre or Bearpaw formations of Montana, drill cores from which disintegrate with visible rapidity and are reduced to a shapeless pile in a few minutes. That surface tension phenomena, and colloidal and dilatation behaviors enter into the process is strongly probable, and it is hoped that an experimental study can be undertaken later.

Another possibility is that crystallization of salts from the sea water may tend to break up the rock in the water-level zone. Occasionally, during quiet weather, there is a sufficient evaporation to concentrate the solution and leave residues of sodium chloride and other salts, but this does not appear to be an important process since the salts are washed away almost as rapidly as they accumulate.

DISCUSSION AND SUMMARY

Alternative Explanations: It needs to be reiterated that the process of water leveling, while it is a powerful accessory in effecting a striking leveling of bench surfaces and in widening those benches, and thus in some degree and on favorable rocks does indeed produce benches, is probably in most places on Oahu operating on the flatter parts of coastal kerfs produced by other processes, such as wave quarrying. It is the purpose of this paper, however, to describe the typical water-leveled surface. For this type of bench floor no other explanation seems adequate. Wave quarrying, subject to the structure of the rock, develops a shore profile with a broadly rounded nip, and a vertical to strongly outsloping curve passing below sea level. Ramp abrasion tends to produce a profile comparable to that of a beach formed of the materials by which the abrasion is carried on, and often at the margin of its action cuts a sloping kerf into the adjacent rock. Where wave quarrying and ramp abrasion merge and somewhat combine characteristics the slope and forms are intermediate. Wave planation, in the sense of degradation of a surface below sea level, to approach the level of effective wave movement, can obviously not be invoked to explain a kerf of such limited width and with generally higher elevations on more exposed points. Both wave quarrying and ramp abrasion are eliminated by the levelness of the bench surface in question and by the presence of the rampart.

The only other process producing surfaces of such levelness is that of solution benching, to be described in another paper. This process operates on calcareous rock and is conditioned by splash or spray levels in similar fashion, but is limited more narrowly to 4 or 5 feet above sea level. Moreover, the rampart zone is missing, the down-cutting is limited less by the outlet level than by other factors, and there is a very distinctive pitted zone inland from the solution bench, which is entirely missing on the tuff coasts where the water-leveling process is dominant. The solution-benching process will not explain the benches here described and the two processes are quite distinct, despite certain similarities.

Origin of Bench: The sequence of events in forming water-leveled bench surfaces is somewhat as follows. Within the zone which can be reached by waves or heavy spray action, differential weathering of rock such as tuff produces pits and irregular depressions. Weathering is aided by wind action, wash, and other erosional processes. Wave quarrying may also produce undrained depressions. The essential feature about any depressions produced by any means within this zone is that wave or spray action clears it of debris, contrary to the condition of most depressions on higher or inland slopes. Given such pits, or a rough bench due to merging of such pits, in this zone, which is higher on exposed coasts, lower on protected coasts, the retention of water pools initiates the water-leveling weathering process. Given time, such a process alone would produce a kerf along the coast. Other processes have doubtless played a part; a kerf roughed out by pool weathering would doubtless be trimmed, rounded and enlarged by wave quarrying. Lack of debris except at the mouths of small streams or at the ends of this type of coast adjacent to beaches, makes ramp abrasion a subordinate auxiliary.

Significance of Elevation: From this discussion it will be apparent that the evidence one may derive from the water-leveled benches as to the exact amount of emergence is indecisive, a fact developed by more intensive observation since the eustatic bench was described in 1925. This does not by any means eliminate the probability that there was a stand of the sea at an elevation less than the 25 feet of the stand designated as Waimanalo by Stearns, however, since there is evidence of other sorts on both the high islands and the atolls, which is not affected by the present discussion. Because of the vertical range of water-leveling action it is inevitable that the present coastline would display both benches water leveled at the optimum level in relation to the present sea, and also benches inherited from an earlier stand, though still subject to the process.

Present Condition: It is the writer's belief from close study of the entire coast of Oahu that the present benches affected by water-leveling were mostly cut when the sea was somewhat higher than it is now. There is no doubt that they are still being leveled and slowly lowered by the process. It seems likely that some of the narrower benches represent an optimum if not a terminal level of pool weathering, but it appears more likely when the amazing expanse of the Manana Island bench is considered that much of the distinctive cutting was done at a higher stand of the sea and probably more largely by wave quarrying. It seems un-

FIGURE 13: Water-leveled patches in dike formation, shore of North Mokulua island, off Lanikai, Oahu. Areas between dikes are least resistant, with the center parts of the dikes next, the dike selvages being most resistant to the particular weathering conditions in operation here.

likely, on a coast initially exposed to the waves, that pool weathering would develop a bench in its appropriate zone more rapidly than would wave quarrying develop a kerf in its proper zone. It is therefore believed that the present condition of the tuff coasts is one of emergence, in which wave quarrying has succeeded in cutting away the merged bench in some places, but in which, along most of the coast, the pool weathering gives to the bench an abnormal aspect of levelness. It should be emphasized that the above statement applies specifically to water-leveled benches; in subsequent papers it will be shown that there are benches on Oahu shores due to other processes which probably do not indicate emergence but which are now being cut in distinctive relationship to present sea level.

Marine Bench-Forming Processes
II, Solution Benching

CHESTER K. WENTWORTH
Board of Water Supply, Honolulu, Hawaii

Outline

INTRODUCTION

Résumé of Previous Paper: The general purpose of these studies of marine bench-forming processes on Oahu shore has been outlined in an earlier paper.[1] That paper included a brief description of the Oahu shoreline, a map showing distribution of basalt, tuff, limestone, and beach sand around the coast, a discussion of wave action, and a list of the chief bench-forming processes. In the body of the paper, water-leveled benches were described in detail as a feature developed mainly on tuff

---

1. C. K. Wentworth, "Marine Bench-Forming Processes: Water-Level Weathering." *Journal of Geomorphology*, Vol. 1, pp. 6-32, 1938.

Reprinted from the *Journal of Geomorphology* 2:3-25 (1939), by permission of Mrs. Juliette Wentworth and Columbia University Press.

coasts, with minor expression on coasts of weathered dike complex. It was shown that the process of water-level weathering operates at elevations from two to twenty feet above sea level, where water is thrown as spray frequently enough to maintain a pool but not in such quantity as to bring about continual washing and disturbance. It was also emphasized that water-level weathering is essentially a process which trims, modifies, and strikingly levels surfaces of tuff, but is probably not a dominant factor in the initial production of a kerf cut against the land. Moreover, though it is recognized that the zone of its more effective action is higher on exposed points and lower on sheltered inlet coasts, it appears that the precise level of any particular patch of water-leveled bench can by no means be used to give a direct measure of the amount of change in sea level. Because of the vertical range of its activity it is evident that any given area of bench, water-leveled in relation to a particular position of the sea, might continue to be affected, perhaps less strongly, after a slight change in relative level of the sea, either a rise of one or two feet, or a fall of even five to ten feet. Under these limitations, it is believed that the water-leveled surfaces on the tuff coasts of Oahu do not in themselves give definite local evidence of any particular amount of recent emergence, though it is thought that the kerf on which the surfaces are developed probably accords with other, more specific evidences in indicating a recent emergence of a few feet.

Scope of Present Paper: In the following pages are described certain benches, nips, and related features which are being developed on limestone coasts of Oahu in rather precise relationship to the present level of the sea, and which are thought to be due to solution by fresh water. Study of these solution benches has been carried on as a component part of the writer's shore-bench research in holiday time. It represents a contribution to general understanding of geologic processes in Hawaii, with application to the geology of water supply, but is quite independent of official studies carried on for the Honolulu Board of Water Supply.

Types of Shore Profiles: Prime requisite for development of the solution bench or nip is a limestone coast. In Hawaii there are two chief sorts, reef limestone composed chiefly of coral and calcareous algae, and detrital limestone formed from beach or dune sand or gravel composed of fragments of coral and calcareous algae, mollusc shells, and calcareous parts of various other organisms. The solution bench is found on both

types of limestone but is more typically and extensively developed on
the reef limestone. This is probably because the bedded structure and
less perfect induration of some of the detrital limestone tends to favor
a structural control of bench forms and the process of wave quarrying
and ramp abrasion.

The exact form of shore profile developed by solution on limestone
apparently depends on steepness of the initial shore, and on the relative

FIGURE 1: View of solution bench, looking along northwest coast of
Ulupau Head toward Moku Manu island. Inland is the nip and pitted
zone of the limestone platform, from which rises a bluff cut in alluvium
and talus breccia. In the foreground is an inlet cut across the bench.

activity of solution by rainwater on the surface as compared to fresh
ground-water just above sea level. For convenience the two end forms
will be called the bench profile and the nip profile, though each partakes
in some degree of the features of the other, and there is complete transition between them with every intermediate form. The bench profile
commences at the seaward margin with a level bench, the edge of which
rises fairly steeply from the water, a few inches to three feet above mean
sea level. This bench may be from five to fifty feet wide, and its inland
margin is fairly sharply marked against the front of a frayed and grad-

ually rising pitted zone. With higher pit bottoms and generally greater spacing between pits this zone rises in fifty feet or more to a level of six to fifteen feet above the sea and is usually delimited inland by mantling formations of sand, alluvium, or other detritus, which overlies the limestone and which is kept somewhat stripped back by storm wave action (Figure 1).

The nip profile is one in which the chief feature is a marked notch cut back into a limestone shore at one to three feet above sea level. Seaward

FIGURE 2: Detail of solution nip profile, on Oahu coast near Laie.

from the nip there may be a bench of the solution type several feet wide, or there may be practically no bench but merely a rugged, irregular step, rounding off into the sea with a general slope near thirty to forty degrees. This surface is commonly riddled with sea urchin borings and usually carries a slight growth of sea weed. Above the deepest landward indentation of the nip is a marked overhanging roof slightly curved at approximately forty-five degrees and making an overhang of three to ten feet. On many coasts the seaward edge of this overhanging visor is only a foot thick and the profile turns back to a somewhat pitted upper surface rising gently landward (Figure 2). The significant difference between the bench profile and the nip profile is that the latter cannot be wholly formed by solvent action of rain water in pits because of the marked overhang, though in many instances the associated bench is evidently conditioned in an identical manner.

SOLUTION BENCHES

Regional Distribution: The most extensive development of solution bench shore on Oahu occurs on the Waianae coast and continuing about three miles east from Kaena Point on the north coast and a greater distance east from Barber's Point toward Pearl Harbor. At least half of the whole length of the Waianae Coast from Barber's Point to Kaena Point is of this type though there are many interruptions by sand beaches or by basalt headlands toward the northwest end. Solution benches are also found in four other chief localities: the Waialua-Haleiwa coast; the coast extending around Kahuku Point; parts of Mokapu Peninsula; and various stretches of the south coast from Honolulu to and including parts of the Pearl Harbor shore. Both windward and leeward coasts are included, and the distribution is wholly fixed by the exposure of limestone in the present coast line. Most, if not all, of the solution bench, discussed in this paper is part of the "lower bench" described by Stearns.[2] However, the "lower bench" of Stearns includes low bench units of other origin and in view of this fact the designation of "lower" and "upper" benches, even for descriptive purposes, seems objectionable to the writer. The total length of limestone shore is fifty-two miles, or thirty-one per cent of the entire shoreline of the island. From this length should be subtracted a small fraction for shore benches of the abrasion ramp and wave-quarried type, which in a few places displace or modify the typical solution bench.[3]

General Features: The general succession of zones constituting the typical solution bench profile is indicated in accompanying profiles (Figure 3, especially profile A). These show greater regularity and smaller range of elevation than does the water-leveled bench previously described. At the seaward margin of the solution bench the water in calm weather rises and falls against a frontal slope of fifty to ninety degrees. Not uncommonly the margin is dressed by the breaking off of large blocks of reef limestone, evidently undermined by wave quarrying. Most commonly the seaward edge of the bench is not appreciably higher than the

2. H. T. Stearns, "Shore Benches on the Island of Oahu, Hawaii." *Bull. Geol. Soc. Amer.,* Vol. 46, pp. 1467-1482, 1935.
3. C. K. Wentworth, Op. cit., Figure 1, 1938.

general surface, though it does carry a more conspicuous and a more lush growth of sea weed. In a few places, usually at a projecting angle of the shore, the seaward part is slightly higher and steps downward by low terraces to the normal bench both laterally and to landward.

The normal bench surface commonly shows variations of elevation of not over three to six inches in an area fifty feet wide by one hundred

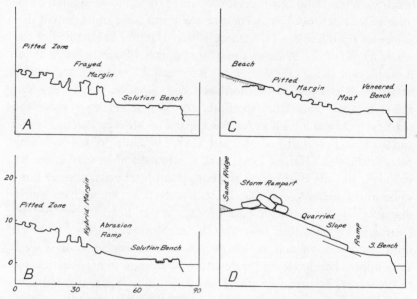

FIGURE 3: Shore profiles drawn to approximate scale from notebook sketches. A. Normal profile. B. Profile with slight abrasion ramp modfication. C. Profile with beach on land side and with moat and veneered zone, Kawela. D. Steep, quarried type of profile with slight bench at water's edge, south of Brown's Camp.

feet in length. The most systematic changes of level from slightly higher to slightly lower parts are by low terraces laterally along the shore. Another common form is a system of low terraces arranged as concentric festoons around a slightly higher part of the bench which has been developed at a projecting point, or at a point where a funnel or inlet has persistently favored a greater splash or surging of waves (Figures 7 and 8).

Size and Form of Solution Bench: Nearly continuous stretches of solution bench on the Waianae Coast, east of Kaena on the north coast, near Waimea Bay, in the Kahuku area, and at Mokapu Peninsula reach a quarter to a half mile in length. Most of these are broken by inlets developed along major joints so that unbroken units of bench are usually not over two or three hundred feet long. Also, along many such coasts the channels developed along such joints, or by other means, are avenues by which basaltic or calcareous gravel is brought down onto the bench, with the result that rounded potholes or abraded furrows are formed, or areas of abrasion ramp are developed, all of which break the continuity of the solution bench proper (Figure 1).

Few if any solution bench units reach a width, from water line to inner margin, of more than sixty to eighty feet on a straight coast, though solution-leveled salients longer than this are found in several places. The prevailing width of the bench, where well developed, is perhaps fifteen to twenty feet, with the more conspicuous parts reaching forty to fifty feet.

In a few places a well-marked solution bench on limestone, formed in relation to the present sea, is known at elevations as high as three feet above mean sea level. Rudely widened flats, due to merging of bottoms of pits and akin to solution benches are also formed as high as five or six feet above sea level locally. All such examples are restricted to a few square feet, immediately adjacent to narrow inlets, or salients, where wave splash persistently reaches exceptional heights. No large areas of wide bench more than three feet above sea level are known though locally some sizable areas reach this level. The general elevation of conspicuous areas of bench is from one to two feet.

The elevation of a solution bench on shores exposed to full tidal fluctuation is probably never less than one foot, but bench and nip levels around enclosed, brackish lagoons like that of Mokapu Peninsula are less, only a few inches.

The level of nip, on nip profile coasts where the shelf or bench is narrow or absent is more variable, ranging up to three or four feet commonly, and in rare instances to five feet or more. It is notable on such a coast that sea urchins and green algae flourish on the shelf or narrow bench, but that in the zone extending one or two feet above the deepest nip the rock is pink with encrusting calcareous algae. Above this level, the rock is whiter, still freshly etched, a condition which gradually gives way higher up to a dark gray color. In summary, it may be emphasized that the solution bench, if ten or more feet wide, is, without significant exception, formed between one and three feet above mean sea level, and hence furnishes one of the most definite sea level indicators known.

Pitted Zone: At the inner margin of the bench, water which rolls over the surface splashes up on a clean, moderately rough surface which rises to the rims and spikes of the pitted zone. In places a single spike may stand alone on the bench, its three or more sides the curved remnants of pool interior surfaces. Often the rims run out a few feet on the bench before being merged with its level. In other places the margin of the pitted zone may rise one to three or four feet as a nearly unbroken wall for a few feet, with numerous pits in its upper surface but with no pits truncated by the invading bench (Figure 4).

The pitted zone ranges generally from ten to fifty feet wide (Figure 5). It is perhaps best described starting from the landward edge. Here the exposed limestone surface is rough in detail, though often not deeply indented and typically a dark gray in color. The structures of various types of coral, certain encrusting algae, and often of included masses of cemented sand or gravel are clearly indicated in color and relief. Breaking the surface are a few pits of rounded outline, which are somewhat undercut around the margins. The larger pits are flat bottomed indicating a tendency to become widened, rather than deepened, locally. Commonly the depth below the general surface is not over a foot and the diameters range from one to five feet. Toward the sea, the pits become more numerous and more closely spaced, frequently with two or more merged in groups. The general surface is less in evidence, giving way to triangular and shard-like remnants, sharp-crested, ragged rims and spikes. The bottoms and sides of pools have roughened but somewhat fresher-appearing surfaces; the tops of the remnants are fragile, honeycombed, and extremely rugged.

The pools are deeper below the tops of rims and the bottoms are progressively cut lower as one proceeds seaward down the frayed margin toward the solution bench itself. This frayed margin often consists of a zone ten to thirty feet wide, in which pools with rims still nearly complete, drain successively from one to another through gaps cut by the encroachment of one pool on another. Not uncommonly the undercut margin of one invades the similar side of another, forming a perforation, but with the upper part of the rim intact as a miniature natural bridge. Not uncommonly a small remnant of pitted zone becomes isolated and forms a low stack with slightly undercut margins.

Form of Nip: The landward margin of the solution bench is sharply marked except in the few places where it grades into an abrasion ramp,

FIGURE 4: Solution bench and pitted zone on Waianae Coast south of
Puuo Hulu Kai.

FIGURE 5: Detail of pitted zone, with moat and veneered zone in upper
left of picture. West of Kawela Bay.

which in turn develops its own distinctive nip. In most places the land-ward margin is a fairly simple, nearly straight, or broadly curving line. Such rims and spikes as project beyond the general line are clearly distinguished as such, and subject to relatively rapid removal. The nip itself is usually sharply curved, and bare of green vegetation though often coated with pink, encrusting algae. The surface texture indicates solution and etching, rather than abrasion. Along many well-marked, solution bench coasts, the nip involves no overhang, the surface merely turning up nearly to vertical along the rims and spikes of the margin of the

FIGURE 6: Veneered solution bench with pits remaining in it. The young people are collecting marine shells. South of Makua.

pitted zone. In other places there is a slight undercutting of the nip which suggests either a slight mechanical wave attack or perhaps an ascendency of solution action at the bench level over that in the pitted zone margin, developed since the solution bench has been formed. Such shore profiles are transitional to those described below as solution nip shores.

Minor Details, Modifications, and Destruction: Two chief minor features are found on the solution bench. Not uncommonly there are pits, or

over-deepened furrows, around the margins of which algae grow luxuriantly, and which are often floored by calcareous gravel (Figure 6).
These possibly represent places where solution by fresh water had gone
too deep, before the particular site had become generally accessible to
the overwash of salt water. It is indeed surprising that there are not more
of these, and that the inhibitory effect of sea water has been so effective.

These pits may become greatly enlarged by potholing, where they
manage to trap coarse detritus, and wave action reaches them effectively.
In many other places, and certainly more typically on extensive bench

FIGURE 7: Algal terrace rims, with remnant of pitted zone at right. Waianae Coast.

areas, the pits tend to become filled by sand and gravel, and narrowed
at the top by growth of algae and other sorts of organisms. Eventually,
by growth of algae over trapped sand and encrustation by calcareous
algae, the bench surface may be restored, and the presence of a pit wholly
obscured.

Another prominent feature in many places consists of series of rims
in a festoon-like configuration, which serve as margins of successive
terrace pools, similar to those of hotsprings and other lime depositing
waters. These usually spread laterally, progressively downward from a
central area where sea water is thrown slightly higher and more frequently than elsewhere and serve as the focus of distribution (Figure 7).
This focus may be either an exposed point, or the apex of a funnel or

fissure cutting the bench margin (Figure 8). The rims themselves consist of rock, due in part to algae growth and in part to protection of earlier reef rock. On some benches it is readily seen that certain of the rims are remnants of the margins of pits of the pitted zone but on a mature bench the rims appear generally to be modified to the form of algal terrace rims.

In a number of places in the pitted zone, or on potholed abrasion ramp surfaces, as well as on potholed patches of basalt coast, one sees former pits or potholes in which groups of pebbles or small blocks are

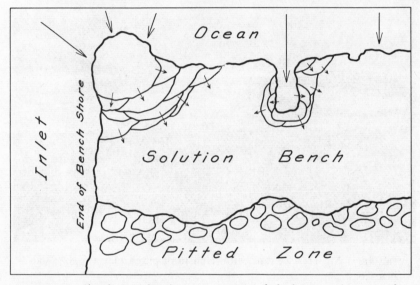

FIGURE 8: Sketch map showing arrangement of algal terrace rims around points of active splashing, one a salient and one an inlet. Conventionalized from actual bench near Mokapu Landing.

firmly cemented in place, often with calcareous sandstone forming a matrix, or associated with cemented, red-brown silt. That these represent a break in history in clear, but one hardly is justified in regarding these as evidence of general unconformity. It seems more likely that the cementing took place under the cover of some temporary and unusual beach sand accumulation, or in some cases when a pitted area of coastal rock was covered by a fan or delta of terrigenous silt and gravel carried out in some torrential streamflow.

One of the factors which occasionally results in aberrant forms on the

bench is the presence inland of a formation which yields hard rock
debris or of hard boulders in the limestone itself which are released by
its destruction. These in any case tend to promote pothole abrasion, and
where they are in the limestone are responsible for various grotesque
remnant forms. (Figure 9)

Owing to changes in local conditions or to the natural evolution of

FIGURE 9: Solution bench showing algal rims around pool margins and
other features, somewhat complicated by lag boulders of basalt, both
from boulder-bearing reef rock and from basalt cliff. South coast of
Mauna Lahilahi.

the shore, the solution bench undergoes destruction locally in several
different ways. It may be cut away laterally by the enlargement of joint
or stream controlled inlets where strong abrasion takes place below the
bench level. (Figure 10) It may also be modified and eventually destroyed by ramp abrasion, starting with a small beach of detritus at the
level of the bench, or by the enlargement of potholes or furrows
started on the bench. Such processes of bench destruction are often
noticeable at the ends of bench shores, where they lie open to encroachment by adjacent beaches and beach processes. Benchs may occasionally
be broken and started on the way to destruction by wave quarrying which

displaces blocks of various sizes; this is most common with benches cut in sandstone.

Solution Nip Shores: The other type of profile to be described here is the nip profile. This differs from the solution bench profile chiefly in that the whole profile is shortened in such a way that the pitted zone is developed on the upper surface of the roof or visor which overhangs the nip and inner margin of the solution bench. There is no frayed margin of the pitted zone transitional down to the level of the solution

FIGURE 10: Reef rock coast, attacked dominantly by abrasion, with boulders in abrasion inlet in foreground and storm ridge of boulders in background. Coast rock slightly pitted in places but marked mostly by abrasion adjacent to furrowed joint line. North coast east of Kaena Point.

bench, and the development of the bench and nip require an explanation somewhat modified from that offered for the normal bench profile. (Figure 11)

Commencing from the seaward side, the nip profile starts usually with a rugged rock surface rising from the water at an angle of about forty-five degrees and becoming gentler in slope one or two feet above the mean level of the sea. This surface is usually much cut by sea urchin

borings and in many places in a view from above as much as one-third
to one-half the area is seen to be taken by sea urchins occupying such
borings, one to three or four inches beneath the surface. In some places
the slight bench which occurs just above the water's edge, which will
here be called the sea-urchin shelf, is cut below a somewhat higher
solution bench of the ordinary sort, which may be from five to forty
feet wide. In others, the sea-urchin shelf runs immediately back and
curves into the main nip of the coast, reaching its greatest depth at an

FIGURE 11: Solution bench and nip, showing form of latter. View
southward toward Nuuanu Pali, from east coast of Mokapu Peninsula.

elevation of one to three, or even four feet above sea level. In those
places where there is a distinct solution bench back of the sea-urchin
shelf, the nip is cut lower and is more sharp angled, where it rises directly from a sea-urchin shelf it partakes of the ruggedness of the shelf
and has a gentler curve.

Wave Conditions: In extremely quiet weather the sea may rise and fall
with scarcely any water reaching most of the surface of the bench. Under ordinary wave conditions, the sea swells and splashes so as to send
water rippling a few inches deep across the width of the bench and
dashing amongst the lower and incomplete pits of the frayed margin of

the pitted zone. Rougher seas send sea water well up on the entire frayed margin and into many of the pools of the pitted zone, and the stripping back of the sand or alluvial cover and the position of large loose blocks makes it clear that in the more severe storms strong wave action sweeps across the entire area of bare rock.

In some places, where the solution bench is developed on sandstone, rather than reef rock, the typical form is somewhat modified by joint-controlled wave quarrying. At such places also it is common to find large blocks flung back toward the landward edge of the bare rock. (Figure 3, profile D)

Organisms and Reef Growth: The solution bench, as will be shown below, is a surface which, by definition, is subject to almost constant wash by sea water. To it would truly apply the phrase "awash in a calm sea." The writer has occasionally seen surfaces of solution bench actually dry, but these conditions are somewhat exceptional, probably a combination of very calm sea and low tide, and do not occur daily on most benches. In general the seaward part of the surface of the bench is well covered with sea weed and a lesser cover extends to the inland margin. Associated with the more conspicuous green algae are calcareous algae and a varied assemblage of echinoids, gastropods of various types, and other marine organisms. A small area blasted free of all organisms was found luxuriantly covered by sea weed (genus Sargassum) ten months later.[4]

Growth of these organisms is favored by certain distinctive conditions. Among these is a persistent, but in general not a violent movement of sea water. Because of steep front of the bench and the bare rock surface at the landward edge, the bench is generally free of sand or other rock detritus found on beaches. Where such detritus is more abundant near the mouths of streams, or at inlets where accumulation is favored, the increased abrasion and movement of debris results in elimination or notable reduction of the veneer of organisms on the bench. It is probable that the flora and fauna of these benches is very similar to that of shallow reef surfaces in the same region, but no detailed study has been made. Indeed, in casual parlance the benches are called reefs and probably generally regarded as such by most frequenters of the coast. Moreover a certain amount of true reef veneer is found on them.

As mentioned above, there are fairly deep pools in some places in the bench. In places where considerable amounts of hard detritus are avail-

4. A. Greendale, Manuscript Report on Preliminary Studies of Bench Organisms. 1935.

able and wave action is suitable, the bench tends toward destruction, but in others such pools tend to become filled and gradually bridged over. This is brought about by the more luxuriant growth of algae along any such margin where clear water is adjacent and partly by the binding action of such algae on the accumulating sand. Algae also tend to develop along festoon-like lines which serve as terrace rims controlling the spreading of sea water from the points at which it most commonly and abundantly reaches the bench surface. These lines are built up and reinforced by trapped sand and other debris and in turn furnish a foundation for further fixation of algal growth.

Critical examination at times of favoring low tide shows in places a fairly extensive veneering of the outer, or seaward part of the bench surface by growth of reef-forming organisms. In certain places the outer belt shows active growth, as distinguished from a landward, lower and much more barren belt. While it may be that the landward belt has been somewhat reduced by solution and is a true solution moat, it is also clear that fairly active building is in progress in the outer belt on a surface originally produced by the solution bench process. This is probably akin to the lithothamnium ridge described by Mayor and others.[5]

Through all these processes, organisms, chiefly algae, tend to preserve and even to rebuild the bench, always up to the limit of access of sea water. Hence, organisms work in close harmony with the solvent action of fresh water which is regarded as the primary cause of the bench. Whether the growth and decay of organisms, biochemical processes, exert a significant effect on the composition of sea water which might function selectively in dissolving or preserving the calcareous rock, is not yet known conclusively.

Composition of Water: As a check on the possible correctness of the solution hypothesis, the water in pools in the pitted zone has been systematically examined on a number of occasions. Since the chief consideration is whether the water which habitually is found in such pools is sea water from spray, or is rain or land water, the determination is most conveniently made in terms of density. A few samples were collected in bottles and rough picnometer determinations made in the laboratory, but later the tests were expedited by construction of a simple wooden hydrometer with a slender neck to allow convenient reading to the nearest one hundredth of the range from fresh water to sea water.

5. J. E. Hoffmeister, "Geology of Eua, Tonga." *Bishop Museum,* Bull. 96, pp. 7-9, 1932.

This could be used under all field conditions and gave immediately the relative percentages of sea water and fresh water in a sample from a given pool. Fresh water can be regarded as derived from rain or seepage from adjacent saturated ground. Water of varying degrees of salinity may be either a mixture of appropriate amounts of fresh and salt water, or may be the result of solution in rain water of salt residues left in pools by evaporation.

At any rate the essential factor is the content of calcium carbonate, which is well known to be approximately at the saturation point in warm surface layers of the ocean.[6] Broadly, it has been assumed that in this latitude the capacity of sea water to dissolve limestone is negligible, and that the capacity of any given mixture of waters to dissolve limestone is a direct function of its percentage of fresh water, reaching a maximum with pure rain water.

Various determinations show that following heavy rains the pools are often filled with pure rain water across the full width of the pitted zone. At the seaward margin such rain water flows from one pool to the next toward the sea, and a given pool near the water line may be the recipient of both fresh water from higher pools and of sea water gently or strongly splashed into it from the seaward side. Under such conditions any composition may be produced and continually modified.

When strong waves wash over the bench and the pitted zone, the water even in the pits farthest landward may be as saline, or with evaporation, more saline than sea water. While it thus appears that at various times, the water of pools may be of any composition, it has been found in general that the pools contain water less saline than sea water and hence more effective for solution of the limestone. Such conditions may obtain for days, or even weeks at a time on the pitted zone, but it is inconceivable that fresh water stands on the solution bench itself for more than a few hours. This is apparently the controlling factor in forming the solution bench and the determination, in a given place, of its elevation.

Comparison of Solution and Water-Level Benches: In order to afford a compact picture of the contrast between the two benches already described, the following table is presented:

6. J. Johnston, and E. D. Williamson, "The Rôle of Inorganic Agencies in the Deposition of Calcium Carbonate." *Jour. Geol.*, Vol. 24, p. 729-750, 1916.

Characteristic	The Water-Level Bench	The Solution Bench
Kind of Rock	Chiefly tuff; weathered dike complex in places.	Reef limestone, less distinctively detrital limestone.
Elevation	Mostly 5 to 15 feet. Small patches to 25 feet.	Mostly 2 or 3 feet; with only small areas to 5 or 6 feet, very exceptionally.
Area	10 to 30 feet wide generally, up to several hundred feet long.	10 to 30 feet wide, to several hundred feet long.
Levelness	Local variations of a few inches only.	Only one or two inches variation, except as terraced by algal rims.
Rugged, etched rampart zone	Typically present.	Wholly missing, not essential to process.
Inland margin	Nip and cliff.	Pitted zone, with or without nip.
Prevalent water condition	Water maintained in pools, but large areas often dry.	Whole bench washed, small areas rarely dry.
Organisms	No algae generally on bench; small fish and invertebrates in pools.	Luxuriant growth of algae, with fish and variety of invertebrates.

SUMMARY

Origin of Solution Bench: The bench here described, like the water-leveled bench previously dealt with, suggests by its levelness from front to rear, and by the lack of marks of mechanical abrasion, that it is due to some sort of quiet aqueous action. Moreover, the transition from slightly pitted to fully pitted and thence to progressively destroyed limestone at the landward margin makes the conclusion unavoidable that the process which forms the bench and that which produces the pits in the shore limestone are essentially the same.

In the writer's early consideration of this bench it was at first thought that fixation of the bench level and the change from pitting attack at higher levels and evident cessation and protection at lower levels was accomplished in some way by the veneer of organisms, and in his early notes the bench was called the organic veneer bench. As a tentative hypothesis it was thought that the sea water might in the higher, bare area have a capacity for solution of limestone which would be reduced or destroyed on the bench proper through the use of carbon dioxide by growing marine plants. It was further thought that the water in higher pools might at times carry the products of decay of plants and animals which would give it an increased solvent power. That such decay goes on in such pools is easy to observe.

As further observations were made, however, it appeared that a more adequate cause was the action of fresh water, which is subject to progressive inhibition through the persistent invasion of lime-saturated sea water at levels determined by the local wave and splash conditions. The tests of salinity by the density method, mentioned elsewhere, seem to indicate clearly that the higher bench is commonly invaded by fresh water and that for days at a time pools in it carry water with a considerable capacity to dissolve limestone. They also show that near the edge of the pitted zone the pools and generally broken surface are increasingly subject to substitution of sea water for fresh water, with the result that such pools must suffer solution to a reduced extent. On the bench itself,

FIGURE 12: Pitted zone at top of reef rock, visor, and solution nip, margin of Nuupia Pond, on Mokapu Peninsula.

only the combination of extraordinary rains, with extreme low tide and very quiet wave conditions can freshen the water for very short periods, bringing about solution only at a vanishingly slow rate.

From this explanation of the formation of the solution bench, we may proceed to interpret the solution nip. Perhaps this explanation may be most evident in the case of such a low nip, with overhanging visor, as is found around Nuupia Pond on Mokapu Peninsula. (Figure 12) Here the nip cannot be regarded as formed from a degraded pitted zone, since the latter overhangs the former. However, since the water of the lagoon is subject to very slight wave action, and the nip is clearly akin to the solution bench rather than the result primarily of abrasion, it seems evident that it is due to the action of fresh water. At times there is a considerable addition of fresh water to the pond so that it is probably less salt than sea water, but it is doubted if the fresh water, despite its lesser density would remain long unmixed on the surface. A more plausible view suggests that it is the fresh water which forms a shallow body in the rocks just at sea level that is primarily responsible.

Thus, it appears reasonable to suppose that the solution nip in various places is fixed in its position at the level where fresh ground-water tends to emerge and below which the water in the rocks is essentially of the composition of sea water.

It is of interest to estimate possible rates of formation of the solution bench, though only certain limiting assumptions can be made. Rainfall on the limestone shores of Oahu probably does not, on the average, exceed twenty-five inches. It is doubtful if any pitted zone area is so arranged that with moderate or heavy rain there would be retained in pits more than twenty-five per cent of the total. On the other hand, some pitted zones may be subject to action of seepage from higher alluvium. If we can assume that so much as six inches of rain per year is retained in pools and dissolves sufficient limestone to reach saturation this would approximate the removal of .00002 feet of limestone per year.[7] Average slope of the frayed edge of the pitted zone is perhaps five feet in fifty feet, or ten per cent. Reduction at .00002 feet per annum would thus be equal to horizontal widening of the bench at a rate of .0002, or one foot per five thousand years. This rate is maximum for rainfall on the bench alone, but might be increased notably by passage over the bench of sheet wash and seepage water from the land. Widths of existing benches seem to demand much more rapid formation than this.

Relation to Other Bench Processes: In an earlier paper on Oahu benches[8] it was pointed out that several types of benches are in process of formation or modification on Oahu today, and that each has its best development where local rocks and shore conditions favor it and do not favor other processes. It naturally follows that where there is local interference with the conditions conducive to the dominant bench of a particular coastal section, the other types of benches tend to develop, according to the type of aberrant condition.

7. On assumption of .12 grams $CaCO_3$ per liter. (F. W. Clarke, "Data of Geochemistry," *U.S. Geol. Surv.* Bull. 770, p. 131, 1924.)
8. C. K. Wentworth, Op. cit., p. 12, 1938.

The typical development of the solution bench is on reef limestone, where the limestone rises to an elevation five to fifteen feet above sea level, and is overlain only by fine-grained marine or terrestrial detrital material which is readily stripped back and which leaves no coarse, resistant lag fragments. The first departure from ideal conditions occurs where the limestone is of detrital origin, with stratification planes and more regular joint planes. In such rock, though the solution bench develops fairly well, there are often places where wave-quarried surfaces, plucking out of blocks, and the like are in evidence, these processes being controlled by the stratum and joint planes. Not uncommonly on such shores, large joint blocks are dislodged and subsequently have marginal areas of solution bench cut against them.

In many places the solution bench is interrupted where a stream reaches the coast and discharges coarse, durable detritus over the bench. At such a point abrasive action commences; if the amount of debris is sufficient to form a beach, the solution bench is modified to the form of an abrasion ramp adjacent to and under the beach; if the debris is small in amount the pieces are likely to become trapped in pits or fissures and to result in potholing action.

Large basalt blocks and boulders are also left on the bench, as lag from alluvium which has been stripped back by waves, and as soon as these are subject to wave action, potholing or other abrasive action is likely to interrupt the normal solution-benching process locally. In places there are prominent joint planes in the reef limestone which may become widened as waves move through them. They further tend to be places of accumulation of coarse material, often largely calcareous, which in turn forms a pocket beach and may develop a considerable cove in which abrasive attack on the rock is dominant. (Figure 10) Similar coves, or inlets, may be formed where a large block has been quarried out by wave action.

Some solution benches once fairly well developed have been from time to time partly covered by sand washed on them from laterally adjacent beaches or from sand ridges inland from them. Such benches suffer abrasion which is sufficiently prolonged destroys the characteristic surface markings. In certain localities the limestone on which the solution bench is developed either contains basalt blocks and boulders washed or rolled out on the reef as it grew, or tuff fragments incorporated in various ways, or if it is a detrital limestone it may contain layers or pockets of basalt boulders. In any case such a rock yields a lag accumulation of non-soluble fragments which tend to develop a potholing action or a ramp abrasion if sufficiently abundant. Or, prior to the release of the non-soluble fragments they stand in relief above the general surface of the widening bench and to some extent modify its development. The most remarkable example of this condition is on the coast of Mokapu Peninsula, east of Mokapu Landing, where blocks of tuff up to twenty-five feet in diameter are exposed in the eroded reef limestone and stand at a level slightly above the solution bench surface. This stretch of coast, with this and other remarkable features, will be described in a later paper.

SOURCE AND VARIATION OF HAWAIIAN LITTORAL SAND[1,2]

RALPH MOBERLY, JR., L. DAVID BAVER, JR.,[3] AND ANNE MORRISON[4]
Hawaii Institute of Geophysics, University of Hawaii, Honolulu, Hawaii

ABSTRACT

Hawaiian littoral sand is a mixture of detrital and organic grains, whose relative abundance depends on recency of vocanism, intensity of weathering in the hinterland, and vigor of growth of marine organisms. The size and sorting of the beach sands vary by island, quadrant, locality, and season in relation to exposure to tradewind-driven waves, to storms, and to reef configuration.

Detrital components are mainly fresh grains of basalt, but weathered grains may be preserved on some sheltered coasts. Sands rich in olivine grains from lava phenocrysts or in black basalt glass are significant locally. Calcareous organic grains in general order of abundance are Foraminifera, mollusks, red algae, Echinoids, corals, and *Halimeda*. Most of the sediment on the widest and shallowest fringing reef flats, and on the beaches behind them, does not originate on the reef flats, but rather comes from organisms washed in across the reef edge.

INTRODUCTION

This report contributes to our still imperfect knowledge of beach materials in tropical areas and in Hawaii in particular.

The initial investigations of the organic components of the calcareous sand, including most of the testing of a variety of techniques, were by Mrs. Morrison, and the later work, involving a larger number of unknown samples and most of the ecologic field studies, were by Mr. Baver.

SETTING

Each of the major Hawaiian Islands (fig. 1) is formed of one or more huge shield volcanoes built from the Pacific sea floor by countless successive thin, intermittent extrusions of basaltic lavas (Stearns, 1946). Relatively small quantities of more alkalic lavas erupted late in the histories of some volcanoes. Areas above sea level of the older volcanoes are being reduced by erosion, and by isostatic sinking because these lava piles are a local load on the earth's crust. Locally the shoreline has been extended by secondary volcanic activity, by deposition of detritus at stream mouths, and by the growth of shallow-water marine organisms. The present beach systems of the major islands of Kauai, Niihau, Oahu, Molokai, Lanai, Maui, and Hawaii are determined by local combinations of recency of volcanism, type of bedrock and weathering, reef development, exposure to waves and currents, and sea level changes of the recent

[1] Manuscript received August 12, 1964.
[2] Contribution No. 84 of the Hawaii Institute of Geophysics, University of Hawaii.
[3] Present address: 2283 Hearst Avenue, Apt. 22, Berkeley, California.
[4] Present address: 1008½ West Green Street, Urbana, Illinois.

geologic past (Shepard and others, 1963; Inman, Gayman, and Cox, 1963; Moberly, 1963a).

SEDIMENT ATTRIBUTES
Grain-size Parameters

About 2400 sediment samples collected from the coastal areas of the larger Hawaiian Islands have been analyzed for grain-size distribution by sieving to $\frac{1}{2}\phi$ sizes. Most of these samples were obtained from the backshore, foreshore, and shallow nearshore environments of beaches whose profiles were measured quarterly for $1\frac{1}{2}$ years. Some additional samples are from dunes and from offshore areas as deep as 30 feet, or from beaches between those visited quarterly, and sampled generally in the surf uprush near apparent sea level. In table 1 the median diameters of 1525 beach samples are shown, by island quadrant, and overall. Where several samples were analyzed from the same part of the beach, and which had been collected during the same visit, only one analysis is used for the purposes of table 1, so as not to bias the results unduly.

Hawaiian beaches are mainly of sand of medium grain-size (classification of Wentworth, 1922, as modified in Dunbar and Rodgers, 1957; parameters of Inman, 1952), although their sediment actually ranges from gravel to sandy mud. Many beaches, especially on Molokai, have coarse sand, and many, especially on Maui, have fine sand.

VARIATION

With a few exceptions, the relationship of grain-size to exposure appears to be closely related to climate and to wave and current energy. Rainfall and resultant intensity of weathering increase with elevation and with exposure to the

Reprinted from the *Journal of Sedimentary Petrology* 35(3):589–598 (1965), by permission of R. Moberly, Jr., and the Society of Economic Paleontologists and Mineralogists.

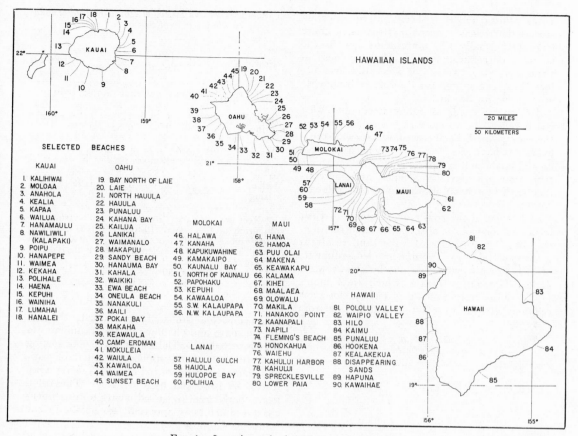

Fig. 1.—Locations of selected Hawaiian beaches.

trade winds. Almost all the energy available in the nearshore environment of Hawaii arrives as ocean waves from one of these four sources (fig. 2):

I. Northeast trade wind waves, possibly present all year, are largest in late spring through late fall. They approach from the northeast or east with heights of 4 to 12 feet and a period of 5 to 8 seconds.

II. North Pacific swell, generated by North Pacific winter and early spring storms. The waves approach from the northwest, north, or northeast with heights of 8 to 14 feet and periods of 10 to 17 seconds.

III. Kona storm waves are generated by local, or "kona," storms, most commonly in the late winter and early spring. These wind-driven waves vary greatly in direction and size, but most commonly approach from the southwest with heights of 10 to 15 feet and periods of 8 to 10 seconds.

IV. Southern swell, very long and low waves from Antarctic winter storms, arrive in

our summer and early fall. These waves approach from the southeast to southwest with heights of 1 to 4 feet and periods of 14 to 22 seconds.

Except for Hawaii Island, with its continuing volcanism that inhibits continued development of weathering on land or of reefs near shore, the islands generally have their beaches with finest grain sizes on their windward, or northeastern, coasts (table 1). Apparently this is due to the high trade wind controlled rainfall along windward-coast hinterlands, which allows deep chemical weathering so that, for the most part, detritus finer than sand-size, as well as colloids and solutions, are formed and transported to the shore (Inman, Gayman, and Cox, 1963; Moberly, 1963b, 1963c). Moreover, the sand produced on the windward reefs is subjected to persistent working by trade wind waves of heights and periods that vary little, and so the sand is quickly sorted and reduced in size.

There also are wide reef areas along the south shores of Oahu and Molokai, but the beaches of those coasts have coarse and poorly sorted sands. During and after severe, infrequent kona storms detritus is carried by streams in spate from the normally drier hinterlands down to the shore, and reef fragments are broken loose in shallow water. However, the waves die down before these coarse and poorly sorted fragments are thoroughly worked.

The coarse sands on many north and west coasts reflect the strong surf generated there by the winter North Pacific swell. Coasts with these exposures have the longest and widest beaches on all islands and, except on Hawaii Island, have reefs that are narrower, deeper, and more irregular, if present at all, than on south and east coasts.

A division of the coasts on the basis of their local geomorphology also shows some relationship between exposure to waves and resultant grain size (table 2). The fine-grained sediments of bays are not winnowed out by strong wave action. The sorting figures, which are Inman's (1952) phi-deviation measure, show a close correlation between wave action and sorting from

TABLE 2.—*Size and sorting of Hawaiian littoral sand in relation to local geomorphic setting*

Features*	Reef	Intermediate	Open	Bays and Harbors	Deltas
All islands, summer waterline samples only					
No.	124	91	47	49	19
Median**	0.97	1.15	1.22	1.70	0.87
Sorting	0.68	0.58	0.52	0.68	0.97
All islands, any season, trios of onshore, waterline, and offshore samples per beach					
No.	354	183	363	96	42
Median	1.26	1.39	1.35	1.94	1.48
Sorting	0.66	0.49	0.46	0.71	0.71

* Reef profiles vary. "Reef" herein is restricted to submarine profiles where 10-foot ($\sim$3 m) depth of water is more than 500 feet ($\sim$150 m) from shore, and "Open" is where 10-foot depth is less than 200 feet ($\sim$60 m) from shore.
** Median: $Md\phi = \phi50$
Sorting: $\sigma\phi = \frac{1}{2}(\phi84 - \phi16)$ (Inman, 1952)

the well-sorted sands of open coasts through intermediate and shallow-reef environments, to the protected bays. Deltas also have poor sorting because the stream-supplied sediment of various grain sizes is deposited at a rate faster than it can be reworked by the waves. The trend from coarser reef-coast sediments to finer open-coast sediments is apparent, especially in the waterline samples.

The increased coarseness of sand on beaches in the winter is shown by the low median-ϕ values in table 3. The range varies from island to island, but generally is about an increase of $\frac{1}{2}\phi$ size.

Grain shape and roundness were estimated from standard illustrations (Pettijohn, 1957, p. 56; Shepard and Young, 1961, p. 199) for each ϕ size of about 300 samples, and for a random split of the whole sample for the remaining 2100-odd samples. The consistency of grain shape, especially of calcareous sands, is undoubtedly

TABLE 1.—*Relationship of littoral sand grain-size to quadrant of exposure*

Quadrant:	Windward	Southeastern	Leeward	Northwestern	All
(median size in phi-units and mm)					
Kauai					
Samples	58	54	70	92	274
Mdϕ	1.17	1.82	1.50	1.26	1.41
Mdmm	0.47	0.27	0.35	0.42	0.38
Oahu					
Samples	224	77	107	133	521
Mdϕ	1.52	0.73	0.89	0.66	1.09
Mdmm	0.35	0.60	0.54	0.63	0.47
Molokai					
Samples	16	54	81	32	183
Mdϕ	1.82	0.63	0.82	0.96	0.88
Mdmm	0.28	0.65	0.57	0.51	0.54
Lanai					
Samples	17	10	0	11	38
Mdϕ	1.79	1.77	—	0.89	1.48
Mdmm	0.29	0.29	—	0.54	0.35
Maui					
Samples	35	0	258	81	374
Mdϕ	2.42	—	1.79	1.21	1.72
Mdmm	0.18	—	0.29	0.43	0.30
Hawaii					
Samples	37	20	78	0	135
Mdϕ	1.28	0.28	1.59	—	1.31
Mdmm	0.41	0.85	0.33	—	0.40
All					
Samples	387	215	594	329	1525
Mdϕ	1.70	0.99	1.44	1.00	1.31
Mdmm	0.31	0.50	0.37	0.50	0.40

TABLE 3.—*Seasonal variation in average median grain size of Hawaii beach sand*

	Phi Median Diameter of Winter-Summer Waterline Pairs	
	Winter November Through March	Summer June Through September
Kauai	0.87	1.42
Oahu	0.54	1.32
Molokai	0.28	0.88
Lanai	1.35	1.51
Maui	0.98	1.84
Hawaii	0.61	0.94

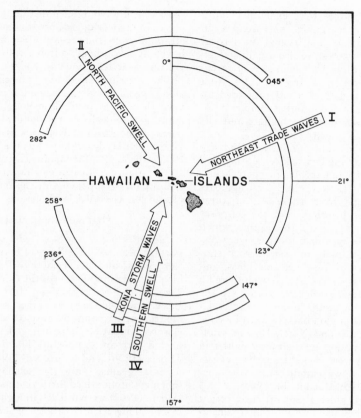

FIG. 2.—Hawaiian waves.

related to the generally low degree of variation of calcareous components from beach to beach in Hawaii, as discussed in the final section of this paper. For calcareous sands, about 30 to 40 percent of the grains of a sample were oblate and 40 percent were bladed. Ten percent, or a little more, were equant, and 10 percent, or less, were prolate. Although grains of any composition might be present in almost any shape, generally the Foraminifera were oblate and the grains abraded from calcareous algae were chiefly bladed, ranging to prolate. Mollusk fragments were mainly bladed and oblate grains. As the detrital component of clastic basalt increased, so did the percentage of equant grains.

Nearly all grains coarser than very fine sand were subrounded to rounded, reflecting both the ease with which basaltic and calcareous sands abrade in the surf zone (Moberly, MS.), and the original shape of some Foraminifera.

After a better understanding of the composition and shapes of calcareous grains was gained, several Hawaiian beach and offshore samples were analyzed in an Emery sedimentation tube. As compared to a quartz standard size, olivine grains fell faster and most calcareous grains fell slower. Slowest of all were fragments of the calcareous green alga *Halimeda* and of mollusk shells.

COMPOSITION
Detrital Components

Sand in the shoreline areas of Hawaii is composed of two general types of grains mixed together in proportions that vary from one locality to the next. Light-colored calcareous grains of biochemical origin, the fragments of skeletal parts of certain marine invertebrate animals and algae, contrast with dark-colored siliceous grains of detrital origin, originating from the land after weathering and erosion. A simple method used to determine the proportion by weight of each component in a particular sample was to dissolve in cold dilute hydrochloric acid the calcareous grains of a weighed random split of the sample, and then to weigh the washed and dried insoluble residue. Of 2084 local samples treated by this method, the results from one sea level sample are illustrated in figure 3 for each of 90 beach systems in Hawaii.

The insoluble residues were examined under binocular and petrographic microscopes in order to establish the composition of the detrital component, and these results also are illustrated in figure 3. Most grains were sand size, or rarely were gravel. However, a few samples from Molokai and Lanai deltaic coasts protected by shallow reefs contained muds composed of clays, iron-oxide accretionary bodies, and silt too fine to identify optically.

The remaining insoluble grains of sand-size are all from pre-existing bedrock (excepting rare sponge spicules or fragments of arthropod shells), either fragments of the rock itself or fragments of specific minerals from rock. All of these grains are volcanic in origin. For the purposes of this study three types of lithic grains, which actually intergrade into one another, were distinguished. Some grains are of fresh microcrystalline lava, some are of fresh volcanic glass, and some grains are more or less altered from these by chemical weathering. Fresh lava grains are the most abundant lithic grains in most samples. Of these grains, basalt predominates except in some East Molokai, Maui, and North Hawaii sands where most lithic grains are distinctly lighter in color and probably were eroded from the mugearite and hawaiite flows capping the volcanoes there (Stearns, 1946; Macdonald, 1960).

Glass grains are most abundant near recent eruptions where they make the so-called "black-sand" beaches, as on the southern coasts of Hawaii Island. Where some flows entered the ocean, explosions caused by the generation of steam from molten lava in contact with water ripped apart the chilling advancing edge of the flow. The resulting ash and lapilli of black basalt glass often formed a littoral cone (Wentworth and Macdonald, 1953), to be eroded and redeposited as glassy beach sands.

Originally, the monomineralic sand grains undoubtedly were lava phenocrysts or crystal ejecta in tuffs, because medium or coarser-grained holocrystalline igneous rocks are exposed over less than 1 percent of the surface of the islands. Olivine is the most common of these grains in Hawaii by far, both as unweathered phenocrysts and as detrital grains of sand-size. Beaches at Hanauma Bay, Oahu, and near South Point, Hawaii, are distinctly green in color from the high olivine content in streaks of sand deposited placer-fashion near the waterline. Black opaque grains of magnetite-ilmenite and dark-gray to gray-green transparent grains of augite are common only locally. A few beaches contain some labradorite plagioclase from nearby flows of hawaiite or alkali basalt with abundant feldspar phenocrysts. Quartz and the potash feldspars, the most common minerals of sands in most places in the world, are absent along local shores, although some quartz is present near the coast in the hydrothermally altered caldera of Koolau volcano near Kaneohe and Kailua, Oahu.

The distribution of detrital grains of sand along the shores of the Hawaiian Islands follows very closely the bedrock geology of the hinterlands, as is revealed in the detailed maps and reports of the series of Bulletins of the Hawaiian Division of Hydrography (Stearns and Vaksvik, 1935, through Macdonald, Davis, and Cox, 1960). Figure 3 illustrates the range of detrital and organic components in the mid-beach samples of 90 selected beach systems.

Organic Components

Identification Procedures.—Most of the important beaches of the State of Hawaii are highly calcareous, and a special effort was made to identify the components of the calcareous grains. Two of the writers, Mrs. Morrison and Mr. Baver, independently examined samples several months apart, and because their results were closely compatible it is believed the results reported here are significant. The descriptions by Thorp (1936) and Ginsburg (1956) of clastic organic grains, and the carbonate staining schemes summarized by Friedman (1959) and Warne (1962) were utilized in identification, and tested along with a variety of additional techniques. The following descriptions refer chiefly to the final methods used.

Each operator commenced with an examination of skeletal material of known invertebrate animals and marine algae that live in local shallow waters and were assumed to be potential contributors to the sand. For example, among corals, *Pocillopora, Porites,* and *Montipora* were included because of their abundance in Hawaiian waters. Identified specimens of these coral genera were crushed with a sledge hammer to fragments in the range of sand size (2.0 > 0.062 mm). The sand grains of each coral were then abraded in a jar mill for periods of time from 6 hours to 6 days. After abrasion the sand was washed, sieved, and studied. Unstained *Porites* and *Montipora* grains could be identified as fine as fine-sand size (to 0.125 mm), but in grains finer than 0.125 mm the characteristic porous structure was lost. Unstained *Pocillopora* was difficult to identify except on edges of the coral head, and abrasion increased the difficulty. Known Echinoid tests and spines, mollusk shells, calcareous algae, and Foraminifera tests were abraded and their structure studied in a similar manner.

Areas of active coral and algal growth were examined by skin and SCUBA diving, and offshore sand samples collected in those areas were studied. Familiarization with the known biota was beneficial in the identification of the organic components of those samples, and subsequently in the unknown beach sands.

Selective staining was a further aid in identification. The calcium carbonate polymorph aragonite is stained gray to black upon brief exposure to Feigl's solution, whereas calcite is not (Friedman, 1959). Corals and the green alga *Halimeda* contain aragonite, but Foraminifera, red algae, and Echinoids contain calcite, and mollusks may contain both (Chave, 1954; Lowenstam, 1954; Revelle and Fairbridge, 1957).

In practice the operator obtained a random split of the main sample with a microsplitter. The split fractions were washed carefully but not given a preliminary etching bath with hydrochloric acid, then placed in coded test tubes, stained by immersion for 1 minute and 15 seconds in Feigl's solution, and dried at 25°C. In nearly all instances this treatment stained the aragonitic grains but not the calcitic ones. An exception in a few samples was that Feigl's solution did not stain aragonite grains already stained a red-brown or pink color from iron-oxide-rich muds.

Quantitative Determination.—Each operator approached the problem of converting observed and identified grains to approximate volume percentage of composition in a slightly different way. After mechanical analysis to $\frac{1}{2}\phi$ sizes, and calculation of the median grain size, one operator combined the two sieve-holdings totaling one phi in which the median fell. This was the modal phi-fraction as well, in all but the poorest sorted gravelly samples. A split of these grains was stained and mounted, and each grain intercepted on a patterned traverse of the whole slide was counted once. Because all grains were nearly the same size, this type of counting would approximate the volume of components in the modal size. Moreover, the operator was seldom confronted with grains finer than 0.125 mm, and therefore was spared that obvious source of identification error. The chief bias of this first method is that there is some sorting of components by size. For example, a small, solid, and well-rounded Echinoid fragment may have the same hydraulic behavior as a larger, porous and disk-like foraminiferal test.

The second operator stained and mounted a split of the entire sample, and counted points moved under the cross-hairs by a device similar to that used by Chayes (1949). This approximation of the compositional volume would have been improved had thin-sections been prepared,

but the operators preferred to mount whole grains in tacky "Caedex" or "Vaseline" for rapidity and in order to observe surface features. There is good correlation if the sample is well-sorted both to size and shape, as most of these were. Otherwise the count becomes biased in favor of smaller, flatter grains.

A series of 400 or more points falling on calcareous grains was counted for each sample except those with predominantly detrital grains, in which a systematic traverse of the whole slide might have produced a total of less than 400 points counted on calcareous grains. After a few weeks each sample was counted a second time, with comparable results (within 10% probable error of a frequency of 10%, curves of Rittenhouse, 1940) on 149 of the 170 samples observed. For the 21 samples with a significant difference between the first and second counts, the second count was assumed to be the better because of experience gained in identification; for the samples with comparable counts, percentages were calculated from the sum of the two counts.

Some samples selected had a high percentage of grains too fine to be identified, and in those cases samples from the same location collected at different seasons, usually winter, were examined, and a coarser sample selected in substitution for otherwise summer-season samples. It is assumed that the identification of the coarser sand was representative of the beach, and that the finer-grained samples would have approximately the same percentages of constituent particles, if they could have been identified. Actually, some grains characteristically are of a single size, such as whole Foraminifera, and may have been discriminated against by this method of substituting coarser samples.

About 100 samples were examined by the first operator, Mrs. Morrison, who was interested in changes across the reef and beach, or by seasons. The second operator, Mr. Baver, examined 170 waterline samples, usually summer, representing all Hawaiian shorelines. Ninety of these, illustrating the composition of the most significant beaches in Hawaii, are shown in figure 3. In nearly all instances where the same sample was examined by both operators the results were closely comparable.

For the islands as a whole, Foraminifera predominate in most beaches, followed by mollusks and red algae, then Echinoids. It is rather a misnomer to speak of "coral sand," as coral is a poor fifth in general order. Only *Halimeda*, so important in the Bahamas and the Western Pacific islands (Lowenstam and Epstein, 1957; Emery, Tracey, and Ladd, 1954), and insignifi-

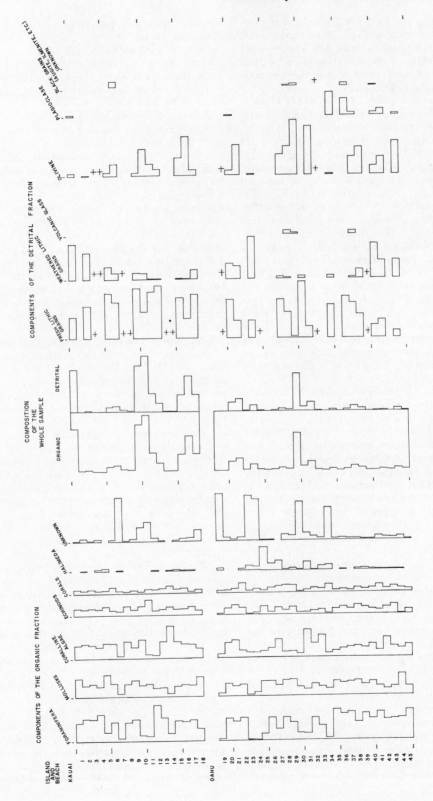

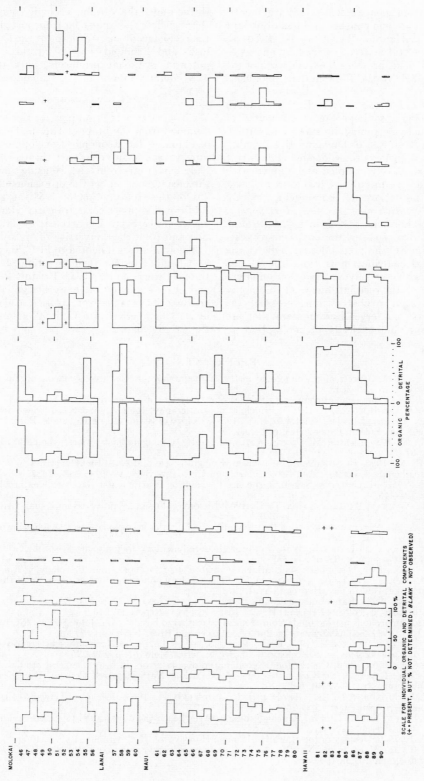

FIG. 3.—Composition of Hawaiian littoral sand. Numbers are keyed to locations in figure 1.

cant amounts of sponge spicules, crab fragments, and similar rare components, are less abundant than coral in Hawaiian beach sands. Of course the coral skeletal material, helped by encrustations of red algae, provides the framework of the reefs inhabited by the Foraminifera, mollusks, and Echinoids.

Source of Calcareous Sands.—Ecologic studies of Foraminifera, so important as a source of sand, are only beginning in Hawaiian waters. On Kahala Reef, east of Diamond Head, Oahu, sediment and algae on the wide and shallow reef flat were extensively sampled and stained with Rose Bengal dye to indicate living protoplasm. Although both large Foraminifera, mainly *Amphistegina*, *Heterostegina*, and *Marginopora*, and smaller Foraminifera, such as *Quinqueloculina* and *Spiroloculina*, are present as empty tests in the sediment, the preponderant bulk of the foraminiferal contribution is from the larger-sized genera. Yet no living large Foraminifera were found on the reef flat, but were commonly alive in a sand-covered channel crossing the reef. At least the larger Foraminifera that are so important volumetrically do not appear to thrive under the variable ecologic conditions of the reef flat; they must be transported in from the reef edge, along with most of the living mollusks and Echinoids and all of the corals. Of potential sediment producers, only the algae were common inhabitants of Kahala reef flat.

ACKNOWLEDGMENTS

The greater part of support for this study was obtained from the State of Hawaii Department of Planning and Economic Development, whose interest was financed in part through an urban planning grant from the Housing and Home Finance Agency, under the provisions of Section 701 of the Housing Act of 1954, as amended. Additional support came from the Harbors Division of the State Department of Transportation and from the University of Hawaii.

The writers are indebted to F. P. Shepard and T. Chamberlain for their direction of much of the field work, and to T. C. Bryant, P. Gilbert, and other students for many of the laboratory analyses. The manuscript has been read critically by T. Chamberlain and G. P. Woollard, whom the writers thank.

REFERENCES

CHAVE, K. E., 1954, Aspects of the biogeochemistry of magnesium: 1. Calcareous marine organisms: Jour. Geology, v. 62, p. 266–283.

CHAYES, F., 1949, A simple point counter for thin-section analysis: Am. Mineralogist, v. 34, p. 1–11.

DUNBAR, C. O., AND RODGERS, J., (1957), Principles of stratigraphy. John Wiley & Sons, New York, 356 p.

EMERY, K. O., TRACEY, J. I., JR., AND LADD, H. S., 1954, Geology of Bikini and nearby atolls. Part. I: Geology: U. S. Geol. Survey Prof. Paper 260-A, p. 1–265.

FRIEDMAN, G. M., 1959, Identification of carbonate minerals by staining methods: Jour. Sedimentary Petrology, v. 29, p. 87–97.

GINSBURG, R. N., 1956, Environmental relationships of grain size and constituent particles in some South Florida carbonate sediments: Am. Assoc. Petroleum Geologists Bull., v. 40, p. 2384–2427.

INMAN, D. L., 1952, Measures for describing the size distribution of sediments: Jour. Sedimentary Petrology, v. 22, p. 125–145.

INMAN, D. L., GAYMAN, W. R., AND COX, D. C., 1963, Littoral sedimentary processes on Kauai, a sub-tropical high island: Pacific Sci., v. 17, p. 106–130.

LOWENSTAM, H. A., 1954, Factors affecting the aragonite:calcite ratios in carbonate-secreting marine organisms: Jour. Geology, v. 62, p. 284–332.

LOWENSTAM, H. A., AND EPSTEIN, S., 1957, On the origin of sedimentary aragonite needles of the Great Bahama Bank: Jour. Geology, v. 65, p. 364–375.

MACDONALD, G. A., 1960, Dissimilarity of continental and oceanic rock types: Jour. Petrology, v. 1, p. 172–177.

MACDONALD, G. A., DAVIS, D. A., AND COX, D. C., 1960, Geology and ground-water resources of the island of Kauai, Hawaii: Hawaii Div. Hydrography, Bull. 13, 212 p.

MOBERLY, R., JR., 1963a, Rate of denudation in Hawaii: Jour. Geology, v. 71, p. 371–375.

———, 1963b, Coastal geology of Hawaii: Hawaii Inst. Geophys., Report 41, 216 p.

———, 1963c, Amorphous marine muds from tropically weathered basalts: Am. Jour. Sci., v. 261, p. 767–772.

PETTIJOHN, F. J., 1957, Sedimentary rocks. 2nd ed., Harper and Bros., New York, 718 p.

REVELLE, R., AND FAIRBRIDGE, R., 1957, Carbonates and carbon dioxide, *in* Hedgpeth, ed., Treatise on marine ecology and paleoecology, v. 1, Ecology: Geol. Soc. America Mem. 67, p. 239–296.

RITTENHOUSE, GORDON, 1940, Curves for determining probable errors in heavy mineral studies, *in* Trask, P. D., Chm., Report of the Committee on Sedimentation: Natl. Research Council, Div. Geology and Geography Ann. Rpt. 1939–40, p. 97–101.

SHEPARD, F. P., MOBERLY, R., JR., OOSTDAM, B. L., AND VEEH, H., 1963, Beaches of Hawaii, *abstract:* Geol. Soc. America Special Paper 73, p. 240.

SHEPARD, F. P., AND YOUNG, R., 1961, Distinguishing between beach and dune sands: Jour. Sedimentary Petrology, v. 31, p. 196–214.

STEARNS, H. T., 1946, Geology of the Hawaiian Islands: Hawaii Div. Hydrography, Bull. 8, 106 p.

STEARNS, H. T., AND VAKSVIK, K. N., 1935, Geology and ground-water resources of the island of Oahu: Hawaii Div. Hydrography, Bull. 1, 479 p.

THORP, E. M., 1936, Calcareous shallow-water marine deposits of Florida and the Bahamas: Carnegie Inst. Washington Pub. 452, Papers Tortugas Lab., v. 29, p. 37–119.

WARNE, S. ST. J., 1962, A quick field or laboratory staining scheme for the differentiation of the major carbonate minerals: Jour. Sedimentary Petrology, v. 32, p. 39–91.

WENTWORTH, C. K., 1922, A scale of grade and class terms for clastic sediments: Jour. Geology, v. 30, p. 377–392.

WENTWORTH, C. K., AND MACDONALD, G. A., 1953, Structures and forms of basaltic rocks in Hawaii: U. S. Geol. Survey, Bull. 994, 98 p.

Section 2

The Hawaiian Environment: The Land

INTRODUCTION

> While these volcanic mountains are still extend-
> ing their limits, in one part of the group, in
> others those changes are finely illustrated
> which they undergo through the action of water,
> gradual decomposition, and other allied causes;
> and these effects are in every state of progress:
> in some instances, the slopes retain the even
> surface of the most recent lava stream; in others,
> they are altered in every feature, the heights
> worn down, the whole surface gorged out with
> valleys, and the depth of the furrowings of time
> indicate that the several islands differ widely
> in the length of the period since they were
> finished by the fires, and left to the action
> of the elements.
>
> J. D. Dana, 1849, *United States Exploring*
> *Expedition*, vol. 10, *Geology*

Climate, location, landforms, earth materials, soil,
and altitude all combine to create the varied physical
environment found in the Hawaiian Islands. Once land
has appeared above the sea, it is attacked by agents
of weathering and erosion: chemical weathering or
decomposition, solution, running water, and wave action.
How rapidly land above sea level becomes worn down
depends on the composition of the rock and soil, the
rate of weathering, the amount and seasonality of rainfall, the steepness of the slope, and the covering of
vegetation.

In this section Blumenstock and Price discuss the
climate of the Hawaiian Islands, Sherman discusses the
genesis of soils, and Doty contrasts pioneer populating
processes on land and in the sea. Finally, the paper
by Krajina summarizes vegetation profiles which reflect
the various ages and physical characteristics of the
islands.

CLIMATES OF THE STATES: HAWAII[1]

David I. Blumenstock[2] and *Saul Price*[3]

Hawaii, alone of the fifty states, is completely surrounded by the ocean and entirely within the tropics.
Both of these factors contribute significantly to its
climate, as do also its division into separate, widely
spaced islands and its topographic diversity.

The islands of the State are the easternmost members of the Hawaiian Island chain. This chain extends
for a distance of nearly 2,000 miles from Kure Atoll
and Midway Islands at the northwest to the island of
Hawaii at the extreme southeast end. In longitude, the
Hawaiian chain reaches from 178° to 154° W; in latitude,
from 28° to 19° N. The islands of the State of Hawaii
cover a far smaller range: from 160° to 154° W and
from 22° to 19° N. They occupy a narrow zone 430 miles
long.

There are six major islands in the State. From
west to east these are Kauai, Oahu, Molokai, Lanai, Maui,
and Hawaii. Taken together with the much smaller islands
of Niihau and Kahoolawe, their total area is 6,424 square
miles, about 30 percent greater than that of Connecticut.

---

[1]This article was adapted by S. Price from D. Blumenstock and S. Price, 1967, Climates of the states: Hawaii,
Climatography of the United States No. 60-51, U.S. Department of Commerce, 27 p. Additional information and
detailed statistics may be obtained from the National
Weather Service.

[2]Weather Bureau Pacific Area Climatologist
(deceased).

[3]NOAA Regional Climatologist for the Pacific Basin.

The islands of the State of Hawaii are summit portions of the long range of volcanic mountains that
comprise the Hawaiian chain. Kauai, in the west, is
geologically the oldest of the six major islands and is
therefore most strongly eroded, as is evidenced by the
deeply cut Waimea Canyon in the western half of the
island and by the broadly eroded valley lands in the
eastern half. Hawaii, in the east, is geologically the
youngest. Its dominant physiographic features are the
large mountain masses of Mauna Loa and Mauna Kea, both
of which rise to over 13,000 feet above mean sea level
and have suffered only slight erosion. The four major
islands lying between Kauai and Hawaii are intermediate
in age and in the amount of erosion to which they have
been subjected. All the islands are bordered in some
areas by fringing coral reefs, and all have coasts that
consist in part of sea cliffs, some of which are 300
to 3,000 feet in height.

The mountainous nature of Hawaii is indicated by
the fact that 50 percent of the State lies above an
elevation of 2,000 feet and 10 percent lies above,
7,000 feet. However, the heights of the mountains vary
greatly from island to island, as is shown by the following tabulation:

ISLAND	MAXIMUM ELEVATION (feet)
Hawaii	13,796
Maui	10,023
Kauai	5,243
Molokai	4,970
Oahu	4,025
Lanai	3,370

Almost half the area of Hawaii lies within 5 miles
of the coast. Only about 5 percent, on the island of
Hawaii, is more than 20 miles inland. Because of this
extreme insularity, the marine influence upon the climate

is very great, yet the mountains, especially the massive
ones on Hawaii and Maui, strongly modify the marine effect with the result that semicontinental conditions
are found in some localities. The result is climatic
conditions of great diversity.

THE CLIMATIC SETTING

Year in and year out, the most prominent feature
of the circulation of air across the tropical Pacific
is the trade-wind flow in a general east-to-west direction. In the central North Pacific the trade winds blow
from the northeast quadrant and represent the outflow of
air from the great region of high pressure, the Pacific
Anticyclone, whose typical location is well north and
east of the Hawaiian Island chain. The Pacific High,
and with it the trade-wind zone, moves north and south
with the sun, so that it reaches its northernmost position in the summer half-year. This brings the heart of
the trade winds across Hawaii during the period from
May through September, when the trades are prevalent
80 to 95 percent of the time. From October through
April, Hawaii is north of the heart of the trade winds.
Nevertheless, the trades still blow across the islands
much of the time, though with a frequency that has
decreased to 50 to 80 percent, in terms of average
monthly values.

The dominance of the trades and the influence of
terrain give special character to the climate of the
islands. Completely cloudless skies are rare, though
much of the time the dense cloud cover is confined to
the mountain areas and windward slopes, while the leeward lowlands have only a few scattered clouds. Showers
are very common; while some of these are very heavy,
the vast majority are light and brief--a sudden sprinkle
of rain, and that is all. Even the heavy showers are of
a special character in that they are seldom accompanied

by thunder and lightning. Indeed, many people who have
lived only in Hawaii have no real notion of the violence
of mainland thunderstorms as evidenced by the lightning
and crashing thunder that are their typical accompaniment. Finally, the trade winds provide a system of
natural ventilation much of the time throughout most of
the State, and bring to the land, at least in the lower-
lying regions, the mildly warm temperatures that are
characteristic of air that has moved great distances
across the tropical seas.

But the trades, though dominant, are not the only
major dynamic element in the climatic setting of Hawaii.
Major storm systems may influence all parts of the islands, and in some areas topographically sheltered from
the trade winds there is a local exchange of air between
land and sea on a rhythmic, diurnal basis. There is
also the fundamental diurnal cycle of night and day, but
because Hawaii is in such a low latitude this cycle shows
less variation in length than is found in any other state.

Major storms occur most frequently from October
through March. During this period there may be two,
three, or as many as six or more major storm events in
any particular year. Such storms typically bring heavy
rains and are sometimes accompanied by strong winds, at
least on a local scale. The storms may be associated
with the passage of a cold front--of the leading edge
of a mass of relatively cool air that is moving from
west to east or from northwest to southeast. The storms
may also be associated with a large eddy or area of low
pressure. Moist, warm air swirling into such eddies
produces tremendous clouds and torrential rains. Other
meteorological circumstances under which heavy storms
occur will be described later in this report.

The land-and-sea circulations are on a far smaller
scale than the circulations of the major storm systems.
The exchange of air often is confined to areas of a

few square miles or tens of square miles. Circulations
of this kind are most common on south and west coasts,
in locations that are to the leeward with reference to
the trade winds and topographically sheltered from them.
The Kona Coast of Hawaii, the Lahaina district on Maui,
the Ewa-Waianae Coast of Oahu, and the Barking Sands
area of Kauai are among the localities in which these
circulations are common. These circulations have a
well-marked diurnal rhythm, in response to the day-to-
night reversal in the temperature contrast between land
and sea. Between forenoon and early evening, air moves
inland on a sea breeze. Sometimes these sea breezes
are fairly brisk. During the night and until shortly
after sunrise the air drifts back from land to sea.
The return drift is usually very gentle, so gentle that
it can barely be felt.

Underlying the land-and-sea circulations are the
diurnal rhythms of illumination periods which contribute
to the changes in temperature, variations in air pressure, variations in cloudiness and rainfall, and the
pace and rhythm of many other facets of the changing
weather.

There is only a slight variation in length of night
and day from one part of Hawaii to another, since the
major islands of the State all lie within a narrow
latitude band. The variations at Honolulu are therefore
generally representative of those of the State as a
whole. Table 1 shows these variations in terms of the
length of the longest and shortest days and compares
them with variations at other cities in the United
States. In each instance, two values are given: one
representing the length of day from sunrise to sunset;
the other, the length of day including the periods
before sunrise and after sunset when the twilight is
sufficiently bright to permit normal outdoor activities
without artificial illumination.

TABLE 1

CITY	NORTH LATITUDE	LONGEST DAY*				SHORTEST DAY*			
		Without twilight		Including twilight		Without twilight		Including twilight	
		Hrs.	Min.	Hrs.	Min.	Hrs.	Min.	Hrs.	Min.
Anchorage	61°	19	20	24	0	5	30	7	30
Seattle	48°	16	0	17	20	8	20	9	30
St. Louis Washington, D.C.	39°	15	0	16	0	9	20	10	20
Los Angeles Atlanta	34°	14	30	15	30	9	50	10	50
Brownsville Miami	26°	13	40	14	30	10	30	11	20
HONOLULU	21°	13	20	14	10	10	50	11	40

* In hours and minutes, to the nearest 10 minutes.

The relatively slight variations in the length of
the daylight period in Hawaii as contrasted with other
states, together with the smaller annual variations in
the altitude of the sun above the horizon, result in
relatively small variations in the amount of incoming
solar energy from one time of the year to another. The
solar energy that pours into the upper atmosphere above
Hawaii each day decreases by only a third from time of
maximum, in early June, to time of minimum, in late
December. But at Washington, D.C., the daily receipt
of energy at time of maximum is 3 times as great as it
is at time of minimum, while at Anchorage it is 20 times
as great.

This small variation in solar energy partly explains
why seasonal changes in temperature are so slight
throughout much of Hawaii. The other principal reason
is the virtually constant flow of fresh ocean air across
the islands. The surface waters of the open ocean around
Hawaii have an average temperature range from a minimum
of 73° or 74° F between late February and early April
to a maximum of 79° or 80° F in late September or early
October. Just as the temperature of the ocean surface
varies comparatively little from season to season, so
also does the temperature of air that has moved great
distances across the ocean. And so the air brings with
it to the land the mild temperature regime characteristic of the surrounding ocean.

The rugged configuration of the islands produces
marked variations in conditions from one locality to
another. Air swept inland on the trade winds or as
part of storm circulations is shunted one way and another
by the mountains and valleys and great open slopes. This
complex, three-dimensional flow of air results in striking differences from place to place in wind speed,
cloudiness, and rainfall. Together with variations in
the elevation of the land, it is responsible for differences in air temperature. Thus the climatic pattern

reflects not only such dynamic elements as the trade-wind
flow, the passage of storms, and the seasonal rhythms of
daylight and of solar heating, but also the static element of topography.

THE GENERAL CHARACTER OF HAWAIIAN CLIMATE

The native Hawaiians recognized only two seasons.
Kau was the fruitful season, the season when the sun was
directly or almost directly overhead, the weather was
warmer, and the trade winds were most reliable. *Hoo'ilo*
was the season when the sun was in the south, the weather
was cooler, and the trade winds were most often interrupted by other winds. Modern analysis of the climatic
records shows the soundness of this Hawaiian system of
seasons, although a slight modification of the old definitions is necessary. Whereas the Hawaiians' seasons
were six months long, *kau* extending from May through
October and *hoo'ilo* from November through April, it is
more accurate to recognize a winter season of seven
months (October through April) and a summer season of
only five months (May through September). Under this
arrangement summer is very definitely the warmer season,
the season with an overwhelming dominance of trade winds,
and when widespread rainstorms are rare. Also throughout the lowlands summer is the drier season in terms of
average monthly rainfall, except on the Kona (leeward)
Coast of the island of Hawaii.

In terms of variations in climatic conditions from
one part of the State to another, the most striking
contrasts are those in rainfall. At one extreme, the
annual rainfall averages 20 inches and less in leeward
coastal areas and near the summits of the very high
mountains, Mauna Loa and Mauna Kea on Hawaii. At the
other extreme, the annual average exceeds 300 inches
along the lower windward slopes of these high mountains
and of Haleakala on Maui and at or near the summit of

the lower mountains of Kauai, Oahu, and western Maui. The
complexity of the rainfall pattern and the sharpness of
the rainfall gradients are evident from the annual precipitation maps (Plates 1 and 2).

The temperature regime is not as variable from place
to place as is rainfall, but there are nonetheless major
geographic differences, chiefly as the result of variations in elevation. The upper slopes of the high mountains lie well above the usual cloud zone, and there are,
accordingly, moderately wide swings in temperature from
day to night. Thus in summer at an elevation of 8,000
feet (above mean sea level) it is not unusual to have
daytime temperatures in the middle 60s and nighttime
temperatures in the 40s, while in winter the range is
typically from the 50s to near freezing or below. Diurnal
temperature ranges are far narrower in the lowlands, with
daytime temperatures commonly in the 70s and 80s and
nighttime temperatures in the 60s and 70s. Both in the
lowlands and at elevations up to about 4,000 feet the
temperature differences from winter to summer are only
4° to 8° F in terms of differences in the mean daily
maximum and mean daily minimum. The values for Lihue,
Honolulu, and Hilo (given in the following section) are
representative of lowland conditions everywhere, except
on the very dry west coasts where both the diurnal and
seasonal variations are slightly greater.

In the general the Hawaiian climate is characterized
by a two-season year, with mild and fairly uniform temperature conditions everywhere except at high elevations,
by strikingly marked geographic differences in rainfall,
by generally humid conditions and high cloudiness except
on the driest coasts and at high elevations, and by a
dominance of trade-wind flow especially at elevations
below a few thousand feet. How conditions differ from
season to season and place to place is discussed in more
detail in the following sections.

Mean Annual Precipitation, Inches

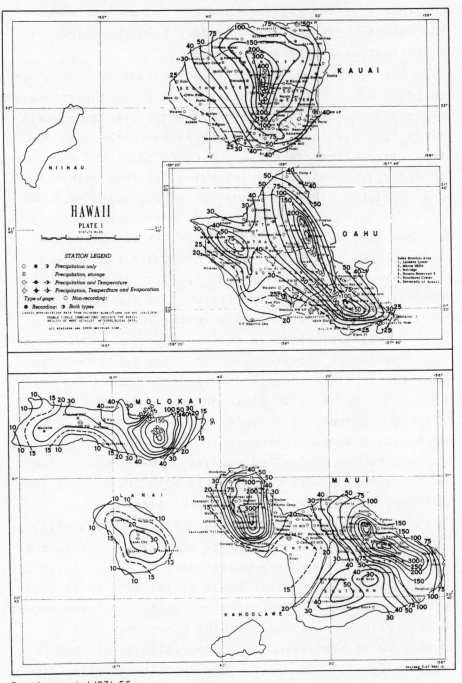

Based on period 1931-55

Isolines are drawn through points of approximately equal value. Caution should
be used in interpolating on these maps, particularly in mountainous areas.

Mean Annual Precipitation, Inches

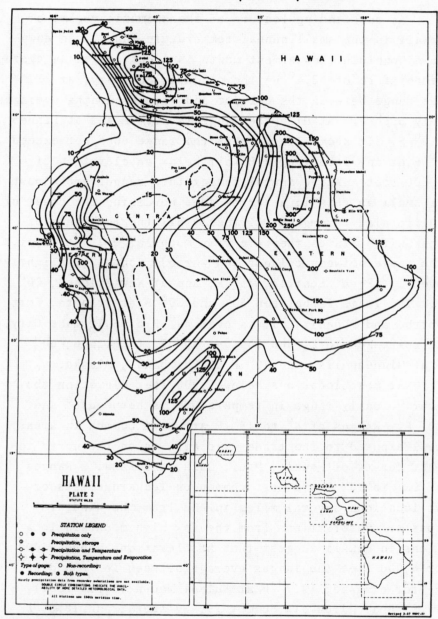

Based on period 1931-55

    Isolines are drawn through points of approximately equal value. Caution should
be used in interpolating on these maps, particularly in mountainous areas.

TEMPERATURE

An outstanding feature of the climatic regime of
Hawaii is the small annual temperature range. In downtown Honolulu the warmest month is August, with an average
temperature of 78.4^o F; the coldest, February, at 71.9^o F.
The range between the coldest and warmest months averages
only 6.5^o F. At Hilo the range is 5.0^o F and at Lihue,
8.0^o F. It seems likely that the range does not exceed
9° F at any location in Hawaii below an elevation of
5,000 feet. While annual temperature ranges are almost
as small as this in a narrow zone bordering the coast of
California, throughout virtually all the remainder of
the United States they are very much larger. At Miami
the range between coldest and warmest months is slightly
over 13° F; at Seattle, 23° F; and at New Orleans, 26°
F. The range is between 30° and 39° F at Atlanta, Fort
Worth, and Phoenix. It is over 40° F at Salt Lake City,
Detroit, New York, and Boston, 50° F at Chicago, 60°
F at Minneapolis, and 70° F at Fairbanks, Alaska.

At most locations below 5,000 feet elevation the
average daily range in temperature is between 8° and
20° F. Ranges of 8° to 15° F are most common in areas
well exposed to the trade-wind air, as on the north to
east coasts of Hawaii, Maui, Oahu, and Kauai. Ranges
of 15° to 20° F are most common on leeward coasts or
at locations several miles inland from the windward
coasts. Observations from the few high mountain locations in Hawaii suggest that at elevations above 5,000
or 6,000 feet the ranges average between 16° F and 20°
F--for example, 19.7^o F at Kulani Mauka (8,300 feet),
17.2^o F at Haleakala Summit (9,960 feet), and 18.8^o F
at Mauna Loa Observatory (11,150 feet). At neither
these elevations nor lower ones is there more than a
few degrees' difference between the average daily ranges
in winter and those in summer.

The rate at which the average temperature decreases
with increasing elevation is illustrated by comparing

the mean monthly temperatures, for January and August,
at a series of stations on the island of Hawaii, as
shown in Table 2.

All of these stations except Hilo are on the slopes
of Mauna Loa, and all but the observatory are on the
east to northeast slope, well exposed to trade-wind air.
The observatory is on the north slope of Mauna Loa.
From these and other temperature values it appears that
the average decrease in mean monthly temperatures upslope is about 3° F per thousand feet. However, the
actual decreases in monthly means vary from 1° F to as
much as 6° F because of marked local differences in
cloudiness, the effect of local winds, and differences
in exposure to the trades.

The highest temperature ever recorded in the State
is 100° F, at Pahala on Hawaii. Temperatures above 95°
F are infrequent, however, even in dry and relatively
cloudless areas such as the leeward coasts, and the 100°
F reading at Pahala may have occurred under special
circumstances. Except in the dry leeward areas, temperatures of 90° F and above are uncommon.

The lowest temperature "officially" recorded in
Hawaii is 14° F, observed at the summit of Haleakala.
However, temperatures at higher elevations on the upper
slopes and summits of Mauna Kea and Mauna Loa may fall
below this value. At times these regions are covered
with snow during the winter season, occasionally for
extended periods. It is possible that under favorable
circumstances cold air formed immediately above this
snow cover on clear nights drains down into local depressions and accumulates to sufficient depths to cause
temperatures of 5° F or lower even at the standard
observational height of 5 feet above the ground.

In exposed locations on the mountains, however, the
cold air formed locally is often swept away and replaced
by the far warmer air that is carried across and around
the mountains by the upper winds; and the local winds

TABLE 2

STATION	ELEVATION ABOVE SEA LEVEL (feet)	MEAN JANUARY TEMPERATURE (°F)	MEAN AUGUST TEMPERATURE (°F)
Hilo	40	71	76
Olaa	280	70	75
Mountain View	1,530	65	70
Hawaii National Park	3,971	58	64
Kulani Camp	5,190	53	58
Mauna Loa Observatory	11,150	41	47

that tend to move downslope at night and upslope during
the day also have the effect of inhibiting the formation
of extremely cold air.

At elevations below 1,000 feet, the lowest nighttime temperatures of record have been in the 50s, except
in relatively cloudless areas such as central Maui and
the leeward coasts, where temperatures in the high 40s
have been known to occur. Here again, however, these
are extreme values, and it is possible for several years
to pass before temperatures below 50° F are experienced
in any locality near sea level.

In general, lowland temperature conditions in all
but the driest areas are well represented by the values
for Honolulu, Hilo, and Lihue, as shown in Table 3.
Conditions in the driest areas are well represented by
the values for Mana, Kauai; Waianae, Oahu; and Lahaina,
Maui--all of which lie on leeward coasts in areas that
are very dry and relatively free of cloud.

It is noteworthy that in these dry areas, as
throughout Hawaii, August and September are the warmest
months of the year, August tending to be the warmest on
Kauai, the northernmost island of the State, and September the warmest on Hawaii, the southernmost island.
The occurrence of highest temperatures in late summer
and early autumn is typical of areas that are overlain
by fresh ocean air a high percentage of the time.

WINDS

As in all mountainous areas, the wind conditions
in Hawaii are exceedingly complex. Though the trade
winds are fairly constant in speed and though they blow
a high percentage of the time across the adjacent sea
and onto the bordering lands, the relatively uniform
trade-wind flow is distorted and disrupted by the mountains, hills, and valleyways. In addition, there are
local wind regimes along many of the coasts and on the

TABLE 3

TEMPERATURE (°F)

STATION	JANUARY			AUGUST			EXTREMES	
	Mean	Mean Maximum	Mean Minimum	Mean	Mean Maximum	Mean Minimum	Maximum	Minimum
Honolulu	72.5	79.1	65.8	79.4	84.9	73.8	92	55
Hilo	70.8	78.7	62.8	75.8	83.1	68.4	94	53
Lihue	70.9	78.2	63.5	78.4	83.9	72.8	90	50
Mana	70.3	79.0	61.4	78.0	88.0	68.0	95	48
Waianae	71.8	81.1	62.5	80.3	89.5	71.1	96	50
Lahaina	71.3	80.7	61.8	77.8	87.4	68.1	93	52

mountain slopes, and these local regimes may either reinforce or oppose the general flow of air depending on the
local circumstances. Finally, in some weather situations
the trade winds are replaced by other general winds, some
of which are not nearly so uniform in direction or speed.
For all these reasons average wind-speed values are in-
formative only in a broad descriptive sense, and it is
necessary to consider a variety of wind situations even
to begin to describe realistically the true wind conditions.

Over the ocean around Hawaii average wind speeds
are highest during the summer trade-wind period. During
the summer months (May through September) the ocean winds
exceed 12 miles an hour 50 percent of the time. These
winds are from the northeast quadrant 80 to 95 percent
of the time. During the winter (October through April),
when trade winds are not quite as prevalent, wind speeds
are in excess of 12 miles an hour about 40 percent of
the time. It is during this winter season that light
variable winds are most frequent, and this more than
balances the fact that winter is also the time of occasional very strong winds--winds stronger than those
experienced during the summer except for the rare tropical storm or hurricane occurring in the summer period.

When the trade winds are moderate or strong--
generally in excess of 14 miles an hour--they dominate
the flow of air across wide reaches of the lowlands. In
contrast, light trade winds are commonly felt only along
the eastern to northern coasts of the islands and in
exposed locations in the hills. With such light trades,
leeward coasts, even those not sheltered from the trades,
may experience a diurnal cycle of land and sea breezes;
and in more sheltered areas, as on the Kona Coast of
Hawaii and in the Kihei area on Maui, these local sea
and land breeze circulations occur not only when the
overall wind is light, but also when the trade winds
are moderate to strong. It should be noted also that

diurnal variations in wind speed, as well as in direction,
occur. Even during periods of pronounced trade winds,
speeds over the open ocean or in well-exposed areas will
usually reach their maximum during the afternoon and
diminish considerably, or even die off from time to time,
during the night.

Because wind conditions at any one time may vary
from place to place, the frequencies at any one point
are not representative of conditions everywhere in Hawaii.
Nonetheless, the frequencies from the International Airport, Honolulu, give a general notion of the variations
in wind speed and direction that are experienced in many
land locations, not including locations at well-exposed
headlands or in the hills or mountains. Wind frequencies
at the airport during the 10-year period 1951 to 1960
are summarized in Table 4.

As these frequencies indicate, extremely high winds
are unusual at most locations in Hawaii. However, where
the trade winds funnel through broad saddle areas, like
Maui's central valley, Molokai's Hoolehua district, and
the Waimea area of Hawaii Island, their speeds are consistently higher than those shown in the table. On a
few exposed headlands and in mountain passes so oriented
as to catch and concentrate the full force of the trades,
winds above 40 m.p.h. may occur on several days each
month of the year. In nearly all other locations,
however, such winds occur only occasionally, and then
only as the result of a major storm, the passage of a
cold front, or an unusual local situation.

Major storms are chiefly events of the winter season. They may yield very high winds from any direction.
At Honolulu airport, wind speeds resulting from these
storms have on several occasions exceeded 60 m.p.h. over
a period of 1 to 2 minutes, and 80 m.p.h. momentarily
in gusts. It seems reasonable to assume that at such
times 100 m.p.h. speeds have been attained locally near
sea level, although speeds that high have actually been

TABLE 4

WIND DIRECTION	WIND DIRECTION FREQUENCIES (%)		WIND SPEED (m.p.h.)	WIND SPEED FREQUENCIES (%)	
	January	August		January	August
NNE to E	50	93	0-12	68	38
ESE to S	19	4	13-24	29	58
SSW to W	10	<1	25 and over	2	3
WNW to N	20	3			
Calm	2	1			

measured at only a very few points in the State. In any
major wind-producing storm the extreme wind speeds may
vary radically from one place to another, owing both to
the peculiarities of the storm, and to the effects of
terrain. It is not unusual to have maximum speeds of
only 35 or 40 m.p.h. in one locality and much higher
speeds in a restricted area only a few miles away. The
nature of these winds and their extent and frequency are
discussed in the separate section on storms, below.

The local situations that produce occasional violent
winds are not always completely understood, even though
the general causes of these winds can be surmised. These
are local winds of very limited extent. In almost all
instances the areas affected appear to have been down-
wind of topographic features such as deep mountain passes,
which have therefore been held responsible for further
increasing the speed and turbulence of winds already
stronger than usual. In these areas the winds must
sometimes reach speeds of 60 to 100 miles an hour, for
they have been known to do considerable structural
damage and to blow down well-rooted trees, as well as
power lines designed to withstand high wind loads. The
inhabited areas chiefly affected are those that lie on
the lee side (relative to the actual wind) of mountain
ranges--such as Oahu's Wahiawa and Kaneohe areas, relative to the Waianae and Koolau mountains, respectively,
and the Lahaina coast, relative to the high mountains
of West Maui. It is likely that these winds also occur
in, but are less frequently reported from, more sparsely
settled areas on the slopes of the mountains of Hawaii
and Maui, or near the mouths of canyons along the base
of these mountains and those of the other islands. They
are, however, known best in the settled areas of Kula
and Lahaina on Maui.

The Kula winds are strong downslope winds. They
occur in the Kula district along a section of the lower
slopes on the west side of Haleakala. According to

observations by inhabitants of the area, the winds tend
to be strongest in the zone that lies between 2,000 and
4,000 feet above sea level. In this zone there may be
episodes of downslope winds with speeds of over 40 m.p.h.
as often as twice a year. However, winds with speeds
in excess of 60 m.p.h. probably occur only once every
4 or 5 years, on the average.

The Lahaina winds also seem to be downslope winds,
but of somewhat different character from those of Kula.
In the Lahaina area they have been given the name "lehua
winds" for the tree which grows in that locality and
with whose red blossoms the air is filled when these
strong winds blow. They issue from the canyons at the
base of the main mountain mass of western Maui, where the
steeper canyon slopes meet the more gentle piedmont slope
below. These winds have been reported from both the
western and southwestern side of the West Maui mountains. In their milder form they may occur once every
1 or 2 years, on the average. Much less frequently,
however--perhaps every 8 to 12 years or so--they are
extremely violent, with wind speeds whose effects suggest
that they may reach 80 to 100 m.p.h. or even more. They
have been known to demolish buildings, to uproot trees,
and to cause severe lodging throughout whole fields of
sugarcane. That they are partly downslope winds is
evident from their being hot and dry. However, the
mountains of western Maui are less than 6,000 feet high
as contrasted with the 10,000-foot height of Haleakala,
and it seems likely that these local Lahaina winds are
caused in large part by the funneling of strong trade
winds through certain of the mountain gorges.

Aside from the more violent mountain winds, there
are light to moderate mountain winds in many areas on
the larger mountains of Hawaii and Maui and in a few
local areas in the smaller mountains of the other islands
of the State. The usual regime is to have upslope winds
by day and downslope winds by night, and this circulation

takes its place with that of the sea-and-land breezes
in coastal locations as a finer, yet important, feature
of the overall wind regime of Hawaii.

HUMIDITY AND CLOUDINESS

Because of Hawaii's valleys, hills, and mountains,
the moisture distribution within the air that moves across
the islands is far from uniform, even at one level in
that air. A few major features of that distribution,
however, are evidenced again and again, and they give
coherence to the observed variations in humidity and
cloudiness.

Under trade-wind conditions, there is very often
a pronounced moisture discontinuity at heights of between 4,000 and 8,000 feet above sea level. Below these
heights the air is moist; above it is dry. The break
occurs in association with a temperature inversion that
is typically embedded in the moving trade-wind air, and
represents a large-scale feature of the Pacific Anticyclone. From the surface up to the inversion, the
temperature decreases with increasing height in a quite
uniform manner. The moisture is well distributed
throughout this lower layer, and the moisture content
of the air is relatively high. At the inversion the
temperature increases by several degrees, sometimes
quite suddenly. These higher temperatures may extend
upward for several hundred feet before the temperature
begins once more to decrease upward, as is most usual
in the atmosphere. The significance of the inversion
climatically is that it tends not only to produce a
lower, more moist layer as against a higher, more dry
layer, but also to suppress the vertical movement of
air and hence to restrict cloud development to the zone
beneath the inversion.

When the inversion is present, as it is 50 to 70
percent of the time, its height fluctuates from day to

day. Most often, however, it is between 5,000 and 7,000
feet. And on trade-wind days when the inversion is well
marked, the clouds develop most markedly below these
heights, and only occasional cloud masses break through
the inversion and extend upward. With an inversion these
towering clouds form chiefly along the mountains in particular local situations, for example, where the incoming
trade-wind air is crowded together as it moves up a
valleyway and is at the same time forced up over the
mountains to heights of several thousand feet. The over-
all result is a complicated cloud pattern, typically with
scattered to broken clouds above the lowlands at a fairly
uniform height on the windward coasts and with more dense
cloud masses along the mountains; these clouds are also
generally of uniform height, but with smaller masses that
bulge upward here and there.

On days when there is no inversion, the vertical
development of clouds is commonly much greater. There
may then be towering clouds at sea as well as over the
land. There is still, however, a tendency for the maximum cloud development to occur along the mountains, and
here individual clouds are especially likely to tower
upward to heights of 15,000 feet or more. When there is
a storm or other disturbance in or near the islands, the
cloud pattern may become very complicated, often with
very high cirrus clouds in different arrangements, with
layered or cellular cloud decks beneath them at heights
of 8,000 to 15,000 feet, and with masses of cumulus clouds
rising from near the surface upward to 30,000 to 50,000
feet. At the other extreme, there are occasional days
without an inversion when the sky is almost cloudless,
and a few times a year it is possible to scan the entire
sky without seeing a single cloud.

According to standard definitions of cloudiness,
clear represents 3/10 or less of the entire sky dome
covered with cloud, *partly cloudy*, 4/10 to 7/10, and
cloudy, 8/10 or more. With reference to these definitions,

throughout the lowlands in windward areas in the islands
the sky is cloudy about 40 to 60 percent of the time
during the daylight hours and clear 15 to 20 percent of
the time. In downtown Honolulu, which is to the leeward of a low mountain range, these values are 27 percent
cloudy and 25 percent clear during the daylight hours.
In leeward locations, well screened from the trade winds,
as along the west coasts of Maui, Kauai, and Oahu, the
percentage of clear daylight conditions ranges from 30
to 60 percent, and cloudy conditions decrease to less
than 20 percent. However, in these leeward areas, as
in those to the windward, the cloudiness increases
rapidly as the mountains are approached.

In general, windward areas tend to be cloudier
during the summer, when trade winds and trade-wind clouds
are more prevalent, while leeward areas--which are less
affected by trade-wind cloudiness--tend to be cloudier
during the winter, when general storms and frontal passages are more frequent.

Leeward coasts and lowlands are actually sunnier
than the foregoing percentages suggest, since a large
part of the reported sky cover consists of clouds that
lie over the mountains to windward, but may not obscure
the sun or the sky nearer overhead.

The cloudiest zones of all are at and just below
the summits of the mountains of Kauai, Oahu, Molokai,
Lanai, and western Maui; and at elevations of 2,000 to
4,000 feet on the windward sides of Haleakala, Mauna
Loa, and Mauna Kea. In these locations, conditions are
cloudy more than 70 percent of the time.

In contrast, the areas of least cloud include the
high mountains above about 8,000 feet. Here the skies
are normally clear between late evening and forenoon,
but tend to become cloudier during the middle part of
the day. The description by Price and Pales (1959)
of the usual regime at the Mauna Loa Observatory
(11,150 feet above sea level) is representative of most

high mountain locations:

> . . . A typical day at the Observatory
> may dawn bright and clear. Visibility is
> excellent. Peaks on other islands 80 miles
> distant and more are distinguishable with-
> out difficulty. The trade inversion lies
> several thousand feet below, and trapped
> beneath it are the clouds and the bulk of
> the water vapor, dust, and haze. In the
> clear atmosphere, insolation is intense
> . . . .
>
> By early afternoon, moister air appears
> to be seeping upward along the mountain.
> The humidity increases and fractocumuli
> (broken cumulus clouds) advance up the
> slopes. In the next hours the observatory
> may be briefly enveloped in fog or light
> rain; but by evening the clouds have dis-
> sipated and the conditions which opened
> the day return. Nights are generally
> clear.

The usual clarity of the air in the high mountains
is associated with the low moisture content of the air.
Except for periods when general storms envelop the upper
slopes and summits in cloud and rain, or when moist air
drifts upslope from below on sunny afternoons, the relative humidity is generally below 40 percent, and it
often falls to 10 or even 5 percent. Such low humidities
are characteristic of the zone above the inversion that
separates the lower and upper air.

Below the inversion, in the lowlands and along the
lower mountains, the relative humidity commonly averages
70 to 80 percent in windward areas and 60 to 70 percent
in leeward areas. Winter relative humidities are somewhat higher than summer ones, and in terms of daily

variations the maximum values occur with the minimum
temperatures, during the late night and early morning.
Nighttime values in the cooler and rainier areas often
exceed 90 percent, but are more frequently between 70
and 80 percent in the leeward lowlands and other drier
localities. Afternoon values are commonly between 60
and 70 percent in windward and upland regions and not
infrequently between 50 and 55 percent in the drier,
warmer coastal zones; they seldom fall below 40 percent
anywhere at elevations below the trade-wind inversion.
Thus, except on the high mountains, the general regime
in Hawaii is one of high humidities as compared with
conditions in most other states.

RAINFALL

If the islands of the State of Hawaii did not exist,
the average annual rainfall upon the water where the
islands lie would be about 25 inches. Instead, the
actual average is about 70 inches. Thus the islands
extract from the air that passes across them about 45
inches of rainfall that otherwise would not fall. That
the mountains are dominantly responsible for this added
water is evident from the annual rainfall maps, which
show the tremendous depths of rainfall deposited in
mountainous areas in the average year. In many mountainous areas of the State these depths exceed 240 inches,
or 20 feet. On Mt. Waialeale, on Kauai, the annual
average reaches the extraordinary total of 486 inches--
over 40 feet. This is the highest recorded annual
average rainfall in the world.

An average of 70 inches of rainfall over Hawaii is
equivalent to not quite 8,000 billion gallons of water
per year. This is more than 10 times the annual water
use in the State of something over 700 billion gallons.
Of this total, irrigation accounts for 74 percent; industrial uses (chiefly for cooling) account for 19

percent; and domestic and miscellaneous uses, for the
remaining 7 percent.

   With actual water requirements running less than
10 percent of the water supplied annually by rainfall,
it may seem strange that there are major problems of
water supply in many parts of Hawaii. However, not only
are there very substantial water losses due to evaporation, transportation, runoff, and percolation into the
porous lavas, but also the rainfall distribution is
exceedingly uneven. There are very few areas elsewhere
in the world and none elsewhere in the United States
where rainfall gradients are as steep as they are in
Hawaii. In a great many places in Hawaii the rainfall
increases 25 inches for each mile traversed along a
straight line. In a very extreme instance, the gradient
is 118 inches per mile along the 2-1/2 mile line from
Hanalei Tunnel to Mt. Waialeale on Kauai. These steep
rainfall gradients and the presence of very dry areas
as well as very wet ones result in an overall abundance
of water, but with great surpluses in some areas and
great deficiencies in others. The major problem of
water supply is therefore one of development and distribution, rather than of a general water shortage.

Annual Rainfall Patterns

   The distribution of mean annual rainfall on the
six major islands is shown on the accompanying maps
(Plates 1 and 2). These are largely self-explanatory,
but a few general comments will serve to bring out features of the annual pattern that are not evident.

   The zones of highest rainfall on the flanks of
the three large, high mountains--Haleakala, Mauna Loa,
and Mauna Kea--are at elevations of 2,000 to 4,000 feet.
In contrast, on the other mountains, all of which are
less than 6,000 feet in maximum elevation, the highest
rainfall is along or near the summit or crest line. The

difference lies in the fact that the incoming ocean air
that is the source of rain usually flows across the lower
mountains, but around the higher mountains. It is significant in this regard that the trade-wind inversion,
which tends to suppress vertical lifting of the air, is
usually above the level of the crests of the low mountains and is never above the level of the crests of the
high mountains.

The driest areas are on the upper slopes of the
highest mountains, on leeward coasts, or in leeward locations in the interior of the islands, as in central
Maui. In the driest of these areas the average annual
rainfall is less than 10 inches, and in one area, around
Kawaihae Bay near the northern end of the west coast of
Hawaii, the rainfall is less than 7 inches.

In many areas of intermediate rainfall, the natural
landscape indicates great aridity. Thus xerophytic
(drought resistant) plants, widely scattered across
otherwise barren ground, are sometimes found in areas
in which the annual rainfall is 100 inches or more.
This seeming anomaly is the result of very high infiltration rates into the volcanic rocks and soils; the
water that falls as rain moves rapidly downward to great
depths in the regolith (loose material overlying solid
rock or earth) and is available to the plants only to
a sharply limited extent. Areas of this kind are most
commonly found on the relatively young island of Hawaii.

Seasonal Variations in Rainfall

At elevations below 2,000 feet throughout the State
(except for the Kona Coast of Hawaii), winter is the
season of highest average rainfall. This is evident
from the data for selected lowland stations given in
Table 5.

The contrast in rainfall between the rainier winter
season and the drier summer season is generally most

TABLE 5

STATION	ELEVATION (feet)	AVERAGE MONTHLY RAINFALL (inches)		WETTEST MONTH		DRIEST MONTH	
		Winter Season (Oct.-April)	Summer Season (May-Sept.)	Month	Inches	Month	Inches
Mana, Kauai	11	2.60	0.78	Jan.	4.06	July	0.56
Lihue, Kauai	207	5.41	3.05	Jan.	6.45	June	2.29
Waialua, Oahu	32	3.30	0.95	Feb.	4.81	June	0.72
Honolulu, Oahu	12	2.74	0.94	Jan.	3.86	June	0.62
Hana, Maui	130	6.88	4.49	Dec.	8.19	June	3.46
Lanai City, Lanai	1,620	3.59	1.97	Jan.	4.62	June	1.42
Hilo, Hawaii	40	13.31	9.48	Mar.	15.45	June	6.80
Haina, Hawaii	461	6.69	3.45	Mar.	8.56	June	1.92

pronounced at low elevations in the areas with low annual
rainfall, as at Mana and Honolulu. The contrast is least
in areas of higher annual rainfall, as at Hilo. Further,
within the extremely rainy areas above 2,000 feet elevation, the winter rainfall maximum disappears in many
localities and instead there is fairly uniform, abundant
rainfall in all months of the year. Thus at Kukui, Maui,
at an elevation of 5,788 feet, the average monthly rainfall is 32.81 inches in winter and 33.49 in summer, with
April the wettest month (40.78) and October the driest
(23.33). The average annual rainfall at Kukui is slightly over 399 inches. Finally, in the very high mountains
where conditions are dry, winter is again the rainier of
the two seasons, although only slightly so. This is
indicated by the observations at Mauna Loa Observatory
(11,150 feet), where, with an annual precipitation of
about 21 inches, winter precipitation averages 1.8 inches
per month and summer precipitation averages 1.6.

The Kona Coast of Hawaii has a unique seasonal rainfall regime. The summers are wetter than the winters.
At Napoopoo, for example, the average monthly rainfall
in winter is 2.80 inches, while the average in summer
is 3.70. November is the driest month, with an average
of 2.06 inches. September is wettest, with an average
of 3.90 inches. Napoopoo is at an elevation of 400 feet
and has an average annual rainfall of 38.05 inches. The
summer maximum on the Kona Coast is associated with the
facts that (1) in the well-protected Kona area, which
lies to the leeward of Mauna Loa and Mauna Kea, there
is a distinctive local circulation, with daytime onshore
breezes that yield fairly regular and sometimes heavy
showers as they ascend the mountain slopes, and which
appear to be more intense in summer than winter; and
(2) the winter storms that contribute the bulk of the
average annual rainfall in other lowland regions of the
State contribute less rain to the Kona Coast.

Diurnal Variations in Rainfall

In the lowlands at all times of the year, rainfall
is most likely to occur during the nighttime or in the
morning hours and least likely to occur during midafter-
noon. Correspondingly, not only is rainfall more frequent at night, but also the total nighttime fall averages
more than the total daytime fall when the two 12-hour
periods are compared. The values worked out for Honolulu
by Loveridge (1924) are representative. They show that
59 percent of the annual rainfall total falls, on the
average, between 8 p.m. and 8 a.m. In general this
diurnal variation is far more pronounced in summer than
in winter, especially with respect to rainfall frequency.
Thus in summer, rainfall is about twice as frequent during the very late night and early morning hours (3 to 8
a.m.) as during the late morning and early or middle
afternoon (11 a.m. to 4 p.m.).

The more pronounced diurnal variation in summer is
associated with the fact that most summer rainfall consists of trade-wind showers, and these showers are most
apt to occur at night. In winter most of the rainfall
in the lowlands occurs in general storm situations,
which are as likely to take place during the daytime as
at night.

It seems reasonable to suppose that at elevations
of a few thousand feet, where trade-wind showers contribute very substantially to the total rainfall in
winter as well as in summer, the nighttime rainfall
maximum is better marked in winter than it is in the
lowlands. However, on the very high mountains above
the trade-wind inversion, the diurnal cycle appears to
be reversed. Judging from the Mauna Loa Observatory
observations, the late afternoon is the time when light
rains are most apt to occur as the accompaniment of
moist air carried upward by the upslope wind.

Rainfall Variability and Drought

In most parts of the tropics the rainfall is highly
variable from one year to another. Hawaii is no exception. Even in areas where the monthly rainfall averages
are all above 10 inches, the rainfall of particular
months may vary by 200 to 300 percent from one year to
another, and there may be very occasional months with
only 1 or 2 inches of rain.

The great annual variability in rainfall is evident
from the extreme values at several different stations
during their periods of record. In downtown Hilo, in
79 years of record, the highest annual total was 207
inches; the lowest 72. At Honolulu, in 62 years, the
extreme values were 46 inches and 10 inches; at Mana,
Kauai, 61 years, 48 and 5 inches. During a period of
only 23 years at Kukui, Maui, the extremes were 578
and 250 inches.

Rainfall variability is far greater during the
winter, when occasional storms contribute appreciably
to rainfall totals, than during summer, when trade-wind
showers provide most of the rain. In January, Hilo has
received less than 0.2 inches of rain, but also more
than 50 inches; Honolulu has received as little as 0.12
and as much as 18 inches. Even Kukui, with an average
January rainfall of 24 inches, has received as little
as 1.5 inches. The highest January total in 23 years
at Kukui was 58 inches. The extreme August rainfall
totals have a much smaller range. At Hilo the range
was from 2 to 38 inches. At Honolulu it was from 0.2
inches to 4 inches. At Kukui during 23 years it was
from 10 to 88 inches.

With such wide swings in rainfall it is inevitable
that there are occasional droughts, sometimes with severe
economic losses. The drought years are the ones in which
the winter rains fail, in which there are only one or
two or even no rainstorms whatsoever of real magnitude.

Although such a deficiency of winter storms can affect any portion of the State, it hits hardest the normally dry areas which depend chiefly on winter rains and receive little rain from the trade-wind showers. In these localities the small amount of rainfall that occurs during the usual dry summer season is insufficient to prevent severe drought. Severe droughts are usually limited to an area of 50 square miles or so, but even so they may be very costly even in irrigated areas because of the increased water costs, and, where irrigation is not practiced, they may destroy or severely damage the crops or range grasses.

One of the winters of record when the rainfall was decidedly below average throughout most of Hawaii was that of 1925-1926. At Honolulu during this period, every month from November through April experienced below-average rainfall, and the total for the 5-month period of January through May was less than 3 inches. For 100 consecutive days during the drought there was not as much as 0.3 inch of rainfall on any one day at Honolulu and on only 2 days was there as much as 0.2 inch. Daily rainfall amounts of this magnitude are insignificantly small so far as any real benefit to crops is concerned, especially in a tropical area where water losses through evaporation and transpiration are high. During this drought period there were severe water shortages in many areas of Hawaii, although some areas received appreciably more rain than Honolulu. Drought damage was greatest on rangeland and in truck-crop and pineapple areas, where irrigation was not being practiced.

Rainfall Intensities

Torrential rainfall is moderately common in all parts of Hawaii except the very high mountains, although it has been known to occur even there. Yet it is also true that in Hawaii very light showers are extremely

frequent in most localities. On windward coasts, for
example, it is usual to have 6, 8, or even 10 brief
showers in a single day, no one of which is heavy enough
to produce 0.01 inch of rain. This seeming contradiction
is explained by the fact that the usual run of trade-wind
weather yields many light showers in the lowlands, whereas the torrential rains are associated with other weather
regimes: with a local thunderstorm or with a major storm.

Extreme rainfall intensities are high in Hawaii.
To take the most extreme instance of record, during the
storm of January 24-25, 1956, over 38 inches of rain fell
within a 24-hour period at the plantation office of the
Kilauea sugar plantation on Kauai, out of a storm total
of 43.5 inches. During the same storm 6 inches of rain
fell during a single 30-minute period and about 11 inches
fell in 1 hour. The 38-inch value for 24 hours is con-
servatively low, because the gauge was already overflow-
ing when it was emptied for the first time. The 6-inch
value is correct within 1 or 2 tenths of an inch; the
11-inch value for 1 hour is an estimate only--again
because of overflow--and may be as much as an inch higher.

These extraordinary high rainfall intensities and
totals appear to have occurred when a current of moist,
unstable air, converging as it moved up a narrowing
valley, was at the same time forced to rise abruptly
over steep mountains nearby. However, such special topographic circumstances are not essential to the occurrence
of torrential rains. In November 1931 Moanalua, Oahu,
received 15.2 inches of rain within 3 hours; Hana, Maui,
has had as much as 28 inches in 24 hours; Opaeula, Oahu,
26 inches; and Hilo, 19 inches, even though none of these
places, nor many others with comparable amounts, are
situated in topographic surroundings conducive to the
occurrence of very high rainfall intensities. In fact,
it is true in Hawaii that the most copious storm rains
frequently occur in localities which do not have the
greatest average rainfall, and it is not uncommon during

such storms for relatively dry areas to receive within
a single day, or even a few hours, totals approaching
their mean annual rainfall.

At Honolulu the greatest 24-hour fall in 55 years
of record was that of March 5-6, 1958, when 17.41 inches
of rain was recorded at the Federal Building in the downtown area. The gauge at which this total was recorded
is situated well away from local topographic influences
that might cause excessive rainfall, a fact that was
evident from the distribution of maximum storm amounts
(discussed under "Storms," below). The second greatest
fall of record in downtown Honolulu was 13.52 inches
in 24 hours; the third, 8.07 inches. In general all
stations in Hawaii for which there are as many as 50
years of record have experienced daily rainfalls of at
least 8 inches, and the majority have experienced falls
of 12 inches or more. These values are comparable to
or greater than those for the great majority of stations
in the Gulf area, which is the principal area in the
mainland United States in which extreme rainfalls are
of the same magnitude as those in Hawaii, especially for
periods of a few hours or more.

These torrential rains, falling on Hawaii's steep
slopes and small drainage basins, often generate flash
floods that erode fields and cause landslides and damage
to crops and, with increasing frequency, to homes, as
residential development continues to encroach on flood
plains.

Fog Drip

Mountain slopes and crests within the cloud belt
are frequently exposed to contact with fog or cloud
mists carried on the wind. Experiments atop Lanai
Hale, highest point on the island of Lanai, suggest that
this "fog drip" may contribute two-thirds as much water
to vegetation and soil in that area as does rainfall
itself--and proportionately more when rainfall is light.

In fact, on occasion, substantial quantities of "fog
drip" have been collected during periods when no measur-
able precipitation was recorded in rain gauges at the
site.

STORMS

For many purposes it is convenient to think of
Hawaiian weather in a very much simplified way, in terms
of trade-wind and nontrade-wind conditions. Most of the
time the weather is dominated by the trade winds. There
are light to moderate trade-wind showers on windward
coasts. In the rainier mountain areas these showers are
often moderate to heavy and may merge with one another
to produce continuous rain for hours on end. In the
leeward areas occasional light trade-wind showers may
drift over from the mountains to windward, except that,
in such completely sheltered lees as the Kona Coast of
Hawaii, sea breezes ascending the mountain slopes may
produce light to occasionally heavy showers in the late
afternoon and early evening. The upper slopes of the
highest mountains are predominantly clear except for
occasional intrusions of moist air from below, when light
rains may fall, especially in the afternoon.

Nontrade-wind conditions are quite different. When
the winds are light and variable, moist air may move
slowly onto the islands from directions roughly perpendicular to the coastline. The convergence of these
onshore currents, coupled during the daytime hours with
the heating of the mountain slopes and island interiors,
produces an ascent of moist air, deep cumulus clouds,
heavy showers, and sometimes lightning and thunder. At
other times there may be major storm disturbances, as
when a cold front crosses the islands or when a large
cyclonic storm system passes by. Major storms may produce
heavy rains in many localities, and even on several different islands, all at the same time. They produce snow

and ice in the high mountains, and sometimes even hail.
They are frequently accompanied by strong winds, whose
directions are usually different from that of the trade
wind. Storm episodes, on either a minor or a major
scale, usually occur during a breakdown in the trades
(although some of Hawaii's heaviest rains have occurred
when trade winds were overlain by low-pressure areas
higher in the atmosphere); and though they are relatively
infrequent, they are an important and integral part of
the total weather scene.

Intense Local Storms

Intense local rainstorms other than those that occur
under trade-wind conditions are small features that seldom cover more than a few square miles and sometimes
less than a single square mile. They occur most typically in the late afternoon or early evening. In some areas
in which there are well-developed sea breezes, such as
Kona, Hawaii, they are common occurrences, especially
in summer. In most areas, however, they are apt to
occur on only a few days a year when the overall winds
are light and variable, and under the conditions described just above--the converging of onshore currents
and island heating. Storms of this character may occur
at any time of the year.

Intense local storms are sometimes accompanied by
lightning and thunder, which also occasionally accompany
very intense rainfall along a cold front moving across
the islands. Lightning and thunder of the violence
common in most areas in the conterminous United States
are, however, quite uncommon. In the lowlands, storms
accompanied by audible thunder occur only 5 to 10 times
a year, on the average. Thunderstorms are reported from
somewhere in the State on 50 or so days a year, more
often in winter than in summer. Judging from the fact
that lightning is visible over the mountains decidedly

more often than over the lowlands, it is likely that
thunderstorms on mountain slopes are more frequent than
in the lowlands. Even in the mountains, however, tremendous claps of thunder are rare.

Waterspouts and other funnel clouds are not uncommon
in the Hawaiian area. About 20 of them are reported in
the average year, although it is likely that at least
as many more are sighted but not reported. Often they
are accompanied by towering cumulus clouds and rain,
although they have also been observed under trade-wind
conditions. Occasionally a waterspout will drift onshore
and do some damage, usually quite minor but at times
severe, as at Kaumakani, Kauai, in December 1967 and at
Kailua-Kona in January 1971. Small tornadoes have been
known to form over the islands with the same effect,
but these phenomena appear to be far less violent than
the worst of their counterparts in the conterminous
United States.

Hail falls somewhere in Hawaii between 5 and 10
times in the average year. Almost always it is quite
small--1/4 inch or less in diameter--but on several
occasions hail the size of marbles and discs about 5/8
inch in diameter, have been reported. Trees and crops
have been battered by hail from time to time, but this
is an infrequent occurrence and the areas affected are
small. Many lifelong residents of Hawaii have never
experienced hail in these islands.

Major Storms

There are four classes of disturbances that produce
major storms affecting Hawaii. Sometimes a cold front
sweeps across the islands, bringing with it locally
heavy showers and gusty winds. Sometimes a storm eddy,
or Low, moves past, bringing widespread heavy rains,
often accompanied by strong winds. These Lows are known
as Kona storms, a term originally reserved for the slowly

moving subtropical cyclones that occasionally enter the
Hawaiian area, but now increasingly applied by the local
public to any widespread rainstorm accompanied by winds
from a direction other than that of the trade winds.
They include situations in which the low-pressure area
is not well marked, but instead consists of a low-pressure
trough into which air feeds from either side. The third
class of disturbance is the true tropical storm, of which
the hurricane is the most intense. These storms are
rare, but they may pass close enough to the islands to
yield heavy rains, high winds, and great waves upon the
coasts. Also meriting treatment as a separate and fourth
class of disturbance are the instances of severe weather
attributable to low-pressure systems (Lows and troughs)
in the upper atmosphere. Of particular interest are
those which occur when the presence of trade winds in
the lower atmosphere would appear to contraindicate the
likelihood of extensive heavy rain.

These four kinds of major disturbances are not
always well defined. Nonetheless they are convenient
classes for descriptive purposes.

Cold-front Storms

During some winter seasons as many as six, eight,
or more well-defined cold fronts moving in from the
northwest may sweep across two or more islands of the
State. In other years, there may be only one or two.
Because of its location at the northwest end of Hawaii,
the island of Kauai commonly has a few more cold-front
storms each year than do Oahu and the other islands,
for sometimes the southernmost edge of a front will
barely encroach upon Kauai and will move on eastward
without reaching as far as Oahu. At other times, cold
fronts that pass Kauai or Oahu may dissipate before
reaching the southern islands.

When a cold front passes, there may be heavy rains.
Typically these rains are spotty, with several inches

falling in some areas and only fractions of an inch or
none in others. Winds may be strong and gusty, with
directions commonly from the south to southwest in advance of the front, and from the north to northwest after
it passes. The cool air that follows the passage of the
front brings relatively cloudless skies. In the lowlands,
nighttime temperatures may drop to near 60° F or lower.
Afternoon temperatures are commonly in the middle 70s.

The winds accompanying a cold front are usually
brisk, but they may be more than merely brisk in some
localities. Perhaps once every three or four years, on
the average, a cold-front storm will produce winds strong
enough to do scattered damage to trees, crops, and houses.
At times the damage has been much more severe, particularly when strong southwesterly winds in advance of a
fast-moving cold front have been made even stronger and
gustier by topography. Such was the destructive wind-
storm of January 13-14, 1970, which resulted in the
greatest dollar damage ever reported in the State for a
single weather event ($6.84 million, $4.48 million of it
to Schofield Barracks, in central Oahu). Oahu also
recorded its highest wind of record--a gust of 96 m.p.h.
at Kaneohe Marine Corps Air Station. From time to time
cold-front passages have given rise in the vicinity of
the islands to damaging waterspouts or tornadoes, such
as those of January 1971, and to falls of hail. Cold
fronts that move as far southward as the high mountains
Haleakala, Mauna Kea, and Mauna Loa often deposit snow
on their upper slopes.

Kona Storms

Kona storms, like cold-front storms, are features
of the winter season. They are so called because they
often bring winds from *Kona* or leeward directions. The
rainfall in a well-developed Kona storm is more widespread and more prolonged than in the usual cold-front

storm; and if the Kona storm is accompanied by high winds,
the winds are usually steadier, more prolonged, and not
as strong as the more extreme winds of the cold front.
Kona-storm rains are usually most intense in an arc or
band extending from south to east of the storm and well
in advance of its center. An entire winter may pass
without a single well-developed Kona storm near enough
to the islands to affect their weather. More often,
however, there are one or two such storms a year, and
rarely four or five.

Kona rains last from several hours to several days.
The rains may continue steadily, but the longer-lasting
ones are characteristically interrupted by intervals of
lighter rain or even partial clearing, as well as by
intense showers superimposed upon the more moderate
regime of continuous, steady rain. The storms of November
1955 and of March 1958 are examples of two different
types of Kona storms that brought extreme amounts of rain.

On November 8 and 9, 1955, a major storm system was
centered about 275 miles north-northwest of Kauai. Warm,
moist air moving around this storm system, poured across
Kauai. Heavy rains began on Kauai about noon on November
8. These rains continued for 20 to 24 hours and produced
rainfall that totaled 3 to 10 inches throughout the
eastern and northeastern sections of the islands. This
particular band of very heavy rains moved southeastward
down the island chain, with totals of 3 or 4 to over 12
inches on the islands of Oahu, Molokai, Lanai, Maui, and
Hawaii on November 9 and 10. Meanwhile, the storm system
had moved in such a manner as to bring a new flow of
fresh, moist air across Kauai. On November 11 and 12
there were tremendous rains on Kauai, bringing total
falls of up to 20 inches in 14 hours. This second rain
episode, coming shortly after the heavy rains of two days
before, caused severe local flooding. Together the two
rainstorms caused damage of more than $100,000 on Kauai
alone.

The band of torrential rainfall that produced the
second storm episode on Kauai also moved down the island
chain, but with distinctly less rainfall than had occurred before. Totals varied widely, from no rain at all
in some localities to as much as 5 or 6 inches in others.

The storm of March 1958 was different in character.
On the evening of March 4, moist air from the south began
to flow across Oahu, with the air edging inward along a
line of convergence. This was a slow, steady flow, without high-speed winds, but, as the air continued to con-
verge, clouds built up to heights of 40,000 to 50,000
feet and torrential rains set in. Aircraft pilots
reported that the clouds lay in a concentrated band
squarely across the island. At first the rains were
moderate, though steady. The very heavy rains began at
one o'clock on the morning of the following day and continued with only brief periods of slackening until around
six o'clock on the morning of the sixth. During the
storm the rainfall totals on Oahu ranged from 5 to 24
inches, with 17.41 inches in a 24-hour period in downtown Honolulu. There was severe local flooding in several different areas. Mountain and hill slopes still in
their natural vegetated state stood up amazingly well.
Damage from this storm totaled $400,000.

Hurricanes and Tropical Storms

Between August 1950 and the present (January 1972)
four true hurricanes, with winds of 74 m.p.h. or more,
came sufficiently close to affect the Islands. However,
prior to about 1947 observations over the surrounding
oceans were too sparse to permit identification of hurricanes with certainty, and early records mention several
severe storms that might have been hurricanes. But
Hawaii's first known true hurricane was Hiki, a small
intense storm which in August 1950 passed just to the

north of the islands. It produced maximum measured winds
of 68 m.p.h. in the State and rains that were locally
very intense, but damage from the storm was relatively
slight. In September 1957, hurricane Della passed well
to the south of the islands yet sufficiently close to
produce very heavy swell on southern Kauai, with breakers
of sufficient height and strength to cause local damage.
Again in 1957, on December 1, hurricane Nina, moving
from the south, approached within 120 miles of Kauai
and brought high winds, heavy rains, and damaging waves
to that island, especially along the south coast. Damage,
chiefly from waves, totaled $100,000. Finally, in early
August 1959, hurricane Dot passed to the south of the
eastern and central islands of Hawaii, then swung northward and crossed Kauai. Damage totaled $6 million,
chiefly on Kauai, as was reported in the August 1959
issue of *Climatological Data, Hawaii*.

Although true hurricanes seldom strike Hawaii, and
only four have done so since 1950, at least as many
others have passed within 200 miles or so during the
past decade. Tropical storms are more frequent. These
are similar to hurricanes but with more modest winds,
below 74 m.p.h. Because weak tropical storms resemble
some Kona storms in the winds and rains that they produce,
and because early records do not permit distinguishing
clearly between them, it has been difficult to estimate
the average frequency of tropical storms. However,
studies based on weather satellite photographs now suggest that, on the average, a tropical storm will pass
sufficiently close to Hawaii every year or two to affect
the weather in some part of the State.

Unlike cold-front and Kona storms, hurricanes and
tropical storms are not limited to the winter season.
They are most likely to occur during the last half of
the year, from July through December.

Storms Associated with Upper Level Lows

Severe weather in the Hawaiian area is at times
attributable to low-pressure areas which are well developed in the upper atmosphere (rather than near sea
level) and are not related to cold fronts, Kona storms,
or tropical storms. The weather which accompanies these
upper Lows or troughs--towering cumulus clouds, thunderstorms, intense and widespread rain--often resembles that
of a Kona storm and may be mistaken for one, except for
the absence of the persistent, and sometimes strong,
southerly winds that frequently accompany Kona storms.

The surface winds during these events may be from
almost any direction, and are often light; but some of
the most torrential rains associated with low pressure
aloft have occurred when trade winds were present in
the lower atmosphere. The early months of 1965 were
marked by several episodes of this kind. Of these, the
most severe was a post-seasonal rainstorm which, during
the first few days of May, moved through the island chain
from the west, swelling streams on Kauai and Oahu into
torrents that swept away homes and bridges, washed out
fields and roads, and disrupted telephone and power
lines. Total damage, most of it on Oahu, reached $1
million.

Meteorologically, the storm resembled several earlier ones of that year, in which groups of thunderstorms
developed beneath an upper low-pressure trough. Apparently augmented by the ascent of the coexisting north-
easterly trade winds over the steep Koolau Range, the
most intense rains were concentrated in the central
portion of Oahu's windward coast, between Punaluu and
Kailua. Hardest hit by flash flooding was Kahaluu,
where 100 families were evacuated and acres of fruit and
garden crops were destroyed. Several gauges at higher
elevations overflowed at 24 inches during the second day
of rain. One of these (Waiahole) recorded 4.25 inches
in a single hour, 6 inches in 2 hours, and over 8.75

inches in 3 1/2 hours. Punaluu, a town on the coast,
measured over 5 inches of rain on each of three successive days. On Kauai, where an Anahola gauge registered
12 inches in 2-1/2 hours, the Hanalei and Wainiha rivers
overflowed, and some upper fields of the Lihue Sugar
Company were damaged.

Snow and Ice

Several times a year, on the average, and almost
always between October and May, major storms may deposit
a foot or more of snow on the upper slopes of one or more
of Hawaii's highest mountains--Haleakala, Mauna Kea, and
Mauna Loa. After an especially heavy fall, patches of
snow may extend to as low as 7,000 feet, but snow below
about 11,000 feet quickly vanishes, since even winter
air temperatures in the Hawaiian area are ordinarily
above the freezing point even to altitudes of 13,000
feet and higher. Hence there is no perennial snow cover
on these mountain summits. Once every few years, a Kona
storm, cold front, or upper Low, accompanied by heavy
rain at lower elevations and unusually low temperatures
in the upper air, will produce an intense ice storm at
elevations above 7,000 or 8,000 feet, coating roads and
structures thickly with ice and snapping power lines.
Haleakala summit appears to be particularly vulnerable
to these ice storms. However, the intense solar heating
and the warm air ordinarily present even at those elevations, eliminate within a few days all traces of even
the most severe ice storm.

CLIMATIC REGIONS OF HAWAII

It is convenient to recognize seven climatic sub-
regions in Hawaii. These are defined chiefly by the
major physiographic features of the State and by location with reference to windward or leeward exposure.
Since one region grades into another, it would be

misleading to attempt to draw sharp boundaries between
adjacent regions. In general, however, the regions and
their characteristics are as follows:

1. Windward lowlands, generally below 1,000 feet
on the north to northeast sides of the islands. This
region lies more or less perpendicular to the prevailing
flow of the trade winds, and is moderately rainy, with
frequent trade-wind showers. Partly cloudy to cloudy
days are common. Temperatures are more nearly uniform
and mild than in other regions.

2. Leeward lowlands, except for the Kona Coast of
Hawaii which has a distinctive climate. In these areas
daytime temperatures are slightly higher and nighttime
temperatures are slightly lower than in windward locations. Dry weather prevails except for occasional light
trade-wind showers, which drift over from the mountains
to windward, and for periods of major storms. In some
leeward areas an afternoon sea breeze is common, especially in summer.

3. Interior lowlands, on Oahu and Maui. In the
northeast these lowlands have the character of the windward lowlands; in the southwest, of leeward lowlands.
The central areas are intermediate in character, and,
especially on Oahu, are sometimes the scene of intense
local afternoon showers from deep clouds that form as
a result of local heating of the land on days when the
trade winds are weak or absent.

4. The Kona Coast of Hawaii. This is the only
region in which summer rainfall exceeds winter rainfall.
There is a marked diurnal wind regime, with well-developed and reliable land and sea breezes, and a high frequency of late afternoon or early evening showers,
especially in summer. Conditions are somewhat warmer
and decidedly drier than in windward locations.

5. Rainy mountain slopes on the windward side.
Rainfall and cloudiness are very high, with considerable
rain both winter and summer. Temperatures are equable.

Humidities are higher than in any other region.

    6. <u>Lower mountain slopes on the leeward side</u>.
Rainfall is greater than on the adjacent leeward lowlands,
but distinctly less than at the same level on the windward side, except that the zone of maximum rainfall
usually occurs just to leeward of the crests of the
lower mountains. Temperature extremes are greater
than on the rainy slopes of the windward sides of the
mountains, and cloudiness is almost as great.

    7. <u>High mountains</u>. Above 2,000 or 3,000 feet on
the high mountains of Mauna Kea, Mauna Loa, and Haleakala,
rainfall decreases rapidly with elevation. Near the
summits of Mauna Loa and Mauna Kea, rainfall is scant
and skies are clear a high percentage of the time. Humidities may reach very low values--5 percent or less--
at times. The lowest temperatures in the State are
experienced in this region, with values below freezing
being common.

CLIMATE AND THE ECONOMY OF HAWAII

In 1971 Hawaii had a resident civilian population
of about 770,000. In terms of dollar income the Federal
Government is the principal employer, chiefly because
of the importance of Hawaii as the Pacific center for
the military departments. Tourism within the past few
years has grown rapidly to second in importance in dollar
value. Aside from these activities, the economy of the
Islands is based chiefly on agriculture and on commerce
and industry.

The location of Hawaii in mid-Pacific is the primary
reason for its logistic and strategic importance as a
site for military establishments. However, the mild
weather and excellent flying conditions are contributing
factors.

The principal agricultural commodity is sugarcane.
Cane occupies about 240,000 of the 1.3 million acres of

agricultural land. It is raised on all the islands
except Lanai and Molokai. In 1970 it accounted for
about 50 percent of the dollar value of all crops.
Sugarcane is a 2-year crop in Hawaii and most of it is
raised under irrigation. The abundance of water and the
genial warmth of the area make it an ideal climate for
this crop.

Pineapples are the second most important crop.
They occupy about 65,000 acres (1970) and are grown on
all islands except Hawaii. This crop occupies lands
that are generally dry, because it requires little water
and, during the ripening period, much sunshine. The
crop requires 18 to 20 months between planting and har-
vesting.

Sugar and pineapple lands are in the lowlands,
generally below 2,000 feet. In contrast, the rangelands
that support the livestock industry occupy chiefly the
higher elevations. About one million acres are in
ranchland, mostly on Hawaii and Maui. Except where
small herds are maintained for dairying, ranchlands are
in the drier areas.

Other agricultural products of the State include
dairy products, poultry, tropical fruits, macadamia
nuts, coffee, and vegetables. Coffee is grown on the
Kona Coast, where the wet summer and the dry period of
early winter are especially favorable to its production.
Vegetables include almost the full range of truck crops
that are common on the Mainland, although the quantities
raised are not sufficient to meet the needs of the local
economy.

The climate is a principal basis for the tourist
industry of the State. Tourism is by far Hawaii's most
rapidly growing industry, in both number of visitors
and revenue. The mild temperatures are an asset, as
are the low rainfall and generally sunny conditions in
such leeward locations as Waikiki and Kona. The trade-
wind breeze is also an important element because on the

warmer days it makes conditions far more pleasant than
the temperature and humidity alone would indicate.   In
the Honolulu area, for example, temperatures of 80° F
or above occur less than 0.5 percent of the time under
conditions when the humidity is as high as 70 percent
and there are not at least moderate trade winds.   August,
September, October, and November are the only months when
such conditions occur more than 1 percent of the time.

In general the climate of Hawaii, especially in the
lowlands, favors many kinds of agricultural, commercial,
and industrial enterprises.   In most areas the summers
are warm but not hot.   Private residences have large open
and screened areas, to take advantage of natural air
movements; but most of the newer office buildings, hotels,
and apartment houses have central air conditioning.   The
winters are warm, and homes are unheated, except in the
mountains.   There is abundant water for domestic, industrial, and agricultural uses in all but the driest parts
of the State.

BIBLIOGRAPHY

Department of Water and Land Development, State of
    Hawaii. 1961. Pan evaporation data, State of
    Hawaii, Honolulu.

Feldwisch, Walter F. 1941. Supplementary climatic
    notes for the Hawaiian Islands. Climate and man,
    yearbook of agriculture, p. 1216-1221.

Jones, Stephen B. 1939. The weather element in the
    Hawaiian climate. Ann. Assoc. Amer. Geogr.
    29(1):29-57.

Landsberg, H. 1951. Statistical investigations into
    the climatology of rainfall on Oahu. Met. Monogr.
    1(3):7-23.

Leopold, Luna B. 1949. The interaction of trade wind
    and sea breeze. J. Met. 6(5):313-320.

Loveridge, Elmer F. 1924. Diurnal variations of pre-
    cipitation at Honolulu, Hawaii. Mon. Weath. Rev.
    52:584-585.

Price, Saul. 1966. The climates of Oahu. Bull. Pacif.
    Orchid Soc. Hawaii (December 1966).

Price, Saul, and Jack C. Pales. 1959. The Mauna Loa
    High-Altitude Observatory. Mon. Weath. Rev. 87:
    1-14.

Solot, Samuel B. 1950. Further studies in Hawaiian
    precipitation. U.S. Weather Bureau Research Paper
    No. 32.

Stidd, C. K., and Luna B. Leopold. 1951. The geo-
    graphic distribution of average monthly rainfall,
    Hawaii. Met. Monogr. 1(3):24-33.

Taliaferro, William J. 1958. Kona rainfall. Hawaii
    Water Authority, Honolulu (September 1958).

————— 1959. Rainfall of the Hawaiian Islands.
    Hawaii Water Authority, Honolulu (September 1959).

Water resources in Hawaii. Hawaii Water Authority,
    Honolulu (March 1959).

TROPICAL SOILS OF THE HAWAIIAN ISLANDS

G. Donald Sherman[1]

The soils of the Hawaiian Islands possess most of the morphological characteristics of soils occurring in tropical regions throughout the world. Tropical soils owe their characteristics to intense mineral decomposition and a wide range of mineral transformation occurring in their development. The processes of mineral transformation and the types of secondary minerals formed are controlled by the weathering environment, including the integrated influence of climate, vegetation, drainage, parent material, and time. Hawaiian soils in their development reflect the intensity of chemical decomposition of primary minerals and, in some instances, secondary minerals resulting from their parent materials, and the synthesis of new secondary minerals from released constituents or by alteration of crystalline structural units by addition, rearrangement, or degradation of constituents. The development of soil profiles or horizons reflects a sequence of secondary mineral formation each reaching or approaching an equilibrium with its weathering environment.

Formation of Hawaiian soil occurs on parent materials which vary greatly in geological age. There is thus a wide range of time of exposure to soil mineral weathering processes. The Hawaiian Islands are the result of volcanic action which is estimated to have begun nine million years ago. They have been progressively built up by continuous volcanic activity which

---

[1]Senior Professor Emeritus of Soil Science, University of Hawaii.

continues today with the intermittent eruptions of Mauna
Loa and Kilauea on the island of Hawaii. Volcanic materials are the result of both lava flows and pyroclastic
depositions. These materials are subject to weathering
in situ, transport by wind and water as in the case of
volcanic ash, or erosion after soil development following mineral weathering which forms the alluvial depositions in the lowlands, plateaus, and offshore areas.
The wide range of mean annual rainfall (5 to 500 inches)
provides, with time, considerable potential for both
mineral-weathering and soil-formation activities. The
older islands of Kauai, Oahu, Molokai, and West Maui
have had post-erosional eruptions which have in many
instances buried weathered surfaces (soils) and provided a surface far more susceptible to the processes
of mineral weathering and rapid soil formation than the
original surface. Rapid soil development and intense
mineral decomposition in post-erosional lavas are due
to two factors: the lavas have been more susceptible
to weathering either because they consist of fine-grain
minerals or of ultrabasic rocks like melilite basalt
with a low silica content; or pyroclastic eruptions
have deposited volcanic ash over fairly wide areas.
The latter has had a tremendous influence in recharging
the surface with both bases and soluble silica even
where the depositions are rather thin.

As a result of these environmental and geological
factors, soil genesis in the Hawaiian Islands has
produced a wide range of soil types, which have a
similarity to soils in other tropical regions. Soils
representing many of the great soil groups are found
in the Hawaiian Islands. Indeed, the Hawaiian Islands
have as many soil series as several of the largest
states of the continental United States. Each group
consists of numerous soil families which represent a
range of soil-horizon development under a specified
weathering environment, but without regard to parent

material. Each soil family consists of many series
representing the influence of various parent materials
and local factors of development. The series is the
mapping unit. The classification and geographic distribution of Hawaiian soils has been reported by Cline
(1955). A new comprehensive system of soil classification is presently being published by the Soil Survey
staff of the Soil Conservation Service, U.S. Department
of Agriculture.

Mineral transformations occurring in soil formation
are reflected in both the physical and chemical properties of the soil. These properties to a large extent
determine the horizon differentiation of the soil profile. The horizons of the soil profile reflect the
accumulation of organic matter in the surface horizon,
the A horizon, which can be further characterized by
its physical, chemical, and mineralogical properties.
These characteristics provide a fairly wide range of
subsoil horizons, the B horizon, which reflects mineral
composition. The horizons lie over the subsoil zone
which, although it may be weathered, does not reflect
the effect of the surface environment and retains its
geological structure and fabric. The soil profile does
not reflect either the structure or fabric of the original geological material from which it has developed.

Mineralogical properties also play a role in the
type and sequence of vegetation which are found in the
Hawaiian Islands. The growth of staghorn fern *(Glei-
chenia linearis)* and melastoma *(Melastoma malabathrium)*
requires the intake of large amounts of aluminum, and
thus these plants are found growing on soils having a
high concentration of free aluminum, such as is found
in bauxitic soils (Moomaw et al., 1959).

SOIL WEATHERING ENVIRONMENT AND SOIL GENESIS

Processes of soil formation in the Hawaiian Islands
are facilitated by: (a) a year-round warm climate in

which weathering processes are continuous; (b) a porous
surface which provides for the maximum infiltration of
water, providing excellent conditions for solution,
chemical reactions, and leaching; (c) the presence of
physical conditions that permit unimpeded internal
drainage, which is essential to leaching of dissolved
constituents; and (d) parent materials which are susceptible to the processes of mineral decomposition.
Under these conditions the major processes of soil
formation, *leaching* and *weathering*, function at their
greatest degree of effectiveness. Their action is
restricted only by the limitations of the climatic
environment or the physical conditions imposed by the
nature of the parent material.

The islands range in elevation from sea level to
a little over 13,000 feet, on Mauna Loa and Mauna Kea
on Hawaii. As elevation increases, the mean annual
temperature drops and seasonal and daily ranges of
temperature widen. Rainfall varies from 5 to more than
500 inches annually. Its distribution ranges from a
rather uniform pattern of rainfall throughout the year
to one of strongly alternating wet and dry seasons.
Cyclonic storms, which occur with the development of
low pressure troughs, bring heavy rainfall of 3 to 10
inches at least once a year, and are the major sources
of rainfall in dry areas. They are important to soil
development as they provide a means of extensive leaching of soil-forming materials in these areas.

The wide range of climatic conditions provides a
unique situation as far as tropical soil development
is concerned. Only Indonesia offers a similar situation
in tropical regions.

COMPARISON OF SOIL FORMATION IN THE HAWAIIAN ISLANDS
WITH THAT OCCURRING IN SOILS OF TEMPERATE REGIONS

In the soils of the Hawaiian Islands mineral decomposition of parent material has progressed to a point

approaching complete decomposition of all primary
minerals. New minerals have been synthesized by the
recombination of released constituents forming an amorphous mineral system which in time crystallizes into
identifiable secondary minerals. Even minerals resistant to decomposition, such as magnetite and ilmenite,
have decomposed or been altered by oxidation. The lack
of quartz in the parent rocks of the Hawaiian Islands
has led to the formation of soils which owe their
physical and chemical properties to clay-sized particles,
secondary crystalline and noncrystalline alumino-silicate
minerals, and to hydrated silicates, oxides, and hydroxides of aluminum, iron, and titanium. Soil profile
morphological characteristics are related to the physico-
chemical properties of the dominant secondary minerals
that have developed as the result of soil mineral weathering. Soils have developed in the Hawaiian Islands
which can be characterized as having properties associated with one or more of the following types of
secondary minerals: (a) montmorillonite; (b) halloysite; (c) allophane and allophane-like minerals; (d)
amorphous hydroxides and hydrous oxides of aluminum,
iron, and titanium; and (e) various combinations of
subcrystalline and crystalline hydroxides and oxides
of aluminum, iron, and titanium.

In Cline's (1955) classification of Hawaiian soils,
each soil has a mineralogical composition common to its
great soil group. The variable is the concentration
of the minerals or their degree of development, and
the characteristics depend on the properties of the
dominant minerals. Due to the concentrations of secondary minerals and near-complete decomposition of the
minerals of the parent material, the role played by
organic matter, texture, and the parent material in
determining soil characteristics and properties is very
minor indeed.

Soils of temperate regions do not undergo the same degree of mineral weathering and decomposition. Soil development in these regions is only in the initial stages of mineral weathering, and mineral decomposition is limited to primary minerals which are easily susceptible to weathering. As the result of limited decomposition, secondary clay minerals, amorphous hydrous hydroxides and oxides of iron, and the hydrous amorphous silicate of aluminum occur in relatively low concentrations. The texture or the size of the mineral grains or aggregates is one of the main physical characteristics of the soil. Because the soil has a limited secondary mineral fraction, organic matter provides an adsorptive complex for cation plant nutrients and a material which holds soil moisture. Thus, the soils of the temperate zone derive their basic physicochemical properties from their textural class (sand, silt, loam, etc.), inorganic chemical composition, and the concentration of organic matter which has accumulated in the surface horizon. The concentration of organic matter, clay, soluble salts, carbonates, and colloidal sesquioxides are distinguishing properties in the horizons of temperate-region soils.

While weathering plays a major role in the formation of tropical soils, with leaching as the limiting factor, in temperate regions leaching plays a major role and weathering, a weak to strongly modifying role. In tropical soils secondary mineral products determine the morphological characteristics of the soil. In the development of soils in the temperate regions the leaching of soluble materials, the contribution of vegetation to the composition of the organic matter, and the persistence of the physical characteristics of the parent material determine the morphology of the soil profile.

PEDOGENESIS OF TROPICAL SOILS

The processes of soil formation are influenced by
the same physical and environmental conditions as is
mineral weathering. The mineral products of decomposition are determined by the integrated processes of *weathering* and *leaching*. The factors which govern and control
the course of weathering and leaching (W x L), are:
climate, drainage, parent material, specific surface
or size of units exposed, the nature and type of surface
of the unit, time, and internal environment as related
to moisture, temperature, and pressure. The composition
of the products of mineral weathering depends on the
integrated action of all seven factors. When one considers the depth of the weathering crust of the earth,
both the external environment and the internal environment must be considered. The former has a tremendous
effect on the surface and near-surface portion where
soil formation occurs; the latter controls the weathering processes in the substrates, or geological
weathering.

In soil formation one is interested in only those
weathering and leaching conditions which occur in
exposed earth surface and near-surface materials
effectively influenced by the surface environment.
It is in that shallow area that the maximum effect of
the daily and seasonal fluctuations of surface temperatures, wetting and drying, hydration and dehydration,
oxidation and reduction, and freezing and thawing occur.
The result of weathering and leaching processes under
these conditions is a horizon differentiation of layers
which follow the topographical surface. This horizon
differentiation is the development of the soil profile.
Vegetation modifies the surface environment and contributes organic material to the surface, and, on decomposition, accumulates in the surface horizon giving it

a distinguishable characteristic. This layer provides
a medium in which the activity of microorganisms extends
the effect of vegetation on the processes of weathering
and leaching.

The product of pedogenesis is the soil profile,
which consists of an arrangement of horizons. Soil
classification is based on the characteristics and
arrangement of these horizons.

In all tropical regions, including the Hawaiian
Islands, the interpretation of soil development is
impossible without some appreciation and knowledge of
the rate of soil development and its approximate time
scale. In the interpretation of soil development in
temperate regions, little consideration is given to
these factors (rate and time) because the weathering
process proceeds at such a slow rate that a static
condition is assumed. In tropical regions weathering
proceeds so rapidly that profound changes result in a
very short time period. These changes can be identified, and the information utilized to predict other
changes. A sudden change in environmental conditions,
such as that resulting from removal of natural vegeta-
tive cover by man's activities, can produce a profound
change in the soil profile, as well as in the physical,
chemical, and mineralogical properties of the soil.
Some of these changes can be recorded not in centuries
but in years and months. Of greater importance is the
less dramatic change which occurs, slowly but progressively, in a system outwardly considered static but
in reality in a state of dynamic equilibrium. The
system is not static because it responds rapidly to
changes in environmental conditions.

The rate of soil formation on volcanic ash depositions under rainfalls exceeding 100 inches is extremely
rapid. Shallow soils have developed on the 1924
Kilauea volcanic ash deposition subject to 200 inches
of rainfall annually, while on the 1855 deposition on
Mauna Loa there is only the very first indication of

mineral decomposition. The former is covered with a
dense ohia *(Metrosideros)* and tree fern *(Cibotium)*
forest. The fern produces acid organic matter which
enhances the processes of mineral decomposition. The
latter is covered with lichen and a few small tree
ferns, with only an occasional ohia tree. Volcanic
ash, because of small particle size, weathers rapidly.
The great specific surface area which is exposed to
chemical action provides the conditions for the rapid
decomposition of the primary minerals. Furthermore,
as volcanic ash weathers the infiltration rate of water
increases at its surface and the rate of water percolation (drainage) through the deposition continues to be
rapid. These are ideal conditions for rapid decomposition of minerals. In addition, segregation as to size
and mineral composition of individual units of volcanic
ash materials must be considered. In pyroclastic eruptions, heavier and larger particles fall near the vent,
and light, siliceous glass and ash particles are thrown
considerable distances from the vent. The 1960 eruption
at Kapoho on the island of Hawaii provided the opportunity to observe the segregation of materials around its
vent.

There are two types of lava flows in Hawaii, aa
and pahoehoe. Aa flows are cindery with chunks of lava
of variable sizes, and the cinders and rock fragments
are porous due to the gaseous nature of the flow. These
characteristics make this type of lava susceptible to
weathering. While it is not so susceptible to mineral
decomposition as volcanic ash, it weathers rapidly
and in most cases gives rise to stony soils. Pahoehoe
flows are extremely resistant to weathering. In most
instances weathering is confined either to a shallow
zone of initial weathering or to massive saprolitic
weathering where the original fabric of the rock is
identifiable. Nakamura and Sherman (1965) described
this type of weathering in the mugearite rocks of West
Maui.

Two features of Hawaiian volcanic activity have a profound effect on soil development: extensive pyroclastic eruptions at the summits of volcanoes as they approach a dormant or inactive stage, and ultrabasic post-erosional flows. Volcanic ash eruptions are well exhibited by the numerous cinder cones on the slopes of Mauna Kea and Haleakala and in the craters of these volcanoes. The surface for miles around each mountain peak is covered with a blanket of successive layers of volcanic ash. The soils on these ash blankets range from 6 inches to more than 20 feet in depth. Soil development is restricted to these layers, as the underlying rock formations are either unweathered or are weathered saprolite, usually halloysitic, after basalt or andesite.

On the geologically older islands, Oahu, Kauai, Molokai, and West Maui, post-erosional flows occurred a million or more years after the last eruption of the major volcanoes. These eruptions produced both types of lava flows and ended with pyroclastic eruptions. The lavas were ultrabasic melilite basalt, nepheline basalts, and other low silicate-containing rock materials. Because the material was extremely low in silicate concentration but high in concentration of bases, it was susceptible to rapid chemical decomposition. Furthermore, most of the materials exposed to soil weathering were either cindery aa flows or pyroclastic materials. Thus, both physical and chemical conditions were conducive to extremely rapid mineral decomposition. The desilication of these materials is extremely rapid where there is high annual rainfall or in situations which favor rapid leaching of the soluble products of weathering. Rapid desilication has led to the formation of almost silicate-free oxide soils of aluminum, iron, and titanium (Sherman and Alexander 1958).

The two unique properties described above have provided a situation where time has less relevance than

might be expected. Other weathering factors are almost
unaffected by time in the expression of their influence
on soil weathering. An anomaly exists in both mineral
weathering and soil formation in that both have progressed
more rapidly and are at a more advanced stage on the
relatively recent and youthful parent materials than on
the geologically older rock formation. In fact soil
development is very shallow on exposed rock 8 to 9 million years old. The soils formed have abrupt boundaries
with older rocks. The soils occur as a blanket over
unweathered rock, as exhibited in the road cuts between
Hanapepe and Waimea on the island of Kauai or on the
Kunia road just north of the junction, west of Waipahu
on Oahu. On the Kunia road, near the golf course, one
can see alluvial fans that developed as the result of
erosion of volcanic ash deposited on eroded valley
surfaces. The road crosses fans, and one can easily
see the overlay of volcanic ash on an older fossil soil.
The fossil soil is so near the surface that the present
soil has developed a subsoil horizon in it. This condition exists in much of the Wahiawa (Oahu) soil, as on
the field of the Poamoho Experiment Station. In other
cases the soil has developed on deep layers of post-
erosional flow. Volcanic ash, which can be deposited
over vast areas, has had a profound influence on soil
formation and has in some cases interrupted the time
scale of weathering.

SOIL-MINERAL SEQUENCES IN HAWAIIAN SOILS

Mineral weathering is the strongest factor in
influencing soil formation in the Hawaiian Islands, and
a sequential relationship between the type of soil which
is formed and the dominant mineral component has been
identified. Tanada (1951) first indicated that the
concentration of kaolin clay minerals decreased with
increasing rainfall over an annual range of 20 to 200

inches. Subsequent research has shown that this rate of
kaolin decomposition represents the broadest range of
rainfall-kaolin decomposition occurring in the islands.
The report opened up a new concept of the role of the
formation and decomposition of secondary minerals in
soil formation, and can be looked upon as a milestone
in the development of our present-day knowledge of soil
science.

Shortly before Tanada's report, Jackson *et al*. (1948)
developed the concept of a sequential relationship of
clay-size minerals as related to their susceptibility
to weathering. These workers recognized 13 stages of
mineral groups, of which the most resistant are dominant
in Hawaiian soils: the minerals of the kaolin, iron
oxide, aluminum oxide, and titanium oxide groups (stages
10 to 13, respectively). Sherman (1949) developed the
concept of a sequential relationship of soil development
to mineral development, based on the chemical composition
of surface horizons. When wet and dry periods alternate,
iron and titanium oxides increase with rainfall, and
silicon and aluminum decrease. When rainfall is continuous and the soil is always moist, aluminum increases
with increasing rainfall, titanium oxide increases
slightly, and silicon and iron oxides decrease.

Sherman (1952), in a subsequent report, developed
a sequential relationship between soils and their
mineral composition. As mineral decomposition increases,
secondary mineral composition changes, and there is a
corresponding change in the morphological characteristics
of the soil. The graphic presentation of current
thinking on the sequential relationship of the soil-
mineral relationship with increasing weathering is
shown in Figure 1. Certain basic factors are shown
in this relationship which have not previously been
reported. The most important change in thinking comes
through the recognition of the important role played by

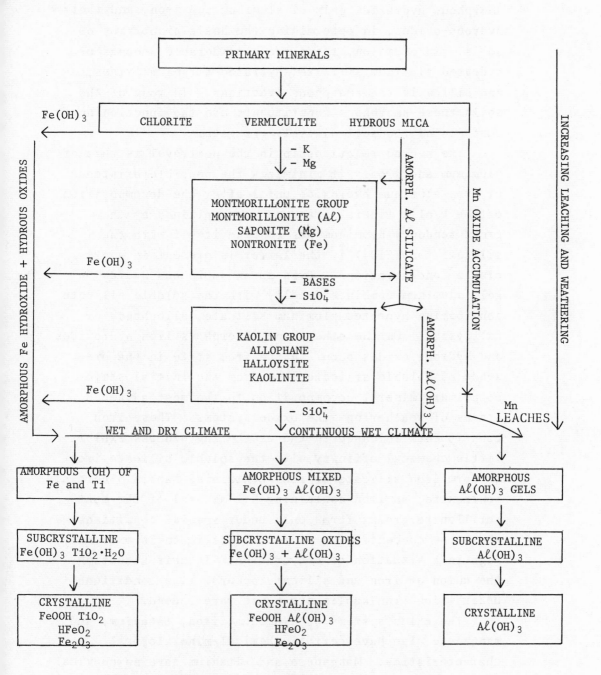

Fig. 1. Secondary mineral formation as related to leaching and weathering.

amorphous hydroxide gels of aluminum and iron, and their
hydrous oxides, in determining the basic properties of
soils. In addition, there are considerable amounts of
hydrated aluminum silicate, hydrated titanium oxides,
and silica in the amorphous fractions. In most of the
soils these amorphous constituents are the functioning
surfaces of the soil-mineral aggregate.

The second relationship in the portrayal is that of
aluminum and iron. It minimizes the possible existence
of free aluminum hydroxide until after the decomposition
of the kaolin minerals, and can be explained by the
great tendency aluminum has to bind itself with the
silicate ion (SiO_4^-) if the latter is present in appreciable concentrations. Even as an amorphous hydroxide
gel, aluminum combines readily with the soluble silicate
ion forming hydrated aluminum silicate, allophane, or
halloysite. On the other hand, amorphous iron hydroxides
and hydrous oxides occur in the free state in the presence of soluble silicate iron from the initial stages
of primary mineral decomposition to the most advanced
stages of weathering--the oxide systems. These iron
constituents released in the weathering process exhibit
little chemical affinity with the soluble silicate iron
to form iron silicate or iron-containing kaolin minerals.
Nontronite, an iron-containing 2:1 mineral of the montmorillonite group, forms only under special conditions
where the concentration of soluble silicate is extremely
high in a situation of dehydration. In this situation
the union of iron and silicate occurs. The conditions
under which iron-kaolin occur are rare indeed.

The oxide systems of aluminum, iron, titanium, and
manganese also have certain chemical-mineralogical
characteristics. Manganese and titanium have no chemical
affinity for soluble silicate iron and thus do not enter
into the crystal lattice of clay minerals. Manganese
occurs in two stable forms in Hawaiian soils: $(MnO)_n \cdot$
$(MnO_2)_n \cdot (H_2O)_n$ and MnO_2 , with the former predominant.

In the former there is an isomorphic substitution of
cobalt for manganese in the crystal lattice and probably
other cations of relatively similar ionic sizes. Manganese oxides begin to appear in the soil as free entities
with the formation of montmorillonite. Their obvious
presence occurs with the peak of kaolinization when they
can be identified as layers, coatings, concretions,
rhyzo concretions, and nodules. Manganese oxides disappear with the decomposition of the kaolin minerals
and are absent in bauxitic soils.

Titanium, like manganese, forms oxides rather than
combining with soluble silicate ions in the processes
of mineral decomposition. The titanium is released
from titanium-containing primary complex ferromagnesium
silicates and oxides. Katsura *et al.* (1962) have shown
that the resistant mineral ilmenite weathers. Walker
(1964) separated a clay colloid fraction containing
45 percent TiO_2 with further indication of the weather-
ability of the titanium-containing minerals. In the
free hydrous colloidal state it exhibits a strong affinity to form titano-ferric oxides. The dehydration of
a colloidal system containing hydrous constituents of
iron and titanium usually results in an approximate
1:1 combination of the two elements. Free anatase
($TiO_2 \cdot H_2O_n$) occurs only when titanium exceeds the
concentration of iron hydroxide and hydrous oxides,
which occurs in the titaniferous clay subsoils near
Koloa junction on the island of Kauai.

Aluminum hydroxide crystallizes to gibbsite or
remains as a hydrated amorphous hydroxide when the
soluble silicate iron concentration becomes low or nil.
Gibbsite differentially crystallizes from the other
constituent of a mixed gel system. Bates (1959) has
described this separation which accounts for the occurrence of gibbsite as relatively pure mineral aggregates.
Thin sections of these aggregates show that iron and
titanium oxides are occluded in the crystallization

process but neither substitute for nor chemically combine
with the aluminum hydroxide.

Iron hydroxide and hydrous oxides have a strong
affinity for titanium, forming titano-iron oxide minerals
when conditions are favorable. In this, crystallization
of goethite ($HFeO_2$) occurs in the presence of aluminum
hydroxide as isomorphous substitution of Al^{+++} for Fe^{+++}
The late Professor Matsusaka showed in unpublished data
that this substitution can amount to 11 percent. Similar
substitution has not been shown in other iron oxide
minerals.

An understanding of these relationships is essential
to the interpretation of the soil-mineral systems which
develop in tropical soil formation. In the following
discussion the generalized systems will be described,
followed by an account of different soils and the systems to which they belong, as they apply to Hawaiian
soils.

THE 2:1 CLAY MINERAL SYSTEMS

No other soil-mineral system has been studied so
extensively as that of the 2:1 clay mineral system. In
the weathering processes of Hawaiian soils, the formation of these clays has been dominated by the high
concentration of magnesium in the soil solution. These
magnesium concentrations give rise to 2:1 clay minerals
with Mg in the trioctahedral position, a Mg isomorphic
substitution in the crystal lattice, and a high percentage of magnesium base saturation in the cation exchange
complex. The clays formed have the following characteristics: (a) a high capacity to swell when wet and
to shrink on drying; (b) large external and internal
surface areas; (c) high cation exchange capacity; (d)
high buffering capacity; and (e) ease of dispersion
related to organic matter content, exchange capacity,
and percent magnesium saturation. Shrinking and swelling

lead to the formation of medium to large cracks in the
soil on drying and a churning action when wet. On meeting they produce surface bulges and clay exudation.
Swelling and shrinking prevent the formation of horizons.

The ease of dispersion appears to be related to
three soil characteristics. In the dispersed state it
puddles readily and infiltration of water is nil after
swelling. Soil structure is poorly developed; on drying,
the soil forms huge clods of clay which are extremely
unstable on wetting. On dispersion, the organic colloids
move to the surface of the soil peds causing the black
color of the soil. Soils having more than 30 percent
magnesium saturation are black and exhibit all the
characteristics of the montmorillonite clay. Below
30 percent magnesium saturation, the soils are first
brown in color and finally red. This change is associated with the decomposition of the montmorillonite
clay and the formation of kaolin clays. When soils
become dominantly red the kaolin clays are dominant and
the magnesium saturation drops to below 20 percent as
described by Uehara and Sherman (1956).

There is little evidence of development of hydrous
mica clays in Hawaiian soils as a part of the natural
sequence of mineral development in weathering. The
parent material on the whole is low in potassium-bearing
minerals. The only evidence of appreciable hydrous
micas is found in the cemented volcanic ash beds surrounding Salt Lake crater on the island of Oahu. There
is considerable evidence of the secondary formation of
hydrous mica, however, in soils having an overlay of
volcanic ash from pyroclastic eruptions of post-erosional
volcanism. Hydrous mica is found in soils subject to
heavy rainfall and in soils that have attained an advanced stage of mineral weathering. Volcanic ash
deposited on the surfaces of weathered soil is the
source of soluble silica and potassium, which, with
the hydrous hydroxide of aluminum, have synthesized the

hydrous micas in a soil-mineral assemblage. Figure 2
is a diagram of an example of the cycling and the synthesis of hydrous mica produced by the rapid decomposition of the minerals of volcanic ash overlay deposition.

The Kapoho eruption of 1960 on the island of Hawaii
showed that vegetation will survive a volcanic ash
deposition. Plant roots that survive absorb released
potassium, which would otherwise escape clay mineral
syntheses, and is utilized by the plant as a nutrient.
It is returned to the soil as the leaves are shed. In
this way the potassium in the system is consumed because
it is recycled through the plant. Silicon is similarly
recycled. These processes ensure a relatively high
concentration of silicate and potassium ions, which
are essential for the stable existence of synthesized
hydrous mica. Rex *et al.* (1969) have suggested that the
origin of micaceous minerals is from wind-blown materials
of continental deserts deposited in rain from the tropo-
sphere. In the opinion of this author this is not a
satisfactory explanation, as the occurrence of hydrous
mica is associated only with post-erosional eruptions.
It does not occur in soils of highly weathered volcanic
ash of the younger islands even when annual rainfall
exceeds 200 inches.

KAOLINIZATION

Climatic conditions are favorable for the formation
of kaolin clay minerals on most of the geologically
older islands (that is, Kauai, Niihau, Oahu, Molokai,
Lanai, Kahoolawe, and West Maui, and the lower dry
slopes of Kohala on Hawaii). Kaolin clays also have
formed in dry areas, where there are only 10 to 30 inches
of annual rainfall, on the volcanic ash deposits on the
younger islands. Usually the peak of kaolinization
occurs at 20 to 30 inches of rainfall where the rainfall
comes in a period of two to four months. The surprising

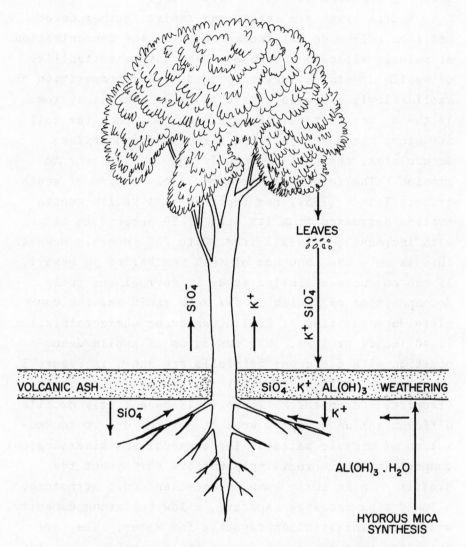

Fig. 2. The role of an overlay of volcanic ash and
mineral cycle of vegetation in the formation
of hydrous mica.

degree of mineral weathering is due to the fine texture
of the parent material and the occurrence of cyclonic
storms at least once a year. The latter provide the
leaching required for rapid weathering.

Kaolin clays are stable and resist further decomposition. They do not decompose until the concentration
of soluble silicate decreases. The inherent stability
of kaolin crystal structure spreads the decomposition of
kaolin slowly timewise toward an oxide mineral system.
If the oxides that develop are aluminum, then the soil
structure becomes firmer and firmer; if iron oxide
accumulates, the soil becomes friable and subject to
erosion. The former is the more likely course of weathering. Tanada (1951) has reported that kaolin concentration decreased from its peak of 80 percent to nil
with increasing rainfall from 20 to 200 inches. However,
this is only one sequence of soil weathering in Hawaii.
If one conducts a similar study in ferruginous soils,
decomposition of kaolin is far more rapid and the complete decomposition of kaolin can occur where rainfall
is 40 inches or less. Various rates of kaolin decomposition with different rainfalls are shown in Figure 3.

Kaolin soils of tropical regions are often called
"tropical red earths." These soils have little profile
differentiation except a weak A_1 horizon due to accumulation of organic matter. The chemical and mineralogical
composition are surprisingly uniform throughout the
profile. These soils have an excellent soil structure,
a low cation exchange capacity, a low buffering capacity,
and a high infiltration capacity for water. They are
among the most manageable soils in the world. Hawaiian
kaolinite soils are unusual in their high concentration
of manganese oxides. The highest concentration of
manganese is found in Wahiawa (Oahu) soils, especially
near Schofield, where it exists as surface encrustations,
concretions, and nodules. The area receives 45 to 60
inches of rainfall a year.

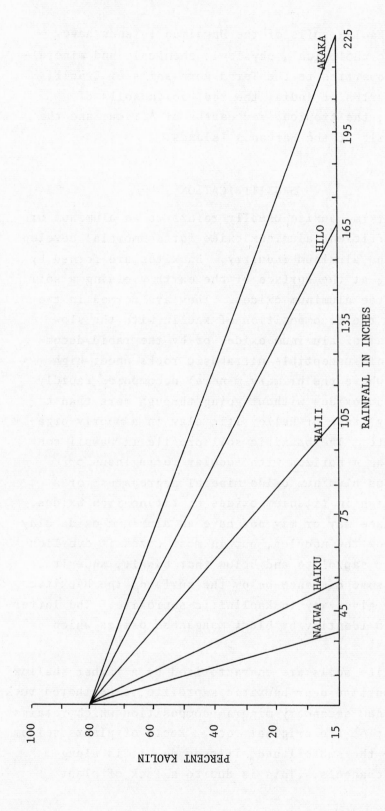

Fig. 3. The effect of rate of mineral decomposition and rainfall on the rate of decomposition of kaolin minerals.

The kaolin soils of the Hawaiian Islands have
similar morphological, physical, chemical, and mineralogical properties to the Terra Roxa soils of Brazil,
the red earths of India, the red kaolin soils of
Australia, the tropical red earths of Africa, and the
kaolin soils of the Barbados Islands.

BAUXITIFICATION

The term bauxite usually refers to an aluminum ore
having sufficient aluminum oxide for commercial development in the aluminum industry. Bauxites are formed by
weathering at the surface of the earth yielding a soil
rich in free aluminum oxides. They are formed in two
ways: by the decomposition of kaolin with the slow
development of aluminum oxide, or by the rapid decomposition of susceptible ultrabasic rocks under high
rainfall where the primary mineral decomposes rapidly
to aluminum oxides without going through more than a
transitory stage of halloysitic clay in a poorly organized state. The bauxitic soil profile in Hawaii consists of an A horizon with nodular ferruginous or
ferruginous-aluminum oxide mineral aggregates, or a
surface high in titanium oxides or titano-iron oxides.
This surface may or may not have an aluminum oxide clay
layer below the nodules, but in most cases it overlies
a bauxitic saprolite and below that basalt, andesite,
etc. At some distance below the surface, the bauxitic
saprolite gives way to kaolinitic saprolite. The latter
is easy to identify by black manganese oxides which
coat rocks.

Bauxite soils are characterized by a rather shallow
surface horizon over bauxitic saprolite, a weathered rock
having a new secondary mineral composition which retains
the fabric of the original rock. Roots of plants seldom
penetrate the subsoil and, if they do, it is along
drainage channels. This is due to a lack of plant

nutrients rather than to aluminum toxicity. Such plants
as the aluminum accumulators staghorn fern, melastoma,
and Java plum *(Eugenia cuminii)*, and the aluminum toler-
ator *Rhodomyrtus* thrive on these soils and, when some
plant nutrients are present, they grow vigorously, as
on the slopes of Kilohana Crater, Kauai. Bauxitic soil
occurs over much of the eastern half of Kauai in areas
receiving in excess of 50 inches of rainfall, and in the
Haiku and Kahakuloa areas of Maui. Hawaiian bauxitic
soils have been described by Sherman (1958), and Sherman
et al. (1967).

FERRUGINOUS-TITANIFEROUS SOIL-MINERAL FORMATION

The Hawaiian Islands are one of the few places in
the world where certain soils contain over 20 percent
titanium oxide. These soils are a type of laterite
in that they indurate on exposure to dehydration. The
process of induration, as far as iron and titanium
oxides are concerned, is one of crystallization of
amorphous hydrous oxides of iron and titanium and is
not due to residual enrichment by leaching and erosion
of soluble and light materials. No soil changes more
in its morphological characteristics than does this soil
on exposure and induration. In its usual state, under
natural forest cover, the soil profile shows little
horizonal differentiation, with only a surface accumulation of organic matter. The soil is a friable loam,
but under hard rubbing between thumb and finger it
moistens and becomes greasy, indicating that it is an
amorphous hydrous oxide clay. This friable soil overlies either a kaolin clay which is an unconformity or
unweathered rock. The clay has developed from a lava,
whereas these soils have formed on surface volcanic
ash deposits. The bulk density of the soils is approximately 1.0.

On dehydration this soil develops a dense surface
layer with a bulk density exceeding 2.0. The layer has

a purplish color. It usually retains its friable
characteristics in the subsoil with a transition layer
to the dense surface horizon. The friable subsoil
layer retains its amorphous hydrous oxide composition.
In the surface horizon the hydrous oxides of both iron
and titanium crystallize to various oxides such as
goethite, hematite maghemite, titano-maghemite, pseudo-
brookite, and other titano-iron oxide compounds. The
increase of titanium in the surface is difficult to
explain. One's first reaction is to assume that it is
the result of enrichment through leaching of aluminum
and silicon, both of which have decreased in concentration to nil in the dense A_2 horizon. However, the
ratio Fe:Ti has changed, indicating an addition of
titanium oxide--which is also suggested by the high
concentration of colloidal hydrous titanium oxide present
in the transitional A-B horizon. Fujimoto *et al.* (1948)
and Walker (1964) have separated a colloidal fraction
containing more than 40 percent titanium oxide from
this horizon. This would provide a form of titanium
that is mobile, and since these soils occur on sloping
benches on mountain slopes it seems reasonable to propose
that the colloidal titanium oxide is brought toward the
surface by capillary rise of soil solution pushed by
a zone of saturation at a greater elevation. On dehydration the titanium oxide forms crystalline titano-
iron oxides. Particle density is 2.2 in the subsoil
horizon and 4.2 in the dense layer. In the profile
covered by vegetation, particle density is similar to
the subsoil horizon and little heavy mineral is present.
The evidence, then, is against the concept of residual
enrichment by removal, because the indurated areas can
be surrounded by soils covered with vegetation.

In a sense the indurated profile fits Mohr's (1944)
description of a laterite profile in its sequence of
horizons. The indurated ferruginous horizon (in this
case ferruginous titaniferous) is underlain by a

ferruginous layer which is not undurated. This in turn
is underlain by a gibbsitic bauxitic horizon which occurs
in a thin aggregated layer above a kaolin clay.

These soils are susceptible to erosion when vegeta-
tive cover is removed either by fire or overgrazing.
The erosion-scarred lower slopes along the Waimea Canyon
(Kauai) road occur in this type of soil. The entire
soil of at least one-third of the area has been removed,
leaving barren, unproductive, weathered rock surfaces.

HYDRATED AMORPHOUS MINERAL-SOIL FORMATION

Soils formed on volcanic ash deposits that receive
rainfall in excess of 20 inches are composed of amorphous aluminum silicate and hydroxides and hydrous
oxides of aluminum and iron. These soils are characterized by low bulk densities ranging from 0.1 to 0.9.
They contain large amounts of water, and the soils
belonging to the hydrol humic latosol contain over 300
percent water in field conditions. Even under these
high moisture conditions the soils handle relatively
heavy equipment. Almost all the sugarcane from the
Hilo and Hamakua coasts of Hawaii is grown on this type
of soil.

Amorphous soils can be divided into two groups:
(a) those that contain both amorphous hydroxide and
oxides of aluminum and iron and hydrated aluminum
silicates; and (b) those that contain only amorphous
hydroxides and hydrous oxides. The latter contain
what Bates (1959) has defined as a highly hydrated,
mixed (Al, Fe, Si, Ti) gel of hydroxides and hydrous
oxides. On dehydration, these soils undergo a change
of state by crystallizing to light-colored aggregates
of gibbsite and dark-colored magnetic aggregates of
maghemite and allophane, as described by Sherman (1957).
The change is irreversible. Soils of the former group
will not undergo an extensive change of state and for

all practical purposes can rehydrate to their former
condition.

There is a marked difference in the physical properties of the two types of soils. The nonsilicate type
has a nonsticky, smeary or buttery consistency, while
those having amorphous silicates have a much firmer
consistency. The nonsilicate amorphous oxide soils
have a weak positive charge. They cannot be dispersed
with alkaline dispersal agents because the increased
hydroxyl concentration causes the crystallization of
aluminum hydroxide to gibbsite in sand-size mineral
aggregates. Even treatment with hydrogen peroxide to
remove organic matter causes crystallization to take
place. Most of these soils are leached of bases, but
in spite of their seemingly impoverished state they
support a heavy vegetation, often including aluminum-
accumulating plant species.

The amorphous soils of the silicate-containing
form have a dark A horizon. The organic matter content
of the surface ranges from 8 to 12 percent. Both surface and subsoil horizons have textures of friable silt
loam to silty clay loam. They are porous and leach
rapidly.

Nonsilicate amorphous soils have a dark surface
horizon containing from 12 to 20 percent organic matter.
The subsoils are stratified due to successive volcanic
ash deposits and interperiods of soil formation. The
profiles are deep and usually lie as a blanket over
lava rocks of earlier volcanic activity.

Nonsilicate amorphous soils have the unusual characteristic of a clay layer at the bottom of the soil
profile. This clay layer does not follow the surface
topography of the soil but rather the topography of
the bottom of the soil profile, which conforms to the
undulating surfaces of the lava rocks.

A zone of saturation forms in the soil profile

just above the unconformity. Leaching silicate ions
accumulate in this zone of saturation and 2:1 montmorillonite clays form by the resilication of the free amorphous aluminum hydroxides. This is the first record of
a horizon in the soil which does not follow the surface
topography. It is shown diagrammatically in Figure 4.

RESILICATION

Chemical weathering of minerals is a progressive
desilication process. It depends on free drainage.
If poor drainage develops, then the soluble silicate ion
concentration increases and resilication of free hydroxides, hydrous oxides, amorphous aluminum silicate, and
amorphous constituents on the surfaces occurs, forming
2:1 or 1:1 clay minerals. The white halloysitic clays
of Hanalei Heights, Kauai, were formed because of poor
drainage of amorphous oxide soils. These soils are
saturated with water, and iron oxide is reduced and
removed, leaving a halloysite clay containing some mineral aggregates of gibbsite of the former soil.

THE SOILS OF THE HAWAIIAN ISLANDS

The soils of the Hawaiian Islands are described
below, following, with some modifications, the scheme
proposed by Cline *et al.* (1955). The soils are grouped
according to their genesis, degree of weathering and
stage of development, and the dominant minerals and
accessory minerals in each. Recognition of the amorphous soils as a soil group is a departure from Cline's
original classification. The author wishes to make it
clear that this is not an effort to reclassify soils
or to present a new classification but rather to describe
soils as a natural body and to show the processes of
their formation.

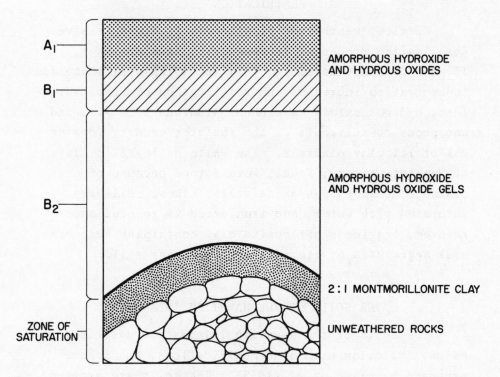

Fig. 4.   The position of clay layer formed in zone
           of saturation above porous rocks.

A.   Soils of Arid and Semi-Arid Regions

1. *Red Desert Soils*

These soils are formed where the climate is very
dry and there is not sufficient vegetation for the accumulation of organic matter. The clays are kaolinitic,
indicating that chemical weathering has occurred. Leaching has been sufficient to remove calcium carbonate,
which is deposited in sheets above the unweathered rocks
below. Leaching is probably due to the regular occurrence of heavy rains associated with cyclonic storms.
Unlike other Red Desert soils there is no accumulation
of clay in the B horizon due to the *in situ* formation
of kaolin clay and its stability in regard to dispersion.

There is one soil family, Kawaihae, with the following profile characteristics. The A_1 horizon is very
weak, thin, and reddish brown, probably formed from the
weathering of a thin deposition of volcanic ash or
cinders. This overlies unweathered rocks coated with
$CaCO_3$ leached from the A_1 horizon. Soils of the Red
Desert group are found on the islands of Hawaii, Maui,
and Oahu.

2. *Reddish Brown Soils*

These soils are formed under slightly higher rainfall conditions than are the Red Desert soils. Distribution of rainfall is better and there is more vegetation, giving rise to an A_1 horizon showing accumulation
of organic matter. Chemical weathering is limited, and
what has occurred has given rise to kaolin clays. Base
saturation is high throughout the profile. Leaching
has been sufficient to remove the carbonates to the
lower portion of the soil where they are precipitated
as coatings on rocks. The formation of 2:1 clays occurs
where internal drainage is slightly impeded. Gypsum
occurs in some of the subsoil, especially near eruption
vents. The chemical composition of the rock and soil are
similar, and little weathering has occurred.

Waikaloa is the only soil family in the group. In
a typical profile, the A_1 horizon is a dark reddish brown
to dark brown, 8 to 12 inches thick, with a high organic
matter content, and the soil reaction is neutral to
slightly alkaline. The A_1 horizon is underlain by a B
horizon 10 to 18 inches in thickness. The B horizon is
lighter in color, being yellowish brown; it has a weakly
prismatic structure and is near neutral in reaction.
Usually $CaCO_3$ and sometimes $CaSO_4$ are found below the
B horizon and occasionally in the soil solum; they are
never in excess of a few percent and usually coat pebbles
or stones.

B. Soils High in Amorphous Hydrated Mineral Constituents

1. *Tropical Reddish Prairie*

These soils have many of the profile characteristics
of other prairie soils in mineral composition and degree
of weathering as exhibited by their low silica-sesquioxide ratio of 0.5 to 0.7. They are termed "tropical"
to designate their state of weathering. These soils are
formed where rainfall is moderate (25 to 70 inches a
year). They have a well-established grass cover and a
high organic matter content; they have formed on fairly
deep deposits of volcanic ash. The soil is highly
weathered, but the rocks covered by the volcanic ash
are unweathered. The profiles are characterized by
their extreme friability. There is considerable variability within each soil family due to the wide range
of geological age of the different ash eruptions;
variation occurs within very short distances depending
on the age of the cinder cone and the degree of segregation of materials in ash distribution. Rainfall has
not been sufficient to leach out the somewhat minor
differences due to the influence of the parent material.

There are three soil families in this group: Pahala,
Waimea, and Naalehu. In the Waimea family there is a

thick (14 to 16 inches), brown or dark brown A_1 horizon with a high organic matter content of 8 to 12 percent. It is slightly acid in reaction and has a very
friable, weak, granular structure. The B horizon is a
gradual transition of the A_1 horizon but is richer in
color, usually dark to light yellowish brown. The soil
solum can be as deep as 4 feet. Base saturation is
high, especially in exchangeable calcium. Silicate
concentration is low due to extensive weathering and
leaching. The silica-sesquioxide ratio is well below
1.0. Cation exchange capacity is high, 40 to 70 milli-
equivalents per 100 grams. The high hydration suggests
that this soil is composed of amorphous aluminum-silicate
clays, probably allophanic, some poorly organized halloysite, and amorphous hydrous oxides. The apparent texture is a silty clay loam, and the real texture is a
clay. These soils seldom have a pH as low as 6.0.

2. *Latosolic Brown Forest Soils*

The latosolic Brown Forest soils result from an
extension of the same soil-forming processes that developed the Tropical Reddish Prairie soils, but they have
formed under more intense weathering and leaching,
reflected in a greater acidity and a lower base saturation. These characteristics are due to generally higher
rainfall, ranging from 40 to 120 inches a year. These
soils are formed on volcanic ash. Rapid desilication
has been the typical characteristic of the weathering
process, and the products of weathering are amorphous
aluminum silicates and hydroxide gels, and hydrous
oxides of aluminum and iron. These soil constituents
are to some extent protected from dehydration by the
wide distribution of rainfall and lack of periods of
drought.

There are four soil families: Hanipoe, Puu Oo,
Maile, and Olinda. The typical profile of the Maile
soil family is as follows: The soil has a dark brown

A_1 horizon about 12 inches thick and has an organic
matter content of more than 8 percent. This horizon
is acid, with a pH of 5.0. The granular structure is
moderately firm. The subsoil is a reddish brown, silty
clay, but, like that of all the amorphous soils, the
true texture is a very fine clay. There is a high
aluminum content and a low silica-sesquioxide ratio
(about 0.3).

3. *Amorphous Humic Latosol Having Aluminum Silicates
    (Humic Latosol)*

This is a modification of Cline's (1955) grouping
and represents an effort to separate the amorphous soils
which have a bonding between Al and Si and those in
which Al and Si exist as free hydroxide and hydrous
oxides. The soils of the Humic Latosol group have low
bulk density, a criterion associated with predominantly
amorphous constituents. Because it does not dry irre-
versibly, it is assumed that the Al and Si linkage exists
in the amorphous system. These soils differ from those
that are oxidic in composition in such physico-chemical
properties as cation exchange, buffering capacity, and
reaction to addition of phosphate. There are three
families: Paauhau, Ookala, and Kapoho.

The soil profile of the Ookala family clearly
shows its transitional character. The soils of this
family in dryer locations take on characteristics
approaching clays of the kaolin group. They do not
exhibit irreversible dehydration and there is a suggestion of smeariness, a property of amorphous hydroxide
gel soils. Both these properties become more pronounced
as the wetter range of these soils is approached. On
dehydration the soils dry to hard aggregates which
break into angular aggregates with sharp edges. There
is little evidence of the segregation of gibbsite on
drying. The range of rainfall annually is from 70 to
150 inches. The A_1 horizon consists of a 0- to 10-inch

layer, which is a dark, reddish brown, silty clay loam
with strong granular structure. It has a reaction of
pH 5.0 to 5.5 and contains 12 to 18 percent organic
matter. There is a gradual transition into the B
horizon, which is a reddish brown, silty clay loam with
a weak, fine, granular structure. The parent material
is weathered volcanic ash. In some areas it lies on a
thin layer of lava which overlies a fossil soil formed
on an older deposition of volcanic ash. The acidity
of the subsoil is similar to that of the surface.

4. *Amorphous Hydroxide and Hydrous Oxide Soils
    (Hydrol Humic Latosol)*

These soils belong to the Hydrol Humic Latosol
group which have a bulk density of less than 1.0. Their
properties are unique; indeed, many soil scientists
consider them unbelievable. The dark layers contain
heavy minerals, while the lighter-colored intervening
layers do not. Bulk densities are extremely low, ranging from 0.09 in the subsoil to 0.5 at the surface;
their water-holding capacity is often over 300 percent
in field conditions. They are smeary or buttery in
consistency and have a weak positive charge, and they
also have the property of irreversible drying due to
crystallization of the amorphous materials to gibbsite
and magnetic iron oxides. These soils form under rainfall ranging from 100 to 400 inches a year on a series
of volcanic ash deposits with different strata reflected
in the profile. Current thinking is that each stratum
underwent soil formation and soil weathering before
deposition of the materials of the next pyroclastic
eruption.

The soils have weathered under intense leaching
conditions. Internal drainage is unimpeded except
above the zone of contact with underlying lava rocks.
Here, a saturation zone is developed that slows up
movement of soluble silicate ions sufficiently to permit

the synthesis of 2:1 clays in a layer which follows the topography of the rock-volcanic ash contact zone. This is further evidence suggesting how delicate the balance must be relative to the concentration of soluble silicate ion for its reaction with aluminum hydroxide to form allophane or alumino-silicate clay minerals. In the soil solum the soluble silicate is removed so rapidly that the silicate ion and aluminum never appear in the solution in concentrations or conditions favoring their union.

Bates (1959) and Sherman (1957) have described the differential crystallization of gibbsite on dehydration. If moist soil is exposed in an open container, the crystalline aggregate can be seen forming in the soil. Dehydration, an increase in hydroxyl concentration, and oxidation can cause the aluminum hydroxide to polymerize to gibbsite even in relatively acid soil conditions. The crystalline soil formed by dehydration is more acid than it was when in the form of an amorphous hydroxide gel. There is no validity to statements that the amorphous hydroxide and oxides have the same chemical and physical properties as their crystalline forms.

There are four soil families in this group: Hilo, Akaka, Honokaa, and Kealakekua. A profile of the Akaka soil family follows: This soil in its native state has an A_0 horizon of 2 to 4 inches of very acid organic matter (pH 3.0) derived from staghorn fern. Staghorn fern is an aluminum accumulator, and its growth is extremely abundant on these soils. The A_1 horizon is a dark, gray-brown, silty clay varying from 5 to 9 inches in thickness; it has some firmness when dry but is smeary when wet. It is extremely acid, with a pH range of 4 to 5, and it contains up to 20 to 25 percent organic matter. These soils do not have a true B horizon but a subsoil of alternating bands of dark, reddish brown and grayish to grayish brown, silty clay. Each probably represents an artifact of a fossil soil.

The dark layer contains more organic matter than the
lighter colored layer. The organic matter content is
as high as 6 percent in the subsoil. Numerous root
channels are lined with deposits of aluminum hydroxide,
which on drying become gibbsite. Roots encased in gibbsite have been removed from these soils. This layer is
very acid, as low as pH 4.5 and seldom above pH 5.2.
The exchangeable bases are low, with Ca^{++} and K^+ the
lowest. Depth of the subsoil varies from 4 feet to
over 20 feet and lies over a layer of weathered saprolite
boulders of the unconformity on older lava flows. Just
above the contact zone is a 6-inch layer of gray silty
clay consisting of 2:1 clay minerals.

C. Soils Having a Predominance of Crystalline
Secondary Minerals

1. *Dark Magnesium Clays (Tropical Black Earths)*
This group of soils is rich in montmorillonite
clays forming under conditions in which magnesium is
the dominant ion in the soil solution. These soils
have a high exchangeable magnesium saturation and a
Ca:Mg ratio approaching 1.0. The soils have self-
mulching surfaces, but they develop wide cracks in dry
summers and swell when they are wet. This property
makes them unsatisfactory for homesites when they occur
on slopes, because the soils are unstable. The churning
action of swelling and shrinking results in many slick-
ensides on the surfaces of large aggregates of soil due
to the orientation of the clays. The base saturation
is high, and most of the profiles have nodules and
nodular forms of gypsum crystals. Rosette forms are
found occasionally. These soils are similar to the
Regur soils of India and the "cracking clays" of the
Gezira area of Sudan.
There is one soil family, Lualualei. The A_1 horizon of 3 to 4 inches consists of a self-mulching, dark
gray clay which is friable when dry and plastic and

sticky when moist. It has an alkaline reaction of pH
7.5 and a low organic matter content of 2.0 percent.
The B_1 horizon is a dark gray clay, 20 to 24 inches in
thickness. It has a coarse blocky structure. The
aggregates often have slickenside surfaces. It is
alkaline, as is the surface. The B_2 horizon consists
of a massive, dark gray clay having some white spots
of gypsum. It is extremely hard when dry and very
sticky and plastic when wet. The reaction is more alkaline than the upper part of the profile. This layer
is often 20 to 24 inches in thickness. The C horizon
is a marine clay or, if on slopes, a weathered lava
rock formation.

2. *Low Humic Latosol (Tropical Red Earths)*

Soils of the Low Humic Latosol group are latosolic
soils formed in dry to moderately humid areas with a
climate in which there is a long dry season. The accumulation of organic matter in the surface horizon is
small, as it is limited by seasonal growth of plants
and high temperatures. The soils have an A_1 horizon
that is weak to moderately developed, depending on the
annual rainfall. The main weathering process in their
formation is kaolinization. The peak of kaolinization
occurs in the dryer families, Molokai and Lahaina. In
addition, these soils are manganiferous. The peak of
manganese accumulation occurs in those receiving moderate rainfall of 40 to 50 inches. These soils are
formed on cindery lava flows, volcanic ash deposits on
geologically older islands, ultrabasic lava of post-
erosional flows, alluvial materials, and coral limestone. There are six soil families: Molokai, Lahaina,
Wahiawa, Kahana, Kohala, and Waialua. They are typical
of all red kaolinitic clay soils of tropical regions,
and almost identical with the Terra Roxa soils of Brazil
and the Red Earths of India. The genesis of the soils
has been described by Sherman and Alexander (1958) and

Fernandez and Sherman (1963).

The modal soils of the group are those of the
Molokai family. The A_1 horizon is a dark red, 2- to
4-inch layer of silty clay. It has a weak granular
structure and is friable. It shows no evidence of an
appreciable accumulation of organic matter, although it
may contain as much as 2 percent. It has a uniform B
horizon, usually a red silty clay with a weak, coarsely
prismatic structure. The B horizon may have numerous
black manganese oxide concretions. The parent material
usually is a kaolinite saprolite. The soil reaction is
near neutral throughout the profile in a virgin profile,
but may be very acid (pH 3.7) after 30 to 40 years of
agricultural use because of the low buffering capacity
of the kaolin clay, which is often 80 percent of the
soil. The soil has a remarkably stable soil structure,
with the aggregates often functioning as single units
due to their encasement by an amorphous iron oxide surface. The chemical composition of the soil is extremely
uniform. The silica-sesquioxide ratio, which is 1.6 to
1.8 for Molokai, ranges from 1.1 to 2.0 in the group.
Infiltration capacity is very high. These soils are
more than 50 percent kaolin clay, which is the peak
concentration of kaolin mineral accumulation in soils
formed under conditions of free drainage.

3. *Humic Latosol*

The soils of this group are formed in wetter climates than the Low Humic Latosols. There is no long
dry season to restrict vegetation. Two characteristics
distinguish them: their strong, prominent A_1 horizon,
which indicates an accumulation of organic matter; and
soil weathering in which kaolin minerals decompose to
form hydroxide and oxide minerals of aluminum and iron.
The kaolin content of these soils is less than 50
percent. There are two soil families: Kaneohe and
Honolua. The latter is transitional to the amorphous

soils. The soils of this group are formed on lavas and
volcanic ash deposits of post-erosional eruptions on
Oahu and Kauai, and on basalts and andesite rock covered
with volcanic ash on Hawaii and Maui. On Oahu and Kauai
much of the volcanic ash may have been deposited as an
alluvium prior to weathering.

In the Kaneohe family there is a prominant A_1
horizon, often a foot in thickness, of a dark, reddish
brown silty clay with a strong, stable, medium-granular
structure. At ordinary moisture levels this structure
is firm and resists dispersion. The horizon is strongly
acidic, with a pH as low as 4.0. It has a high organic
matter content of 8 percent or more. The B horizon is
a red silty clay of variable thickness, usually related
to the depth of the fine volcanic ash which is the
parent material of most of these soils. It has a fine
to medium blocky structure. It is friable when wet and
is nonplastic.

These soils are highly leached and very acid. Their
base saturation is low, due to the peculiar characteristics of the surface aggregates which act as units. A
pH of 3.6 has been measured in these soils at the foot
of the Pali on Oahu.

4. *Aluminous-Ferruginous Latosol (Ferruginous Bauxitic
    Soils)*

These soils were separated from Cline's classification group on the basis of additional information.
In many cases the soils are bauxite, in that they
contain sufficient aluminum oxide to be a commercial
source of aluminum. Usually they have a surface horizon
either of a titaniferous ferruginous oxide clay or of
nodular iron oxides containing varying amounts of aluminum oxide. These soils have been strongly weathered
and intensely leached of all silicates. The total
SiO_2 may be as low as 0.5 percent, with 2 to 4 percent
as the average. There is no indication of silicate

clays. They are strongly acid soils formed under conditions of heavy rainfall of 75 to 200 inches and
unimpeded drainage. Poorly drained areas of these soils
have kaolin clays. The soils are resistant to erosion;
cultivation of crops has been practiced on extremely
steep slopes without fear of erosion, and road cuts
show no evidence of erosion. These soils are base
depleted, with sodium the highest base owing to deposition by ocean spray in rain water. These soils occur
on post-erosional volcanic lavas and ash of the volcanic
series of the eastern half of Kauai, and in the Haiku
and Nakalele point areas of Maui. Three soil families
are recognized: Halii (formerly Humic Latosol), and
Haiku and Puhi (formerly of the Humic Ferruginous Latosol
group).

In the Halii soils there is a surface A_1 horizon
of ferruginous aluminous nodules of which 60 to 80
percent are larger than 4 mm in diameter. The nodules
have highly polished surfaces and when broken reveal a
block surface shell of hematite with either mixed oxides
of aluminum and iron or some gibbsite. These nodules
were described by Sherman *et al.* (1969). The remaining
material is ferruginous bauxitic clay. The surface
horizon is predominantly iron oxide; it is grayish
brown when wet and considerably lighter in color when
dry. The B_1 horizon underlying the A_1 is a clay of
variable thickness. This clay is weakly smeary. It
contains some nodules that are smaller than those of
the A_1 horizon. It lies over a bauxitic saprolite
which ranges in depth from a few feet to over 30 feet
on the slopes of Kilohana Crater (Kauai). These lie
abruptly over kaolinite saprolite, after basalt. The
change is indicated by the presence of a manganese
oxide coating in the pores of the weathered saprolite.
The saprolite is soft and can be cultivated for crop
production with the addition of fertilizer. All these
soils require the application of calcium silicate for

the growth of crops other than those of plants which
accumulate or tolerate aluminum. The Halii soils were
described as soils by Sherman *et al.* (1967) and as a
bauxitic ore by Sherman *et al.* (1968). In some of the
wetter areas where these soils occur, iron oxide pans
occur around the bauxitic saprolite.

5. *Humic Ferruginous Latosol (Titaniferous Ferruginous
   Soils)*

   The soils of this group are characterized by high
iron and titanium oxide content and the capacity to
indurate on exposure. In this respect they have the
basic properties of the laterite. The soils are strongly
weathered to the oxide stage. They are well desilicated:
there is little evidence of the existence of silicate
clays except in the less weathered members of the group.
Aluminum has also been removed to a large extent from
the soil, but it occurs in the lower horizon as gibbsite
aggregates and nodules. These soils are formed under
30 to 70 inches of rainfall. The climate includes a
long dry period which can dehydrate the exposed surfaces.

   These soils, in their natural state with a vegeta-
tive cover, have a profile of little differentiation
except for the dark A_1 horizon and a friable silt loam
subsoil usually lying over a lava unconformity or an
impervious halloysite clay. The soil solum has a low
bulk density. On exposure, either by man's activities
or by fire, a tremendous change occurs in the soil
profile. The surface horizon indurates and becomes a
massive, dense, reddish purple horizon with a high
bulk density. This is underlain by a brightly colored
transitional A-B horizon which is in turn underlain by
the light-colored, friable, low bulk density subsoil
of the original soil. These are profound changes in
morphological characteristics, far greater than those
utilized as criteria in systems of soil classification.

   Induration develops very rapidly. On sites pur-

posely exposed to climatic elements, there are definite
indications of induration in as little as one year's
time, and induration has occurred on the sides of road
cuts in even shorter periods of time. The highest bulk
density measured, 2.98, was taken from the side of an
irrigation ditch which showed no evidence of erosion.
High bulk density is produced by crystallization of the
amorphous iron and titanium oxides. Induration is
caused by the same process. In crystallization the
mineral aggregates increase in size and concretions
develop. The high concentration of titanium oxide in
the surface horizon is explained by movement of these
constituents. Both iron and titanium are concentrated
from hydrated, colloidal, mobile forms. The evidence
for this type of concentration is as follows: (a) the
lack of heavy minerals in the soil before induration
and their presence after induration--particle density
2.2 vs. 4.2, respectively; (b) the increase in crystal
aggregate size from less than 0.8 microns to more than
30 microns; (c) the formation of pea-size concretions;
(d) the formation of magnetic iron oxides; and (e) the
presence of a colloidal fraction in the A-B horizon
containing over 40 percent TiO_2. Walker (1964) has made
a detailed study of these profiles and their profound
changes.

Three soil families are recognized in this soil
group: Naiwa, Mahana, and Kolekole. The modal profile
of the Naiwa soil (Maui) is as follows: "A_1, 0-3 inches,
dark red silt loam; moderate medium granular structure;
very friable; moderate volume weight; pH 4.5 to 6.0,
roots numerous. A_2 horizon 3 to 8 inches, dark red
(purplish tinge) silt loam, massive; very firm or firm
to break but may be crushed with fingers to a silty
powder when dry or moist. pH 4.5 to 6.0; few roots;
very high volume weight. A_3, 8 to 11 inches, red silt
loam similar to A_2 but has a weak blocky structure and

not so high a volume weight. B, 11 to 21 inches red
fine sandy loam or silt loam; moderate to weak fine
blocky structure; loose or very friable when moist and
non-plastic when wet; pH 4.0 to 5.5; few roots present.
B_3 or C_1, 21 to 36 inches red fine sandy loam or silt
loam containing gray, yellow, or brown weathered rock
fragments that retain their original structure but may
be crushed between the fingers; pH 4.0 to 5.5. C_2, 36
inches . . ." (Cline 1955:437). This profile represents a site where induration has been due to grazing
rather than exposure.

6. *Hydromorphic Latosol (Resilication)*

This group of soils has poor drainage which probably developed after an initial weathering stage when
drainage was not impeded. In the advanced stages of
weathering, drainage became impeded and, at least for
periods of time, the soil was saturated with water.
Iron oxides were reduced and removed. Amorphous aluminum hydroxides were resilicated and formed a white
halloysite clay. Nodules of gibbsite remained, but
their surfaces were converted to a thin coating of
halloysite clay. The largest area of these soils occurs
on the mountain ridge east of Hanalei Valley, Kauai.
There is one soil family recognized, the Koolau.

In the Koolau soil profile from Kauai, the A_1
horizon consists of a dark gray, silty clay, 6 to 8
inches in thickness. It is a moderately granular,
friable, nonsticky, nonplastic clay. It is mainly a
titaniferous oxide-halloysite clay containing some
organic matter. The B horizon is a white, silty clay
containing some gibbsite nodules. It ranges from 2 to
25 feet in depth. It has a uniform, very fine, weak
granular structure. The clay turns a light gray color
on drying. It is nonplastic. The B horizon lies on
saprolite rocks or on an iron oxide pan as much as 4
inches thick. The white clay is halloysite (kaolin).

The entire profile is very acid (pH 4.0 to 4.5) and it
has a low base saturation. The stability of the clay
is due to soluble silicate concentration in the soil
solution.

D. Soils of Imperfect Drainage (Lowlands)

This is a minor group of soils. Each profile is
restricted by the degree of poor drainage. Four types
are recognized: (a) soils having an impeded drainage
which are water saturated during short intervals of
the year; (b) soils in which the surface has good drainage but the subsoil has a water table; (c) soils in
which the water table is at or near the surface; and
(d) paddy or flooded soils. All of these soils have a
high base saturation and are chiefly montmorillonite
clays. All are characterized by exchangeable magnesium.
Since most of them occur on alluvial deposits, the original parent material is variable. The soil profile is
a sticky, plastic clay with little differentiation. In
the zone of water saturation there is extensive mottling.

E. Immature Soils

These soils occur in locations where they have had
either no time to weather or insufficient rainfall and
time to permit sufficient soil genesis to yield a profile. Each soil reflects the properties of the parent
material.

1. Lithosols represent the most important group,
as forests, grass, and crops grow on them. These soils
are the unweathered surfaces of cindery flows in areas
receiving more than 75 inches of rainfall distributed
throughout the year. Many tree crops such as macadamia
nuts, papaya, guava, coffee, etc., are grown on these
soils, and a commercial lumber industry is being initiated in these areas.

2. Regosols are represented by two very minor groups of soils. They are of unweathered volcanic ash and coral sand.

3. Bog soils on tops of mountains and the sorts of saline estuaries represent other minor groups of soils.

THE EVOLUTION OF HAWAIIAN SOILS

Despite the great variation in the processes of soil formation (weathering and leaching) and in the rate of soil formation in the Hawaiian Islands, it is possible to trace the past and predict the future behavior of these soils. Soils have been described in terms of their stages of development with an age connotation by Mohr (1944): (a) fresh, (b) juvenile, (c) virile, (d) senile, and (e) latent. The author would change the last stage to the "oxide" stage.

The terms *virile* and *senile* were introduced by Mohr to convey the concept of the degree of weathering involved. The former term denotes a phase of increasing specific surface; the latter, a phase in which specific surface is decreasing. In the initial stages of weathering, that is, of clay mineral formation, including the development of an amorphous fraction, there is a continuous increase in specific surface. Reactivity of soil constituents is greatest during this phase. Parent material is predominant, and most of the soils can be classified as lithosols or regosols, and designated basaltic lithosol and so forth. Soil development passes from the virile phase to the senile phase as soon as it begins to lose specific surface area. Loss of specific surface area occurs with the development of such mineral aggregates as concretions and nodules which function as a unit, and by crystallization of amorphous hydroxides and hydrous oxides to crystalline hydroxides and oxides with an increase in unit size

(Sherman *et al.* 1968). Oxide soils are in a stage when
secondary mineral aggregates are quite apparent, the
aggregates often more than 4 mm in diameter. The juvenile stage is distinguished from the fresh by the
occurrence of a soil differentiation profile.

Figure 5 is a diagrammatic representation of soil
development on volcanic ash, from the fresh to the oxide
stage. The geographical distribution of soils in the
Island chain clearly demonstrates the sequence of phases.
The geologically recent islands of Hawaii (except the
Kohala area) and East Maui do not have soils in either
the senile or oxide stage. Soils of the Latosolic
Brown Forest and Tropical Reddish Prairie types occur
only on recently deposited ash. Soils of the Low Humic
Latosol, Humic Ferruginous Latosol, and Aluminous Humic
Latosol types, on the other hand, occur on the geologically older surfaces of West Maui, Lanai, Molokai, Oahu,
and Kauai. Cline (1944) has previously pointed out
the relationships.

CONCLUSIONS

The tropical soils of the Hawaiian Islands are
not unique, but the Islands form a natural laboratory
for tropical soil science because within short distances
the scientist can study soil properties which are world
wide in their application.

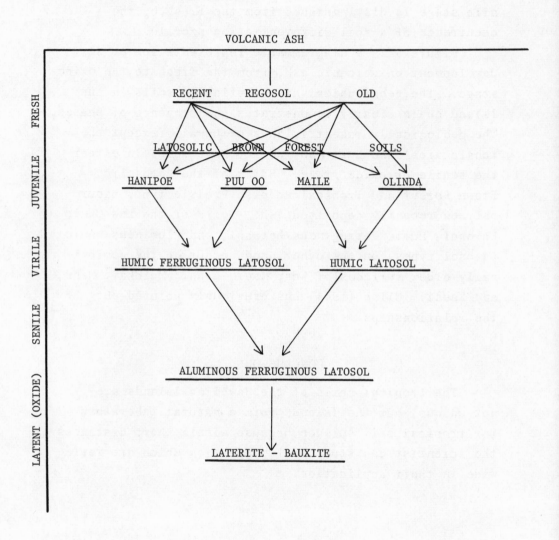

Fig. 5. Diagrammatic representation of the evolution
         of Hawaiian soils.

REFERENCES

Bates, T. F. 1959. Rock weathering and clay formation
     in Hawaii. Miner. Ind. (State College, Pa.) 29:1-6.

Cline, M. G. 1955. Soil survey, Territory of Hawaii,
     islands of Hawaii, Kauai, Lanai, Maui, Molokai, and
     Oahu. Washington, U.S. Gov't. Printing Office,
     U.S. Soil Conservation Service. Soil Survey Series,
     No. 25, 644 p.

Fernandez, N. C., and G. Donald Sherman. 1963. Cer-
     tain morphological, mineralogical, and chemical
     properties of four soils of the Molokai family.
     Philipp. Agric. 47:168-182.

Fujimoto, G., G. Donald Sherman, and Ada C. Chang. 1948.
     The chemical composition of the separated mineral
     fractions of a Ferruginous Humic Latosol profile.
     Proc. Soil Sci. Soc. Amer. 13:166-169.

Jackson, M. L., A. Tyler, A. L. Willis, G. A. Bourbeau,
     and R. P. Pennington. 1948. Weathering sequence
     of clay-size minerals in soils and sediments.
     J. Phys. Chem. 52:1237-1260.

Jenny, H. 1941. Factors of soil formation. McGraw-
     Hill, New York.

Katsura, T., I. Kushiro, S. Akimoto, J. L. Walker, and
     G. Donald Sherman. 1962. Titanomagnetite and
     titanomaghemite in a Hawaiian soil. J. Sediment.
     Petrol. 32:299-308.

Mohr, E. J. C. 1944. Soils of the equatorial regions.
     Edward Bros., Ann Arbor, Michigan.

Moomaw, J. C., M. Nakamura, and G. Donald Sherman. 1959.
     Aluminum in some Hawaiian plants. Pacif. Sci.
     13:335-341.

Nakamura, M., and G. Donald Sherman. 1965. Genesis
     of halloysite and gibbsite from mugearite on the
     island of Maui. Hawaii Agric. Exp. Sta. Bull.
     62, 36 p.

Rex, R. W., J. K. Syers, and M. L. Jackson. 1969.
     Eolian origin of quartz in soils of Hawaiian Islands
     and in Pacific sediments. Science 163:277-279.

Sherman, G. Donald. 1949. Factors influencing the
     development of lateritic and laterite soils in the
     Hawaiian Islands. Pacif. Sci. 3:307-314.

————— 1952. The genesis and morphology of the alumina-rich laterite clays. *In* Problems of clay and laterite genesis. Symposium, St. Louis, Missouri, 1951. American Institute of Mining and Metallurgical Engineers, New York.

————— 1957. Formation of gibbsite aggregates in Latosols developed on volcanic ash. Science 125: 1220-1221.

————— 1958. Gibbsite-rich soils of the Hawaiian Islands. Hawaii Agric. Exp. Sta. Bull. 116, 24 p.

Sherman, G. Donald, and L. T. Alexander. 1958. Characteristics and genesis of Low Humic Latosol. Proc. Soil Sci. Soc. Amer. 23:168-170.

Sherman, G. Donald, J. D. Cady, H. Ikawa, and N. E. Blomberg. 1967. Genesis of the bauxitic Halii soils. Hawaii Agric. Exp. Sta. Tech. Bull. 56, 46 p.

Sherman, G. Donald, and H. Ikawa. 1968. Soil sequences in the Hawaiian Islands. Pacif. Sci. 22:458-464.

Sherman, G. Donald, H. Ikawa, and Y. Matsusaka. 1969. Aluminous-ferruginous oxide mineral nodules in tropical soils. Pacif. Sci. 23:115-122.

Sherman, G. Donald, J. L. Walker, and H. Ikawa. 1968. Some of the mineral resources of the Hawaiian Islands. Hawaii Agric. Exp. Sta. Bull. 138, 34 p.

Soil Survey Staff. 1960. Soil classification--a comprehensive system--7th approximation. U.S. Dept. Agric., Washington, D.C.

Tanada, T. 1951. Certain properties of the inorganic colloidal fraction of the Hawaiian soils. J. Soil Sci. 2:83-96.

Uehara, G., and G. Donald Sherman. 1956. The nature and properties of the soils of the red and black complex of the Hawaiian Islands. Hawaii Agric. Exp. Sta. Tech. Bull. 32, 31 p.

Walker, J. L. 1964. Genesis of ferruginous laterites in Hawaii. Hawaii Inst. Geophys. Report No. 10, 406 p.

CONTRAST BETWEEN THE PIONEER POPULATING PROCESS ON LAND AND SHORE[1]

MAXWELL S. DOTY

Botany Department, University of Hawaii, Honolulu, Hawaii

INTRODUCTION

The east rift of the volcano, Kilauea, (Fig. 1) on the Island of Hawaii erupted in 1955 and sent streams of lava into the sea. As the lava fields cooled and the pioneer communities became established on them, an opportunity thus was provided both to record these pioneer events as they took place and to experimentally test various hypotheses. The purpose of the present article is to present some of the results of this observation and experimentation and some of the inferences drawn.

The oldest prehistoric lava rock lands and shores of Hawaii bear slow-to-change populations that are nearly in equilibrium with the environment. For the present work, such populations are considered to represent climax communities, and the present work is conceived primarily as a study of the initial events leading toward such climax communities. The first populants to appear on a new surface are designated pioneer colonizers and, if through ecesis they form an enduring community, they are accepted as having formed, thus on the new surface, pioneer communities.

Most studies of the pioneer population process on lava have been concerned with the rate in reference to the type of surface, ash, a'a or pahoehoe (*e.g.*, Forbes, 1912; Wentworth, 1938; Eggler, 1941, 1963; Tagawa, 1963; Skottsberg, 1930, 1941; Robyns & Lamb, 1939), the collection of dust or debris (Forbes, 1912; Eggler, 1941), moisture (Robyns & Lamb, 1939; Eggler, 1963), the availability of disseminules (Griggs, 1933; Rigg, 1914; Eggler, 1963; Tagawa, 1966), or nitrogen (Griggs, 1933; Tezuka, 1961; Eggler, 1963). It is well known (*e.g.*, Tagawa, 1965) that as seral progression takes place a species first increases and then decreases in abundance. Also the idea is widely held (*e.g.*, Whitford, 1949; Tagawa, 1965) that order, non-random distribution, contagiousness or overdispersion,

[1]Financial support for this work has come largely from NSF grant G-1992 and AEC contract AT(04-3)-235.

Reprinted from the *Bulletin of the Southern California Academy of Sciences* 66(3):175–194 (1967), by permission of the author and the publisher.

tends to appear out of the at first random distribution of the elements in a population.

Factors in population development on new lava surfaces that have not been studied much are age of the lava; its inherent physical or chemical nature, heat and stability. Actually the above authors and biological studies of others on lava surfaces have been almost entirely concerned with events on land related timewise to scores of years.

There are few studies of the above-mentioned phenomena beginning with the still hot lava flows and covering their first few years. Such studies are especially rare for marine sites. While Martin (1913) and Rigg (1914) did consider the marine environment, they described only the destruction of vegetations by the volcanic events. The late Dr. E. Yale Dawson was one of the first to compare the marine vegetations appearing on new lava with the mature vegetations and, also, with the vegetations on old lava denuded by the volcanic events. This he did some nine months after the eruption at San Benedicto Island in the Revillagigedo Islands at 20 deg. North Latitude, off the west coast of Mexico.

The results of four sets of observations or experiments are considered here. They were begun on the 1955 Hawaiian lava flows as they cooled. Two sets are from the intertidal region and are paired, respectively, with two similar situations from the terrestrial habitat. One of these two contrasting sets of phenomena concerns the results of population experiments in reference to the age and chemical nature of the substratum. The second concerns the population process principally in reference to the cooling of the lava flows and, especially in the intertidal region, the stabilization of their surfaces.

The historic lavas of Hawaii are (Macdonald, 1949) olivinaceous basalts and are generally black in contrast to many of the older prehistoric lavas, which are brown. Lava reaches the place where it solidifies and cools under different conditions of pressure, temperature and movement such that locally several lava types may be formed which are superficially quite different from one another. This was true of the 1955 lava that was poured out onto the surface. However, it has been recognized (Macdonald & Katsura, 1961) that the 1955 lava types are all very much alike from the chemist's point of view. Macdonald (1959:55) analyzed three samples of the 1955 lavas where they had entered the sea and decided there was no evidence, contrary to some beliefs, that lava was altered in its chemical nature by having been cooled in sea water.

PIONEER POPULATION IN RESPECT TO
CHEMICALLY DIFFERING SUBSTRATA

Experimentally the common different types of 1955 lava, including those described in Table I and those of different age and nature mentioned above, were exposed to seeding in uniform habitats. The experiments were carried out on land and in the intertidal region or subtidally within a meter of the lowest level to which the tides recede. For experimental exposures on land, the different types of lava were placed on a concrete walkway in a glass house mist room and seeded densely but randomly with a mixtures of disseminules of the organisms reported upon below. For the experimental exposures in the sea, similar chunks of the different lava types were set in concrete poured in wooden boxes, the corners of which were reinforced with iron. This preparation was placed on the reef at Waikiki in Honolulu where the water was about a half meter deep at low tide. Several somewhat similar experimental embeddings were made in concrete poured *in situ* on intertidal lava shores of both historic and prehistoric ages.

At various intervals the experimentally exposed rocks for both the marine and terrestrial studies were observed and the populations on them noted. Throughout, observation indicated the variations in light, temperature and air or sea-water were random and slight within different portions of any one experimental area or set of experimental lava chunks. These environmental variations were not correlated with the population events. The experiments were not carried on long enough to permit observing the results beyond the pioneer population stages.

The marine situation can be dismissed quickly. Throughout, in all cases, very much the same populations developed on all surfaces exposed in a given environment, even including the concrete, wood and iron used to facilitate the experimental exposure of the different lava types.

In regard to the terrestrial situation a much more complex result was obtained. Native lore in Hawaii includes "everybody knows that red volcanic cinders are better for such crops as orchids than black." Evidence for this of an experimental nature is slight. In reference to rate of population some lava types are thought to become more quickly populated. However, the environment is so often different in the natural situations that reliable conclusions cannot be drawn from field observations alone. With these things in mind, the mist-room experiment mentioned above was carried out.

To initiate this experiment, a non-sterile mixture of powdered leaflets, sporangia and spores of *Nephrolepis exaltata* (a fern) was scattered over the arranged rocks in the spray room. Growth was allowed to go on with at least weekly observation. Obviously a random assortment of the almost ubiquitous *Scytonema hofmannii* (a blue-green alga), *Campylopus exasperatus* (a moss) along with *Phyllanthus niruri* and *Euphorbia hirta* and *E. glomerifera* (both genera of flowering plants) was eventually seeded onto the rocks if not actually planted at the same time inadvertently. All of these organisms are common on lava substrata in the 1955 lava flow area.

In this experiment, the three rock types used can be taken to represent (but remotely, indeed) "soils" formed as lava flows decay and change with respect to the oxidation state of the iron in them and the solubility or leachability of their minerals increases. One might say this was a series leading from a freshly exposed lithosol toward a more mature lateritic soil, *i.e.*, a series leading from the black dense crystalline rocks (BC) to the black low-density glassy rock (BG) and on to the red low-density glassy rocks (RG).

TABLE I

Measurements of pioneer communities on lava types

The different olivinaceous basalt rock types used from the 1955 lava flows were: "BC," black crystalline dense; "BG," black glassy light weight; and "RG," red glassy light weight. *Scytonema hofmannii* was most of the algae; *Nephrolepis exaltata* most of the fern; and *Phyllanthus amarus*, *Euphorbia hirta* and *E. glomerifera* most of the flowering plants listed as "all others."

Rock type	Density, approx.	Milligrams per square centimeter of upper horizontal surface				Organism or total for all
		Dry wt.	Chl. —a	Total chl.	Total pigs.	
BC	2.9	—	.79	3.02	3.06	Algae
			.01	.01	.02	Fern
			—	—	—	All others
		.02	.80	3.04	3.09	Total
BG	1.2	—	.58	2.17	2.26	Algae
			.18	.22	.26	Fern
			.11	.09	.12	All others
		.17	.87	2.19	2.34	Total
RG	1.3	—	.47	1.31	1.37	Algae
			.12	.34	.34	Fern
			.11	.17	.19	All others
		.96	.71	1.81	1.90	Total

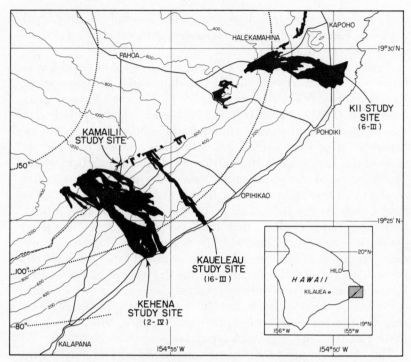

Figure 1. Map of the 1955 lava flows from the east flank of the volcano, Kilauea, on the Island of Hawaii, *i.e.*, the shaded area on the inset. The principal study sites are indicated as are the dates in 1955 when the flow stopped moving at its seaward end. Isohyets show as dotted lines with the rainfall in inches. Topographic contours are shown as thin solid lines with the elevations in feet.

The results after ten months of growth are summarized in Table I, related to the "area" of rock used. The area was determined from the vertically cast shadow of the particular rock concerned. The lava is extremely porous and irregularly so; this makes the measurement of surface area very difficult and makes the removal of the microscopic pioneer organisms next to impossible on any quantitative basis. For this latter reason, pigment content of the rocks and their populations was determined by a modification of the Creitz & Richards (1955) technique and used as a measure of the populations obtaining.

In gross aspect (Fig. 2) the populations on the different rock types were strikingly different at the close of the experiment. Flowering plants dominated the red rocks with but a few ferns and very little apparent algal material. Ferns dominated the black glassy rocks with but very few flowering plants and only a little algal material. The black crystalline rocks were dominated by algal coatings with very little else present.

Among the quantitative results measured (Table I) and qualitative observations, five conspicuous relationships to the series of rock types, BC, BG to RG, are evident. 1) The most obvious gross aspect was (Fig. 2) the shift from a blue-green algal population, to a fern population, and to the situation where flowering plants were dominant. This is in correlation with what one can observe less well on the same sort of rocks in the field, and which field observation led us to this experiment done under uniform glass-house conditions. These results are also in line with the observation of the seral events in the field: *i.e.*, 2) the organisms that first form a community are the algae, then the ferns and lastly the flowering plants. It is also, 3), in line with the degree of development of primary producers to be expected on a series of soil types leading from lithosols to lateritic soil. Finally, 4) the dry weight increases and, 5) the pigment total quantities decrease through the series (while there were several rocks in each other category only one BG rock survived the viscisitudes of experimental science; thus confidence in the values given for this rock type is low).

The closed nature of the algal community and gradually less closed natures of the fern and flowering plant populations may explain the gradual reduction in plant pigments through the series. In time, as a closed cover would be more nearly achieved in nature, the pigment standing crops of the fern and flowering plant communities might have come to exceed that of the algae. Otherwise, one must give consideration to the idea that the ferns, and in turn the flowering plants, are more efficient in the conversion of photosynthate to accumulated material (dry weight) or are more efficient in their use of the chlorophyll molecule than are the algae. Perhaps there is some truth in all of these possibilities.

Pioneer Population in Respect to Physically Differing Substrata

In the field the time course of pioneer community establishment was followed on the 1955 lava flows themselves. In respect to their initial stages, while not realized at the time, it became likely that slow cooling of the rock on land and the change toward a stable surface in the sea were the most conspicuous physical influences. In the discussion that follows, the related events leading to the pioneer marine communities are discussed first and then the events leading to the pioneer terrestrial communities.

Marine Pioneer Communities

Community establishment was studied only insofar as macroscopic algae were concerned by following events on the 1955 intertidal lava flow surfaces (Fig. 1) for ten years. While there is almost explosive boiling of sea water as the hot lava reaches the sea, the surface is soon cool and within a month densely populated with algae. The algal populations on nearby prehistoric flows, kept under observation as control surfaces, underwent a seasonal progressive set of changes, but otherwise, except for catastrophic events, the events were not the same as those on the 1955 surfaces. Since this work is published elsewhere (Doty, in press) in some detail only sufficient detail is given below to provide a basis for the discussion to follow.

As commonly reported elsewhere (*e.g.*, Northcraft, 1948; Fahey & Doty, 1949; Fahey, 1953; Dawson, 1954), on the 1955 flows the most conspicuous and first element to appear as a macroscopic pioneer populant is *Enteromorpha* followed by other genera such as *Ectocarpus, Cladophora* and *Polysiphonia*. These same genera are the first populants on all surfaces newly exposed to the sea, *e.g.*, on boat hulls of various compositions, on prehistoric lava and on historic lavas as well. Dawson (1954) made a particular note of this in respect to the populations on old lava nine months after the previous populations had been removed by pumice scouring. Also the same organisms are the pioneers despite the time of year the above chemically and physically different surfaces are exposed either as a result of catastrophic events or as pioneer exposure events. These latter are not much different in this case but the terms are used here to distinguish between the case where an advanced population is destroyed by catastrophic events and the pioneer organisms reappear, and the case where the substratum is newly brought into the sea, the pioneer exposure events. This latter occurs whether rocks from the shore are placed in the sea for the first time, or whether lava flows into the sea.

The pioneer colonizers first appear over a wider range than that in which they mature. The immature thalli form dense coatings on the rocks with the individual thalli almost adjacent like the hair in a fur. As time goes on, and as these thalli mature, they become reduced in their vertical range and sharply restricted in their up-

Figure 2. Selective vegetation of 3 different lava types illustrated by a photograph of the populations that developed on them in a spray room following
random seeding. A black crystalline rock such as that in the right hand may
remain nearly barren or become covered with algal growths; one that is black
but glassy, as in the case of the other hand-held example, can be expected to
become dominated by ferns; and red glassy lava, such as that on the ground
directly below the right hand, can be expected to become dominated by flowering
plants.

ward and downward limits, disappear from some parts of their
ultimate range and, as mature thalli, release reproductive structures where they still persist as tufts separated a few centimeters
from each other. The pioneers are replaced in time by slower-
growing and later-appearing algae.

Zonation on these lava flows arises in time as a result of the seral
processes such as described above. In the intertidal region zonation
is seen as different bands one above the other, each with narrow
vertical and relatively wide horizontal limits and each dominated
by different organisms. As a rule several such bands or zones can
be seen at low tide on a vertical shore. Doty (in press) describes this
process as it occurs on the 1955 lava flows and it need suffice here

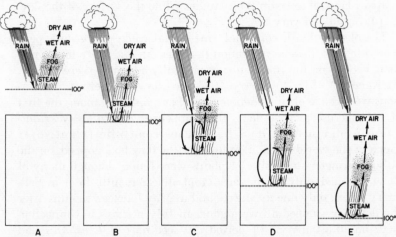

Figure 3. The putative relationship between rain and the cooling of a molten lava flow. During the phase labeled "C" the constantly moist warm surface becomes relatively densely populated with a polyglot vegetation that cannot exist earlier ("A") on the hotter rock or later ("E") on the intermittently very dry rock. This flush of vegetation is characteristic of lava flows and is followed by the changes that lead to a soil and vegetation normal to the climate of the region. During the stages represented by "D," the transition from "C" to "E," the pioneer communities become established and, depending upon the physical nature of the substratum, may display considerable vertical zonation by the time the stage represented by "E" is reached.

to say that as the sere moves along, the communities and zones become more discrete and more stable in their content and place on the shore.

Terrestrial Pioneer Communities

Events on lava flows leading to establishment of the pioneer community on land are very different timewise from the marine area events and, of course, different in respect to the organisms concerned. When the lava first stops flowing (Fig. 3A) and for perhaps a week afterwards, the surface is over 100 deg. C. Rain falling is instantly converted to steam. Any spores or seeds falling on the surface would be killed by the high temperature and nothing grows. When rain falls, such an area is immediately cloaked in a fog bank. When there is no rain, the air is clear immediately and there is no lingering of steaming or fog. While the general idea of moisture availability has been considered by many, the role of the heat in the flow itself has not, it seems. Perhaps this is because so few ecologists have had the opportunities so often readily available in recent years in Hawaii to begin their studies while the surface of the flow is still liquid and very hot.

The observation is commonly made that when plants do appear there is a first flush of vegetation that dies out and it is a long time, then, before communities and a consistently advancing sere appear. At Kamaili* (Fig. 1) on the 1955 lava flows numerous observations were made of this phenomenon. For example, among the first of the macroscopic populants there appeared *Erechtites valerianifolia*, an almost ubiquitous herbaceous composite (plant) over much of the world. Nine months after the flow had stopped, on the 10 square meter study site, 21 plants were found. Though many of these bloomed, only three were found alive 2 months later in February, 1956; only one in March, and in May fourteen months after the flow had stopped all were gone. In July perhaps in connection with an unusually moist period, 10 seedlings of *Erechtites* had appeared, but these were all gone by November and none appeared again during the study. This phenomenon was observed elsewhere on the flows from this eruption and in the case of other plants as well, *e.g.*, in the case of *Nephrolepis exaltata* and *Metrosideros polymorpha*, respectively, the most common fern and tree in the area.

The casual observation that, after sitting on the sun-hot dry rocks at Kamaili, one would find cameras, notebooks and pants wet on the underside led the author to consider this water problem further. This phenomenon two and a half years after the flow had stopped was apparently caused by hot air saturated with water coming out of the flow, but on such a hot clear sunny day no fog was formed as the air cooled and was wafted away diluted by the passing breeze. While formerly fog was an almost constant feature of this site, and for two years appeared with each rain shower, its appearance during the last part of this period was associated with only a few nearby spots and eventually even then only with heavy rain. By 1960, for some few years no steaming had been observed under any conditions. The duration and the nature of these events and phenomena, summarized in Figure 3, are widely variable. Variations in time as well as in the return of water to the air and the surface phenomena described depend on the rainfall in the district and the physical properties of the lava surface itself. From all ob-

*MacDonald (1959) gives a detailed pictorial account of the origin of the flow as a crack among the cucumber plants in a garden and development of this site in his Plates 10 through 15. Doty and Mueller-Dombois (1966) include more of the biological details related to the ideas derived from the study of this site.

servations combined, including some made on the 1965 lava flow that covered the floor of Napau Crater in Hawaii Volcanoes National Park, I am led to the following explanation of this commonly observed initial-flush phenomena as observed in Hawaii.

About two weeks after the flow had stopped moving (Fig. 3B) the 100 deg. C temperature level is not on the surface but a few centimeters below the surface. Fog is produced immediately with each rain shower and it persists for successively longer periods for a given amount of rainfall as more heat is transferred, thus, out of the flow surface and the 100 deg. C level falls more and more deeply within the flow. The steam must repeatedly sterilize the surface; though during dry spells the surface temperature may fall to biologically tolerable levels. Spilling water on the surface at this stage produces a surprising explosion of steam which may turn into a small fog cloud if the humidity is high enough or, if the humidity or water volume is low, there may be only a violent hiss as the water is converted to steam which in turn dissolves in the air without forming fog. Peck *et al.* (1964) describes the temporary lowering of the temperature near the surface by rainfall and cooling water pumped into drill holes and, also, the rates at which temperatures have been measured to fall in the 1963 eruptive lava nearby from the same volcano, Kilauea. Also, the scale- or sand-like products of exfoliation that can be seen on the surfaces by this time may at least in part be enhanced by this reaction with water.

Likewise the time lapsing before the next, the first biotic, stages (Fig. 3C) may vary but often the first biotic stages appear within 3 months. At this time the 100 deg. C level is sufficiently far down in the rock that only fog or water-saturated hot air returns to the surface following a rain. Rain falling on the flow percolates to the level where it is converted to steam and rises. However, most of it condenses and percolates again to the hot region below. This recycling process, from which in this stage some water vapor gets into the air as fog, keeps the moisture and temperature conditions on the surface between biologically tolerable limits and identifiable populants appear. As related elsewhere, the first are most commonly blue-green algae which are, like *Scytonema hofmannii* the most common among them, tolerant of wide ranges of temperature and moisture.

Previous stages (represented by Figs. 3A and 3B) are characterized by the lava surfaces being barren and dry and by fog production ceasing almost as soon as a rain ceases. The stage represented

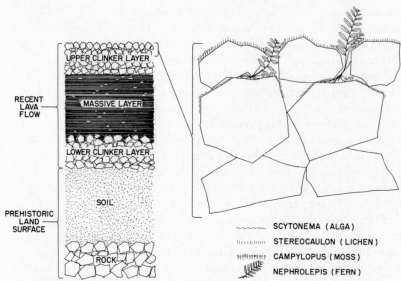

UPPER CLINKER LAYER

MASSIVE LAYER

RECENT
LAVA
FLOW

LOWER CLINKER LAYER

SOIL

PREHISTORIC
LAND
SURFACE

ROCK

~~~~~   SCYTONEMA (ALGA)

||||||||| STEREOCAULON (LICHEN)

CAMPYLOPUS (MOSS)

NEPHROLEPIS (FERN)

Figure 4. A section through a recent a'a lava flow, on the left, overlaying a prehistoric well developed soil. The upper clinker layer is that which would eventually give rise to a new soil layer with a climax vegetation on it. At the right is illustrated the arrangement of the pioneer communities to be expected on the lava flows at the lower elevations in Hawaii.

by Figure 3C is characterized by the appearance of blue-green algae, by the surface remaining moist longer after a shower and by the slower appearance and longer persistence of steaming or fog production after a shower has passed.

As the stage represented by Figure 3C wears on, mosses appear and, in the shade, liverworts and ferns. Primary leaves of *Nephrolepis exaltata* and unidentifiable dicotyledons were found at the Halekamahina site at about 200 feet elevation on August 15, 1955, five months after the eruption but they did not mature. Colonies of flowering plants come to thrive rooting in cracks and the crevices between folds of lava. They are a wide variety in Hawaii varying in time of appearance, in just what species appear and in just what population densities obtain. Their success may be promoted by the earlier-mentioned exfoliated fine material accumulated by gravitation or as Eggler suggested (1941) by wind. *Scytonema hofmannii* is always preeminent among the algae. It has been observed to be infested with fungi at this time. *Campylopus* species (Miller, 1960) are preeminent among the mosses and *Nephrolepis exaltata* is the fern with but rare exceptions. *Spathoglottis plicata* (an orchid), the *Erechtites* and the *Metrosideros*, both mentioned above, are pre-eminent among the plants.

As the next stage (Fig. 3D) draws on, the abundance of vegetational elements wanes. Fog production in this stage (Fig. 3D) is much less and in time comes to appear only after the heaviest of showers or more prolonged rains. Yet on a flow at this stage one learns, as reported above, that a great deal of water may be being brought to the surface where the bottoms of everything sitting on the flow quickly become wet. The water is leaving as hot high-humidity air that may form wisps of fog in mid air as it cools. Except where moist algal or moss patches remained, the surface of the rock became hot in the sun with 150-odd degree Fahrenheit temperatures being measured. However since some flowering plants persisted, such as those listed below, it would seem the redistillation process was keeping the root zone moist. New disseminules falling during this period would undoubtedly die during the dry hot periods.

Four biological phenomena were apparent at Kamaili in this stage represented by Figure 3D. First, minute white flecks of what later proved to be the podetia of the lichen *Stereocaulon vulcani* heralded the arrival of this stage two years after the flow had stopped. The case history of *Erechtites* represents a second phenomenon: after its initial flush this annual plant disappeared completely from the study area. Though the plants produced seed, it is presumed that the seedlings could not persist long enough on the now-dry hot surface, after germinating during a rainy period, for their roots to penetrate to moist depths. A third phenomenon pertained to the longer-lived plants such as *Metrosideros*. Actually as *Erechtites* disappeared these first woody-based perennials, seedlings of the tree *Metrosideros*, were seen. The original plants often died back to their crowns and presumably sent up new shoots during the next more prolonged rainy period.

The fourth phenomenon in the stage represented by Figure 3D was one of succession in the cryptogamic communities. While the first appearing *Scytonema hofmannii* was cleanly and clearly typically this species, fifteen months later some patches had conspicuous fungus infections in their sheaths. While the first community to become established was algal and of *Scytonema hofmannii*, blackened areas of *Stigonema* eventually became conspicuous. Sometimes low dense coatings of *Stigonema* are formed on the sunny upper surfaces of the pahoehoe among the podetia of the *Stereocaulon vulcani* and are formed so extensively that for areas a decimeter or so in extent, 30 to 50 per cent of the rock surface is black. This, it would seem, would be a replacement of the primary blue-green pioneer colonizer, *Scytonema*, by the secondary and morphologically more complex colonizers, *Stigonema*, and this in turn by *Stereocaulon*.

The phenomenon of succession would seem to have been expressed also in the moss genus *Campylopus* alone, at least by a succession of forms. The first to appear was dark green dense tufts in the crevices between folds of lava nine months after the flow had stopped. It was identified by Dr. H. A. Miller as *C. boswelli*. This was not found again but in the same environment 2 months later the moss was *C. densifolius*. At sixteen months *C. exasperatus*, ubiquitous on lava in this region, was becoming widespread and *C. densifolius* was not refound.

Nephrolepis exaltata went through a period of maximum conspicuousness and declined to a much less conspicuous state during the first 3 years of the stages related to Figures 3A through 3D. It appeared that during the dry stage "D" few or no new thalli developed.

It would appear that during the final stage studied at Kamaili and represented hypothetically by Figure 3E, the water arriving as rain is soon lost to the plants. The hot zone, if present at all, is so far down in the rocks that plants with small root systems would be in dry rock most of the time. The flows in the study areas in this stage no longer steam after a rain, and presumably the water is lost largely by percolation. The surface is very variable and extreme in reference to heat and water.

Seral development (Fig. 3E) is largely maturation of the cryptogamic communities, especially in respect to vertical zonation. This is partially illustrated in Figure 4 which shows, among other things, the typical pioneer communities of cryptogams established at Kii (Fig. 1) on a clinker-covered flow. Here a long-persisting fern may be found to have arisen from a prothallus that grew near a protuberance from the under surface of a large lava chunk or from a pendant lava finger extending stalactite-like from the lower surface of a broken-open lava blister roof, on pahoehoe, or underside of an unusually large clinker. Rain falling on the lava percolates through slowly and may drip* for a long time from such lower

---

*Such drippings collected in leaves and shells were a major source of drinking water for the Polynesians in this district.

surfaces making them ideal places for fern prothallus development.

As Figure 4 shows, when zonation develops *Stereocaulon vulcani* covers the upward protruding rock surfaces with *Stigonema* between the podetia. *Campylopus exasperatus* tends to fill in between when the surface is a little lower, perhaps where wind velocities are lower but there is hardly less light. *Scytonema hofmannii* persists as the dominant deeper in the flow but where lighted from the surface. The occasional fern or *Metrosideros* completes the complement of organisms persisting generally on the 1955 lava flow areas and other plants are rare at this stage.

Change on the flows since 1959 has been slow, hardly any population or visible change at all has appeared in the lowest and driest areas though a dense vegetational cover of mosses had developed by 1960 at Kamaili, the wettest (120 inch rainfall) study site. The pioneer communities can be seen to have developed vertical zonation at this stage and to have become stable.

DISCUSSION

Conditions are extremely variable at the different sites where observation for this study was done. For example, in the above no distinction has been drawn between pahoehoe and a'a flows and (Fig. 1) a two-fold variation in rainfall is to be expected. The temperature varies much more uniformly at these sites. Most of the study, which the in-places-putative Figure 3 summarizes, was made on a pahoehoe flow at the 950 foot Kamaili study site. Much of that upon which Figure 4 was based was from repeated observation at this site but even more of it was derived from study of a much drier site at about the 50 foot elevation in the Kii area on a clinker-covered a'a flow. Our purposes here have been merely to describe the early changes in reference to the interrelationships between water, residual heat in the lava and the biotic events as useful in pointing out the striking difference between the early events of succession on the land and in the sea.

In the marine environment it would appear that the pioneer algal communities appear with little difference correlatable with the chemical nature of the substratum as long as, in this case, the substratum is stable. This is in general agreement with the relative success of different antifouling paints composed to flake off as attached organisms grow. By contrast, in the terrestrial environment, different types of botanical organisms develop on the different types of lava. The experimental phenomena on terrestrial materials (Table I) seem related both to the phylogenetic complexity of the organisms and to the degree that the rock is of soil-like nature.

On land it is commonly reported that a lava flow supports one or a few relatively lush growths of flowering plants and then, with succeeding crops declining greatly, may become relatively barren. As seen in Hawaii an explanation of this phenomenon seems to be present in the transferring of heat out of the lava by steam. Some explanation for the first community being blue-green algae is provided in this hypothesis while not excluding the older idea that the blue-greens are nitrogen fixers and thus are the pioneers rather than the non-nitrogen fixing plants. That is, they are more tolerant of the heat and dryness extremes that characterize an otherwise barren yet-hot lava flow, than are the plants. No such heat phenomenon is present in the marine environment and the pioneer communities lead on more directly to the secondary communities. At least the intertidal lava faces are cooled so quickly the effect, if there is one, is outside the operational limits of such pioneer-population studies as this.

It seems that the pioneer communities on land (from the stage represented by Figure 3E and beyond it) ameliorate and stabilize conditions by holding water at the surface where it leads to evaporational cooling, and by producing shade. Thus they lead to the next stage, that of an herbaceous ground cover and an admixture of trees such as found on the oldest prehistoric flows, in correlation with the prolongation or stabilization of moisture and lowering the high temperature extremes.

There is further evidence such conditions are brought about by the successively more impressive development of the above-mentioned communities of cryptogams and *Metrosideros* in Hawaii. In Hawaii much of the surface of the 1750 Kaimu lava flow just above Kaimu Bay is still in this cryptogam-*Metrosideros* stage. On such land it must take at least 500 to 1000 years for a practical climax population to appear on a new lava flow. This time varies greatly especially in regard to moisture. Tagawa (1964) suggests 700 years is required. In contrast, if the surface is stable in the intertidal region, it may take little more than five or ten years; though change seems to be noticeable for much longer. This latter has not been determined with any degree of precision and was not an element in the present study.

On land there is evidence that over the many years it takes a climax population to develop, as Forbes (1912) and Skottsberg (1941) suggested, there is a succession of blue-green algae, lichens, mosses, ferns and flowering plants. This is also a succession of phylogenetically more advanced botanical organisms. There is evidence from the experimental work that the series is related to the freeing of ions to move in the substratum, *i.e.*, they would hardly be free to move in the crystalline basalt and much more free to move in the vitreous material or in a mature soil. Intertidally, succession is of different algae in several phyla. The successive kinds to appear are different in growth form (*e.g.*, crusts succeed other attached forms) or rate of growth and maturity (*e.g.*, rapidly developing forms appear first). There is no evidence that the intertidal igneous substrata change in time and the populations then change accordingly.

In both types of habitat the pioneer colonizers appear over a wider range than that in which they persist if they come to form a community. As the pioneer communities become established, in both cases vertical zonation occurs in reference, perhaps, to exposure to air and water, and in both cases the populations become more stable as this zonation becomes more pronounced. In the case of the marine populations perhaps this zonation is caused (Doty, 1946) by tidal control of the exposure to sea and air. In the terrestrial environment, other factors such as tolerance of the different moisture and light conditions are causative, the heat factor having been ameliorated.

These observations and conclusions support the thesis that pioneer organisms arrive by chance and colonize unless something kills or removes them. They tend to be killed or removed outside of the range in which they become pioneer communities, vertically zoned, both on land and in the intertidal region. This idea of development of vegetations from negatively contagious (random) to contagious has been commonly accepted in reference to horizontal distribution. With the above recognition of vertical zonation (storeying) phenomena in these pioneer communities we can extend this concept to this new dimension.

SUMMARY

Field observation and experimentation over a ten-year period in reference to the 1955 lava flows in Hawaii has facilitated comparative and descriptive studies of the pioneer population phenomena.

Achievement of stability of surfaces in the sea is a major factor in community development beyond the subclimax stages whereas actual chemical nature of the substratum is less important. On land the chemical and physical nature of a lava flow is important as is water availability. Rain water seems to play a major role in removing heat from the surface of a hot lava flow, and in this process a warm moist root bed is provided for a time, perhaps accounting for the early flush of vegetation often reported to appear and disappear on lava flows. The well known change from random distribution to non-random distribution during seral development is extended by the present observations to include vertical zonation in the pioneer communities.

Literature Cited

CREITZ, G .I., and F. A. RICHARDS
1955. The estimation and characterization of plankton populations by pigment analysis. III. A note on the use of millipore membrane filters in the estimation of plankton pigments. J. Mar. Res. 14: 211-216.

DAWSON, E. YALE
1954. The marine flora of Isla San Benedicto following the volcanic eruption of 1952-1953. Allan Hancock Foundation Publ. Occas. Paper 16: 1-25.

DOTY, M. S.
1946. Critical tide factors that are correlated with the vertical distribution of marine algae and other organisms along the Pacific Coast. Ecology 27: 315-328.

(In press.) Pioneer intertidal population and the related general vertical distribution of marine algae in Hawaii.

DOTY, M. S., and D. MUELLER-DOMBOIS
1966. Atlas for bioecology studies in Hawaii Volcanoes National Park. University of Hawaii, Hawaii Bot. Sci. Paper No. 2. 510 pp.

EGGLER, W. A.
1941. Primary succession of volcanic deposits in southern Idaho. Ecol. Monographs 3: 277-298.

1963. Plant life of Paricutin Volcano, Mexico, eight years after activity ceased. Amer. Midl. Nat. 69: 39-68.

FAHEY, E. M.
1953. The repopulation of intertidal transects. Rhodora 55: 102-108.

FAHEY, E. M., and M. S. DOTY
1949. Pioneer colonization on intertidal transects. Biol. Bull. 97: 238-239.

FORBES, C. N.
1912. Preliminary observations concerning the plant invasion on some of the lava flows of Mauna Loa, Hawaii. Bernice P. Bishop Mus., Occas. Paper 5:15-23.

GRIGGS, R. F.
1933. The colonization of the Katmai ash, a new and inorganic "soil." Am. J. Bot. 20: 92-113.

MacDONALD, G. A.
1949. Petrography of the island of Hawaii. U.S. Geol. Survey, Prof. Paper 214-D.
1959. The activity of Hawaiian volcanoes during the years 1951-1956. Bull. Volcanologique Ser. II, Vol. 22: 1-70.

MacDONALD, G. H., and T. KATSURA
1961. Variation in the lava of 1959 eruptions in Kilauea Iki. Pacific Sci. 15: 358-369.

MARTIN, G. C.
1913. The recent eruption of Katmai Volcano in Alaska. National Geographic Magazine 24: 131-181.

MILLER, H. A.
1960. Remarks on the succession of bryophytes on Hawaiian lava flows. Pacific Sci. 14: 246-247.

NORTHCRAFT, R. D.
1948. Marine algal colonization of the Monterey Peninsula, California. Amer. J. Bot. 35: 396-404.

PECK, DALLAS L., JAMES G. MOORE and GEORGE KOJIMA
1964. Temperatures in the crust and melt of Alae lava lake, Hawaii, after the August 1963 eruption of Kilauea Volcano — a preliminary report. U. S. Geol. Survey Prof. Paper 501-D, pp. D1-D7.

RIGGS, B. G.
1914. The effect of the Katmai eruption on marine vegetation. Science n s. 40: 509-513.

ROBYNS, W., and S. H. LAMB
1939. Preliminary ecological survey of the island of Hawaii. Bull. Jard. Bot. Brux. 15: 241-293.

SKOTTSBERG, C.
1930. The flora of the high Hawaiian volcanoes. Fifth Int. Bot. Congress, Cambridge: 16-23.
1941. Plant succession on recent lava flows in the island of Hawaii. Gotteborgs Kungl. Vetenskap-och Vitterhetssamhalles Handlinger Sjatte fojden, ser. B., Bd. 1, no. 8. 32 pp.

TAGAWA, H.
1963. Investigation of pattern in plant communities. I. Pattern in *Carex kobomugi* Ohwi population. Jap. J. Ecol. 13: 10-15.
1964. A study of the volcanic vegetation in Sakurajima, Southwest Japan. I. Dynamics of vegetation. Mem. Fac. Sci., Kyushu Univ., Ser. E (Biology) 3: 165-228.
1965. A study of the volcanic vegetation in Sakurajima, Southwest Japan. II. Distributional pattern and succession. Japanese J. of Bot. 19: 127-148.
1966. A study of the volcanic vegetation in Sakurajima, Southwest Japan. III. Trap sampling of disseminules on the lava flow and the culture experiment of some pioneer mosses. Sci. Repts., Kagoshima Univ. No. 15: 63-83.

TEZUKA, Y.
1961. Development of vegetation in relation to soil formation in the volcanic
island of Oshima, Izu, Japan. Japanese J. Bot. 17: 371-496.

WENTWORTH, C. K.
1938. Ash formations on the island of Hawaii. 3rd Spec. Rpt. Hawaii. Volcano
Observatory viii + 183 pp., Honolulu.

WHITFORD, P. B.
1949. Distribution of woodland plants in relation to succession and clonal
growth. Ecology 30: 199-208.

BIOGEOCLIMATIC ZONES ON THE

HAWAIIAN ISLANDS[1]

Vladimir J. Krajina[2]

The vegetational aspects of the Hawaiian Islands are
rather unique by their vastly endemic flora. However,
many introduced plants, which are becoming widely distributed now, constitute such biotic elements that the
vegetational units are quite comparable with those of
other tropical areas. Furthermore, in the Hawaiian
Islands the environmental parts of their ecosystem units
are such that they are repeatedly occurring in many
other tropical mountainous regions with similar tropical, subtropical mesothermal, microthermal, and even
alpine (polar) climates. These environmental complexes,
by their climatic, edaphic, geologic, and topographic
factors, constitute great educational assets that
should be available to those who would like to study
them as a scientific basis especially for multiple land
use. They need to compare them with those of other
similar regions. In this respect, the Hawaiian Islands
possess much greater variation of climates and their
respective biogeoclimatic zones than any other lands of
the United States.

---

[1]Paper presented at the 14th Annual Meetings of
the American Institute of Biological Sciences (AIBS)
for the Ecological Society of America at the University
of Massachusetts on August 27, 1963. A preliminary form
of this paper was presented at the Hawaiian Botanical
Society meeting on June 4, 1962. Manuscript received
Sept. 3, 1963. Hawaiian plant common names were
checked with Pukui, M. K., and S. H. Elbert, Hawaiian-
English Dictionary (1957).

[2]Professor of biology and botany, The University
of British Columbia, Vancouver 8, B.C., Canada, and
Honorary Associate in Botany, B. P. Bishop Museum.

From the *Hawaiian Botanical Society Newsletter* 2(7):93–98 (1963), by permission of the author.

Table 1. Biogeoclimatic Zones on the Hawaiian Islands

Zonal Group	No.	Zone Letters	Zone Name	Altitude in feet	Main Exposure	Annual precipitation in ins.	Clouds	Mean annual temperature $^{\circ}$F
Semiarid and subsemiarid tropical	(1)	A	kiawe - pili - bristly foxtail	Less than 1000 on lee sides, or very low windward lands	SW	Less than 25	Very rare	75-76 (maximum over 90)
	(2)	B	koa haole - panini - kakonakona	Less than 3000 on lee sides, less than 1000 on windward sides	SW	25 - 40	Rare	72-75
Subhumid tropical and subtropical (low elevations)	(3)	C_1	guava - lantana - pukeawe - palaa - yellow foxtail	Less than 3000 on lee sides, on windward sides less than 2000	None	40 - 60 *)	Occasional	71-75
	(4)	C_2	koa - guava - pukeawe - ohelo	2500-4000	SW	40 - 60 *)	Frequent	60-68
Humid tropical and subtropical (mesothermal)	(5)	$D-K_1$	koa - Boston fern - basket grass - Hilo grass	Less than 3000 on lee sides, less than 2000 on windward sides	None	60 - 75 *)	Very frequent	70-74
	(6)	$D-O_1$	ohia lehua - hapuu - uluhe - wawaeiole	Less than 4000 on windward sides	NE	75-100 *)	Common	60-73
	(7)	$D-C_a$	olapa - lapalapa - hapuu - ekaha - ohiaku	Less than 6000 on windward sides	NE	100-140 *)	Dense	60-70
	(8)	$D-C_b$	lapalapa - oha wai - hapuu - ape	Less than 6000 on windward sides	NE	140-200 *)	Rainy	60-65
	(9)	$D-C_c$	Oreobolus - Panicum - Plantago - Lobelia	2000-5800 feet	NE	200-466	Extremely rainy	60
	(10)	$D-O_2$	ohia lehua - amaumau - Boston fern - uluhe	6000-6500 (Maui, Hawaii)	NE	75-100 Snow extremely rare (in winter)	Common	50-55
	(11)	$D-K_2$	koa - Boston fern - uluhe - brackenfern	6500-8000 (Maui, Hawaii)	NE	60-75 Snow very rare (in winter)	Frequent	50
Subhumid mesothermal (high elevations)	(12)	E - K	koa - mamani - pukeawe - ohelo - brackenfern - lovegrass	4000-8000 (Maui, Hawaii)	None	40-60 Snow very rare (in winter)	Occasional	50
Subsemi-arid micro-thermal (subalpine)	(13)	E - M	mamani - naio - pukeawe - pilo - ohelo - kukainene	7000-10,000 (Maui, Hawaii)	None	20-40 Snow occasionally (in winter)	Rare	40
Alpine	(14)	E - L	lichen - moss - bentgrass - silversword	10,000-14,000 (Maui, Hawaii)	None	15-30 Snow frequent in winter and may remain in sheltered places all year	Very rare	32

*) Note: In the zones C_1, C_2, $D-K_1$, $D-O_1$, $D-C_a$, and $D-C_b$ relatively more frequent

Climate	Prevailing soil-forming processes	Zonal soils	Dominant plant indicators	Vegetation cover	Land use
Semiarid marine tropical	Calcification and leucinization	Red Desert	Prosopis chilensis (kiawe) Heteropogon contortus (pili), and Setaria verticillata (bristly foxtail)	Xerophytic savanna thorn-scrub grassland	Irrigated sugar cane, vegetables, banana, papaya, mango. Winter grazing (after rains).
Subsemi-arid marine tropical	Laterization and leucinization	Reddish Brown	Leucaena glauca (koa haole), Opuntia megacantha (panini), and Panicum torridum (kakona-kona)	Xerophytic thorn scrub forest	Irrigated sugar cane up to 1,200 feet, pineapple above, vegetables, banana, papaya, mango. Taro in inundated places. Grazing especially after winter rains.
Subhumid marine tropical	Laterization and leucinization	Low Humic Latosols	Psidium guayava (guava), Lantana camara (lantana), Styphelia tameiameiae (pukeawe), Sphenomeris chusana (palaa), and Setaria geniculata (yellow foxtail)	Mixed xerophytic and mesophytic scrub forest	As above. Macadamia and litchi (marginally). Taro in inundated places. Grazing whole year. Forest when cultivated.
Subhumid marine subtropical (mesothermal)	Laterization and melanization	(Low) Humic Latosols	Acacia koa (koa), Psidium guayava (guava), Styphelia tameiameiae (pukeawe), and Vaccinium spp. (ohelo)	More or less open mixed xerophytic and mesophytic forest	Too cool for sugar cane or pineapple. Grazing is major use. Forest when cultivated.
Humid marine tropical	Laterization and melanization	Humic Latosols	Acacia koa (koa), Nephrolepis exaltata (Boston fern), Oplismenus hirtellus (basket grass), and Paspalum conjugatum (Hilo grass)	Mixed mesophytic and xerophytic forest (closed)	Non-irrigated sugar cane; limited pineapple. Macadamia, litchi. Grazing. Forest of better qualities when cultivated.
Humid marine tropical (or sub-tropical)	Laterization, weak podzolization, and melanization	Podzolic Humic Latosols	Metrosideros polymorpha (ohia lehua) Cibotium spp. (hapuu), Dicranopteris spp. (uluhe), and Lycopodium cernuum (wawaeiole)	Mesophytic marine tropical and subtropical forest	Forest reserve for water-shed management. Grazing in some cleared portions. Excellent forest under silviculture.
Very humid marine subtropical or tropical	Podzolization and gleization of laterized soils	Hydrol humic latosols (weakly up to strongly podzolized)	Cheirodendron trigynum (olapa), Cheirodendron platyphyllum (lapalapa), Cibotium spp. (hapuu) Elaphoglossum spp. (ekaha), and Mecodium recurvum (ohiaku).	Hygrophytic marine subtropical and tropical rainforest.	Water-shed. Good forest.
Rainy marine subtropical or tropical	Podzolization and gleization	Strongly podzolized hydrol humic latosols	As in D - Ca, and additionally: Cheirodendron dominii (lapalapa), Clermontia spp. (oha wai), and Gunnera spp. (ape).	Hygrophytic marine subtropical and tropical rain forest rich in bryophytic epiphytes	Water-shed
Extremely rainy marine subtropical	Gleization	Alakai Bog Gleysols	Oreobolus furcatus, Panicum spp., Plantago spp., and Lobelia spp.	Chamaephytic alakai bog	Water-shed.
Humid marine subtropical (warmer)	Podzolization and laterization	Latosolic Brown Forest Soils	Metrosideros polymorpha (ohia lehua), Sadleria spp. (amarmau), Nephrolepis exaltata (Boston fern), and Dicranopteris spp. (uluhe)	Mesophytic subtropical forest	Water-shed. Forest.
Humid marine mesothermal (cooler)	Podzolization and laterization	Latosolic Brown Forest Soils	Acacia koa (koa), Nephrolepis exaltata (Boston fern) Dicranopteris spp. (uluhe), and Pteridium aquilinum (brackenfern)	Mixed mesophytic and xerophytic more or less open forest.	Grazing. Forest (under silviculture).
Subhumid marine mesothermal	Weak podzolization and weak laterization	Latosolic Brown Forest Soils	Acacia koa (koa), Sophora chrysophylla (mamani), Styphelia spp. (pukeawe), Vaccinium spp. Pteridium aquilinum (brackenfern), and Eragrostis spp. (lovegrass)	Mixed meso-phytic and xerophytic more or less open scrub forest (chap-arral-like)	Grazing. Potential forest (under silviculture).
Subsemiarid microthermal (Subalpine)	Not yet stabilized	Lacking, only lithosols and regosols (volcanic)	Sophora chrysophylla (mamani), Myoporum sandwicense (naio), Styphelia spp. (pukeawe), Vaccinium spp. (ohelo), and Coprosma spp. (kukainene)	Xerophytic scrub (more or less open)	National Park.
Semiarid tundral	Not stabilized	Lacking, volcanic lithosols and regosols only	Lichenes, Musci, Hepaticae, Agrostis spp. (bentgrass), and Argyroxiphium spp. (silversword)	Semiarid barren alpine tundra	National Park.

cloudiness may substitute for the lower precipitation than indicated in these zones.

Certain ecological observations and studies carried
out on the Hawaiian Islands were published by Rock
(1913), Hosaka (1937), Egler (1939, 1947), Robyns and
Lamb (1939), Hartt and Neal (1940), Ripperton and Hosaka
(1942), Skottsberg (1942), Schwartz and Schwartz (1949),
and Fosberg (1961).

Fourteen Hawaiian biogeoclimatic zones (Table 1)
are outlined according to field studies carried out by
the author in 1961-62. They are modifications of the
ten vegetation zones of Ripperton and Hosaka (1942),
later applied and further elaborated by Schwartz and
Schwartz (1949).

The geologically younger islands, Maui and Hawaii,
differ from those of the other islands or their parts
which are geologically much older. Their differences
are great not only in their environmental complexes but
also in their vegetational and pedological products.
Thus, the Hawaiian Islands yield a great chance to study
the effect of time on both vegetation and soil development.

Each of the fourteen Hawaiian biogeoclimatic zones
has several distinct habitats which are under the control of either topographic, geologic, or biotic factors.
In response to these factors, the habitats are usually
represented by distinct plant communities. The number
of such ecosystem units is increased by cultivated
stands of introduced trees which have frequently great
influence upon the structure of the original vegetation
units. The other introduced plants (herbs and shrubs)
also have their great influence upon the changes of the
environmental factors. These ecosystems, indigenous
as well as introduced, need to be studied in the future.

LITERATURE CITED

Egler, F. E.   1939.   Vegetation zones of Oahu, Hawaii.
    Emp. For. J. 18:44-57.

_____   1947.   Arid southeast Oahu vegetation, Hawaii.
    Ecol. Monogr. 17:383-435.

Fosberg, F. R.   1961.   Guide to excursion III, Tenth
    Pacific Science Congress. University of Hawaii.
    207 p.

Hosaka, E. Y.   1937.   Ecological and floristic studies
    in Kipapa Gulch, Oahu. B. P. Bishop Mus. Occ. Pap.
    13(17):175-232.

Hartt, C. H., and M. C. Neal.   1940.   The plant ecology
    of Mauna Kea, Hawaii. Ecology 21:237-266.

Ripperton, J. C., and E. Y. Hosaka.   1942.   Vegetation
    zones of Hawaii. Hawaii Agric. Exp. Sta. Bull.
    89:1-60.

Rock, J. F.   1913.   The indigenous trees of the Hawaiian
    Islands. Honolulu. 518 p.

Robyns, W., and S. H. Lamb.   1939.   Preliminary ecolog-
    ical survey of the island of Hawaii. Jard. Bot.
    Brux. Bull. 15:241-293.

Schwartz, C. W., and E. R. Schwartz.   1949.   A recon-
    naissance of the game birds in Hawaii. Board of
    Commissioners of Agriculture and Forestry,
    Territory of Hawaii. Honolulu. 168 p.

Skottsberg, C.   1942.   Plant succession on recent lava
    flows in the island of Hawaii. Göteborgs
    VetenskSamh. Handl. Följd., Ser. B, 1(8):1-32.

Section 3

The Hawaiian Environment: The Sea

INTRODUCTION

Come back and dwell in Hawai'i-of-the-green-back,
A land that was formed in the ocean,
That was drawn up from the sea,
From the very depths of Kanaloa,
The white coral of the ocean caves that was
    caught on the hook of the fisherman,
The great fisherman of Kapaahu,
The great fisherman Kapu-he'e-ua-nui.

Polynesian myth in *Vikings of the Sunrise*
by Peter H. Buck

The sea is an omnipotent influence on all aspects of
island life. Ocean currents and temperatures determine
to a large extent the climate of the islands (see
Blumenstock and Price, Section 2), and tides and waves
sculpture the land forms (see papers by Wentworth and
by Moberly, Baver, and Morrison, in Section 1). The
influence of these factors and of the physical structure of the offshore waters on the marine biota are
discussed in this section in the papers of Brock and
Chamberlain, Gosline, and Doty.

The sea also absorbs most of the solar energy
reaching the earth. A measure of the rate of utilization of solar energy and inorganic nutrients by photosynthesizing organisms is one of the most important
phenomena to be considered in evaluating the biota of
the marine biochore. Kohn and Helfrich had an unusual
opportunity to compare primary productivity in a marine
environment with that of an adjacent terrestrial area
subject to approximately the same insolation. The
effect of that productivity on the animals in the
intertidal zone is discussed by Kohn, who not only
demonstrates a rather simple, three-step food chain
involving mollusks and polychaete worms on solution
benches, but also shows how the diversification of
niches can lead to the maintenance of populations of
large numbers of closely related sympatric species.

281

A Geological and Ecological Reconnaissance off Western Oahu, Hawaii, Principally by Means of the Research Submarine "Asherah"[1]

VERNON E. BROCK and THEODORE C. CHAMBERLAIN[2]

ABSTRACT: In November 1965 a combined geological and ecological reconnaissance of the sea floor off western Oahu was undertaken using a variety of methods and techniques to maximize both the range and reliability of the information obtained. Bottom topography and fish concentrations were surveyed with a precision echo sound recorder for which the transducer was towed in a streamlined housing below the research ship. Photographic bottom surveys were also made with an automatic stereo-camera system, and some bottom dredging and trawling were undertaken to secure samples of the bottom and the biota. Direct visual observations were also made using a small research submarine largely in the depth range of 25–180 meters.

The dominant geological features were a series of submerged, wave cut, largely sand covered terraces separated by rocky escarpments. The major terraces were an upper one terminating seaward at approximately 60 meters, an intermediate one from 70 to 120 meters, and a deep one beginning from a shoreward depth of 180 meters or deeper.

Patterns of littoral sand movement were observed to be southerly in the region between Kaena Point and Kepuhi Point with a substantial movement offshore. It was estimated that approximately 10,000 cubic yards of calcareous sand move seaward and are deposited annually on the inner portions of the deep terrace.

Associated with the escarpments were large and discontinuous aggregations of fish and, on the upper and intermediate terraces, extensive beds of the clam *Pinna muricata*. The observed patterns of distributions may be a response to the localized accumulation of food. Organisms which make nocturnal vertical migrations in adjacent deep water may be swept shoreward by surface currents and become trapped on the terraces. The collection of planktonic organic material in the thermocline where the water increases rapidly in density with depth may be a mechanism for the localized accumulation of particulate food of value to the clams.

The simultaneous use of a variety of observational techniques in an area provided non-identical and independent observations of the same situations. This served to confirm the information obtained and to add new and significant detail.

DURING NOVEMBER OF 1965 a reconnaissance of the sea floor geology and of the marine ecology off western Oahu, Hawaii was made using a remotely operated stereo-camera system, a precision echo sounding recorder, biologic and geologic dredges, and, most importantly, a two-man deep-diving research submersible vehicle.

Surface support was supplied by the University of Hawaii's 90-ft research vessel, the "Teritu." The intent of the investigation was to make a series of direct observations of the geomorphology and the biota by means of the submersible vehicle and to correlate with these observations data collected at the same time and in the same area by means of conventional, indirect data-gathering techniques (submarine photography, biologic and geologic dredging, etc.). The experiments were successful: 15 deep dives were made with the research submarine, most to 180

[1] Contribution 283, Hawaii Institute of Marine Biology. Manuscript received September 12, 1967.

[2] Department of Oceanography, Hawaii Institute of Geophysics, University of Hawaii, Honolulu, Hawaii 96822.

meters; 500 black and white and an equal number of color photographs were taken, some from the remote surface controlled stereo-camera, some from the submarine; 20 bathymetric profiles were run normal to the coast by the "Teritu" and numerous geological and biological specimens were collected from the terraces and escarpments by the various dredges and trawls. The following report summarizes these data and compares their relative merits for geological and biological reconnaissance surveys.

AREA OF INVESTIGATION

The area of investigation was chosen mainly with the intent of selecting oceanographic and meteorologic conditions that would be optimum for handling a small, research submarine. Since the submarine diving operations necessitated surface towing of the vehicle, and since the replenishment of compressed air, recharging of

the battery bank, and maintenance required moving alongside the mother ship, a leeward coast was necessary. Secondary requirements in the selection of the area of investigation were connected with the land-based logistical support of the entire operation over a 10-day period.

Because of the prevailing easterly tradewinds and the resulting near permanency of a lee coast along western Oahu, it was possible to meet the above requirements in an area of intensely interesting submarine features and a poorly known biota. Consequently a 14-kilometer length of coast along western Oahu, from Kaena Point to Kepuhi Point, was chosen for the reconnaissance (Figs. 1 and 2). This area provided ideal lee operating conditions during November; it was within ½ hour by boat from Pokai Bay, a replenishment harbor just to the south; it was a single isolated geological unit or cell in regard to the littoral circulation of sand; and

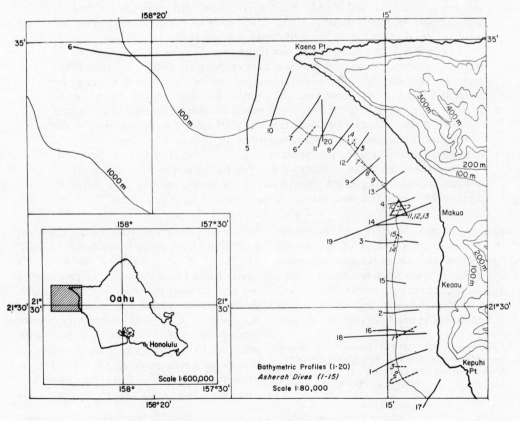

FIG. 1.   Location chart.

FIG. 2. View from above Kaena Point. The seafloor is delineated from the water's edge to and beyond the escarpment between the Mamala and Lualualei terraces. Sand channels and reef rock outcrops are shown. (Drawing by Ken Shutt.)

it contained numerous, well developed submarine terraces and escarpments that could be correlated with ancient stands of the sea, as recorded in recent borings made on the Ewa Plain 20 miles to the south.

ENVIRONMENTS

Oceanographic

SURFACE CURRENTS: The Hawaiian Islands are located on the northern edge of the Pacific North Equatorial Current, a westerly-flowing component of the large anticyclonic circulatory pattern that dominates the North Pacific Ocean. Within a few hundred miles of the Hawaiian Islands the surface currents all set toward the western quadrant, generally with a drift of about $\frac{1}{2}$ knot. As this large mass of water flows past the Hawaiian Islands it breaks up on the downstream side of the islands into large, semi-permanent eddies, some cyclonic and others anticyclonic. Superimposed upon these eddies, and in some cases completely dominating the surface circulations, are strong tidal currents.

About 10 miles off western Oahu the surface water appears to consistently move south, in conformation with the general flow of water from the east through the Kauai Channel, and join the circulation of an anticyclonic eddy about 20 miles in diameter located about 20 miles directly offshore at southwest Oahu (Latham, 1967). The velocity of the near-Oahu portion of this eddy was measured by Latham and found to be about $\frac{1}{2}$ knot to the south.

Nearer shore the surface currents have been found to reverse themselves semi-diurnally in accordance with the tides. During flood tides there is generally a flow of water to the south just west of Kaena Point, and to the southeast, south of the point. These currents have been measured at about $1\frac{1}{2}$ knots (Latham, 1967). However, immediately adjacent to the coast, both north and south of Kaena Point, there is a persistent drift of water of 1–2 knots that follows the coastline to a convergence point some few miles west of Kaena Point. These northwest-setting currents are more intense during ebb tide and have been measured at a maximum of 5 knots (Laevastu et al., 1964).

During the diving operations with the "Asherah" a nearly constant set to the north and west was encountered. The drift of this current varied, but $\frac{1}{2}$ knot was not uncommon even to depths of 180 meters.

WAVES: Wave energy reaching the western coast of Oahu can be approximately represented by four wave types related to predominant meteorological conditions within the Pacific Basin:

(1) *Kona Wind Waves:* Generated by local westerly storms; period 7 seconds, direction of approach SSW, height 2.4 meters, frequency of occurrence[3] 9.5%, generally during the winter months.

(2) *North Pacific Swell:* Generated by the passage of low pressure areas across the Northern Pacific Basin; period 13 seconds, direction of approach NNW, height 3.4 meters, frequency of occurrence 89%, generally during the winter months.

(3) *Southern Hemisphere Swell:* Generated by low pressure areas in the Southern Hemisphere; period 15 seconds, direction of approach S, height 0.9 meters, frequency of occurrence 53%, entirely during the summer months.

(4) *Tradewind Waves:* Generated by the easterly tradewinds; period 8 seconds, direction of approach E and NE, height 2.4 meters, frequency of occurrence nearly 100% but, due to the sheltering effect of Oahu, of minor importance in the area of investigation.

The currents that lie within the breaker zone, and which are of prime importance in the alongshore transport of littoral sand, are dependent upon the wave regime and consequently vary greatly in direction and speed. Waves from the northwest quadrant (generally North Pacific Swell) create southeastwardly flowing currents; waves approaching from the southwest quadrant (generally Southern Hemisphere Swell and Kona Wind Waves) produce currents flowing toward the northwest. Current speeds vary from less than $\frac{1}{10}$ knot to about $\frac{1}{2}$ knot.

THERMAL STRUCTURE: The island of Oahu centered at 21°30′ north latitude is in tropical water with a permanent surface isothermal layer. The long term (1936–1956) average temperatures within a 250-mile radius of Oahu are given in Table 1, together with the range for depths from the surface to 2000 meters.

It will be noted from Table 1 that the greatest range in temperature occurs between 200 and 300 meters. These are the depths where the thermocline is ordinarily found. However, the thermocline fluctuates in depth depending upon

[3] Per cent of the year during which each wave type occurs.

TABLE 1

AVERAGE TEMPERATURE DATA FOR AN AREA WITHIN A 250-MILE RADIUS OF OAHU, HAWAII*

DEPTH IN METERS	TEMPERATURE (DEGREES C)	TEMPERATURE RANGE (DEGREES C) + OR −
0	24.6	2.2
50	24.1	2.5
100	22.3	2.3
200	16.7	4.7
300	12.4	3.7
500	8.2	2.7
800	4.8	0.6
1000	4.2	0.7
1500	2.8	0.2
2000	2.1	0.2

* From Dr. B. C. Heezen.

the stirring effects of the wind or lack thereof, and the depths through which it fluctuates will show a greater temperature range than depths above or below. A protected lee area such as the Waianae coast of Oahu, because of reduced strength of the prevailing tradewinds, may have a shallower mixed layer. During the "Asherah" dives in this area, the location of the thermocline was inferred by noting the depth at which both visual ranges were minimal and the greatest apparent concentration of particulate matter occurred. On this basis the thermocline was between 70 and 100 meters. No vertical temperature profiles were obtained at the time of the diving operations.

Geologic

The main Hawaiian islands lie toward the southeastern limit of the Hawaiian Ridge, a large, positive, geomorphic feature built up of shield-shaped basaltic domes along a 1,600-mile fissure in the north-central Pacific Ocean. Neither the age nor the geologic history of the Hawaiian Ridge is well known, but recent investigations have indicated a Tertiary age for most of the Ridge, with a developmental sequence starting in the northwest and proceeding to the southeast. The growth of the Ridge has been accompanied by large scale subsidence; superimposed upon this subsidence have been major Tertiary and Quaternary eustatic sea level fluctuations due to tectonic deformation of the Pacific Basin and intense continental glaciation. The result of these positive and negative shifts of sea level has been the formation of numerous marine terraces, reef horizons, and beaches, now found at various positions from several thousands of feet below to several hundreds of feet above the present sea level.

Oahu, the center of population and site of the present investigations, is the third largest of the Hawaiian Islands with an area of 604 square miles. The island was built up above sea level by the emergence and coalescing of two large volcanoes, the Koolau Volcano on the east and the Waianae Volcano on the west. Today the remnants of these two volcanoes form the Koolau and Waianae mountain ranges respectively, between which lies the Schofield Plateau, a flat, low plateau consisting of alluvious and thinly-bedded lava flows. On the north and south flank of the island are wide coastal plains.

Along western Oahu, the geology is completely dominated by the deeply eroded remnants of the Waianae Volcano. The center of volcanic activity of this volcano was a caldera near Kolekole Pass at the head of Lualualei Valley. From this caldera and from the rift zones extending from it, large amounts of fluid lava were extruded over many millions of years. The older extrusions were thin, fluid, pahoehoe flows; the later flows were massive, adesitic aa.

The main extrusive activity of the Waianae Volcano terminated several millions of years ago; the cessation of major eruptions was followed by deep erosion of the volcano and later by a few secondary eruptions of small magnitude near the caldera. During the initial period of erosion the major valleys were formed; some, such as Lualualei, were graded to stands of the sea over 600 meters below the present sea level. With subsequent and continued subsidence of Oahu these major valleys were drowned, and eventually thick sections of reef, lagoonal, and beach sediments were deposited.

The present geomorphology of the western coast of Oahu is dominated by the deeply eroded valleys described above. Between these valleys, sharp spurs extend down to the sea and offshore as submarine ridges. These spurs and their offshore extensions act as effective barriers to the alongshore transport of nearshore sand and other sediment. Consequently the nearshore environment is divided into littoral units or cells between which little exchange of sand occurs, and within which the amount of sand produced is in equilibrium with the amount of sediment lost from the cell. Contributions of littoral sand are from coastal streams and from the disintegration of calcium carbonate skeletal remains on the reef flats; losses of littoral sand are by offshore sedimentation into deep water, and to a lesser extent by paralic deposition and by the landward migration of beach dunes.

The coastal zone between Kaena and Kepuhi points, the area of the present study, is essentially one large littoral cell; there appears to be very little nearshore sand transport around either point. The cell is dominated by the large Makua Valley located in the center of the cell; the major reservoir of beach sand is located at the mouth of this valley. Above sea level there are probably no fewer than four well-developed ancient sea level stands preserved, the most pronounced at $+8$ meters. Below sea level there are at least five additionally preserved sea level stands, at -18, -55, -90, -550, and -1100 meters (Stearns, 1966:23).

Biologic

The nature of the sea floor in the area of investigation has been described elsewhere. As an environment it is a series of sand-covered terraces paralleling the trend of the coast and backed by discontinuous escarpments. In places, the sand covering on the terraces is thin and the epifauna scant, even where the rock is bare due possibly to sand scouring. This is most apparent in shallow water from 10 to 30 meters in depth. In depths of 30 meters or less there are some areas with a vigorous growth of hermatypic corals. There are extensive beds of the clam *Pinna muricata* on the sand-covered terraces in depths between 35 and 100 meters, and occasionally on rocky areas numerous vasiform coral colonies, possibly a *Montipora*, are found in 60 to 80 meters of water.

The sand-covered terraces, other than areas of *Pinna* beds, have little apparent life. Some dredging on the terraces resulted in the collection of numerous heart urchins *Brissus latecarinatus*. There were also very few fishes over the terraces. The escarpments had in general an abundant fauna of fishes and invertebrates.

Areas of some of the terraces have a scattered covering of rubble with attached algae as deep as 90 meters. Algae also were noted on the escarpment areas. Where the escarpment was deeper than 90 meters it appeared to lack algal growth and had a poorer epifauna as compared with the escarpments in shallower water. At all depths, in holes and small caves, an abundant fauna was noted of fishes and invertebrates characteristic of their environment.

RECONNAISSANCE TECHNIQUES

"Asherah" Operations

To obtain the maximum amount and the highest quality of scientific data during the investigations it was felt that, simultaneously with the use of the "Asherah," other techniques should be employed to measure biologic and geologic parameters. Consequently, while the "Asherah" was diving, the "Teritu" was engaged in bathymetric or photographic surveys or geologic and biologic dredging operations in the same general area. (For equipment specifications see the APPENDIX.)

The "Asherah" was moored each night alongside the "Teritu" off Makua Valley. During the night her batteries and compressed air tanks were recharged. The daily procedure was to take the "Asherah" in tow with a 16-foot power boat early each morning and proceed to the proposed diving locality. Upon reaching the diving site the "Asherah" was released, made ready for diving, and boarded. Each dive lasted for from 2 to 3 hours and generally two dives were made a day. During the time the "Asherah" was actually under water she was accompanied on the surface by a 13-foot power boat with which she maintained direct and continual communications. From November 1 through November 5, 15 dives were made.

Remotely Controlled Stereo-Photography

While the "Asherah" and her accompanying small boats were actually engaged in diving operations, the "Teritu" was also employed in data collection. Each area transversed underwater by the "Asherah," as well as additional interesting areas, were photographed from the surface by the "Teritu." Edgerton, Germeshansen and Grier cameras were used, depth-controlled by a pinger unit mounted on the camera frame and monitored by the Precision Echo Sonic Recorder aboard the "Teritu." A stereo-(double-)camera arrangement was employed, and both black and white and color film were used. In all, 500 pairs of photographs were taken at depths of 120 to 300 meters.

Echo Sounding

Numerous continuous echo sounding profiles were made by the "Teritu" prior to, during, and subsequent to the "Asherah" dives. The equipment used consisted of an EDO echo sounder towed outboard in a Braincon streamlined housing and a GIFFT recorder (Precision Echo Sonic Recorder). Because of the high degree of sensitivity of the recording unit, it was possible to record fish schools and micro-relief on the various submerged terraces, and consequently the echo sounding profiles were instrumental in determining the diving localities for the "Asherah." Twenty of the best echo sounding profiles are shown in Figures 3a–3d, their localities in Figure 1; these records form the basis for the bathymetric chart shown in Figure 4. Three of the echo sounding profiles (Nos. 4, 10, and 11) show excellent examples of fish populations, and consequently are reproduced in Figures 5, 6, and 7.

Geologic Dredging

Numerous attempts to dredge rock from the various marine terraces and escarpments were made by the "Teritu." Heavy pipe dredges with chain bridles were used connected to the ship by $3/8$-inch steel wire, but the light "A" frame and sheeving system of the "Teritu" prevented heavy strains being put on the system. Dredging on the outer edge of the Penguin Banks Shelf, just north of Kepuhi Point, recovered reef rock fragments with freshly broken surfaces. These samples came from depths of from 50 to 60 meters and probably represent the outcrops marking the boundary between the Penguin Banks and Mamala shelves. Similar reef rock fragments were obtained at depths of 120 meters on the Mamala Shelf off Makua Valley.

Attempts to break rock off the major escarpment between the Mamala and Lualualei shelves

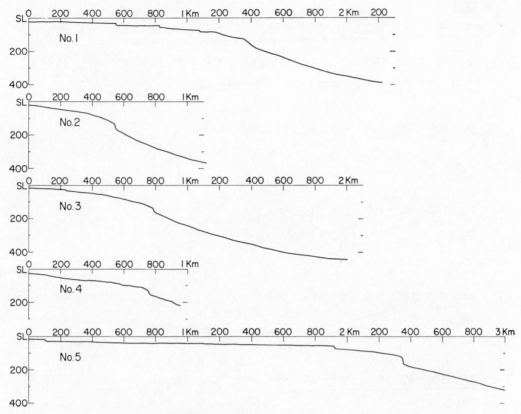

FIG. 3a. Bathymetric profiles Nos. 1–5. See Figure 1 for locations.

met with failure. In each case the ship had to be backed to recover the dredges and the cutting edge of the dredge was frequently bent.

Trawling

A standard shrimp try trawl was tested as a collecting device in the general area of the "Asherah" operations, but deeper and south of the area off Pokai Bay. The trawl was hauled twice in about 350 meters of water and took a scant catch with a good deal of damage to the net. The echo sounding record had indicated a smooth bottom. The tension on the cable reached one ton, overloading the ship's generator. A new net was rigged and shot in a sand channel off Pokai Bay which was presumed to be free of obstructions. The gear was towed perpendicularly to the trend of the coast offshore beginning in 20 meters of water and ending in about twice that depth. A large catch was taken of nearshore fishes, including a female *Dasyatis*

hawaiiensis whose weight must have exceeded 100 kilograms even though the fishing time was quite short. Again the net was badly damaged.

Both the dredging and trawling operations indicated that the "Teritu" was quite inadequate for this use.

MARINE GEOLOGY

Geomorphology

The submarine geomorphology between Kaena and Kepuhi points, is dominated by a series of marine terraces separated by escarpments. From the "Asherah" it was possible to discern at least three distinct levels:

(1) An upper level terminating seaward at a depth of approximately 60 meters.

(2) An intermediate level extending from about 70 meters down to approximately 120 meters.

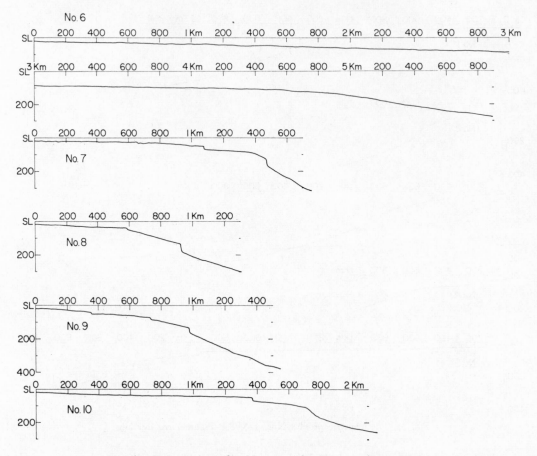

Fig. 3b. Bathymetric profiles Nos. 6–10. See Figure 1 for locations.

(3) A deep level extending from about the diving limitation of the "Asherah" (180 meters) seaward. These marine terraces observed from the "Asherah" correspond fairly well with the submarine terraces recorded by Ruhe et al. (1964) in their careful analysis of the shorelines and submarine terraces of Oahu. It is known from work done by Stearns (1966) and by Ruhe et al. (1964) that a shoaler terrace also exists in the depth range of 5–18 meters, but this terrace was above the general working range of the "Asherah" during the present investigation.

It is not the purpose of this paper to attempt to refine on the depth limitations computed by Ruhe for each of the submarine terraces around Oahu. Interested readers should refer to his work cited above or to several of H. T. Stearns' works on the same subject. However, it is our

purpose to describe certain features of these terraces that lay beyond the ability of these earlier workers because of the previous lack of means for direct visual observation.

The most striking feature of the submarine geomorphology off northwestern Oahu as observed by the "Asherah" was the escarpment between the lower and intermediate terrace levels (here equated to the Lualualei and Mamala shelves, 247–932 meters and 75–124 meters, respectively, of Ruhe et al., 1964). After viewing firsthand this major escarpment and the submarine terraces it separates, it seems no wonder that the depth determinations for the various shelves around Oahu have such a wide range: the near vertical nature of this escarpment prevents accurate determinations of its features by echo sounding, it is cut in many places by wide sand channels that grade gently

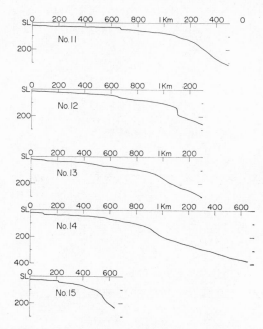

FIG. 3c. Bathymetric profiles Nos. 11–15. See Figure 1 for locations.

from one terrace to another, and the escarpment is almost completely burried by nearshore sand for almost one-half its length—from Makua Point to Kepuhi Point.

Figure 2 shows the relationship of this deeper escarpment to the upper terrace levels and generally to the land topography. Figure 9 shows a detailed picture at a point slightly north of Makua Valley. Generally this escarpment between the Lualualei and Mamala shelves is much more pronounced in the area north of Makua Valley. In places it is perfectly vertical for over 30 meters with caverns and indentations in the lower levels and in some localities large boulders at the base. The amount of sand in the offshore zone increases to the south (as explained in the section on Littoral Processes below), and this increase in offshore sand partially masks the base of this escarpment and, far to the south near Kepuhi Point, completely obliterates it. Starting at about Makua Valley, large spillways or canyons cut through the escarpment and, together with the sand spilling over the rim and fragments from the escarpment itself, form immense talus slopes (Fig. 9). On most of the dives directly to 180 meters the "Asherah" alighted on a 10°–15° talus slope

which dropped off seaward into darkness and extended upward and shoreward to the base of steep cliffs or over broken outcrops of rock to the Mamala Shelf.

In the area of investigation it would be almost impossible to fix the depth of the inshore edge of the Lualualei Shelf by means of echo soundings: the sand and talus deposits are probably tens of feet in thickness and completely bury the inner portion of the shelf. Just south of Kaena Point, where the base of the escarpment is covered with large boulders, the depth is approximately 186 meters. These boulders most probably are the remnants of a boulder beach; together with the near vertical escarpment above them they possibly represent the strand line and sea cliffs for a very prolonged stand of the sea. The age of the Lualualei Shelf is not known, but its possibly warped and titled surface (Ruhe, 1964) and the recovery from it of a possible Miocene fauna (Menard, Allison, and Durham, 1962) would indicate mid-Tertiary. Irrespective of the absolute age, a long period of stability of the sea level is indicated by the massive nature of the escarpment observed from the "Asherah." A continuation of this escarpment can be traced around most of western and southern Oahu.

The upper edge of the escarpment described above terminated abruptly in a nearly horizontal marine terrace. The seaward or deeper edge of this terrace generally was encountered at depths of about 120 meters, but ranging from approximately 100 to 140 meters in depth. Landward the terrace continued for hundreds of meters, finally terminating against a very broken line of irregular outcrops. Figure 8 is a representation of this intermediate terrace (here referred to as the Mamala Shelf) at a depth of about 90 meters. The nature of the outcrops defining its inner edge is shown as well as some of the surface features of the shelf. The outcrops themselves were very interesting as many had large caves in their seaward sides and were 3 to 6 meters in height and perhaps twice that in diameter. A definite delineation of these outcrops, generally parallel to the shoreline, could be seen. A representation of this delineation is attempted in Figure 8.

It was possible to trace the Mamala Shelf landward in some areas to depths of less than

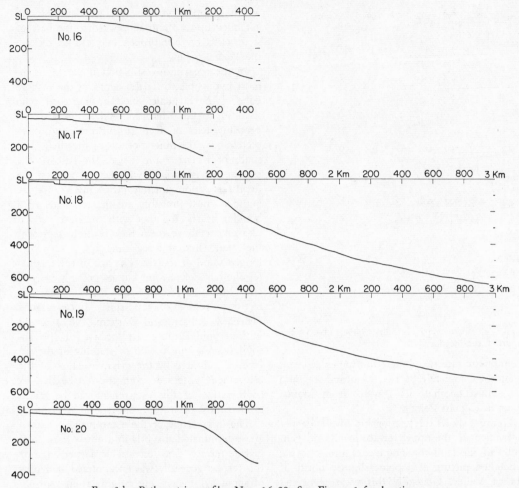

Fɪɢ. 3d. Bathymetric profiles Nos. 16–20. See Figure 1 for locations.

70 meters, but usually landward of about 75 meters another terrace level commenced, probably equated to the Penguin Banks Shelf of 55 meters depth as defined by Stearns (1966). The inner edge of this shelf was not explored with the "Asherah."

Both the Mamala and Penguin Banks shelves were very flat and, approximately south of Makua Valley, were covered extensively with patches and channels of sand. These masses of sand were generally irregular but connected into river-like masses 30 or more meters in width, which continued across the shelves and through cuts in the escarpments down to the diving limit of the "Asherah." On the Mamala and Penguin Banks shelves, the sand channels and sand patches were rippled; generally the

ripples were elongated normal to the channel axis irrespective of the meandering of the channel. Usually the sand bodies were not below the general level of the shelves, except where the sand bodies passed through the various escarpments.

Lithology

Due to the limitations of the "Asherah" it was not possible to collect rock samples at the time visual observations were made. Nor was it possible to use heavy rock dredging gear aboard the "Teritu." Consequently, an adequate lithologic sampling program could not be undertaken.

Nevertheless, rock samples were dredged

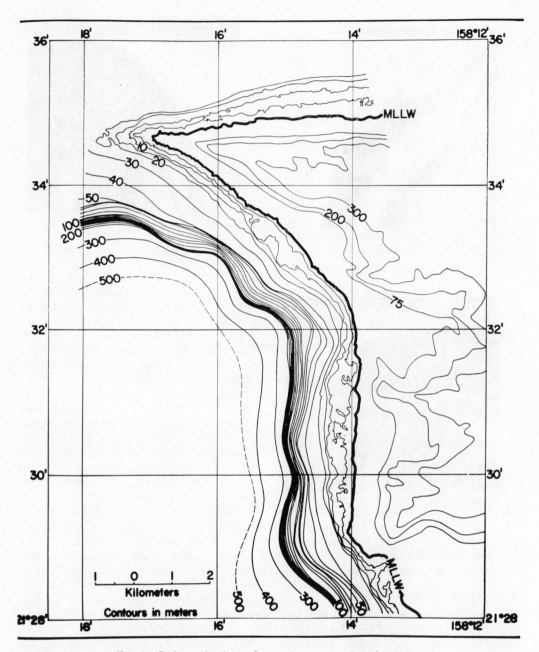

FIG. 4. Bathymetric chart of area just north of Makua Valley.

from the escarpment between the Penguin Banks and Mamala shelves. These samples were all well indurated reef limestone. No basaltic cobbles nor pebble-size fragments nor basaltic outcrops were seen on the Penguin Banks or Mamala shelves.

The rounded boulders observed at the base of the escarpment between the Lualualei and Mamala shelves and the escarpment itself appeared to be basalt, though no samples were taken of either. Fragments of basalt were numerous in the channels cutting through this

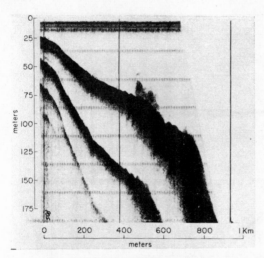

FIG. 5. Fathometer record No. 4.

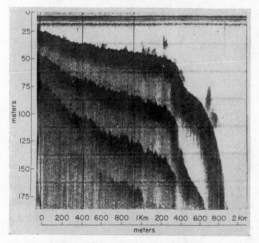

FIG. 6. Fathometer record No. 10.

escarpment and on the talus-like slopes on the inner edge of the Lualualei Shelf.

Nearshore and Offshore Sedimentation

Generally the coastal area between Kaena and Kepuhi points (herein called the Makua Cell) is one littoral unit or cell, that is, a zone in which the beaches are essentially in equilibrium, and the sand produced within or transported into the cell is just balanced by the sand lost to deep water sedimentation (Chamberlain, in press). Very little sand is transported around either Kaena or Kepuhi points.

The sand, nearshore and on the beach, is continually shifting in response to the wave and

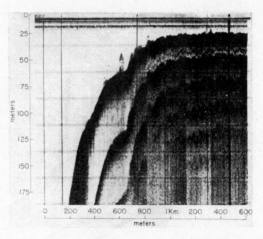

FIG. 7. Fathometer record No. 11.

current regime, both on and offshore and alongshore. But usually there is a net, yearly, alongshore transport of sand to the south under the influence of the North Pacific Swell—high, powerful waves arising from the northwest gradient more than one-half of the time. These are mainly winter waves, and consequently most of the southward transport of sand takes place during that season.

As a result of these littoral processes, the sand-size particles, produced on the reef or carried onto the beaches from the hinterland by the intermittent streams of the area, are carried southward in the littoral cell and piled up on the southernmost beaches, and offshore against the northern side of Kepuhi Point.

The dives in the "Asherah" revealed that by no means all of the nearshore sand moves within the surf zone and on the beach to the south, but rather, a very substantial amount moves directly offshore, across the various marine terraces and escarpments into deep water. In Figure 2 an attempt is made to indicate these patches and channels by which sand is moved directly offshore.

The sand-size particles that make up the beaches, and the nearshore and offshore sand bodies between Kaena and Kepuhi points are of various composition and from various sources. Generally the sand is of medium grain-size and well sorted. Most of the constituents are remains of reef organisms; a small percentage of lithogenic components are present in the form of crystal grains of olivine and

FIG. 8. Mamala Terrace at 100 meters. Shown are reef rock outcrops, the terrace, and some of the commoner fishes. (Drawing by Ken Shutt.)

weathered basalt fragments. Samples from the area of Keawaula Beach have shown the organic constituents to be mainly the remains of benthic Foraminifera, with lesser amounts of fragments of Mollusca and calcareous algae; various amounts of coral and echinoid debris are also present (Moberly and Chamberlain, 1964:137). A general discussion of the constituents of

Hawaiian beach sands can be found in the report by Moberly et al. (1965).

As can be seen from the composition, most of the sand-size particles are produced in the nearshore zone by disintegration of reef-associated organisms. Their route of transportation is unknown but probably complex. Some of the particles move onto the beaches and, as the beaches are eroded and accreted during the year, the particles migrate onshore and offshore, but year after year they are set in the direction of net alongshore transport, that is, to the south. Just north of Kepuhi Point, thick, extensive sand deposits attest to this southerly migration. During periods of intense northwesterly waves, strong littoral currents deflected seaward by Kepuhi Point as they flow southward, probably carry large quantities of this material nearshore and offshore, where it completely buries the various offshore terraces and escarpments at least down to 180 meters, the diving limitation of the "Asherah." A similar littoral cell a few miles to the south (Kahe) has been well studied and shows a similar nearshore sand circulatory pattern (Chamberlain and Marine Advisers, 1964).

The masses of sand lying on the Penguin Banks and Mamala shelves, and the accumulations of calcareous sand on the inner edges of the Lualualei Shelf at the base of the deeper escarpment must be explained in a somewhat different manner. It is quite possible that little of this sand has ever been on the beaches. Most of it, except that in the larger channels connected to the nearshore zone, is probably produced *in situ* on the deeper terraces, and by some process, yet unclear, it progresses seaward across the shelves, eventually spilling down onto the Lualualei Shelf. The larger sand channels on the deeper terraces may well be located relative to strong, offshore currents that develop within the Makua Cell during periods of storm. But most of the sand observed from the "Asherah" is moving slowly downslope under the influence of gravity, disturbed occasionally by the orbital velocity of large waves in the unidirectional flow of periodic bottom currents. Where the escarpments are very steep, for example, between the Mamala and Lualualei shelves, the calcareous sand simply spills over the escarpment edge and falls down upon various ledges and finally upon the inner edge of the Lualualei Shelf.

The quantity of sand within the Makua Cell has been estimated previously at approximately 5×10^5 cu yd (Chamberlain, in press). However, in light of the observations made from the "Asherah," this estimate is probably too low by a factor of two, perhaps even by an order of magnitude. Assuming this amount (say, 10^6 cu yd) to be a sand reservoir essentially in equilibrium with the present geologic and oceanographic conditions, then the yearly addition of new sand to this reservoir must be balanced by the yearly loss of sand from the reservoir. The yearly production or input of sand-size particles per length of coast along western Oahu is not known, but from the analyses made just to the south at Kahe, the total yearly production, or introduction, of sand into the Makua Cell is probably less than 10,000 cu yd. Nevertheless, since the principal loss of sand from the Makua Cell is to deep water sedimentation, this figure means that approximately 10,000 cu yd of sand are deposited yearly onto the inner portions of the Lualualei Shelf. The distance that this sedimentation extended out onto the Lualualei Shelf could not be ascertained from the "Asherah" due to depth restrictions, but sand-size particles were photographed on the shelf down to below 600 meters.

BENTHIC ECOLOGY AND FISH COMMUNITIES

Information on the kinds, distributions, and associations of organisms were obtained through four more or less complementary investigations: (1) by dredging and trawling, (2) by precision echo sounding, (3) by submarine photography with an automatic camera system, (4) direct observations from a research submarine.

The submarine was limited to depths of 180 meters or less and, while the other methods of investigation were not thus limited, the discussions concern observations from about 180 meters to about 25 meters. Few observations were made in water shallower than this. The nature of the bottom and its topography is described in detail in the section on geomorphology. Considered as an environment the area comprised two major biotopes: terraces, generally sand covered, and rocky areas, either outcrops of reef rock or near-vertical rocky escarpments separating the terraces. Of the latter, the important ones were a line of outcrops and low escarpments at 70 meters and massive escarpments with crests at 120 meters or deeper, paralleling the coast. Associated with the rocky areas were an abundance of fishes and in places a rich epifauna also.

The Communities of the Rocky Areas

Figures 5, 6, and 7, reproducing the actual sounding traces of the bottom, also show, more faintly and somewhat separated from the bottom, traces of what were subsequently demonstrated to be concentrations of fish. These were located generally at or above escarpment crests or over outcrops of reef rock. These concentrations of fish were investigated by cruising in the "Asherah" near the sea floor, along and across the escarpments near where the soundings were made. In addition, photographic transects were made both obliquely to the trend of the coast and at a right angle. These ran from shallow to deep water in order to minimize direct contact of the camera system with the bottom.

The visual observations made from the "Asherah" provided a dramatic contrast to the photographic ones obtained with the automatic camera system. Visual observations confirmed the indication given by the echo sounding record in finding major, but highly discontinuous, concentrations of fish associated with the escarpment crests. This was not true of the photographic transects. Fish were photographed on only a few frames of the hundreds exposed, and those photographed were species that commonly rest on the bottom or swim very near the bottom. The greatest number of fish were photographed in a few instances when the camera system was in contact with the bottom, being dragged along so that photographs were taken parallel with the sea floor.

Observations from the "Asherah" on the relative abundance of some species, suggested that the fish community associated with outcrops of reef rock at about 70 meters differed from that associated with the deeper escarpment crests further offshore at depths of 120 meters or more. The damsel fish *Chromis verater* ap-

peared to be the most abundant species about the outcrops of reef rock. The little bass *Caesioperca thompsoni* was common in small loose schools on the face of these outcrops. *Heniochus acuminatus* was also common, frequently as individuals, but sometimes in small groups. The surmullet *Parupeneus bifasciatus* was also common near the basal portion of the outcrops or around rocks in the vicinity, but not in schools.

The angel fish *Holocanthus arcuatus* was observed as scattered individuals over rocky areas, usually very close to the bottom. The most abundant butterfly fish observed was *Chaetodon miliaris;* however this species was less numerous than the damsel fish *Chromis verater* in the rocky outcrop environment. See Figure 8.

Both *Naso hexacanthus* and *Seriola dumerilli* were observed in schools at both the outcrops of reef rock and the escarpments. The schools of *Naso* appeared to be smaller and more open in the shallower water. *Naso* schools above the crest of the deep escarpments, near large aggregations of *Chaetodon miliaris,* had the following characteristics. The schools were roughly spherical, about 3 to 7 meters across, and moved slowly between 5 and 15 meters off the bottom. The individual fish appeared to be 35 to 70 cm in length and swam rather closely together.

Seriola dumerilli were observed in roving schools of a few dozen fish. Individual fish in the schools were estimated to be larger than 70 cm and less than 150 cm in length.

Mention has been made of aggregations of *Chaetodon miliaris* above the crests of the escarpments. These occurred over a relatively small area of bottom, usually less than 50 meters across, which was somewhat elevated (by 5 meters or less) above the general height of the escarpment crest. The aggregation, or school, extended upward into the water column from 15 to 40 meters. Individual fish were 12 to 25 cm in length and appeared to be separated by distances of 0.5 to 2 meters or more apart. The fish were close to the bottom but confined to the rocky elevated portions. They did not occur down over the face of the escarpments and the diameter of the aggregation appeared to be less with increased distance from the bottom. The individual fish were in easy motion, both vertically and horizontally, but the aggregation as a whole appeared to be fixed over a specific area of the bottom. It is this feature which suggests that the large number of fish be considered an aggregation rather than a school. See Figures 5, 6, 7, 8, 9, and 10.

The schools of *Naso hexacanthus* also appeared to be oriented with respect to the aggregation of *Chaetodon miliaris* but not nearly as tightly as the latter appeared to be oriented to the sea floor topography. The *Naso hexacanthus* schools were located peripherally to the aggregation of *Chaetodon miliaris* and over the terrace rather than beyond the face of the escarpments. However, schools of the deep water snapper *Etelis carbunculus* did occur peripherally in relation to the *Chaetodon miliaris* aggregation at the level of the terrace, or deeper in open water beyond the escarpments. This species was not observed in shallower water, but it was also observed near the crest of the escarpments or beyond in deeper water where no aggregations of *Chaetodon miliaris* occurred.

These aggregations did not occur continuously along the crests of the escarpments, but appeared to occur wherever an elevated rocky area broke

FIG. 9. Escarpment between the Mamala and Lualualei terraces at 200 meters. The "Asherah" is shown off the face of the escarpment and a fish aggregation above the crest. (Drawing by Ken Shutt.)

the crest profile. While the face of the outcrops of reef rock had had an abundant population of fish, there was a scant population along the face of the escarpments. The commonest species was an unidentified priacanthid-like fish that appeared to dwell in shallow holes on the face of the escarpments at distances of 10 meters or more apart. Small carangids were occasionally observed at all depths studied on or beyond the face of the escarpments. There were cavities of various sizes in the rocky areas. Those of apparent depth were usually thickly crowded by myripristids and holocentrids. *Holocentrus scythrops* or a species very much like it appears to be common. Spiny lobsters were also common and, while no certain identification of the species was made, *Panulirus japonicus* would at least be anticipated to occur since it appears to be commoner in deeper water within the range of SCUBA. Spiny lobsters were sighted in depths greater than 140 meters. A large moray eel, resembling *Gymnothorax flavimarginatus*, was seen at a depth of 150 meters adjacent to a cavity in the rock.

The Terrace Community

For the most part the terraces were covered by sand with little apparent epifauna. Fish were also largely absent. A large school of kawakawa (*Euthynnus yaito*) was observed, apparently foraging over a rubble- and sand-covered area about 150 meters deep. The fish were very near the bottom, less than a meter above it. Rays, probably *Dasyatis hawaiiensis* and certainly *Aetobatus narinari,* were not infrequently sighted on or over sandy areas. A very large *Dasyatis hawaiiensis* was taken in a small trawl at a depth of less than 50 meters off Pokai Bay from a sand bottom, and dredging at between 150 and 75 meters largely in sand north of Kepuhi Point resulted in an abundant catch of the heart urchin *Brissus latecarinatus* and many fragments of shells from the hatchet clam *Pinna muricata.* While the heart urchin is normally buried in the sand and is therefore not detectable visually, very extensive beds of the clam were observed from the "Asherah" and by submarine photographic transects off western Oahu and elsewhere in depths between 35 and 100 meters. One such clam bed observed from the "Asherah" was at least 500 meters across.

Subsequently, a bed which had an extent of more than 1500 meters was photographed during a submarine camera transect in an area between Maui and Lanai at a depth of 70 to 80 meters. As is characteristic for this genus, the clams were buried deeply in the substrate with the lip of the shell protruding. Individual clams were close together, appearing to be almost in contact.

The Neritic Community

Observations of the biota thus far have concerned benthic organisms, and suggest that distributions of fish are related to bottom topography. Very few fish were observed high above the bottom. However, concentrations of plankton and particulate matter, possibly organic, were observed from the "Asherah" well above the bottom and also near it, at depths of 70 to 100 meters. It was assumed that these concentrations, causing a substantially reduced visual range, were located at the bottom of the mixed layer, at the thermocline. Temperature measurements were not taken to confirm this assumption.

Discussion

The ecological observations from the "Asherah" together with the data obtained by echo sounding, submarine photography with automatic cameras, and trawling and dredging suggest the existence of two major biotopes—the terraces, and the rocky outcrops and escarpments—and that each of these contains two recognizable subdivisions. For the terrace biotope these are: (1) the sand-covered flats, and (2) the extensive beds of *Pinna muricata,* which could be better characterized as a biocoenosis. Its investigation would likely be rewarding.

The biotope of rocky outcrops and escarpment includes two subdivisions—the outcrops of reef rock characterized by *Chromis verater* and the less abundant *Caesioperca thompsoni,* and the escarpments characterized by large aggregations of *Chaetodon miliaris* and small schools of *Etelis carbunculus,* as well as other species. The observed patterns of distribution are difficult to understand in detail, but two general hypotheses are proposed, in part to provide a basis for future investigations of these matters. One hypothesis concerns the bathymetric distribution of *Pinna muricata,* and the other, the aggregations of *Chaetodon miliaris* and associated species.

Occasional specimens of *Pinna muricata* are found in quite shallow water, essentially just below the low tide level. The shallowest beds observed from the "Asherah" were about 38 meters deep, and SCUBA divers have reported beds as shallow as 25 meters. The deepest beds observed from the "Asherah" off western Oahu were at about 100 meters. This may not, of course, represent the downward extension of the range of this species. As shown in Table 1 the average temperature to and including depths of 100 meters is from 24.6° to 22.3°C, with a low temperature of 20.0°C at 100 meters. At 200 meters the average temperature is 16.7°C with a range of plus or minus 4.7°C. This is the maximum range for the water column. The temperature variation is less in either shallower or deeper water, becoming markedly less for depths in excess of 500 meters. There may be an association between the depths of abundant occurrence of *Pinna muricata* and the lower part of the mixed layer. *Pinna* is a filter feeder, and the lower part of the mixed layer may have a higher concentration of organic particulate material since such material, unless mobile, tends to settle. The sinking rate would decrease at the bottom of the mixed layer because of an increase in density of the water. As mentioned earlier a marked reduction in visual range was sometimes noted at depths between 70 and 100 meters. Upon going deeper the transparency of the water increased abruptly, with a change in visual range from 10–15 meters to 40 meters or more. If the lowest portion of the mixed layer did have a higher concentration of particulate food, the bathymetric range through which it passed may be the bathymetric range of the clam beds, with a possible additional qualification that the decrease in temperature with depth may establish an independent lower limit to the distribution of the clam.

The striking aggregations of *Chaetodon miliaris* observed over certain topographic features of the deep escarpment must relate to some essential advantage that this behavior provides in this locality. *Chaetodon miliaris* is the commonest butterfly fish in Hawaiian waters and was considered to be a coral reef fish. Its abundant occurrence in depths of 120 meters

FIG. 10.   An aggregation of fish at 140 meters. A close view of a fish aggregation similar to that in Figure 9. (Drawing by Ken Shutt.)

and more was surprising. However, with the exception of *Etelis carbunculus, Caesioperca thompsoni, Chaetodon tinkeri* and possibly *Holocentrus scythrops* and one or two others, the list of fish species observed from the "Asherah" (see Table 2) are common either in nearshore reef environments or in near-surface waters. With a few additions, the fish fauna at depths to 180 meters was essentially a selected portion of a nearshore reef fish fauna.

Many of the species of fish listed in Table 2 are normally found about rocky areas in shallow

TABLE 2

A LIST OF SPECIES OF FISH OBSERVED FROM THE "ASHERAH"

SPECIES	ABUNDANCE	REMARKS
Dasyatis hawaiiensis	sighted occasionally	Over or on sand bottom.
Aetobatus narinari	sighted occasionally	Over or on sand bottom.
Gymnothorax flavimarginatus	not common	Living in holes. Other species probably present but not identified.
Holocentrus spp.	common	Living in or adjacent to cavities in rock. H. scythrops may be an abundant species.
Myripristis spp.	common	Habits similar to Holocentrus.
Caesioperca thompsoni	common	More abundant on nearshore escarpment face in small loose schools.
Apogon or Holocentrus spp.	dominant	Large schools of small reddish fishes (4–5 cm). Very abundant near bottom.
Seriola dumerilii	abundant	In medium-sized schools, usually in motion.
Carangids	common	Both scattered fish and small schools observed as deep as 180 meters. More than a single species involved. Not obviously part of the escarpment community.
Etelis carbunculus	abundant	In small scattered schools of 10–30 fishes frequently over deep water beyond top of outer escarpment.
Mulloidichthys pflugeri	not common	
Parupeneus bifasciatus	common	Seen more frequently about inner escarpments. Not obviously a part of the escarpment community.
Holocanthus arcuatus	common	Scattered over rocks near bottom.
Heniochus acuminatus	common	Usually seen individually or in small groups somewhat further from bottom than Holocanthus arcuatus.
Chaetodon tinkeri	rare	A rare deepwater Hawaiian endemic butterfly fish known heretofore only from single type.
Chaetodon miliaris	dominant	An indicator species for the escarpment community.
Chromis verater	abundant to dominant	Most abundant about nearshore escarpments. Near rocks, not high in water column.
Naso hexacanthus	dominant	In large- to medium-sized schools frequently well off bottom.
Euthynnus yaito	sighted occasionally	Few large schools observed feeding over submerged beach terrace. Not part of escarpment community.
Canthigaster cinctus	rare	Few sighted near bottom.

water and apparently find both shelter and food in a rocky environment. *Chaetodon miliaris* is such a species in nearshore areas. It is possible that *Chaetodon miliaris* occurs in major aggregations well off the bottom in the deepwater environment as a response to a plankton feeding regime. Isaacs and Schwartzlose (1965) suggested that vertically migrating zooplankton are swept over shoal areas such as banks during the night when they move upward in the water column, and then are trapped against the bottom on their downward migration with the approach of day. They may be thereby especially vulnerable to predation by fishes. A mechanism of this nature would not, however, explain the highly discontinuous distribution of fish laterally along the crest of the escarpments. It is also difficult to see what advantages would accrue through aggregating upwards of 40 meters above the bottom, in some instances over a rocky area not more than 5 meters above the average height of the escarpment crest.

Aggregations of fish do occur over rocky mounds on a much smaller scale in shallower water. Immature *Dascyllus albisella* do this over individual coral heads and seek concealment in the branches of the coral when alarmed. However, it is unlikely that the very large aggregations of *Chaetodon miliaris* use for shelter the features of bottom topography above which they aggregate. This statement would also apply to *Chromis verater*.

Fish concentrations on or over banks and in the vicinity of oceanic islands have long been noted by fishermen. Tuna fishermen in the eastern tropical Pacific have found concentrations of tuna in the vicinity of offshore banks regularly enough to make such topographic features of special interest (Bennett and Schaefer, 1965).

Four hypotheses have been offered to explain the apparent greater abundance of marine life about such topographic features, three of which would apply to banks as well as islands. The margins of continents, under many circumstances, would have similar effects on the abundance of marine life. The four hypotheses, which are not mutually exclusive, are as follows: (a) nutrients from land runoff (Gran, 1931); (b) vertical movement of water transporting nutrients into the euphotic zone (Moore, 1949); (c) increased productivity through the growth of benthic algae in relatively shallow depths (Sargent and Austin, 1949); (d) the trapping of deep scattering layer organisms (Isaacs and Schwartzlose, 1965).

A discussion of the first three of these possible mechanisms, which involve means by which the primary production is increased, is presented by Jones (1962) in connection with the discovery of larger standing crops of zooplankton as the Marquesas Islands are approached.

The pattern of fish concentrations as observed off western Oahu seem to accord best with a food resource which may be provided by the trapping of deep scattering layer organisms as suggested by Isaacs and Schwartzlose (1965). However, if this is the correct hypothesis, the observed relation among topographical features, fish concentrations, and deep scatters is a complex one, and is affected by elements that are not obvious.

CONCLUSIONS

1. At least three well-defined terraces were discernible from the "Asherah" (Fig. 1): (a) the Lualualei Terrace deeper than 180 meters, (b) the Mamala Terrace at depths of 70 to 120 meters, and (c) the Penguin Banks Terrace shoaler than 70 meters.

2. Vertical and near-vertical rock escarpments separate the Mamala Terrace from the Lualualei Terrace. In many places these escarpments were over 35 meters high and north of Makua Valley there were areas of rounded boulders at their bases; in some areas caves were present (Fig. 9). Between the Penguin Banks Terrace and the Mamala Terrace a broken line of reef rock outcrops extended up above the level of the terraces. These outcrops were from 5 to 10 meters in height and generally aligned parallel to the shore (Fig. 8).

3. Associated with these bottom structures were communities of the benthic biota. There appeared to be two major biotopes, the terraces and the rocky outcrops and escarpments. Each of these biotopes was separable into two portions based on the presence or absence of dominant species.

The terraces were largely sand covered, rather barren of fishes or obvious benthic fauna except for extensive beds of a hatchet clam *Pinna muricata,* which were both extensive enough and dense enough to constitute a biocoenosis.

The escarpments lying between the Lualualei Terrace and the Mamala Terrace had at irregular intervals large concentrations of fish associated with features of the crest. Concentrations of fish were also observed with the reef rock outcrops between the Mamala Terrace and the Penguin Banks Terrace. These concentrations appeared to differ significantly in both dominant species and the proportions of other species.

4. The majority of the species of fish and those most abundant within the range of depths observed from the "Asherah" were species common or abundant in shallow water.

5. Offshore transport of calcareous sand was evident to the diving limit of the "Asherah" (180 meters). On the Mamala and shoaler shelves, large sand "channels" and interconnected sand patches were present (Figs. 1 and

3). Seaward these sand channels spilled over the Lualualei escarpment or through gullies in that escarpment down into the Lualualei Terrace. In most places the inner edge of the Lualualei Terrace was buried with thick masses of nearshore calcareous sand mixed with escarpment talus of pebble and cobble size (Fig. 9).

6. The amount of offshore sand increased markedly from north to south; near Kepuhi Point all of the escarpments and terraces were completely buried and a single sand slope of about 5° extended from 25 meters to the depth limit of the "Asherah."

APPENDIX
EQUIPMENT SPECIFICATIONS

"Asherah"

The research submarine "Asherah" was leased from the Electric Boat Division of General Dynamics for a period of one week. Accompanying the submarine was a 3-man operating and maintenance crew and equipment to keep all systems functioning. She was 17 feet long with a spherical pressure hull 5 feet in diameter at the anterior end attached to a cone-shaped afterpart which was floodable and housed batteries, compressed air tanks, and ballast tanks.

She was rated for a maximum depth of 600 feet and for an operating period of 10 hours. Other data include:

Crew: 2, an operator and an observer
Propulsion: 2 side-mounted, 2-hp motors
Power: 24-volt storage batteries
Life support: 48 man-hours endurance (CO_2 absorbent and compressed oxygen)
Viewports: six 5-inch minimum diameter, 90° truncated cone, 2-inch-thick plexiglass; and one 2-inch skylight of 1-inch plexiglass in hatch
Weight in air: 8,500 pounds

Through a "pinger" mounted on the hull of the submarine and a directional hydrophone on board the 13-foot power boat, the approximate position of the "Asherah" was monitored throughout a dive.

Where the nature of the diving investigation permitted, the dive was begun at its deepest point, that is at 180 meters, in order to get the submarine down into cool water as soon as possible. This was desirable since in near-surface waters the temperature inside the craft, together with 100% humidity, made her uncomfortable. For this reason, near-bottom observations were taken from deep to shallow water. Both the operator and the scientific observer aboard the vehicle used the viewports and exchanged information on their observations. In addition, a portable tape recorder was used to record what was seen; however, because of the ambient noise level, the tapes were difficult to understand on playback. Photographs in monochrome and color were taken through the viewports with cameras impervious to moisture such as the Nikonos. While the "Asherah" had an external automatic camera, this was in operating condition for only a few of the dives near the termination of the program. While few of the photographs were of good quality, many were adequate to confirm visual observations.

Stereo-Photographic Equipment

The following photographic equipment, purchased from Edgerton, Germeshausen and Gier, Inc., 160 Brookline Avenue, Boston, was used throughout the "Asherah" diving operations: two 35-mm cameras, Model 200; light source, Model 210; and camera mount, Model 240.

A pinger system monitored by the "Teritu's" echo sounding recorder was used to record the camera's distance from the bottom. Its components consisted of a driver (Model 220), and a transducer (Model 221).

The entire camera system, including pinger, was powered by silver cell batteries.

Kodak TRI-X film was used for all black and white photography, Echtochrome MS film for all color photography.

Echo Sounding Equipment

The echo sounding equipment used aboard the "Teritu," and by means of which the bathymetric profiles were made, consisted of: GIFFT Transceiver: 800 watts peak power at 12 kilocycles, ALPINE *Precision Echo Sonic Recorder* (PESR), and BRAINCON towed "V" Fin incorporating an EDO transducer.

Geologic Dredges

The rock dredges were made of ¼-inch iron pipe, 14 inches in diameter and cut into 3-foot lengths. An iron grating was welded across one end and a 4-foot chain bridle attached to the other end. The cutting edges of the dredges were sharpened and tempered.

REFERENCES

BENNETT, E. B., and M. B. SCHAEFER. 1960. Studies of physical, chemical, and biological oceanography in the vicinity of the Revilla Gigedo Islands during the "Island Current Survey" of 1957. Int.-Am. Trop. Tuna Comm. Bull. 4(5):219–257.

CHAMBERLAIN, T., and MARINE ADVISERS. 1964. Analysis of Littoral Processes, Kahe, Oahu. Prepared for Hawaiian Electric Company, Honolulu, Hawaii, 62 pp.

GRAN, H. H. 1931. On the conditions for the production of plankton in the sea. Rept. Internatl. Council Expl. Sea 75:37–46.

ISAACS, JOHN D., and R. A. SCHWARTZLOSE. 1965. Migrant sound scatterers: Interaction with the sea floor. Science 150:1810–1813.

JONES, E. C. 1962. Evidence of an island effect upon the standing crop of zooplankton near the Marquesas Islands, Central Pacific. J. Internatl. Council Expl. Sea 27:3.

LAEVASTU, T., et al. 1964. Coastal Currents and Sewage Disposal in the Hawaiian Islands: Hawaii Inst. Geophys. Tech. Rept., 64-1, 101 pp.

LATHAM, R. C. 1967. Kauai Channel Currents. Master of Science Thesis, University of Hawaii, 128 pp.

MENARD, H., E. ALLISON, and J. DURHAM. 1962. A Miocene terrace in the Hawaiian Islands. Science 138:896–897.

MOBERLY, R., et al. 1965. Source and variation of Hawaiian littoral sand. J. Sed. Petrology 35(3):589–598.

MOBERLY, R., and T. CHAMBERLAIN. 1964. Hawaiian Beach Systems. Hawaii Inst. Geophys. Rept. 64-2.

MOORE, H. B. 1949. The zooplankton of the upper waters of the Bermuda area of the North Atlantic. Bull. Bingham Oceanogr. Coll., Vol. 12, Article 2, 97 pp.

RUHE, R. V., J. M. WILLIAMS, and E. L. HILL. 1964. Shorelines and submarine shelves, Oahu, Hawaii. J. Geol. 73:485–497.

SARGENT, M. C., and T. S. AUSTIN. 1949. Organic productivity of an atoll. Trans. Am. Geophys. Union 30:245–249.

STEARNS, H. T. 1966. Geology of the State of Hawaii. Pacific Books, Palo Alto, California. 266 pp.

VERTICAL ZONATION OF INSHORE FISHES IN THE UPPER WATER LAYERS OF THE HAWAIIAN ISLANDS[1]

William A. Gosline

Department of Zoology, University of Hawaii, Honolulu, Hawaii

Abstract. The Hawaiian Islands are in the trade wind belt; they have about a 1-m tide. Along open coasts the effect of the tide on the zonation of inshore fishes is minor compared to that of the surge. Above sea level, pools depend primarily on wave splash for replenishment. The higher splash pools have few species of fishes, and those that occur there are ecologically well differentiated. On the exposed rocky benches just above sea level, there is usually abundant seaweed, but one herbivorous blenny is the only fish that lives there.

For some 6 m or more just below sea level on open coasts horizontal water movement frequently scours the bottom, often with the abrasive action of sand added. The bottom here is of rock or sand. Most of the species of the area are herbivores which graze on such short algal stubble as exists on the rocks. Indeed, in both species and individuals, the maximum number of herbivorous fishes would seem to occur in this zone.

In the quiet water offshore from, and just below the surge zone the best live coral formations in the Hawaiian waters grow. Here there is also a far greater diversity of fishes than in the surge-scoured area above. Data on the zonation of fishes below this point are scarce. Preliminary information suggests that the differentiation of the fish fauna at deeper levels is far more gradual, and that there is still a considerable number of species to at least half a mile in depth.

Around the high Hawaiian Islands the waters protected by fringing reefs appear to have a mixed zonal fauna containing partly surge zone fishes, partly fishes that come in from quiet, deeper water, and partly forms restricted, so far as known, to such areas.

INTRODUCTION

After 16 years of collecting and observing fishes in Hawaiian waters, it seems well to bring together information obtained on vertical zonation. Though such a summary raises more questions than it answers, it has a number of justifications. In the first place, reports on vertical zonation in fishes are rare, and those that exist deal for the most part with deep-water forms, e.g., Grey 1956. Second, the development and perfection of self-contained (SCUBA) diving gear in the last 20 years has greatly facilitated direct observation of the marine environment down to nearly 100 meters. Third, Hawaiian zonation seems to be rather different from temperate region zonations usually discussed.

With regard to the work upon which this paper is based, several limitations should be noted. Thus, all observations refer to daytime only. Certain Hawaiian fishes seem to make inshore migrations at night, e.g., the blenny *Entomacrodus marmoratus* (see Strasburg 1953), the tiger shark

(*Galeocerdo cuvieri*) and certain jacks (*Caranx*); conversely, certain others move offshore, e.g., the bigeyes (*Priacanthus*) and menpaches (*Myripristis*). However, this about summarizes present knowledge of nocturnal conditions. Second, only adult and half-grown fishes will be dealt with. It may well be that the eggs and larvae occur at different depths from the juveniles and adults, but too little is known about this to warrant discussion. Third, no attempt has been made to analyze possible seasonal differences in the depth zonation of fishes. If there are such in Hawaii, they are not obvious. Fourth, available knowledge concerning Hawaiian fishes dwindles rapidly with depth. Aside from the dredge-haul records in Table I most of the present paper is based on the author's personal observations, which do not extend below 30 meters. Finally, the three available sources of information used here—poison stations, sight records, and dredge hauls—are not exactly comparable to one another. Rotenone poison stations kill primarily those fishes that retreat into bottom cover at the approach of danger; large, free-

[1] Contribution No. 230, Hawaii Marine Laboratory.

Reprinted from *Ecology* 46(6):823–831 (1965), by permission of the author and Duke University Press.

TABLE I. Depth zonation of some Hawaiian inshore bottom-inhabiting fishes

Family and species[a]	Splash zone[b]	Surge zone[c]	Reef-protected zone[d]	Sub-surge zone[e]	Fishes dredged in 30 to 200 m of water[f]
Synodontidae					
Synodus variegatus...........			+	+	+
S. binotatus............				+	+
Saurida gracilis..........			+		+
Trachinocephalus myops.......					+
Muraenidae					
Uropterygius knighti..........		+	+		
U. fuscoguttatus........			+		
U. supraforatus........			+		
Anarchias allardicei..........			+		
A. leucurus..........			+	+	
Muraena pardalis............		+			
Echidna polyzona............		+	+		
Gymnothorax eurostus........		+	+	+	
G. flavimarginatus........		+	+	+	
G. petelli............		+	+	+	
G. steindachneri........			+		
G. undulatus............			+		
G. melatremus............				+	
G. gracilicaudus........				+	
Xenocongridae					
Kaupichthys diodontus........				+	
Chilorhinus platyrhynchus.....					+
Moringuidae					
Moringua macrochir.....			+	+	
Congridae					
Conger marginatus...........		+	+	+	
Ariosoma bowersi.......		+	+	+	+
Ophichthidae					
Muraenichthys cookei.......		+	+		
Schultzidia johnstonensis.....			+		
Callechelys luteus.......			+		
Cirrhimuraena macgregori.....			+		
Myrichthys maculosus........			+		
Phyllophichthus xenodontus....			+	+	
Leiuranus semicinctus........			+	+	
Caecula platyrhyncha........			+	+	+
Caecula flavicauda............			+	+	+
Fistulariidae					
Fistularia petimba............			+		
Aulostomidae					
Aulostomus chinensis........			+		
Macrorhamphosidae					
Macrorhamphosus gracilis.....					+
Syngnathidae					
Doryrhamphus melanopleura...			+		
Syngnathus balli.............			+		
Ichthyocampus erythraeus......					+
Holocentridae					
Holocentrus lacteoguttatus......	+	+	+	+	+
H. spinifer...............				+	
H. tiere.................				+	
H. scythrops.............				+	
H. xantherythrus........				+	
H. diadema.............				+	
Holotrachys lima...........		+	+		
Myripristis multiradiatus.....		+	+		
M. argyromus...........		+	+		
M. berndti..............				+	
Antigoniidae					
Antigonia eos.............					+
Bothidae					
Eothus pantherinus..........			+		
Bothus mancus............			+		+
Parabothus chlorospilus.......					+
Taeniopsetta radula...........					+

Family and species[a]	Splash zone[b]	Surge zone[c]	Reef-protected zone[d]	Sub-surge zone[e]	Fishes dredged in 30 to 200 m of water[f]
Engyprosopon hawaiiensis.....					+
E. xenandrus................					+
Pleuronectidae					
Samariscus triocellatus.......			+	+	
S. corallinus................					+
Poecilopsetta hawaiiensis.....					+
Soleidae					
Aseraggodes kobensis..........				+	
Serranidae					
Pteranthias longimanus........				+	+
Pseudochromidae					
Pseudogramma polyacantha....			+	+	
Kuhliidae					
Kuhlia sandvicensis.........	+	+	+		
Priacanthidae					
Priacanthus cruentatus........		+			
Apogonidae					
Apogon erythrinus...........		+	+	+	
A. maculiferus............			+	+	+
A. waikiki..............			+	+	
A. snyderi..............			+	+	
A. menesemus...........				+	+
A. brachygramma........				+	
Pseudamiops gracilicauda......				+	
Mullidae					
Mulloidichthys samoensis......		+	+		
M. auriflamma...........			+		
Parupeneus porphyreus.......		+	+	+	
P. chryserydros...........			+		
P. multifasciatus.........			+	+	
P. bifasciatus............				+	
P. pleurostigma...........				+	
Scorpididae					
Microcanthus strigatus........		+			
Chaetodontidae					
Centropyge potteri............				+	+
C. fisheri................					+
Heniochus acuminatus........					+
Chaetodon miliaris...........		+	+	+	+
C. lunula............			+	+	
C. auriga............			+	+	
C. fremblii............			+	+	
C. unimaculatus........				+	
C. multicinctus........				+	
C. corallicola........					+
Cirrhitidae					
Paracirrhites cinctus..........		+		+	
P. forsteri............				+	
P. arcatus............				+	
Cirrhitus alternatus........		+		+	
Cirrhitoidea bimacula........			+		
Pomacentridae					
Dascyllus albisella.........				+	
Abudefduf sindonis.........	+	+			
A. sordidus............	+	+	+		
A. imparipennis..........	+	+	+		
A. abdominalis..........		+			
Electroglyphidodon johnstonianus				+	
Pomacentrus jenkinsi........				+	
Chromis ovalis............		+		+	
C. verater............				+	
C. vanderbilti........				+	
C. leucurus............				+	+
Labridae					
Cheilio inermis.............			+		
Bodianus bilunulatus........				+	

TABLE I (continued)

Family and species[a]	Splash zone[b]	Surge zone[c]	Reef-protected zone[d]	Sub-surge zone[e]	Fishes dredged in 30 to 200 m of water[f]
Labroides phthirophagus				+	
Cirrhilabrus jordani					+
Cheilinus bimaculatus					+
Pseudochelinus octotaenia				+	
P. tetrataenia				+	
P. evanidus				+	+
Thalassoma umbrostigma	+	+	+		
T. duperreyi		+	+	+	
T. ballieui		+	+	+	
Gomphosus varius				+	
Coris flavovittata		+	+		
C. venusta		+	+	+	
Stethojulis axillaris		+	+	+	
Novaculichthys bifer			+		
Marcopharyngodon geoffroyi			+		
Anampses cuvieri		+	+	+	
A. godeffroyi				+	
Halichoeres ornatissimus				+	
Scaridae					
Calotomus sandvicensis				+	
Scarus dubius			+	+	
S. perspicillatus			+	+	
Parapercidae					
Osurus schauinslandi					+
Trichonotidae					
Crystallodytescookei		+	+		
Limnichthys donaldsoni				+	
Zanclidae					
Zanclus canescens				+	
Acanthuridae					
Acanthurus sandvicensis	+	+	+	+	
A. guttatus		+			
A. leucopareius		+	+		
A. nigrofuscus		+	+	+	
A. nigroris		+	+	+	
A. olivaceus				+	
Ctenochaetus strigosus				+	
Zebrasoma flavescens				+	
Naso lituratus					+
Eleotridae					
Eviota epiphanes			+	+	
Gobiidae					
Kelloggella oligolepis	+	+			
Bathygobius fuscus	+	+	+		
B. cotticeps		+	+		
Zonogobius farcimen		+	+	+	
Quisquilius eugenius		+	+	+	
Q. aureoviridis				+	
Gnatholepis anjerensis				+	
Fusigobius neophytus				+	
Callionymidae					
Callionymus decoratus				+	+
Synchiropus rubrovinctus					+
Tripterygiidae					
Tripterygion atriceps		+	+		
Blenniidae					
Exallias brevis				+	
Cirripectus lineopunctatus		+			
C. variolosus		+	+		
C. obscurus		+	+		
Entomacrodus marmoratus	+	+	+		
Istiblennius zebra	+				
I. gibbifrons		+	+		
Enchelyurus brunneolus		+			
Brotulidae					
Brotula multibarbata		+	+	+	+
Microbrotula nigra				+	
Carapidae					
Carapus homei				+	+
Scorpaenidae					
Taenianotus triacanthus			+		+
Pterois sphex					+
Dendrochirus brachypterus			+		+
Iracundus signifer					+
Peloropsis xenops					+
Helicolinus rufescens					+
Scorpaenodes parvipinnis			+		
S. guamensis		+	+		+
Scorpaenopsis gibbosa		+	+		
S. cacopsis					+
S. altirostris					+
Merinthe macrocephala					+
Scorpaena ballieui		+	+		
S. coniorta		+			+
S. coloratus					+
Caracanthidae					
Caracanthus maculatus				+	
Dactylopteridae					
Dactyloptena orientalis					+
Pegasidae					
Pegasus papilio					+
Balistidae					
Balistes bursa				+	
Melichthys buniva				+	
Monacanthidae					
Pervagor spilosoma				+	+
Cantherines sandwichiensis				+	
Ostraciontidae					
Ostracion lentiginosus		+	+	+	
Lactoria fornasini			+	+	
Aracana aculeata					+
Canthigasteridae					
Canthigaster amboinensis		+	+		
C. jactator		+	+		
C. cinctus					+
Antennariidae					
Antennarius bigibbus		+		+	+
A. drombus		+		+	
Phrynelox cunninghami					+
Ogcocephalidae					
Halieutaea retifera					+

[a] The species names and the order in which the families and genera are listed are those of Gosline and Brock (1960); species within genera are in order of depth.

[b] Comprises the pools caused by intermittent waves or spray; species list based on Strasburg (1953, p. 109 to 110).

[c] Comprises open coastal areas of continuous or nearly continuous, horizontally moving surge; species list based on two rotenone poison stations, one off Kaena Point and the other off Makapuu Point, Oahu—maximum depth of water 4 meters.

[d] Species list based on two rotenone poison stations, one from along the edge of a cut in the reef off Hauula Park and the other from a small semienclosed bay near Kahuku, Oahu—maximum depth 5 meters.

[e] Species list based on two rotenone poison stations run from boats, one in 8 to 12 meters of water outside the Waikiki reef and the other off Waimea, Oahu, in 10 to 25 meters of water.

[f] Species list based on hitherto unreported fishes dredged by the *Miss Honolulu* plus those published by Gilbert (1905; the numerous species recorded by Gilbert only from water deeper than 200 meters are not included).

swimming fishes that react to rotenone by abrupt departure from the area are rarely taken. On the other hand the observer in the water (Brock 1954) tends to notice the larger, less secretive fishes and is generally surprised to find how many small or crevice-living fishes, e.g., eels, are killed by poison in an area he has been carefully observing. Fortunately, the results from sight transect records and from rotenone stations can be checked against one another, for some of each have frequently been made in the same area. The few relatively deep-water dredge hauls have still a different bias. Most bottoms around Oahu are not only rocky but rugged (Gilbert 1905, p. 577). Dredge hauls, however, effectively sample only the sand and rubble bottoms. This ecological restriction of dredge-haul samples is difficult to evaluate, since no hard-bottom material from similar depths is available. (In Table I fishes regularly occurring in splash pools and all of those that have been dredged in Hawaiian waters between 30 and 200 meters have been listed. In addition, all species from certain selected rotenone poison stations have been tabulated; the basis for selection here has been for successful stations run within and not between the zones they are supposed to represent. It is hoped and believed that Table I gives a moderately good, though by no means all-inclusive representation of the commoner Hawaiian inshore bottom fishes. A number of the observations discussed elsewhere in the paper are not included in Table I.)

THE HAWAIIAN INSHORE MARINE

ENVIRONMENT

The Hawaiian Islands extend some 1,600 miles from east-southeast to west-northwest (Zimmerman 1948; Gosline and Brock 1960). As with all oceanic islands, there is no continental shelf, although a certain amount of benching has occurred (Wentworth 1938, 1939; Stearns and Vaksvik 1935, p. 37 to 39). Runoff from the land seems to have slight effect on the inshore environment except in a few semienclosed areas, e.g., Pearl Harbor, Kaneohe Bay. Associated at least in part with the paucity of runoff is a general clarity of the water. Temperatures are fairly warm. Offshore around Oahu, the island from which the great majority of the data for the present paper was gathered, surface temperatures range only between 75°F in March and 81°F in September; a virtually isothermal layer extends down from the surface to about 80 m in March and 50 m in September (Leipper and Anderson 1959). Finally, the whole Hawaiian chain lies in the zone of the northeast trades. These blow at 10 to 20

knots for half to three quarters of the year. Only a few of the high islands form sufficient obstruction to the trades to provide a lee; on the other hand these same high islands are close enough together to form wind funnels and hence increased wind intensity in the channels between them. During the winter, the southern (leeward) shores are subject to heavy surge action originating in local storms that break up the trade wind regime.

The western half of the Hawaiian chain is made up entirely of low atolls. There, the islands are formed of calcareous beach rock, sand, and rubble. The eastern members of the chain (principally Kauai through Hawaii) are high, volcanic islands fringed only in part by reef; elsewhere, except for benching, the slope of the islands above and below sea level is about the same. There is no abrupt transition along the chain from atolls to high islands. All were once volcanic; it is merely that at the older, western end of the chain calcareous material precipitated from sea water has covered over the basalt, which has eroded away, sunk, or both. Oahu is something of a special case among the Hawaiian Islands in that a good proportion of its shore line has been affected by human activities of various sort, from dredging (Moberly 1963) to fishing.

So far as the fishes themselves are concerned, all of the inshore forms are of Indo-West Pacific derivation (Ekman 1953). Though the Hawaiian fish fauna may be somewhat impoverished by Central Pacific standards, it is not more than slightly disharmonic, i.e., unbalanced (Gosline 1955; Gosline and Brock 1960). There appears to be no great difference between the fishes of the eastern and western end of the chain.

VERTICAL ZONATION

In the account that follows an attempt will be made to relate differences in the vertical distributions of fish species to certain physical factors that vary with depth. It seems well to introduce this relationship by a brief discussion of the kind of vertical zonation that occurs in Hawaiian fishes.

There are of course major groups, e.g., the blennies (Blenniidae), restricted to shallow waters; and others found only in deep water, e.g., in Hawaii the Ogcocephalidae, with every conceivable type of intermediacy represented. More instructive, however, are those instances where different members of a single genus have different vertical distributions. Only enough of the clear-cut examples in this category will be cited to demonstrate that no simple pattern can be fitted to such data.

There are some fish genera in which the Hawaiian species seem to replace each other at adjacent depths. Thus the eggs, juveniles, and adults of the goby *Bathygobius fuscus* all live in high pools or reef-protected areas, whereas *B. cotticeps* has only been taken along open rocky coasts in areas of continuous water where there is frequently heavy surge. Somewhat lower down, the half-grown and adult goatfishes of the genus *Mulloidichthys* form another replacement series. The silvery *M. samoensis* is the shore form, coming into water of a few feet of depth in reef-protected areas, followed farther out by the pinkish *M. auriflamma*, with the large red *M. pflugeri* the deepest-water member of the series. Unlike *Bathygobius*, however, the larval *Mulloidichthys* are planktonic; whether or not there is a differential depth zonation in the larvae of its three species is unknown.

Another sort of vertical differentiation is that in which a genus has one species that comes distinctly farther into shallow water than others. (The converse of this—where one species penetrates into distinctly deeper water—is probably equally common but less well known.) The squirrel fish *Holocentrus lacteoguttatus* is an example in which apparently all but the larval stages may be found in the surge zone and in surge pools; however, *H. lacteoguttatus* also extends down through the vertical ranges of other species of the genus and has been taken in dredge hauls (Table I). *Acanthurus sandvicensis* is unique among Hawaiian surgeonfishes in that the larvae come in to the highest available pools to transform and then work their way back out to sea with growth (Randall 1961); the depth range of the adults, however, is approximately that of the genus *Acanthurus*, except *A. thompsoni*.

One can only summarize these different zonal relationships by saying that they are complex. The factors that cause these differences in zonation are unknown.

In dealing with the physical factors of the environment, it seems best to start with open rocky coasts. Reef-fringed shores present complications that will be discussed subsequently; and sand, on the high Hawaiian Islands is a somewhat discontinuous as well as a secondary phenomenon (Moberly 1963).

On the open coasts which surround the majority of the high Hawaiian Islands, a primary physical factor influencing the shore environment from the highest pools to some 10 to 20 m below sea level is wave action. Tides are wholly secondary. The difference between high and low tides in Hawaii is about a meter. On a relatively calm day the difference between the crest of a breaking wave and the trough following it is equal to that, and

with heavy surge may go to three to four times as much (cf. Wentworth 1938, p. 10 to 12).

Three examples will perhaps bring home the difference in importance between the waves and tide in Hawaii. 1)—During my first year I selected an exceptionally low tide for a class collecting station, locating in advance an appropriate "tide pool" on the lee (Waianae) coast. However, on the appointed day the surge had risen; the whole area of the "tide pool" was a continuous mass of white water and it was not even possible to locate the pool selected. 2)—On another (the Waimea) coast, many of the benches slightly above high tide are ordinarily covered with a heavy growth of algae. In some years, however, there has been during the summer an exceptional period of 2 or 3 weeks of calm water. At the ends of such periods these benches have been covered with dead, brown, rotting vegetation. 3)—On the same (Waimea) coast a juvenile fish of the bass-like species *Kuhlia sandvicensis* was found in a pool on top of a sheer drop into the sea of about 5 m. Since *K. sandvicensis* is not a fish that travels over land, there seems no convincing way it could have gotten into the pool except via wave action against the rock face.

Because of the above and countless other examples that could be given, descriptive terms based on wave action, e.g., splash pools, surge zone, etc., would seem to be far more appropriate for open Hawaiian coasts than those associated with tides. An added consideration is this. The splash pools may have essentially the same fishes but be considerably higher above mean tide level on an open, windward shore, e.g., along the Molokai (Kaiwi) Channel coast of Oahu, than in a semiprotected area, e.g., Hanauma Bay (cf. Wentworth 1938, p. 30).

The surge, however, continues its primary effect on the inshore area for some distance below as well as above mean tide level. Over deep water, of course, any particle at the surface moves principally up and down as the wave itself passes by horizontally. But as a wave moves into shallower water there comes a point at which the water itself moves almost horizontally (cf. King 1963, p. 200). At and inshore from this point the horizontal movement of the water will not only carry suspended objects with it but will roil up and carry along bottom particles, e.g., sand. This horizontal wave motion, which begins in depths considerably greater than that in which the wave breaks, results in a scouring action on the bottom wherever there is sand in the area.

Along open coasts the growth of corals and macroscopic algae is low in this surge-affected zone, even on hard bottoms. The depth and extent to which the sweeping, scouring action of the surge will be effective will depend upon the degree to which the coast is protected by reef and whether it is on the windward or lee side of an island. Everywhere, however, an area of unscoured bottom in quiet water is sooner or later reached (cf. Trask 1955). It is in the upper levels of such quiet water that the most luxuriant growth of coral occurs in Hawaii. Sometimes, in semi-protected areas like Hanauma Bay this may take place at a mere 3 to 8 m depth; in heavy surge areas off headlands, however, such coral growth as occurs is probably restricted to depths of 20 m or more.

Before dealing with the sharp zonal boundary between fishes in the surge-affected areas and those living in the quiet water below, certain major differences between the upper and lower limits of the surge-affected area itself must be noted.

At the upper limit and generally well above high tide level, the first standing water to be encountered is in spray pools. These may be largely fresh water at some times and dry at others. They contain no fishes. Only slightly lower, however, fishes begin to appear. In general, from the uppermost inhabited pools down to sea level the pools become larger, deeper, more frequently replenished by sea water, and richer in plant and animal life.

Though there is no distinct line of demarcation between the lowermost surge pools and the surge-affected shores of the open ocean, two factors usually differentiate them. One is that the pools tend to form somewhat protected pockets behind the shore face against which the main force of the waves is expended. The other is that such pools are usually too small for permanent residence and too difficult of access for larger fishes to encourage transient foraging; in any event, medium and large fishes are rarely found in such pools. Both of these reasons perhaps contribute to an explanation of why surge pools so often serve as incubators for juvenile fishes. In sum, it seems well in a study of fish zonation to differentiate the frequently isolated pools (Table I, "Splash zone") from the seaward-facing slope of the surge zone (Table I, "Surge zone").

The few species inhabiting the upper splash pools are ecologically well distinguished from one another. Here only four of the predominating forms will be mentioned: a blenny (*Istiblennius zebra*) and a goby (*Bathygobious fuscus*), both rather small fishes which become adult and breed in the pools; and the bass-like *Kuhlia sandvicensis* and a surgeonfish, *Acanthurus sandvicensis*, both

larger species using the pools as an incubator for the young, which move back out to sea as they grow up. *Istiblennius* and *Bathygobius* rest on the bottom; the former frequently jumps across from pool to pool (Strasburg 1953), and *Bathygobius* is said to do so (Hiatt and Strasburg 1960) p. 104). *Kuhlia* and *Acanthurus*, by contrast, are free swimming and appear to need continuous water to get about. The main sources of food of the four species are quite different, though all are opportunists. *Istiblennius* scrapes precipitated detritus (leptopel) from the bottom with its close-set, hair-like teeth (Strasburg 1953). *Acanthurus* juveniles nip off the tips of delicate algal fronds with incisiform teeth (Randall 1961). *Bathygobius* is a generalized bottom-feeding carnivore (Hiatt and Strasburg 1960, p. 104). Juveniles of *Kuhlia* are omnivorous, eating everything from algae to terrestrial animals that get swept into the pools (Tester and Takata 1953); they differ from *Bathygobius* in being mostly midwater feeders and will rise to the surface for floating insects, etc.

Aside from the splash and surge pools there is only one habitat above the frontal slope that is inhabited by any Hawaiian fishes. This is the weed-covered but otherwise periodically exposed lower bench where another blenny, *Entomacrodus marmoratus*, and that species only, is frequently encountered (Strasburg 1953).

The frontal slopes of open shores and such wave-scoured areas of the bottom as extend out from below them have a fish fauna that is richer in species than that of the surge pools but much more limited than that of the quiet, deeper water below (Table I). The whole zone is subject, at least at times, to heavy surge pounding and, in places at least, to scouring by sand, coral rubble, etc.

Much of the frontal slope, at least on basalt shores, is covered with a thin veneer of a pink coralline alga, *Porolithon* (see Strasburg 1953, p. 88). Along the top of this *Porolithon* zone lives the sea urchin *Podophora atrata* and one or more species of grapsoid crabs (Edmondson 1946). Lower down, the face of the frontal slope is often riddled with the borings of the urchin *Echinometra mathei*. The sea urchin *Podophora* and the coralline and other algae in the area may form a potential food source to fishes; however, they live so high in the splash zone as to have a very limited availability. In any event I have never seen fishes feeding on them. Below mean water line in the surge zone, the rocks are neither riddled with urchins nor conspicuously covered with algae. Such algae as cover the rocks are in the form of a short fuzzy nap; preliminary experiments by Randall (1955, p. 250) indicate that the shortness of the algae in this zone is due to grazing, especially by fishes.

Living on and in this surge-affected zone is a number of small carnivorous fishes such as the damselfishes *Abudefduf imparipennis* and in places *A. sindonis,* the wrasse *Thalassoma umbrostigma,* and the goby *Bathygobius cotticeps.* Larger carnivores like the jacks, *Caranx,* undoubtedly enter the area from time to time. But the great majority of fishes in this zone are grazers or detritus feeders. The damselfish *Pomacentrus jenkinsi* is a detritus feeder as are the blennies of the genus *Cirripectus.* All of the fishes mentioned above except *Caranx* somehow live most of their lives in the surge zone, retreating to holes, etc. for protection. However, on a relatively quiet day (which is the only kind of day one can observe the surge area), the most conspicuous fishes are the grazing surgeonfishes and parrot fishes. Several kinds of surgeonfishes occur here. The relatively large *Acanthurus guttatus* is generally found farthest inshore in areas of white water. Tremendous schools of adult *A. sandvicensis* may be seen outside the white water zone, cropping the rocks somewhat like a flock of sheep. The parrotfishes around Oahu tend to be more solitary, probably because they are avidly speared for food, but on the less frequented leeward Hawaiian Islands they also form great shoals. The parrotfishes bite pieces off the rock and coral, whereas the surgeonfishes nip off any strand of alga close to its base. At its face value the observed aggregations of moderate to large fishes in the surge zone would indicate a rather rich habitat. This may, however, be an observational artifact arising from the circumstance that the calmer periods permitting a swimmer to observe in this zone also present the principal opportunities fishes have to graze there. (Conversely, it may be that the presence of as much algae as there is in the surge zone is due to the fact that the grazers can only occasionally manage to crop it.)

With regard to the few carnivorous fishes living in the surge zone, the question arises of whether this paucity is due to the physical or to the biological environment or to both. Several comments have a possible bearing on but provide no solution to this question. First, where any sand is available in a generally rocky surge zone, additional, burrowing carnivores are found, for example, the eel *Uropterygius knighti* and the small trichonotid *Crystallodytes cookei.* Whether they find food as well as shelter in a loose bottom is unknown. Second, large offshore carnivores could presumably come into the surge zone along with the grazers

on calm days. Around the high Hawaiian Islands they do not seem to do so, but this may be because of human fishing pressure (compare Hiatt and Strasburg's 1960 account of the fauna of Marshallese surge channels). Finally, one of the principal permanent surge zone residents, *Abudefduf imparipennis,* has a diet rather highly restricted to one species of worm; on the other hand a suggestion that this same species may have problems of coping with the physical environment is suggested by the fact that the only large aggregation of ripe individuals ever taken was from a protected area well out of the surge (both of these are unpublished observations).

So far as the bottom-inhabiting fishes are concerned the greatest vertical differentiation is between the surge-scoured zone and the deeper, quieter water below. As already noted, the latter area has the best coral growth in Hawaii. The variety of both food and shelter for small fishes is greatly increased and the total number of species goes up accordingly. One rather striking exception to this increase in number of fish species in deeper water should be noted, namely that the grazers and detritus feeders tend to drop out. For example, none of our blennies are known from water deeper than perhaps 20 m. The surgeonfishes have only one species in depths over 75 m, and that is the apparently carnivorous *Acanthurus thompsoni* (Randall 1956).

In these quiet waters below the effects of wave action, the surge zone fishes are sometimes replaced by others of the same genus, e.g., the eel *Uropterygius knighti* by other species of *Uropterygius* and the related *Anarchias* (Table I). Sometimes the replacement is on a generic level; thus the damselfishes of the genus *Abudefduf* are mostly found in the surge zone while those of the genera *Chromis* and *Dascyllus* are largely quiet water forms. At still other times whole families drop out, e.g., the blennies; and others come in, e.g., in Hawaii, the groupers (Serranidae). A far commoner phenomenon than any of these, however, is to have a family or genus represented by one species in the surge zone and several in the quiet water below, e.g., the wrasses (Labridae), butterflyfishes (Chaetodontidae), angler fishes (Antennariidae), etc.

Turning now to sandy areas, the same surge vs. sub-surge zone distinction is present, though perhaps less clear-cut and certainly less well investigated. Thus, a couple of poorly known species seem to be limited to the surge zone, i.e., the dragonet *Pogonymus pogognathus* and the flatfish *Engyprosopon arenicola* (incorrectly synonymized with the deeper water *E. hawaiiensis* by Gosline and Brock 1960). The burrowing trichonotid *Crystallodytes cookei* of the surge zone has on at least one occasion been taken in deeper water along with the related *Limnichthys donaldsoni,* and the burrowing eel *Caecula platyrhyncha* occurs principally in the surge zone, but also, with *C. flavicauda,* in deeper water.

Though the distinction between a Hawaiian open-coast surge zone and an adjacent one of deeper quiet water is sharp, the impression should not be given that it is absolute. There are some Hawaiian fishes that seem to range more or less indiscriminately from the upper surge zone down to 50 m or more of depth; the surgeonfish *Acanthurus sandvicensis,* the damselfish *Pomacentrus jenkinsi,* and the butterflyfish *Chaetodon miliaris* are examples. (It may have some significance that in Hawaii these three species are the commonest forms of their respective families.)

However, on open coasts the mixing of surge zone and sub-surge zone fishes is minor compared to that which occurs in areas of coast protected by a fringing reef. Behind such a reef all sorts of combinations of surge zone and sub-surge fishes occur depending on the amount of protection afforded by the reef. Thus the pomacentrid *Dascyllus albisella* normally found in the deep water beyond the effect of the surge may occur abundantly in quiet water a few feet in depth in reef-protected Kaneohe Bay. Again the sand-burrowing eel *Ariosoma bowersi* has been taken from a well-protected surge pool in 1½ m of water and has also been dredged from 100 m. Examples of this sort could be multiplied at length. Perhaps more interesting is the fact that in addition there is a number of species that have yet to be taken anywhere in Hawaii except behind fringing reefs. The burrowing eel *Muraenichthys cookei* and the blenny *Istiblennius gibbifrons* are examples. In these and other instances no particular reason for the restriction can be suggested. In still other examples, however, species seem to be limited to habitats only found behind reefs. Thus, the eleotrid *Asterropteryx semipunctatus* seems to be restricted in habitat to holes in silt around the base of dead coral.

Around the high Hawaiian Islands the reef-protected coasts are important but by no means universal. On atolls, however, a great portion of whatever shallow-water habitats exist are reef protected. Indeed, on such atolls there is frequently a species replacement of those forms found on the lagoon side and the offshore side of any reef. Such a differentiation is at best incipient in Hawaii, though it does seem to be exemplified by

the anchovy species pair *Stolephorus purpureus* and *S. buccaneeri.*

In depths greater than 30 m a whole series of fishes are known that have never been seen or taken at lesser depths. Some such species are members of families otherwise well represented in shallower water. The hawkfish *Oxycirrhites typus* and apparently the butterflyfish *Chaetodon tinkeri* (compare Hubbs and Rechnitzer 1958) are examples. Sometimes, as with the Hawaiian scorpaenids and flounders, there are a few inshore species but the majority are deep-water forms. Finally there is a whole host of families only known from Hawaii in deep water. In some instances, as apparently with the Peristediidae, etc., these families are everywhere restricted to deep water, but other families, e.g., the Lutjanidae and Serranidae, are elsewhere abundantly represented by inshore forms.

The vertical zonation beyond the surge zone in Hawaii seems to be gradual so far as known. Thus the burrowing eel *Caecula flavicauda,* fairly common in some areas at 16 m, has also been dredged from sand in 250 m of water. As to the deeper-water species, the serranid *Caesioperca thomsoni* seems to be restricted, so far as observed, to waters of over 70 m off Waikiki but has been seen at some 25 m of depth a few miles along the coast. On the basis of this and other quite scanty data it appears that "deep-water" species may come in to relatively shallow areas under certain ecological conditions. However, far too little is known of zonation below 30 m to draw definite conclusions. One point can be made with some assurance. There is every indication from dredging (Gilbert 1905), from the fishes taken off the 1950 lava flow (Gosline, Brock, Moore and Yamaguchi 1954), and from deep-water shark catches (unpublished data) that an abundant fish fauna occurs around the Hawaiian Islands to depths of at least half a mile. Evidence of the variety of this fauna is the 30 families of fishes so far known in Hawaiian waters only from depths greater than 200 m (Gilbert 1905).

Acknowledgments

Under the auspices of the Bernice P. Bishop Museum, the *Miss Honolulu* made a series of dredge hauls for shells in the summer of 1959. The fishes from these hauls were picked out by T. Matsui and, through the kindness of the Bishop Museum, turned over to me. They form the major portion of the dredge-haul data reported here.

My colleagues, B. S. Muir and R. Moberly, Jr. have made constructive comments toward the improvement of the manuscript, for which I am deeply grateful.

Literature Cited

Brock, V. E. 1954. A preliminary report on a method of estimating reef fish populations. J. Wildl. Mgmt. 18: 289-308.

Edmondson, C. H. 1946. Reef and shore fauna of Hawaii. Bernice P. Bishop Mus. Spec. Pub. 22: 1-381. (Revised Edition)

Ekman, S. 1953. Zoogeography of the sea. Sidgwick and Jackson, London.

Gilbert, C. H. 1905. The aquatic resources of the Hawaiian Islands. Part II, Section II. The deep-sea fishes. Bull. U. S. Fish Comm. 23(2): 575-713.

Gosline, W. A. 1955. The inshore fish fauna of Johnston Island, a Central Pacific atoll. Pacific Sci. 9: 442-480.

—— and V. E. Brock. 1960. Handbook of Hawaiian Fishes. University of Hawaii Press, Honolulu.

——, ——, H. L. Moore and Y. Yamaguchi. 1954. Fishes killed by the 1950 eruption of Mauna Loa. I. The origin and nature of the collections. Pacific Sci. 8: 23-27.

Grey, M. 1956. The distributon of fishes found below a depth of 2000 meters. Fieldiana: Zoology 36(2): 77-337.

Hiatt, R. W., and D. W. Strasburg. 1960. Ecological relationships of the fish fauna on coral reefs of the Marshall Islands. Ecol. Monogr. 30: 65-127.

Hubbs, C. L., and A. B. Rechnitzer. 1958. A new fish, *Chaetodon falcifer*, from Guadalupe Island, Baja California, with notes on related species. Proc. California Acad. Sci. (4)29(8): 273-313.

King, C. A. M. 1963. An introduction to oceanography. McGraw Hill, New York.

Leipper, D. F., and E. R. Anderson. 1950. Sea temperatures, Hawaiian Island area. Pacific Sci. 4: 228-248.

Moberly, R., Jr. 1963. Coastal geology of Hawaii. Hawaii Institute of Geophysics Report No. 41, 215 pp. Mimeographed.

Randall, J. E. 1955. A contribution to the biology of the Acanthuridae (surgeonfishes). University of Hawaii Ph.D. Thesis. 422 p.

——. 1956. A revision of the surgeonfish genus *Acanthurus*. Pacific Sci. 10: 159-235.

——. 1961. A contribution to the biology of the convict surgeonfish of the Hawaiian Islands, *Acanthurus triostegus sandvicensis*. Pacific Sci. 15: 215-272.

Stearns, H. T., and K. N. Vaksvik. 1935. Geology and ground-water resources of the Island of Oahu, Hawaii. Hawaii Div. Hydrography, Bull. 1. 479 p.

Strasburg, D. W. 1953. The comparative ecology of two salariin blennies. University of Hawaii Ph.D. Thesis. 266 p.

Tester, A. L., and M. Takata. 1953. Contribution to the biology of the aholehole, a potential baitfish. Hawaii Industrial Research Advisory Council Grant No. 29, Final Report. 54 p.

Trask, P. D. 1955. Movements of sand around Southern California promontories. Beach Erosion Bd., Tech. Mem. No. 76. (Not seen)

Wentworth, C. K. 1938. Marine bench-forming processes: water-level weathering. J. Geomorphol. 1: 6-32.

——. 1939. Marine bench-forming processes. II, solution benching. J. Geomorphol. 2: 3-25.

Zimmerman, E. C. 1948. Insects of Hawaii. Vol. 1. Introduction. University of Hawaii Press, Honolulu.

PIONEER INTERTIDAL POPULATION AND THE RELATED GENERAL VERTICAL DISTRIBUTION OF MARINE ALGAE IN HAWAII [1]

MAXWELL S. DOTY

Botany Department, University of Hawaii, Honolulu, Hawaii

On the island of Hawaii lava flows have run down the slopes of the active volcanoes and into the sea in both prehistoric and historic times. The events leading to establishment of their marine algal populations have been followed closely on several 1955 flows [2] (Fig. 1) with comparative observations being made on nearby prehistoric shores. The nature of the observations made and the major conclusions are reported here for these events, which seem to have been nearly ideal demonstrations of a number of major ecological phenomena. Likewise the opportunity is seized to describe the general vertical distribution pattern of the mature algal communities in this tropical part of the world, something that has not been done previously in this detail.

Without going into the possible tide level relationships of the different apparently dominant species (Fig. 2), generally *Ahnfeltia concinna* (*19682* [3])) is the highest-growing conspicuous macroscopic alga on a prehistoric steep basalt shore in Hawaii. This species forms a yellow bunchy cover on the rocks with individual fronds often 25 centimeters long. At a distance it reminds one [4] familiar with North Atlantic coasts of the similarly located yellow-brown stands of *Fucus* or *Pelvetia*. Such horizontally extensive populations with sharply defined upward and downward limits and seen one above the other are called zones. In a place where wave action dominates tidal action, as generally true in Hawaii, there are usually but 3 major intertidal zones. Note the variation in their standing crops with elevation and their often-sharp upper and lower limits in the successive zones as indicated in the 'blown up' part of Figure 3A.

The zone just below the *Ahnfeltia* is generally of about the same width as the *Ahnfeltia* zone itself. It is usually (between the parallel heavy lines in Fig. 2) one of several sorts: merely for the most part black rock; populated with *Ulva fasciata*; populated with *Ralfsia pangoensis* (*13201*) above and the *Ulva* below, or dominated by crustose corallines which seem to be largely *Porolithon onkodes*. Of course there are locations where there are mixtures of all three or other species. *Caulacanthus ustulatus* (*20074*) occurs here, too. Sometimes this zone is subdivided with the rock of the lower part coated with crustose coralline algae, the upper part with non-coralline algae. The corallines low

---

[1] Contribution no. 264 from the Hawaii Institute of Marine Biology. Financial support for this work from U.S. National Science Foundaticn grant G-1992 and U.S. Atomic Energy Commission contract AT-(04-3)-235, Project Agreement no. 4, is gratefully acknowledged.

Acknowledgement is also made here of the conscientious assistance rendered this and other of the author's phycological research problems by Dr. Josephine Koster, though she was certainly not always aware of the considerable value nor the application of the help given.

[2] The area of concern is near 19° 30' N and 154° 30' W.

[3] Such numbers are the author's collection numbers and appear on the labels of the voucher specimens.

[4] Dickie (1876: 454) also mentions this resemblance when writing of the algae collected on the island of Hawaii, at Hilo, by H. N. Moseley on the Challenger Expedition.

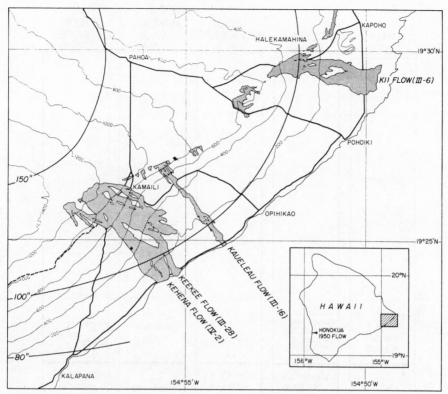

Figure 1. Map of the 1955 lava flow from the east rift of the volcano Kilauea on the island of Hawaii (see inset) in the Central Pacific Ocean. The dates on which the seaward end of the lava ceased to flow are indicated along with the names of the individual flows studied. The light topographic contour lines indicate elevation above sea level in feet. The dark contour lines indicate annual rainfall in inches.

in this zone (Fig. 3A) may be rough-surfaced or produce small Porolithon-type [5] (*13202*) heads. Such animals as *Podophora pedifera* (sea urchin), *Drupa ricinus* (shelled gastropod), and *Helcioniscus exaratus* (limpet), when present, are here.

The next zone down (below the two heavy parallel lines in Figs. 2 & 3A) is comparatively as broad as or even broader than the two above together. It is underlain by smooth crustose coralline algae, often covered with a *Gelidium* (*13194*) and yet smaller species. At the lowest common level of the waves, the dense *Gelidium* cover rather abruptly terminates. When working on prehistoric shores the abrupt upper limit of this alga (Fig. 3A) provides a convenient level from which to measure vertical distribution; when under water the abrupt lower edge is similarly useful.

About 2 meters below the bottom of the *Gelidium* an algal stubble becomes dominant and is conspicuous for at least 5 meters on down. Conspicuous elements in this stubble are *Dictyota friabilis* (*13199*) and a *Griffithsia* (*13240*) as well as the small algae commonly found in the *Gelidium* communities and especially well developed in pools. *Pocilopora*,

<hr>

[5]) The only saxicolous melobesioid coralline identified in this environment on the new solid substratum has been *Porolithon onkodes* (Heydrich) Foslie.

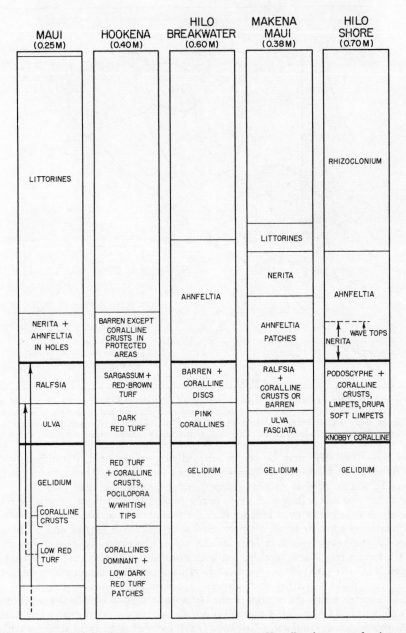

Figure 2. The vertical distribution patterns common to mature Hawaiian shore areas for three places on the island of Hawaii and two places on the nearby island of Maui. The distance in meters given at the top of each strip is the distance between the two horizontal dark lines across it and, thus, provides a scale for that strip. The necessity for different scales in this area where the tidal phenomena are relatively uniform is correlated with differing degrees of wave action.

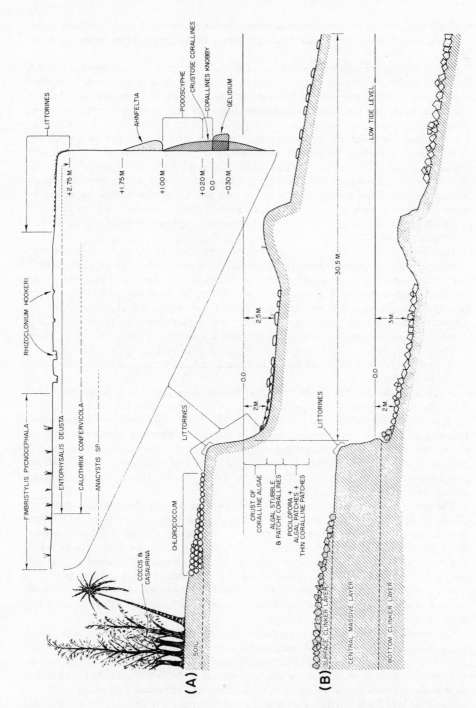

Figure 3. Profiles through shores on the island of Hawaii from the levels that are definitely terrestrial to those that are about 6 meters below low tide line. The vertical distributional features of the populations are drawn to scale but not the horizontal and geological details. (A) Represents a mature shore near Hilo with insets to show in greater detail the distributions of various intertidal and near-shore populations. (B) Represents an idealized section through a shore formed by the erosion of a lava flow perhaps one year old as described in the text for the 1955 Kehena and Kaueleau flows.

the only conspicuous coelenterate coral seen, appears regularly at about 3 meters below low tide level with the individual heads perhaps 3 meters apart down to the -8 meter level.

No really sharp limits below the bottom of the *Gelidium* have been observed in Hawaii. From the results of dredging it appears that the algal standing crop may actually increase once depths below those affected by wave action are reached. The crustose corallines extend on below the *Gelidium*-covered zone (Figs. 2 & 3A), often completely covering all consolidated rock surfaces down to a depth of 1 to 1.5 meters below low tide line. They extend much further down (certainly beyond -100 meters) but as a gradually thinner cover, becoming yet thinner and covering the surface less completely as greater depths are reached. Preliminary explorations in a small research submarine to depths of -160 meters and the results from dredging indicate the species are not greatly different from those nearer the surface though some, such as *Codium phasmaticum*, appear to be more abundant in deeper water and others, such as *Codium mammilosum*, are restricted to subtidal levels. In the greatest depths most remaining species are merely more delicate and further apart.

The observations on the 1955 lava where it went into the sea were made not only to provide a record of events but to provide a series of special observations to test certain hypotheses concerning the development of intertidal populations. These hypotheses are, largely, concerned with the separation and distinction of succession and periodicity, the events in zonation, the regulation of climax formation, and classification of the different algae and other organisms according to the part they play in the populating process. Testing, observation, and experimentation elsewhere (Northcraft, 1948; Fahey & Doty, 1949; Fahey, 1953) have been concerned with surfaces such as concrete, old rock, or wood brought to the sea for the first time, denuded surfaces, and (e.g., Williams, 1965) glass slides.

In the intertidal regions of the Hawaiian Islands there are historic lava flows dated from about 1750 down to the present. None of them has quite the same population on it as is to be found on the adjacent, probably much older, undated or prehistoric lava shores. This is a problem for, in studies elsewhere, intertidal observation has led us to expect five or six years for the climax situation to become established. Indeed, perhaps because of the few years involved, some have said that in the case of intertidal populations there was 'direct development' of the mature or climax population. Fahey reviewed (1953) this situation briefly.

The initial hypotheses were that this phenomenon of slow development toward a climax situation was related to the chemical or physical composition of the lava. These hypotheses were unsupported or negated by a few simple experiments and measurements. For example, chunks from recent and old lava flows of different dates, composition, and physical surface were seated in concrete blocks, sometimes enclosed in wooden forms, and exposed in the sea. It was found that the pioneer and secondary populants that did appear during the course of the experiment developed about the same on all surfaces exposed, including the wood and concrete. The chemical, physical, and age differences seemed to have no influence.

Chemically the hot lava, being cooled in contact with sea water (Macdonald, 1959) at the Kaueleau site, was not altered. Samples of the water washing the rocks shortly after they had begun to develop algal populations had about the same phosphate content as samples of water from offshore or that washing the prehistoric shores. Again, chemical differences were not found to substantiate the chemical difference hypothesis.

The 1955 lava flows ran into the sea along a shore (Fig. 1) where there was very little sand. Shortly after the flows had cooled, extensive beaches of black sand were seen extending along the shores to the left and right of the new lava flows. Uniform samples of the water washing the intertidal surfaces were taken from near the 1955 flows and from near the much older undated flows. These revealed a measurably larger amount of sand and sediment in the water from the new flow areas. Rigg (1914) and Dawson (1954: 10) both comment on the denuding action of such volcanic pumice and sand on nearby populations. In our case, no such observation of the removal of old nearby populations was made. With time, as determined by successive observation, this sand moved off or away (initially often moving inland) from these first formed beaches. As it has moved away so have the algal populations become established and stable.

Not finding chemical nature or sand erosion a factor, a different hypothesis finally arose after following the populations on these 1955 intertidal lava flow surfaces for some time. This is to the effect that the substratum must be so stabilized that it will remain effectively constant for at least the five or six years we expect it takes a climax population to appear. Here a small dated flow that has not yet worn back to the general coast line does not bear a sere-wise mature population. Surely large flows, like the flow nearby which went into the sea in 1961, will form permanent contour modifications that will be populated with a climax population in some years. The 1750 flow on the island of Maui should be studied in this regard. Erosion of the 1955 lava shores was rapid and, in some cases, several meters of the new lava surface were removed in but a few months. In passing, it may be noted that the Honokua 1950 lava flow (see inset in Fig. 1) at Hookena was so worn back, in late 1955, that in many places the massive basalt face of the prehistoric flow under it was again exposed to the sea and on it was a well established algal population. We note too that the breakwater around the harbor at Hilo thirty odd miles away and which was made of large stones in recent years now bears a more mature population than one would expect if it were a lava flow of similar age and exposure.

Stability of the shore is not restricted to the solid rock of the massive part of a lava flow (Fig. 3). As indicated by the contrast between Figures 3A and 3B, there is a change in the boulders on the euphotic sea bottom with time as well. Not only did the rocks in the sea fronting the Kehena flow become smaller, more closely packed, and more rounded, they also became more completely populated, largely by crustose algae. Early visits to the area were marked by recorded notes of the frequency with which stones were seen thrown by wave action beyond the splash of the water itself. Likewise, moving stones were often seen while skin and SCUBA diving. The author observed stones, adjudged to be of 7 to 12 centimeter dimensions, in the turbulent water at 0.3 to 0.7 meters off the bottom during a period of unusually rough seas while swimming under the larger breaking waves after having been washed off the study area. Observations have not been made in the water at this place under just such conditions during the last few years, but the impression is that the closely packed stones on the bottom are fewer, more uniformly dense, of rounded contour, more mechanically stable in form, and not moving as freely as they did during the first two years of the study. Again, the populations on them developed as the available surfaces became more stable.

In June, 1955, one of the dominant algae on the 1955 lavas was *Liagora maxima* [6]). It was present both on prehistoric lava near the 1955 Keekee flow (*12801*) and on the 1955 Kehena flow (*12802* & *12806*). This alga was much less evident in November (*13032*) and in December, 1955, than it had been earlier in June and August, and by February and March, 1956, none was seen at all. However, in May and in July, 1956, it was again

---

[6]) The verification of the determination of this species by Dr. Isabella Aiona Abbott is gratefully acknowledged.

abundant (*13235*). This we regard as an manifestation of seasonal progression or periodicity rather than as pioneer colonization without ecesis.

Our study has been rewarding in connection with observations that bear on the problem of distinguishing seral progression. As illustrated in Figure 4, the first macroscopic populants on the newly cooled lava were fine green filaments later shown to be *Enteromorpha*. Specifically they were not identifiable further than to genus. These populations were very hard to reach consistently for measurement or collection.

A subsequent and more consistent study was possible when portions of the flow surface broke away and disappeared. In these cases, one of which is illustrated as the record B in Figure 4, regardless of time of year or vertical position in the intertidal region, the same *Enteromorpha* appears as a fine, hair-like, rather uniform coating on such 'fresh' surfaces. Certainly this catastrophic phenomenon induces a subclimax in consideration of the whole area, yet on the particular fresh lava surface just exposed the *Enteromorpha* is a pioneer. In time the *Enteromorpha* matures into isolated tufts of mature thalli (*13149*) that may eventually become somewhat brownish with the development of epiphytic diatoms. Then it disappears as succession takes place.

Ectocarpus breviarticulatus (*12798*, *12803*) can be expected to appear (Fig. 4C) shortly after the *Enteromorpha* has appeared and with it but also alone at still higher intertidal levels. This was seen to happen at several sites. While the *Ectocarpus* at first may be diffusely spread over the surfaces, intermixed with the hair-like coating of *Enteromorpha*, it also becomes restricted to small tufts. The tufts become fewer and larger as time goes on. In age the lower tufts of *Ectocarpus* may become intermixed with a *Cladophora*, the tufts of which, other than for color, are quite similar macroscopically.

While the *Ectocarpus*, all the time it remains, is the highest macroscopic alga, a blue-green coating began to appear conspicuously on the rocks above the *Ectocarpus* in December, 1955, six months after the flow had cooled.

The series of events illustrated in Figure 4 was progressive. The blue-green algal population gradually became more dense and could be readily detected in its lower reaches even when dry. At first it was seen as a blue-green sheen only when wet. Concurrently *Littorina pintada* became progressively more abundant. Lower down the same events were true for the high-growing limpet, *Helcioniscus exaratus*. *Ralfsia pangoensis* and the crustose corallines appeared as small spots over a wide vertical range, became larger, tended to completely cover the surface in a smaller vertical range, and became fertile. The corallines often developed erumpent edges where adjacent crusts closed together. The early populants *Ectocarpus*, *Chnoospora minima* (*13102*, *13237*), and the various Chlorophyta were gone by 1958 (Fig. 4K) except on an occasional spot where a chunk of lava had recently broken away.

As time goes on, the pioneers became replaced by other algae and zonation (Fig. 4) became evident and more stable as longer-lived organisms appeared. We have gained the impression that with excessive abrasion during storms, many of the zoned organisms are removed. In fact, so many may be removed irregularly and replaced by pioneers that zonation becomes obscured. It would seem this catastropich process is related to that which holds some areas in a subclimax condition semi-permanently but this is not, e.g., in the case illustrated in Figure 5, a phenomenon peculiar to new lava flows.

The finger-shaped point of rock some 7 meters broad and perhaps 4 meters thick which jutted into the sea some 20 meters and bore the surface repeatedly studied, photographed, and measured to provide most of Figure 4, almost completely disappeared between visits early in 1961. Perhaps this is related in part to removal of the bottom clinker layer (Fig. 3B) and undermining as the depth alongside increased. Even before that time, disclimatic events had disrupted the study and such climax genera as *Sargassum*

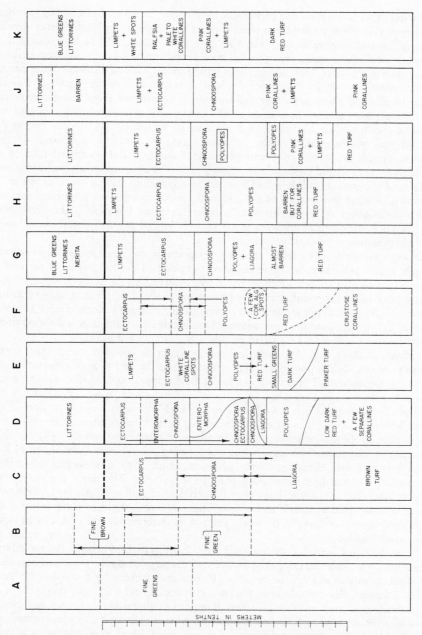

Figure 4. Population changes in time on a vertical 1955 lava surface extruded into the sea and observed as follows: A & C at Kaueleau (respectively), 21-VI-1955 and 15-VIII-1955; and at Kehena (respectively), B, 30-XII-1958; D, 21-XII-1955; E, 24-III-1956; F, 16-V-1956; G, 14-VII-1956; H, 18-VIII-1956; I, 10-XI-1956; J, 20-IV-1957; K, 30-XII-1958. The base line for measurement was the top of the particular population across which on the figure a dark horizontal line is drawn. This corresponded in general with a set of recognizable physical features of the shore but the physical features changed from time to time as erosion took place.

never did develop there. Of this point there remains only an isolated islet perhaps 2 meters in diameter which is constantly washed over by the waves at high tide. Other sizeable protrusions and seaward faces of the 1955 lava flows were noted to have disappeared between visits. As a result, by 1966 the flow at Kehena was hardly an irregularity in the outline of the shore. Undoubtedly, this rapid wearing back of the flows to the general island contour is a major reason for the lack of bays in this youngest part of Hawaii.

In the series of phenomena observed through 1961, we feel there was demonstrated seral progression as *Sargassum echinocarpum* (*17021*), *S. obtusifolium* (*17022*), and the crustose coralline algae became well established (at Kaueleau, Fig. 1) only during the second year of observation of the 1955 flow surfaces. *Corallina sandwicensis* (*13236*) became present as dense fertile hemispheres at Kehena, as did occasional tufts of an *Alsidium* sp. (*13239*) and *Lophosiphonia villum* (*13233*) at their characteristic high elevations. This seral progression, while it had resulted in populations having some of the more conspicuous algae and animals of the climax situation, had not yet progressed very far either qualitatively or quantitatively. On more protected, less rapidly abraiding, areas and in pools the populations were much more advanced toward the climax situation and the standing crop was higher.

No one has yet been successful in determining the precise quantities of algae on such rough, nearly perpendicular, intertidal shores exposed to the full sweep of the surf as these shores in Hawaii, but simple comparative observations showed that though forms conspicuous in climax populations were present and fertile in 1961, e.g., crustose coralline algae, the cover is still not as dense as it is on prehistoric adjacent shores. Thus one would not say balance between the most advanced undisturbed communities and the environment had been achieved, i.e., a climax situation does not yet exist.

Certain qualities, e.g., the red algal species *Ahnfeltia concinna*, coelenterate corals, and the brown *Ralfsia pangoensis*, were absent during the first year of observation. Of these during the second year small patches of *Ralfsia* appeared. *Ahnfeltia* was first noted at the Kaueleau site in December, 1959, about four and a half years after the surface had cooled. These two qualities have been found sparsely developed on the surfaces of the 1950 Honokua flow (Fig. 1, inset) five years old at the time of observation. By April, 1962, tufts of *Ahnfeltia concinna* 7 to 8 cm tall were conspicuous on the 1955 Kaueleau lava flow study point. This alga, while not forming a band, was quite abundant here though not frequent elsewhere on the 1955 lava. Much of the flow surface inland from the study point had been removed during the seven years. The material removed was largely loose clinker material, but some of the clinkers or chunks of massive lava removed must have weighed at least a metric ton. This removal is slight in comparison to the complete removal of most of the study point at the Kehena site and which event closed the present study.

It can be stated here that the idea of Fahey, Northcraft, and others, that the pioneer organisms, e.g., *Enteromorpha*, *Polysiphonia*, and *Ectocarpus*, may be occasional organisms in climax situations seems to be borne out by our observations. To this group we would add *Cladophora*. *Enteromorpha* after 1961 was restricted to but a few spots on some of the population-wise most advanced surfaces. It appears in abundance, however, as a pioneer coating over any new surface such as is formed when a piece of the flow is broken away by the waves. *Ectocarpus breviarticulatus*, on the other hand, may remain as a rather regularly predictable populant of the highest intertidal regions for a year or more even when, as at Kehena (Fig. 4), it is not being held as on the breakwater at Hilo (Fig. 5) in a disclimax by scouring. It is much less conspicuous on older surfaces and absent for the most part on prehistoric flows where *Ahnfeltia concinna* is abundant in a position which would seem suitable for this *Ectocarpus* otherwise. It is to be noted that the more

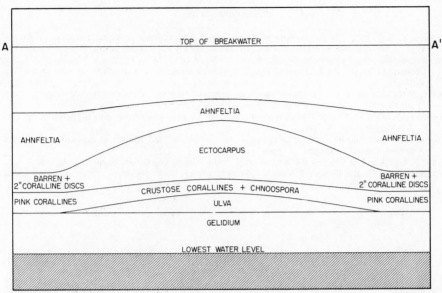

Figure 5. Proportionate diagram of algal vertical distribution on a scoured wave-exposed projecting angle of the breakwater at Hilo, Hawaii, in relation to the adjacent less scoured and less wave-exposed portions of the same breakwater. Scouring is maximal at the center and reduced toward both A and A'.

permanent crustose colonizers, e.g., *Ralfsia pangoensis* and the crustose corallines, appear as small spots and grow so as to occupy most of the surface. In doing so, they leave less and less space free such as that on which the frondose or short-lived earlier populants grew.

For comparison with the seral state of the Kehena study area, the vertical distribution of the populations (Fig. 2) on two Maui Island and two Hawaii Island prehistoric shores and on the large stable stones of the Hilo breakwater are shown. The Hilo shore sites depicted in Figures 2 and 3A were near each other and of similar exposure and form. The difference may be said to represent the seral development yet necessary before the climax is attained and the differing wave action. As determined elsewhere on artificially denuded or introduced stable surfaces this may require five or six years, but on Hawaiian lava flows it can be expected to require more than ten. Yet an initial remark in this paper, to the effect that the communities on historic flows (say, 100 years old) are generally different from those on adjacent prehistoric flows, would indicate this process, which in its pioneer phases is so quick, may be measured in its later phases in terms of a few centuries as in the case of terrestrial communities.

SUMMARY

The populations of the seaward intertidal ends of the 1955 lava flows in Hawaii were studied during the first few years of their development. Different seral phenomena were recognized such as pioneer colonization, succession, disclimax, and subclimax. The term climax is used as a practical term to denote existence of an equilibrium between the populations and the environment. Appearance of the climax situation seems to be related to stability of the substratum for a period at least as long as six to ten years, but even populations on surfaces as old as 100 years are different from some that are on adjacent prehistoric surfaces.

LITERATURE CITED

DAWSON, E. Yale. 1954. The marine flora of Isla San Benedicto following the volcanic eruption of 1952—1953. Allan Hancock Foundation Publications Occasional Paper number 16, 25 pp., 5 plates.

DICKIE, GEORGE. 1876. Notes on algae collected by H. N. Moseley, M.A., of H.M.S. 'Challenger,' chiefly obtained in Torres Strait, Coasts of Japan, and Juan Fernandez. Journal of the Linnean Society 15: 446—486.

FAHEY, ELIZABETH M. 1953. The repopulation of intertidal transects. Rhodora 55: 102—108.

—— & MAXWELL S. DOTY. 1949. Pioneer colonization on intertidal transects. Biol. Bull. 97: 238—239.

MACDONALD, GORDON A. 1959. The activity of Hawaiian volcanoes during the years 1951—1956. Bulletin Volcanologique Ser. II, Vol. 22: 1—70.

NORTHCRAFT, RICHARD D. 1948. Marine algal colonization of the Monterey Peninsula, California. American Journal of Botany 35: 396—404.

RIGG, B. G. 1914. The effect of the Katmai eruption on marine vegetation. Science n. s. 40: 509—513.

WILLIAMS, LOUIS G., and DONALD I. Mount. 1965. Influence of zinc on periphytic communities. American Journal of Botany 52: 26—34.

Primary Organic Productivity of a Hawaiian Coral Reef[1]

ALAN J. KOHN

Osborn Zoological Laboratory, Yale University, and Hawaii Marine Laboratory, University of Hawaii

AND PHILIP HELFRICH

Department of Zoology and Entomology, University of Hawaii

ABSTRACT

Primary organic productivity was determined by measuring changes in oxygen concentration of sea water flowing over a fringing coral reef at Kapaa, Kauai, Hawaii. Prevalence of a rather strong, unidirectional current facilitated use of this method.

Determinations were made both in summer (July) and winter (November). The reef is autotrophic, as were two previously studied atoll reefs in the Marshall Islands. Gross primary productivity is about 2,900 g C/m²/yr. This is in impressive agreement with results obtained on the atoll reefs, which are the only previous measurements of coral reef productivity.

All three results are considerably higher than determinations of productivity of open ocean waters. The authors attribute this difference to photosynthesis by benthic algae on the coral reef platform.

INTRODUCTION

The attention of many oceanographers has in recent years been directed toward measurement of rates of biological productivity of the oceans. Riley (1941) summarized data available at that time, most of which had been obtained from the North Atlantic Ocean. More recently, studies of primary organic productivity have been extended to other parts of the open ocean (Steemann Nielsen 1952, 1954, and others; see also Fleming and Laevastu 1956) and to coral reefs.

Prior to the investigation reported in this paper, the only definitive data on coral reef productivity were those provided by Sargent and Austin (1949, 1954) and Odum and Odum (1955) for atoll reefs in the Marshall Islands.

The present paper provides comparable

[1] Contribution No. 92, Hawaii Marine Laboratory. This research was supported by grants from the Society of the Sigma Xi, the Hawaiian Academy of Science, and the Lihue Plantation Co., Ltd. Appreciation is expressed to W. J. Newhouse for surveying the algal flora; to T. S. Austin, G. E. Hutchinson, and G. A. Riley for criticism of the manuscript; to D. C. Cox and F. E. J. Fry for helpful discussion; to M. S. Adachi for preparation of the figures; and to W. J. Atkinson for technical assistance.

data for a fringing reef in the Hawaiian Islands. It will be shown that (1) the rate of organic production on the reef is sufficient to meet the needs of the consumer organisms present, and (2) the rate of gross primary productivity is of the same order of magnitude as those reported in the two Marshall Islands studies. These rates are considerably higher than those reported for open oceans and, with one exception, somewhat higher than those reported for even the most productive coastal waters. An explanation is advanced to account for this discrepancy.

Location and description of the reef

The investigation was carried out on North Kapaa Reef, at Kapaa, on the windward (east) coast of the island of Kauai (Fig. 1). The reef was visited in October and November of 1955, and in July, 1956.

North Kapaa Reef extends for about 4,000 feet fringing an approximately north-south shoreline (Fig. 2). Its southern boundary is a small stream and stone jetty. A small embayment of deep water which approaches a steeply sloping shore marks its northern limit. The reef reaches a maximum width of 1,400 feet near its southern end and gradually narrows to 500 feet at the northern end.

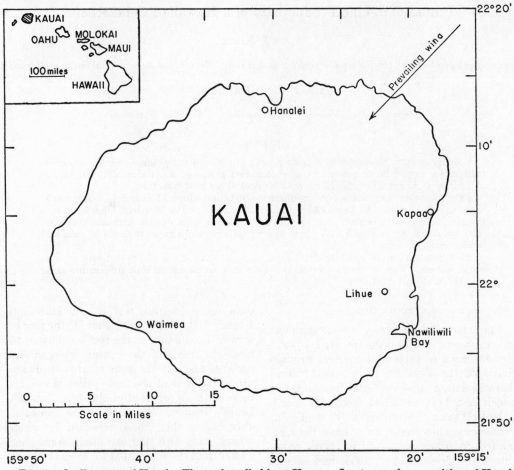

FIG. 1.   Outline map of Kauai.   The reef studied is at Kapaa.   Inset map shows position of Kauai (hatched) in the Hawaiian Islands.

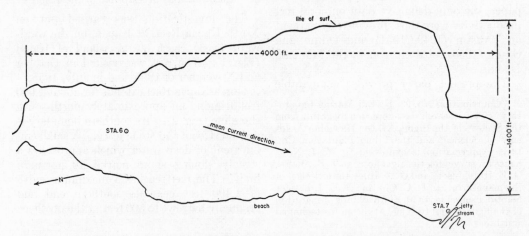

FIG. 2.   Outline map of North Kapaa Reef, showing stations, mean current direction, and important topographic features.

Depth of water over the reef varies from 6 to 173 cm above mean sea level. Mean depth was calculated to be 79 cm. This datum represents the average of 107 measurements of depth with respect to mean sea level made by the Lihue Plantation Co., Ltd.

The substratum is characterized by irregular areas of living and dead coral, coral rubble, and sand. The distribution and abundance of benthic organisms vary with the nature of the substratum. A detailed survey of the flora and fauna was not made; however, the general distribution and abundance of prominent organisms were noted (Helfrich and Kohn 1955). Benthic algae, which are of special interest, are represented chiefly by the genera *Acanthophora*, *Lyngbya*, and *Padina*. Other genera of large plants present are *Ulva*, *Halimeda*, *Sargassum*, and *Amansia*. The encrusting *Porolithon*, *Goniolithon*, and *Lithothamnion* occur especially toward the seaward edge of the reef.

Investigations of currents over the reef revealed a definite pattern. A rather strong, unidirectional current prevails. Fifty-two determinations in October and November of 1955 gave a mean current velocity of 24 cm/sec and a mean heading of 220°T. Twenty determinations in July, 1956, gave a mean velocity of 22 cm/sec and a mean heading of 218°T. The current is thus approximately parallel to the coastline and to the prevailing northeast trade winds. At the southern end of the reef the current is deflected out to sea by the jetty (Fig. 2) and reached a maximum velocity of 44 cm/sec. (Measurements of currents at this station [Sta. 7] were not included in average velocities and headings.)

Vertical diurnal tide range is only about 1.8 feet in the area under consideration. Calculations made for the authors by D. C. Cox, Senior Geologist, Hawaiian Sugar Planters Experiment Station, showed that the volume of water moved on and off the reef with change in tidal phase does not cause a significant tidal current. This was verified by plotting observed current velocities against time and tidal phase (Fig. 3). These graphs show significant increases in mean

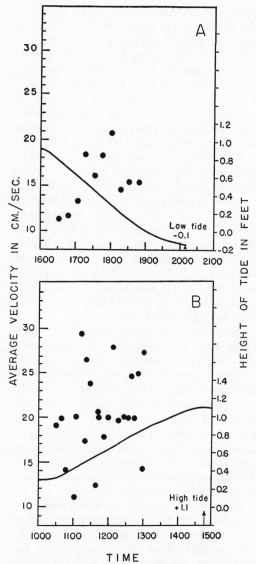

FIG. 3. Individual determinations of current velocity (●), and height of tide (——), plotted against time of day, showing absence of relationship between current velocity and phase of tide. A, 29 October 1955. B, 30 October 1955.

current velocity with time; however, it should be noted that the determinations on 29 October were made while the tide was falling, while those on 30 October were made during rising tide.

METHODS

Two stations (Sta. 6 and 7) were established on the reef such that a line drawn between them was approximately parallel to the mean current direction (Fig. 2). Distance between the stations was 861 meters.

Each of the determinations of current velocity cited above consisted of recording the time required for a fluorescein dye spot to travel a distance of 5 m. Current direction was determined by sighting with a compass from the point of release of the dye spot to its position after traveling 5 m.

Water samples were collected in 300-ml glass-stoppered bottles at intervals over a 24-hour period. Samples were taken at a depth of approximately six inches below the surface. They were fixed immediately for determination of dissolved oxygen by the Winkler method. The samples were kept in darkness and titrated upon return to the laboratory 2–3 days later. Replicate samples of 50 ml were titrated with 0.01 N sodium thiosulfate standardized with potassium biniodate (Harleco).

In the November series, records for a single cycle were obtained. In July, data were obtained for two successive 24-hour cycles.

Water temperature at each station (Fig. 4A) and incident light intensity (Fig. 4B) were measured simultaneously with collection of each water sample in the July series. A Norwood Director exposure meter placed on a level surface on the shore near Sta. 7 was used to measure incident light. At times of intermittent cloudiness series of readings were taken and averaged. Meter readings were converted to foot-candles by multiplication by the appropriate factor. Data on cloud cover (Fig. 4B, 5A) as well as other weather data were obtained from the Weather Bureau Pacific Supervisory Office in Honolulu, through the courtesy of D. I. Blumenstock. All Weather Bureau observations were made at Lihue, Kauai, approximately ten miles south of Kapaa.

RESULTS

Observations of 27–29 July 1956

In the July series of observations an effort was made to test the methods used by comparison of productivity during two successive 24-hour cycles. The results are summarized in Figure 4. Water temperature fluctuated diurnally at both the upstream

station (Sta. 6) and the downstream station (Sta. 7), as shown in Figure 4A. Maximum and minimum temperatures and diurnal ranges at both stations are given in Table 1. The greater amplitude of fluctuation at Sta. 7 is attributed to the increased surface/volume ratio of the water as it flows from the open ocean across the shallow reef platform.

Measurements of incident light and the extent of cloud cover are shown in Figure 4B.

Results of oxygen determinations at each station are shown graphically in Figure 4C. At both stations a diurnal cycle of oxygen concentration is apparent. The greater amplitude at Sta. 7 is attributed to biological activity on the reef platform.

The mean observed current velocity in July was 22 cm/sec. The time required for water to pass from Sta. 6 to Sta. 7 was close to one hour (3910 sec.). Therefore, the curve for Sta. 6 in Figure 4C has been shifted to the left by one hour, according to the convention suggested by Odum (1956). This enabled analysis of the data in such a way as to make possible the determination of rates of primary organic production (photosynthesis) and consumption (respiration) on the reef. This method was first used by Sargent and Austin (1949, 1954).

Since the mean compass bearing of Sta. 7 from Sta. 6 was 218°T. and the mean current direction was 220°T., the two stations utilized were virtually on a line coinciding with the mean current direction, and no correction for angle of current was necessary.

The mean rate of change of oxygen concentration in milliliters per centimeter of reef normal to the current (*i.e.* in a strip 1 cm wide between the two stations) is given by the formula

$$\text{mean depth (cm)} \times \text{velocity (cm/sec)} \\ \times \text{ mean change in oxygen between} \\ \text{stations (ml/cm}^3) = \text{mean change in} \\ \text{oxygen over reef (ml/cm/sec)} \quad (1)$$

Substitution in Equation (1) of observed values for mean depth and mean current velocity gives

$$79 \times 22 \times (\text{ml/L}_{\text{Sta. 7}} - \text{ml/L}_{\text{Sta. 6}})$$

$$\times 10^{-3} = \text{ml/cm/sec.} \quad (2)$$

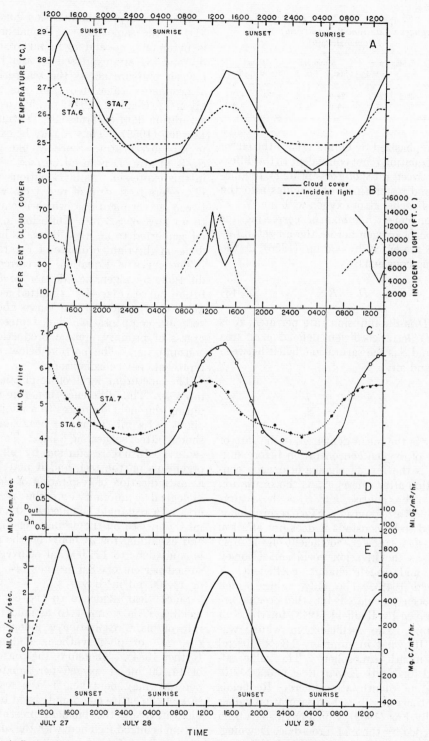

FIG. 4. *A*, Sea surface temperatures at Sta. 6 and 7. *B*, Incident light and cloud cover. *C*, Oxygen concentration at Sta. 6 and 7. *D*, Diffusion of oxygen across the air-sea interface. *E*, Production and consumption of organic matter. Data from North Kapaa Reef, 27–29 July 1956.

TABLE 1. *Temperature (°C) maxima, minima, and ranges at stations 6 (upstream) and 7 (downstream)*

	Maximum		Minimum		Range	
	Sta. 6	Sta. 7	Sta. 6	Sta. 7	Sta. 6	Sta. 7
27–28 July	27.2	29.1	24.9	24.3	2.3	4.8
28–29 July	26.4	27.1	25.0	24.1	1.4	3.0

As emphasized by Odum (1956) the curve of this equation is not equivalent to the difference between rates of gross primary productivity and respiration but includes also the result of exchange of oxygen with air.

A convenient method of correcting for diffusion of oxygen across the air-sea interface is presented by Odum (1956) in the following equations:

$$D = KS \qquad (3)$$

where D is the diffusion rate per area, K is the gas transfer coefficient defined on an area basis, and S is the saturation deficit between water and air.

$$K = \frac{z(q_m - q_e)}{S_m - S_e} \qquad (4)$$

where z is the mean depth, q_m is the rate of change of oxygen concentration before sunrise, q_e is the rate of change of oxygen concentration after sunset, S_m is the saturation deficit before sunrise, and S_e is the saturation deficit after sunset. Since respiration is assumed to be constant it does not affect q.

The gas transfer coefficient K is also known as the invasion coefficient (Dorsey 1940), and the exchange coefficient, E (Redfield 1948). The only values which have been calculated for the oceans are those given by Redfield (1948) for the Gulf of Maine. The coefficient in winter was 13×10^6, and in summer, 2.8×10^6 ml $O_2/m^2/month/atmosphere$. The value calculated for North Kapaa Reef is 3.3×10^6 ml $O_2/m^2/month/atmosphere$. Redfield's calculations were based on saturation values given by Fox (1909), which have since been superseded by those of Truesdale, Downing, and Lowden (1955). Use of the data of Fox's tables in the calculation for North Kapaa Reef would increase K by about 15%.

In order to plot the diffusion curve (Fig. 4D) in the same units as Equation (2), z is in meters, q_m and q_e in ml/m³/hr, and S_m and S_e are expressed as the head of oxygen pressure across the sea surface, in atmospheres, calculated from the formula given by Redfield (1948: p. 355) using the saturation data of Truesdale, Downing, and Lowden (1955). Thus K may be expressed in ml/cm/sec/atm. Since S, like S_m and S_e, is in atm, D is in ml/cm/sec. The cm in this expression, as in Equations (1) and (2), refers to a strip of reef 1 cm wide between the two stations, which is equivalent to an area of 8.6 m². Diffusion may thus be converted to an areal basis, as has been done on the right ordinate of Figure 4D.

The curve of Equation (1) corrected for diffusion by algebraic addition of the diffusion curve (Fig. 4D) is plotted as Figure 4E. The portion of the curve above the zero or compensation line represents an excess of primary organic production over consumption. The portion below the line represents net consumption.

The nocturnal level of respiration is of interest. The difference between stations during the night decreases to a minimum of about -1.4 ml $O_2/cm/sec$ near sunrise (or shortly after, suggesting a lag). This represents nocturnal respiration by all of the organisms on the reef, and it may be used as an indication of respiration of the entire biological community on the reef. The area of a rectangle bounded by 0 and -1.4 ml $O_2/cm/sec$ on the ordinate of Figure 4E and extending for 24 hours on the abscissa is equivalent to 121,000 ml of oxygen consumed per cm ($= 8.6$ m²) per 24-hour day, or 14,100 ml/m²/day.

Since clear evidence to the contrary is lacking, it is simplest to assume that the rate of plant respiration is independent of the rate of photosynthesis (Odum 1956, Ryther 1954). Therefore, the consumption of 14,100 ml of oxygen per square meter per day may be taken as the respiration rate of the entire community, and it reflects quantitatively the biomass present. This datum is introduced here with the suggestion of possible future correlations between measurements of biomass and rates of metabolism of biological communities.

TABLE 2. *Net production and consumption in ml O_2/cm on North Kapaa Reef, 27–29 July 1956*

Based on graphical integration of areas above (production) and below (consumption) 0-line in Figure 4E.

	Net production	Net consumption
27–28 July	73,700	45,600
28–29 July	64,600	46,700

In order to compare net production and consumption on the reef, the curve of Figure 4E was graphically integrated. Values for net production (area above 0 line) and net consumption (area below 0 line) are given for the two days studied in Table 2. Inspection of Table 2 and Figure 4E shows reasonable similarity of the data for successive days, thus affirming the validity of the method. The first sample collected was at 1200 on 27 July. In order to obtain a complete cycle for this date, the time of the 0 intercept was taken as the average (0916) of the observed times on 28 July (0920) and 29 July (0912). For this reason, the portion of the curve for 27 July between 0916 and 1200 is shown as a dotted line in Figure 4E. Mean net production was about 69,200 ml and mean net consumption about 46,600 ml of oxygen for a 24-hour day. There is thus a mean excess of 22,600 ml of oxygen per day.

The rate of primary production of living substance is of greater interest than the rate of exchange of oxygen *per se*. Therefore, in the conversion to areal units on the right ordinate of Figure 4E, milliliters of oxygen have been converted to milligrams of carbon by the simplified photosynthesis equation,

$$CO_2 + H_2O = (CH_2O) + O_2 \qquad (5)$$

The daily excess of 22,600 ml of oxygen is equivalent to 12,100 mg of carbon, by which production exceeds consumption per centimeter of reef normal to the current per day. In areal units, the excess is about 1,400 mg C/m^2/day.

Production averaged 4,300, and consumption 2,900 mg C/m^2/day, giving the production excess of 1,400 mg C/m^2/day. In summer, a significantly greater amount of organic matter is thus produced on the reef over that which is consumed. Thus, the reef is self-sufficient, or autotrophic, at least during this part of the year. The excess is presumably stored on the reef as organic biomass.

In order to determine gross primary productivity, the entire curve (Fig. 4E) above the baseline (-1.4 ml O_2/cm/sec) was graphically integrated. This represents 133,000 ml O_2/cm/day for the only complete cycle covered by the observations (28 July). This is equivalent to about 71.3 g C/cm/day, or 8.3 g C/m^2/day. The ratio of gross primary productivity to community respiration (P/R) is 1.1.

If this rate of production were maintained throughout the year, annual productivity would be 3,000 g C/m^2.

Observations of 25 November 1955

The results of the initial study, made 25 November 1955, are summarized in Figure 5. Temperature measurements taken at this time were too few to permit construction of curves of diurnal fluctuation and diffusion. Those obtained were about 1.5°C lower than corresponding values in July.

Incident light measurements were not made in the November series, but the extent of cloud cover for the period under consideration has been plotted in Figure 5A. In the field notes it was stated that the "data were collected on a day throughout which the sun shone brightly."

Results of determinations of oxygen concentrations at each station are shown graphically in Figure 5B. The diurnal cycle at both stations is apparent, as is the greater amplitude of the curve for Sta. 7, which is expected from increased biological activity on the reef platform.

The mean observed current velocity in November was 24 cm/sec. Time required for water to pass from Sta. 6 to Sta. 7 was one hour (3590 sec). Therefore, the curve for Sta. 6 in Figure 5B has been shifted to the left one hour. Since the mean current direction was close to the compass bearing of Sta. 7 from Sta. 6, correction for angle of current was not necessary.

The rate of change in oxygen concentra-

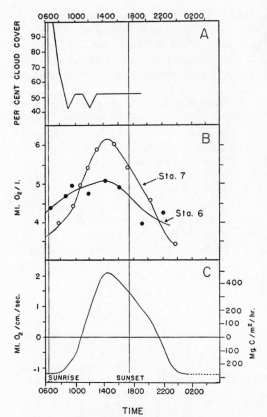

FIG. *A*, Cloud cover. *B*, Oxygen concentration at Sta. 6 and 7. *C*, Production and consumption of organic matter (not corrected for diffusion). Data for North Kapaa Reef, 25 November 1955.

tion between stations throughout the 24-hour cycle is plotted in Figure 5C. This graph is not directly comparable with Figure 4E, since the latter has been corrected for diurnal fluctuation of diffusion, while the former has not.

The nocturnal level of respiration in Figure 5C is about -1.2 ml/cm/sec. Since diffusion is in the direction of air to water at night, its effect is to reduce the apparent difference in concentration between Sta. 6 and Sta. 7. Thus the observed rate of respiration is probably too small. The actual rate probably approaches closely the July rate of -1.4 ml/cm/sec, or consumption of 14,100 ml/m²/day.

Graphic integration of the curve (Fig. 5C) gives uncorrected values of 47,100 ml O_2/cm/sec net production and 46,900 ml O_2/cm/sec net consumption. In the July series of observations, correction for diffusion resulted in increasing net productivity by 20.7% and increasing net consumption by 11.5%. If this discrepancy applies also in winter, daily production is probably somewhat greater than daily consumption. Thus in winter as well as in summer, sufficient organic matter is produced on the reef to meet the demands of the consumer organisms present.

Gross productivity, as calculated from the uncorrected curve (Fig. 5C) is 103,100 ml O_2/cm/day. In the July series, correction for diffusion raised the calculated gross productivity by 19.5%. Application of this factor to the November result gives a corrected gross productivity of 123,200 ml O_2/cm/day. This is equivalent to 7.7 g C/m²/day, somewhat lower than the 8.3 g/m²/day for July.

If the calculated summer and winter values are each assigned one-half year, annual gross primary productivity is calculated to be 2,900 g C/m².

Efficiency of gross production

Determinations of solar radiation made by the writers were not sufficiently numerous to support an estimate of photosynthetic efficiency. Records of insolation obtained at the Hawaiian Sugar Planters Association Experiment Station in Honolulu indicated 7.15×10^6 cal/m²/day for 30 July 1956. Using the energy equivalent of the July production datum of 8.3 g C/m²/day, efficiency of gross productivity was calculated to be 1.1%. This is lower than the value of 5.8% measured on an atoll reef (Odum and Odum 1955) but somewhat higher than other marine communities. Riley (1941) calculated values of 0.55–0.82% efficiency for phytoplankton in Long Island Sound.

DISCUSSION

In previous quantitative determinations of primary productivity of coral reefs, no corrections for diffusion of oxygen have been made. For this reason, the directly comparable uncorrected curve for North Kapaa Reef are shown in Figure 6. In Figure 6A,

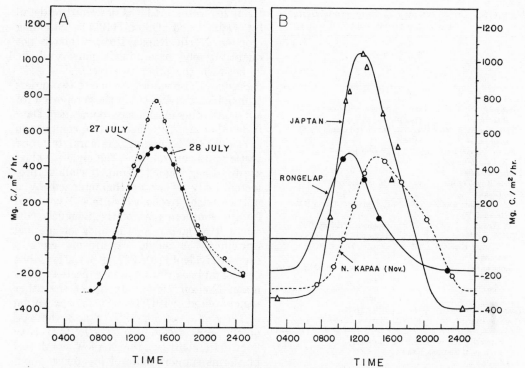

Fig. 6. Production and consumption of organic matter. A, North Kapaa Reef, 27 July 1956 and 28 July 1956. B, North Kapaa Reef, 25 November 1955; reef at Japtan Island, Eniwetok Atoll; and reef at Bokujarito Island, Rongelap Atoll. Data not corrected for diffusion. Data from Japtan and Bokujarito are from Odum and Odum (1955) and Sargent and Austin (1954), respectively.

the two cycles observed on North Kapaa Reef in July have been superimposed to facilitate comparison. The curves obtained by Sargent and Austin (1949, 1954), Odum and Odum (1955), and for North Kapaa Reef in November have been recalculated in terms of mg C/m²/hr and included in Figure 6B.

It is noteworthy that the peaks of production for the three determinations made on North Kapaa Reef (27 and 28 July and 25 November) are in very close agreement. All three fall between 1400 and 1430. They are later, however, than those obtained by Sargent and Austin (1949, 1954) at Rongelap (before noon) and by Odum and Odum (1955) at Japtan (about 1230). Sargent and Austin (1954) point out that a morning peak is reasonable in the light of results obtained by Kostytschew et al. (1926, 1930), who observed that the rate of photosynthesis both in land and water plants reached a maximum before noon and then

declined. Yonge, Yonge, and Nichols (1932) also observed this phenomenon in reef corals.

Odum and Odum (1955) explain that the lag between sunlight intensity and oxygen production may be partially due to location of photosynthesizing organisms beneath the surface of the calcareous reef surface, sand, and coral polyps. This also seems the best explanation for the occurrence of a lag in peak production at North Kapaa Reef. However, it does not explain why the peak at Kapaa is later than at Japtan. The discrepancies in time of peak production in these investigations seems sufficient to suggest that this aspect requires further investigation, especially with regard to the extend of oxygen production and its rate of diffusion from primary producers within coral and other types of substratum.

The three coral reefs that have been studied all show a daily excess of production of organic matter over consumption.

TABLE 3. *Gross primary organic productivity of marine environments*

Location	Gross productivity g C/m²/yr	Reference
Coral Reefs		
Rongelap Atoll, Marshall Is.	1500 (1800)[1]	Sargent and Austin (1954)
Eniwetok Atoll, Marshall Is.	3500 (4200)[1]	Odum and Odum (1955)
North Kapaa Reef, Kauai, Hawaii	2900	Present paper
Turtle Grass Bed		
Long Key, Florida	4650	Odum (1956)
Open Ocean		
Off Rongelap Atoll, Marshall Is.	28	Sargent and Austin (1954)
Off Hawaii	37	Steemann Nielsen (1954)
Off Hawaii[2]	21	Doty and Oguri (1956)
Off Hawaii (Inshore waters)[3]	123	Doty and Oguri (1956)
Sargasso Sea	167	Riley, Stommel, & Bumpus (1949)
Georges Bank	309	Riley, Stommel, & Bumpus (1949)
Long Island Sound	470	Riley (1956)
Benguela Current	167–912	Steeman Nielsen (1954)

[1] With estimated correction for diffusion.
[2] Average of Stations 1 and 2.
[3] Station 3.

Sargent and Austin (1954) reported net production of 0.5 g C/m²/day, and Odum and Odum (1955) 9 g C/m²/day. The mean net production in the present study, corrected for diffusion, is 7.9 g C/m²/day.

In the second column of Table 3, the annual values of gross productivity reported by Sargent and Austin (1954) and Odum and Odum (1955) are listed. These values were not corrected for diffusion. For North Kapaa Reef, the diffusion correction represents an increase of 19.5%. This factor has been applied to the Marshall Islands data to give an estimate of corrected gross productivity. These values are placed in parentheses in Table 3.

Two important aspects of these data merit further discussion. First, the present authors are impressed by the fact that all three of the coral reefs thus far studied show gross productivity values of the same order of magnitude, when determined by the flow method. The highest value differs from the lowest by a factor of about two. Sargent and Austin (1954) described the reef at Rongelap as appearing "rather barren of plants." The rich biota of Japtan

Reef, Eniwetok Atoll, is described in detail by Odum and Odum (1955). Standing crop on North Kapaa Reef, although not quantitatively determined, may well lie in between the other two reefs.

Second, these values are one to two orders of magnitude greater than those reported for almost all other marine environments. Data from other areas are included for comparison in Table 3. Excluding the coral reef and turtle grass communities, the highest values are for Long Island Sound, a shallow, protected body of water characterized by a nutrient-rich, freshened surface layer, and for the southern part of the Benguela current. The latter is a locality of marked upwelling. A single experiment gave a rate equivalent to 1387 g C/m²/yr, but considerable variation was expected (Steemann Nielsen 1954). In all of the other regions cited, with the probable exception of Doty and Oguri's (1956) Sta. 3, the base of the euphotic zone is above the ocean floor. In contrast, the shallow coral reef platforms support more or less dense populations of benthic algae. Productivity due to phytoplankton of neighboring oceanic water is extremely low. It is apparent that the extremely high gross primary productivity of coral reefs is attributable to photosynthesis by benthic algae on the reef platforms.

The extensive substrate area covered by a shallow layer of constantly flowing sea water is concluded to be the major factor responsible for the productivity of coral reefs being two orders of magnitude higher than adjacent oceanic waters. The substrate enables the growth of large attached algae, as well as algae which live within the substratum in a strongly illuminated region of the sea. In some regions, attached phanerogams play an important role. The strong constant flow of water provides these plants with a continual source of nutrients. The plants in turn promote a rich community of large and small animals confined to the same surface. Communities of adjacent areas may also benefit, as indicated by higher phytoplankton productivity of Hawaiian inshore waters (Doty and Oguri 1956).

The highest gross primary productivity

value reported for a marine community is 4650 g $C/m^2/yr$ (Odum 1956). It was obtained at a depth of three feet in a bed of turtle grass (*Thalassia*), which is undoubtedly the primary source of this productivity.

SUMMARY

Primary organic productivity was determined by measuring changes in oxygen concentration of sea water flowing over a coral reef at Kapaa, Kauai, Hawaii. Prevalence of a rather strong, unidirectional current facilitated use of this method. Determinations were made both in summer (July) and in winter (November).

The reef is autotrophic, that is the rate of organic production is sufficient to meet the requirements of the consumer organisms present. This was also found to be the case on two atoll reefs in the Marshall Islands, on which studies of this type had previously been made.

Gross primary productivity was calculated to be 2,900 g $C/m^2/yr$. This is in impressive agreement with data obtained by Sargent and Austin (1954) and Odum and Odum (1955) on the atoll reefs.

The ratio of gross productivity to community respiration was calculated to be 1.1. Efficiency of gross productivity was calculated to be 1.1%.

Except for a rather specialized turtle grass community, the primary productivity of coral reefs is far greater, on an areal basis, than all other marine environments that have been studied. The authors attribute this difference to photosynthesis by benthic algae on the reef platforms.

REFERENCES

DORSEY, N. E. 1940. Properties of ordinary water substance. New York, Reinhold. 673 pp.

DOTY, M. S., AND M. OGURI. 1956. The island mass effect. J. Cons. Int. Explor. Mer, **22**: 33–37.

FLEMING, R. H., AND T. LAEVASTU. 1956. The influence of hydrographic conditions on the behavior of fish. FAO Fish. Bull., **9**: 181–196.

FOX, C. J. J. 1909. On the coefficients of absorption of nitrogen and oxygen in distilled water and sea water, and of atmospheric carbonic acid in sea water. Trans. Faraday Soc., **5**: 68–87.

HELFRICH, P., AND A. J. KOHN. 1955. A survey to estimate the major biological effects of a dredging operation by the Lihue Plantation Co., Ltd. on North Kapaa Reef, Kapaa, Kauai. Preliminary Report. 31 pp. (Mimeographed. Available from the authors.)

KOSTYTSCHEW, S., AND V. BERG. 1930. Untersuchungen über den Tagesverlauf der Photosynthese in Transaukasien. Planta, **11**: 144–159.

KOSTYTSCHEW, S., AND S. SOLDATENKOW. 1926. Der tägliche Verlauf und die specifische Intensität der Photosynthese bei Wasserpflanzen. Planta, **2**: 1–19.

ODUM, H. T. 1956. Primary productivity in flowing waters. Limnol. & Oceanogr., **1**: 102–117.

ODUM, H. T., AND E. P. ODUM. 1955. Trophic structure and productivity of a windward coral reef community on Eniwetok Atoll. Ecol. Monogr., **25**: 291–320.

REDFIELD, A. C. 1948. The exchange of oxygen across the sea surface. J. Mar. Res., **8**: 347–361.

RILEY, G. A. 1941. Plankton Studies. III. Long Island Sound. Bull. Bingham Oceanogr. Coll., **7**: 1–93.

———. 1956. Oceanography of Long Island Sound, 1952–1954. IX. Production and utilization of organic matter. Bull. Bingham Oceanogr. Coll., **15**: 324–344.

RILEY, G. A., H. STOMMEL, AND D. F. BUMPUS. 1949. Quantitative ecology of the plankton of the western North Atlantic. Bull. Bingham Oceanogr. Coll., **12**: 1–169.

RYTHER, J. H. 1954. The ratio of photosynthesis to respiration in marine phytoplankton algae and its effect upon the measurement of productivity. Deep-Sea Res., **2**: 134–139.

SARGENT, M. C., AND T. S. AUSTIN. 1949. Organic productivity of an atoll. Amer. Geophys. Union Trans., **30**: 245–249.

———. 1954. Biologic economy of coral reefs. Bikini and nearby atolls, Part 2. Oceanography (biologic). U. S. Geol. Surv. Prof. Paper 260-E: 293–300.

STEEMANN NIELSEN, E. 1952. The use of radioactive carbon (C^{14}) for measuring organic production in the sea. J. Cons. Int. Explor. Mer, **43**: 117–140.

———. 1954. On organic production in the oceans. J. Cons. Int. Explor. Mer, **49**: 309–328.

TRUESDALE, G. A., A. L. DOWNING, AND G. F. LOWDEN. 1955. The solubility of oxygen in pure water and sea-water. J. Appl. Chem., **5**: 53–62.

YONGE, C. M., M. J. YONGE, AND A. G. NICHOLS. 1932. Studies on the physiology of corals; VI, the relationship between respiration in corals and the production of oxygen by their zooxanthellae. Sci. Repts. Great Barrier Reef Exped., **1**: 213–251.

THE ECOLOGY OF *CONUS* IN HAWAII*

Alan J. Kohn[1]

Department of Zoology, Yale University, and Hawaii Marine Laboratory, University of Hawaii

TABLE OF CONTENTS

INTRODUCTION

Members of the gastropod genus *Conus* (Prosobranchia: Conidae) are among the most conspicuous invertebrates on the coral reefs and marine benches that fringe the Hawaiian Islands. At least 21 species of *Conus* are known to occur in these habitats.

Investigation of these natural populations was stimulated by the existence of such a large number of closely related species in a restricted environment. This phenomenon is not unique to *Conus*, for many other genera of marine invertebrates are also characterized by large numbers of sympatric species in tropical regions. The gastropod genera *Cypraea*, *Mitra*, and *Terebra* are represented by 30-50 species in Hawaii (Edmondson 1946). A non-molluscan example is the snapping shrimp genus *Alpheus*, represented by 30 species in Hawaii (Banner 1953). The evolution of such genera has contributed to a marked enrichment of the tropical littoral epifauna. Here the number of species approaches ten times that of temperate regions (Thorson 1956).

Although these assemblages are well-known to systematists, no previous comparative ecological studies are known to the present writer. The objective of the study reported here was to describe the ecological niches of the species, to determine the extent of isolation between ecologically similar species, and thus to elucidate the mechanisms that permit a large number of closely related species to survive and retain their identity in a narrow environment.

* Contribution No. 113, Hawaii Marine Laboratory.
[1] Present address: Department of Biological Sciences, Florida State University, Tallahassee, Florida.

This paper is the first in a projected series reporting the results of ecological observations on natural populations of *Conus* in different areas, with emphasis on the Indo-West Pacific region. The research reported here was carried out while the author was a fellow of the National Science Foundation.

Financial aid was also received from the Higgins Fund and the Director's Fund, Sheffield Scientific School.

Gratitude is expressed to G. E. Hutchinson, Sterling Professor of Zoology, Yale University, for inspiration and guidance. Special thanks for the collection of material are due Dr. A. H. Banner, Mr. C. E. Cutress, Mr. R. M. Gray, Mr. E. C. Jones, Miss Alison Kay, Mr. R. A. McKinsey, Mr. C. M. Stidham, Mr. R. Sheats, and Miss Shirley Trefz. Miss Marian Adachi assisted in many phases of the work. Members of the staff of the Hawaii Marine Laboratory rendered much helpful assistance. Appreciation is expressed to Dr. J. L. Brooks, Dr. E. S. Deevey, Dr. W. D. Hartman, Dr. R. H. MacArthur, and Dr. G. A. Riley for helpful discussion and criticism of the manuscript, and to Dr. E. Mayr for examination of preliminary data. All of the algae mentioned were identified by Dr. A. J. Bernatowicz. The writer is also indebted to Mr. W. G. VanCampen for translating the paper by Takahashi (1939). Mechanical analyses of substratum samples were carried out at the Connecticut Agricultural Experiment Station, where Dr. T. Tamura, Dr. P. Waggoner, and the staff of the Department of Soils gave much assistance. The help of Mrs. Nancy Kimball in the preparation of the figures is gratefully acknowledged. The author is especially grateful to Dr. Olga Hartman for identification of the polychaetes discussed in the section on food and feeding. Without her willing and patient attention to a collection of partly digested, fragmentary remains of polychaetes, the food analyses presented here would not have been possible.

THE GENUS *CONUS* IN HAWAII

Of 45 species of *Conus* previously reported from the Hawaiian area, 32 are known from two or more specimens collected alive and are thus considered to be valid constituents of the Hawaiian marine fauna. Ecological observations on 25 of these, listed below, will be reported in this paper. Eighteen species were collected by the writer in the subtidal coral reef (noted by *) and intertidal marine bench (noted by +) habitats to be discussed in detail below, The specific names used are those given by Kohn (1959).

> *Conus abbreviatus* Reeve*+
> *Conus catus* Hwass *in* Bruguière+
> *Conus chaldaeus* (Röding)*+
> *Conus distans* Hwass *in* Bruguière*+
> *Conus ebraeus* Linné*+
> *Conus flavidus* Lamarck*+
> *Conus imperialis* Linné*
> *Conus leopardus* (Röding)
> *Conus lividus* Hwass *in* Bruguière*+
> *Conus marmoreus* Linné*
> *Conus miles* Linné*+
> *Conus moreleti* Crosse
> *Conus nussatella* Linné
> *Conus obscurus* Sowerby
> *Conus pennaceus* Born*+   (Fig. 1)
> *Conus pertusus* Hwass *in* Bruguière
> *Conus pulicarius* Hwass *in* Bruguière
> *Conus quercinus* Solander
> *Conus rattus* Hwass *in* Bruguière*+
> *Conus retifer* Menke+
> *Conus sponsalis* Hwass *in* Bruguière*+
> *Conus striatus* Linné*
> *Conus textile* Linné
> *Conus vexillum* Gmelin*+
> *Conus vitulinus* Hwass *in* Bruguière*

Most of the species listed are widely distributed throughout the Indo-West Pacific region. One species, *Conus abbreviatus,* is believed to be endemic to the Hawaiian archipelago. It is closely related to *Conus coronatus* Gmelin, which occurs in other areas of the central and western Pacific.

Conus nanus Broderip is here regarded as conspecific with *C. sponsalis,* but the Hawaiian populations probably constitute a valid subspecies. All specimens of *C. marmoreus* known from Hawaii agree with the description of *C. bandanus* Hwass *in* Bruguière. Most systematists consider the latter a variety of *C. marmoreus,* but the Hawaiian populations probably constitute a valid subspecies.

THE HABITAT OF *CONUS*

Marine benthic communities may be separated into two principal types, "those that tolerate or re-

FIG. 1. Photograph of *Conus pennaceus* Born. Length of shell about 35 mm. Photograph by C. E. Cutress.

quire exposure to the atmosphere and occupy stable and usually hard substrata exposed to the full force of the air with each important fall of tide," and "those that do not tolerate exposure to the atmosphere and are practically always submerged in water" (Clements & Shelford 1939: 323).

The present paper deals primarily with the ecology of natural populations of *Conus* which occupy habitats of these two types, marine benches and coral reef platforms, respectively. Notes on species occupying other habitats will also be included.

THE MARINE BENCH HABITAT

The geomorphology of emerged marine benches in the Hawaiian Islands has been discussed in detail by Wentworth (1938, 1939). These benches result from the single or combined action of processes designated by Wentworth as solution benching, water-level weathering, ramp abrasion, and wave quarrying.

SOLUTION BENCHES

In the Hawaiian Islands, solution benches occur where the shoreline is composed of reef rock and calcareous sandstone. On Oahu, this type of shore comprises 52 miles, or 31% of the coastline (Wentworth 1938). A detailed description of the characteristics and formation of solution benches is given by Wentworth (1939). A typical shore profile is shown in Fig. 2A.

Unbroken units of bench are ordinarily a few hundred feet long and 5-70 ft in width. The bench platforms are very flat. "The normal bench surface commonly shows variations of elevation of not over three to six inches in an area fifty feet wide by one hundred feet in length." (Wentworth 1939.) The outer edge of the solution bench rises more or less steeply from the water. The bench surface is ordinarily a few inches to 3 ft above mean sea level, and there is no raised rampart at the seaward margin. The bench itself is usually reef limestone, which consists of the firmly lithified skeletons of coral and calcareous algae. On the sloping outer edge, calcareous algae and, to a lesser extent, corals, contribute active building of the bench out from shore.

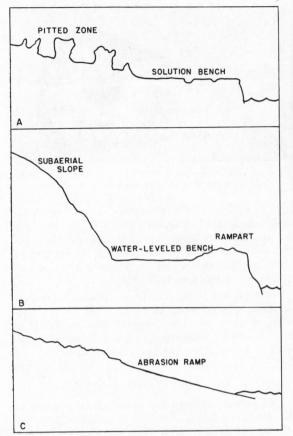

FIG. 2. Profiles of Hawaiian marine benches. A. solution bench. B. Water-leveled bench. C. Abrasion ramp bench. Modified from Wentworth (1938, 1939).

Other organisms, chiefly echinoids, are a destructive force in the same region.

The shoreward edge of the bench is sharply delimited by the front of a zone of pitted limestone (Fig. 3), ordinarily 10-50 ft in width and rising to a height of one to several ft above the bench surface. Wentworth (1939) presents evidence to show that this type of bench is formed chiefly by dissolution of the shoreward zone of pitted limestone by rain water, which collects in its pools; wave quarrying may finally produce the flat surface.

Details of solution benches selected for study are as follows:

Kahuku, Oahu (Sta. 5). The solution bench at Kahuku (Figs. 3, 4) is typical of the formation and was thoroughly investigated. It extends for several hundred feet along shore and is 40-80 ft wide. The bench surface is about one foot above mean sea level and is completely exposed for periods of up to four hours at tides of +0.2 feet[1] or less when seas are fairly calm. The coast here is exposed, and trade winds are ordinarily quite strong (about force 5). At high tide, the bench is strongly awash, and observations on it are not possible. The bench platform,

[1] All tidal data are referred to O datum = mean lower low water and are from Coast and Geodetic Survey Tide Tables.

FIG. 3. Photograph of solution bench at Kahuku, Oahu (Station 5). The width of the bench (left to right) is about 60 ft. The seaward margin of the zone of pitted limestone is visible at the left.

which is of solid reef limestone with a few potholes, is covered by a well developed algal turf. Zonation of algae across the bench is present. The landward portion is characterized by *Laurencia* sp., *Sargassum polyphyllum* J. Agardh, and *Microdictyon setchellianum* Howe; the central portion, by *S. polyphyllum*, *S. echinocarpum* J. Agardh, and *Halimeda discoidea*, Decaisne; and the seaward portion, by *S. echinocarpum*, *H. discoidea* and *Dictyosphaeria cavernosa* (Forskål) Børgesen. *Lyngbya majuscula* Harvey ex Gomont and *Cladophoropsis membranacea* (C. Agardh) Børgesen are also of common occurrence.

Nanakuli, Oahu (Sta. 11). On the leeward coast of Oahu, a limestone shore with solution benches extends, with interruptions, from Nanakuli Beach to the northern end of Nanakuli town, near Maile Head (Fig. 4). The bench is generally 50 ft or less wide, although at the end of one section it is about 100 ft. This is a very short section, however, and the bench there occupies less than one-half acre. The bench platform is about one foot above sea level, but it is less often exposed than is the bench at Station 5, described above. This is due to a prevailing heavy swell in the region, so that even at low tide large waves breaking over the bench may make collecting impossible. The algal turf is as well developed here as at Station 5. *Valonia aegagropila* C. Agardh is the dominant species. *Jania capillacea* Harvey, *Sargassum* sp., and *Padina* sp. are common. Zonation of algae was not studied, but it was not obvious.

Gastropods other than *Conus* common on solution benches are *Mitra litterata* Lamarck, *Haminoea aperta* Pease, and *Cypraea caputserpentis* Linné. A number of sea anemones are abundant. The most conspicuous Crustacea are xanthid crabs, snapping shrimp, and hermit crabs. The microfauna is especially rich. Prominent are amphipods, isopods, harpacticoid copepods, polychaetes, and Foraminifera.

WATER-LEVELED BENCHES

A formation typical of palagonite tuff and weathered basalt shores in Hawaii is the water-leveled bench, the characteristics and origin of which are dis-

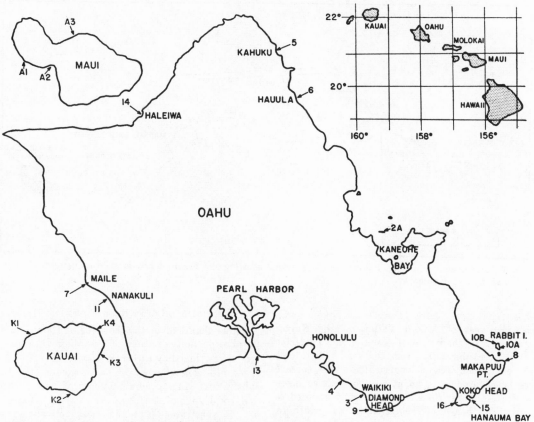

FIG. 4. Maps of the Hawaiian Islands showing location of stations. Stations lacking locality data on maps are: 2A, Sand (Ahuolaka) Island; 4, Ala Moana; 13, Ft. Kamehameha; Al, Olowalu; A2, Maalaea Bay; A3, Lower Paia; K1, Milolii; K2, Poipu; K3, Kapaa; K4, Moloaa.

cussed in detail by Wentworth (1938). Benches of this type may be 10-12 ft above sea level on exposed coasts, but are only 2-3 ft above sea level in sheltered places. Most of them are less than 100 ft wide. A steep subaerial slope landward of the bench is characteristic (Fig. 2B).

Unlike the solution bench, water-leveled benches are characterized by a well-developed rampart (Fig. 2B) of slightly higher rock at the seaward edge. The outer face of this zone is a steep cliff, characteristically occupied by echinoids. Landward of the rampart is the water-leveled bench proper. Its surface may be quite smooth or bear vertical irregularities of the order of a few inches to a foot. These are often due to differences in hardness of the dipping beds of tuff on which this type of bench is most often found.

Water-leveled benches which were given special study were as follows:

Lower Paia, Maui (Sta. A3). A fairly typical water-leveled bench near Lower Paia, Maui (Figs. 4, 5) was visited on 5 August 1956. The shore profile at this station is similar to that shown in Fig. 2B. The seaward face of the rampart zone is steep. The rampart zone (Fig. 5) averages about 15 ft wide. Its surface is irregular and is covered by a luxuriant algal turf, composed of many species. The water-

FIG. 5. Photograph of water-leveled bench at Lower Paia, Maui (Station A3) from subaerial slope. The 100-sq ft quadrat is outlined. Tide pools and rampart are also visible.

leveled part of the bench (Figs. 2B, 5) is about 15 ft wide and quite smooth. It bears a low algal turf which binds some sand. The tide was extremely low (—0.2 ft) during the period of observation, and this region was quite dry. Landward of it are large tide pools 1-2 ft deep (Fig. 5).

Milolii, Kauai (Sta. K1). Two broad marine

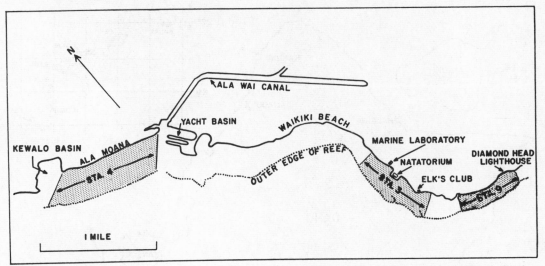

Fig. 6. Outline map of the south shore of Oahu, showing the nearly continuous fringing reef, Stations 3, 4, and 9, and landmarks.

benches fringe the shore at each end of a small beach, just east of Milolii Valley on the Napali (north) coast of the island of Kauai (Fig. 4). This region is accessible only from the sea. Four days were spent in the area in August 1955. The surface of the bench studied is about one foot above mean sea level. At minus tides it is completely exposed to the air. The benches reach a maximum width of about 200 ft. The algal turf of the platform is very low and does not present a "healthy" appearance. The dominant species is *Wurdemannia miniata* (Lamarck and DeCandolle) Feldmann and Hamel. Other species observed were *Dictyosphaeria* sp., probably young *D. cavernosa* (Forskål) Børgesen, *Gelidiella* sp., *Jania capillacea,* and *Valonia aegagropila.* At about 110 ft from shore a low pink encrusting alga, probably *Porolithon* sp., is present, and it continues to the seaward edge. The differences in flora between Station K1 and the solution benches may be due to the absence of heavy surf over most of the former.

ABRASION RAMP BENCHES

The distribution and formation of abrasion ramp benches on Hawaiian shores has not been treated in detail, but Wentworth (1938) includes a photograph of one. The formation is found on limestone and/or tuff shores. Abrasion is caused by washing of sand and gravel back and forth across the bench by waves. The result is a rather smooth sloping surface extending from below the low tide line often to several feet above it (Fig. 2C). A dense but low algal mat, usually of a varied flora, is typically present. Abrasion ramp benches are limited in size and constitute only a minor portion of shorelines. Three such benches were visited, Station 10A, on the southern shore of Rabbit (Manana) Island; Station 16, near Kawaihoa Point, on the eastern end of Maunalua Bay, Oahu; and Station A2, west of Kihei on Maalaea Bay, Maui (Fig. 3).

THE SUBTIDAL CORAL REEF PLATFORM HABITAT

More than half of the shoreline of Oahu and comparable portions of some of the other Hawaiian Islands are fringed by rather narrow coral reefs. These reefs are characterized by a predominantly sandy substratum. Living coral, patches of bare limestone and coral rubble also comprise varying proportions of the substratum, but the most actively growing corals and coralline algae are typically found at the outer edges and on the reef slopes. The reef platforms are typically subtidal and variable in depth, being usually 2-10 ft below mean sea level. Occasionally portions of the reef platform are exposed at low spring tides. The platform of some reefs is raised at the outer edge, but this rampart is often not well developed. A general discussion of Hawaiian coral reefs is given by McCaughey (1918). A typical reef fringes the south shore of Oahu, interrupted only by dredged channels and the drainage of streams. Investigation was concentrated on sections of this reef near the laboratory, noted as Stations 3 and 9 (Fig. 6). Additional collections were made at Station 4.

Brief descriptions of Stations 9 and 3, based on field notes, follow. They emphasize, respectively, the characteristics of the reef normal to the shore and parallel to the shore. The ecological notes on *Conus* which are included will serve as an introduction to the quantitative data presented below.

Diamond Head, Oahu (Sta. 9). The fringing reef on the Honolulu side of Diamond Head may be roughly divided into four zones. Zone (1) is an intertidal area of moderate surf which breaks over a substratum of detrital limestone. Landward of this zone, above the high tide limit, is a narrow sand beach. A dense growth of many species of algae occurs in zone (1), except in the bare limestone surge channels and tidal pools. This region takes the form of an abrasion ramp bench, 30-50 ft wide, which slopes to seaward. No *Conus* were observed here, but this is perhaps due to the convenience of the area to shell collectors.

Zone (2) comprises the broad submerged reef platform, 2-6 ft below 0 tide datum. The substratum is characterized by areas of coral rubble, coral heads and sand, more or less intermingled. This region comprises most of the width of the reef, which reaches a maximum of about 1,500 ft. The areas with substratum of coral rubble are extensive. Conspicuous benthic algae are absent. These areas are also barren of large gastropods, probably because of lack of shelter provided by the pieces of rubble, which are readily moved back and forth by wave action. Scattered coral heads, usually bearing only a small colony of living coral, harbor a variety of invertebrates, including *Conus pennaceus* on the sand beneath. *C. rattus* and *C. imperialis* are occasionally epifaunal on dead coral. Sandy areas interspersed with reef limestone outcrops form the typical habitat of *Conus flavidus* and *C. lividus*, which are usually epifaunal. *C. abbreviatus* is also found, usually burrowing in sand in these areas.

Zone (3), which is variable in width, is characterized by large areas of dead coral reef, which appear to be eroding. The surface areas of these regions are often near the 0 tide datum and hence are often dry at low tide. At high tide, surf over these areas is heavy. *Conus rattus* is occasionally found, and *C. ebraeus* sometimes occurs on the vertical edges of the eroding coral areas, or in small crevices of sand below. Channels 4-6 ft deep and normal to the shore separate these areas near the outer edge of the reef and broaden into extensive areas with sand substratum just inshore. *Conus pulicarius* is found typically beneath the surface of the sand. Reef fishes abound about the steep edges.

Zone (4) is the zone of heavy surf at the outer edge of the reef, where coral flourishes. Environmental conditions precluded extensive observations. The most common alga at Station 9 was *Lyngbya majuscula*. *Sargassum, Hypnea, Codium,* and others were also common.

Waikiki, Oahu (Sta. 3). The wide fringing reef at Station 3 appeared to offer a wide variety of microhabitats. The collecting area extended about 1,000 ft north, and about 2,500 ft south, from the Waikiki Branch of the Hawaii Marine Laboratory (Fig. 6). The width of the reef is about 600-1,000 ft. Inshore areas of the southern portion, to about the Elks Club, are characterized by more or less abundant coral rocks set in sand or sand-rubble substratum. *Conus lividus* and *C. flavidus* are often common. *C. abbreviatus* sometimes occurs in the larger sandy areas between coral rocks. Much of the reef area to seaward is eroding dead coral reef, as at Station 9, and *Conus* is generally absent. At the seaward edge of the reef are sandy areas, with some limestone outcrops. The reef slope is gentle and quite sandy. Although the area appears suitable, *Conus* occurs only occasionally. This area can be visited only on

calm days, and the usually heavy surf may make this portion of the habitat unsuitable for the snails. *C. flavidus* and *C. distans* have been found however. The latter typically occurs at reef edges and generally in rougher water than the other species of *Conus*.

From the Elks Club (Fig. 6) to just north of the laboratory, the substratum is quite different. An inner reef, shoreward of a dredged channel, is limestone bench and rubble and devoid of *Conus*. The outer reef is generally deeper, being 3-8 ft below MLLW. Sand is the dominant substratum, but coral heads are abundant and there are some rubble areas. *C. lividus, C. flavidus,* and *C. ebraeus* occur but are rather sparse. *C. distans* is sometimes found at the outer edge.

The northern portion of the area sampled supported a richer fauna. The substratum was of coral heads and rocks, reef limestone, and rubble areas. A detailed discussion of this region was given by Edmondson (1928). *Conus pennaceus* occurred under rocks in sand. Epifaunal species included *C. rattus, C. flavidus, C. lividus, C. ebraeus,* and *C. abbreviatus,* none of which was uncommon. This area especially provided sites for attachment of *Conus* egg capsules. Subsequent to the investigation, however, much of this area was dredged, and the inshore portion covered by a sand beach, to create an area for swimming.

Other reefs studied were essentially similar to the two described. Helfrich & Kohn (1955) and Kohn & Helfrich (1957) discussed the characteristics of Station K3. Extensive collecting was also carried out at reefs on Oahu at Maile (Sta. 7) and Ala Moana (Sta. 4). The location of the more important reef stations is shown in Fig. 4.

LIFE HISTORY OF *CONUS*

An account of spawning and larval development of *Conus* in Hawaii is in preparation and will be published elsewhere. Therefore, only information of ecological importance will be presented here.

SPAWNING SITE AND SEASON

Egg capsules of at least 12 species of *Conus* have been collected in Hawaii, chiefly by Ostergaard (1950) and by the writer and colleagues.

Coral reef platforms, but not marine benches, provide suitable attachment sites for egg capsules of *Conus*. Of 36 egg masses collected in the field, 29 were recorded from reef platforms. An almost complete absence of records from marine bench habitats suggests that spawning is unsuccessful there. This is probably due to the absence of protected pools in which egg capsules may be deposited without being subject to desiccation at low tide and/or torn away by heavy surf at high tide. Recruitment of bench populations is probably from pelagic veliger larvae which have been carried from other areas and are washed onto marine benches in condition to settle and assume the benthic mode of life.

All of the capsules were found between the months of February and August, although search for them was not confined to, or emphasized during, this period. The data suggest that most species of *Conus* spawn during about the same part of the year. The spawning season of most species for which more than one egg mass has been collected is rather extended over the period between the months cited. The most complete data are for *C. pennaceus,* of which 12 egg masses were collected, all in the months of May, June, July and August. The data are probably sufficient to establish the breeding season as continuing through these months.

REPRODUCTION AND LARVAL DEVELOPMENT

As is typical in the Prosobranchia, the sexes are separate in *Conus.* The male possesses an extensible penis. Copulation was not observed. In spawning, eggs are released from the genital aperture and pass ventrally over the foot in a temporary groove to the prominent aperture of the nidamental gland on the sole. There the capsular material is extruded, enclosing a number of eggs. The capsule is attached to a hard substratum, typically under a coral rock, or to the underside of the rock itself. Illustrations of the egg capsules of *Conus* are given by Ostergaard (1950). A number of capsules (3-78, in 12 species studied) are deposited to form a cluster. The number of eggs per capsule varied from 40 to 11,400 in 5 species studied.

In 4 species studied (*C. vitulinus, C. abbreviatus, C. imperialis, C. quercinus*), the trochophore stage is entered at 2-6 days, and the veliger stage at 6-10 days, after spawning. Larvae hatch as veligers about two weeks after spawning. These observations are in agreement with those of Ostergaard (1950), who also reported development of 4 other species, which hatched 12-16 days after spawning. Almost all of the eggs in a capsule develop completely, and no nurse eggs were observed.

With the exception of one species, the length of the pelagic stage could not be determined. The maximum survival time of free-swimming veligers in the writer's laboratory was 9 days. Metamorphosis was observed only in *Conus pennaceus,* which has an extremely short free-swimming stage of less than one day. On the second day after hatching, metamorphosis is virtually completed and the young snail begins to craw about on its foot. These juveniles survived for periods of up to 20 days, but no significant growth was observed after hatching. The nature of the food at this stage is unknown. Protozoa abounded in the cultures. Thorson (1946) concluded that all prosobranch larvae known from the Oresund feed on phytoplankton, and he calculated the theoretical maximum diameter of the food to be 5-45μ. The mouths of *Conus* veligers measured were of about the same diameter as the esophagus of the smaller larvae measured by Thorson. Thus the larvae of *Conus* probably depend for food on phytoplankton, nannoplankton and detritus. Examination of squash preparations of *C. pennaceus* a few days after settling revealed the presence of radula teeth. These differ in form from the adult teeth, being shorter in pro-

portion to the thickness, and they are probably not functional. Thus neither the method of feeding nor the food is known at this stage of the life history.

POST-LARVAL DEVELOPMENT AND GROWTH

It was possible to study post-larval development only in *Conus pennaceus.* At hatching, the larvae of this species are several times as large as those of other species, measuring about 1.3 mm in shell length.

A rough estimate of the rate of post-larval growth was obtained in the following manner. Four clusters of egg capsules of *Conus pennaceus* were collected in a large tide pool adjacent to Station 9 on 13 August 1955, and additional clusters were observed but not removed. Adults collected at the same time ranged from 33 to 37 mm in shell length. On 30 November, 3.5 months later, 8 specimens of *C. pennaceus* were collected in the same tide pool. Of these, 6 were probably hatched from egg capsules the previous summer (Fig. 7). On 27 December, 41 specimens of *C. pennaceus* were collected in this tide pool.

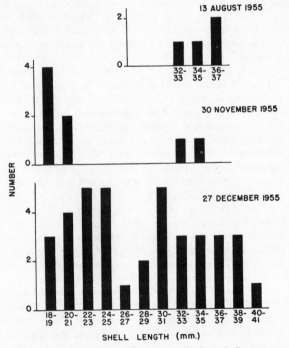

FIG. 7. Length-frequency distribution of *Conus pennaceus* at Station 9, 13 August-27 December 1955.

The length-frequency distribution of the December population is also shown in Fig. 7. Although bimodality suggesting two age classes is evident, it is quite possible that all of the specimens were spawned the previous summer. The minimum at 26-27 mm may not indicate separation of two age classes, because of the large number of specimens of greater length collected. If these were older specimens, most of them probably would have been collected from the tide pool on previous occasions. As noted above, the breeding season is long. The mean shell length of first age-class individuals in November was 19 mm, with S.D. = 6.3 mm. In December, mean shell length was 28 mm, with S.D. = 7.7 mm. The mean mean growth rate was thus 5-6 mm/month during the first 3.5 months. During the next month the mean increment was 5 mm.

It was not possible to obtain any other growth data of this type, since such isolated populations are exceptional. Shells of a number of specimens of *Conus ebraeus, C. abbreviatus,* and *C. sponsalis* from a marine bench (Sta. 5) were marked with a diamond point vibrator and returned to their natural habitat. Of these, three specimens, all *C. ebraeus,* were recovered after 133-221 days following release. The growth increments ranged from 0.3-0.6 mm shell length and 0.2-0.4 g wet weight per month. Although only these data are available, they presumably give the correct order of magnitude of growth of older individuals.

If the growth rates cited hold for other species, it may be concluded that, in species comparable in size to *Conus pennaceus* and *G. ebraeus* (Fig. 9), several millimeters per month in shell length are added during the first few months, the rate later falling off to a few tenths of a millimeter per month.

ABUNDANCE AND POPULATION DENSITY OF *CONUS*

Darwin (1859: 319) pointed out that most species of animals are characterized by being rather rare. Since species of *Conus* are not exceptions, and because time available for collecting was limited, several of the less abundant species are represented by rather small samples. In order to determine the ecological relationships of the species, the data presented in this report have therefore been subjected to appropriate statistical analyses.

As MacArthur (1957) has shown, the expected abundance of the rth rarest species in the community of a single habitat which has been adequately sampled, and in which ecological niches are nonoverlapping and continuous, is

$$\left(\frac{m}{n}\right) \sum_{i=1}^{r} \left(\frac{1}{n-i+1}\right) \qquad (1)$$

where m = the total number of individuals, n = the number of species, and i = the species rank. All of the data on abundance of *Conus* have been presented in comparison with the distribution expected according to this theory.

The Marine Bench Habitat

Solution Benches. The population of *Conus* at Station 5 was the densest stable population studied on Oahu. Eight species were collected, of which *C. ebraeus* was the most abundant. In 61 quantitatively sampled 100-sq ft quadrats, four species were collected. The relative abundance of species is shown in Fig. 8. If only data from the quantitatively sampled areas are included (Fig. 8A) a homogeneous population or single community is indicated by agreement

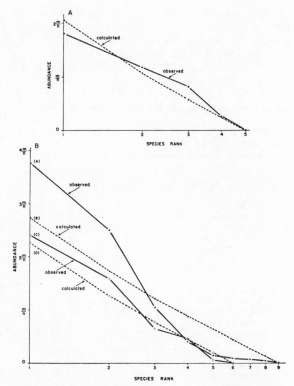

Fig. 8. Abundance of species of *Conus* at Station 5. A. Data from quantitatively sampled quadrats. m = 136, n = 4. Species rank: 1 = *ebraeus*, 2 = *abbreviatus*, 3 = *sponsalis*, 4 = *chaldaeus*. B. Curves (A) and (B), data from all collections at Station 5. m = 500, n = 8. Curves (C) and (D), data from all collections, but with exclusion of three species characteristic of other habitats. Explanation in text. m = 484, n = 5. Species rank: (A) and (B) 1 = *ebraeus*, 2 = *abbreviatus*, 3 = *sponsalis*, 4 = *chaldaeus*, 5 = *lividus*, 6 = *flavidus*, 7 = *rattus*, 8 = *pennaceus;* (C) and (D) 1 = *ebraeus*, 2 = *abbreviatus*, 3 = *sponsalis*, 4 = *chaldaeus*, 5 = *rattus*.

of the observed curve with the expected distribution for the community of a uniform habitat.

Curve (A) in Fig. 8B is based on summation of results of all 18 collecting trips made to Station 5. The slope is steep, since common species are too common and rare species too rare. The curve is therefore not in good agreement with the theoretical distribution (Curve B), and a heterogeneous population, or the inclusion of occupants of more than one habitat, is indicated. The heterogeneous aspect of the total population may be explained as follows: Three of the species included occur more typically in habitats other than the solution bench platform. All three, *Conus pennaceus, C. flavidus,* and *C. lividus,* are typically subtidal species, which are rarely exposed by receding tide, and they occur much more commonly where such a habitat is provided, as will be shown below. If the abundance curve is plotted without these species, the resulting line (C) is considerably straighter and approaches the theoretical curve (D) more closely. It is therefore apparent that the sparse occurrence of three species which are more typical residents of a different habitat contributes to the heterogeneity shown by the curve (A) for total abundance at Station 5.

The mean density of *Conus* on this bench is 2.2 individuals/100 sq ft, based on the 61 quantitatively sampled quadrats. The mean population density of species censused in quadrats is shown in Table 1A.

TABLE 1. Population Density of Species of *Conus* at Two Marine Bench Stations.

Species	Mean number per 100 sq. ft. (=9.3m.²)
A. Station 5	
Conus ebraeus..................	1.02
Conus abbreviatus..............	0.66
Conus sponsalis................	0.41
Conus chaldaeus................	0.15
	2.24
B. Station K1	
Conus abbreviatus..............	0.85
Conus ebraeus..................	0.55
Conus sponsalis................	0.48
Conus catus....................	0.24
Conus chaldaeus................	0.18
Conus rattus...................	0.09
Conus flavidus.................	0.03
Conus retifer..................	0.03
	2.44

The mean biomass of all species was calculated to be about 0.6 g dry organic matter/100 sq ft, or 0.065 g/m².

The species differ in size. Length-frequency distributions are shown in Fig. 9. The population is essentially an adult one, and juvenile specimens are rarely found. Despite numerous collecting trips at all times of year, no egg capsules of *Conus* were ever found.

At Station 11, nine species of *Conus* were collected, of which *C. sponsalis* was the most abundant. In eight 100-sq ft quadrats, quantitatively sampled in September, four species were present, with mean density of 5.5 individuals/100 sq ft and abundances as shown in Fig. 10. The curve shows that the observed number of *C. sponsalis* (38) is much higher than that expected in a homogeneous population containing the observed numbers of the other species.

An even denser population was observed on 29 November 1955. At this time, counts of two areas, each of but one sq ft, were 3 and 7 individuals of *Conus sponsalis*. No other species were present. This abundance (= 500/100 sq ft) was present only on the extremely wide area of bench described above.

This high density of *Conus sponsalis* is believed to be related to the fact that the individuals were much smaller (mean length 13.5 mm) than elsewhere (mean length 22.1 mm at Sta. 5). Length-frequency distributions of specimens collected at Station 11 in September and November are shown in Fig. 11A. The September population is unimodal. However, the

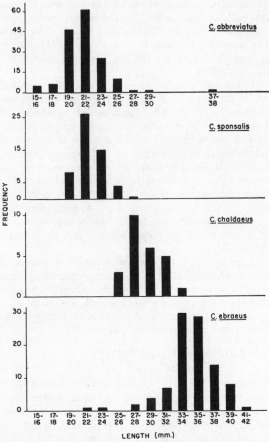

FIG. 9. Length-frequency histograms of the dominant species of *Conus* at Station 5.

November population is bimodal, with an absence of individuals of 12-13 mm. This suggests that a new age class of 6-11 mm individuals has been added to the population. Unfortunately, no information is available on the reproductive cycle of *C. sponsalis*. However, egg capsules of many species of *Conus* are found in summer and if eggs were laid in August, hatching might take place in September, with settling of pelagic veliger larvae in October giving rise to a dense population of juvenile individuals in November. Although no egg capsules were found at Station 11, the bench is interrupted by rather deep, somewhat protected pools, which may provide suitable spawning sites. Alternatively, larvae may arrive in numbers from other areas in settling condition.

Population density varied greatly in the area of Station 11. Particularly densely populated sections were quantitatively sampled by the transect method. In these regions, two transects of eight quadrats gave the mean density of 5.5 individuals (of four species)/100 sq ft. The maximum observed density of about 500 juveniles/100 sq ft has been mentioned.

On other occasions, searches of 0.63 and 1.25 man-hrs resulted in only one and three specimens, respectively. Since the time required to sample a 100-sq ft quadrat was usually 5 minutes (0.08 hr), this

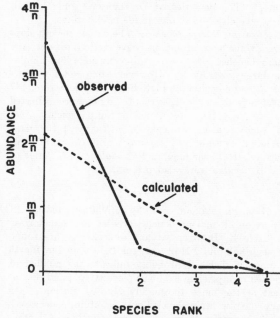

FIG. 10.   Abundance of species of *Conus* at Station 11.   Data from quantitatively sampled quadrats.   m = 44, n = 4.   Species rank: 1 = *sponsalis*, 2 = *chaldaeus*, 3 = *ebraeus*, 4 = *rattus*.

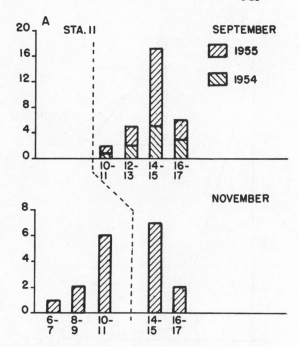

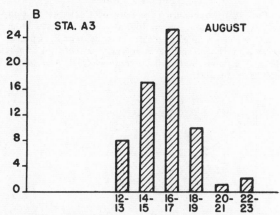

FIG 11.   Length-frequency histograms of *Conus sponsalis*.   A, Station 11.   B, Station A3.

factor can be used to convert time-relative to space-relative density.   A search of 0.63 man-hr would thus cover 7,900 sq ft and 1.25 man-hrs 15,600 sq ft. Corresponding densities are 0.01 and 0.02 individuals/ 100 sq ft, respectively.

Water-leveled Benches.   Six species of *Conus* were collected at Station A3, of which *C. sponsalis* was by far the most abundant.   The abundance of species is plotted in Fig. 12.   Fig. 12A represents total abundance, and 12B the abundance in a single quantitatively sampled 100-sq ft quadrat on the water-leveled part of the bench (Fig. 4).   Both curves show an obvious inflection point, which is caused by the relatively great abundance of *C. sponsalis*.   Disagreement with the calculated theoretical distribution suggests a heterogeneous population.

Density on the water-leveled bench at Station A3 was second only to that in the two 1-sq ft quadrats sampled at Station 11.   At Station A3, only the single quadrat was sampled.   However, this represented a considerable fraction of the total available area (Fig. 4).   One specimen of *Conus flavidus* and 25 *C. sponsalis* were present in this area.

The length-frequency distribution of *Conus sponsalis* at Station A3 is unimodal (Fig. 11B).   The population is probably an adult one, although the individuals are not as large as those at Station 5.   The relative superabundance of *C. sponsalis* cannot therefore be ascribed to an influx of first age class juveniles.   Since the observations were made on 5 August, during the probable spawning season, this is even less likely.

Marine benches do not in general provide suitable

sites for deposition of egg capsules of *Conus*.   However, a specimen of *C. catus* was collected at Station A3 in spawning condition, as evidenced by the deposition of an egg capsule which was attached to the shell after collection.

Station K1.   At Station K1, all *Conus* present in 33 quadrats, each of 100 sq ft, were counted.   Eight species were present in the area sampled, of which the most abundant was *C. abbreviatus*.   Relative abundance of species is shown in Fig. 13.   The distribution calculated from Equation (1) is also included, and the data are seen to be in excellent agreement with it.   This supports the observation that the habitat is a rather uniform one, with a homogeneous population, or single community, of *Conus*.

The solution bench at Station 5 was the only area

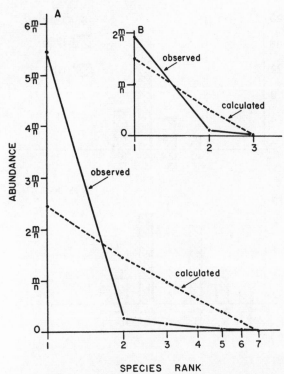

FIG. 12. Abundance of species of *Conus* at Station A3. A, Total data. m = 166, n = 6. B, Data from quantitatively sampled quadrat. m = 26, n = 2. Species rank: A. 1 = *sponsalis*, 2 = *rattus*, 3 = *catus*, 4 = *flavidus*, 5 = *abbreviatus*, 6 = *chaldaeus*; B. 1 = *sponsalis*, 2 = *flavidus*.

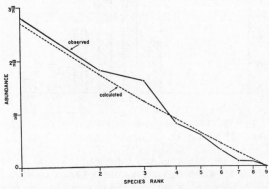

FIG. 13. Abundance of species of *Conus* at Station K1. Data from quantitatively sampled quadrats. m = 81, n = 8. Species rank: 1 = *abbreviatus*, 2 = *ebraeus*, 3 = *sponsalis*, 4 = *catus*, 5 = *chaldaeus*, 6 = *rattus*, 7 = *flavidus*, 8 = *retifer*.

sampled more intensively than Station K1. The three most abundant species are the same at the two sites, although the order is different. The mean density of all *Conus* species at Sta. K1 is 2.44 individuals/100 sq ft, based on the 33 quantitatively sampled quadrats. The mean density of each species is shown in Table 1B. The mean density of *C. abbreviatus* is higher, while that of *C. ebraeus* is lower, than at Sta-

tion 5. The densities of *C. sponsalis* and *C. chaldaeus* are about the same at the two stations.

Abrasion Ramp Benches. The rather smooth sloping surface and attendant wave action of abrasion ramp benches provide a rather unfavorable habitat for large gastropods. However, some shallow crevices provide shelter at high tide. A total of but 47 specimens of seven species of *Conus* were collected in five field trips to abrasion ramp benches. On all such benches studied, *C. rattus* was the most abundant species. *C. sponsalis* and *C. abbreviatus* were relatively common, and *C. chaldaeus, C. flavidus,* and *C. lividus* were also present.

SUMMARY

Data on abundance and population density of *Conus* on all marine benches studied are summarized in Table 4. Between six and nine species are found in such habitats. However, the figures in the fourth column of Table 2 probably indicate the number of species comprising a homogeneous population, at least at the more thoroughly studied stations. On very narrow water-leveled and solution benches, *C. sponsalis* is the dominant species, and only 1-3 other species may be present. Wider benches are occupied by proportionally greater numbers of species. As will be shown below, the species are then distributed non-randomly across the bench platform from shore to seaward edge.

TABLE 2. Summary of Abundance and Population Density of *Conus* on Marine Benches

Station	Width of Bench (ft.)	Total Number of Species	Number of Species in Quadrats	Number of Quadrats Sampled	Density (No./100 sq. ft.)	Most Abundant Species
Solution Bench Stations						
5..........	60	8	4	61	2.24	*ebraeus*
11..........	40	9	4	8	5.5 (0.01*-500)	*sponsalis*
Water-leveled Bench Stations						
K1..........	200	9	8	33	2.44	*abbreviatus*
A3..........	15	6	2	1	26	*sponsalis*
Abrasion Ramp Bench Stations						
Total........	...	6	..	0	1.0*	*rattus*

*Calculated from time-relative density.

The species of greatest abundance is variable among benches of similar, as well as different, geological origin. Abrasion ramp benches were not studied in detail, hence data from them are combined in Table 2. However, *Conus rattus* was the most abundant species at all three such benches visited, and it may be termed typical of this formation. This species was of minor importance on both solution benches and water-leveled benches.

Sampling of a large number of 100-sq ft quadrats at Stations 5 and K1 indicated that a fairly stable population of 2-2.5 individuals/100 sq ft may be expected on solution benches and water-leveled benches. Other areas sampled quantitatively were those in which extremely large populations were observed by inspection. Conversion of time-relative to space relative density suggests a lower limit of population density on marine benches of about 0.01 individual/ 100 sq ft.

THE SUB-TIDAL REEF PLATFORM HABITAT

Inspection of a number of coral reef platforms led to the conclusion that the abundance and distribution of *Conus* in these habitats are characterized by patchiness. This not unexpected phenomenon must be considered in interpreting the data presented in this section and in the following one on distribution.

In Figs. 14-17, data on abundance at the four thoroughly sampled reef stations are presented. No one species is most abundant on all of the reefs. At each station, however, either *Conus flavidus* or *C. lividus*, or both, represent one or both of the two most abundant species. This is in marked contrast to marine bench stations where, as has been shown above, these two species occur infrequently.

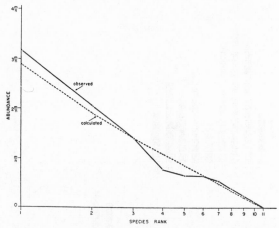

FIG. 15. Abundance of species of *Conus* at Station 4. m = 78, n = 10. Species rank: 1 = *lividus*, 2 = *flavidus*, 3 = *abbreviatus*, 4 = *imperialis*, 5 = *ebraeus*, 6 = *rattus*, 7 = *vitulinus*, 8 = *sponsalis*, 9 = *chaldaeus*, 10 = *vexillum*.

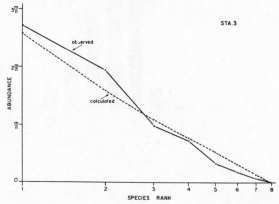

FIG. 14. Abundance of species of *Conus* at Station 3. m = 182, n = 9. Species rank: 1 = *flavidus*, 2 = *lividus*, 3 = *ebraeus*, 4 = *abbreviatus*, 5 = *rattus*, 6 = *imperialis*, 7 = *striatus*.

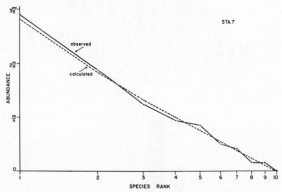

FIG. 16. Abundance of species of *Conus* at Station 7. m = 182, n = 9. Species rank: 1 = *sponsalis*, 2 = *lividus*, 3 = *ebraeus*, 4 = *flavidus*, 5 = *pennaceus*, 6 = *abbreviatus*, 7 = *rattus*, 8 = *distans*, 9 = *chaldaeus*.

At only one of the adequately studied reef stations is the most abundant species neither *Conus lividus* nor *C. flavidus*. At Station 7, the most abundant species was *C. sponsalis*. This is attributed to substratum factors, which will be discussed in detail below.

At all stations, agreement of the results of analysis of abundance data with the curve calculated from Equation (1) is sufficient to justify the conclusion that the subtidal reef platform constitutes a single rather than composite habitat, which supports a homogeneous community or interspecific population of *Conus*. The striking agreement of the observed and calculated curves for Station 7, which is the closest of any census thus far analyzed in this manner (MacArthur, personal communication), is probably fortuitous.

Population Density. Population density of *Conus* was more difficult to study directly on subtidal reef

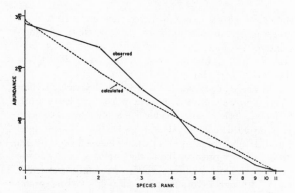

Fig. 17. Abundance of species of *Conus* at Station 9. m = 187, n = 10. Species rank: 1 = *flavidus*, 2 = *pennaceus*, 3 = *lividus*, 4 = *abbreviatus*, 5 = *pulicarius*, 6 = *ebraeus*, 7 = *imperialis*, 8 = *vexillum*, 9 = *rattus*, 10 = *marmoreus*.

platforms than on marine benches. This was due both to technical difficulties and to the obvious patchiness of the populations. During most field trips,

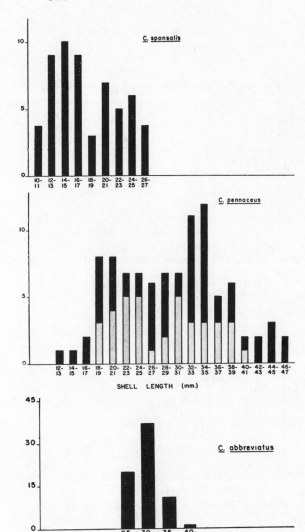

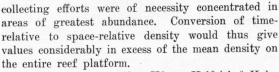

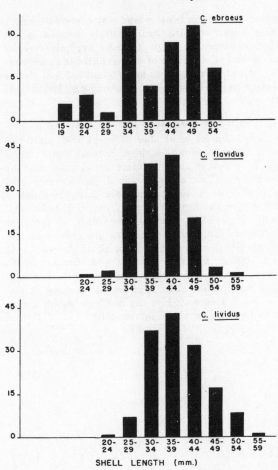

Fig. 18. Length-frequency distribution of *Conus* species at four reef stations. Stippled portion of *C. pennaceus* histograms represent collection at Station 9, 27 December 1955. See Fig. 7.

collecting efforts were of necessity concentrated in areas of greatest abundance. Conversion of time-relative to space-relative density would thus give values considerably in excess of the mean density on the entire reef platform.

At one reef station (Sta. K3, see Helfrich & Kohn 1955) transects of known area were sampled quantitatively. The results (Table 3) show that the mean population density of all species in the area sampled was 0.16 individual/100 sq ft. This is lower by an order of magnitude than the density on marine benches. This relationship is probably generally valid, although favorable parts of reef platforms may support local populations which approach those of marine benches in density.

The mean biomass of *Conus* in the quantitatively sampled areas at Station K3 was calculated to be 0.06 g dry weight organic matter/100 sq ft (0.0065 g/m²). Although the population density on marine benches is about 15 times as large as on reef platforms, the biomass of *Conus* is only ten times as

TABLE 3. Population Density of *Conus* at Station K3.

Area Sampled (sq. ft.)	Species	Density (No./100 sq. ft. =9.3 m.²)
3,000........	*C. ebraeus*	0.07
	C. abbreviatus	0.07
	C. chaldaeus	0.03
	C. flavidus	0.03
		0.20
3,000........	*C. ebraeus*	0.10
1,200........	*C.* (species not noted)	0.17

Mean Density of All Species=0.16

great. Although the comparisons are extremely rough, the discrepancy is probably real. Comparison of Figs. 9 and 18 clearly shows the prevalence of larger individuals in the populations occupying reef habitats. The mean shell length of two species common in both habitats is compared in Table 4. These values are 13% and 54% larger in reef platform than in marine bench populations of *C. ebraeus* and *C. abbreviatus*, respectively. This may reflect the more equable environmental characteristics of the former habitat. The mean shell length of *C. sponsalis* on reefs was 17.8 mm. In bench populations, mean shell length ranged from 13 to 22 mm. The explanation may be that *C. sponsalis* occupies those parts of reef platforms where conditions most closely approximate those of marine benches.

TABLE 4. Mean Shell Length of Reef and Bench Populations of *Conus ebraeus* and *C. abbreviatus*.

| | LENGTH IN MILLIMETERS | | | |
| | All Reefs | | Sta. 5 (bench) | |
	Mean	S.D.	Mean	S.D.
C. ebraeus...	39.0	9.7	34.6	3.2
C. abbreviatus	32.7	3.1	21.3	3.5

Except for the growth studies reported above, collection data were not analyzed for seasonal variations, since observations were made only during a single complete annual cycle.

COMMUNITY DIVERSITY AND HETEROGENEITY

The similarity of the species composition of different populations may be conveniently measured by an index of diversity given by Koch (1957):

$$I = \frac{t-n}{n(P-1)} \tag{2}$$

where n = the total number of species represented, P = the number of populations or communities sampled, and t = the arithmetic sum of $n_1, n_2, n_3, \ldots$ n_p, which are the numbers of species in each population or community. If I is low, the species composition differs greatly from population to population. I approaches unity with increasing similarity of the populations compared.

This index was calculated separately for the four most thoroughly sampled reef stations (Sta. 3, 4, 7, and 9) and the four most thoroughly sampled bench stations (Sta. 5, 11, K1, and A3). In both cases, I was 0.58. Comparison of total collections from all bench stations with those from all reef stations gave I = 0.61. The three indices are so similar that there would appear to be no greater ecological difference between the reef and bench habitats than among different reefs, or among different benches. This is misleading, however, since the index used measures only similarity of qualitative species composition.

Consideration of quantitative data concerning the relative abundance of species in different habitats suggests a different interpretation. It has been shown that individual reefs and benches generally support homogeneous populations of *Conus* (Figs. 8, 10, 12-17). Inspection of these graphs shows that three species, *C. sponsalis*, *C. ebraeus*, and *C. abbreviatus*, are rather consistently the most abundant species on

marine benches, while two entirely different species, *C. lividus* and *C. flavidus,* are dominant at almost every reef station.

A comparison of the relative abundance of all species at all reef and bench stations is shown in Fig. 19. Of the 18 species considered, 6 are proportionally more abundant on marine benches than on reef platforms. In 4, the discrepancy in abundance between the two types of habitats is at least one order of magnitude. Twelve species are relatively more abundant on reefs than on benches. The discrepancy is at least one order of magnitude in 8 of these.

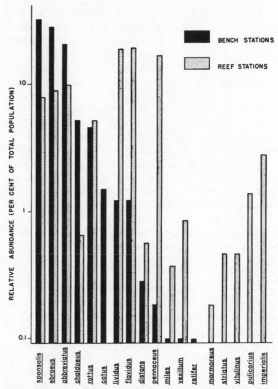

FIG. 19. Relative abundance of *Conus* species at all bench stations (solid histograms) and all reef stations (stippled histograms).

A more quantitative measure of community heterogeneity, H′, based on information theory, is given in Equation (3), which is modified from Margalef (1956):

$$H' = I_{m(AB)} - \left(\frac{I_{m(A)} + I_{m(B)}}{2}\right) \tag{3}$$

in which

$$I_m = \frac{1}{m} \log \frac{m!}{m_1! \cdot m_2! \cdot \ldots \cdot m_s!} \tag{4}$$

where m = the number of individuals of all species, m_1 = the number of individuals of the most abundant species, and m_s the number of the rarest species. The subscripts are equivalent to the values on the abscissas of Figs. 8, 10, and 12-17 and the values can be determined from data given in the graphs.

In Equation (3), A and B signify different communities. Equation (3) can be expanded for application to more than two communities. Equation (5) gives H′ for four communities, A, B, C, and D:

$$H' = I_{m(ABCD)} - \left(\frac{I_{m(A)} + I_{m(B)} + I_{m(C)} + I_{m(D)}}{4} \right) \quad (5)$$

sampled bench stations (Figs. 8, 10, 12, 13), H′ = 0.19.

Application of Equation (3) to summations of abundances at the four most thoroughly sampled reef stations (combined as community "A") and the four most thoroughly sampled bench stations (combined as community "B") gave H′ = 0.84.

The low heterogeneity of the *Conus* communities at individual stations has been demonstrated above. In addition, a low value resulted when the measure of heterogeneity introduced by Margalef (1956) was calculated for summed abundance data from four reef stations. Calculation from summed data from four benches gave a similar low value. However, comparison of summed data from four reefs with summed data from four benches resulted in a high value, indicating marked heterogeneity between the communities of *Conus* in these two kinds of habitats.

To summarize, two types of habitats, reef platforms and marine benches, were distinguished on the basis of observational data presented in the previous section. The data reported in the present section are interpreted as justifying this separation by indicating its significance to the gastropods under consideration, as well as to the investigator.

LOCAL DISTRIBUTION OF *CONUS*

MARINE BENCHES

Distribution of *Conus* across bench platforms was studied by the transect method. Two parallel lines, marked at 10-ft intervals and 10 ft apart, were secured across the bench from inshore edge to near the seaward margin. Ten-foot square areas of the platform were thus delimited. In each transect series, all of the *Conus* visible in each 100-sq ft area were counted. Counts were made at night, when the gastropods were actively crawling about on the bench. For convenience, it was assumed that all of the snails in the study areas were visible from above and none were buried in the algal turf or under stones or coral, as is often the case in the daytime.

Solution Benches. Distribution of *Conus* species, based on data from transects made at Station 5, is shown graphically in Fig. 20. Only the four most abundant species at Station 5 were observed in the transects. The populations of these species are not randomly distributed across the bench platform from pitted zone to outer edge. Interspecific differences are apparent from Fig. 20. Although *C. abbreviatus* is the more abundant, it and *C. sponsalis* are similarly distributed (Wilcoxon test: P ≫ .05). Most of the populations of these two species occupy a strip within 20 ft of shore, independently of the width of the bench. In contrast, the peak density of *C.*

Application of Equation (5) to the abundance data presented (Figs. 14-17) for populations of *Conus* at the four most thoroughly sampled reef stations gave H′ = 0.09. For the four most thoroughly

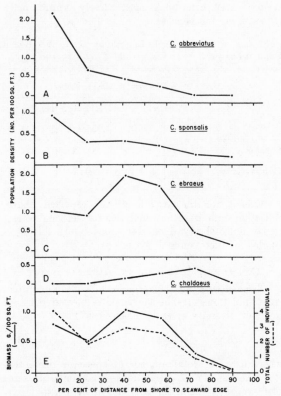

Fig. 20. Distribution of species of *Conus* across bench at Station 5. Each point to the left of 90% represents the average of 8 or 9 transects. The points at 90% represent the average of 5 transects. If width of bench varied from 60 ft at transect site, data were adjusted to a width of 60 ft.

ebraeus occurs about halfway across the bench. Lower densities occur near shore and near the outer edge. The density peak of the least abundant species, *C. chaldaeus,* is nearer the outer edge, but the edge itself is not occupied. This species rarely occurs in the shoreward zone occupied by *C. abbreviatus* and *C. sponsalis.* Wilcoxon tests showed that the distribution of *C. ebraeus* differs significantly from that of *C. sponsalis* (P< .05) and from that of *C. chaldaeus* (P< .01).

The biological significance of this pattern of distribution will be discussed below. The total density of all species of *Conus* tends to decrease toward the outer edge. Fig. 20E shows this distribution in density as well as in terms of dry weight, excluding shells.

At Station 11, the distribution of *Conus sponsalis* across the bench is shown in Fig. 21 to be essentially similar to that at Station 5. Most of the population occupies the more protected shoreward portion of the bench. The striking difference between the populations at Stations 5 and 11 is the virtual absence of *C. ebraeus* and *C. abbreviatus* at the latter (Fig. 10), although the type of habitat afforded seems suited to these species.

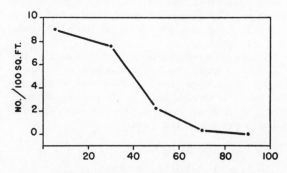

Fig. 21. Distribution of *Conus sponsalis* across bench at Station 11. Data from transects.

Water-leveled Benches. The patterns of distribution across the bench at Station K1, as determined by transecting (Fig. 22), are also quite similar to those at Station 5. As at Station 5, the distribution of *Conus sponsalis* and *C. abbreviatus* are not significantly different from each other (P ≫ .05). The distribution of *C. ebraeus* differs significantly from that of *C. sponsalis* (P< .01) as well as from that of *C. chaldaeus* (P< .01).

A striking difference between the distribution patterns at Stations 5 and K1 is that although the bench at Station K1 is three times as broad as Station 5, the four dominant species occur in bands which are only about twice as wide as those at Station 5. Since population density is similar, the density peaks of *C. abbreviatus* and *C. sponsalis* are therefore considerably higher at Station K1 (5.8 and 3.5, respectively) than at Station 5 (2.3 and 0.9, respectively). Thus, in contrast with Station 5, a broad area of bench platform is present which is occupied only by *C. chaldaeus* of the four dominant species under consideration.

In this region, four other species were found. The most abundant was *Conus catus*. Densities of the others, *C. rattus*, *C. flavidus*, and *C. retifer*, were very low. Thus three of the species characteristic of the solution bench habitat do not extend to the seaward portion of the broad water-leveled bench at Sta. K1 but are replaced there by four other species, only one of which is common.

The density distribution of all species is shown in Fig. 22G. The density peak is relatively nearer shore than at Station 5. Total density decreases toward the seaward edge at both stations.

Station A3. Search of the rampart zone at Sta. A3 revealed no specimens of *Conus*. In addition to *Morula tuberculata*, which is the dominant gastropod, the only other common large gastropod was *Mitra*

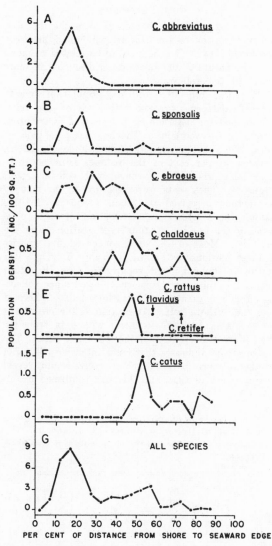

Fig. 22. Distribution of species of *Conus* across bench at Station K1. Data represent the average of two transects.

litterata. The factor which excludes *Conus* from this microhabitat is not known. Almost all of the specimens of *Conus sponsalis* were collected on the flat water-leveled platform. They were found with the shells partly buried in the algae-sand turf, and they thus apparently avoid desiccation during the day. The other species, in contrast, were found more typically on the inner margin of the rampart and level bench platform, or in other sites where the irregular tuff provides shelter during the day. These species may be too large to obtain adequate protection from the thin algal mat. The heterogeneity shown by the abundance curve (Fig. 12) can be accounted for by these microhabitat differences. It is of interest that the single specimen of *C. flavidus* collected in the quadrat was only 13 mm long, less than one-half the normal adult length of this species.

REEF PLATFORMS

The most apparent characteristic of the distribution of *Conus* on reef platforms, patchiness, has been mentioned above. It is believed to be related primarily to the nature of the substratum, discussed in more detail in the following section.

Technical difficulties and low population density on reef platforms precluded the use of the transect method for determining patterns of distribution normal to the shoreline. The less exact method of noting the approximate site of individual specimens, in terms of per cent of the distance from shore to outer edge where the specimen was collected, was employed. These data were recorded in the field by the method described by Kohn (1956a). In this manner the approximate distribution of 274 specimens of 11 species at four reef stations was determined. Most of the data concerned five species at three stations, as shown in Table 5. Data for Station 7 are tabulated separately. At the other stations, samples were somewhat biased since collecting effort was greater on the inshore half of the reef than the offshore half. At Station 7, the effort was not so biased, and the similarity with data from the other stations suggests that the latter are valid. The evidence thus indicates that more intensive collecting on the offshore parts of other reefs would reveal *Conus* in low density, and this was confirmed by inspection.

TABLE 5. Distribution of Five Species of *Conus* Across Reef Platforms at Stations 3, 7, and 9.

Per cent of Distance From Shore to Outer Edge	abbreviatus		flavidus		lividus		ebraeus		sponsalis		Total
Sta.	7	T	7	T	7	T	7	T	7	T	
0- 30.........	4	8	6	26	12	23	7	10	2	2	69
30- 60.........	0	4	6	16	10	18	2	10	20	20	68
60- 90.........	3	3	3	5	4	5	7	8	29	29	50
90-100.........	1	2	0	0	3	4	1	2	2	2	10
	8	17	15	47	29	50	17	30	53	53	197

T=Stations 3+7+9

The distribution patterns normal to the shore of *Conus abbreviatus, C. flavidus, C. lividus,* and *C. ebraeus* do not differ significantly from each other in the samples observed (P ≫ .05). The distribution of *C. sponsalis* at Station 7 may differ significantly (P > .05) from that of *C. ebraeus* and thus from those of all other species. This variation, however, is in the opposite direction from that observed on marine benches, where *C. sponsalis* characteristically occupies the shoreward zone (Figs. 20-22). On the subtidal reef platform at Station 7, the bulk of the population of this species occupies the central region of the reef (Table 5). This is probably due to the infrequency of suitable substratum nearer shore, as will be discussed below.

The distribution patterns of *Conus lividus* and *C. flavidus,* two closely related species which are also

similar in size, are strikingly similar, but some of the predominance of inshore individuals may be due to sampling bias.

The total density of all species is similar over most of the reef platform from shore to outer edge (Table 5). The total density decreases as the breaker line is approached, but sampling bias is also in this direction. The downward trend in the first three figures in the right hand column of Table 5 is probably not significant.

It may be concluded, then, that over most of the area of reef platforms the distribution of *Conus* is patchy, or clumped, and is not related to distance from shore or breaker line. In the zone of surf and very close to shore, however, *Conus* is less abundant, although present in low density.

SUBSTRATUM

MARINE BENCHES

By definition, a habitat must possess uniformity with respect to an important quality (Andrewartha & Birch 1954: 28). In the case of marine benches, uniformity is in the physiography of the bench platform, which constitutes the substratum of the species under consideration. This substratum is hard, rather smooth, and covered with an algal turf which may vary markedly in density. The algae, if sufficiently dense, bind sand, which is of importance because its presence increases the amount of residual water retained on the bench at low tide, and because it provides a medium into which *Conus* may burrow in order to escape desiccation or heavy wave action.

The substratum is of importance not only to adult *Conus*, but also to the pelagic veliger larvae. The importance of certain attributes of the substratum in the settling of pelagic larvae of certain other benthic marine invertebrates has been demonstrated by Wilson (1952, 1955), and this is likely to be the case in *Conus* also. Peculiarities of the substratum of marine benches may attract larvae of some species and not of others and thus determine qualitatively the species composition of the population of this habitat. The possibility of obtaining direct evidence relevant to this hypothesis was remote. However, it is probably one of a number of density-inactive mechanisms (Nicholson 1955) which determine the specific composition of populations of *Conus* on marine benches.

The hypothesis that the microhabitats of different species differed with respect to substratum preferred by the adults is more amenable to study. The predominant substratum of marine benches is the hard, algal-matted reef limestone noted above. In addition to the zonation of distribution discussed in the previous section, variations of substratum exist which may further differentiate microhabitats. These are patches of bare limestone or tuff which do not support an algal turf, and patches of sand, which usually fill shallow depressions in the bench platform. In the latter, benthic algae may or may not be present. The association of various species of *Conus* with these regions is summarized in Table 6A.

TABLE 6. Proportion of Populations of *Conus* Species Associated with Different Types of Substratum.

A. Marine Benches

Species	Sample Size	Bench with Algal Turf, Binding ± Sand		Sand Pockets or Patches on Bench		Bare Limestone or Turf	
		No.	%	No.	%	No.	%
C. sponsalis........	211	189	90%	10	5%	11	5%
C. abbreviatus.......	96	63	65%	25	26%	6	6%
C. ebraeus..........	97	63	65%	15	15%	17	18%
C. rattus...........	45	28	62%	5	11%	11	24%
C. chaldaeus.......	29	13	45%	8	28%	8	28%
C. catus...........	11	5	45%	2	18%	4	36%
	489	361	74%	65	13%	57	12%

B. Reef Platforms

Species	Sample Size	Sand		Reef Limestone' with or without Algal Turf		Dead Coral and Coral Rubble	
		No.	%	No.	%	No.	%
C. pulicarius.......	12	12	100%	0	0%	0	0%
C. abbreviatus.......	73	57	78%	13	18%	3	4%
C. lividus..........	133	86	64%	29	22%	18	14%
C. ebraeus..........	54	33	61%	11	20%	10	19%
C. flavidus.........	130	73	56%	34	26%	23	18%
C. imperialis.......	23	11	48%	6	26%	6	26%
C. sponsalis........	61	23	38%	24	39%	14	23%
C. rattus...........	37	8	22%	14	38%	15	40%
	659	405	61%	160	25%	94	14%

C. *Conus pennaceus* on Reef Platforms

	Sample Size	SAND		Reef Limestone, with or without Algal Turf	Dead Coral and Coral Rubble
		Visible From Above	Under Rocks		
day........	79	2	70	3	4 (all under rocks)
night........	57	30	0	26	1 (visible from above)
Total........	136	32 (102)	70	29	5
Per cent.....		75%		21%	4%

Most individuals of all species are found on the most abundant kind of substratum, algal turf on hard bench platform. A certain proportion of each species "spills over" onto the other types of substratum available. This frequency is significantly less in *Conus sponsalis* than in the other species. *C. abbreviatus* utilizes sandy areas more often than *C. sponsalis* (P< .01). *C. ebraeus* utilizes bare regions of bench more often than *C. abbreviatus,* but the difference is probably not significant (P = .08). Substratum preferences of other species do not differ significantly from one another.

The particle size distribution in samples of sand from several stations was determined by the use of graded sieves, in order to detect possible interspecific differences in preference for sand of diffrent mechanical proprties. The methods used varied but slightly from those of Holme (1954).

Since sand particles are subject to sorting by wave action, larger particles might be expected to dominate in samples taken near the outer edge of benches. Application of Wilcoxon tests to data from

Stations 5 and K4 showed that *Conus ebraeus* is associated with somewhat coarser sands than *C. abbreviatus* (P = .05). However, mechanical properties of the sand probably do not vary sufficiently to provide different microhabitats with respect to this factor.

Sandy areas are more common on reef platforms than marine benches. The small areas of sand on benches may limit the density of some species of *Conus*. *C. pennaceus* is found rarely on benches, but it is common in habitats where sand is abundant, as the animals typically remain in sand under rocks during the day. Other species of *Conus* which occur in low densities on marine benches (e.g. *C. lividus, C. flavidus*) may be limited indirectly by the absence of sandy substrata which are required not by them but by the species on which they prey (see section on Nature of the Food of *Conus* on Marine Benches).

REEF PLATFORMS

The predominance of a sand substratum and the absence of extensive living coral characterize the platforms of Hawaiian fringing reefs and distinguish them from those of typical atoll and barrier reefs.

The nature of the substratum associated with 659 individuals of the 9 most abundant species of *Conus* on reef platforms is summarized in Table 6B. Most of the specimens (61%) of all the species collected on reef platforms occupied sandy substrata. From 12% to 14% of the populations were found on each of the other types of available substrata: bare limestone, limestone with algal turf (combined in Table 6B), and coral (including coral rubble and dead coral). The relative abundance of the available types of substratum was not measured, but sand is by far the most prevalent. Thus, as is the case on marine benches, most of the population of *Conus* occupies the most abundant type of substratum.

Specific Differences of Substratum. Conus pulicarius is probably entirely restricted to a sandy substratum. Although the sample size in Table 6B is small, it is supported by similar unpublished data from other regions where this species occurs. *C. pulicarius* typically occurs in areas of reefs characterized by sand bottom and the absence of limestone outcrops and growing coral. Individuals are usually partly or completely buried during the day. At night, they actively crawl about through the sand, leaving a broad track which is visible from above and facilitates collection. In quiet water, these tracks are often visible the next morning, and they may lead to the discovery of completely buried individuals.

Conus flavidus and *C. lividus,* the two most abundant species on reef platforms, also occur predominantly on sand substrata but are commonest in areas of sand patches and smaller pockets among solid substratum. These two species do not differ significantly from each other with respect to the types of substratum utilized (P = .15; see Table 20). Both species are predominantly epifaunal, and individuals are rarely found even partly buried in the substratum during the day.

Conus abbreviatus is also primarily a sand dweller when it occurs on reef platforms. It will be recalled that this species also occupies sandy regions of marine benches significantly more often than do the other species present. *C. abbreviatus* also burrows in sand on reef platforms significantly more often (P< .01) than the other species, with the exception of *C. pulicarius*.

The proportions of different types of substratum utilized by *Conus ebraeus* on reef platforms do not differ significantly from those of the other predominantly sand-dwelling species just discussed (Table 6B). This species is also typically epifaunal, but some individuals are found partially buried in the substratum.

Conus pennaceus is also primarily associated with a sand substratum. However, in contrast to the other species, the substratum of *C. pennaceus* is altered by the diurnal activity cycle. The substratum of 79 specimens collected during the day and 57 collected at night is shown in Table 6C. During the day, specimens are characteristically found on (37%) or partly buried in (63%) sand under basalt or coral rocks. At night, the snails actively crawl about on the surface of the sand or on reef rock, and they are visible from above. The substratum of *C. pennaceus* thus differs qualitatively from those of the other sand dwellers, which are found uncommonly under rocks.

The number of specimens of *Conus sponsalis, C. imperialis,* and *C. rattus* found on other types of substratum exceeds the number found on sand. Most of the specimens of *C. sponsalis* listed in Table 6B were collected at Station 7, where it is the most abundant species of *Conus. C. sponsalis* occurs sparsely or not at all on the other reefs studied (Figs. 14-17). The substratum of a large area of Station 7, particularly where *C. sponsalis* is common, consists of rather smooth limestone, which supports an algal turf, and dead coral, which presents a rough surface but is apparently being smoothed by wave quarrying. The former type of substratum especially is similar to that of marine benches, where *C. sponsalis* is also abundant. It is therefore not surprising that, when such a substratum is available on an otherwise predominantly sandy reef platform, it should be occupied by a population of *C. sponsalis*. Only a few scattered individuals of *C. sponsalis* are found on reefs which lack extensive areas of this type of substratum.

Conus rattus is also found more often on lithified than on sandy substrata, and in this respect probably does not differ significantly from *C. sponsalis* (P = .08). The numbers of these two species found on each of the substratum-types listed in Table 6B are significantly different, however (P = .02), in the samples collected.

Analysis of Particulate Sediments. The five most abundant species of *Conus* on subtidal reef platforms are characteristically associated with the sand moiety of the substratum. It was therefore of interest to determine the properties of the particulate sediments and the distribution of *Conus* with respect to these properties.

The sediments are almost entirely biogenic, comprising chiefly Foraminifera tests, fragments of coral, mollusk shells, echinoid tests and spines, and calcareous algae. Small amounts of olivine are often present, especially at Station 9, located at the foot of Diamond Head (Fig. 6), which takes that name from the local term "Hawaiian diamonds" for olivine.

Sediments associated with seven species of *Conus* on reef platforms were analyzed. *C. lividus* was found to be associated with somewhat coarser sediments than *C. flavidus* (Wilcoxon test: P = .05). However, all species are associated with sediments with extremely variable particle size distribution in the sand-gravel range. It therefore seems likely that, on reef platforms as on marine benches, there is no niche diversification of *Conus* species with respect to the particle size distribution of the sand moiety of the substratum.

EFFECTS OF ENVIRONMENTAL STRESSES

As Prosser (1955) has recently stated, "Determination of the importance of specific variations requires (a) the careful observation of ecological niches of subspecies and species occupying overlapping habitats, and (b) physiological tests of the effects of environmental stresses."

In order to test the effects of some environmental stresses on the species of *Conus* that inhabit marine benches, experiments on the effect of strong water currents and low oxygen tension were carried out. In addition, observations on activity with respect to desiccation will also be reported. The environment of the subtidal reef platform habitats is in general more equable than that of intertidal marine benches.

TEMPERATURE

Water temperatures ranging from 22.8 to 28.3°C were recorded at marine bench stations. The extreme range is probably somewhat greater, especially in shallow pools at low tide. Seasonal fluctuations appeared to be extremely small. Sea temperatures ranging from 22.0 to 29.1°C were measured on reef platforms. More extensive data for Station 3 were published by Edmondson (1928), who reported extremes of 21.5 and 29.0°C.

Analyses of diurnal fluctuations of temperature at Station K3 have been published elsewhere (Kohn & Helfrich 1957). On successive days in summer, ranges of 24.3-29.1°C and 24.1-27.1°C were recorded. The amplitude of diurnal temperature fluctuation thus closely approaches the annual range of variation on at least some reefs.

Temperature is not a limiting factor to species tolerant of the prevailing range, and population densities do not affect, and are not affected by, temperature. The qualitative species composition of populations of *Conus* in Hawaii may, however, be determined at least in part by the temperature regimen. The Hawaiian Islands represent the highest latitudes at which most of the species present are known to occur. The fauna of islands at lower latitudes, where sea temperatures are higher, is richer. Some species may be excluded from the Hawaiian area by temperatures below their tolerance limits. However, most regions nearer the equator which have been studied lie closer to the Indonesia-Melanesia center of distribution, and distance from this center is also a factor of major zoogeographical importance.

EXPOSURE TO AIR AT LOW TIDE

Marine benches, but not reef platforms, are subject to periodic exposure to air at times of low tide. Therefore, only a limited range of depth of water is available on marine benches at low tide, ranging from 0 (hereafter noted as "exposed") to about a foot in tidal pools.

A certain fraction of the population of each species of *Conus* was found to be left exposed at low tide, when the bench platform may not be awash for periods of up to four hours (Table 7). The frequency of exposure is significantly higher in *C. sponsalis* than in all other species (P< .01), mainly because the sample contains the large population at Station A3, which was entirely exposed. This dense population, and the virtual absence of *C. abbreviatus,* has been noted above. *C. abbreviatus* may be unable to withstand the long periods of exposure to air required for habitation of Station A3.

TABLE 7. Proportion of Populations of *Conus* Species Exposed to Air at Low Tide.

Species	Sample Size	Number Exposed	Per Cent Exposed
C. sponsalis	144	79	55%
C. abbreviatus	83	29	35%
C. chaldaeus	31	10	32%
C. ebraeus	73	21	29%
C. catus	28	8	29%
C. rattus	47	8	17%

Data from all marine bench stations.

The low proportion of the population of *Conus rattus* which is out of water at low tide is probably due to the fact that this species occurs more often on abrasion ramp benches than on other types. Since these slope into the sea, they are more often awash at low tide than the horizontal platforms of solution benches and water-leveled benches.

All species of *Conus* observed by the writer tend to remain quiescent in the daytime. On marine benches, the algae-sand turf provides shelter from heavy wave action at high tide, when the entire bench is awash, and the residual water it retains at low tide reduces the danger of desiccation for the smaller species (*C. sponsalis, C. abbreviatus*) during the day. If the turf is dense enough and sufficient sand is

present, the shells may be completely buried. Larger species (*C. ebraeus, C. chaldaeus*) find shelter in shallow crevices or under pieces of coral rubble in the daytime.

In order to ascertain whether different species occupy different microhabitats with respect to depth of water at low tide, the proportion of each species population partly buried or otherwise sheltered was determined. The samples were rather small and excluded completely buried individuals. Nevertheless, the frequency of burrowing in *C. abbreviatus* is significantly greater than in any of the other species (P< .01). This is probably due at least in part to the preference of this species for sandier regions of the bench platform, where burrowing can be more easily accomplished. Proportions of populations of other species buried during the day did not differ significantly from each other in the samples examined.

Although seemingly unsuitable shelters that are vacant can always be found on marine benches, the density of available sheltered sites, and the ability of *Conus* to locate them when needed, may be a limiting factor of population size in some cases.

Heavy wave action, a prominent environmental factor on marine benches, is generally absent from subtidal reef platforms except near the outer edge. Large waves are broken by the outer edge of the reef, and wave action on the platform is rarely so heavy as to interfere with collecting or observation, even at high tide.

ACTIVITY RHYTHMS

At night, especially at low tide, the snails are typically up on the surface of marine bench platforms, moving actively about. This activity rhythm persists when *Conus* is maintained in laboratory aquaria. Degree of expansion of the foot, movement of the siphon, and movement of the entire animal are much greater at night than in the daytime, even if the aquaria are illuminated at night. Rhythmicity of activity in nature is thus probably at least partly endogenous.

Alternating periods of light and darkness are important to many marine invertebrates because they synchronize rhythms of locomotor and other activities (Brown *et al.* 1953). In the field, no interspecific differences in activity with respect to light or time of day, which might lead to reducing the possibility of interspecific competition, were noted. Enhanced activity may be correlated with the immediate presence of food, as Ohba (1952) observed in *Nassarius,* and as was shown in *Conus striatus* in the laboratory (Kohn 1956b).

The relationship of tidal fluctuation to locomotor activity in *Conus* is probably complex. Observations were hampered by the fact that most marine benches are accessible only at low tide. Maximum activity was observed during low spring tides at night. At such times, waves may not break over solution benches for periods of several hours. The retention of much residual water by the algae-sand mat and the absence of solar radiation probably make the problem of desiccation negligible.

The initial movements of *Conus,* which begin after sunset, are mostly vertical, being directed out of the daytime hiding place up onto the bench platform. This behavior pattern is illustrated from field observations which comprised counts made in seven 100-sq ft quadrats at Station 5 at intervals over a 4-hr period in the evening. No *Conus* were visible on the bench platform at 1800 hrs, but by 2030, 17 specimens of four species had become active and were crawling about on the surface of the 700-sq ft area studied. By 2200, three additional individuals had also become active. Time of low tide (−0.2 ft) was 2023. Ohba (1952) noted activity peaks of *Nassarius* in tide pools at times when agitation of the water ceased on the receding tide and was renewed on the rising tide. In the present study, however, the bench had been exposed since before 1800. The rhythm is probably timed so that increased activity begins when two factors, darkness and absence of strongly flowing water, become favorable.

Since heavy wave action made observations on benches impossible except at low tide, experiments designed to measure the ability of *Conus* to withstand strong currents were carried out. Individuals of the four species dominant on marine benches were subjected to artificially created currents of 20, 100, 175 and 210 cm/sec. The ability to withstand the currents was found to be roughly correlated with size, in that *C. ebraeus,* which is larger than the other species (Fig. 9), is the most tenacious. The tenacity of *C. sponsalis, C. abbreviatus,* and *C. chaldaeus* is similar, although individuals of the last named species are somewhat larger (Fig. 9).

These data may offer a partial explanation of the observed pattern of distribution on solution benches (Fig. 20). The two smallest species are less able to withstand strong currents generated by waves breaking over the bench. By occurring chiefly on the landward portion, they are probably able to spend more time seeking food between high tides. The larger and heavier *Conus ebraeus,* on the other hand, being better able to withstand strong currents, may find a wider area of bench within its optimal habitat.

The ability of *Conus chaldaeus* to withstand strong currents in the experiments was comparable only to that of *C. sponsalis* and *C. abbreviatus.* In size, *C. chaldaeus* ranks between these species and *C. ebraeus* (Fig. 9). The experimental data thus do not help to explain the distribution pattern of *C. chaldaeus,* which characteristically occurs at the more seaward portion of marine benches. However, the data may suggest a possible explanation for the small population size of this species at Station 5, where wave action is more violent than at Station K1 and other collecting sites.

Reef Platforms. Diurnal activity cycles are difficult to observe on reef platforms. Most specimens were collected during the day, when they are typically quiescent. Little apparent difference in activity is observable in the field in the case of typically epifaunal species such as *Conus lividus* and *C. flavidus.* However, both of these species probably feed only at night, as will be shown below, and they are therefore presumably most active then.

Diurnal differences in the activity of *Conus pennaceus* are more readily observable, as alluded to in the previous section. This species is almost always found on or partly buried in sand under rocks during the day (Table 6C). At night, however, the snails leave that microhabitat to crawl about on the surface of the sand or on coral or limestone. Of 60 specimens of *C. pennaceus* collected at night, three were found crawling about out of water. Exposure to air is insignificant as an environmental stress on reef platforms, however. Exposed individuals of other species were found even more rarely or not at all.

OXYGEN REQUIREMENTS

Diurnal cycles of solar radiation and semidiurnal tidal cycles are factors leading to large fluctuations in oxygen concentration in the sea water on Hawaiian marine benches. Amplitude of fluctuation is greatest at low tide. At mid and high tides, oceanic water breaking over the bench in surf is probably always saturated. During daytime low tides residual water on the bench platform becomes supersaturated with oxygen due to photosynthesis by the dense mat of attached algae. At night low tides, oxygen content of residual water is reduced by respiration of both plants and animals.

Determinations of oxygen concentration *in situ* were made at three marine bench stations. Determinations were made by the Winkler method. The highest concentration measured was 7.68 ml O_2/l, and the lowest was 0.97 ml O_2/l, or only 19% of saturation.

It was thought that the nocturnal minimum might represent an environmental stress on *Conus.* In an attempt to determine the oxygen requirements of *Conus* and the ability to survive low oxygen tension, experiments on three of the four dominant species on marine benches were carried out in a simple respirometer. The results of three experiments, each with 14-20 specimens of *C. ebraeus,* and six experiments, each with 16-20 specimens of *C. chaldaeus,* are summarized in Fig. 23. Seven experiments with *C. abbreviatus* had erratic results, and they have not been included in Fig. 23. Indeed, all results were rather erratic, as indicated by the large standard errors. Some of this variation may be due to diurnal and tidal cycles in rate of respiration, such as have been reported in other gastropod genera by Sandeen, Stephens & Brown (1954).

The data in Fig. 23 suggest that *Conus ebraeus* and *C. chaldaeus* are probably physiological adjusters rather than regulators with respect to oxygen. That is, the rate of consumption varies with the environmental concentration rather than remaining relatively constant (Prosser 1955).

Three respiratory rate determinations of *Conus*

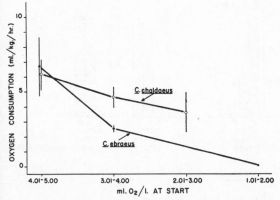

FIG. 23. Rates of oxygen consumption of *Conus* at different oxygen concentrations. Vertical lines indicate standard error of mean.

ebraeus in water containing 1 03-1.19 ml O₂/l, near the lowest *in situ* concentration measured, showed no detectable uptake of oxygen over a period of 6 hrs. Nevertheless, all animals survived the experiment. On marine benches, oxygen concentration is probably never so low for so long a time. In addition, the typical activity cycle of *Conus* tends to obviate danger of hypoxia. When the snail crawls about out of water on the bench platform, a thin layer of water over the ctenidia ensures diffusion of oxygen from the air as the concentration in the water is reduced by passage of oxygen into the tissue.

Reef Platforms. Like temperature, oxygen concentration of the water over subtidal reef platforms undergoes diurnal fluctuation of lower amplitude than on marine benches. A graphic presentation of the diurnal cycle of oxygen concentration at Station K3 has been published (Kohn & Helfrich 1957). The minimum concentration recorded (at 0300) was 3.58 ml O₂/l, equivalent to 77% saturation. Midday values ranged to 7.27 ml O₂/l, or 168% saturation. A few determinations of oxygen concentration were also made at Stations 3, 7, and 9. The maximum value observed was 8.91 ml O₂/l (197% saturation) recorded at Station 7.

Dissolved oxygen is probably never in short supply to *Conus* on reef platforms. However, individuals of several species burrow into the sand substratum. Below a centimeter or so, these sands are usually gray. This reducing environment probably does not adversely affect *Conus*, however, since the inspiratory organ, the siphon, projects above the water-sand interface and draws a stream of oxygenated water over the ctenidia.

FOOD AND FEEDING

The Feeding Process

Members of the genus *Conus* are known to have a unique feeding mechanism (discussed in detail by Bergh 1896, and Hinegardner 1957, 1958) and are known to be predatory (Alpers 1932a, Kohn 1955). The feeding process in piscivorous species has been de-

scribed elsewhere (Kohn 1956b). Alpers (1932b) studied the feeding process in *C. mediterraneus* Hwass in Bruguière, which feeds on polychaetes. He concluded erroneously that *Conus* ejects venom into the water in the vicinity of the prey, and he was not able to discern the function of the radula teeth.

Feeding of several of the vermivorous species which occur in Hawaii was observed in the laboratory. In *Conus abbreviatus* and *C. ebraeus,* the manner of injecting the radula tooth and accompanying venom do not differ from that described (Kohn 1956b) for *C. striatus.* However, the radula tooth is not held by the proboscis after injection. Rather, the proboscis retracts quickly, leaving the tooth in the prey. The mouth then expands and the paralyzed prey is engulfed. However, as will be noted below, other vermivorous species do retain the radula tooth within the proboscis and use it to draw the impaled prey into the mouth, as does *C. striatus.*

The method of feeding is somewhat different in *Conus pennaceus,* which, as will be shown, feeds on other mollusks. When the prey is stung, the radula tooth is completely freed from the proboscis. In contrast with the vermivorous species, not one, but up to six radula teeth may be injected into the same prey organism. If the prey is an opisthobranchiate mollusk with an internal shell, it is usually swallowed whole. The shell is presumably later regurgitated, since it is usually too large to pass into the intestine. When the prey is a prosobranch, or an opisthobranch with a large external shell, the shell is not swallowed. Rather the mouth of *C. pennaceus* is applied to the aperture of the shell of the prey after stinging. This position is maintained for 15 min-1 hr, following which the shell, now empty, falls away. Presumably the venom acts on the columellar muscle during this time, relaxing its attachment to the shell and allowing the soft body to be removed intact from the shell and swallowed. The feeding process was observed to be essentially identical in *C. textile.*

Digestion. After the prey has been completely swallowed, it lies in a large, distensible organ variously termed the crop (Clench & Kondo 1943) or esophagus (Speiseröhe of Bergh 1896; Ösophagus of Alpers 1931). Usually no digestion takes place in this organ, although enzymes may leak anteriorly from the intestine, causing some. Since there is no mechanism for trituration, prey in the esophagus is usually in a good state of preservation and identification is thus facilitated. The junction of the esophagus and intestine is marked by the entrance of two large ducts from the digestive glands. The prey is gradually moved from the crop into the intestine, where digestion and absorption occur. Fecal matter is not usually compacted into pellets but is excreted as undigested remains.

The piscivorous species represent an exception to the course of digestion just described, as noted by Kohn (1956b). Considerable digestion occurs in the anterior portion of the alimentary tract. The food swallowed is proportionally much larger than that

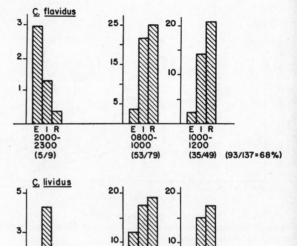

eaten by the other species, and the lower parts of the tract are not very distensible.

TIME OF FEEDING

Feeding takes place at night and usually not during daylight hours. This was demonstrated in the following manner. In analyses of alimentary tract contents, the position of food in the tract was recorded. Since the time of collection was noted, the position of food in the tract could be plotted against time of day. Food frequency histograms for the three dominant species on marine benches are shown for pertinent times of day in Fig. 24. Data from all marine bench stations are included. Data for three species on reef platforms are presented in Fig. 25. At other times of day (during afternoon and early evening) the proportion of snails with empty alimentary tracts was so high that it was not profitable to collect and examine large numbers of them.

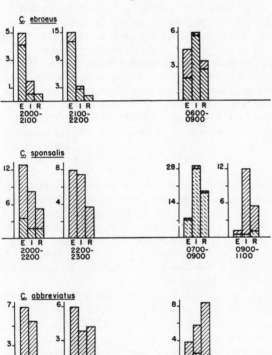

STA. 5   STA. A3   ALL OTHER STATIONS

FIG. 24. Food in alimentary tracts of *Conus* collected at marine bench stations at different times of day. E = esophagus. I = intestine. R = rectum.

In Figs. 24 and 25, alimentary tracts are divided into esophagus (E), intestine (I), and rectum (R). The esophagus and intestine are quite distinct organs (Bergh 1896, Alpers 1931), while the rectum is somewhat arbitrarily considered as the region between the last curve of the intestine and the anus. The dat from marine benches show that, in all three species,

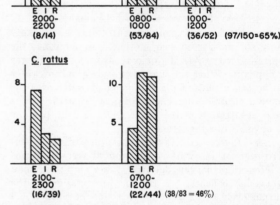

FIG. 25. Food in alimentary tracts of *Conus lividus, C. flavidus,* and *C. rattus* at different times of day. E = esophagus. I = intestine. R = rectum.

the crops contain the largest number of food organisms at night. By mid-morning, food has largely passed from the esophagus into the intestine and rectum, and incidence of esophagus contents is greatly reduced.

Of the dominant reef platform species, evidence of time of feeding was obtained for *Conus flavidus, C. lividus,* and *C. rattus,* as shown in Fig. 25. Nocturnal records for *C. flavidus* and *C. lividus* are probably too few to be meaningful. That feeding takes place at night in *C. flavidus* is plainly shown, however, by the low incidence of prey in the esophagus during the day. In *C. lividus,* the data are less clear-cut. This may be due to a slower rate of digestion, or some feeding may take place during daylight hours. *C. rattus* is plainly a nocturnal feeder. At night, prey organisms are found chiefly in the esophagus, while during the morning their remains occupy the lower regions of the alimentary tract.

The number of specimens examined which had food in the alimentary tracts is also indicated in Fig. 25. About two-thirds of the population of both *Conus*

TABLE 8. Prey Organisms Consumed by Vermivorous Species of *Conus* at Marine Bench Stations

	sponsalis				abbreviatus		ebraeus			chaldaeus			rattus	lividus			flavidus		miles	distans
Station...	5	11	A3	T	5	T	5	11	T	5	11	T	T	5	11	T	5	T	T	T
No. Specimens Examined	45	51	92	258	158	243	94	5	122	25	12	59	79	10	1	24	6	10	1	2
Nereis jacksoni Kinberg var.	—	6	5	30	—	—	—	—	—	—	—	—	—	—	—	—	—	—	—	—
Perinereis helleri Grube	15	14	—	32	19	20	104	3	115	—	—	—	13	—	—	—	—	—	—	—
Platynereis dumerilii (Audouin & Edwards)	2	2	6	10	2	3	—	—	—	17	16	45	—	—	1	1	—	—	—	—
Nereid sp. 350	1	2	1	4	—	—	—	—	—	—	—	—	—	—	—	—	—	—	—	—
Unidentified Nereidae	—	—	1	1	1	1	—	—	—	—	—	—	—	—	—	—	—	—	—	—
Total Nereidae	18	24	13	77	22	24	104	3	115	17	16	45	13	—	1	1	—	—	—	—
Lysidice collaris Grube	2	3	3	11	5	27	—	—	—	—	—	—	—	—	—	—	—	—	1	—
Palola siciliensis (Grube)	—	—	—	—	—	—	3	3	7	4	—	8	—	—	—	—	—	—	—	—
Eunice antennata Savigny	—	1	1	2	1	2	—	—	—	—	—	—	12	—	—	—	—	—	—	—
Eunice (Nicidion) cariboea (Grube)	—	5	30	36	8	10	—	—	—	—	—	—	1	—	—	—	—	—	—	—
Eunice filamentosa Grube	1	—	—	1	2	3	—	—	—	—	—	—	—	—	—	—	—	—	—	—
Marphysa sanguinea (Montagu)	—	—	1	1	1	3	—	—	—	—	—	—	—	—	—	—	—	—	—	—
Eunice afra Peters	—	—	—	—	—	—	—	—	—	—	—	—	—	—	—	—	—	—	—	1
Unidentified Eunicidae	1	—	—	1	1	1	—	—	1	—	—	—	—	—	—	—	—	—	—	—
Lumbrinereis sarsi (Kinberg)	2	3	8	14	10	11	—	—	—	—	—	—	—	—	—	—	—	—	—	—
Arabella iricolor (Montagu)	—	—	—	—	—	4	—	—	—	—	—	—	—	—	—	—	—	—	—	—
Total Eunicea	6	12	43	66	28	61	3	3	8	4	—	8	13	—	—	—	—	—	1	1
Nicolea gracilibranchus (Grube)	—	—	—	—	—	—	—	—	—	—	—	—	—	1	—	4	—	2	—	—
Terebellid sp. 837	—	—	—	—	—	—	—	—	—	—	—	—	—	—	—	—	—	3	—	—
Cirriformia semicincta (Ehlers)	—	—	—	—	—	—	—	—	—	—	—	—	—	—	1	—	—	—	—	—
Polydorid sp. 1500	—	—	—	—	—	—	—	—	—	—	—	—	—	—	—	—	—	1	—	—
Unidentified annelids	—	1	3	6	4	4	1	—	1	—	—	—	—	—	—	2	—	1	—	—
Total Annelids	24	36	59	149	45	89	108	6	124	21	16	53	26	1	1	8	—	7	1	1
Total Identified Food	24	36	59	149	54	89	108	6	124	21	16	53	26	3*	1	16†	—	7	1	1
Unidentified Food	1	1	1	4	1	3	—	—	—	—	—	—	—	—	—	3	—	1	—	—

Data from Stations 5, 11, and A3 are entered separately as noted.   T = Data from all bench stations.
Numbers in body of table indicate numbers of polychaete species at left found in alimentary tracts of *Conus* species at top.
Chief references used in the identification of the polychaetes were Abbott (1946), Hartman (1940, 1944, 1948), Holly (1935), Fauvel (1927), Okuda (1937), and Treadwell (1906, 1922).
*Includes one specimen definitely identified, and one tentatively identified, as *Ptychodera flava laysanica* Spengel.
†Includes five specimens definitely identified, and three tentatively identified, as *Ptychodera flava laysanica* Spengel.

flavidus and *C. lividus,* and about one-half of the population of *C. rattus* succeed in capturing food each night.

Investigation of the rate of passage of food through the alimentary tract of *Conus abbreviatus* showed that the food starts passing into the intestine after about 1.5 hrs in the esophagus. After about 3 hrs, fecal matter is present in the rectum. From 12-24 hrs after feeding, the alimentary tract is completely emptied. Therefore, gastropods observed with empty tracts in the afternoon may or may not have fed the previous night.

NATURE OF THE FOOD OF *Conus* ON MARINE BENCHES

Solution Bench Stations. Of the eight species of *Conus* present at Station 5, five, including the four dominant species, were found to feed exclusively on polychaete annelids. Of the less abundant species, *C. flavidus* feeds predominantly on polychaetes but may occasionally take an unsegmented worm. *C. lividus* feeds on the enteropneust *Ptychodera flava* but consumes polychaetes as well. *Ptychodera* is a sand-dwelling worm and is uncommon on marine benches. Both *C. flavidus* and *C. lividus* prefer Terebellidae among the polychaetes. These worms are also typically sand dwellers, building tubes on the sides of rocks partly buried in sand. The low abundance of *Ptychodera* and terebellids on benches may limit the populations of *C. lividus* and *C. flavidus* in this habitat.

Conus pennaceus was earlier reported (Kohn 1955) to feed on other gastropods. Small species of the type on which *C. pennaceus* thrives (especially *Haminoea*) are abundant on benches, so the low density of *C. pennaceus* does not seem the result of limited food supply. Rather, *C. pennaceus* is probably limited by lack of sufficient sand in which to burrow during the day.

Contents of alimentary tracts of 343 specimens collected at Station 5 were determined by dissection of fixed specimens or collection of fecal matter from living individuals. From these, 210 prey organisms were identified, 199 of them to species. All eight species of *Conus* are represented in the sample, but food remains were not found in any alimentary tracts of the few *C. rattus* and *C. pennaceus* examined. The results are summarized in Table 8, which also includes totals from other bench stations for comparison.

These data show that at Station 5, *Perinereis helleri* is the primary food of the three most abundant species of *Conus*. *C. ebraeus* eats this species almost exclusively, while *C. abbreviatus* especially feeds on other polychaetes as well. Members of the superfamily Eunicea (only the families Eunicidae, Lumbrinereidae, and Arabellidae are represented) are eaten about as often as nereids. *C. sponsalis*, on the other hand, is more restricted to nereids. This may reduce the possibility of competition for food between these two species, which feed in the same zone of the bench. Most of the population of *C. ebraeus* is found feeding in the central portion of the bench (Fig. 20) and is thus seeking *P. helleri* in a different place from *C. sponsalis* and *C. abbreviatus*.

The food of the fourth commonest species, *Conus chaldaeus,* is strikingly different. *C. chaldaeus* also feeds exclusively on a single species of nereid, but its food is *Platynereis dumerilii*, which occurs predominantly toward the outer edge. A large substratum sample collected near the outer edge at Station 5, adjacent to two specimens of *C. chaldaeus*, contained the following Nereidae:

Platynereis dumerilii	16
Nereis jacksoni	14
Perinereis helleri	1
Unidentified epitokes	3

Thus *P. dumerilii* is an order of magnitude more abundant than *P. helleri* near the outer edge. The prey species of *C. chaldaeus* is thus correlated with the distribution pattern across the reef platform, as both prey and predator are less abundant near shore.

The three most abundant species of *Conus* exert an active demand on the local population of *Perinereis helleri*. If this demand were found to exceed the immediate supply of the prey species, it could be said that the three predator species compete with each other for this food, at least in areas of distribution overlap.

Food organisms were found in about 60% of all alimentary tracts of specimens examined from Station 5. Since specimens were collected at all hours, and since feeding has been shown to take place only at night, it is possible that some individuals had defecated remains of the previous night's meal before being examined. A mean of one polychaete per

gastropod per night is a reasonable estimate of feeding rate.

The mean density of the *Conus* species that feed on *Perinereis helleri* is 2/100 sq ft. Since *P. helleri* constitutes about 74% of their diet, these species consume an average of 1.5 individuals of *P. helleri*/100 sq ft/night, or 0.17/m.²/night. Substratum samples taken about halfway across the bench contained the densities of nereids shown in Table 9. At the calculated feeding rate, about 28 years would be required to exhaust the observed population of *P. helleri,* considering no replacement.

TABLE 9. Population Density of Nereidae and Eunicea Halfway Across Station 5.

Species	No. counted in 625 cm.²	No./m.²	Eaten by *Conus* /m.²/day
Perinereis helleri	121	1,940	0.17
Nereis jacksoni	267	4,270	
Platynereis dumerilii.	7	112	
All Eunicea	4/30 cm.²	1,300	

Although the smaller *Nereis jacksoni* was more abundant than *Perinereis helleri* at Station 5, it was not found to be eaten by *Conus*. Elsewhere it is eaten by *C. sponsalis* (Table 8).

The feeding habits of the species at Station 11 are shown in Table 8 to be essentially similar to those at Station 5. In addition, the few specimens of *Conus rattus* collected there were found to consume both nereid and eunicid polychaetes. The single specimen of *C. catus* collected had an empty alimentary tract.

No quantitative samples of polychaetes at Station 11 were analyzed. However, *Perinereis helleri* was observed to be common. Each of two samples, representing a few square centimeters of substratum surface, contained 9 polychaetes, of which 3 and 5, respectively, were *P. helleri*. Standing crop is probably of the same order as at Station 5.

Water-leveled Bench Stations. Alimentary tracts of 92 specimens of *Conus sponsalis* from Station A3 were analyzed. Of these, 90 were collected between the hours 0700 and 0900. Polychaete remains were found in 55 specimens. The frequency distribution of remains in alimentary tracts is shown in Fig. 24. The low frequency of esophagus contents indicates that feeding had ceased some time before collection, probably at or before dawn. Most of the remains are seen to be in the intestine and/or rectum. This is in essential agreement with data from other stations.

Fifty-two of the specimens examined contained remains of one polychaete in each, two contained remains of two polychaetes each, and one contained remains of three polychaetes. It may be concluded that most individuals succeed in capturing one polychaete per night.

The nature of the food of *Conus sponsalis* at Station A3, shown in Table 8, differs markedly from that of other bench stations. The primary prey organism is not a nereid, but the eunicid, *Eunice (Nicidion) cariboea*. *Perinereis helleri* was not found to be eaten at all (but its presence at Station A3 was not ascertained). This resulted in eunicids far exceeding nereids in the prey of *C. sponsalis* at Station A3, in contrast with other stations studied. This may be correlated with the fact that *C. abbreviatus,* which generally (Table 8) feeds on eunicids more often than nereids, is virtually absent from Station A3. It may be conjectured that where the two co-occur, they compete for eunicids, with the result that *C. abbreviatus* is the more successful, and *C. sponsalis* is forced to eat nereids, which are possibly less desirable as food. When *C. abbreviatus* is excluded for other reasons from a microhabitat where *C. sponsalis* does occur, the latter species would then be able to exploit eunicids as food.

As for other polychaete feeders at Station A3, remains of *Eunice antennata* were found in three of the seven specimens of *Conus rattus* which were examined, and the single *C. abbreviatus* had fed on a *Lysidice collaris*.

The food of *Conus catus* has previously been shown to be small fishes, chiefly blennies and gobies, and the feeding process has been briefly described (Kohn 1956b). Remains of fishes were found in two of the three specimens collected at Station A3. One of the fishes was identified as the goby, *Bathygobius fuscus*. The other was too poorly preserved to permit identification. The food of *C. catus* at bench stations is summarized in Table 10.

TABLE 10. Prey Organisms Consumed by *Conus catus* at Marine Bench Stations.

	Sta. K1	All Bench Stations
No. Specimens Examined.....	13	24
Bathygobius fuscus (Rüppell)..	2	3
Istiblennius gibbifrons (Quoy and Gaimard).............	3	3
Unidentified fishes...........	2	5
Total Fishes.............	7	11
Unidentified fecal matter.....		1

Only small samples of most species from Station K1 were examined for alimentary tract contents. The expected prey organism, *Perinereis helleri,* dominated in *Conus sponsalis* and *C. ebraeus*. Nine of 10 food organisms isolated from *C. abbreviatus* were *Lysidice collaris*. Thirty-eight specimens of *C. rattus* were analyzed. Eleven contained remains of *P. helleri,* one, *Eunice antennata,* and the remaining 26 were devoid of identifiable food. Results of analysis of alimentary tracts of 13 specimens of *C. catus* are shown in Table 10. The single specimen of *C. retifer* was found to have an empty alimentary tract. However, other members of its subgenus (*Cylinder*) feed exclusively on other gastropods, and it is likely that *C. retifer* does also.

Polychaetes did not appear as abundant as on solution benches, but no quantitative samples were collected. *Perinereis helleri* and *Lumbrinereis* sp. 239 were observed to be present. Three of the eight species of *Conus* collected feed primarily on *P. helleri*. It is not known whether the demand exceeds the immediate supply and, therefore, whether food is the requisite which governs population size. The possibility of competition for food between *C. catus* and the other species present is entirely precluded, as it feeds on fishes.

FOOD PREFERENCE

Of the species of *Conus* characteristic of the marine bench habitat, *C. sponsalis* and *C. abbreviatus* have been shown to be most similar to each other with respect to feeding habits and pattern of distribution. Both species feed exclusively on polychaetes. Frequency of different prey species found in alimentary tracts is shown in Table 8. If data from all marine benches studied are combined (Column T), polychaetes of the superfamily Euniceca comprise 68%, and Nereidae 26% of the diet of *C. abbreviatus*. The diet of *C. sponsalis* consists of 44% Euniceca and 52% Nereidae. Although feeding habits are rather similar, the difference between the two species is significant ($P = 10^{-3}$) in the samples analyzed.

Polychaetes of both groups are abundant (Table 9). The observed differences in feeding frequency may be accounted for by two alternative hypotheses: (1) *C. abbreviatus* is better adapted to feeding on eunicids, which burrow into limestone and coral, than on nereids, which occur epifaunally among the holdfasts of algae. Conversely, *C. sponsalis* is better adapted to feeding on nereids than eunicids. (2) *C. abbreviatus* exhibits active preference for eunicids over nereids, and *C. sponsalis* prefers nereids to eunicids.

Comparison of results of food studies at Station A3 with other stations provided at least some evidence in favor of the view that, where the two species co-occur, *C. abbreviatus* is the more efficient predator on eunicids.

The second hypothesis was tested experimentally in a choice chamber, following the method of Van Dongen (1956). The chamber was a lead-sheathed wooden sea water table 125 × 58 cm in area and 8 cm deep (Fig. 26). Polychaetes were placed in Bull Durham bags, which were secured to the chamber floor. The water current thus passed over the polychaetes and then over the snails. All stimuli received by *Conus* from the polychaetes were thus of a chemical nature. Actual predation was prevented by the cloth bags, from which snails were unable to extract the polychaetes. In each experiment, one or two polychaetes were placed in each bag, and 12-59 specimens of a single species of *Conus* were placed at a distance of 88 cm from the goal (Line cd, Fig. 26).

Experiments were usually begun in late afternoon and allowed to continue overnight, to coincide with the snails' normal food-seeking regimen. A few of

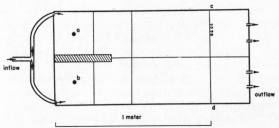

Fig. 26. Choice chamber for determination of food preferences of *Conus*. Lines were marked on floor of chamber as shown. During an experiment, fresh sea water was admitted to the chamber equally through the two inflow tubes. Outlets were located 1 cm above the chamber floor, so that a uniform depth of 1 cm of water was maintained in the chamber. A wooden partition (hatched) 40 cm in length partially separated the two portions of the chamber. This served to prevent mixing of stimuli and alteration of choice by snails. Food chambers are shown at a and b. Line cd is the starting line along which snails were placed at outset of an experiment.

the experiments with *Conus sponsalis* were allowed to run 40 hrs. At the termination of an experiment, snails were scored as having reached to within 25-50 cm of the goal, less than 25 cm, or adjacent to the food chamber. In the summary of results (Table 11), all three categories are summed.

TABLE 11. Summary of Results of Food Choice Experiments with *Conus sponsalis* and *C. abbreviatus*.

Number of Experiments	Number of Snails	Nereidae* Chosen	Eunicidae Chosen
C. sponsalis			
6	222	42	28**
2	61	22	2***
Total 8	283	64	30
C. abbreviatus			
2	87	17	35**

Figures in body of table indicate number of snails choosing polychaete listed above in choice chamber experiments.
    * = *Perinereis helleri*
   ** = *Eunice antennata*
  *** = *Palola siciliensis*

Table 11 shows that, given equal choice of both, *Conus abbreviatus* chooses the eunicid (*Eunice antennata*) more often than it chooses the nereid (*Perinereis helleri*). *C. sponsalis* chooses the nereid (*P helleri*) more often than either of the eunicids tested (*E. antennata, Palola siciliensis*). The difference in preference for eunicids and nereids between *C. sponsalis* and *C. abbreviatus* is highly significant (P< .01).

Comparison of Food in Nature and Choice Experiments. A comparison between the experimental choices and food in nature is made in Table 12. Since the percentages given do not permit direct comparison between the experiments and nature, the ratios of eunicids to nereids for *Conus abbreviatus* and *C. sponsalis* are included. Variation of the relative frequency of predation on nereids and eunicids in nature from the frequency of choice in the experiments is

significant for *C. sponsalis* (P = .05) but not for *C. abbreviatus* (P ≫ .1).

TABLE 12. Comparison of Results of Choice Chamber Experiments with Food Habits of *Conus sponsalis* and *C. abbreviatus* in Nature.

	Food in Nature (all marine benches)	Choice in Experiments
C. sponsalis		
Nereidae......	52%	23%
Eunicea.......	44%	11%
Ratio E:N.....	1:1.3	1:2.1
C. abbreviatus		
Nereidae......	26%	20%
Eunicea.......	68%	40%
Ratio E:N....	2.6:1	2.0:1

Comparison of data for nature and experiments shows that the food of *Conus sponsalis* and *C. abbreviatus* in nature is reflected in the choice experiments. The partition of the environment into different but overlapping microhabitats which occurs with respect to food may therefore be maintained by active preference of different prey species by the two predator species.

The hypothesis that *Conus sponsalis* is better adapted to feeding on nereids than eunicids was not amenable to experimental test. It has been suggested, however, that information bearing on this question might be gained from study of radula morphology (Peile 1939).

Although the anterior extremities of radula teeth show considerable variation throughout the genus *Conus,* the teeth may be grouped in two categories with respect to the posterior portion, or base. In the first, the base is simple and of more or less greater diameter than the shaft, thus forming a terminal knob. The base in the second group is characterized by the presence of a forward projecting cone (Fig. 27).

Fig. 27. Radula tooth of *Conus abbreviatus*. The forward projecting cone is visible at the left.

Peile (1939) made the plausible suggestion that this cone might serve to retain the tooth within the proboscis when prey is attacked. It was shown, however, that *C. striatus* which does not possess such a cone, retains the tooth in the proboscis in feeding (Kohn 1956b).

It will be shown below that the presence of the forward projecting cone is generally correlated with feeding on eunicid and other tube-dwelling polychaetes in nature. Eunicids, unlike nereids, live in burrows in coral and reef rock, and the basal cone may well aid the predator in extracting the worm from its burrow.

TABLE 13. Prey Organisms Consumed by Vermivorous Species of *Conus* at Subtidal Reef Stations. Numbers in body of table indicate number of polychaete species at side found in alimentary tracts of *Conus* species at top.

	sponsalis			abbreviatus				ebraeus				chaldaeus		miles		rattus			distans	
Station...	7	R	T	3	9	R	T	3	9	R	T	R	T	R	T	15	R	T	R	T
No. specimens examined....	64	72	330	19	24	99	342	15	8	55	199	4	106	11	20	18	55	149	19	21
Nereis jacksoni Kinberg var........	4	4	34	—	—	—	—	—	—	—	—	—	—	—	—	—	—	—	—	—
Perinereis helleri Grube...........	3	3	35	—	—	—	20	—	1	6	136	—	5	—	—	7	7	21	—	—
Platynereis dumerilii A. & E.......	3	3	13	—	—	—	3	—	—	—	—	2	98	—	—	—	1	1	—	—
Nereid sp. 350...................	1	1	5	—	—	—	—	—	—	—	—	—	—	—	—	—	—	—	—	—
Unidentified Nereidae............	1	1	2	—	—	—	1	—	—	—	—	—	—	—	—	—	—	—	—	—
Total Nereidae.................	12	12	89	—	—	—	24	—	1	6	136	2	103	—	—	7	8	22	—	—
Lysidice collaris Grube..........	6	6	17	—	—	9	36	—	—	2	2	—	—	5	16	—	—	—	—	—
Palola siciulensis (Grube)..........	—	—	—	1	—	—	1	14	8	29	44	—	14	—	—	—	—	—	—	—
Eunice antennata Savigny.........	1	1	3	5	10	20	22	—	—	—	—	—	—	1	1	3	17	29	1	1
Eunice (*N.*) *cariboea* Grube........	—	3	39	—	—	4	14	—	—	1	1	—	—	—	—	1	1	2	—	—
Eunice afra Peters...............	—	—	—	—	—	—	—	—	—	—	—	—	—	—	—	4	9	9	12	13
Marphysa sanguinea Montagu.....	—	—	1	1	1	3	6	—	—	—	—	—	—	—	—	—	—	—	—	—
Eunice filamentosa Grube.........	—	—	1	—	—	—	3	—	—	—	—	—	—	—	—	—	—	—	—	—
Unidentified Eunicidae...........	—	—	1	1	—	1	2	—	—	—	1	—	1	—	—	—	—	—	—	—
Lumbrinereis sarsi (Kinberg)......	2	3	17	—	—	—	11	—	—	—	—	—	—	—	—	—	—	—	—	—
Arabella iricolor (Montagu)........	—	—	—	—	—	5	9	—	—	—	—	—	—	—	—	—	—	—	—	—
Total Eunicea..................	9	13	79	8	11	43	104	14	8	32	48	—	15	6	17	8	27	40	13	14
Eurythoe complanata (Pallas)......	—	—	—	—	—	—	—	—	—	—	—	—	—	—	—	—	—	—	—	—
Unidentified Annelids............	1	1	7	—	—	—	4	—	—	1	2	—	—	—	—	—	—	—	—	—
Total Annelids.................	22	26	175	8	11	43	132	14	9	39	186	2	118	6	17	15	35	62	13	14
Total Identified Food............	22	26	175	8	11	43	132	14	9	39	186	2	118	6	17	15	35	62	13	14
Unidentified Food...............	2	2	6	—	—	—	4	—	—	—	—	—	1	—	—	—	—	—	1	1

SUMMARY OF FOOD OF *Conus* IN

THE MARINE BENCH HABITAT

Conus abbreviatus and *C. sponsalis*, both of which possess the small cone at the base of the radula tooth, feed on polychaetes which belong to different groups, the Nereidae and Eunicea, and differ ecologically as noted above. Although there is overlap (63%), the difference in numbers of the two groups of prey organisms eaten by *C. abbreviatus* and *C. sponsalis* is highly significant ($P = 10^{-3}$). Comparison by individual species of the food eaten by these two *Conus* species on all bench stations (Table 8) revealed overlap of only 25% and the probability of only 10^{-6} that the polychaetes preyed on represented random samples from the same population. Differences between the species composition of the food of *C. sponsalis* and *C. abbreviatus* are thus sufficiently great that competition for food is unlikely.

Of the other species which occur in the marine bench habitat, *Conus ebraeus* and *C. chaldaeus* do not possess the forward projecting cone on the radula tooth. Both species are extremely oligophagous. Nereids comprise 85% of the food of *C. chaldaeus* and 93% of the food of *C. ebraeus*. The two species do not differ significantly in the proportion of the diet comprised by nereids ($P = .24$). In striking contrast to this, however, is the specific nature of the prey eaten, as shown in Table 8. In the samples collected on all marine benches, the only nereid eaten by *C. ebraeus* was *Perinereis helleri*, while the only nereid eaten by *C. chaldaeus* was *Platynereis dumerilii*. Despite the fact that both predators are typically found on the same benches, and with overlapping distributions, they were never found to eat the "wrong" polychaete in the bench habitat.

Unfortunately, no choice experiments were carried out in order to test the possibility of differences in active preference of prey species by *Conus ebraeus* and *C. chaldaeus*. It is likely that the specific differences in prey are correlated with differences in the ecology of the prey species. In Table 9 *Perinereis helleri* was shown to be two orders of magnitude more abundant than *Platynereis dumerilii* about halfway across the bench at Station 5, where *C. ebraeus* is maximally abundant. Nearer the outer edge, where *C. chaldaeus* reaches its peak density, *P. dumerilii* is an order of magnitude more abundant than *P. helleri*.

R = All reefs; T = All stations; * = All from Station 4; + = Equals Total.

vexillum			vitulinus	imperialis	pulicarius		flavidus				lividus					
9	R	T	T*	R+	9	R+	3	9	R	T	3	7	9	R	T	Station
13	16	17	4	31	11	20	47	56	182	192	32	46	34	216	240	No. Specimens Examined
—	—	—	—	—	—	—	—	—	—	—	—	—	—	—	—	*Nereis jacksoni* Kinberg var.
—	—	—	—	—	—	—	—	—	—	—	—	—	—	—	—	*Perinereis helleri* Grube
—	—	—	—	—	—	—	—	—	—	—	1	5	—	11	12	*Platynereis dumerilii* A. & E.
—	—	—	—	—	—	—	—	—	—	—	—	—	—	—	—	Nereid sp. 350
—	—	—	—	—	—	—	—	—	—	—	—	—	—	—	—	Unidentified Nereidae
—	—	—	—	—	—	—	—	—	—	—	1	5	—	11	12	Total Nereidae
—	—	—	—	—	2	2	5	5	24	24	—	—	—	—	—	Capitellid sp. 1040
—	—	—	—	—	—	—	—	—	11	11	—	—	—	—	—	*Thelepus setosus* Quatrefages
6	9	9	—	—	—	—	13	5	22	22	—	—	—	1	1	*Polycirrus* sp. 660
—	—	—	—	—	—	—	—	—	2	5	—	—	1	1	1	Terebellid sp. 837
—	—	—	1	—	—	—	10	17	32	34	2	—	—	7	11	*Nicolea gracilibranchus* (Grube)
5	6	6	—	4	—	—	—	—	—	—	—	—	—	1	2	Unidentified Terebellidae
—	—	—	—	—	—	—	23	22	67	72	2	—	1	10	15	Total Terebellidae
—	—	—	—	—	—	—	—	—	5	5	—	—	—	1	1	Polydorid sp. 1500
—	—	—	—	—	—	—	—	—	1	1	—	1	1	4	5	*Cirriformia semicincta* (Ehlers)
11	15	15	1	4	—	—	—	—	—	—	—	—	—	2	2	*Lygdamis nesiotes* (Chamberlin)
—	—	—	—	—	—	—	—	—	—	—	—	—	—	3	3	*Sabellastarte indica* Savigny
—	—	—	—	11	—	—	1	3	4	5	—	1	—	2	3	Unidentified Annelids
11	15	15	1	15	—	—	29	30	101	108	3	7	2	33	41	Total Annelids
—	—	—	—	—	—	2	—	—	—	—	—	—	—	—	—	*Thalassema* sp.
—	—	—	—	—	—	—	1	—	1	1	13	5	8	28	33	*Ptychodera flava laysanica* Spengel
—	—	—	—	—	—	—	—	—	1	4	2	5	6	29	32	*P. flava laysanica* Spengel (tentative identification)
—	—	—	—	—	—	—	—	—	—	—	—	—	1	1	1	*Octopus* sp.?
11	15	15	1	15	2	4	30	30	106	113	18	17	16	90	106	Total Identified Food
2	—	2	1	2	—	3	7	5	18	21	5	10	6	39	42	Unidentified Food

Conus rattus, the other vermivorous species characteristic of marine benches, does possess the basal cone on the radula tooth. It feeds predominantly on eunicids (Table 8) and in the proportion of Eunicea eaten does not differ significantly from *C. abbreviatus*. However, the specific nature of the food of these two species is significantly different ($P = 10^{-6}$). In fact, the nature of the food of each vermivorous species of the marine bench habitat differs significantly from that of all others at the 1% level. Thus these species, as well as *C. catus* which eats only fishes, avoid interspecific competition for food in the bench habitat.

Nature of the Food of Conus on Subtidal Reefs

Of the 16 species of *Conus* collected by the writer on reef platforms, 10 were found to feed exclusively on polychaetes. These are *C. abbreviatus*, *C. ebraeus*, *C. sponsalis*, *C. rattus*, *C. imperialis*, *C. chaldaeus*, *C. vexillum*, *C. distans*, *C. vitulinus*, and *C. miles*. Polychaetes constitute more than 90% of the food of *C. flavidus*, which occasionally consumes an unsegmented worm. Polychaetes comprise about 50% of the food of *C. lividus*, which feeds also on an entero-

pneust. *C. pulicarius* feeds on polychaetes and echiuroids, as far as is known. *C. pennaceus* and *C. marmoreus* feed on other gastropods, and *C. striatus* feeds on fishes.

VERMIVOROUS SPECIES

Species Typical of Marine Benches Which Occur also on Reef Platforms. The species composition of the food of the vermivorous species of *Conus* which occur on reef platforms is given in Table 13 for a sample of 784 specimens of 13 species. From these, 360 prey organisms were identified, 254 of them to species. Most of the records are determinations of alimentary tract contents of fixed specimens. A few represent collection of fecal matter from living individuals. Total data for certain species include records from marine bench and deep water habitats for comparison.

The more diversified food on reefs in comparison with marine benches is made possible by the addition of the sand substratum microhabitat on reef platforms. All of the prey species listed in Table 13 but not in Table 8 are associated with the sand substratum. All but one of the polychaetes eaten by

Conus on marine benches were found to be present and eaten on reef platforms. The limestone outcrops and coral of the reefs provide abundant burrowing sites for eunicids. Nereids, however, are not common on the reefs, except where an algal turf is present on exposed limestone. This is especially reflected in the feeding habits of *C. sponsalis, C. abbreviatus, C. ebraeus,* and *C. rattus. Perinereis helleri* is the dominant prey of each of these species on marine benches (Table 8), but it is much less important to all four on reefs, where it is less abundant.

On reef platforms, *Conus sponsalis* is often found in regions of dead coral and reef limestone which support an algal turf and nereids, as well as eunicids. Both groups of polychaetes are eaten by *C. sponsalis,* in frequencies which do not differ significantly from those eaten by marine bench populations of this species.

No nereids were found in alimentary tracts of 99 specimens of *Conus abbreviatus* collected on coral reefs. This is as expected, since on reef platforms *C. abbreviatus* is not found on the algae-matted areas where some nereids occur. *Eunicea,* which commonly burrow into any available limestone on coral reefs (Hartman 1954), apparently constitute the entire diet of *C. abbreviatus.* The frequency of different polychaete species eaten differs significantly between bench and reef populations of *C. abbreviatus.* This is due largely to the predominance of *Eunice antennata* as prey in the latter habitat.

The food of *Conus ebraeus* in reef habitats also varies from that on marine benches in the direction of increased concentration on a species of eunicid. In contrast with the previous species, however, *C. ebraeus* feeds chiefly on *Palola siciliensis* and does not eat *Eunice antennata.*

The most obvious difference between the ecological niches of *Eunice antennata* and *Palola siciliensis* is that the latter species is typically found in more dense limestone. This observation is correlated with the fact that the mandibles are larger and stronger in *Palola* than in the other genera of *Eunicea.* (This has been discussed by Hartman (1954), who suggests that *Palola* may be the most destructive of the *Eunicea* to coral reefs. Following the same criterion, *Lysidice, Eunice, Marphysa, Lumbrinereis,* and *Arabella* would follow in order of decreasing destructiveness.) Filamentous algae were observed in intestines of *E. antennata.* These are perhaps the boring forms recently discussed by Odum & Odum (1955). The food of *P. siciliensis* was not determined. Takahashi (1939) concluded that several eunicids inhabiting coral reefs are omnivorous, consuming sand, diatoms, crustaceans, and algal fragments.

Conus chaldaeus occurs rather rarely on reef platforms. *C. rattus,* on the other hand, is about as common as it is on marine benches. As in other species common to both habitats, eunicids are consumed significantly more often than nereids (P = .03) by reef than bench populations of *C. rattus.*

In summary, there is virtually no qualitative difference in the specific nature of the prey eaten by those species of *Conus* common to both the reef and bench habitats. The frequencies of the different species eaten vary considerably, however, and are correlated with differences in substratum characteristics of the two habitats.

Typical Reef Platform Species. The most abundant species of *Conus* on subtidal reef platforms were shown (Figs. 14-17, 19) to be *C. flavidus* and *C. lividus.* Prey organisms recovered from alimentary tracts of about 200 specimens of each of these species are listed in Table 13. It is readily apparent that *C. flavidus* feeds almost exclusively on polychaetes, that the largest single item in the food of *C. lividus* is the enteropneust, *Ptychodera flava,* and that these species feed only occasionally or never on nereids and eunicids.

Tubicolous polychaetes comprise almost the entire diet of *Conus flavidus.* About two-thirds of these are members of the family Terebellidae. The other main prey species is an unidentified species of the family Capitellidae. The terebellids on which *C. flavidus* feeds live in tubes which are usually attached to the under sides of coral rocks or pieces of rubble resting in sand. The intestines of these polychaetes are usually filled with extremely fine sand particles. The terebellids are probably selective deposit feeders, selection apparently being effected by the tentacles.

Conus flavidus consumes enteropneusts only occasionally. In contrast, *Ptychodera flava* constitutes about 50% of the diet of *C. lividus.* Since it has no hard parts, *P. flava* is particularly difficult to identify in the partially digested state. The reddish eggs, which are apparently refractory to the digestive enzymes of *Conus,* aided identification of the females eaten. However, a number of *C. lividus* alimentary tract contents, which appeared to be remains of *Ptychodera,* could not be positively identified. These are entered separately in Table 13, but they are included in "total identified food."

The ecological niche of *Ptychodera flava* differs markedly from those of the terebellids on which *Conus lividus* feeds less often. Although all are deposit feeders in the same habitat, *P. flava* moves slowly about through the sand. It appears to be a nonselective feeder, ingesting in the manner of an earthworm. A wide range of sand particle sizes is found in its alimentary tract. As there is no apparent mechanism for trituration, the particle size distribution in the tract is presumably identical with that of the environment, but this was not determined.

The feeding of *Conus lividus* on *Ptychodera flava* was observed in the laboratory. When both were placed in a dish of sea water, the rostrum, but not the proboscis, of *Conus* was extended. When the mouth touched the worm, the latter was engulfed without being stung. During the entire engulfment process, which lasted only about 15 sec, the *Ptychodera* continued its normal peristaltic pulsations. This method of feeding may not be duplicated in nature. The observed presence of radula teeth in the alimentary tract with food remains indicates that *C. lividus* stings *Ptychodera* as well as polychaetes before feeding.

Other Reef Species. The remaining six reef-inhabiting vermivorous species together comprise only about 6% of the total population of *Conus* in this habitat. It was possible to collect and analyze only small samples, but the results obtained are of considerable interest and are included in Table 13 for completeness.

The most common of these species is *Conus imperialis*. Only two prey species were found in analyses of alimentary tract contents and recovery of fecal matter of 31 specimens. One of these was the eunicid, *Marphysa sanguinea*, which is also eaten to some extent by other species of *Conus*. Notes on the ecology of this polychaete were recorded by Abbott (1946), who stated that "this species has been found only in limited areas of the pond [Wailupe Fish Pond, Oahu] where the bottom is sandy and the salinity close to that of sea water. Here it occurs under rocks, and does not appear to burrow deeply into the sand. It has not been found in regions where a soft mud bottom prevails."

The more common prey of *Conus imperialis* is the amphinomid polychaete *Eurythoe complanata*. Although this species is the most conspicuous polychaete on Hawaiian coral reefs, it was never found to be eaten by any other species of *Conus*. *Eurythoe* possesses extremely abundant large setae, which easily penetrate human skin and cause a burning sensation. They may possess a venom (Halstead 1956). Nevertheless, intestines of *C. imperialis* were often observed literally packed with these setae. The polychaete is typically found under rocks or in crevices in coral. Its food is unknown.

On several occasions, specimens of *Eurythoe complanata* were fed to *Conus imperialis* in the laboratory. The stinging operation is typical. Like *C. striatus*, *C. imperialis* uses its radula tooth as a harpoon. The tooth is not freed from the proboscis, but the impaled prey is drawn into the mouth by rapid contraction of the proboscis.

Only four prey organisms were recovered from the alimentary tracts of 20 specimens of *Conus pulicarius* which were examined. These were sufficient to show that the food of this species is not restricted to polychaetes. Two of the food organisms were of the species of capitellid eaten by *C. flavidus*, but the other two were of the echiuroid worm, *Thalassema* sp. Both of the latter were regurgitated by the snails after capture. At least one of the echiuroids was alive when regurgitated. This suggests that *Thalassema* may not be stung before being swallowed by *C. pulicarius*.

All of the other four vermivorous species of *Conus* collected on the reefs may be restricted to Eunicidae for food, although the samples examined were small. The primary food of *C. distans* is *Eunice afra*. This polychaete was found most commonly completely buried in coral rocks or in coral or other calcareous

encrustation on basalt boulders. *C. miles* feeds chiefly on *Lysidice collaris*, and *C. vexillum*, on *Eunice antennata* and *Marphysa sanguinea*. A single specimen of *E. afra* was recovered from the alimentary tract of *C. vitulinus*.

The large differences in the specific nature of the prey of the vermivorous species of *Conus* on reef platforms would seem to virtually preclude the possibility of interspecific competition for food. It was nevertheless of interest to obtain some information on the abundance of the prey species.

In order to determine the species and abundance of polychaetes associated with, or burrowing into, limestone, coral and coral ruble, sample blocks of substratum were removed from reefs and placed in sea water in sealed jars. When the oxygen tension decreased, the polychaetes were attracted out of their burrows and eventually fell to the bottom of the jar. After 2-3 days, the contents of the jar were fixed in 10% formalin. Cracking of pieces of coral revealed few or no polychaetes remaining within the blocks after this treatment. Dry weight, volume and surface (projection) area of the blocks were determined. Polychaetes equal to or greater than 0.3 mm in maximum diameter were identified and preserved.

The results of samples from Stations 3 and 7 treated in this manner are shown in Table 14. In suitable areas on reefs eunicids are seen to be extremely abundant. It is difficult, however, to assess the density of polychaetes over the entire reef platform, since the relative areas of different types of substratum could not be adequately measured. The data in Table 14 probably give the correct order of magnitude for areas with a predominantly lithified substratum.

MOLLUSCIVOROUS SPECIES

Two species of *Conus* found on subtidal reef platforms appear to feed exclusively on other gastropod mollusks. The species composition of their prey, as well as that of *C. textile*, found rarely on reefs, is shown in Table 15. In addition to specimens collected on reefs, total data include material collected in deeper water.

At least 13 species of prosobranchiate and opisthobranchiate gastropods were recorded from alimentary tract analyses of 146 specimens of *Conus pennaceus*. The most common food species is the bubble shell, *Haminoea crocata*. Second commonest is the small prosobranch, *Phasianella variabilis*. Since the shells of prosobranchs are not swallowed, the identification of partly digested remains was extremely difficult. About half of the prey organisms were identified to species, but this was not possible in some which were represented only by radulae and/or opercula.

Feeding of *Conus pennaceus* on *Haminoea crocata*, *Terebra gouldii* Deshayes, and *Cypraea maculifera* (Schilder) was observed in the laboratory. A specimen of *Cypraea moneta* Linné was not eaten, however, when left in a tank with two *C. pennaceus* for 24 hr. *C. pennaceus* did not prey on other species of *Conus*,

TABLE 14. Abundance of Polychaetes Associated with Hard Substrata on Reefs.

Sample No.	Station	Area (cm.²)	Species	Number Present
1269	7	50	*Eunice (Nicidion) cariboea*	6
			Cirriformia semicincta	2
			Eunice antennata	1
			Unidentified Polychaetes	6
				—
			Total	15
			Density of Large Polychaetes	3,000/m.²
			Density of Eunicidae	1,800/m.²
			(Number of Polychaetes <0.3 mm. diameter in sample	51)
1276	3	129	*Eunice antennata*	5
			Palola siciliensis	4
			Lysidice collaris	3
			Eunice (Nicidion) cariboea	2
			Cirriformia semicincta	1
			Eurythoe complanata	1
			Platynereis dumerilii	1
				—
			Total	17
			Density of Large Polychaetes	1,300/m.²
			Density of Eunicidae	1,100/m.²

although several were retained in the same aquaria for several months.

The most striking aspect of the food of *Conus marmoreus* is that it appears to consist entirely of other species of *Conus*. Remains of *Conus* species were found in alimentary tracts of five of the seven specimens of this rather rare species which were examined. On 31 March 1956, Mr. Charles Sueishi observed a specimen in the act of feeding on *Conus abbreviatus* near Station 11. Dissection revealed the remains of a second *C. abbreviatus* in the intestine. On 6 July 1956, the writer observed a specimen in the act of feeding on *C. lividus* at Station 9.

A specimen of *Conus textile* collected at Station 15 by Miss Valerie Lang contained the radula sheath, operculum, and other remains of a *Conus pennaceus* in its alimentary tract. Another specimen, which had just eaten a *Conus striatus*, was collected by Dr. C. M. Burgess near Makua, Oahu. One other gastropod, a *Morula ochrostoma* (Blainville), was identified from the alimentary tracts of *C. textile* examined. In the laboratory, specimens of *C. textile* were observed to sting and consume *C. abbreviatus*, *C. ebraeus*, *C. lividus*, *Cypraea caputserpentis*, *Cypraea moneta*, *Turbo intercostalis* Menke, *Thais aperta* Blainville, and *Drupa morum* Lamarck, but they did not sting *C. flavidus* or *Helcioniscus argentatus* Nuttall.

PISCIVOROUS SPECIES

Conus striatus occurs sparsely on Hawaiian reef platforms. Remains of fishes from the five specimens which were examined could not be identified. A goatfish (*Parupeneus* sp.) is known to be eaten by *C. striatus* in Micronesia (unpublished data). The other known piscivorous species, *C. catus* and *C. obscurus*, were not collected by the writer on reef platforms, but

TABLE 15. Food of Molluscivorous Species of *Conus* on Reefs.

	C. pennaceus All Reefs	*C. marmoreus* All Reefs	*C. marmoreus* Total	*C. textile* All Reefs	*C. textile* Total
No. Specimens Examined...	146	3	7	2	10
Haminoea crocata Pease	24	—	—	—	—
Haminoea sp. cf. *H. aperta* Pease	2	—	—	—	—
Haminoea sp. 1057	1	—	—	—	—
Phasianella variabilis Pease	12	—	—	—	—
Dolabrifera olivacea Pease	7	—	—	—	—
Gastropod sp. 1963	4	—	—	—	—
Gastropod sp. 1964	4	—	—	—	—
Trochus intextus Kiener	3	—	—	—	—
Turbo intercostalis Menke	2	—	—	—	—
Pleurobranchus sp. 1064	2	—	—	—	—
Gastropod sp. 988	2	—	—	—	—
Natica marochiensis Gmelin	1	—	—	—	—
Conus abbreviatus Reeve	—	1	3	—	—
Conus lividus Hwass in Bruguiere	—	1	2	—	—
Conus sp.	—	—	1	—	—
Conus pennaceus Born	—	—	—	1	1
Conus striatus Linne	—	—	—	—	1
Morula ochrostoma Blainville	—	—	—	—	1
Unidentified Gastropods	7	—	—	—	3
Total Gastropods	71	2	6	1	6
Unidentified Food	23	1	1	1	1

References consulted in the identification of the mollusks in this table were Edmondson (1946), Ostergaard (1955), Pease (1860), and Pilsbry (1917, 1920).

Ostergaard (1950) reported the former species from Station 3.

SUMMARY OF FOOD AND FEEDING IN THE SUBTIDAL REEF HABITAT

Modifications of radula teeth which can be correlated with increased frequency of feeding on tube-dwelling polychaetes are present in many of the vermivorous species of *Conus* characteristic of the subtidal reef platform habitat. A forward projecting cone on the base, which may aid in retaining the tooth in the proboscis while the prey is extracted from its tube, is present in the two dominant reef species, *C. flavidus* and *C. lividus*. The former preys almost exclusively on tube-dwelling Terebellidae. Polychaetes preyed on by *C. lividus* are chiefly terebellids, but the dominant food species is the enteropneust *Ptychodera flava*. In addition to the basal cone, both *C. flavidus* and *C. lividus* possess a backward projecting spur on the shaft of the radula tooth, about one-third of the length from the base. Peile (1939) suggested that this structure may serve to prevent the tooth from being forced back into the proboscis on the impact of the sting.

The chief differences in the radula teeth of *Conus lividus* and *C. flavidus* are that the latter is shorter and is finely serrate (in disagreement with Peile 1939), while the former has a long shaft and no serrations. There is no obvious adaptive significance to these differences; nevertheless, the difference in nature of the food of the two species is highly significant ($P < 10^{-6}$).

The characteristics of the radula teeth of *Conus*

sponsalis, C. abbreviatus, C. ebraeus, and *C. rattus* were discussed above. Differences in the feeding habits of these species on reef platforms are apparent from inspection of Table 13. The feeding habits of *C. abbreviatus* and *C. rattus* are most similar to each other, but even these differ highly significantly (P = 10^{-6}) in the samples examined.

Conus imperialis, C. miles, C. vexillum, and *C. vitulinus* all possess the forward projecting cone on the base of the radula teeth. All feed primarily on polychaetes which either burrow into coral (Eunicidae) or live under rocks or in crevices (*Eurythoe*). The presence of the cone is therefore correlated with the habit of feeding on burrowing polychaetes, and it may well serve the function of aiding in the extraction of the worm from its tube, as suggested by Peile (1939). Distinct differences in the nature of the food of all of these species is also apparent from Table 13, although the samples are rather small for rigorous statistical analysis.

Conus distans, which also feeds on burrowing eunicids, does not possess the basal cone on the radula tooth, but the terminal knob is extremely large and may have the same function. The food of *C. distans* is similar to that of *C. rattus,* but the differences between them are highly significant (P< 10^{-3}).

On reef platforms as on marine benches, the nature of the food of each vermivorous species of *Conus* differs significantly from that of all other species. Thus these species avoid competition for food among each other. In addition, they are completely ecologically isolated, with respect to food, from *C. pennaceus,* which feeds only on a large number of other gastropods. Two other molluscivorous species, *C. marmoreus* and *C. textile,* occur only very rarely on reef platforms. *C. striatus* is the only piscivorous species collected by the author on the reefs, although small numbers of *C. catus* also occur in this habitat.

AMOUNT OF FOOD EATEN

Thorson (1956) has recently called attention to the need for more information on the quantity of food consumed by predators in order to understand the dynamics of benthic communities. A few data on predatory benthic fishes show that the daily food consumption is equal to 3-5% of the weight of plaice (Dawes 1930, 1931). Smith (1950) calculated rates of 1.1-2.4% in benthic fishes of Block Island Sound. Among the gastropods, young, growing specimens of *Polinices duplicata* Say, feeding on *Gemma gemma* Totten, consumed about 7% of their own weight per day. The rate in older *Polinices* was about 5% (Turner 1951). Higher rates of 10-25% were calculated for other predatory gastropods by Thorson (1958).

In the data on *Conus* which follow, dry weight of the predator (excluding shell) is compared with dry weight of the prey. Dry weights of *Conus* were measured following heating at 100°C for 48-96 hr, or by estimation from "alcohol weight" using the con-

version given by Holme (1953). Dry weights of polychaetes were determined by the method of Holme.

Enough specimens of *Perinereis helleri* were available to establish the relationship between maxilla length and body weight. Thus the weight of the prey organisms could be determined even if only the maxillae were found in the alimentary tract of the predator. Using data obtained with this method as well as from direct weighing of intact polychaetes found in crops, the amount of food (17 *P. helleri*) consumed by 17 adult *Conus ebraeus* was calculated to average 0.0049 ± 0.0005 g. Dry weight of the predators was 0.43 ±0.02 g. Since the daily feeding rate was estimated to be one polychaete per snail, the daily food consumption of *C. ebraeus* is equal to about 1% of its own body weight. Average quantitative food consumption of the four dominant species of *Conus* on marine benches, in per cent of body weight per day, was:

C. sponsalis	4.6%
C. abbreviatus	3.4%
C. chaldaeus	1.2%
C. ebraeus	1.2%

The two smaller species consume proportionately more food per day than the larger species. The rates are somewhat lower than those cited above for other predatory gastropods. The reason is probably that all of the other figures are for temperate species, many of which do not feed in winter. Since the time available for feeding is shorter, the feeding rate during the season is likely to be higher than in a tropical gastropod such as *Conus*, which feeds at a constant rate throughout the year.

PREDATION ON *CONUS*

The extent of predation on *Conus* is difficult to evaluate. In the course of collecting trips, freshly dead fragments of *C. catus, C. rattus, C. abbreviatus,* and *C. flavidus* were observed on marine benches. In some cases, shells had been broken into many pieces so recently that most of the pieces were present within a few square centimeters. On reef platforms, shell fragments of freshly killed specimens of 11 species of *Conus* were collected. Fragments of the relatively thin-shelled *C. pennaceus* were found most often. Surprisingly, fragments of the extremely thick-shelled *C. flavidus* were second commonest. These cases are believed due to predation. The identity of the predators is not known, but parrot fishes (Scaridae) and the zebra eel, *Echidna zebra* (Shaw) are possibly responsible.

Other organisms, including the other species of *Conus* mentioned in the previous section, other gastropods (*Cymatium*), and starfish (*Asterope*), were observed to prey on *Conus* in the laboratory.

Cymatium nicobaricum Röding readily attacked *Conus* in laboratory aquaria. A large specimen (shell length 84 mm) devoured specimens of *C. ebraeus, C. abbreviatus,* and *C. catus.* Dead *C. ebraeus* were also eaten. In one case, a live *Conus ebraeus* was attacked by *Cymatium nicobaricum* about 20 min after the two were placed in the same aquarium. The predator introduced its proboscis into the aperture of the *Conus* shell, and apparently began to rasp off pieces of the foot with its radula. This position was maintained for 9 days, after which the empty *Conus* shell was released. *Cymatium*, which is represented by several species in Hawaii, is a likely predator of *Conus* in nature.

Although specimens of the starfish *Asterope carinifera* Lamarck were kept for months in aquaria with several species of *Conus*, predation was observed only rarely. It is not known whether *Asterope* preys on *Conus* in nature. The starfish is not very common, and its habitat is often not shared by *Conus*. Both *Asterope* and *C. ebraeus*, which the starfish ate in the aquarium, were however found at Station 13.

Xanthid crabs also attacked *Conus* in laboratory aquaria. The attacks usually resulted in the outer lip of the shell being broken off. Crabs were never observed to succeed in killing the gastropods, probably because the latter could retract farther into the shell, and the older portions of the shell were too thick for the crabs to break. However, laboratory observations were made only on two thick-shelled species, *C. lividus* and *C. flavidus*. Crabs may prey more successfully on some of the thinner-shelled species.

Two species of fishes, a wrasse, *Stethojulis axillaris* (Quoy and Gaimard) and a goby, *Chlamydes cotticeps* (Steindachner), were reported by Strasburg (1953) to feed on the eggs of *Conus* in Hawaii. The problem of predation on larvae remains unstudied. Large numbers of free-swimming veligers are undoubtedly consumed by carnivorous planktivores. Many newly settled larvae probably fall prey to brittle stars (*Ophiocoma* spp.) which abound on the reefs.

FOOD CHAINS AND TROPHIC STRUCTURE OF THE COMMUNITY

The polychaetes on which the dominant marine bench species of *Conus* feed are mainly herbivorous. At Station 5, *Perinereis helleri* was found to feed chiefly on the blue-green alga, *Lyngbya majuscula*. Alimentary tracts of specimens collected at night were often full of the filaments of this alga. Eunicids also feed on *Lyngbya* as well as on other algae .

Since predation on adult *Conus* may be assumed to be negligible, a short food chain of three steps is indicated. Since the numbers of species at the two higher trophic levels are large, increased efficiency associated with a restricted diet can be achieved without detracting from community stability (MacArthur 1955).

Data presented above for biomass of polychaetes and *Conus*, together with dry weights of algal samples collected about halfway across the bench at Station 5, were used to calculate the biomass pyramid for the algae-polychaete-*Conus* food chain shown in Fig. 28. The dominant alga in the sample was *Laurencia* sp. Since this does not appear to be eaten by the polychaetes under discussion, only *Lyngbya majuscula*, which represented 7% of the algae sample, is included in the pyramid.

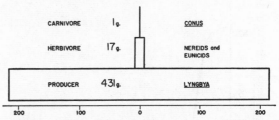

FIG. 28. Pyramid of biomass for the algae-polychaete-*Conus* food chain at Station 5.

For this food chain, the ratios of standing crop between trophic levels are herbivores/producers 4% and carnivores/herbivores 6%. It is to be noted that these ratios apply only to the single food *chain* considered and not to the entire community or food *web*.

ECOLOGICAL NOTES ON OTHER SUBTIDAL HABITATS

The most important habitats of *Conus* in the Hawaiian Islands are the intertidal marine benches and subtidal reef platforms which have been discussed in the previous sections. The relatively fragmentary ecological information which has been gained concerning species which occur chiefly in other habitats is summarized in the following paragraphs.

Conus quercinus. Certain limited regions off the shore of Oahu, usually in bays, are characterized by vast areas of sand substratum uninterrupted by coral heads or limestone outcrops. Wave action is usually comparatively light, and the salinity is often somewhat reduced by the proximity of streams. Portions of such areas may be a foot or two above the 0 tide datum, forming a sand spit. Station 2A, Sand (Ahuolaka) Island, in Kaneohe Bay (Fig. 4), is such a formation. The habitat of *C. quercinus* appears to be restricted to areas of this type, at least at certain seasons. The writer's observations are in agreement with those of Bryan (1915), who stated "they (*C. quercinus*) appear to prefer the muddy brackish water conditions at the harbor mouth to a life on the coral reef in the open sea." The species is often common where it occurs, but its distribution in shallow water is probably limited by the sparse occurrence of favorable habitats about the Hawaiian Islands and by seasonal differences in habitat.

Collections made by the writer confirmed a marked seasonality of *Conus quercinus*, which had been verbally reported to him by a number of collectors. Collecting trips to Station 2A made by the writer between July, 1954, and June, 1956, are noted by closed circles in Fig. 29. A marked seasonal fluctuation in abundance, with maxima annually in February and March, is apparent. Since no quantitative sampling of the area was done, the absolute amplitude of the maxima is not meaningful.

The biological significance of the fluctuation in numbers of *Conus quercinus* is in reproduction.

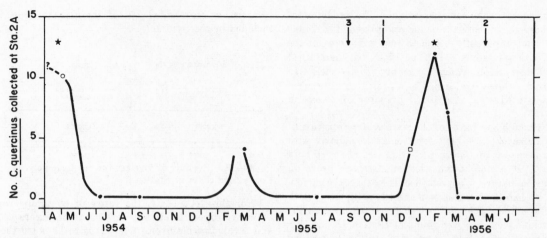

FIG. 29. Seasonal changes in abundance of *Conus quercinus* at Station 2A. Stars indicate observation of spawning of *C. quercinus* at Station 2A (1956) or in laboratory soon after being collected at Station 2A (1954). Closed circles indicate collecting trips by the author. Additional trips, during which no *C. quercinus* were seen, were made in August, 1954, and August, September, November, and December, 1955, but the exact dates were not recorded.

Explanation of vertical arrows: 1. Collection of one specimen in sampan channel, Kaneohe Bay, depth 10 ft, by A. H. Banner. 2. Collection of two specimens off Barbers Point, depth 160 ft, by R. Sheats. 3 Collection of two specimens in Bay ½ mile south of Hapuna Beach, Hawaii, depth 15-20 ft, by R. A. McKinsey.

Spawning was observed at Station 2A in February, 1956. A number of specimens collected at Station 2A in April, 1954, by staff members of the Hawaii Marine · Laboratory, spawned in laboratory aquaria late the same month. The population apparently migrates to Station 2A from deeper water in early spring for spawning. The egg capsules are typically attached to the alga, *Acanthophora orientalis*. The adults then presumably return to deeper water. Specimens at Station 2A were collected in 2-10 ft of water and were most abundant in 2-5 ft. Other, "out of season" collection records from deeper water are also noted in Fig. 29.

Analysis of alimentary tract contents of 34 specimens of *Conus quercinus* revealed the commonest prey organism to be the enteropneust, *Ptychodera flava*, remains of which were found in 13 specimens. Two specimens contained remains of the sabellid polychaete, *Sabellastarte indica*. These were the only identifiable prey organisms. *Ptychodera flava* was extremely abundant at Station 2A; densities of several individuals per square foot were not uncommon.

Conus leopardus. The habitat of *Conus leopardus* is similar to that of *C. quercinus*, but the former species usually occurs in somewhat deeper water. It is rarely collected at depths of less than 10 ft. The deepest record known to the author is a specimen collected in 120 ft off Pearl Harbor, Oahu, by R. Sheats on 2 February 1956. Sand is the typical substratum, but specimens are also found on mixed sand-rubble bottoms.

No definitely identifiable food organisms were found in alimentary tracts of ten specimens which were examined. Remains in one specimen were tentatively identified as *Ptychodera flava*. The feeding of

C. leopardus on *P. flava* was observed in the laboratory. Within a few seconds after the enteropneust was introduced into an aquarium containing a *C. leopardus*, the latter became active, extending its siphon and waving it about in the water. Several minutes later, the orange rostrum extended and began to engulf the *Ptychodera*. At no time was the proboscis visible. The prey was apparently never stung, since rhythmic contractions of the proboscis, collar and trunk regions persisted until engulfment was complete, some 18 min later.

Conus leopardus is the largest species of the genus in Hawaiian waters, the shell lengths of some specimens exceeding 200 mm. However, its radula and venom apparatus are extremely poorly developed. The radula teeth of a 160-mm specimen measured only 0.9 mm in length, comparable to those of an adult (40-mm) *C. lividus*. It is just possible that the radula, which is an extremely specialized apparatus in other species of *Conus*, is vestigial in *C. leopardus*. It must be recalled however, that some species with well developed radula teeth do not always sting the prey prior to feeding.

Conus moreleti. No identifiable food organisms were found in alimentary tract contents of 6 specimens of *Conus moreleti* which were collected in depths of 10-40 ft off the leeward (west) coast of Oahu. However, this species, which is rather similar to *C. lividus*, is probably vermivorous.

Conus obscurus. Nine specimens collected at depths of 15-35 ft off leeward Oahu were examined. Remains of an unidentified fish were present in one. Attempts to observe the feeding process in the laboratory were not completely successful. Introduction of a fish into the vessel with the snail usually evoked extension of the proboscis. In only one instance was a radula tooth ejected, however. The fish, a specimen of *Bathygobius fuscus,* escaped and was not swallowed but died a few minutes later, presumably from the effects of the venom.

Conus textile. Specimens were collected rarely on the reefs and at depths of 10-75 ft. Results of alimentary tract examinations are included in Table 15.

Conus miles. This species occurs occasionally on reefs and benches but is somewhat more common in deeper water. Individuals on reefs are usually larger, however. Specimens collected in 35-40 ft off leeward Oahu were found to have fed on *Lysidice collaris.* (Most of the specimens of *C. moreleti, C. obscurus, C. textile* and *C. miles* discussed in this section were collected by R. M. Gray, R. A. McKinsey and C. M. Stidham.)

DISCUSSION: ECOLOGICAL NICHES AND ECOLOGICAL ISOLATION

Odum (1953) satisfactorily defined ecological niche as "the position or status of an organism within its community and ecosystem resulting from the organism's structural adaptations, physiological responses, and specific behavior." The ecological niche is multidimensional.

In the preceding sections of this paper, the species of *Conus* inhabiting Hawaiian coral reefs and marine benches have been compared with respect to some of the dimensions of niches. The purpose of this discussion is to state concisely all comparative data. From these data, evidence of ecological isolation, or its reciprocal, the overlap of ecological niches, will be evaluated.

Formulation of the theory that ecological isolation is the result of interspecific competition is due to Volterra (1926; see also D'Ancona 1954). Since Gause (1934) clearly showed that this theory was applicable to experimental populations, the postulate that in a stable community each species occupies a different ecological niche and that two or more species with the same ecological requirements cannot coexist has become known as Gause's principle (Odum 1953), Gause's hypothesis (Gilbert, Reynoldson & Hobart 1952), or, more properly, the Volterra-Gause principle (Hutchinson 1953). In such experiments, only one species finally survives in a population by inhibiting the population(s) of the other species initially present more than its own.

Although the process of competition can thus be observed in experimental populations, it is very difficult to do so in natural populations. The reasons for this are that (1) if the process occurs in nature, its rate may be very slow, and (2) it is often difficult to make the necessary determination of the behavior of a species in the absence of its presumed competitor in completely natural populations. It should be pointed out that the demonstration of niches which overlap with respect to one or more dimensions does not prove the occurrence of competition. This seems to have been overlooked by some authors (e.g. Test 1945, Odum 1953). In its most satisfactory definition, competition requires common exploitation of a limited requisite. Furthermore, mechanisms by which even species whose niches overlap with respect to limited requisites can avoid severe competition have been pointed out by Hutchinson (1953). Severe competition is used here to mean competition leading to the elimination of the less successful species.

Despite the inherent difficulties, interspecific competition has been observed in nature, particularly in birds, on a few occasions (Mackenzie 1950, Pitelka 1951, S. D. Ripley, verbal communication). The rarity of such cases, together with the invocation of other factors, led Andrewartha & Birch (1954) to a general theory of population ecology without introduction of the concept of competition. A number of studies of natural populations containing ecologically similar species provide strong evidence of a less direct sort in favor of the operation of interspecific competition in nature. Additional evidence has been derived from studies of geographical replacement of species with "too slight ecological dissimilarity" (Svärdson 1949a, 1949b).

In all carefully studied stable populations containing two or more ecologically similar species, more or less subtle differences in the ecological niches of these species have been elucidated, thus demonstrating the validity of the Volterra-Gause principle in nature. Ecologically *similar* species are just that and not ecologically *identical.* It can be stated with Gilbert *et al.* (1952), that these observations support the hypothesis that "in a population of a species, mechanisms which reduce competition between it and populations of other species tend to persist."

In the experimental studies of the Volterra-Gause principle, avoidance of interspecific competition was shown to be the result of such competition. In many natural populations ecologically similar species coexist because of reduction or avoidance of competition. In this way, the evidence from natural populations favors the hypothesis that the process of competition, leading to the avoidance of competition, operates in nature, most probably as a selection pressure.

This evidence has been derived from studies of natural populations which contain ecologically similar species of many kinds, including flatworms (Beauchamp & Ullyott 1932), fruit flies (Da Cunha, Dobzhansky & Sokoloff 1951), copepods (Hutchinson 1951), mollusks (Test 1945), fishes (Daiber 1956), amphibians (Dumas 1956), birds (Lack 1945, 1947), and mammals (McCabe & Blanchard 1951, Johnson 1943).

Except for a few papers which consider only one dimension of the ecological niche, e.g. zonation (Fischer-Piette 1935, Eslick 1940), the work of Test (1945) is the only previous such study of marine gastropods known to the writer. It deals with herbivorous limpets, of the genus *Acmaea.* Test's work differs from most of the others listed, and is more similar to the present study, in that it deals with

TABLE 16. Summary of Ecological Characteristics of Species of *Conus* on Marine Benches.

	sponsalis	*abbreviatus*	*ebraeus*	*chaldaeus*	*rattus*	*catus*
Relative abundance at all bench stations.............	1	2	3	4	5	6
Population density on a solution bench (Sta. 5) (no./100 sq. ft.).............................	0.41	0.66	1.02	0.15	0.02*	0.00
Population density on a water-leveled bench (Sta. K1) (no./100 sq. ft.).............................	0.48	0.85	0.55	0.18	0.09	0.24
Population density at abrasion ramp stations* (no./100 sq. ft.).............................	0.25	0.21	0.00	0.07	0.33	0.00
Distance from shore of density peak at Sta. 5 (% distance across bench)........................	8%	8%	50%	73%	——	——
Distance from shore of density peak at Sta. K1 (% distance across bench)........................	22%	18%	26%	48-70%	47%	53%
Per cent of population on substratum of algal turf on bench, binding ± sand........................	90%	65%	65%	45%	62%	(45%)
Per cent of population on sand patches on bench.....	5%	26%	15%	28%	11%	(18%)
Per cent of population exposed to air at low tide.....	55%	35%	29%	32%	17%	29%
Per cent of population partly buried in substratum during day...................................	30%	63%	31%	42%	10%	(44%)
Ability to withstand strong water currents (exp't'l.) (arbitrary units).............................	+	+	++	+		
Active period in nature and in laboratory............	All species actively crawl about at night, are quiescent during day					
Per cent of diet represented by Nereidae............	52%	26%	93%	85%	50%	Eats Only
Per cent of diet represented by Eunicea.............	44%	69%	6%	15%	50%	Fish

*Calculated from time-relative density.

more than two ecologically similar sympatric species. As many as 17 species of *Acmaea* coexist in a broad region of the California coast. Test was able to show diversification of the ecological niches of these species, despite the demonstration of varying degrees of overlap in one or more dimensions of the niches. Only quite recently have similar studies been extended to large numbers of sympatric species in other groups, namely insects (Cooper & Dobzhansky 1956; Da Cunha, El-Tabey Shehata & de Olivera 1957) and birds (Betts 1955).

A total of 18 species of *Conus* were collected by the writer on Hawaiian coral reefs and marine benches. Of these, 16 were collected on reefs and 13 on benches, dispersed among these habitats as previously discussed. On marine benches, 6 of the 13 species present are characteristic of the habitat, and only these are included in the following discussion of ecological niches. Of the others, two represent unique collection records, and five are occasionally found on benches but are more typical of the reef habitat. The factors which probably limit their abundance on benches have been discussed above.

The ecology of the species of *Conus* inhabiting marine benches is complicated by the fact that the whole life cycle is not passed in the same habitat. Recruitment of all species is predominantly from pelagic veliger larvae which are washed onto benches from other areas of origin, particularly subtidal reefs, where conditions for spawning are more favorable.

The ecological requirements of pelagic larvae and newly metamorphosed young are unknown and are extremely difficult to study. Because of their small size, newly settled larvae are virtually impossible to observe in nature. Attempts to raise young from eggs in the laboratory generally failed. Veligers usually hatched and swam about freely but died before settling to the

crawling mode of life. The food at these early stages is unknown. Veligers are probably plankton or seston feeders. It is not known whether or not newly settled larvae immediately assume the carnivorous habit, or at what stage the venom apparatus becomes functional.

Requisites which govern population density of pelagic veligers and newly-settled young stages may affect the observed adult population densities reported here. Predation may well be an important factor. These statements are, however, not based on positive evidence. The hypothesis was not amenable to investigation in the time available, so adult populations only were studied. The evidence to be summarized in Tables 16-20 suggests that adults of all species studied are sufficiently isolated ecologically that interspecific competition does not limit population densities.

In Table 16, all characteristics of ecological niches studied are summarized for the six most abundant species of *Conus* on marine benches. All of these species also occur in the subtidal reef habitat, although usually in considerably lower abundance. In Table 17, data for the 8 most abundant species on subtidal reefs are similarly summarized.

In order to determine the significance in niche differentiation of interspecific differences with respect to dimensions of niches, the results of statistical analyses of all observed ecological data relating to these species are summarized in Tables 18-20. In the right column of these tables the category of relationship of *Conus* to a number of environmental factors is listed. The statistical test applied to the data and the probability of the samples of the two species having been drawn at random from the same population are given in the second and third columns, respectively. Probabilities in most cases are extremely low. However, it is not legitimate to attribute all

TABLE 17. Summary of Ecological Characteristics of Species of *Conus* on Subtidal Reefs.

	flavidus	*lividus*	*pennaceus*	*abbreviatus*	*ebraeus*	*sponsalis*	*rattus*	*imperialis*
Relative abundance at all reef stations............	1	2	3	4	5	6	7	8
Population density on a reef platform (Sta. K3) (no./100 sq. ft.).................	0.03	—	—	0.07	0.09	—	—	—
Per cent of population on sand substratum..............	56%	64%	75%	78%	61%	38%	22%	48%
Per cent of population on reef limestone substratum.....	26%	22%	21%	13%	20%	30%	38%	26 %
Per cent of population on coral, rubble and rough coral bench substrata.........	18%	14%	4%	4%	19%	23%	40%	26%
Dominant component of particulate sediments.....	coarse+very coarse sand		coarse sand	coarse+very coarse sand				fine to coarse sand
Per cent of population buried or under rocks during day.	15%	10%	100%	54%	27%	13%	14%	8%
Per cent of diet represented by Nereidae................	—	—	—	—	15%	46%	23%	—
Per cent of diet represented by Eunicea.................	—	12%	—	100%	82%	50%	77%	27%
Per cent of diet represented by Terebellidae.............	64%	14%	Eats only Gastropods	—	—	—	—	—
Per cent of diet represented by all polychaetes...........	96%	39%		100%	100%	100%	100%	100%
Per cent of diet represented by enteropneusts...........	4%	61%						

of the differences solely to the dimensions of the niches. If the degree of overlap is large, chi-square (but not Wilcoxon) tests may indicate significant differences if the sample also is large. A hypothetical case is illustrated in Fig. 30. In both both A and B, the probability that the two samples were drawn at random from the same population is the same. The ecological significance of the two situations is, however, quite distinct. Because of differences in position of the curves on the abscissa, competition between N_1 and N_2 for the requisite represented is much less likely in B than in A. Competition does not necessarily take place in either case.

For this reason the degree of overlap of the species with respect to each dimension is also included in Tables 18-20. In entries where the interspecific differences are highly significant, and where per cent overlap is large, the biological significance is less than the low probabilities might imply. That is, the possibility of competition is not virtually precluded.

Inspection of Table 16 shows as a first approximation that *Conus sponsalis* and *C. abbreviatus* are ecologically more similar to each other than to the other species in the table. These species are also similar in absolute abundance and in size. They are closely related systematically, usually being placed in the same subgenus (*Virroconus*). The results of statistical analyses of all observed ecological data relating to these two species are summarized in Table 18. Population densities are similar at the two most thoroughly studied bench stations, but they differ significantly when all marine benches are considered. The great difference in abundance on different reefs is due to the fact that *C. sponsalis* is much more abundant than *C. abbreviatus* at Station 7 and less abundant at all other

TABLE 18. Statistical Analyses of Ecological Data: Comparison of the Ecological Niches of *Conus sponsalis* and *C. abbreviatus.*

Relation of *Conus* to Environmental Factor	Statistical Test	P	Per cent Overlap
1. Relative abundance at Stations 5 and Kl............................	Chi-square	.8	95%
2. Relative abundance on three types of benches........................	Chi-square	<.01	53%
3. Relative abundance on four reefs..	Chi-square	<10⁻⁶	14%
4. Distribution pattern on a solution bench (Sta. 5).................	Wilcoxon	≫.05	80%
5. Distribution pattern on a water-leveled bench (Sta. Kl)	Wilcoxon	≫.05	80%
6. Occupation of different types of substratum on marine benches.....	Chi-square	<.001	62%
7. Occupation of different types of substratum on reefs	Chi-square	10⁻⁵	42%
8. Frequency of burrowing into substratum during day: marine benches	Chi-square	<.01	50%
9. Frequency of burrowing into substratum during day: reefs........	Chi-square	≪.001	42%
10. Frequency of exposure to dry air at low tide on marine benches.......	Chi-square	<.01	67%
11. Nature of food: Frequency of Eunicea and Nereidae eaten on marine benches.........................	Chi-square	<.001	59%
12. Nature of food: Frequency of individual prey species on benches........	Chi-square	10⁻⁶	42%
13. Nature of food: Frequency of Eunicea and Nereidae eaten on reefs......	Chi-square	≪.01	34%
14. Nature of food: Frequency of individual prey species on reefs	Chi-square	<10⁻⁶	25%
15. Food preference in choice experiments.	Chi-square	<.001	48%

Entries 8, 10, and 11, are dependent on 7, 12, and 13, respectively.

reef stations. Both species are almost identically distributed over the benches where both are abundant. Despite the fact that both are common in the same habitat, the two species differ at the 1% level of significance with respect to all other dimensions of the

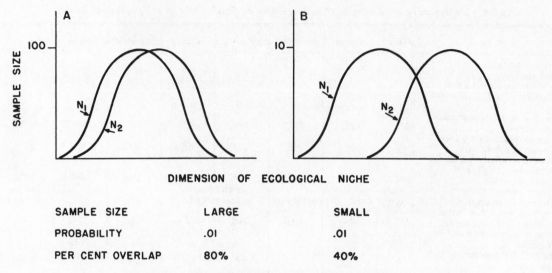

SAMPLE SIZE   LARGE   SMALL

PROBABILITY   .01   .01

PER CENT OVERLAP   80%   40%

N_1 AND N_2 ARE RELATED SYMPATRIC SPECIES

FIG. 30. Hypothetical case indicating the possibility of interspecific competition despite apparent statistically significant difference in niches. Explanation in text.

ecological niches which were investigated. Furthermore, the degree of overlap is small, hence ecological isolation is pronounced, with respect to all other factors.

Conus ebraeus and *C. chaldaeus* are the two species which are most closely related systematically. Both belong to the same subgenus (*Virroconus*) as *C. sponsalis and C. abbreviatus*. Many authors have considered *C. chaldaeus* to be a variety of *C. ebraeus*. This view has persisted among a few recent workers (e.g. Dodge 1953). Usually, however, both are accorded specific rank, and even opponents of this view have acknowledged the absence of intergrades. In Hawaii, the shells of these two species are quite distinct in appearance, much more so than in other parts of their range (Kohn unpublished.).

Furthermore, evidence discussed above and summarized in Table 19 indicates that the microhabitats of *Conus ebraeus* and *C. chaldaeus* are quite distinct, although the two species are typically found together in the marine bench macrohabitat. Since *C. ebraeus* is fairly common on reef platforms, but *C. chaldaeus* is virtually excluded, all of the comparisons in Table 19 are concerned only with marine benches. There the relative abundance, relation to substratum, frequency of exposure to air at low tide, and general nature of the food are very similar. However, striking differences in pattern of distribution across benches and especially in the specific nature of the food are apparent. The degree of overlap between the niches with respect to these two dimensions is extremely small. The two species are thus able to coexist and avoid interspecific competition.

Inspection of Tables 16 and 17 suggests that *Conus ebraeus* is ecologically about as similar to *C. abbreviatus* as it is to *C. sponsalis*. A similar comparison of the ecological data of *C. ebraeus* and *C. sponsalis* was also made. These two species differ

TABLE 19. Statistical Analyses of Ecological Data: Comparison of the Ecological Niches of *Conus ebraeus* and *C. chaldaeus* on Marine Benches.

Relation of *Conus* to Environmental Factor	Statistical Test	P	Per cent Overlap
1. Relative abundance at Stations 5 and K1	Chi-square	.2	71%
2. Relative abundance on three types of benches........................	Chi-square	.03	80%
3. Distribution pattern on a solution bench (Sta. 5).................	Wilcoxon	$<.01$	59%†
4. Distribution pattern on a water-leveled bench (Sta. K1)	Wilcoxon	$<.01$	14%*
5. Occupation of different types of substratum....................	Chi-square	.17	63%
6. Frequency of burrowing into substratum during day	Chi-square	.6	80%
7. Frequency of exposure to dry air at low tide	Chi-square	.6	94%
8. Occupation of particulate sediments with different mechanical properties	Wilcoxon	.05	75%
9. Nature of food: Frequency of Nereidae and Eunicea eaten	Chi-square	.22	83%
10. Nature of food: Frequency of individual prey species..................	Chi-square	$<10^{-6}$	0.5%

Entry 9 is dependent on entry 10.

†Overlap=3% if only 2nd and 3rd quartiles of the distribution shown in Figure 20 are considered.

*Overlap=0% if only 2nd and 3rd quartiles of the distribution shown in Figure 22 are considered.

significantly from each other with respect to almost all of the dimensions of ecological niches which were studied.

Inspection of Tables 16 and 17 suggests that *Conus rattus* is ecologically quite similar to *C. ebraeus*. *C. rattus* is placed in a different subgenus (*Lithoconus* or *Rhizoconus*) from the other bench species. An analysis similar to those of Tables 18 and 19 indicated that differences with respect to several dimensions of the niches of the two species are not significant and that there is considerable overlap. However, the two species are usually not found in the same place, for *C. rattus* dominates the abrasion ramp benches where *C. ebraeus* is absent. Where both occur, *C. ebraeus* is the more successful, judging from absolute numbers of both present on solution benches, water-leveled benches, and reef platforms. The difference between the food of these two species is also highly significant. On marine benches, the food of *C. rattus* is most similar to that of *C. sponsalis* (P = .7 in comparison of families of polychaetes eaten), but the individual species preyed on by *C. rattus* and *C. sponsalis* differ highly significantly (P< 10^{-6}), and the overlap is only 22%.

Of the species of *Conus* characteristic of marine benches, *C. catus* (subgenus *Chelyconus*) was the least abundant. This species was commonest at Station K1, where its greatest density was nearer the outer edge than any other species present (Fig. 22). Samples were too small to provide reliable information on most other characteristics of the niche. However, *C. catus* is completely ecologically isolated from all other species of *Conus* which inhabit marine benches by the nature of its food, which consists entirely of fishes.

Turning to the species characteristic of subtidal reef platforms, it is apparent from Table 17 that *Conus flavidus* and *C. lividus*, the two most abundant species, are very similar ecologically. Since both occur uncommonly on marine benches, only data from reef stations are presented in Table 20, which summarizes the comparative ecology of these two species.

TABLE 20. Statistical Analyses of Ecological Data: Comparison of the Ecological Niches of *Conus lividus* and *C. flavidus* on reefs.

Relation of *Conus* to Environmental Factor	Statistical Test	P	Per cent Overlap
1. Relative abundance on four reefs (Stations 3, 4, 7, 9)	Chi-square	.001	64%
2. Relative abundance on three reefs (Stations 3, 4, 9)	Chi-square	.08	75%
3. Distribution pattern on three reefs.....	Wilcoxon	≫.05	88%
4. Occupation of different types of substratum......................	Chi-square	.15	77%
5. Association with particulate sediments with different mechanical properties.	Wilcoxon	.05	42%
6. Nature of food: Frequency of major groups eaten*	Chi-square	<10^{-6}	12%
7. Nature of food: Frequency of individual prey species eaten.................	Chi-square	<10^{-6}	10%

*Major groups=Terebellidae, other polychaetes, and enteropneusts

On most reefs, the abundance of *C. flavidus* and *C. lividus* is similar. An exception is Station 7, where the latter species was much the more abundant. The significant difference in abundance in the first entry of Table 20 is due entirely to Station 7, as the second entry shows. The nature of, and relation to, the substratum is similar in both species. The most striking difference in the ecological niches of *C. flavidus* and *C. lividus* is in the nature of the food. Frequency differences in the samples examined are highly significant, and degree of overlap is exceedingly low. There is thus little possibility of competition for food.

Extensive overlapping with respect to other environmental requisites may permit competition, however.

A number of vermivorous species occur on reefs in very low population densities. Three of these, *Conus distans*, *C. vexillum* and *C. imperialis*, attain a larger size than almost all of the other species found on the reefs. Specimens of *C. distans* collected ranged from 46 to 131 mm in shell length; the range in *C. vexillum* was 44-85 mm, and in *C. imperialis*, 52-88 mm. These species, as well as *C. miles* and *C. vitulinus*, feed on eunicid polychaetes. Some of these species may be restricted to eunicids for food, but *C. imperialis* also feeds on the amphinomid polychaete, *Eurythoe complanata*. Since the samples collected were small, little statistical information was obtained. However, the data presented in Table 13 suggest striking differences in the specific nature of the prey of these species and, therefore, in that dimension of their ecological niches. The factors influencing population density are not known.

Two salient features of the niche of *Conus pulicarius* serve to isolate this species ecologically from its sympatric congeners. *C. pulicarius* occurs most often in large areas of deep sand on reef platforms, while the more abundant *C. flavidus* and *C. lividus* occur most often on patches of thin sand on reef limestone, or in small sandpockets. Secondly, part of the diet of *C. pulicarius* consists of the echiuroid, *Thalassema*, which as far as is known is not exploited for food by any other species of *Conus*. Information on the ecology of *Thalassema* is not sufficient to determine whether these two aspects of the niche of *C. pulicarius* are related.

The ecological niche of *Conus pennaceus* differs qualitatively from those of the other reef species with respect to both space and food. This species typically remains under basalt or coral rocks on, or partly buried in, sand during the day. Other species are found only rarely in this microhabitat. Competition for food with the numerous vermivorous species is completely avoided, since *C. pennaceus* feeds solely on other gastropods. The two other molluscivorous species, *C. marmoreus* and *C. textile*, are exceedingly rare on the reefs. Data obtained by the author are too few to indicate the extent of overlap with respect to food. However, both *C. marmoreus* and *C. textile* feed at least partly on other species of *Conus* while *C. pennaceus* was never found to eat its congeners.

The wide variety of gastropods on which *C. pennaceus* feeds is further evidence that intraspecific competition is of much greater importance than interspecific competition to this species. For, as Svärdson (1949a) showed, dominant intraspecific pressure causes a species to approach more closely the tolerance limits of its niche. "In this case, the species may be said to go down the slopes of its adaptive peak" (Svärdson 1949a).

Both piscivorous species, *Conus striatus* and *C. catus*, are very rare on Hawaiian reefs. They are ecologically isolated from all of the other species by the nature of their food. Young *C. striatus* may feed on fishes of similar size to those eaten by adult *C. catus,* but the food of adult *C. striatus* is much larger.

The data presented in the preceding paragraphs indicate a high degree of ecological isolation among the species of *Conus* considered. Except where otherwise noted, each marine bench and subtidal reef habitat is a homogeneous one, containing a single community of *Conus,* as evidenced by agreement with the theoretical distribution given by MacArthur (1957). Although such agreement implies non-overlapping niches, this ideal is not completely realized in nature. As MacArthur (1957) showed, however, the distribution expected if niches overlapped randomly would fit the observed data much more poorly.

Ecological isolation results from fractionation of the habitat into microhabitats which differ especially with respect to zone occupied, relation to the substratum, and, especially, nature of the food. The first factor is of much greater importance on marine benches than on reef platforms. In this manner, interspecific competition severe enough to lead to the elimination of some of the species from the habitat is avoided. Such avoidance of competition is a likely result of the process of competition itself (Park 1954). But, as has been noted, direct evidence bearing on this is difficult to obtain from observation of natural populations (see also Mayr 1948).

Pertinent evidence obtained in the present study is that mentioned in connection with *Conus sponsalis,* which sometimes occurs where the ecologically similar *C. abbreviatus* is absent. Here the microhabitat is broadened to include, for example, more extensive use of eunicids for food. Also, *C. rattus* occurs in very low densities where *C. ebraeus* is abundant, but the former is the dominant species on the abrasion ramp type of marine bench, where the latter is absent. Restriction of the vermivorous species to apparently optimal regions of their possible habitats may also indicate the efficacy of interspecific competition, in accord with Svärdson (1949a).

In summary, density-inactive factors of the environment (Nicholson 1955) permit certain species of *Conus* to occur in the marine bench and subtidal reef habitats. Hydrographic characteristics and certain properties of the substratum are likely to be important factors of this type. The number of ecologically closely related species which may occupy a habitat is proportional to the amount of fractionation into microhabitats, which may overlap but are sufficiently distinct that severe interspecific competition is precluded. The process by which these microhabitats are established may be interspecific competition.

The population density is adjusted to certain governing requisites in the environment. Some of the species of *Conus* which occur on marine benches in Hawaii are believed to be limited by the extent of sand substrata suitable for burrowing (*C. pennaceus*) or required by prey organisms (*C. lividus, C. flavidus*). Six other species on marine benches may be termed dominants in this habitat. Of these, the population size of *C. catus* may be limited by the

amount of available food. Population densities of the more abundant species on reefs may also be limited by the amount of available food. Governing requisites of the other species are probably not amount of adult food, space, or predators. Factors which are effective at a pre-adult stage in the life history, which were not amenable to study, are likely to be important.

SUMMARY

The gastropod genus *Conus* has contributed to the enrichment of the number of species of epifaunal marine invertebrates in tropical regions in that it is typically represented by many sympatric species. Ecological observations on 25 species which occur in the Hawaiian Islands are reported. Most of the data concern natural populations of 18 species studied on intertidal marine benches and subtidal coral reefs which fringe much of the coastline of the Islands. Investigations on marine benches were carried out at nine stations on the islands of Oahu, Kauai, and Maui. Eight subtidal reefs on Oahu and Kauai were studied.

Conus populations on marine benches are composed chiefly of adult individuals. A stable population density of about 2.5 individuals/100 sq ft (30/100m^2) may be expected on solution benches and water-leveled benches. Mean density of a few quantitative samples on a reef was 0.16 individual/100 sq ft (2/100m^2). Although populations are much denser on marine benches, spawning is usually unsuccessful there, presumably because of the absence of protected sites for the attachment of egg capsules. Recruitment is from pelagic veliger larvae which originate elsewhere but are carried to benches in condition to settle and assume the benthic mode of life.

Four species (*Conus sponsalis, C. abbreviatus, C. ebraeus,* and *C. chaldaeus*) are usually dominant on solution benches and water-leveled benches. *C. rattus* is the most abundant species on abrasion ramp benches. *C. catus* is also a typical inhabitant of marine benches. *C. distans, C. flavidus, C. lividus, C. miles, C. pennaceus, C. nussatella, C. retifer,* and juvenile *C. vexillum* were also recorded from marine benches.

Conus flavidus and *C. lividus* are the dominant species on subtidal reefs, although at one station *C. sponsalis* was most abundant. *C. pennaceus, C. abbreviatus, C. ebraeus,* and *C. rattus* are also common. Other species recorded from reef stations were *C. imperialis, C. distans, C. chaldaeus, C. marmoreus, C. miles, C. pulicarius, C. striatus, C. textile, C. vexillum,* and *C. vitulinus.*

Values of an index of diversity, which measured similarity of species composition of different populations, differed but little in comparisons a) among the several bench stations, b) among the several reef stations, and c) between reef and bench stations. Quantitatively, however, certain species are characteristically most abundant on benches, while others are most abundant on reefs. Calculation of a measure of heterogeneity gave low values when the *Conus* communities of reefs were compared among each other (H′ = .09) and when the communities of benches were compared among each other (H′ = .19). Comparison of summed reef populations with summed bench populations showed much greater heterogeneity (H′ = .84).

At the most thoroughly studied bench and reef stations, number of species and number of individuals are related in a manner which agrees with the theoretical distribution expected in an adequately sampled, homogeneous community of a single habitat, where niches are non-overlapping and continuous.

Fractionation of the habitat into microhabitats was observed but, as expected intuitively, it is not complete. On marine benches, the species present are non-randomly distributed across the bench platform from shore to seaward edge. The distributions of *Conus sponsalis* and *C. abbreviatus* are similar. Those of all other species differ significantly from each other at the 5% level of probability. The number and biomass of *Conus* decreases from a maximum near the landward edge to the seaward edge.

On reef platforms, the distribution of *Conus* is characterized by patchiness, or clumping, which is correlated with the nature of the substratum. Distribution is not related to distance from shore or breaker line, except that density is low at both extremes. Over most of the reef platform, the observed distribution reflects the uniformity of water movements across the reef.

Differential association with different kinds of substratum on marine benches serves to partially distinguish the microhabitats of *Conus sponsalis* and *C. abbreviatus*, the latter occurring more often in sandier regions. This is correlated with the observation that *C. abbreviatus* burrows in the substratum significantly more often than *C. sponsalis*. Although these two species commonly coexist, only *C. sponsalis* was found on benches or parts of benches exposed to dry air for long periods at low tide.

On Hawaiian coral reefs, most species of *Conus* are most often found associated with sand, the most prevalent type of substratum. Only one species, *C. pulicarius*, is probably entirely restricted to a sand substratum. The two most abundant species on the reefs, *C. flavidus* and *C. lividus*, occur characteristically on patches of sand among solid substratum. *C. abbreviatus*, which occupies sandier regions of marine benches, is also a sand dweller on the reefs. *C. pennaceus* characteristically occurs on or partly buried in sand under basalt or coral rocks during the day but crawls about on the surface of the sand at night. Other species are not commonly found under rocks.

Mechanical analyses of sand suggested no niche diversification with respect to particle size distribution of this moiety of the substratum.

Alimentary tracts of 1,930 specimens of 24 species of *Conus* collected in Hawaii were examined. From these, 1,073 prey organisms were identified, 879 of them to species. Three groups of species within the

genus *Conus* may be distinguished on the basis of the nature of the food: most species feed exclusively on worms, mainly polychaetes. A second group feeds exclusively on other gastropods, and the third group feeds only on fishes. Eleven species, *C. sponsalis*, *C. abbreviatus*, *C. ebraeus*, *C. chaldaeus*, *C. rattus*, *C. distans*, *C. miles*, *C. imperialis*, *C. vexillum*, *C. vitulinus*, and *C. pertusus*, feed exclusively on polychaetes. Samples of the last three named species were rather small, however. Three species, *C. lividus*, *C. flavidus* and *C. quercinus*, feed both on polychaetes and on the enteropneust, *Ptychodera*. *C. leopardus* probably feeds on *Ptychodera*. *C. pulicarius* eats polychaetes and the echiuroid, *Thalassema*. *C. pennaceus*, *C. marmoreus*, and *C. textile* feed exclusively on other gastropods. *C. striatus*, *C. catus* and *C. obscurus* feed only on fishes.

On marine benches, the vermivorous species of *Conus* prey almost exclusively on members of the polychaete family Nereidae and superfamily Eunicea. At one station, the species *Perinereis helleri* was found to be the primary food of the three most abundant species of *Conus*. This polychaete was so abundant, however, that food cannot be said to be in short supply. Interspecific competition for food is therefore not indicated. Species of *Conus* common to both habitats feed proportionately more often on eunicids on reef platforms than they do on marine benches, for nereids are uncommon in the former habitat.

The typically reef-dwelling vermivorous species feed chiefly on polychaetes and enteropneusts associated with the sand moiety of the substratum. Of the two dominant species, *Conus flavidus* eats mainly Terebellidae, and *C. lividus* eats mainly *Ptychodera*.

On marine benches, the dominant species of *Conus* eat polychaetes which feed on algae, forming a three-step food chain. Calculation of a biomass pyramid for this food chain gave an herbivore/producer ratio of 4% and a carnivore/herbivore ratio of 6%.

Predation on *Conus* was difficult to measure. Certain fishes, other gastropods, octopi, crabs and starfishes are possible predators on adults. Predation on free-swimming larvae and newly-settled young is presumably of major ecological significance, but it was not amenable to investigation. Other factors which may also govern population density of the various species are also considered.

Ecological niches, ecological isolation, and interspecific competition in natural populations are discussed briefly. The comparative ecology of the more abundant species of *Conus* is summarized in the discussion, with emphasis on the extent of ecological isolation. Statistical analyses of certain dimensions of the niches of the ecologically most similar species are presented. Limitations of simple tests of significance of differences are noted. Degree of overlap is extremely important in niche diversification.

The adult ecological niche of each species of *Conus* studied differs significantly with respect to at least two of the following characteristics: nature of the food, nature of and relation to the substratum, and zonation or distribution pattern. The last is of particular importance only on marine benches. These differences are concluded to be the primary factors by which the ecological niches of species of *Conus* are differentiated. This is the mechanism which enables the maintenance of populations of large numbers of closely related, sympatric species of *Conus* in tropical regions.

LITERATURE CITED

Abbott, D. P. 1946. Some polychaetous annelids from a Hawaiian fish pond. Univ. Hawaii Res. Publ. No. 23: 5-24.

Alpers, F. 1931. Zur kenntnis der anatomie von *Conus lividus* Brug., besonders des darmkanals. Jena. Zeitschr. Naturwiss. 65: 587-658.

———. 1932a. Zur biologie des *Conus mediterraneus* Brug. Jena. Zeitschr. Naturwiss. 67: 346-363.

———. 1932b. Ueber die nahrungsaufnahme von *Conus mediterraneus* Brug. eines toxoglossen prosobranchier. Pubbl. Staz. Zool. Napoli 11: 426-445.

Andrewartha, H. G. & L. C. Birch. 1954. The Distribution and Abundance of Animals. Chicago: University of Chicago. 782 pp.

Banner, A. H. 1953. The Crangonidae, or snapping shrimp, of Hawaii. Pac. Sci. 7: 3-144.

Beauchamp, R. S. A. & P. Ullyott. 1932. Competitive relationships between certain species of fresh-water triclads. Jour. Ecol. 20: 200-208.

Bergh, R. 1896. Beiträge zur kenntnis der coniden. Nova Acta Ksl. Leop.-Carol. Akad. Naturf. 65: 67-214.

Betts, M. M. 1955. The food of titmice in oak woodland. Jour. Anim. Ecol. 24: 282-323.

Brown, F. A. Jr., M. Fingerman, M. I. Sandeen & H. M. Webb. 1953. Persistent diurnal and tidal rhythms of color change in the fiddler crab, *Uca pugnax*. Jour. Exp. Zool. 123: 29-60.

Bryan, W. A. 1915. Natural History of Hawaii. Honolulu: Hawaiian Gazette Co. 596 pp.

Clements, F. E. & V. E. Shelford. 1939. Bio-Ecology. New York: John Wiley & Sons. 425 pp.

Clench, W. J. & Y. Kondo. 1943. The poison cone shell. Amer. Jour. Trop. Med. & Hyg. 23: 105-121.

Cooper, D. M. & T. Dobzhansky. 1956. Studies on the ecology of *Drosophila* in the Yosemite region of California. I. The occurrence of species of *Drosophila* in different life zones and at different seasons. Ecology 37: 526-533.

Crombie, A. C. 1947. Interspecific competition. Jour. Anim. Ecol. 16: 44-73.

Da Cunha, A. B., T. Dobzhansky & A. Sokoloff. 1951. On food preferences of sympatric species of *Drosophila*. Evolution 5: 97-101.:

Da Cunha, A. B., A. M. El-Tabey Shehata & W. de Olivera. 1957. A study of the diet and nutritional preferences of tropical species of *Drosophila*. Ecology 38: 98-106.

Daiber, F. C. 1956. A comparative analysis of the winter feeding habits of two benthic stream fishes. Copeia 1956: 141-151.

D'Ancona, U. 1954. The struggle for existence. Leiden: W. J. Brill. 274 pp.

Darwin, C. 1859. On the origin of species by means of natural selection. London: J. Murray. 502 pp.

Dawes, B. 1930. Growth and maintenance in the plaice (*Pleuronectes platessa* L.). Part I. Jour. Mar. Biol. Assn. U. K. 17: 103-147.

———. 1931. Growth and maintenance in the plaice (*P. platessa* L.) Part II. Jour. Mar. Biol. Assn. U. K. 17: 877-947.

Dodge, H. 1953. A historical review of the mollusks of Linnaeus. Part 2. The class Cephalopoda and the genera *Conus* and *Cypraea* of the class Gastropoda. Bull. Amer. Mus. Nat. Hist. 103: 1-134.

Dumas, P. C. 1956. The ecological relations of sympatry in *Plethodon dunni* and *Plethodon vehiculum*. Ecology 37: 484-495.

Edmondson, C. H. 1928. The ecology of an Hawaiian coral reef. B. P. Bishop Mus. Bull. 45. 64 pp.

———. 1946. Reef and shore fauna of Hawaii. B. P. Bishop Mus. Spec. Pub. 22, 381 pp.

Eslick, A. 1940. An ecological study of *Patella* at Port St. Mary, Isle of Man. Proc. Linn. Soc. Lond. 152: 45-59.

Fauvel, P. 1927. Polychètes Sédentaires. Faune de France, 16. 494 pp.

Fischer-Piette, E. 1935. Les patelles d'Europe et d'Afrique du nord. Jour. Conchyl. 79: 5-66.

Gause, G. F. 1934. The Struggle for Existence. Baltimore: Williams and Wilkins. 163 pp.

Gilbert, O., J. B. Reynoldson & J. Hobart. 1952. Gause's hypothesis: an examination. Jour. Anim. Ecol. 21: 310-312.

Halstead, B. W. 1956. Animal phyla known to contain poisonous marine animals. Venoms (Amer. Assn. Adv. Sci.): 9-27.

Hartman, O. 1940. Polychaetous annelids. II. Chrysopetalidae to Goniadidae. Allan Hancock Pacific Expeditions 7: 173-287.

———. 1944. Polychaetous annelids. V. Eunicea. Allan Hancock Pacific Expeditions 10: 1-236.

———. 1948. The marine annelids erected by Kinberg, with notes on some other types in the Swedish State Museum. Ark. Zool. 42A: 1-137.

———. 1954. Marine annelids from the northern Marshall Islands. Geol. Surv. Prof. Pap. 260-Q: 619-644.

Helfrich, P. & A. J. Kohn. 1955. A survey to estimate the major biological effects of a dredging operation by the Lihue Plantation Co., Ltd. on North Kapaa Reef, Kapaa, Kauai. Preliminary Report. 31 pp. (Mimeographed. Available from the authors).

Hinegardner, R. T. 1957. The anatomy and histology of the venom apparatus in several gastropods of the genus *Conus*. M.S. Thesis, University of Southern California.

———. 1958. The venom apparatus of the cone shell. Hawaii Med. Jour. 17: 533-536.

Holly, M. 1935. Polychaeta from Hawaii. B. P. Bishop Mus. Bull. 129: 33 pp.

Holme, N. A. 1953. The biomass of the bottom fauna in the English Channel off Plymouth. Jour. Mar. Biol. Assn. U.K. 32: 1-49.

———. 1954. The ecology of British species of *Ensis*. Jour. Mar. Biol. Assn. U.K. 33: 145-172.

Hutchinson, G. E. 1951. Copepodology for the ornithologist. Ecology 32: 571-577.

———. 1953. The concept of pattern in ecology. Proc. Acad. Nat. Sci. Phil. 105: 1-12.

Johnson, D. E. 1943. Systematic review of the chipmunks (genus *Eutamias*) of California. Univ. Calif. Pub. Zool. 48: 63-148.

Koch, L. F. 1957. Index of biotal dispersity. Ecology 38: 145-148.

Kohn, A. J. 1955. Studies on food and feeding of the cone shells, genus *Conus*. Ann. Rept. Amer. Malacol. Union, Bull. 22: 31.

———. 1956a. The ecology collecting sack modified for marine organisms. Turtox News 34: 33.

———. 1956b. Piscivorous gastropods of the genus *Conus*. Proc. Nat. Acad. Sci. 42: 168-171.

———. 1959. The Hawaiian species of *Conus*. Pac. Sci. (In Press).

Kohn, A. J. & P. Helfrich. 1957. Primary organic productivity of a Hawaiian coral reef. Limnol. & Oceanogr. 2: 241-251.

Lack, D. 1945. The ecology of closely related species with special reference to the cormorant (*Phalacrocorax carbo*) and shag (*P. aristotelis*). Jour. Anim. Ecol. 14: 12-16.

———. 1947. Darwin's Finches. Cambridge: University Press. 208 pp.

MacArthur, R. 1955. Fluctuations of animal populations, and a measure of community stability. Ecology 36: 533-536.

———. 1957. On the relative abundance of bird species. Proc. Nat. Acad. Sci. 43: 293-295.

Margalef, R. 1956. Información y diversidad específica en las communidades de organismos. Inv. Pesq. Barcelona 3: 99-106.

Mackenzie, J. M. D. 1950. Competition for nest-s es among hole-breeding species. Brit. Birds 43: 184-185.

Mayr, E. 1948. The bearing of the new systematics on general problems: The nature of species. Adv. Gen. 2: 205-237.

McCabe, T. T. & B. D. Blanchard. 1951. Three species of *Peromyscus*. Santa Barbara: Rood Associates. 136 pp.

McCaughey, V. 1918. A survey of the Hawaiian coral reefs. Amer. Nat. 52: 409-438.

Nicholson, A. J. 1955. An outline of the dynamics of animal populations. Austral. Jour. Zool. 2: 9-65.

Odum, E. P. 1953. Fundamentals of Ecology. Philadelphia: W. B. Saunders Co. 384 pp.

Odum, H. T. & E. P. Odum. 1955. Trophic structure and productivity of a windward coral reef community on Eniwetok Atoll. Ecol. Monogr. 25: 291-320.

Ohba, S. 1952. Analysis of activity rhythm in the marine gastropod, *Nassarius festivus*, inhabiting the tide pool. I. On the effect of tide and food in the daytime rhythm of activity. Annot. Zool. Japon. 25: 289-297.

Okuda, S. 1937. Polychaetous annelids from the Palau Islands and adjacent waters, the South Sea Islands. Bull. Biogeogr. Soc: Japan 7: 257-316.

Ostergaard, J. M. 1950. Spawning and development of some Hawaiian marine gastropods. Pac. Sci. 4: 75-115.

———. 1955. Some opisthobranchiate Mollusca from Hawaii. Pac. Sci. 9: 110-136.

Park, T. 1954. Experimental studies of interspecies competition. II. Temperature, humidity, and competition in two species of *Tribolium*. Physiol. Zool. 27: 177-238.

Pease, W. H. 1860. Descriptions of new species of Mollusca from the Sandwich Islands. Proc. Zool. Soc. Lond. Pt. 27. 1860: 18-36.

Peile, A. J. 1939. Radula Notes VIII. 34. *Conus*. Proc. Malacol. Soc. Lond. 23: 348-355.

Pilsbry, H. A. 1917. Marine Mollusks of Hawaii, I-III. Proc. Acad. Nat. Sci. Phil. 69: 207-230.

———. 1920. Marine mollusks of Hawaii, XIV-XV. Proc. Acad. Nat. Sci. Phil. 72: 360-382

Pitelka, F. A. 1951. Ecologic overlap and interspecific strife in breeding populations of Anna and Allen humming birds. Ecology 32: 641-661.

Prosser, C. L. 1955. Physiological variation in animals. Biol. Rev. 30: 229-262.

Sandeen, M. I., G. C. Stephens & F. A. Brown, Jr. 1954. Persistent daily and tidal rhythms of oxygen consumption in two species of marine snails. Physiol. Zool. 27: 350-356.

Smith, F. E. 1950. The benthos of Block Island Sound. Ph.D. Thesis, Yale University.

Strasburg, D. W. 1953. Comparative ecology of two salariin blennies. Ph.D. Thesis, University of Hawaii.

Svärdson, G. 1949a. Competition and habitat selection in birds. Oikos 1: 157-174.

———. 1949b. Competition between trout and char (*Salmo trutta* and *S. alpinus*). Report, Inst. Freshw. Res., Drottninghom 29: 108-111.

Takahashi, K. 1939. Polychaeta on coral reefs in Palau. Kagaku Nanyo (Science of the South Sea) 2: 18-29. (in Japanese)

Test, A. R. 1945. Ecology of California Acmaea. Ecology 26: 395-405.

Thorson, G. 1946. Reproduction and larval development of Danish marine bottom invertebrates. Medd. Komm. Havundersøg., Kbh., Plankton 4: 523 pp.

———. 1956. Marine level-bottom communities of recent seas, their temperature adaptation and their "balance" between predators and food animals. Trans. N.Y. Acad. Sci. 18: 693-700.

———. 1958. Parallel level bottom communities, their temperature adaptation and their "balance" between predators and food animals. *In* Perspectives in Marine Biology. Berkeley: University of California Press. 67-86.

Treadwell, A. L. 1906. Polychaetous annelids of the Hawaiian Islands collected by the steamer "Albatross" in 1902. U. S. Fish. Comm. Bull. 1903: 1145-1181.

———. 1922. Leodicidae from Fiji and Samoa. Carnegie Inst. Wash. Pub. No. 312: 127-170.

Turner, H. J. 1951. Fourth report on investigations of the shellfisheries of Massachusetts. State of Massachusetts. 21 pp.

Van Dongen, A. 1956. The preference of *Littorina obtusata* for Fucaceae. Arch. Néerl. Zool. 11: 373-386.

Volterra, V. 1926. Variazioni e fluttuazioni del numero d'individui in specie animali conviventi. Mem. Accad. Lincei. Ser. 6. 2: 31-113.

Wentworth, C. K. 1938. Marine bench-forming processes: Water-level benching. Jour. Geomorphol. 1: 6-32.

———. 1939. Marine bench-forming processes. II, solution benching. Jour. Geomorphol. 2: 3-25.

Wilson, D. P. 1952. The influence of the nature of the substratum on the metamorphosis of the larvae of marine animals, especially the larvae of *Ophelia bicornis* Savigny. Ann. Inst. Oceanogr. Monaco 27: 49-156.

———. 1955. The role of micro-organisms in the settlement of *Ophelia bicornis* Savigny. Jour. Mar. Biol. Assn. U.K. 34: 531-544.

Section 4

_____

The Hawaiian Biota

INTRODUCTION

In all the world, the richest, maturest, and at
the same time one of the most extreme cases of
a flora and fauna built entirely out of trans-
oceanic waifs is, if the majority opinion is
correct, the Hawaiian Island group, located
2,000 miles from North America, more than 3,000
miles from the shores of Japan, and over 1,000
miles from any other biologically significant
islands.

Addison Gulick, 1932

The progenitors of all living things in the Hawaiian
Islands came from across the sea. The native terrestrial biota, now estimated at between 10,000 and 15,000
species, probably descended from fewer than 1,000 introductions. Many groups of plants and animals, dominant or abundant on other Pacific islands and on
continents bordering the Pacific, are absent from the
Hawaiian chain; others represent strays or relicts;
and still others which are rare elsewhere are dominant
in Hawaii. Representation of terrestrial organisms
apparently reflects both superior vagility and chance;
those forms most easily transported long distances
by wind, water, or long-ranging seabirds are the most
likely to be represented. The noticeable lack of native
nonflying mammals, land amphibians, reptiles, and fresh-
water fish; the presence of plants which must originally
have had wind-adapted seeds; and the recent captures
of certain insects in air traps over the ocean demonstrate the tenability of the hypothesis.

In this section, Hubbell succinctly summarizes the
characteristics of insular biotas in general, with
special reference to that of Hawaii. Analyses of the
flora by Fosberg, fungi by Baker and Goos, and birds
by Berger detail the characteristics of some elements
of the terrestrial biota. The characteristics of the
marine fauna are discussed in the papers by Kay and
Gosline.

THE BIOLOGY OF ISLANDS

By Theodore H. Hubbell*

MUSEUM OF ZOOLOGY, UNIVERSITY OF MICHIGAN, ANN ARBOR

In so brief a presentation as this must be, only some of the more salient aspects of island biology can be discussed. Ever since the time of Darwin and Wallace, islands have been recognized as natural laboratories for the study of evolution, and by now the literature on the subject is very extensive. The first comprehensive treatment was Alfred Russel Wallace's *Island Life* (1880),[1] one of the classics of biology, still a mine of information, and a landmark from which to measure subsequent progress. In 1965, in a book of the same title, Sherwin Carlquist[2] has summarized our present knowledge of the subject. In what follows I have drawn freely upon his highly readable and well-illustrated account.

What should be stressed, however, is not how much, but how very little we actually know about the biology of islands. Looking back, it is interesting that Wallace, in 1880, thought that enough information was already at hand to make further expeditions and collecting redundant. What was needed, he said, was intensive study of selected islands, and since Britain owned most of the world's islands, the government should post naturalists on some of them to make such studies. Wallace's suggestion was good, though naturally nothing came of it, but his major premise was wrong. We still need to know a great deal more than we do about the species that make up island biotas, not merely for the sake of naming and cataloguing them, but because knowledge of the identities, relationships, distribution, behavior, and ecological roles and requirements of the species is essential for understanding both the evolution of the island biotas and the evolution and functioning of the island ecosystems. No complete inventory of a large island's plants and animals has ever been made, and for various reasons none is ever likely to be made. But even in an archipelago supposedly so well known as Hawaii, every intensive modern study of a group of native animals or plants not only turns up previously unknown species, sometimes in large numbers, but also often reveals unsuspected and sometimes surprising evolutionary and ecological phenomena. Some instances of this will be mentioned later.

Destruction of the native island biotas by man and his introductions is proceeding rapidly in all parts of the temperate and tropical zones, and on many islands is already almost complete. Establishment of nature reserves may save some of the species, but nothing can prevent drastic alteration of the native ecosystems and elimination of a great many of their distinctive plants and animals. In future, most of the endemic species of most islands will be known, if at all, only by specimens in museums. It is therefore both important and urgent that selected island biotas be thoroughly studied while there is still time, and such investigations are highly appropriate for the International Biological Program.

* Director (retired), Museum of Zoology, The University of Michigan, and Chairman, Subcommittee on Systematics and Biogeography, USNC/IBP.

Reprinted from *Proceedings of the National Academy of Sciences* 60:22-32 (1968), by permission of the author and the National Academy of Sciences.

Of all island groups, Hawaii is one of the most interesting biologically. It is also one of those most urgently in need of study, because of the rapidity with which its remarkable native fauna and flora and unique ecosystems are disappearing. The U.S. National Committee for the IBP has approved, as one of its major programs, an intensive study of the biology of this archipelago, and to show why this project has been given such high priority, I shall focus my remarks on *oceanic* islands in general and Hawaii in particular.

The one thing that all islands have in common is their isolation from other land by a water barrier, narrow or wide. That isolation is the key to an understanding of island biology. Upon it depends the train of events that not only ensures that each island biota will differ in some degree from all others, but also gives island biotas as a group the characteristics that distinguish them from those of continental areas.

Aside from being isolated, islands are so various that they cannot be neatly classified. They range in size from almost-continents to mere dots of land, in elevation above the sea from a few feet to more than two miles, in topography from level to extremely rugged, and in climate from very dry to very wet and from arctic to tropical. Islands differ in geologic origin and structure, in age, and in distance from other islands and the mainland. Some are barren; others teem with life. To the biologist, however, the most meaningful question is whether or not an island has ever been connected with a continent. Wallace was the first to show that the nature of island biotas depends on whether such connections have existed, and to distinguish between continental and oceanic islands on biogeographic grounds.

A *continental island*, when it was a part of the mainland, shared the mainland fauna and flora. When it was cut off it was already populated with the same groups of animals and plants, in much the same proportions, as those present on the adjacent continent. Such a biota is said to be *harmonic*, and would in itself, even without corroborative geologic evidence, suffice to prove a former land connection. Thus the presence of primary division fresh-water fishes and the larger mammals, which cannot cross even a narrow arm of the sea, has no other explanation, although their absence does not prove that a connection did not exist. As the age of a continental island increases, some groups originally present may become extinct, and those that persist will follow different evolutionary paths than those taken by their mainland relatives, but traces of the mainland origin of the biota are never completely eliminated. Continental islands are numerous and some of them very large. Many were most recently joined to the mainland during the Pleistocene lowerings of sea level and have biotas very similar to those of the adjacent continental areas. Examples are Ceylon, Sumatra, Java, Borneo, Japan, and Taiwan, with Asian connections; New Guinea and Tasmania, with Australian connections; and Corsica, Sardinia, and the British Isles, with European connections. Other continental islands are much older; thus Australia, the world's largest island or smallest continent, seems to have been briefly joined to Asia in the Cretaceous, and Madagascar, if it was once attached to Africa, has probably been an island at least since Triassic times.

An *oceanic island* is one that has always been an island. Its entire biota has been derived by colonization across a salt-water barrier. Except for strong fliers—birds, bats, and a few insects—all its native plants and animals are the descendants of immigrants that reached the island by floating in sea currents, drifting on natural rafts, being carried by the wind, or being brought by flying creatures, chiefly birds. Organisms differ greatly in their capacity for such dispersal, and only a few of the many kinds of plants and animals present on mainland areas will succeed in reaching an island and establishing themselves there. In the biota of an oceanic island, therefore, some mainland groups are entirely absent and others are disproportionately well represented; such a biota is said to be *disharmonic*. Oceanic islands can have only disharmonic biotas; but old continental islands possess both the remnants of an originally harmonic biota and a newer disharmonic element derived from colonizers that reached it after it became an island.

Darwin and Wallace believed that accidental long-distance dispersal occurred often enough to account for all oceanic island biotas. Their evidence was, however, entirely circumstantial, and for a long time many zoogeographers remained unconvinced that such creatures as land snails and lizards could have crossed wide expanses of ocean. They drew hypothetical former land bridges on their maps, over which their animals could walk or crawl; and since each group needed different ones to explain its distribution, the postulated bridges eventually became so numerous that there would scarcely have been room for water if they had all existed. Except for Panama, the Bering bridge, and a few others, land bridges are today discredited, and the efficacy of long-distance dispersal is well established. Winds probably account for much more transport than was formerly believed. Visher showed that tropical storms could carry small animals and plant propagules over considerable distances. Gressitt and his collaborators, by straining many cubic kilometers of air on long flights over the Pacific, have demonstrated that the air is always full of spores, seeds, and small insects and other arthropods, many of them flightless.

Long-distance dispersal is a very risky affair. The chance of any individual traveler's reaching an island is almost infinitesimally small. But there are millions of involuntary starters, and in this great sweepstakes—to use George Gaylord Simpson's felicitous phrase—even though most must lose, there are bound to be a few winners. Statistically, it is inevitable that, given time enough, every island will be populated. In general, the more distant the island, the fewer organisms, both in number and in kind, will succeed in reaching it and becoming established. Other things are of course involved. Species that are abundant have a better chance than rare ones, more immigrants will reach a large island than a small one, some islands are more hospitable than others, and so on.

The capacity of various kinds of animals and plants for long-distance dispersal can be judged by the maximum sea gaps they are known to have crossed: primary division fresh-water fishes and large mammals, 25 miles; fresh-water turtles and small mammals, except rodents, 200 miles; rodents and some amphibians, land tortoises, and snakes, 500 miles; some lizards, 1,000 miles; and land birds, bats, land mollusks, insects, and spiders, 2,000 miles. Among plants, the conifers, oaks, prunes, and large-seeded forest trees are poor travelers; plants with fleshy, hard-seeded fruits that are eaten by birds, fair to good; ferns, mosses, lycopods, and horsetails, with wind-borne spores, and aquatic plants with seeds that are carried on birds' muddy feet, very good. Best of all plant travelers are those with very minute wind-carried spores or seeds, those with sticky or barbed seeds that cling to birds' plumage, and those with floating seeds or other propagules that are unharmed by prolonged immersion in sea water.

The evolutionary and ecological results of this selection of good travelers for colonizing islands are numerous and fascinating. To draw an imperfect analogy, suppose that in setting up a new human colony on an island, only champion swimmers, winners of yacht races, and successful balloonists were chosen to go, regardless of what else they could do. It would be an oddly assorted group, and its members would have to adapt rapidly and learn new skills to survive. There might be niches that no member of the group could fill. So it is with the plant and animal species that reach islands; they find themselves in a strange environment, in which their capacity for dispersal has little to do with their ability to meet the exigencies that confront them, and might, in fact, even prove a handicap.

As Briggs[3] and many others have pointed out, oceanic islands afford the evolutionary biologist opportunities to examine the results of experiments in natural selection, competition, and distribution that have been carried on by nature for thousands or millions of years. As each founder species becomes established on an island it gives rise to a population which can be expected to embark immediately on its own lines of evolutionary change. Since relatively small populations are usually involved, and because many aspects of the ecology are apt to be different, it may be expected that such change will occur rapidly in comparison to evolution in a mainland situation. As a result, relatively old oceanic islands should possess biotas that show a high degree of evolutionary divergence from others, as indicated both by the percentage of endemism among their species, genera, and families, and the degree of unlikeness of those species to related forms elsewhere.

Carlquist[4] has listed 24 so-called principles of island evolution, derivable from the study of long-distance dispersal and subsequent adaptive evolution among colonists. Omitting those already mentioned, the more important include the following: (1) Successful establishment of a species is probably usually accomplished not by a single but by repeated or simultaneous introductions. A single gravid female animal or monoecious plant brings less genetic material than do several individuals, diminishing the potentialities for rapid adjustment. (2) The new situations encountered dictate the course of immigrants' evolution. Adaptive radiation is certain to occur on an island or archipelago when a small number of immigrant groups is faced by a broad spread of ecological opportunities. If the environment is restrictive or largely preempted, an immigrant stock may evolve to occupy one or a few niches. (3) New growth forms evolve among plants on oceanic islands. Most conspicuously there is a tendency toward increased stature and woodiness. (4) On oceanic islands plants tend to lose dispersal mechanisms and capacity, and volant animals to become flightless. (5) Endemics of oceanic islands often show slight to marked decrease in competitive ability. (6) In waif floras, means for outcrossing become highly developed. Species without potential for outcrossing are probably doomed to short tenure. (7) Natural hybridization achieves positive evolutionary value in waif biotas. (8) Pollination relationships and mechanisms correspond to and change with the availability of insects and other pollinating agents on the islands. (9) Some mutations that would be disadvantageous or lethal in continental environments have a more nearly neutral value in the less competitive island environment.

Everything thus far presented tends to show that although a great deal has been learned about island biology since Wallace's time, we are still in the stage of observation, deduction, and plausible hypothesis. Generalizations such as those just cited describe what can be seen to have happened on islands, but the details of how and why, in terms of genetics, population dynamics, and ecology remain largely unknown. Island ecosystems are simpler than those of continental areas; they are self-contained and unaffected by the shifting tides of population pressure and competition characteristic of the mainland; and they exist in a more uniform physical environment, moderated by the sea. Islands being numerous, isolated, and extremely various, they afford unique opportunities for comparative studies of ecological processes and for ecosystem analysis—even for the experimental testing of evolutionary and ecological hypotheses. Such work has yet to be done.

A new approach to the study of island biology that should prove fruitful was suggested by McArthur and Wilson (1963) in a paper entitled "An equilibrium theory of insular zoogeography," which was later expanded into a book.[5] They assume that an island of given size can support only a limited number of species, and that when this "saturation" point has been reached, further colonization must be balanced by extinction. They also assume that in relation to food resources, selection must act differently at different species densities. They develop the theory that on an uncrowded island with ample food resources, selection will favor gene combinations that maximize food utilization, regardless of wastage; but on a saturated island, where demand exceeds supply, those modifications will be favored that maximize efficiency in the use of what food is available. Models of this kind can lead to predictions that can be tested by observation and experiment.

Let us now turn to Hawaii, our primary focus of interest, to see how its animals and plants exemplify some of the phenomena described, and to explain why their study is so urgent.

Hawaii is one of the most isolated of island groups.[6] It lies in mid-Pacific, astride the Tropic of Cancer, 2,000 miles from California, 3,400 miles from Japan, 450 miles from the nearest small island, and 850 miles from the last atoll in the chain that extends south to the Society and Tuamoto archipelagos. Stretching 1,500 nautical miles, it begins on the northwest with a coral atoll, continues southeast as a string of islets, reefs, and rocks that make up the Leeward Islands, and ends in the main group of Windward Islands that we usually think of as constituting Hawaii. The whole chain is the product of vulcanism that began in the west sometime in the mid-Tertiary and progressed southeastward. The Leeward Islands were once comparable in size to those of the main group, as can be seen from submarine contours, but erosion has reduced them to mere remnants. The seven main islands are relatively young; Kauai and Oahu may first have appeared some 10 million years ago.[7] Hawaii, the easternmost and largest island, is probably no more than one million years old, and is still growing; in the past 100 years the surface of Mauna Loa's vast dome has been raised an average of six feet by lava flows.

Hawaii lies in the path of the trade winds, is surrounded by a warm sea, and has a correspondingly equable climate which, however, varies with elevation from subtropical to alpine. Rainfall is very heavy everywhere in the mountains except at the highest elevations; the summit of Puu Kukui on Maui has more than 300 inches a year, and Mt. Waialeale on Kauai, one of the wettest spots on earth, has an annual average of 540 inches and a recorded maximum (1948) of 624.01 inches, or 52 feet. By contrast, some lowland areas in the lee of the mountains have less than 10 inches of rainfall per year.

The sourthern*part of Maui and most of Hawaii are undissected lava domes, but on northern Maui and the other islands the mountains rise abruptly from marginal lowlands, and have been carved by erosion into fantastically rugged topography, with many deep, narrow valleys separated by knife-edged ridges, and slopes that often approach the vertical. The 13,784-foot summit of Mauna Kea on Hawaii is the highest point in the islands; Haleakala on Maui attains an elevation of 10,025 feet; on Kauai, Oahu, and Molokai the mountain crests are 4,000 to 5,000 feet high. Hawaii's physical diversity is reflected in its variety of biotic communities, adapted to habitats which range from barren, sunbaked lava fields to wet mountain bogs, from rocky cliffs to fertile lowlands, from semidesert to rain forest, and from boreal to subtropical.

In 1948, Zimmerman[8] tabulated the number of native species and subspecies of animals and plants then known from Hawaii (6,753), and the number of immigrant ancestral species (677–700) from which they were thought to have descended (Table 1). Many others have since been discovered, and if all were

TABLE 1. *Estimated numbers of existing endemic and of ancestral Hawaiian species.*

Group	Known species and subspecies (1948)	Probable number of immigrant ancestral species	Average intervals between introductions (thousands of years)
Insects	3,722	233 to 254	21±
Land snails	1,064	22 to 24	217±
Land birds	70	15	333
Ferns and allies	168	135	37
Flowering plants	1,729	272	17
Totals	6,753	677 to 700	

In this table the age of the main islands is arbitrarily assumed to be five million years. The figures are estimates by Zimmerman and collaborators, and do not include several hundred species described since 1948.

* Corrected spelling is "southern."

known, the total might approach 10,000, without, however, greatly increasing the number of ancestral stocks represented. On the basis of an assumed age for the islands of five million years (probably much too low), the average interval between successful colonizations in each of the major groups is shown in the table. The islands were obviously hard to reach by even the best travelers, the flowering plants and insects. Colonizations were probably much more frequent earlier in the islands' history than later; newcomers would have faced less competition, and there may then have been better opportunities for immigration, in the form of island stepping stones that have since disappeared.

One characteristic of long-distance dispersal is its randomness. The postulated 700 ancestors of the native Hawaiian plants and animals came from all quarters of the compass. Indo-Pacific types were most numerous, perhaps because they had a better chance to island-hop. Of the rest, a fair number came from America, others from far north or south, and some belonged to pan-tropical groups. The first-comers must have been plants preadapted to life on bare lava or beaches of volcanic sand. Among them may have been the ancestors of the chief forest tree of the islands, the red-flowered ohia lehua (*Metrosideros*), from the south, and of a shrubby tarweed (*Dubautia*), from America. In Hawaii both are early invaders of fresh lava fields, and both have relatives back home that live in dry, rocky places. The pioneers would create shade and shelter that would permit other less hardy plants to come in, and in time animals would arrive to feed on the plants and each other.

A new island may not be an Eden, but at least it is empty. On the mainlands every plant and animal species has a multitude of competitors and enemies that restrict the expression of its evolutionary possibilities and keep it pruned to fit its biological niche. The early immigrants to an island have left all that behind. They are free, in a sense, to experiment with genetic variations that would have had little chance to survive in the old environment. The evolutionary result is described as adaptive radiation—the separation of the descendants of one ancestral stock into numerous species, adapted to life in a variety of new situations by changes in form, function, and ecological tolerances and requirements.

Adaptive radiation is not something that happens only on islands; it is inherent in the evolutionary process. Islands are, however, especially favorable for observing its operation and results. Best of all are isolated archipelagoes such as Hawaii, because archipelagoes are notorious species-breeders, and species are the entities that adapt to new conditions. The islands of an archipelago, though themselves isolated, are sufficiently close to ensure occasional interchange of species. When a species of one island colonizes another, the two populations are genetically separated, must evolve independently, and will inevitably become increasingly different. Eventually a stage will almost certainly be reached at which if either one invades the other's island, some degree of reproductive isolation will manifest itself. If not already complete, selection is likely to make it so and also to reinforce any tendencies toward different niche specializations that will reduce competition between the two populations. The result is that there are now two species on an island where there was one before. Repetition of this process of invasion, change, and reinvasion increases the number of species in the archipelago as a whole and on each of its islands. When, as in Hawaii, each island is itself divided into many isolated areas of similar environment, the opportunities for speciation and concomitant adaptive radiation are multiplied.

Every oceanic island and island group is unique in some or many ways, and evolution has followed a different course on each, often with remarkable results. It is as though nature, prescient of our need to understand evolution, had set up a series of experiments that have been conducted for thousands or millions of years under a wide variety of conditions, the results of which are now offered for our study. Unfortunately, many of these island laboratories have been or are being wrecked, and the experimental results wiped out before they have been recorded and analyzed by science. Although destruction is already far advanced in Hawaii, we know a good deal about what evolution accomplished there and can learn much more if we hurry. Let us look at a few examples of adaptive radiation in these islands.

The Hawaiian tarweeds, studied by Keck and by Carlquist,[9] are plants of the sunflower family, Compositae, which belong to a group otherwise confined to western North America. The American species have seeds enclosed in a sticky envelope that can adhere to birds' feathers and thus be transported. Most of the American species are annuals, but a few are low woody shrubs that live in dry, open sites on islands off the Californian and Mexican coasts. Long ago some member of this woody group reached Hawaii, where a whole gamut of opportunities lay before it, and where competitors were few. From that original immigrant ancestor there developed an assemblage of species adapted to life in many very unlike situations, and so changed that only a botanist would recognize their kinship to the lowly tarweeds.

One group, members of the already mentioned genus *Dubautia*, spread to all the main islands and split into many species. Most of them kept to the dry places, and of these a few moved up the lava slopes and became small alpine shrubs on the high volcanic summits, with stiff stems and tiny leaves that withstand the fierce drying winds and other rigors of life at high altitudes. Some *Dubautias* moved into the rain forest, where they changed into small trees with large, leathery leaves and trunks up to a foot in diameter. A second group of tarweeds evolved into the elegant silverswords, *Argyroxiphium*—extraordinary yucca-like plants with silvery pointed leaves and a tall spike of flowers. One species grows in the crater of Haleakala on Maui, at 9,000 feet, under extremes of drought, heat, and cold. Its nearest relative, a plant of the same genus, also lives on Maui but under diametrically opposite conditions, in the perpetual clouds and rain on the 5,800-foot summit of Puu Kukui, where the annual precipitation is 300 inches and the ground is a quaking bog. Lastly there is the strange *Wilkesia*, confined to dry valleys on Kauai, a remarkable plant with a cluster of long, spike-like leaves at the top of a tall, spindly trunk, about as unlike a tarweed as it is possible to be.

Similar things happened in many other groups of plants and animals that reached Hawaii. Thus among the land snails of the families Achatinellidae and Tornitellidae more than 1,000 species, subspecies, and local races evolved from about two dozen ancestral species. Almost every valley on the main islands had its own distinctive forms, many of which are now extinct.   Another classic and often cited case of adaptive radiation is that of the honey creepers, birds of the endemic family Drepanididae, described by Amadon and by Baldwin.[10]   From a single tanager-like ancestor there developed nine genera adapted to different modes of life, largely by modifications in the bills and tongues and the associated feeding habits.   In one group the birds have short, parrot-like beaks and stubby tongues, suited for handling tough seeds and digging into wood for insects.   At the other extreme are forms with long, slender, curved beaks used to probe in flowers for nectar and small insects, and with narrow tongues that can be rolled at the sides to form a tube for sucking nectar.   Such beaks and tongues nicely fit the long, curved, tubular flowers of some of the Hawaiian lobeliads visited by the birds, and both the birds and the flowers doubtless evolved together.   A number of the honey creepers are now very rare or extinct.

The Hawaiian drosophilid flies provide an even more striking illustration of insular speciation and adaptive radiation.   Most of what we know about them comes from work done since 1963 by a research team that has studied intensively their morphology, taxonomy, genetics, cytogenetics, ecology, life history, and behavior.[11]   When these studies began, some 300 species were already known— about as many as occur in all of tropical America.   Hardy's 1965 monograph[12] lists over 400, and at least 200 more have since been recognized; conceivably the total number of species in the islands may approach 1,000, in an area less than one tenth the size of Michigan.   All are descended from one or at most two ancestral species.

These Hawaiian drosophilids are extraordinarily different from the mainland species familiar to geneticists.   Some are as large as small horseflies, and many are strikingly colored.   Very few can be reared on the ordinary media;   most of them breed in one or a few species of native plants, or in leaves on the forest floor. Some of the larvae are leaf miners, and others feed on spider eggs.   Many of the Hawaiian flies are very unlike in mainland species behavior.*   Most are secretive, resting in the dense forest undergrowth and darting swiftly downward when disturbed.   This makes them hard to collect, and small vacuum cleaners proved very useful for catching them.   In most drosophilids mating is simple and direct, but many of the Hawaiian species have a prolonged and elaborate courtship, and in some groups the males have complicated mouthparts used for holding the female.   The species are strongly localized;   few occur on more than one island, and most have restricted ranges that may even be single "kipukas," or patches of native forest isolated by lava flows.   Perhaps the greatest surprise was the discovery that the striking morphological diversity among these flies is not matched by chromosomal differences.   In marked contrast to the mainland situation, the species are more easily recognized by their morphology than by their chromosomes.   The karyotypes are relatively invariable throughout large assemblages.   In one group of 22 closely related but easily distinguishable species no changes were detected in the metaphase chromosomes and very few inversions in the giant salivary gland chromosomes, and in four species pairs the species of each pair have apparently identical chromosomes.[13]

Insular evolution sometimes produces extraordinary forms of life, and Hawaii

* Should read: " . . . unlike mainland species in behavior."

has its share of such oddities. To mention only a few, there is the lobeliad *Brighamia*, a cliff plant that rocks back and forth in the wind on a rounded pedestal. There are forest trees that are nothing but overgrown herbs, relatives of beets, amaranths, and four-o'clocks, with trunks that grow, not like those of ordinary trees, but by developing successive rings of secondary cambium in the same way as does a beet. One of the strange Hawaiian insects is the lace-winged neuropteroid *Pseudopsectra cookei*, which has wings but cannot fly, and has developed long, erect, possibly protective spines all over the exposed faces of its closed wings.

Commerce, agriculture, and other human activities are rapidly changing the face of Hawaii and destroying its unique biota at an ever-increasing rate. Already the native lowland plants and animals are gone, replaced by crops, foreign weeds, and introduced insects and other animals. Even the mountains are not safe; their forests are being cleared for grazing land or planted timber, are rooted up by wild hogs and browsed by wild cattle and introduced deer, and are everywhere being invaded by foreign plants and insects that replace the native species. Thus the island ecosystems are being drastically changed, and a great part of the original biota is doomed to disappear. It is therefore both vital and urgent that a concentrated effort be made to learn all we can about the Hawaiian evolutionary experiment while the chance still exists. This is not only important for science; what we discover will help to determine what should be preserved and how best to preserve it. Much of the charm of Hawaii for residents and visitors alike lies in its distinctiveness, which in large part resides in its biotic peculiarities.

The Hawaii Terrestrial Biological Program, already referred to, envisions a detailed, long-term, comprehensive study of the endemic and invading biotas of the Hawaiian Islands, under the auspices of the subcommittees on Systematics and Biogeography and on Conservation of Ecosystems of the U.S. National Committee for the IBP. A planning group met in Honolulu in March 1967, to confer with local biologists, state and government officials, and representatives of the armed services and large land owners, the Bishop Museum, and the University of Hawaii. A task force has been appointed to make detailed plans, establish priorities, seek the necessary funds, and enlist the cooperation of biologists of this and other countries to do the work. It is hoped that the program can be put into operation during 1968.

[1] Wallace, A. R., *Island Life* (London: Macmillan, 1880).

[2] Carlquist, S., *Island Life* (Garden City: Natural History Press, 1965).

[3] Briggs, J. C., *System. Zool.*, **15**, 153 (1966).

[4] Carlquist, S., *Quart. Rev. Biol.*, **41**, 247–270 (1966).

[5] McArthur, R. H., and E. O. Wilson, *Evolution*, **17**, 373–387 (1963); *The Theory of Island Biogeography* (Princeton, N. J.: Princeton University Press, 1967).

[6] The best general description of the origin and history of the Hawaiian Islands and their biota, from which much of the information here presented has been taken, is that by E. C. Zimmerman, *Insects of Hawaii* (Honolulu: University of Hawaii Press, 1948), vol. 1, *Introduction*.

[7] Macdonald, G. A., and W. Kyselka, *Anatomy of an Island* (Honolulu: Bishop Museum Spec. Pub. 55, 1967).

[8] Zimmerman, E. C., *op. cit.*, pp. 63–119.

[9] Keck, D. D., *Occasional Papers Bishop Museum* (Honolulu), **11** (19), 1–38 (1936); Carlquist, S., *Am. J. Bot.*, **44**, 695–705 (1957); Carlquist, S., *Pacific Sci.*, **13**, 195–210 (1959).

[10] Amadon, D., *Bull. Am. Museum Nat. Hist.*, **95**, 151–262 (1950); Baldwin, P. H., *Univ. Calif. Pub. Zool.*, **52**, 285–398 (1953).

[11] Individual papers by H. L. Carson, F. E. Clayton, D. E. Hardy, H. T. Spieth, H. Takada, and L. H. Throckmorton, in *Studies in Genetics*, III (Morgan Centennial Issue), ed. M. R. Wheeler (Austin: Univ. Texas Press, Pub. 6615, 1966).

[12] Hardy, D. E., *Insects of Hawaii* (Honolulu: Univ. Hawaii Press, 1965), vol. 12, *Drosophilidae*.

[13] Stalker, H. D., H. L. Carson, and F. E. Clayton, these Proceedings, **57**, 1280–1285 (1967).

DERIVATION OF THE FLORA OF THE HAWAIIAN ISLANDS

F. R. FOSBERG

Speculation as to the affinities and derivation of the Hawaiian flora has not been lacking in the past. Unfortunately there have been more guesses than careful investigation.

The flora is a small one, typically that of an oceanic island. The total known flora of seed plants is, according to the census which follows, 1,729 species and varieties scattered through 216 genera; that of ferns, 168 species and varieties in 37 genera.

Because of its isolation and high endemism, this flora has always attracted attention, and many competent botanists have worked and written on it. It early had one of the finest general descriptive floras (Hillebrand, 1888) ever written on a tropical region. Yet, according to modern standards we know remarkably little about this flora. Many of the most difficult genera have not been monographed. Some monographs which have been written are so poor that they must be redone. The reputation for polymorphism enjoyed by Hawaiian plants has led taxonomists to avoid undertaking major problems on them.

Especially little has been written specifically on the relationships of Hawaiian genera and species to their relatives elsewhere. Even in the most modern and extensive revisions and monographs one frequently finds no indication that the plants have or do not have relatives elsewhere. It seems that much of the work has been done on the assumption that all Hawaiian plants are isolated endemics.

This has made it very difficult to compile any list of the affinities of Hawaiian groups. It has also made the quality of the compilation very uneven. Wherever possible the compiler has relied on his own knowledge or opinions. Unfortunately, there are many groups with which he has had only superficial contact outside of their Hawaiian representation. In the cases of these, an attempt has been made to find where a competent student has expressed an opinion, or to persuade one to express himself. In many instances the last opinion to be expressed was that of Hillebrand 60 years ago. The writings of Dr. Carl Skottsberg have been freely drawn upon. Most of the recent monographs and revisions have given surprisingly little assistance.

It must be emphasized that the present state of our knowledge permits only the most tentative conclusions as to the relationships and origin of most Hawaiian plants, and that even the numbers of species and varieties are by no means definitely known. Current explorations still yield numerous new ones.

Merely writing down some of these approximations may give them more weight than they deserve. However, it has been considered worth while to compile this summary to bring together the best current information.

The tabular arrangement selected, though more complex than that for animal groups, is, if anything, too simple. It seems that the history of plant distribution in the Pacific may have been more complex than that of animals. Plants have

Author's note: The data compiled in this paper were obtained about 25 years ago, and some of the details may have to be considered in light of work done on the Hawaiian flora since that time.

Reprinted from E.C. Zimmerman, *Insects of Hawaii,* vol. 1, p. 107–119, by permission of F.R. Fosberg, special advisor, tropical biology, Smithsonian Institution; E.C. Zimmerman; and The University Press of Hawaii.

apparently come to Hawaii *from all directions, more or less indiscriminately,* with a preponderance, of course, from the island-rich areas to the southwest. It would be misleading to divide the affinities into Pacific and American, since the Austral group is so strong.

In the tables, where doubt as to two alternatives is expressed by question marks, the least likely of the two has been enclosed in parentheses and the other has been counted in the totaling. In the interest of simplification, question marks have been used only in the most doubtful cases.

The term *Indo-Pacific* is applied to groups following the common distributional pattern of a concentration of species in Indonesia or southeastern Asia and attenuating out into the Pacific, or to groups showing a portion of this distribution: generally, those plants having their affinities to the west and southwest of Hawaii.

Austral is applied to those whose affinities are in the south Pacific, from Australia to Patagonia, but not usually to any extent west of Australia, and not restricted to America. This includes the "Antarctic" element of previous compilers.

American is of obvious circumscription, except that certain plants of far northern connection may be referred to the Boreal category. The Galapagos and Juan Fernandez Islands are regarded as American.

Boreal refers to northern North America and extra-tropical Eurasia. This is not entirely satisfactory, as certain East Asiatic groups should perhaps have a category of their own.

Pantropic includes groups which have such a wide tropical or cosmopolitan distribution that it is difficult or impossible to suggest from which area the original immigrant may have come. A great many of these are groups that are strand or widespread lowland plants.

The *Obscure* category includes such plants as are so isolated as to have no apparent living relatives. There may be some that are placed here only from lack of adequate study. This is certainly true in such ill-classified groups as certain large grass genera, etc. In general, however, these may well be the oldest members of the flora, isolated for so long either that all their relatives have succumbed to competition or to other causes of extinction, or that they have had time to change so completely that evidence of their kinship has been lost.

The philosophy adopted in this tabulation is that actual percentages of the flora are of little significance in speculation on its origin. An attempt has been made to determine by affinities the probable number of original immigrants that established themselves and were the ancestors of the present flora. Countless others may have come, flourished, then become extinct leaving no trace. The indications of the affinities in the tables are on the basis only of these lines of descent. Therefore, the percentages derived from the six general categories of sources do not indicate percentage of the flora but of the original immigrants.

Separate tables have been made for seed plants and Pteridophytes, as their propagules are so different in nature that different principles may well govern their dispersal and distribution. One would naturally expect a much more continuous rain of microscopic fern spores on an isolated island than of heavy seeds or fruits.

Where genera that are widely accepted are here considered as synonyms (or as subgenera) of others, they are placed beneath the accepted genera in parentheses and in italics. Where several genera are considered to represent the progeny of one introduction, the derived ones are placed in parentheses, but not italicized, under that genus believed closest to the original immigrant. Where there are divergent ideas on the number of species and varieties in a group and the compiler has no definite opinion, the least probable number has been added in parentheses, and this number is not incorporated in the totals. Question marks in the first five data columns indicate strong doubt as to numbers. In the columns under "Affinities" they indicate doubt as to direction of affinity. When alone they are counted as one; when in parentheses they are not counted as they are the less likely alternatives.

Introduced species, either recent or aboriginal, have been excluded where the compiler is satisfied that they are introduced.

SUMMARY OF THE HAWAIIAN SEED PLANTS

FAMILY	GENUS	GENERA ENDEMIC (e); NON-ENDEMIC (w)	NO. SPECIES PLUS VARIETIES	NO. ENDEMIC	NO. NON-ENDEMIC	NO. ORIGINAL IMMIGRANTS	Indo-Pacific	Austral	American	Boreal	Pantropic	Obscure
Pandanaceae	Freycinetia	w	1	1		1	1					
	Pandanus	w	1		1	1	1					
Potamogetonaceae	Potamogeton	w	2		2	2			1		1	
	Ruppia	w	1		1	1					1	
Naiadaceae	Naias	w	1		1	1					1	
Hydrocharitaceae	Halophila	w	1		1	1	1					
Gramineae	Agrostis	w	3	2	1	2		2				
	Andropogon	w	1		1	1	1					
	Calamagrostis	w	2	2		2		2				
	Cenchrus	w	3	3		1	1					
	Deschampsia	w	3	3		1				?		
	Digitaria	w	1		1	1	1					
	Dissochondrus	e	1	1		1			1			
	Eragrostis	w	12	12		2		2				
	Festuca	w	1	1		1				?		
	Garnotia	w	1	1		1	1					
	Heteropogon	w	1		1	1					1	
	Isachne	w	2	1	1	2	2					

SUMMARY OF THE HAWAIIAN SEED PLANTS—*Continued*

FAMILY	GENUS	GENERA ENDEMIC (e); NON-ENDEMIC (w)	NO. SPECIES PLUS VARIETIES	NO. ENDEMIC	NO. NON-ENDEMIC	NO. ORIGINAL IMMIGRANTS	AFFINITIES					
							Indo-Pacific	Austral	American	Boreal	Pantropic	Obscure
	Ischaemum	w	1		1	1						
	Lepturus	w	1		1	1		1				
	Microlaena	w	1		1	1	1					
	Oplismenus	w	1		1	1	1					
	Panicum	w	23	23		3			1			2
	Paspalum	w	2		2	2	1		1		1	
	Poa	w	(3)–4	(3)–4		1			?			
	Sporobolus	w	1		1	1					1	
	Trisetum	w	2	2		1				1		
Cyperaceae	Carex	w	9	6	3	6	1	1	2?	1	1	
	Cladium	w	3	2	1	3		2	1			
	(*Baumea*)											
	(*Vincentia*)											
	Cyperus	w	23	16	7	8	3		1		4	
	Eleocharis	w	1		1	1		(?)	?			
	Fimbristylis	w	2	1	1	2	1					1
	Gahnia	w	6	6		2	2					
	Oreobolus	w	1	1		1	1					
	Rhynchospora	w	3	1	2	2	2					
	Scirpus	w	(4)–5	1?	4	(4)–5			4		1	
	Scleria	w	1	1?		1			1			
	Uncinia	w	1		1		1					
Palmae	Pritchardia	w	2–(38)	2–(38)		1	1					
Flagellariaceae	Joinvillea	w	1	1			1					
Juncaceae	Luzula	w	3	3		1					1	
Liliaceae	Astelia	w	12	12		1	1					
	Dianella	w	3	3		1	1					
	Dracaena	w	2–(4)	2–(4)		1	1					
	(*Pleomele*)											
	Smilax	w	2	2		1	1					
Iridaceae	Sisyrinchium	w	1	1		1			1			
Orchidaceae	Anoectochilus	w	2	2		1	1					
	Habenaria	w	1	1		1	1					
	Liparis	w	1	1		1	1					
Piperaceae	Peperomia	w	50	48	2	3	1		1			1
Ulmaceae	Trema	w	1		1	1	1					
Moraceae	Pseudomorus	w	1	1?		1		1				

SUMMARY OF THE HAWAIIAN SEED PLANTS—*Continued*

FAMILY	GENUS	GENERA ENDEMIC (e); NON-ENDEMIC (w)	NO. SPECIES PLUS VARIETIES	NO. ENDEMIC	NO. NON-ENDEMIC	NO. ORIGINAL IMMIGRANTS	Indo-Pacific	Austral	American	Boreal	Pantropic	Obscure
Urticaceae	Boehmeria	w	1	1		1	1					
	Hesperocnide	w	1	1		1			1			
	Neraudia	e	9	9		1						1
	Pilea	w	1		1	1	(?)		(?)		?	
	Pipturus	w	13	13		1	1					
	Touchardia	e	5?	5?		1	1?					
	Urera	w	3	3		2			2			
Santalaceae	Exocarpus	w	3–(5)	3–(5)		1		1				
	Santalum	w	6	6		2		1				1
Loranthaceae	Korthalsella	w	8	6	2	2	1	1				
Polygonaceae	Polygonum	w	1		1	1					1	
	Rumex	w	2	2		1						1
Chenopodiaceae	Chenopodium	w	1	1		1			1			
Amaranthaceae	Achyranthes	w	2	2		1	1					
	Aerva	w	1	1		1	?					
	Amaranthus	w	1	1		1	1					
	Charpentiera	w	3	3		1		1				
	Nototrichium	e	5	5		1		1				
Nyctaginaceae	Boerhavia	w	3		3	3	3					
	Pisonia	w	3	3		2	1		1			
	(*Ceodes*)											
	(*Rockia*)											
	(*Heimerliodendron*)											
Phytolaccaceae	Phytolacca	w	1	1		1			1			
Aizoaceae	Sesuvium	w	1		1	1					1	
Portulacaceae	Portulaca	w	6	4	2	3	1		1		1	
Caryophyllaceae	Sagina	w	1	1		1			?			
	Schiedea	e	45	45		1						1
	(*Alsinodendron*)											
	Silene	w	5	5		1						1
Ranunculaceae	Ranunculus	w	2	2		1		?				
Menispermaceae	Cocculus	w	1		1?	1		1				
Lauraceae	Cassytha	w	1		1	1					1	
	Cryptocarya	w	2	2		1	1					
Papaveraceae	Argemone	w	1	1		1			1			
Capparidaceae	Capparis	w	1		1	1	1					
	Cleome	w	1	1		1			1			

SUMMARY OF THE HAWAIIAN SEED PLANTS—*Continued*

FAMILY	GENUS	GENERA ENDEMIC (e); NON-ENDEMIC (w)	NO. SPECIES PLUS VARIETIES	NO. ENDEMIC	NO. NON-ENDEMIC	NO. ORIGINAL IMMIGRANTS	Indo-Pacific	Austral	American	Boreal	Pantropic	Obscure
Cruciferae	Cardamine	w	1	1		1					1	
	Lepidium	w	(3)–4	(3)–4		2	1					1
Droseraceae	Drosera	w	1		1	1				1		
Saxifragaceae	Broussaisia	e	2	2		1	1					
Pittosporaceae	Pittosporum	w	50	50		1	1					
Rosaceae	Acaena	w	2	2		1		1				
	Fragaria	w	1		1	1			1			
	Osteomeles	w	1		1	1	1					
	Rubus	w	2	2		1			1			
Leguminosae	Acacia	w	3	3		1	1					
	Caesalpinia	w	2		2	2					2	
	Canavalia	w	2	2		1	1					
	Cassia	w	1	1		1	1					
	Entada	w	1?		1	1					1	
	Erythrina	w	1	1		1	1					
	Mezoneurum	w	1	1		1	1					
	Mucuna	w	2		2	2					2	
	Sophora	w	1	1		1		1				
	Sesbania	w	1	1		1		?				
	Strongylodon	w	1		1?	1	1					
	Tephrosia	w	1?		1	1	1					
	Vicia	w	1	1		1			?			
	Vigna	w	3	2	1	2					1	1
Geraniaceae	Geranium	w	6	6		1						1
Zygophyllaceae	Tribulus	w	1		1	1					1	
Rutaceae	Fagara	w	14	14		1	1					
	Pelea	w	94	94		1	1					
	(Platydesma)	e										
Euphorbiaceae	Antidesma	w	6	6		1	1					
	Claoxylon	w	8	8		1	1					
	Drypetes	w	1	1		1	1					
	Euphorbia	w	60	60		1	1					
	Phyllanthus	w	2	2		1	1					
Aquifoliaceae	Ilex	w	1		1	1		1				
Celastraceae	Perrottetia	w	1	1		1	?					
Anacardiaceae	Rhus	w	1	1		1	1					

SUMMARY OF THE HAWAIIAN SEED PLANTS—*Continued*

FAMILY	GENUS	GENERA ENDEMIC (e); NON-ENDEMIC (w)	NO. SPECIES PLUS VARIETIES	NO. ENDEMIC	NO. NON-ENDEMIC	NO. ORIGINAL IMMIGRANTS	Indo-Pacific	Austral	American	Boreal	Pantropic	Obscure
Sapindaceae	Alectryon	w	1	1		1	1					
	Dodonaea	w	18	18?		1					1	
	Sapindus	w	2	2		2	1		1?			
Rhamnaceae	Alphitonia	w	1	1		1	1					
	Colubrina	w	2	1	1	2	1?				1	
	Gouania	w	3	3		1	1					
Tiliaceae	Elaeocarpus	w	1	1		1	1					
Malvaceae	Abutilon (*Abortopetalum*)	w	3	2	1	2			1			1
	Gossypium	w	1	1		1			?			
	Hibiscadelphus	e	4	4		1						1
	Hibiscus	w	10	9	1?	4	2?	1			1	1
	Kokia	e	4	4		1					1	
	Sida	w	2		2	2	1				1	
Sterculiaceae	Waltheria	w	1	1		1			?			
Theaceae	Eurya	w	2	2		1	1					
Violaceae	Isodendrion	e	4	4		1			?			
	Viola	w	7	7		1						1
Thymeleaceae	Wikstroemia	w	14	14		1	1					
Flacourtiaceae	Xylosma	w	2	2		1	1					
Cucurbitaceae	Sicyos	w	8	8		1						1
Myrtaceae	Eugenia	w	4	4		2	2					
	Metrosideros	w	18?	18?		1		1				
Begoniaceae	Hillebrandia	e	1	1		1						1
Halorrhagaceae	Gunnera	w	7	7		1			1			
Araliaceae	Cheirodendron	w	5?	5?		1		1				
	Reynoldsia	w	1	1		1		1				
	Tetraplasandra (*Pterotropia*)	e	10?	10?		1						1
Umbelliferae	Daucus	w	1		1	1			1			
	Hydrocotyle	w	1		1	1					1	
	Peucedanum	w	3	3		1						1
	Sanicula	w	4	4		1						1
	Spermolepis	w	1	1		1			1			
Ericaceae	Vaccinium	w	8	8		1		1				
Epacridaceae	Styphelia	w	2	1	1	1		1				

SUMMARY OF THE HAWAIIAN SEED PLANTS—*Continued*

FAMILY	GENUS	GENERA ENDEMIC (e) ; NON-ENDEMIC (w)	NO. SPECIES PLUS VARIETIES	NO. ENDEMIC	NO. NON-ENDEMIC	NO. ORIGINAL IMMIGRANTS	Indo-Pacific	Austral	American	Boreal	Pantropic	Obscure
Primulaceae	Lysimachia	w	13	12	1	2	1	1?				
Myrsinaceae	Embelia	w	2	2		1	1					
	Myrsine	w	25	25		1?					1	
Sapotaceae	Nesoluma	w	1		1	1	1					
	Pouteria (*Planchonella*)	w	6?	6?		1	1					
Ebenaceae	Diospyros (*Maba*)	w	7	7		1	1					
Plumbaginaceae	Plumbago	w	1		1	1	1					
Loganiaceae	Labordia	e	75	75		2	2					
Gentianaceae	Centaurium	w	1		1	1			1			
Oleaceae	Osmanthus	w	1	1		1	1					
Apocynaceae	Alyxia	w	1	1		1	1					
	Ochrosia	w	1	1		1	1					
	Pteralyxia	e	2	2		1						1
	Rauvolfia	w	7	7		1						1
Convolvulaceae	Breweria	w	2	2		1						1
	Cressa	w	1		1	1			1			
	Cuscuta	w	2	2		1			1			
	Ipomoea	w	9	4	5	7	5				2	
	Jacquemontia	w	1	1		1			1			
Hydrophyllaceae	Nama	w	2	2		1			1			
Boraginaceae	Heliotropium	w	2	1	1	2		(?)	2			
Verbenaceae	Vitex	w	1		1	1	1					
Labiatae	Lepechinia	w	1		1	1			1			
	Phyllostegia (*Stenogyne*)	w e	108	108		1		1				
	(*Haplostachys*)	e										
	Plectranthus	w	1		1	1	1					
Solanaceae	Lycium	w	1		1	1			1			
	Nothocestrum	e	6	6		1			1			
	Solanum	w	7	7		1						1
Scrophulariaceae	Bacopa	w	1		1	1					1	
Myoporaceae	Myoporum	w	1	1		1	1					

SUMMARY OF THE HAWAIIAN SEED PLANTS—*Continued*

FAMILY	GENUS	GENERA ENDEMIC (e) ; NON-ENDEMIC (w)	NO. SPECIES PLUS VARIETIES	NO. ENDEMIC	NO. NON-ENDEMIC	NO. ORIGINAL IMMIGRANTS	AFFINITIES Indo-Pacific	Austral	American	Boreal	Pantropic	Obscure
Gesneriaceae	Cyrtandra	w	110	110		1?	1					
Plantaginaceae	Plantago	w	19	19		2?		2				
Rubiaceae	Bobea	e	4?	4?		1	1					
	Canthium	w	1		1	1	1					
	Coprosma	w	27	27		3?	3					
	Gardenia	w	2	2		2	2					
	Hedyotis	w	76	76		1	1					
	(Gouldia)	e										
	Morinda	w	3	3		1	1					
	Nertera	w	1		1	1		1				
	Psychotria	w	11	10	1	2	1		1			
	(*Straussia*)											
Campanulaceae	Brighamia	e	2	2		1						1
	Clermontia	e	42	42		1		1				
	Cyanea	e	100	100		1						1
	(Rollandia)	e										
	(Delissea)	e										
	Lobelia	w	23	23		1	?					
	(Trematolobelia)	e										
Goodeniaceae	Scaevola	w	12	11	1	1	1					
Compositae	Adenostemma	w	1		1	1	1					
	Argyroxiphium	e	61	61		1						1
	(*Wilkesia*)											
	(Dubautia)	e										
	(*Railliardia*)											
	Artemisia	w	5	5		1				1		
	Aster	w	1	1		1		1				
	Bidens	w	60	60		1		1				
	Gnaphalium	w	1	1		1					1	
	Hesperomannia	e	7	7		1			1			
	Lagenophora	w	3	3		1		1				
	Lipochaeta	e?	55	55		1	1					
	Remya	e	2	2		1			?			
	Tetramolopium	w	20	20		1	1					
Totals 83	216	28e 188w	1,729	1,633	96	272	109	45	50	7	35	28

The table of seed plants yields the following information:

83 families
216 genera
    28; 13 percent endemic
    188; 87 percent non-endemic
1,729 species and varieties
    94.4 percent endemic
    5.6 percent non-endemic
272 original immigrants
    40.1 percent Indo-Pacific
    16.5 percent Austral
    18.3 percent American
    2.6 percent Boreal
    12.5 percent Pantropic and Cosmopolitan
    10.3 percent Obscure

Significantly absent are gymnosperms, *Ficus,* Cunoniaceae, mangroves, *Piper,* Bignoniaceae, Araceae, and the several large predominantly American tropical families. Significantly few are Orchidaceae, palms, Loranthaceae, Lauraceae, Scrophulariaceae. Significantly numerous are grasses and Compositae.

Not evident from the table is the interesting fact that of the American element a far greater part of the species are only slightly distinct from their American relatives (probably indicating geologically recent arrival) than is true for the other elements.

For the Pteridophyte table much of the basic information was kindly supplied by W. H. Wagner, Jr. However, the generic concepts, arrangement of the table and interpretations are those of the compiler.

The Pteridophyte table shows that there are:

10 families
37 genera
    3; 8.1 percent endemic
    34; 91.9 percent non-endemic
168 species and varieties
    119; 64.9 percent endemic
    49; 35.1 percent non-endemic
135 original immigrants
    48.1 percent Indo-Pacific
    3.7 percent Austral
    11.9 percent American
    4.4 percent Boreal
    20.8 percent Pantropic and Cosmopolitan
    11.1 percent Obscure

Most notably absent are *Cyathea* (sensu lata) and *Blechnum.* (*Sadleria,* however, is of blechnoid affinity.)

SUMMARY OF THE HAWAIIAN PTERIDOPHYTES

FAMILY	GENUS	GENERA ENDEMIC (e); NON-ENDEMIC (w)	NO. SPECIES PLUS VARIETIES	NO. ENDEMIC	NO. NON-ENDEMIC	NO. ORIGINAL IMMIGRANTS	AFFINITIES						
							Indo-Pacific	Austral	American	Boreal	Pantropic	Obscure
Psilotaceae	Psilotum	w	2	1	1	1					1	
Lycopodiaceae	Lycopodium	w	13	9	4	9	4		1		4	
Selaginellaceae	Selaginella	w	3	3		3				1	1	1
Ophioglossaceae	Ophioglossum	w	4	1	3	3	1				2	
	Botrychium	w	1	1		1	1					
Marattiaceae	Marattia	w	1	1		1	?		(?)			
Schizaeaceae	Schizaea	w	1	1		1		1				
Gleicheniaceae	Gleichenia (sensu lata)	w	4	2	2	3	2		1			
Hymenophyllaceae	Hymenophyllum (sensu lata)	w	3	3		3	1				2	
	Trichomanes (sensu lata)	w	6	5	1	6	3	2			1	
Polypodiaceae	Adiantum	w	2(?)		2(?)	2(?)	1(?)				1	
	Asplenium (sensu lata)	w	21	12	9	21	13		2	2	2	2
	Athyrium (Diplazium)	w	9	7	2	9	6		2			1
	Cibotium	w	5	5		1	?		(?)			
	Coniogramme	w	1	1		1	1					
	Cystopteris	w	1	1		1					1	
	Diellia	e	8	8		1						1
	Doodia	w	2		2	2		2				
	Doryopteris	w	2	2		1					1	
	Dryopteris (Lastrea) (Ctenitis) (Cyclosorus)	w	25	20	5	25	14		5		2	4
	Elaphoglossum	w	9	9		9	5				2	2
	Histiopteris	w	1		1	1					1	
	Hypolepis	w	1		1	1	1					
	Lindsaea	w	1		1	1	1					
	Microlepia	w	2		2	2	2					
	Nephrolepis	w	4		4	4					4	
	Pellaea	w	1		1	1			1			

SUMMARY OF THE HAWAIIAN PTERIDOPHYTES—*Continued*

FAMILY	GENUS	GENERA ENDEMIC (e); NON-ENDEMIC (w)	NO. SPECIES PLUS VARIETIES	NO. ENDEMIC	NO. NON-ENDEMIC	NO. ORIGINAL IMMIGRANTS	AFFINITIES					
							Indo-Pacific	Austral	American	Boreal	Pantropic	Obscure
	Polypodium (Pleopeltis) (Microsorium) (Grammitis) (Xiphopteris) (Amphoradenium)	w	16	13	3	7	3		1	2		1
	Polystichum (Rumohra) (Cyrtomium) (Phanerophlebia)	w	4	2	2	4	1		1	1		1
	Pteridium	w	1	1		1			1			
	Pteris	w	4	3	1	3	1				2	
	Sadleria	e	(4)–5	(4)–5		1						1
	Schizostege	e	1	1		1						1
	Sphenomeris	w	1		1	1	1					
	Tectaria	w	1	1		1					1	
	Vittaria	w	1		1	1	1					
Marsileaceae	Marsilea	w	1	1		1			1			
Totals 10	37	3e 34w	168	119	49	135	65	5	16	6	28	15

The low percentage of Austral affinities is interesting in view of Dr. Copeland's (1939) derivation of almost all ferns from Antarctica, and in view of the much higher percentage in seed plants. Interesting, also, is the relatively low endemism and, particularly, the low ratio (1.24) of present species and varieties to original introductions.

Tables for the lower cryptogams were not prepared because of the lack of critical knowledge of these groups on the part of the compiler, and also because of the rudimentary state of available information on Hawaiian members of many groups.

These statistics from the two tables clearly support the commonly held idea that the flora is basically an attenuated Indo-Malayan one, but not nearly so predominantly so as previously thought. The American element, on the present basis, is stronger than the most commonly accepted recent view has held.

The picture, on the basis of the small number of original immigrants, the diversity of their origin and the important groups not represented, seems to be that of a flora that has always been insular. It is exactly the type that might be expected to be descended from a random aggregation of chance waifs carried overseas by a combination of factors such as storms, currents and birds. Of seed plants, an average of one successful arrival and establishment every 20,000 to 30,000 years would account for the flora. This is granting an estimate of 5 to 10 million years of above-water history for the entire Hawaiian chain, starting with the islands at the extreme northwest, such as Kure, Midway and Lisianski.

The preponderance of Indo-Pacific affinities seems satisfactorily explained by the number of islands in that direction as compared with the lack of islands to the east and north. The Austral element, too, is more or less in proportion on this basis.

If we resort to land bridges or continents to account for the presence of the Hawaiian flora, then we may well have to build them in all directions.

ENDEMISM AND EVOLUTION IN THE HAWAIIAN BIOTA: FUNGI

Gladys E. Baker[1] and Roger D. Goos[2]

More than eighty years ago Hillebrand (1888) recognized
that the flora of the Hawaiian Islands was unique for its
high percentage of endemic species, now rated as 90-96 percent, exclusive of algae and fungi (Stone 1967). Should
we expect similar findings for the fungi? Why do we have
no data for endemic or Hawaiian fungi? In order to
evaluate endemism in the fungi of Hawaii, it is necessary
to explore the nature of fungi; the fungus population of
Hawaii, its distribution and origin; and the history of
mycology in Hawaii.

By conservative estimate there are at least 50,000
species of fungi in the world (Ainsworth 1968). Other
calculations place the number as high as 200,000 species
(Emmons, Binford, and Utz 1970). Fungi are classified in
several taxonomic groups, all of which are well represented in the Hawaiian Islands. Specifically, these
groups are designated: Myxomycetes, the acellular slime
molds; Phycomycetes, the algal-like fungi; Ascomycetes,
sac fungi; Basidiomycetes, basidium bearers (jelly fungi
such as the local delicacy *pepeiao*, rusts, smuts, and
mushrooms); and Fungi Imperfecti or molds. In 1940
G. K. Parris, then professor of plant pathology at the
University of Hawaii, prepared a check list of fungi in
Hawaii. Although many more species have been recorded
subsequently, even then all groups were on record. If
one compares the numbers of fungus species in Hawaii,
using Parris' data, with numbers known in the world,
figures show:

---

[1]University of Hawaii, Department of Botany, Honolulu, Hawaii 96822

[2]University of Rhode Island, Department of Botany,
Kingston, R. I. 02881

	Hawaii (Parris 1940)	Known (Ainsworth 1961)
Myxomycetes	98	400
Phycomycetes	40	1,400
Ascomycetes	234	15,500
Basidiomycetes	126	15,000
Fungi Imperfecti	185	15,000

The number of species known in Hawaii has been greatly augmented since Parris' compilation, but totals are
still only a fraction of those known. This would probably be true for any geographic area of limited size.

Everyone agrees that fungi are cosmopolitan in their
distribution. In fact, it has been said that "cosmo-
politanism is so commonplace that the taxonomist of
fungi does not use a local flora to identify his plants,
but must have recourse to the whole of the world's
mycological literature if he would be even approximately
correct" (Diehl 1937). Fungi occur from sea level to
above timber line on mountains, within a few miles of
both poles, in fresh and marine waters, as spores and
viable fragments in the air, in soil and in association
with plants and animals, including man, either as commensals or in varying degrees of parasitism.

In the layman's terms fungi are often equated with
yeasts, molds, and mushrooms. Yeasts are rarely seen
because they are microscopic, yet their fermentation
products, both wanted and unwanted, are easily recognized.
One does not need to be in Hawaii for very long to be
aware of mildew or mold problems, especially in rainy
seasons. At the macroscopic level many molds are
readily seen. Toadstools and mushrooms (useful though
untenable terms distinguishing poisonous from edible
fungi) are the most conspicuous fungi. The number of

microscopic fungi undoubtedly outweighs the number of
macroscopic forms. In Hawaii, curiously, the conspicuous, fleshy fungi seemingly are poorly represented. This
may mean only that they are rarely collected, but not
necessarily rare.

Whatever their size, all fungi have some common
characteristics which favor their distribution and
establishment in many habitats. These can be expressed
by one word: versatility. This versatility includes
their nutrition, cell structure, and methods of reproduction. Fungi are heterotrophic organisms (which is
the reason why nearly everyone defines a fungus as an
organism without chlorophyll). In nutritional requirements fungi range from species satisfied by simple substrata to those requiring highly complex substrata. On
a given substrate, or under similar environmental
conditions, one might expect to find the same or closely
related species anywhere in the world. In Hawaii these
expectations are substantiated by fungi found in a
variety of ecological habitats.

Soil is one of the major habitats for fungi.
Ecologically, fungi may be actively growing (permanent
or transitory mycota) or resting until conditions again
permit activity (potentially active mycota). The soil
is a great reservoir of many organisms acting and
interacting. The problem in any microbial soil study is
the difficulty attending determination of what actually
is occurring there, as direct observation is virtually
impossible. Initial steps in understanding activity
in situ are the isolation, estimation of numbers, and
identification of the members of the population.
Quantitatively, a count of several hundred thousand
fungi per gram of soil probably means some 500 lbs of
fungus tissue per acre, calculated on a live-weight basis
(Alexander 1961). Soil counts from a Maui cane field
and from the rain forest on top of Mt. Kaala are in this

range (Baker 1964). Qualitatively, both sites yielded 18
species each. Although the lava cinders at 10,000 ft
on Mt. Haleakala, Maui, returned 22 species, the numbers
per gram were so low as to be uncountable (statistically
not significant). None of these fungi was a new species,
but over the years interesting relationships among
species, habitat, and distribution are noted.

   Penicillium rotundum, which produces ascocarps in
its perfect stage, is now known not only from its
original site in Panama, but from soil of a pasture under
an *Opuntia megacantha* at 1,500 ft near the road to
Mt. Haleakala (Baker 1968), and from beach sand of
McKean Island of the Phoenix group (Steele 1967).
Another Ascomycete, *Chaetomium longirostre*, was first
isolated from soil of Barro Colorado, Panama (Farrow
1954). More than ten years later it was found in a soil
from upper Manoa Valley, Oahu (Baker 1968). Goos (1960)
noted other collections in the interval, which record the
species from India, Costa Rica, and Honduras.

   Fungi, which play an active role in the soil, are
responsible for many biochemical changes. Some of their
metabolic by-products are economically significant,
notably antibiotics and antimycotics, chemicals with
therapeutic value for controlling bacterial and fungal
diseases in man. In a survey of 100 soils (61 forest
and 39 cultivated) Blunt and Baker (1968) screened 175
isolates for antimycotic activity against five human
pathogenic fungi. There was no appreciable difference
in the antimycosis level displayed by forest or cultivated
soil fungi. Only a few fungi showed broad-spectrum
antimycosis against all the test organisms. A high level
of activity among the Phycomycetes was unexpected, as
this group has not been noted for such properties.
Although these tests were conducted *in vitro*, this kind
of antagonistic action presumably goes on in soils everywhere.

   Fungi can be recovered as easily from water as from

soil, although the numbers recovered are always much lower. They inhabit marine, fresh, and polluted waters. Until the survey by Steele during 1964 and 1965, there was no information about marine fungi in the central Pacific (Steele 1967). Almost concurrently a study of marine fungi was carried out by mycologists at the Marine Institute of Miami University in Florida (Roth, Orpurt, and Ahearn 1967). The total number of species isolated was almost identical for the two regions: 133 in the Caribbean and 127 in the Pacific. The major differences were in numbers of samples taken (227 in the Caribbean, 59 in the Pacific) and in the kinds of samples. The Pacific study included more sand samples, which would result in higher numbers. Eleven Caribbean genera were not found in the Pacific, and conversely 29 Pacific genera were unrecorded in the Caribbean. Thirty genera were common to both areas. All groups of fungi except Myxomycetes were found among the Pacific isolates. Neither Ascomycetes nor Basidiomycetes were reported from the Caribbean samples. There were also differences in the predominant species of the two regions. These differences, according to Steele (1967), suggest that the two populations are different, but the components present in both are cosmopolitan species.

Fresh-water fungi in Hawaii also reflect the cosmopolitan distribution of fungi. Sparrow (1965), surveying aquatic habitats, noted the recovery of three fungi known both from mainland bogs and from the Wahiawa bog on Kauai. A keratinophilic water mold, isolated from Kauai and Hawaii, is known in Liberia and Cuba. In all, Sparrow discussed some 50 species of Phycomycetes, 4 of which he considered new species. Probably this distribution record will be tenable until Sparrow spends a semester in Tahiti or some other Pacific locality. It is Sparrow's opinion that the zoosporic Phycomycetes have moved into the Hawaiian Islands virtually unchanged from older, continental land masses and have remained unchanged.

There are very few lakes in Hawaii, but they are not lacking in fungal populations. On the summit of Mauna Kea on the island of Hawaii, there is a small lake, Lake Waiau, situated at an elevation of 13,007 ft. Temperatures there at night drop to the freezing level all year, and in winter it is probably frozen much of the time. This is hardly what one expects in the latitude of the tropics. When the water and bottom ooze were sampled for fungi in 1965 (Baker, unpublished data), a total of 29 species was recovered, representing Phycomycetes, Ascomycetes, and Fungi Imperfecti. This seemed a typical return for water samples. The isolation of a particular ascomycete, *Emericellopsis terricola*, promoted further thought. *Emericellopsis* usually occurs in wet soils, water, or bottom muds of lakes and ponds. *E. terricola* was commonly present in water and lake-bottom samples when a series of ponds and lakes in northwest Montana was under survey (Baker, unpublished data), but no representatives had been recovered in Hawaii from soil or water, either fresh or marine. A comparison of the Lake Waiau population with those known from a series of small lakes and potholes at 3,000 ft in Montana, showed that the Montana population was richer in number of species than the Lake Waiau population. More samples were taken in Montana, and so it is not surprising that these returned 56 species compared with 28 from Lake Waiau. Fourteen species were common to both geographic areas. *E. terricola* was isolated from water and bottom samples taken in both Lake Waiau and Montana. Four additional fungi found in the Lake Waiau bottom sample occur in other Montana aquatic habitats. Here, then, is presumptive evidence that *E. terricola* and the other species of fungi which are common to both areas have strains which are adapted to a given type of habitat. The waters of Lake Waiau, the Montana lakes, and the potholes are alkaline, and all are subject to freezing conditions for the better part of the year. In Montana

it is common knowledge that there are only two seasons:
winter and July.

Specialized spores are characteristic of the aquatic
Fungi Imperfecti called Hyphomycetales. Ingold, Ranzoni,
Petersen, and Tubaki have recovered these fungi from many
regions including England, Africa, California, New York,
Japan, and Jamaica (Nilsson 1964). The Hyphomycetales
live submerged on skeletonized leaves. Their spores are
either long and threadlike in a *C* or *S* shape, or they
are branched with four arms (tetraradiate). Spore shape
is considered an aid to anchorage and establishment in a
new location after passive dispersal. Large numbers of
these spores can be picked up in foam of eddies, around
barriers such as twigs and branches, and below waterfalls.
Hyphomycetales are worldwide in distribution. When
Anastasiou (1964) looked for them in five streams on
Kauai, he isolated a total of 17 species: 16 known and 1
new species.

Another habitat attractive to fungi in the tropics
is the phylloplane--literally an ecological habitat of
leaf surfaces (Ruinen 1961, 1963; Preece and Dickinson
1971). Controlling factors of populations are wetta-
bility of the leaf epidermis, water, and available
nutrients. The organisms constituting the populations,
besides the fungi, include bacteria, nitrogen-fixing
bacteria, algae, Protozoa, actinomycetes, lichens, and
sometimes epiphytic Bryophyta and Pteridophyta. Together,
these constitute a continuous or broken layer over the
leaf surface. Nutrients available are foliar exudates
(minerals, sugars, and organic acids) and leachings,
dust (organic particles), insect excreta, dead cells,
and microbial metabolic products. The population climax
of this ecosystem correlates with leaf senescence.
The mycota of the phylloplane correspond to those of
the soil, representing permanent species (actively growing and sporulating), transient species, and potentially
active species (dormant or resting).

When a survey of Hawaiian phylloplane populations
was made by Marsh (1966), samples were taken from leaves
collected from sea level to 6,000 ft on the island of
Hawaii. Whenever possible, the same leaf species were
used from zone to zone. Marsh isolated 121 species of
fungi, 22 of which he considered dominants. Of these he
felt 8 might represent a permanent mycota. He found virtually no differences between populations on dorsal and
ventral leaf surfaces, as has been claimed, but he did
agree with other phylloplane investigators that the fungi
of the soil and air at a given site were not constituents
of the phylloplane population, which is, therefore, more
or less unique. Marsh concluded that the controlling
factor in species distribution for his samples was climate. The number of species per square centimeter of
leaf surface was in the same range for all samples (1 to
4), but the numbers increased with elevation and attendant
climatic change. The species of the populations were
cosmopolitan fungi, even on the native *Acacia koa*.

Distribution of species on a cosmopolitan basis
extends to other very specialized groups, such as
coprophilous species, pathogenic species, mangrove associated fungi, commensals, nematode-trapping fungi, and
lignicolous fungi. All of these groups are here in
Hawaii, some more frequently represented than others.

Fungi which are adapted for growth on dung (coprophilous) comprise an interesting group. Their spores
are usually dispersed great distances, as they are taken
in with food by animals and are capable of surviving
intestinal passage. This allows for rather rapid transit
of a species if the animals, for example, are migratory
birds. On the top of Mt. Haleakala, Maui, some 10,000
ft elevation, there seems little to support fungus life
in the bare cinders. From these supposedly barren soils
several coprophilous fungi have been isolated, all
recognized species. Many migratory birds land on
Mt. Haleakala, and so the presence of these specialized

fungi is not unexpected. Further dispersal by birds is
quite likely, as Evans and Prusso (1969) have described
recently.

Fungi isolated from dung samples are not necessarily
limited to the substratum. Goos (1962) isolated
Sphaerostilbe repens, an Ascomycete notable for its
rhizomorphs, from soil of banana fields in Costa Rica
and Honduras. The same fungus turned up in 1967 on
horse dung in Hawaii (Baker, unpublished data).

Even more specialized in substrate relationships is
a group of fungi living as commensals in the digestive
tracts of arthropod larvae. Lichwardt (personal communication) finds that many species of this group, the
Trichomycetes, occur in the same "host" in mainland
United States, Hawaii, and Japan. A given species may
occur in Africa, South America, Europe, and parts of
Asia.

The relationship between fungi and mangroves is an
interesting one which Kohlmeyer (1969a) has investigated in widely separated geographic regions, including
Hawaii. According to Kohlmeyer the mangrove fungi fall
into two groups ecologically. One group is marine,
living submerged at least part of the day; the other is
terrestrial, living above the high-tide line. There is
some overlapping of species at the high-water mark.
Some species are definitely host specific. Because
mangroves are introduced plants in Hawaii (Walsh 1967),
the host-specific fungi are thought to have come with
the host in 1902. The distribution of other mangrove
fungi is controlled by water temperature, salinity, and
the nature of the host cells, specifically the cork
cells of seedlings and prop roots. Kohlmeyer's collections here in 1968 extended the known list of Pacific
marine fungi handsomely: he noted 27 species, 22 being
new records for Hawaii and 12 for the Pacific area
(1969b). His collections further pointed to distribution of a given species according to water temperature.

Several species are common to the warm waters of the
Atlantic and the Pacific. Cold-water species are not
found in Hawaii. Mangrove and marine fungi include
species of Phycomycetes, Ascomycetes, Basidiomycetes
(rarely), and Fungi Imperfecti.

The distribution of fungi can be considered in
relation to time as well as space. There is no geological record for fungi in Hawaii and few such records
anywhere. Some of the fossil fungus records, however,
are significant, for they not only place fungi in time
but serve as indicators of climatic conditions at a
given period and place. Dilcher (1963) has described
two epiphyllous fungi from the Eocene of Tennessee.
These fungi are widely known today, especially in warm,
humid areas. Stevens found them in Hawaii (1925). This
implies that these Ascomycetes, *Meliola* sp. and *Asterina*
sp., have been here a long time and that nowhere have
they undergone significant evolutionary change, as
morphologically the fossil forms are easily assignable
to contemporary genera.

Versatility in cell structure allows for remarkable
change in fungal morphology and consequent adaptation of
a fungus to different environments. The fungus filament
is essentially one continuous coenocytic, multinucleate
tube, growing by apical extension. Some fungi are
capable of shifting from this linear tubular form to
single, budding cells, or a yeast phase. This shift
may be related to nutrition, temperature, oxygen level,
or a combination of these. This versatility is especially characteristic of fungi which are invasive
pathogens in man. In soil these fungi live as nonpathogenic filamentous organisms, but, given the opportunity, they become pathogenic for man and assume the yeast
or tissue phase in the human body.

In Hawaii, fungus infections are nonreportable diseases; therefore, it is hard to estimate the frequency
of their occurrence by frequency of infection. There

is evidence that the Hawaiians of old were plagued by
the common filamentous yeasts *Candida albicans,* and
related species. These organisms cause "thrush" in the
mouths of children and other ailments in adults, ranging
from involvement of the skin to disorders of the central
nervous system. This yeast occurs in poi and even today
may be the cause of thrush. Poi is a fine substratum
for fungi and bacteria, well worth microscopic survey.

To determine the distribution of zoopathogenic fungi
in Hawaii, Kishimoto and Baker (1969) made a survey of
361 beach sands and 170 soils associated with bird droppings, for which some pathogenic fungi display affinity.
Such sources are known as geophilic. From the beach
sands they recovered 54 pathogenic or potentially pathogenic species, chiefly etiologic agents of superficial
infections such as athlete's foot, ringworm, and other
dermatomycoses. Of significance was the isolation of
Epidermophyton floccosum which attacks both skin and
nails, and *Cladosporium werneckii* which produces a superficial infection of palmar surfaces. Neither of these
pathogens had been recovered previously from a geophilic
source. Although their occurrence in the sand may be
only transitory, in bits of sloughed-off skin, nevertheless infection could result if opportunity were presented. Recovery of pathogenic species and potentially
pathogenic species was positively correlated with numbers
of persons using the beaches.

The soils associated with bird droppings were
screened for the presence of two systemic pathogens:
Cryptococcus neoformans, a yeast causing meningitis, and
Histoplasma capsulatum, a diphasic fungus with a soil-
inhabiting, nonpathogenic phase and a yeast phase in man.
C. neoformans was known from one Kauai isolation (Ajello
1958). Except for this one report there was no previous
record for these fungi in their natural habitat here.
Kishimoto and Baker recovered 61 isolates of *Cryptococcus neoformans* but no *Histoplasma.* Either the

incidence is too low for chance recovery from 170 samples,
or *Histoplasma* does not occur here. Unexplained is a
single case of histoplasmosis a few years ago in a Makiki
resident who had not left Hawaii.

Dispersal of fungi is related to their mode of
reproduction. The fungi are all spore formers. A study
of the variety of spores produced plus the versatility
displayed in their mechanisms of dispersal could keep
one occupied for a lifetime. Several mycologists have
and do so disport themselves. A spore is really embryonic in function and is the equivalent of any cell with
totipotential for growth and differentiation. Its
longevity is measured in hours to years. The large resting spore of *Histoplasma capsulatum* in the nonpathogenic
or soil phase has survived 500 days in tap water and
160 days at -40°C (Cooke and Kabler 1953). Gregory
(1966) has suggested a dual classification for fungus
spores. One group is aptly called "bide-awhile spores"
(memnospores, meaning "steadfast") which are active
in situ and are passively dispersed. The other group is
designated "go-places spores" (xenospores, meaning
"strangers"). Xenospores are widely dispersed in air or
water by various active launching devices. Memnospores,
are passively transmitted by air currents, by insects,
and other animals, including man. Often animal dispersal
is inadvertent. No matter what kind of spore is
involved, landing and establishment in a suitable environment must be highly subject to chance.

One means of passive dispersal is transport on surfaces to which spores adhere. Countless numbers of such
surfaces must have made contact with the Hawaiian Islands
since man first arrived, the number increasing proportionately with the population and its activity. Out of
curiosity about this kind of transport, a study was made
of the shoes of travelers arriving here by plane and
ship (Baker 1966). Bottom surfaces (soles) were swabbed
before these shoes had contact with Hawaiian soil or

surfaces. When the number of species recovered reached
65, including 3 Phycomycetes, 5 Ascomycetes, and 57 Fungi
Imperfecti, it appeared that the point had been proved.
One culture of *Candida albicans*, potentially pathogenic,
was recovered. All of the isolates were known species,
although some were new records for Hawaii at that time.

Considering the role of "go-places" spores in
Hawaii, good examples are found among the plant pathogens. *Phytophthora parasitica* is a soil-inhabiting
Phycomycete which attacked papaya and other plants.
Infection can be established by a single zoospore swimming in a drop of water. Hundreds of these are freely
produced on the mycelium, waiting for their opportunity.
In addition, *Phytophthora* produces "bide-awhile" resting
spores, ensuring longevity in the soil. A closely
related soil Phycomycete, *Pythium*, is implicated as a
biological factor associated with yield decline of
sugarcane in Hawaii. When Adair (1969) first began to
study this problem, he thought he was dealing with one
species. Then he found a second species, previously
unreported in Hawaii. It has interesting physiological
differences which are reflected in antagonism toward
other soil fungi in fields suffering from yield decline,
for it is parasitic on some of them.

Both memnospores and xenospores may find their way
into the air stream. The distance a xenospore can travel
correlates with its size. The probable flight range,
therefore, can be predicted in relation to size and
distance launched. It has been calculated that if a
medium-sized spore is launched 1 cm in air of normal
turbulence its probable flight range is 850 m, or more
than one-half mile (Gregory 1966). The number of spores
that travel long distances at great heights is probably
small compared with the number released into the air.
Spores have been found at high altitudes by exposing
culture plates from airplanes in trans-Atlantic and
polar flights. The first of such exposures was made by

Charles Lindbergh for the late F. C. Meier of the U. S.
Department of Agriculture (USDA). Only one such study
is known for the Pacific area. In 1947 an obliging pas-
senger flying over the Tasman Sea held coated slides out a
window for five minutes (Newman 1948). Collected on the
slide were pollen grains and spores of several cosmopolitan species of fungi.

Spores released into the air constitute a direct
source of infection in man and also function as fungus
allergens. The number of spores required to bring about
allergic symptoms in a sensitized person is unknown, but
it has been estimated that normal outdoor activity in
three hours might lead to an inhaled dose of 36,000
spores and could reach a level of 120,000 for *Cladosporium*, an imperfect fungus recognized as a worldwide
allergenic agent (Austwick 1966). In Hawaii there is a
high incidence of asthma but a low incidence of pollen
in the air (Myers 1956). Consequently, fungus spores
are suspected of being the allergenic agents. In a
six-months' study of the air spora in the bedrooms of
10 asthmatic patients living in upper Manoa Valley on
Oahu, many fungi were isolated (Oren and Baker 1970).
Alternaria, one of the most frequently cited allergens
on the mainland United States, was of low incidence, but
Cladosporium was dominant. The second-ranking dominant
was *Oidiodendron*, another imperfect fungus. This fungus
is unreported as an allergen in other parts of the world,
although recently a similar *Oidiodendron* species was
described as the etiologic agent of a respiratory infection in India.

If Hawaii supports a diversified mycota, as the
preceding remarks indicate, some of its members should
show relationship with mycota of other geographic regions.
Of 150 Hawaiian specimens examined by Burt (1923), 43 percent were cosmopolitan; 13 percent tropical American; 24.5
percent Philippine, East Asian, and East Indian; and 6 percent North American. According to Goos (unpublished data),

the fungi found in Hawaii appear to have more affinities
with those of Australasia and the East Indies than with
those of North America. For many fungi, the distribution
perhaps correlates with the distribution of a suitable
substratum. This would be particularly true for lignicolous (wood inhabiting) species, as evidenced by some
recent records for Hawaii: *Edmundmasonia* (Fungi Imperfecti), India and Manoa Valley, Oahu; and *Chaetotyphula
hyalina* (Basidiomycetes), Singapore area and Manoa
Valley, Oahu. One of the discomycetes, *Dasycypha citrino-
alba*, described by Cash (1938) occurred on a number of
wood hosts in Hawaii. It was first reported from Java.

The geographic distribution of fungi shows a
striking correlation with the geographic distribution of
mycologists (Ainsworth 1968). It is often as close as a
one-to-one relationship. This not only establishes the
presence of fungi in a given place but explains their
absence in others. It is not surprising to find that the
known distribution of a fungus is based on records from
Cambridge, England, Iowa City, Iowa, and New Delhi, India,
but nowhere in between. Obviously a fungus found at
such widely separated points must occur at intermediate
points. Either there is no one at other locations who
can recognize it, or it has been overlooked.

Three species of the genus *Zygosporium*, an imperfect
fungus, have now been recognized in Hawaii. Of these
Z. masonii was described by Hughes (1951) from the Gold
Coast, Africa, where he collected it on dead coconut
leaves. Next, in 1960, it was reported as an air isolate
over Recife, Brazil, by Batista and Lima, and in 1961
Whaley and Barnett isolated it as a laboratory contami-
nant in West Virginia. Steele (1967) listed three iso-
lations from coastal sands of Kauai, Oahu, and Maui.
It has subsequently been found again in Maui coastal sand
and in soil taken under coconut trees on Raiatea in the
Society Islands (Baker, unpublished data). The second
species, *Z. echinosporum*, has only one Pacific record,

based on a colony growing on a plate exposed for air
spora in Waipahu (Wang and Baker 1967). The recovery of
the third species correlates with the arrival of
Dr. Roger D. Goos in Hawaii. Recently he has found
Z. oscheoides on the petiole of a *Pandanus* leaf picked up
on the University of Hawaii campus.

The records for *Wiesneriomyces javanicus* (Fungi
Imperfecti) are well qualified as a further example of
the coincidence of fungi and mycologists. *W. javanicus*
was collected in Manoa Valley recently by Goos (unpublished data). It was first described from Java in 1907,
next reported from India in 1951, then isolated from
Panama soil in 1967, and now collected in Hawaii in 1968.
Based on the single record from Java, it could have been
argued that this fungus was endemic in Java, and it would
have been nearly 50 years before anyone could have
refuted the suggestion.

The recognition of microscopic fungi requires a
trained person. With an increase in the distribution
of mycologically trained investigators, one can expect
a corresponding increase in knowledge of fungi and their
distribution. This suggests that Hawaii is accruing more
knowledge about its fungi as it accrues more mycologists,
which is certainly true. The pursuit of fungus collecting in Hawaii has been historically sporadic. Most
studies, aside from those concerned with fungi causing
disease in economic plants, have been pursued by visiting
mycologists or others who have been here for relatively
short periods of time. According to Bessey (1943) the
first fungi were collected by A. A. Heller in 1895.
Among other specimens he collected were about two dozen
fungi. Between 1910 and 1920, Charles N. Forbes, a
botanist with the Bishop Museum, made collections of
higher fungi, a selection of which he sent to E. A. Burt,
mycologist at the Missouri Botanical Garden, for identification (Burt 1923). A more directed search for fungi
was made by F. L. Stevens (1925). Stevens was interested

primarily in parasitic fungi--rusts, smuts, and the group
of Ascomycetes called Pyrenomycetes. His report is
still the most important single work on the fungi of
Hawaii. C. L. Shear and N. E. Stevens, from the USDA,
came during the winter of 1927-1928 to study Ascomycetes
in Hawaii. They did not publish their findings, but
their specimens are available for study in the National
Fungus Collections, Beltsville, Maryland. Cash (1938)
studied one group, the discomycetes, from the Stevens and
Shear collections. She designated 5 species as new among
the 34 she described.

Although all major groups of fungi are represented
in Hawaii, certain fungi are poorly represented or conspicuously absent. Among those poorly represented are
the "stinkhorns" (Phallales, Basidiomycetes). These
fungi are dispersed by sarcophagous flies attracted to
the foetid, gloeoid spore masses. Only five species
have been found in Hawaii, four of which have been known
since the early 1900s (Cobb 1906, 1909), and one known
only since the summer of 1969 (Goos, unpublished data).
The fifth one, *Aseroe rubra*, has been collected several
times within the last five years and is now known from
Oahu, Maui, and Molokai. Goos (1970) has reviewed the
history of these five phalloids in Hawaii. Cobb's
interest stemmed from the association of phalloids with
sugarcane roots, on which he regarded these fungi as
parasitic. He carefully recorded the development of the
basidiocarp from the embryonic "egg" stage to maturity,
in illustrations which delineate a perfect growth curve.
He noted the marked ephemeral life of the mature fruit
body. The three species Cobb studied are closely
associated with cane roots. Cane is an introduced plant,
so that it is probable the fungus was introduced with
sugarcane. This suggestion gains credibility by virtue
of a story from Kew Gardens, England. There, a phalloid
fungus appeared in a greenhouse after the introduction
of some tropical plants from Australia.

Even more poorly represented in Hawaii are many of
the fleshy Basidiomycetes (gill fungi, clavarioid, and
poroid fungi). For example, two genera of gill fungi,
Russula and *Lactarius*, so conspicuous and common in
north central and north eastern North America, are
totally absent. The fleshy poroids or boletes are also
unknown. Clavarioid fungi are represented by two small
forms, one of which was collected by Goos as this discussion was being prepared.

If the fleshy fungi as a group are as short-lived as
the phalloids, it is not surprising that there is a
paucity of collections. In addition, their mode of spore
dispersal probably does not lend itself to far-ranging
dissemination.

Climatic differences in relatively close patterns
may account for some distribution patterns (Mäkinen 1969)
In studying the smuts (Basidiomycetes) parasitic on
vascular plants of Hawaii, Mäkinen found the group
relatively limited here. Smuts in Hawaii occur on both
native and introduced plants. Mäkinen was able to discuss 4 native and 11 introduced species by studying
specimens in the herbaria of the Bishop Museum and the
USDA plant quarantine station at Honolulu International
Airport, by surveying vascular plants in the Bishop
Museum herbarium for the presence of smuts, and finally
by his own field collections. He pointed out that fungi
may have macroecological requirements which differ
sufficiently from the host requirements to limit the
fungi but not the host. Because temperature decreases
with elevation the fungus may be affected before the host
is, as Mäkinen noted for some smuts.

The consideration of fungi as plant pathogens is
beyond the scope of this discussion except for one
important aspect: the host-parasite relationship and its
role in endemism. Although Burt (1923) and Stevens
(1925) equated endemism with new species, this concept
is seriously open to question, especially as subsequent

distribution records for species removes many from this
possibility. Endemism is not common among the fungi
(Park 1968), but it does occur. Where it is known, it
usually involves a host-parasite relationship, the fungus
migrating with the host. The limitation of fungus
distribution, then, is that of the host, as illustrated
by the Ascomycete *Cyttaria* associated with southern beech
(*Nothofagus*) (Pirozynski 1968).

If endemism is to be found among fungi in Hawaii,
it is most likely to be represented by species limited to
endemic hosts and their distribution. This relationship
is likely to be highly evolved, with the degree of
parasitism at a minimal level of damage to the host, for
otherwise a virulent parasite would probably eliminate
the host. Stevens (1925) noted 35 epiphyllous, parasitic
Ascomycetes on indigenous Hawaiian plants. Twenty-five
species were on endemic hosts; so Stevens considered
these endemic fungi. The validity of their endemism
rests on their being restricted to Hawaii on these hosts.
This has not yet been established. Stevens' work,
though, offers the best evidence to date for endemic fungi
in Hawaii. What is needed to clarify this question of
endemism in fungi is more study of fungi associated with
the endemic flora, and also more extensive search for
the kinds of fungi said to be endemic.

From the trend of recent data on fungi in Hawaii, it
would appear that there is as yet no compelling evidence
which justifies the use of the designation "Hawaiian
fungi," *sensu strictu*. There is ample evidence that many
fungi of all kinds are here carrying on in their own
illimitable, versatile style in all our ecological habitats. To paraphrase an English mycologist (Bisby 1953),
"the fungi are a vast and confusing assemblage . . .. They
are a challenge to an army of students." In Hawaii the
work is just begun and the army remains to be recruited.
There is need for speedy recruitment (Hubbell 1968) if
the evidence is to be found before the native flora,
fauna, mycota, and unique ecosystems succumb to progress.

LITERATURE CITED

Adair, C. N.   1969.   The relation of *Pythium* species to the growth of a sugarcane variety in Hawaii. Ph.D. dissertation, University of Hawaii, Honolulu. 118 p.

Ainsworth, G. C.   1961.   Ainsworth and Bisby's dictionary of the fungi. 5th ed.   Commonwealth Mycological Institute, Kew, Surrey.   547 p.

————   1968.   The number of fungi.   *In* G. C. Ainsworth and A. S. Sussman, eds.   The fungi.   Vol. 3, p. 505-514.   Academic Press, New York and London.

Ajello, L.   1958.   Occurrence of *Cryptococcus neoformans* in soils.   Amer. J. Hyg. 67:72-77.

Alexander, M.   1961.   Introduction to soil microbiology. John Wiley and Sons, New York and London.   472 p.

Anastasiou, C. J.   1964.   Some aquatic Fungi Imperfecti from Hawaii.   Pacif. Sci. 18:202-206.

Austwick, P. K. C.   1966.   The role of spores in the allergies and mycoses of man and animals.   *In* M. F. Madelin, ed.   The fungus spore.   Colston Pap. no. 18, p. 331-337.   Butterworth and Co., London.

Baker, G. E.   1964.   Fungi in Hawaii.   Hawaiian Bot. Soc. Newsletter 3:23-28.

————   1966.   Inadvertent distribution of fungi.   Canad. J. Bot. 12:109-112.

————   1968.   Fungi from the central Pacific region. Mycologia 60:196-201.

Batista, A. C., and J. A. Lima.   1960.   Un grupo de Fungos da atmostera do Recife.   Instituto de Micologia, Universidade do Recife, Publication no. 297, p. 1-24.

Bessey, E. A.   1943.   Notes on Hawaiian fungi.   Pap. Mich. Acad. Sci. 28:3-8.

Bisby, G. R.   1953.   An introduction to the taxonomy and nomenclature of fungi.   2nd ed.   The Commonwealth Mycological Institute, Kew, Surrey.   143 p.

Blunt, F. L., and G. E. Baker.   1968.   Antimycotic activity of fungi isolated from Hawaiian soils. Mycologia 60:559-570.

Burt, E. A.   1923.   Higher fungi of the Hawaiian Islands. Ann. Mo. Bot. Gdn. 10:179-189.

Cash, E. K. 1938. New records of Hawaiian discomycetes.
    Mycologia 30:97-107.

Cobb, N. A. 1906. Fungus maladies of the sugar cane.
    Hawaiian Sugar Planters' Association Experiment
    Station Report, Bull. no. 5, p. 1-254.

_____ 1909. Fungus maladies of the sugar cane.
    Hawaiian Sugar Planters' Association Experiment
    Station Report, Bull. no. 6, p. 1-110.

Cooke, W. B., and P. W. Kabler. 1953. The survival of
    Histoplasma capsulatum in water. Lloydia 16:252-
    256.

Diehl, W. W. 1937. A basis for mycogeography. J. Wash.
    Acad. Sci. 27:244-247.

Dilcher, D. 1963. Eocene epiphyllous fungi. Science
    42:667-669.

Emmons, C. W., C. H. Binford, and J. P. Utz. 1970.
    Medical mycology. 2nd ed. Lea and Febiger,
    Philadelphia. 508 p.

Evans, R. N., and D. C. Prusso. 1969. Spore dispersal
    by birds. Mycologia 61:832-835.

Farrow, W. M. 1954. Tropical soil fungi. Mycologia
    46:632-646.

Goos, R. D. 1960. Soil fungi from Costa Rica and
    Panama. Mycologia 52:877-883.

_____ 1962. The occurrence of *Sphaerostilbe repens*
    in Central American soils. Amer. J. Bot. 49:19-23.

_____ 1970. Phalloid fungi in Hawaii. Pacif. Sci.
    24:282-287.

Gregory, P. H. 1966. The fungus spore: what it is and
    what it does. *In* M. F. Madelin, ed. The fungus
    spore. Colston Pap. no. 18, p. 1-14. Butterworth
    and Co., London.

Hillebrand, W. 1888. Flora of the Hawaiian Islands.
    Carl Winter, Heidelberg. 673 p.

Hubbell, T. H. 1968. The biology of islands. Proc.
    Nat. Acad. Sci. 60:22-32.

Hughes, S. J. 1951. Studies on micro-fungi. X.
    Zygosporium. Mycol. Pap. no. 44, p. 1-18.

Kishimoto, R. A., and G. E. Baker. 1969. Pathogenic
    and potentially pathogenic fungi isolated from

beach sands and selected soils of Oahu, Hawaii.
Mycologia 61:537-548.

Kohlmeyer, J. 1969a. Ecological notes on fungi in mangrove forests. Trans. Brit. Mycol. Soc. 53:237-250.

_____ 1969b. Marine fungi of Hawaii including the
new genus *Heliascus*. Canad. J. Bot. 47:1469-1487.

Mäkinen, Y. 1969. Ustilaginales of Hawaii. Pacif. Sci.
23:344-349.

Marsh, D. H. 1966. Microorganisms of the phyllosphere,
with particular reference to fungi occurring on
the dominant plants of the biogeoclimatic zones of
the Hawaiian Islands. Master's thesis, University of
of Hawaii, Honolulu. 52 p.

Myers, W. A. 1956. Air-borne molds in Honolulu. J.
Allergy 27:531-535.

Newman, I. V. 1948. Aerobiology on commercial air
routes. Nature 161:275-276.

Nilsson, S. 1964. Freshwater Hyphomycetes. Symb. Bot.
Upsaliens. 18:1-130.

Oren, J., and G. E. Baker. 1970. Molds in Manoa: a
study of prevalent fungi in Hawaiian homes. Ann.
Allergy 28:472-481.

Park, D. 1968. The ecology of terrestrial fungi. *In*
G. C. Ainsworth and A. S. Sussman, eds. The fungi.
Vol. 3, p. 5-39. Academic Press, New York and
London.

Parris, G. K. 1940. A check list of fungi, bacteria,
nematodes and viruses occurring in Hawaii and their
hosts. Plant Dis. Reptr. Suppl. no. 121, p. 1-91.

Pirozynski, K. A. 1968. Geographical distribution of
fungi. *In* G. C. Ainsworth and A. S. Sussman, eds.
The fungi. Vol. 3, p. 487-504. Academic Press,
New York and London.

Preece, T. F., and C. H. Dickinson. 1971. Ecology of
leaf surface micro-organisms. Academic Press,
New York and London. 640 p.

Roth, F. J., Jr., P. A. Orpurt, and D. G. Ahearn. 1964.
Occurrence and distribution of fungi in a subtropical marine environment. Canad. J. Bot. 42:
375-383.

Ruinen, J. 1961. The phyllosphere. I. An ecologically
neglected milieu. Plant and Soil 15:81-109.

_____ 1963. II. Yeasts from the phyllosphere of tropical foliage. Antonie van Leeuwenhoek, J. Microbiol. Serol. 29:425-438.

Sparrow, F. K. 1965. The occurrence of *Physoderma* in Hawaii, with notes on other Hawaiian Phycomycetes. Mycopath. Mycol. Appl. 25:119-143.

Steele, C. W. 1967. Fungus populations in marine waters and coastal sands of the Hawaiian, Line, and Phoenix islands. Pacif. Sci. 21:317-331.

Stevens, F. L. 1925. Hawaiian fungi. Bernice P. Bishop Mus. Bull. no. 19, p. 1-189.

Stone, B. C. 1967. A review of endemic genera of Hawaiian plants. Bot. Rev. 33:216-259.

Walsh, G. E. 1967. An ecological study of a Hawaiian mangrove swamp. *In* G. H. Lauff, ed. Estuaries. American Association for the Advancement of Science, Publication no. 83, p. 420-431.

Wang, C. J. K., and G. E. Baker, 1967. *Zygosporium masonii* and *Z. echinosporum* from Hawaii. Canad. J. Bot. 45:1945-1952.

Whaley, J. W., and H. L. Barnett. 1961. Rare or unusual fungi from West Virginia. I. *Zygosporium masonii*. Proc. W. Va. Acad. Sci. 33:1-4.

The Present Status of the Birds of Hawaii[1]

ANDREW J. BERGER[2]

THE GREAT EXPANSES of open ocean that separate the Hawaiian Islands from the major continental land masses of North America and Asia resulted in the evolution of a number of unique landbirds. Unfortunately, a higher percentage of species of birds have become extinct in Hawaii than in any other region of the world. Approximately 40 percent of the endemic Hawaiian birds are believed to be extinct, and 25 of the 60 birds in the 1968 list of "Rare and Endangered Birds of the United States" are Hawaiian ("Rare and Endangered Fish and Wildlife of the United States, 1968 edition," Bureau of Sport Fisheries and Wildlife, Washington, D. C.). Most of the native birds of Oahu have long been extinct, and few native landbirds are to be found on any of the main islands below 3,000 feet elevation.

Three general groups of birds are found in Hawaii today: endemic, indigenous, and introduced.

ENDEMIC HAWAIIAN BIRDS

Ten families of birds are recognized as having endemic genera, species, or subspecies in Hawaii (although taxonomic dispute still exists regarding the relationship of some Hawaiian forms to closely related North American forms); in addition, one entire family of birds (Drepanididae) is endemic to the Hawaiian chain of islands (Amadon, 1942; Mayr, 1943). An "endemic" form is one that occurs in one region only and is not found in any other part of the world. Ornithologists believe that the ancestors of these birds reached Hawaii from the areas indicated in Figure 1. The endemic Hawaiian birds, listed according to these 11 families, are discussed briefly.

1. Anatidae (ducks, geese, and swans)

The NENE or HAWAIIAN GOOSE (Branta sandvicensis) is endemic to the island of Ha-

waii, and in 1962 birds were first released in the Paliku Cabin area of Haleakala Crater on Maui. There is still debate as to whether or not the Nene originally inhabited Maui.

The Nene was on the verge of extinction in the 1940s, and the species is still included in the list of endangered species. In 1949 a Nene Restoration Program was begun by using a pair of captive birds obtained from Herbert Shipman of Hawaii. This has been a very successful program, and Nene have been raised in captivity both at the Severn Wildfowl Trust at Slimbridge, England, and at the State of Hawaii Fish and Game rearing station at Pohakuloa on the Saddle Road of Hawaii (Elder, 1958).

The program at Pohakuloa has been increasingly effective throughout the years, primarily through the dedicated efforts of Mr. Ah Fat Lee. Over 500 Nene have been raised at Pohakuloa during the period of 1949 through 1968. Most of these pen-reared birds have been released at several known habitats of wild Nene on the slopes of Mauna Loa; a smaller number have been released in Haleakala Crater.

The Nene is a highly specialized goose, adapted for living in a rugged habitat of lava flows far from any standing or running water (Miller, 1937). Among the more noticeable anatomical specializations for this terrestrial life is a reduction in the webbing between the toes. The birds spend much of the time on sparsely vegetated lava flows on Mauna Loa and Hualalai, at elevations between approximately 5,000 and 8,000 feet. Here the birds often build their nests on the lava although typically well concealed in clumps of vegetation. The nests are lined with the birds' own down feathers; the clutch consists of from 2 to 5 eggs.

The KOLOA or HAWAIIAN DUCK (Anas wyvilliana) originally was found on all of the main Hawaiian Islands except Lanai and Ka-

[1] Manuscript received June 13, 1969.
[2] Department of Zoology, University of Hawaii, Honolulu. Supported by NSF Grant GB-5612.

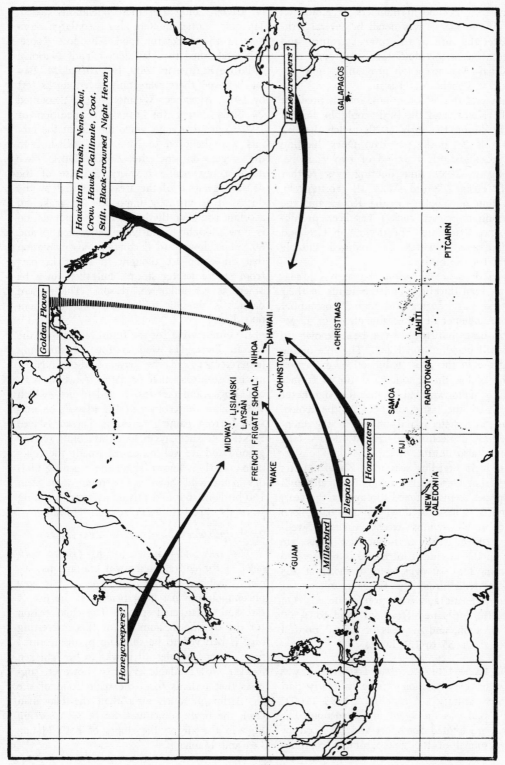

Fig. 1. Map of the Pacific Basin to show regions from which the ancestors of endemic Hawaiian birds are presumed to have originated. The broken arrow indicates the annual migratory flights of the Pacific Golden Plover between Alaska and the Hawaiian Islands.

hoolawe. A decline in numbers of Koloa on most of the islands was noted by several writers after the turn of the present century, and in recent years this duck has been found only on Kauai. A propagation program is now underway at Pohakuloa, Hawaii.

Man probably was the most serious predator on the Koloa, and the birds could be hunted legally during the early 1920s, when the bag limit was 25 ducks per day. Duck hunting was prohibited for a period of two years beginning in 1939, and hunting was further closed during World War II. Fortunately, duck hunting (both for the Koloa and the wintering migratory ducks) has been prohibited since that time. The decline in taro and rice acreages, however, has reduced suitable habitat for the birds.

Wild dogs are known to be serious predators on both ducklings and the adults in their flightless stage during the annual postnuptial molt. A number of other animals (e.g., largemouth bass, bullfrog) have been known to kill small ducklings on Kauai. The role of the mongoose in the great reduction or extinction of the Koloa throughout most of its former range is unknown, but it may be significant that Kauai, the last stronghold of the Koloa, is the only main island on which the mongoose has not been introduced. Wild cats, rats, and pigs also destroy nests.

The main breeding season on Kauai appears to be from December through May, although the species seems to breed throughout the year, inasmuch as nests or downy young have been found in all months except August (Swedberg, 1967). The well-concealed nests are built on the ground. Clutch size is reported to be from 2 to 10 eggs, with a mean of 8.3 eggs for wild birds. The Koloa is tolerant of varying climatic and ecological conditions. On Kauai the birds nest from sea level to 3,500 feet elevation, and in areas of annual rainfall varying from 35 to 125 inches.

The LAYSAN DUCK (*Anas laysanensis*) was in danger of extinction during the early part of this century (Rothschild, 1893–1900). Again man was the agent of destruction. The birds were hunted for sport and for food by the personnel of the guano mining company on Laysan, and, after these operations ceased, Japanese feather hunters also used large numbers of the ducks for food. Theodore Roosevelt established the Hawaiian Islands National Wildlife Refuge in 1909, but Alfred M. Bailey believed there were only seven ducks left by 1912. Alexander Wetmore (1925) counted 20 birds during the Tanager Expedition of 1923. Since that time, when the last of the rabbits were believed to have been killed, both the vegetation and the Laysan Duck have made a remarkable recovery. Because of the dense vegetation of the areas inhabited by the ducks, it is virtually impossible to make an accurate count of the birds, but the population is now thought to fluctuate between 100 and 600. The downward fluctuations in population that do occur are thought to result in part from severe winter storms, but there may be other, as yet unknown, reasons. The present habitat is thought to be adequate for about 600 ducks.

It is imperative for the future welfare of the Laysan Duck (as well as for the surviving honeycreeper and the tens of thousands of nesting seabirds) that predators (such as rats, cats, dogs) and pest insects and plants (which would alter the ecology of the island) be prevented from gaining access to Laysan Island.

Nests of the Laysan Duck are built on the ground and are well concealed among the vegetation. Little is known about the breeding biology in the wild, however. There are more than 150 birds in zoos and private aviaries; breeding pairs also are held at Pohakuloa, Hawaii.

2. Accipitridae (*hawks, kites, and eagles*):

The HAWAIIAN HAWK or IO (*Buteo solitarius*), for entirely unknown reasons, has always inhabited Hawaii only. The bird is now uncommon and has been placed on the list of rare and endangered species. The chief reason for the decline in numbers of this interesting bird is believed to be shooting by uninformed people who consider all hawks to be "chicken hawks." All available evidence, however, suggests that rodents form the main food of the Io. Although much rarer than the Hawaiian Owl, the hawk sometimes can be seen soaring high in the air on the slopes of both Mauna Loa and Mauna Kea.

Few nests of this species have been found and very little is known of its breeding habits. The birds build nests of twigs and sticks in trees, and one author has described a lining made of the stems and fronds of ferns. Two or three eggs are thought to form a clutch.

3. Rallidae (rails, gallinules, and coots):

The LAYSAN RAIL (*Porzanula palmeri*) had a historical life of 116 years. The species was discovered on Laysan Island in 1828, and it probably became extinct in 1944.

The devastation wrought by the rabbits released on Laysan Island in 1903 is well depicted by Alexander Wetmore (1925) after he visited Laysan in 1923 as a member of the Tanager Expedition: "On every hand extended a barren waste of sand. Two coconut palms, a stunted hau tree and an ironwood or two, planted by former inhabitants, were the only bits of green that greeted the eye. Other vegetation had vanished. The desolateness of the scene was so depressing that unconsciously we talked in undertones. From all appearances, Laysan might have been some desert, with the gleaming lake below merely a mirage."

It was estimated that there were about 2,000 rails on Laysan as late as 1915, but Wetmore and his party found only two birds, and the species is thought to have been extirpated there before 1936.

A pair of Laysan Rails was introduced to Midway Island in 1891. A large population had built up by the turn of the century and still existed in 1939. The extermination of the Laysan Rail on Midway, however, was very rapid after the onset of World War II when the U.S. Navy took over, and rats gained access to both Sand and Eastern islands. The last rails were seen on Eastern Island in June of 1944.

The Laysan Rail could easily have been saved from extinction if Government officials had heeded the pleas of ornithologists, but they were unable to obtain the necessary transportation to restock Laysan Island (or other islands) from the Midway population after the vegetation began to recover on Laysan. Although small and flightless, the Laysan Rail was a hardy bird, easily reared in captivity.

Several birds survived the long sea voyage to England in the 1890s.

Like many rails on oceanic islands, the Laysan Rail had evolved into a flightless condition. The birds ate many kinds of insects, the flesh from the carcasses of other birds, and the eggs of the smaller seabirds, such as terns and petrels. Although the rails apparently sometimes broke open the eggs, they are said usually to have waited until Laysan Finches (*Psittirostra cantans*) broke through the shells with their more powerful bills and then chased the finches away to eat the egg contents.

The breeding season apparently extended from late March through July on Laysan, but downy young were seen on Midway in March. The nests were built on the ground or in grass tussocks and were constructed of dried stems and leaves of juncus and other plants. Unlike Mainland rails, which lay large clutches of eggs, the Laysan Rail laid 2 to 4 eggs in a clutch (Baldwin, 1947).

The HAWAIIAN RAIL (*Pennula sandwichensis*) was last collected on the island of Hawaii (near Olaa) about 1864, and was last seen about 1884 (Greenway, 1958, p. 235). Munro (1944, p. 51) believed that this rail "frequented most of the larger islands" and that "it certainly was on Molokai," although there is no good evidence for this belief. The nest, eggs, and newly hatched young were never described.

The causes of extinction of this small (about 5½ inches in total length), flightless rail are unknown, but it seems certain that rats, dogs, and cats played a large role in the extermination of this unique species. Hawaiian chiefs are said to have hunted the rail with bows and arrows.

The GALLINULE (*Gallinula chloropus sandvicensis*) is considered conspecific with the Common Gallinule of North America and Eurasia, although the Hawaiian birds are nonmigratory and have been inhabitants for an unknown length of time. Their distinctness is indicated by their subspecific name. These are birds of fresh-water ponds and marshes, and, because of the continuing disappearance of such habitats in Hawaii, the birds are considered endangered on all islands they still inhabit. They formerly inhabited all of the main islands except Niihau and Lanai. Attempts to reestablish the birds on Hawaii and Maui appear to have been unsuccessful. Essential habitat is being destroyed to make way for housing developments, and mongooses, rats, dogs, and cats are serious predators on the birds. The prospects for survival of this species are considered by personnel of the Bureau of Sport Fisheries and Wildlife as "not good."

The gallinule builds its nest of reeds and other aquatic vegetation. Like its continental relatives, the bird is thought to lay large clutches of eggs (6 to 13). The newly hatched young have red bills and are covered with black down feathers; they are precocial and are able to run about and swim within a few hours after hatching.

The HAWAIIAN COOT (*Fulica americana alai*) also is considered conspecific with the North American members of this widely distributed species. Like the gallinule, however, the Hawaiian birds are nonmigratory and have been inhabitants of the Hawaiian Islands for a long period of time. They are given subspecific designation.

Coots occupy the same general type of freshwater ponds as gallinules, but they prefer more open water. The coot is found on all the main islands, and is especially common on Kauai and at Kanaha Pond on Maui. Munro (1944, p. 54) reported seeing "from 500 to 600 on a lagoon near Lihue, Kauai," in 1891, but nowhere are they so abundant now. One or more birds sometimes can be observed on the reservoir along the Old Pali Road in Nuuanu Valley, Oahu. Coots were on the game bird list until 1939. They are now classified as an endangered species, with an estimated total population of 1,500 birds.

Coots typically build relatively large floating nests of aquatic vegetation. Little is known of the clutch size of the Hawaiian Coot, but it presumably lays fewer than the 8 to 12 eggs of the Mainland birds. The newly hatched chicks are covered with black down except on the head, neck, and throat where the down is reddish-orange. The down is short or absent on the forehead and crown of the head, giving the bird a bald-headed appearance. Like gal-

linule chicks, the young are able to move about shortly after hatching, when the down has dried.

4. Recurvirostridae (avocets and stilts)

The BLACK-NECKED or HAWAIIAN STILT (*Himantopus himantopus knudseni*) is a large (16 inches), striking, black-and-white bird with very long reddish legs. This species is endemic to the islands of Niihau, Kauai, Oahu, Molokai, Maui, and Hawaii, but is now greatly reduced in numbers in most of its former range.

The stilt was considered a game bird until 1941, and still is sometimes shot illegally. The birds also are subject to predation by the mongoose and by feral dogs and cats. A major reason for the decline of this species, however, has been the continual draining of marshes and other wetland areas.

It is estimated that the total population of the stilt now numbers about 1,500 birds, which are found chiefly on Oahu and Maui. One of the major nesting and feeding habitats is at Kanaha Pond on Maui. This marsh area is in constant danger of being filled in because of pressures to enlarge the runways at the Kahului Airport. Another important breeding area is found among the ponds on the Kaneohe Marine Air Station on Oahu; efforts have been made with military personnel to have some of these ponds set aside as a sanctuary for the stilt.

The nest of the stilt is a simple "scrape" made on the ground by the birds themselves; small stones, bits of wood, and other debris often are added to the scrape. The normal clutch is 4 eggs. The newly hatched, precocial young are covered with a coat of variegated brownish down, which makes them very difficult to find after they leave the nest. The young are brooded for some time after hatching, but they run from the nest and hide in the surrounding vegetation when disturbed.

5. Stridgidae (owls)

The PUEO or SHORT-EARED OWL (*Asio flammeus sandwichensis*) differs from most species of continental owls in that it is diurnal in habits. It is found in open grassland (such as along the western part of the Saddle Road of Hawaii), over lava flows, and in forested areas (both ohia and mamane-naio forests), and often it is seen near towns. This species appears to be tolerant of wide climatic extremes—from relatively dry areas (about 20 inches of annual rainfall) to the extremely wet Kokee area of Kauai. The Pueo is resident on all of the main islands of the chain, and it was prominent in Hawaiian mythology.

The Pueo builds its nest on the ground. The females are said to lay from 3 to 6 eggs in a clutch.

6. Corvidae (crows, jays, and magpies)

The HAWAIIAN CROW (*Corvus tropicus*) is endemic to the island of Hawaii only, being found in the Kona and Kau districts. The bird is now rare, and it is estimated that the total population may be no more than 30 birds. In former times, they were much more common and were found at elevations from 1,000 to 8,000 feet. Shooting is probably responsible for the decline of this sole representative of the crow family to have reached the Hawaiian Islands. The effect of the great alteration of the environment on the decline of the species is unknown.

Very little is known about the feeding habits or breeding biology of the Hawaiian Crow. The birds build nests of twigs and sticks, lined with finer plant materials. The eggs have been described as having a greenish background with brown markings around the larger end of the egg. In April 1964, Dr. P. Quentin Tomich (1967) found a nest containing five eggs in an ohia tree.

7. Turdidae (thrush family)

The SMALL KAUAI THRUSH (*Phaeornis palmeri*) is now known to inhabit only the ohia forests in the Alakai Swamp region of Kauai. The size of the remaining population is unknown, but, because of its restricted distribution, this species is thought to be rare and it is included in the list of rare and endangered species, as are most of the endemic Hawaiian birds. Both this thrush and the Hawaiian Thrush (*P. obscurus*) appear to tolerate very little change in environment. Hence the further spread of exotic plants into the depths of the Alakai Swamp must be prevented if the

native birds are to be expected to survive; population levels of goats and pigs also must be controlled.

Nothing is known about the breeding habits of this thrush.

The HAWAIIAN THRUSH (*Phaeornis obscurus*) developed races on all of the main islands except Maui. The races found on Oahu and Lanai are presumed to be extinct; reports of survival of the Molokai race need to be confirmed (Richardson, 1949).

The Kauai race, or the Large Kauai Thrush (*P. o. myadestina*) appears to be even rarer than the Small Kauai Thrush, whereas the Large Kauai Thrush was said by early writers to be the most common forest bird on Kauai in 1891.

The Hawaii race (*P. o. obscurus*) still is fairly common in suitable habitat (Berger, 1969a). The birds inhabit the ohia forests in regions of high annual rainfall, in general above 3,000 feet elevation. The best areas are on the Saddle Road, Stainback Highway, and in the more undisturbed, wet forests of Hawaiian Volcanoes National Park, but this thrush also is found in ohia forests at higher elevations on the Kona coast.

A nest of this species and genus was first found near the Saddle Road on May 11, 1968, by Andrew J. Berger (1969). The nest, built on the trunk of a tree fern less than 5 feet above the ground, contained a single egg which was heavily covered by small, irregularly shaped, reddish-brown markings.

8. Sylviidae (Old World warbler family)

The LAYSAN MILLERBIRD (*Acrocephalus familiaris familiaris*) was one of three species of endemic birds to become extinct on Laysan prior to 1923 because of the destruction of the habitat by the rabbits. How the ancestors of this small bird (about 5½ inches in total length) managed to reach Laysan and Nihoa is, of course, unknown. Because of their Old World affinities, however, it is assumed that they came from Asia and "island-hopped" to reach Laysan and Nihoa islands.

The NIHOA MILLERBIRD (*Acrocephalus familiaris kingi*) has one of the most limited distributions of any bird species: Nihoa con-

tains 156 acres. Personnel of the Bureau of
Sport Fisheries and Wildlife estimated a total
population between 500 and 600 in 1967. The
species is endangered because of its limited
distribution, and it is imperative that rats, cats,
and dogs be prevented from gaining access to
Nihoa and the other islands in the Hawaiian
Islands National Wildlife Refuge.

The birds are secretive in habits, usually
staying in the dense cover afforded by *Chenopodium sandwicheum* (goosefoot) and *Sida
fallax* (ilima). Several nests have been found
in this vegetation, but little else is known about
either the breeding biology or the feeding
habits of the Nihoa Millerbird.

9. *Muscicapidae* (*Old World flycatcher family*)

The ELEPAIO (*Chasiempis sandwichensis*),
important in Hawaiian folklore, has a puzzling
distribution in that races have developed on
Kauai, Oahu, and Hawaii, but there is no evidence that the species was ever found on the
other main islands in the chain (Wilson and
Evans, 1890–1899).

Although not as common as reported during
the early 1900s, the Elepaio has been able to
adapt to man-made changes in the environment as no other endemic landbird has been
able to do. The Oahu race (*C. s. gayi*) is still
fairly common in the mixed forests of the
island, and a small population is resident in
the lowland introduced forest near the head
of Manoa Valley.

The Kauai race (*C. s. sclateri*) is common
in the Kokee State Park area as well as in the
Alakai Swamp. The Hawaii race (*C. s. sandwichensis*) is found both in the wet ohia forests and in the dry mamane-naio forest on
Mauna Kea.

Frings (1968) found that the Oahu Elepaio
defended a territory of 4.9 acres. The nest site
is selected by the female, but both sexes take
part in nest-building activities. The average
height above ground of 32 nests was 25 feet.
The small cup-shaped nests are very neat and
compact, and contain large quantities of spider web, which aids in holding the plant
materials together. The eggs have a white
background covered with reddish-brown spots,
which are concentrated at the larger end of
the egg. The clutch size was 2 eggs in 15 nests

and 3 eggs in one nest. The incubation period
is 14 days, and the nestling period, 16 days.
Frings found the breeding season in Manoa
Valley to extend from mid-January to mid-
June. The season differs on the other islands
for as yet unanalyzed reasons.

10. *Meliphagidae* (*honeyeater family*)

This is a large Old World family, containing 160 species of birds. Two genera and five
species were found in Hawaii, but all except
one species are now thought to be extinct.

The four species of the genus *Moho* had
patches of bright yellow feathers, prized by
the early Hawaiians who used them for their
feather capes and headdresses. The role that
the Hawaiians played in causing the extinction
of the several species of the Oo is unknown,
but it may be significant that the sole known
surviving species (on Kauai) has fewer yellow
feathers than any of the other species. The
evidence also suggests that the Oos, like most
of the other endemic Hawaiian landbirds, are
intolerant to any extensive changes in their
environment. Also unknown is the role played
by the three species of rats in the islands as
predators on the eggs and young of tree-nest-
ing birds; some species of rats are agile climb-
ers and have been seen in tall trees and in
tree ferns in the ohia forests.

The KAUAI OO (*Moho braccatus*), formerly
thought to be extinct, was rediscovered by
Dr. Frank Richardson in 1960 in the depths
of the Alakai Swamp region (Richardson and
Bowles, 1964). The bird is very rare and
nothing is known of its breeding habits.

The OAHU OO (*Moho apicalis*) is thought to
have become extinct within a short period after
1837 (Greenway, 1958, p. 423).

The MOLOKAI OO (*Moho bishopi*) was last
reported in 1904 and is now presumed to be
extinct.

The HAWAII OO (*Moho nobilis*) has not
been reliably reported since 1934 and is listed
as "probably extinct." It is certain that the
birds no longer inhabit the forests where they
were collected in the 1890s, but there are vast
forest areas on Hawaii which have not been
visited by ornithologists, and this species may

still exist in remote and relatively undisturbed areas.

The KIOEA (*Chaetoptila angustipluma*) was a large bird, about 13 inches in total length. Its color pattern was unlike that of any other Hawaiian bird: a black face mask, greenish-brown wings and tail, and a heavily streaked pattern of brown and white feathers on the head, upper back, and underparts. The type specimen was collected by the Pickering and Peale expedition in 1840 on the island of Hawaii, the only known range of the species. According to Munro (1944, p. 88) several additional specimens were collected by Mills about 1859. The species apparently has not been seen since that time.

11. Drepanididae (Hawaiian honeycreepers)

This endemic Hawaiian family exhibits among its numerous species the most striking example of adaptive radiation from an assumed single ancestral species of any bird family in the world. It demonstrates admirably, therefore, the results of evolutionary processes on oceanic islands. That this family of birds has not been studied more intensively in the past can be attributed, in part, to the fact that Charles Darwin visited the Galapagos Islands and not the Hawaiian Islands.

The members of this family reached all of the main Hawaiian Islands, and two species were found on certain of the Leeward Islands in historic times. The tragic remnant population of three individuals of the Laysan Honeycreeper (also incorrectly called the Laysan "Honeyeater"), a race of the Apapane, became extinct in 1923. The finch-billed Laysan Finch and Nihoa Finch still inhabit those respective islands.

It might be noted here that the name "finch" was given to these birds by taxonomists in the 1890s, because they thought that these large-billed birds (as well as some on the main islands) belonged to the finch family (Fringillidae). This interpretation was based almost exclusively on the superficial resemblance in bill shape and size. Later students of Hawaiian birds (particularly Perkins, 1901), concluded that a large number of the endemic Hawaiian birds had evolved from a single ancestral species; all of these were included in the family

Drepanididae (formerly, also, Drepaniidae). No suitable evidence has been found since that time to refute this interpretation, although the possibility exists that we are not dealing, in fact, with a true monophyletic family. Nevertheless, I choose to follow the classification of the Hawaiian Honeycreepers proposed by Amadon (1950). There is a more recent system of classification (Greenway, 1968), but that author had no more information on anatomy or breeding biology than was available to Amadon.

Unfortunately, all of the highly specialized honeycreepers have become extinct on Oahu, Molokai, and Lanai, as have most of those on Hawaii. Kauai, the only island on which the mongoose was not introduced, is the only island which still has all of the endemic birds known to have occurred there. Most of these are confined to the Alakai Swamp region, and many are now rare. The east and northeast slopes of Haleakala also have proven a haven for the survival of unique Hawaiian birds.

One should note that the largest number of species of honeycreepers are now found in two relatively undisturbed wilderness areas: the Alakai Swamp of Kauai and the outer, windward slope of Haleakala. These are areas which have not been much disturbed by wild cattle, nor have they been desecrated by State foresters and ranchers.

Despite the remarkable bill adaptations found in the Hawaiian Honeycreepers, very little is known about this family of unique birds. The nests, eggs, and newly hatched young were never described for any of the extinct species (except for the Laysan Honeycreeper). A nest with eggs of the Palila was found for the first time by Andrew J. Berger in 1968 (Berger, 1969*b*); the first nests of the Akepa and the Creeper to be found were reported by C. Robert Eddinger in 1969. The incubation periods for this family also were first determined by Eddinger in 1969.

A. Subfamily Psittirostrinae

AMAKIHI (*Loxops virens*): This, the second most common living honeycreeper, is found on all of the main islands. The four subspecies are distributed as follows: *L. v. stejnegeri*, Kauai; *L. v. chloris*, Oahu; *L. v. wilsoni*, Maui,

Molokai, and Lanai; *L. v. virens,* Hawaii. The Amakihi is a characteristic bird of the wet ohia forests on the windward slopes of the islands, but it is also a common permanent resident of the dry mamane-naio forest on Mauna Kea. This broad climatic distribution suggests that the Amakihi may be the most adaptable of the surviving species of honeycreepers.

ANIANIAU (*Loxops parva*): This species is endemic to Kauai, and now is limited in distribution to the Kokee and Alakai Swamp regions of the island, where the bird is fairly common. The nest and eggs of this species were first described in 1969 (Berger, Eddinger, and Frings, 1969).

GREATER AMAKIHI (*Loxops sagittirostris*): This bird, which has been called also (inappropriately) the Green Solitaire, had a very short known history. The species was first collected near the Wailuku River on Hawaii in 1892. It was rediscovered by Perkins in 1895, but has not been observed since early in the present century. The early collecting sites probably were near the upper limits of the present sugar cane fields. However, there are extensive cloud forests along the Hamakua Coast of Hawaii where this species might still survive.

CREEPER (*Loxops maculata*): The six subspecies of this small bird with a relatively short bill are: *L. m. bairdi,* Kauai; *L. m. maculata,* Oahu; *L. m. flammea,* Molokai; *L. m. montana,* Lanai; *L. m. newtoni,* Maui; *L. m. mana,* Hawaii. The creeper is a relatively common bird in the Alakai Swamp region of Kauai and on the windward slope of Haleakala Crater, Maui. It is uncommon on Hawaii, rare on Oahu and Molokai, and presumed to be extinct on Lanai. An unusual feature of the Molokai race is that the males are reddish-brown, whereas the males of the other races have yellowish-green or brownish feathers, especially on the dorsal surface.

AKEPA (*Loxops coccinea*): This species differentiated into subspecies on Kauai (*L. c. caeruleirostris*), Oahu (*L. c. rufa*), Maui (*L. c. ochracea*), and Hawaii (*L. c. coccinea*). The Akepa is fairly common in the Alakai Swamp

region of Kauai. It appears to be rare on Maui and Hawaii, and is presumed to be extinct on Oahu. The males of the Hawaii and Maui races have reddish-orange plumage, whereas the Kauai male has a yellow crown and underparts and olive-green back and wings.

KAUAI AKIALOA (*Hemignathus procerus*): This highly specialized honeycreeper with its long (over 2 inches) and strongly decurved bill was long feared to be extinct, but it was rediscovered in the Alakai Swamp region in 1960 by Richardson and Bowles (1964). The bird must be very rare, probably close to extinction, and has been found by very few observers.

AKIALOA (*Hemignathus obscurus*): Subspecies of a second closely related species of Akialoa formerly inhabited Oahu, Lanai, and Hawaii. Those on Oahu and Lanai are certainly extinct, and the Hawaii race is presumed to be extinct.

NUKUPUU (*Hemignathus lucidus*): The strongly decurved bill of the Nukupuu is unique among birds in that the lower mandible is only about half as long as the upper mandible. Subspecies formerly were distributed as follows: *H. l. hanepepe,* Kauai; *H. l. lucidus,* Oahu; *H. l. affinis,* Maui. The Oahu race is extinct; the Maui race was rediscovered in 1967; and the Kauai race is very rare, inhabiting the depths of the Alakai Swamp.

AKIAPOLAAU (*Hemignathus wilsoni*): The upper mandible of this closely related species also is long and strongly decurved but the lower mandible is straight, robust, and only about half as long as the upper mandible. The Akiapolaau has woodpecker-like habits in that it pounds its lower mandible into dead branches and tree trunks, searching for grubs and insects; the birds often forage on branches close to the ground. The Akiapolaau is endemic to the island of Hawaii. The bird is very rare, and, in recent years, has been sighted only in the mamane-naio forest on Mauna Kea, but formerly, at least, the species was found in Volcanoes National Park.

MAUI PARROTBILL (*Pseudonestor xanthophrys*): This remarkable stub-tailed bird with a large parrot-like bill is known to have occurred only at higher elevations on the very wet, windward slopes of Haleakala, Maui. Virtually nothing is known about this rare bird. It was observed in the upper reaches of Kipahulu Valley in August 1967.

OU (*Psittirostra psittacea*): The Ou is a large-billed, yellow-headed bird with a greenish back. The species once inhabited Kauai, Oahu, Molokai, Lanai, Maui, and Hawaii. It is extinct on Oahu, Molokai, and Lanai; Maui is not even listed as part of the former range in most books, and the species has not been seen there for many years. The Ou apparently was last reported seen on Hawaii in 1955. The bird is rare on Kauai but can be found in the Alakai Swamp.

LAYSAN FINCH (*Psittirostra cantans cantans*): This species was first described by S. B. Wilson in 1890. It was undoubtedly because of its omnivorous feeding habits that the Laysan Finch managed to survive the destruction by rabbits of the vegetation on Laysan Island. During the extended breeding season of the seabirds, the Laysan Finch breaks the eggs of the several species of nesting terns, especially, and eats their contents. Wetmore found several dozen Laysan Finches on the island in 1923. The population has increased steadily since that time, and there were between 8,000 and 10,000 Laysan Finches on the island in 1967. Personnel of the U.S. Bureau of Sport Fisheries and Wildlife have since released birds on Southeast Island of Pearl and Hermes Reef; the population is now thought to number between 75 and 100 birds.

The Laysan Finch also was introduced on Midway Island in 1891 and again in about 1905. Bailey (1956, p. 124) wrote, however, that "the disappearance of the finches and the [Laysan] rails was very rapid when rats overran the islands during the war years, and few if any existed on Midway after 1944."

About two dozen Laysan Finches were presented to the Honolulu Zoo in 1966, and a similar number were sent to the University of Michigan.

NIHOA FINCH (*Psittirostra cantans ultima*): This honeycreeper was named "ultima" in 1917 by W. A. Bryan because he thought it

would be the last endemic Hawaiian bird to be discovered. In 1923, however, Alexander Wetmore visited Nihoa and discovered the Nihoa Millerbird.

The Nihoa Finch is a successful species, with an estimated population in 1967 of between 4,800 and 5,000 birds on Nihoa's 156 acres. The survival of the species, however, depends upon maintenance of the native vegetation and prevention of the introduction on the island of rats and other mammalian predators.

PALILA (*Psittirostra bailleui*): The Palila is superficially similar to the Ou, being a large-billed and large-headed bird with a yellow head and throat but with a gray back. The bill of the Palila is dark in color, rather than light, and is differently shaped than the bill of the Ou. The Palila is found only on Hawaii. It had a wider distribution on that island in the past but is now known to occur only in the mamane-naio forests on the slopes of Mauna Kea, in general at elevations above 6,500 feet. The survival of the Palila, therefore, is entirely dependent on the recovery and continued maintenance of this forest. The present tree line is located at approximately 9,300 feet and is gradually receding because of overgrazing by the feral sheep on the State-owned game management areas on Mauna Kea. A superabundance of wild pigs also inhabits this relatively dry forest region.

GREATER KOA FINCH (*Psittirostra palmeri*): This and the next two species of Koa Finch provide ornithologists with a real puzzle. The three species were first discovered and described during the period between 1888 and 1892, all on the Kona slope of Mauna Loa. There are no reliable records of any one of these species having been seen since 1896.

LESSER KOA FINCH (*Psittirostra flaviceps*)

GROSBEAK FINCH (*Psittirostra kona*)

B. Subfamily Drepaniinae

APAPANE (*Himatione sanguinea*): This is the most common of the surviving species of honeycreepers, and it has undergone no important geographic variation. One race (*H. s.*

sanguinea) inhabits all of the six main Hawaiian islands. A second race (*H. s. freethii*) inhabited Laysan Island until becoming extinct in 1923.

The Apapane is the most conspicuous of the native birds in the wet ohia forests on all major islands, in general now above 3,000 feet elevation. It also is found along the Mauna Loa Strip Road in Volcanoes National Park, among both the scattered ohia trees and the groves of koa (Baldwin, 1953). The species rarely moves through the mamane-naio forest on Mauna Kea, and is not known to nest there. The places to observe this species most easily are at Kokee State Park on Kauai, Hosmer's Grove on Maui, and Volcanoes National Park on Hawaii.

CRESTED HONEYCREEPER (*Palmeria dolei*): This remarkably plumaged honeycreeper (totally unlike any other species) once inhabited both Molokai and Maui. The species is extinct on Molokai, and almost nothing is known about the birds on Maui. There they are found in the cloud forest on the northeast slope of Haleakala, presumably at elevations above 5,000 feet.

ULA-AI-HAWANE (*Ciridops anna*): According to Munro (1944, p. 99), the common name means "the red bird that feeds on the hawane" (the native Hawaiian palm, *Pritchardia* spp.). The color pattern of this species, too, was unlike that of any other honeycreeper. The species apparently was first collected about 1859 but it was not described until 1879. Palmer and Munro obtained one specimen from natives in the early 1890s, the last of this species ever reported.

IIWI (*Vestiaria coccinea*): This is the most striking in appearance of the common honeycreepers. The head and body feathers are a brilliant vermillion; there is a white patch in the otherwise black wings; and the long, decurved bill is salmon colored. This species once inhabited all of the main islands. It is extinct on Lanai and probably Molokai, and it is rare and presumably on the verge of extinction on Oahu. On Kauai, Maui, and Hawaii, however, it is still fairly common.

MAMO (*Drepanis pacifica*): The naturalists accompanying Captain Cook first collected this striking yellow and black bird with its very long, decurved, black bill, which was endemic only to the island of Hawaii in historic times. The head and body feathers were black but the rump, upper and lower tail coverts, thighs, bend of wing, and part of the under wing coverts were bright yellow. Munro (1944, p. 91) reported that the birds were still being collected for their yellow feathers in 1880, and that one man shot as many as 12 in one day with a shotgun. The species apparently was last seen in 1899.

BLACK MAMO (*Drepanis funerea*): This jet black bird with white on the wing feathers had an even larger, decurved bill than the Mamo. Endemic to Molokai, the species was discovered in 1893. The last specimens apparently were collected in 1907, and the species is thought to be extinct.

INDIGENOUS HAWAIIAN BIRDS

Indigenous birds are those native to Hawaii but whose normal range of distribution includes a much wider geographical area. Included among these indigenous Hawaiian birds are many seabirds, the Black-crowned Night Heron, and a number of migratory species that spend the nonbreeding season in the Hawaiian Islands. Most of these birds are illustrated in the books by Ord (1967) and Peterson (1961).

BLACK-CROWNED NIGHT HERON (*Nycticorax nycticorax hoactli*): This heron is considered indigenous rather than endemic (see gallinule and coot) because the Hawaiian birds have not been recognized as subspecifically distinct in plumage characters from the American continental birds. This subspecies has a very large breeding range, extending from Washington and Oregon south to northern Chile and south-central Argentina.

The Black-crowned Night Heron, found on all the main islands, inhabits marshes, ponds, and lagoons, where it feeds on aquatic insects, fish, frogs, and mice. The birds roost and nest in trees. The future of this species in Hawaii, like that of the gallinule and coot, is dependent on the preservation of suitable wetland habitat.

The Seabirds

These birds belong to several families of oceanic birds (as indicated below). They breed by the tens of thousands on the Leeward Islands, and certain species nest on the offshore islands of Kauai and Oahu (especially Moku Manu and Manana Island (Fisher, 1948*a*, 1966). The offshore islands are State wildlife refuges, and permission is required before visiting these islands.

A few species nest on the main islands. Red-footed Boobies (*Sula sula*) have established breeding colonies near the Kilauea Lighthouse on Kauai and on Ulupau Head, Oahu. Newell's Manx Shearwater (*Puffinus puffinus newelli*) is known to breed on almost inaccessible cliffs on Kauai. The Hawaiian Dark-rumped Petrel (*Pterodroma phaeopygia sandwichensis*) nests on the walls of Haleakala Crater, Maui, and, in smaller numbers, on Hawaii. Both species are thought to have nested formerly on all of the high islands, and both are listed as endangered species.

Families containing species that nest in the Hawaiian Islands and the species are these:

Diomedeidae (albatrosses or gooney birds)
 Black-footed Albatross (*Diomedea nigripes*)
 Laysan Albatross (*Diomedea immutabilis*)
Procellariidae (shearwaters, petrels, fulmars)
 Wedge-tailed Shearwater (*Puffinus pacificus*)
 Christmas Island Shearwater (*Puffinus nativitatus*)
 Newell's Manx Shearwater (*Puffinus puffinus newelli*)
 Dark-rumped Petrel (*Pterodroma phaeopygia sandwichensis*)
 Bonin Petrel (*Pterodroma hypoleuca*)
 Bulwer's Petrel (*Bulweria bulwerii*)
Hydrobatidae (storm petrels)
 Harcourt's Storm Petrel (*Oceanodroma castro*)
 Sooty Storm Petrel (*Oceanodroma markhami*)
Phaethontidae (tropicbirds)
 White-tailed Tropicbird (*Phaethon lepturus*)
 Red-tailed Tropicbird (*Phaethon rubricauda*)
Sulidae (boobies and gannets)
 Blue-faced or Masked Booby (*Sula dactylatra*)

 Brown Booby (*Sula leucogaster*)
 Red-footed Booby (*Sula sula*)
Fregatidae (frigatebirds)
 Great Frigatebird (*Fregata minor*)
Laridae (gulls, terns, and noddys)
 Sooty Tern (*Sterna fuscata*)
 Gray-backed Tern (*Sterna lunata*)
 Blue-gray Noddy (*Procelsterna cerulea*)
 Brown Noddy (*Anous stolidus*)
 White-capped or Hawaiian Noddy (*Anous minutus*)
 Fairy Tern (*Gygis alba*)

Migratory species

The most conspicuous of these is the Pacific Golden Plover (*Pluvialis dominica*), which spends the nonbreeding season in Hawaii, inhabiting grassy areas in the cities as well as in the mountains. Most of the birds molt into the full breeding plumage before leaving for Alaska, usually in April.

A number of species of ducks and shorebirds also are winter residents in the Hawaiian Islands (see Ord, 1967; Bryan, 1958; and Clapp and Woodward, 1968).

INTRODUCED OR EXOTIC BIRDS

Virtually all of the landbirds that one sees in Honolulu, as well as in lowland areas on all islands, are introduced species: for example, doves, mynahs, white-eyes, cardinals, mockingbirds, linnets (Fisher, 1948*b*; Eddinger, 1967*a*, 1967*b*; Walker, 1967; Warner, 1968). To see endemic birds, one must get into the mountains and the native forests; and few native birds remain on the island of Oahu.

In addition to the 76 species of game birds *known* to have been introduced in the main Hawaiian Islands as of 1967, at least 60 species of non-game birds have been released. These cover the gamut from the Chinese Fishing Cormorant (*Phalacrocorax carbo*) and the Guam Edible-nest Swiftlet (*Collocalia inexpectata*) to a wide variety of passerine birds. Fortunately, most of the introductions have been unsuccessful.

The exact number of birds which have been introduced is uncertain because an unknown number of cage birds have been released illegally by presumably well-meaning, but ignorant, citizens. A surprising number of weaver-finches (family Ploceidae, to which the House Sparrow, *Passer domesticus,* belongs) have been released intentionally by citizens on the slopes of Diamond Head in recent years, and a number of these seem to be established as breeding birds.

The success of an exotic bird introduced into a foreign environment is best exemplified, perhaps, by the Mejiro or Japanese White-eye (*Zosterops palpebrosus japonicus;* family Zosteropidae). According to Bryan (1958, p. 21), the White-eye was introduced to Oahu from Japan in 1929. This species has spread (apparently unaided by man) to all of the main islands; it is found both in the very dry and the very wet habitats, and from sea level to treeline on the mountains of Hawaii and Maui.

Another successful exotic is the Red-billed Leiothrix (*Leiothrix lutea;* family Timaliidae), which was released in 1918 and again in 1928–1929. This species prefers the wetter areas (both native and introduced vegetation), but is now widely distributed on the main islands. It is a common bird in the native forests, where it, as well as the White-eye, may be competing seriously with the endemic birds.

LITERATURE CITED

AMADON, DEAN. 1942. Relationships of the Hawaiian avifauna. Condor, vol. 44, pp. 280–281.

——— 1950. The Hawaiian honeycreepers (Aves, Drepaniidae). Bulletin of the American Museum of Natural History, vol. 95, article 4.

BAILEY, A. M. 1956. Birds of Midway and Laysan Islands. Denver Museum of Natural History, Museum Pictorial No. 12.

BALDWIN, P. H. 1947. The life history of the Laysan Rail. Condor, vol. 49, pp. 14–21.

——— 1953. Annual cycle, environment and evolution in the Hawaiian honeycreepers (Aves, Drepaniidae). University of California Publications in Zoology, vol. 52, pp. 285–398.

BERGER, A. J. 1969*a.* Discovery of the nest of the Hawaiian Thrush. The Living Bird, Eighth Annual, Laboratory of Ornithology, Cornell University.

——— 1969*b.* The eggs and young of the Palila. Condor, vol. 71. In press.

BERGER, A. J., C. R. EDDINGER, and S. C. FRINGS. 1969. The nest and eggs of the Anianiau. Auk, vol. 86, pp. 183–187.

BRYAN, E. H., JR. 1958. Check list and summary of Hawaiian birds. Books about Hawaii, Honolulu.

CLAPP, R. B., and P. W. WOODWARD. 1968. New records of birds from the Hawaiian Leeward Islands. Proceedings of the U.S. National Museum, vol. 124, no. 3640, 39 pp.

EDDINGER, C. R. 1967*a.* A study of the breeding behavior of the mynah (*Acridotheres tristis* L.). Elepaio, vol. 28, pp. 1–5, 11–15.

——— 1967*b.* Feeding helpers among immature White-eyes. Condor, vol. 69, pp. 530–531.

ELDER, W. H. 1958. Biology and management of the Hawaiian Goose. Transactions of the 23rd North American Wildlife Conference, Washington, D. C.

FISHER, H. I. 1948*a.* Laysan Albatross nesting on Moku Manu Islet, off Oahu, T. H. Pacific Science, vol. 2, p. 66.

——— 1948*b.* The question of avian introductions in Hawaii. Pacific Science, vol. 2, pp. 59–64.

——— 1966. Airplane-albatross collisions on Midway Atoll. Condor, vol. 68, pp. 229–242.

FRINGS, S. C. 1968. The breeding biology of the Oahu Elepaio, *Chasiempis sandwichensis gayi.* Unpublished thesis, University of Hawaii.

GREENWAY, J. C., JR. 1958. Extinct and vanishing birds of the world. American Commission for International Wild Life Protection, Special Publication 13, New York.

——— 1968. Drepanididae, Hawaiian honeycreepers. In: Check-list of birds of the world. Vol. XIV. Museum of Comparative Zoology, Cambridge, Massachusetts.

MAYR, ERNST. 1943. The zoogeographic position of the Hawaiian Islands. Condor, vol. 45, pp. 45–48.

MILLER, A. H. 1937. Structural modifications in the Hawaiian Goose (*Nesochen sand-*

vicensis), a study in adaptive evolution. University of California Publications in Zoology, vol. 38, pp. 11–242.

MUNRO, GEORGE. 1944. Birds of Hawaii. Tongg Publishing Co., Honolulu.

ORD, W. M. 1967. Hawaii's birds. Hawaii Audubon Society, Honolulu.

PERKINS, R. C. L. 1901. An introduction to the study of the Drepanididae. Ibis, 1901, pp. 562–585.

PETERSON, R. T. 1961. A field guide to western birds. 2nd ed. Houghton Mifflin Co., Boston.

RICHARDSON, FRANK. 1949. The status of native land birds on Molokai, Hawaiian Islands. Pacific Science, vol. 3, pp. 226–230.

RICHARDSON, FRANK, and JOHN BOWLES. 1964. A survey of the birds of Kauai, Hawaii. Bernice P. Bishop Museum Bulletin 227.

ROTHSCHILD, WALTER. 1893–1900. The avifauna of Laysan and the Hawaiian possessions. R. H. Porter, London.

SWEDBERG, G. E. 1967. The Koloa. State of Hawaii Division of Fish and Game, Department of Land and Natural Resources, Honolulu.

TOMICH, P. Q. 1967. Arthropoda associated with a nest of the Hawaiian Crow. Proceedings of the Hawaiian Entomological Society, vol. 19, pp. 431–432.

WALKER, R. L. 1967. A brief history of exotic game bird and mammal introductions into Hawaii, with a look to the future. Conference of Western Association of State Game and Fish Commissioners, Honolulu, July 19, 1967.

WARNER, R. E. 1961. Hawaii's birds—birth and death of an island biota. Pacific Discovery, vol. 14, pp. 6–13.

———— 1968. The role of introduced diseases in the extinction of the endemic Hawaiian avifauna. Condor, vol. 70, pp. 101–120.

WETMORE, ALEXANDER. 1925. Bird life among lava rock and coral sand, the chronicle of a scientific expedition to little known islands of Hawaii. National Geographic, vol. 48, pp. 77–108.

WILSON, S. B., and A. H. EVANS. 1890–1899. Aves Hawaiienses. R. H. Porter, London.

The Composition and Relationships of
Marine Molluscan Fauna of the Hawaiian Islands[1]

E. Alison Kay[2]

(General Science Department, University of Hawaii, Honolulu, Hawaii)

This is an attempt at a crudely quantitative analysis of the marine molluscan fauna of the Hawaiian Islands. I am also going to try to indicate some relationships, both as the Hawaiian marine mollusks exemplify an insular fauna and as they are phylogenetically related to the fauna of the Indo-West-Pacific.

The marine mollusks of the Hawaiian Islands are among the best known of any insular marine fauna. Extensive collections in the B.P. Bishop Museum, Honolulu, Hawaii, range in time from that accumulated by Andrew Garrett in the 1860's to that of Ditlev Thaanum made between 1895 and 1950. The many amateur shell collectors in the State have explored not only shallow water but with SCUBA equipment depths down to 30 m. Dredgings by the privately owned cabin cruiser "Pele" have provided more than 5000 lots of specimens from depths of 10 m to 400 m. And, finally, my own monthly collection from shallow water stations on Oahu and Kauai have provided much information on the minute mollusks of the intertidal zone and on the opisthobranchs.

Data for comparisons are less accessible and less extensive. Despite the incomplete records, however, I have used only lists which are available*for insular faunas, working on the assumption that while these lists will be augmented, the proportions of the various groups of mollusks represented at the present time will remain about the same. For the Indian Ocean I have used the manuscript list of Winckworth (British Museum (Natural History)) for the Seychelle Islands. For the Pacific Ocean the manifestly incomplete lists of Hedley (1899) for the Ellice Islands and Demond (1957) for micronesian reef gastropods have been useful, as have the more extensive lists of Dautzenberg and Bouge (1933) for French Oceania (the Tuamotu and Society

---

1) This paper was presented to Symposium No. 4, " Evolution, Distribution, and Migration of Plants and Animals in the Pacific Area" at the Eleventh Pacific Science Congress, Tokyo, Japan, 1966.
2) This work was done under the auspices of NSF grant GB 1346. Hawaii Marine Laboratory Contribution No. 274.

* Should read: " ... I have used the only lists available ... "

Reprinted from *Venus* 25:94–104 (1967) by permission of the author and the Malacological Society of Japan.

Islands), OLIVER (1915) for the Kermadecs, and KURODA (1960) for Okinawa. I have used KEEN's (1957) work on the mollusks of the west coast of the Americas and IREDALE and McMICHAEL's (1961) list of mollusks from New South Wales as summaries of continental molluscan faunas, and the list of FAUSTINO (1928) for the Philippine Islands.

Composition

The marine molluscan fauna of the Hawaiian Islands is probably composed of about 1000 species. The check list on which the following discussion is based numbers 898 species but we can expect that with further collection, especially in deep water, the list will be augmented. On the other hand, I do not anticipate the 50 per cent increase which would satisfy the prediction of William Healy DALL who worked with the Hawaiian marine mollusks between 1920 and 1935. DALL's estimate of 1500 species, while reasonable thirty years ago, included many species which modern molluscan systematists, including myself, cannot consider valid today.

The 898 species for which we have collection records are distributed in the following way (Table 1):

Table 1.

Class	No. of Species	% of Hawaiian Marine Mollusca (Rounded off)
Cephalopoda	15	2.0
Amphineura	5	1.0
Scaphopoda	9	1.0
Gastropoda	719	80.0
Lamellibranchia	150	16.0
Total	898	100.0

The Cephalopoda, Amphineura, and Scaphopoda, which account for only about 4% of the marine mollusks, can be briefly summarized. There are four species of chitons representing three families; all occur in shallow water. Twenty-four species of cephalopods representing 13 families were recorded by BERRY (1914); only six species are common in shallow water and one in deep water. The other cephalopods reported are either pelagic or known only from fragments dredged at depths of several hundred meters. There are about nine species of scaphopods, all representing the family Dentaliidae, and all occurring at depths of more than 10 m.

Of the gastropods, 554 or 77 per cent are prosobranchs and 165 or 23 per cent opisthobranchs. I have not included about ten species of marine pulmonates in the figures nor have I included pelagic species such as the pteropods.

The prosobranchs are represented by the three orders as follows (Table 2):

Table 2.

Orders	No. of Species	% or Prosobranchia
Archaeogastropoda	38	7
Mesogastropoda	262	47
Neogastropoda	254	46
Total	554	100%

Seven prosobranch families comprise more than 50% of the prosobranch species in the Islands. These are: the Mitridae—60 species; Triphoridae—50 species; Turridae —45 species; Terebridae—36 species; Cypraeidae—34 species; Conidae—34 species; and Muricidae—30 species.

The opisthobranchs are represented in the following way (Table 3):

Table 3.

Orders	No. of Species	% of Opisthobranchia
Nudibranchia	82	50%
Cephalaspidea	32	19
Pyramidallacea	20	12
Sacoglossa	18	11
Anaspidea	9	6
Notaspidea	4	2
Total	165	100%

About 85% of the opisthobranchs, occur in shallow water, mostly at depths of not more than 3 m; only 25 species (15 per cent) have been collected from depths of more than 10 m. The Doridacea predominate among the nudibranchs, with 54 species representing 66 per cent of that group; the Aeolidacea comprise the other large group of nudibranchs with 30 per cent of the species while the Dendronotacea and Arminacea are represented by only three species.

In the Lamellibranchia 19 superfamilies and 33 families are represented. Six families provide more than 50 per cent of the species: the Arcidae—17 species; Pectinidae—16 species; Mytilidae—15 species; Tellinidae—10 species; Ostreidae—9 species; and Erycinidae—8 species. About 65 species, not quite 50 per cent, of the bivalves have been recorded from shallow water, but of these only 35 are either common or abundant. The Arcidae and Erycinidae are represented by the largest number of species in shallow water with about five species each, while species of the Isognomonidae, Ostreidae, and Veneridae are most abundantly represented. In water more than 20 m in depth the Arcidae are also dominant in so far as species representation is concerned with 10 species, and the Pectinidae, Tellinidae, Carditidae, Lucinidae, and Saxicavidae are represented by six or seven species each. In terms of abundance in deeper water, the members of the Pinnidae are undoubtedly the most numerous; tremendous beds of *Pinna* are apparently a characteristic feature of offshore waters at depths of 30 m or more. In lesser abundance but nevertheless numerous are members of the Tellinidae and Lucinidae.

Attenuation

One of the conspicuous features of the Hawaiian marine molluscan fauna is its attenuate character. The coasts of both New South Wales and western America, which are about the same latitude above and below the Equator as the Hawaiian chain, have molluscan faunas of approximately 2000 species; in the Philippines about 3000 species have been listed, Okinawa, which is close to a continental area, has a molluscan fauna of about 1700 species. The few insular faunas which I have been able to check have an attenuation resembling that of the Hawaiian: 700 species for the Seychelles (Indian Ocean) and 1000 species for French Oceania (the Tuamotu and Society Islands of DAUTZENBERG and BOUGE).

At what level does attenuation occur? All of the classes and orders of marine mollusks are represented and the fauna cannot be considered disharmonic at this level. However, I have estimated that 20% of the families of cephalopods, gastropods, and lamellibranchs which occur in the Pacific basin are absent. Among the cephalopods the lack of any members of the Sepiidae is perhaps the most striking of the familial gaps, while among the lamellibranchs the absence of the Tridacnidae, the well-known family of reef-dwelling giants, is especially noticeable. Other bivalve families which are lacking from Hawaiian waters are the Crassatellidae, Soleniidae, Corbulidae, and Donacidae.

The gaps at the family level among the prosobranch gastropods are perhaps less noticeable than they are among the bivalves. None of the families which are missing contributes significantly to the faunal composition of insular areas within the Pacific basin. The Acmaeidae, Truncatellidae, Turritellidae, Potamididae, Ficidae, Volutidae and Cancellaridae are apparently restricted to continental areas and in the Pacific do not range further west than Fiji in the south or the Marianas in the north. The Vasidae and Haliotidae are represented on several Pacific islands but only by three or four species among the three*families.

At the generic and specific level attenuation becomes even more obvious. Comparison with the* DEMOND's (1957) list of Micronesian reef gastropods, for example, shows that while only 8 per cent of the families are not represented in Hawaiian waters, 22 per cent of the genera and 60 per cent of the species are absent. Such familiar genera as *Monodonta*, *Tectus*, *Lambis*, *Terebellum*, and *Ovula* do not occur in Hawaiian waters, and widespread species such as *Cellana stellaeformis*, *Trochus maculatus* and *Turbo petholatus* are missing.

* Should read: "... among the two families."

* Omit "the" before "Demond's."

The Gastropod-Lamellibranch Ratio

Another feature of the Hawaiian marine mollusks is the high proportion of gastropods and correspondingly low proportion of lamellibranchs present in the fauna: 82 per cent of the total number of gastropods and bivalves is gastropod, 18 per cent lamellibranch (Text-fig. 1). On the coast of New South Wales and in the Philippines there are apparently a* higher proportions of bivalves: 71 : 29 and 63 : 33 per cent gastropods: lamellibranchs respectively. But the Hawaiian Islands are not peculiar in so far as the proportion is concerned: in the Seychelles and Ellice Islands the figures are 82 : 18 gastropod: bivalve while even higher gastropod: lower bivalve proportions are listed for the Kermadecs and French Oceania: 86 : 14 and 87 : 13 respectively.

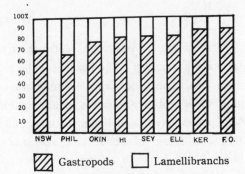

Gastropods   Lamellibranchs

Text-fig. 1. Percentages of gastropods and lamellibranchs estimated from available check lists. NSW—coast of New South Wales; PHIL—Philippines; OKIN—Okinawa; H.I.—Hawaiian Islands; SEY—Seychelles; ELL—Ellice Islands; KER—Kermadec Islands; F.O.—French Oceania (Tahiti and Tuamotus).

The trend toward a higher percentage of gastropods and a correspondingly lower percentage of lamellibranchs appears to be characteristic of insular marine faunas in general. IREDALE (1910) noted the overwhelming majority of gastropods over lamellibranchs in the Kermadecs and observed that* HEDLEY (1899) and MELVILL and STANDEN (1895) recorded the same phenomenon from the Ellice Islands and New Caledonia respectively.

Gastropods are, for the most part, epifaunitic, living upon or associated with rocks, stones, shells, algae, etc.; bivalves are typically infaunal organisms, inhabiting the sandy or muddy surface layers of the sea bottom. THORSON (1957) showed that while the number of epifaunal invertebrate species increases towards the tropics, the number of infaunal species from the arctic to the tropics remains nearly the same, reasoning that the differences could be explained in terms of increased numbers of microhabitats—coral reefs, mangroves, etc.—present in the tropics. The explanation for the high gastropod-low lamellibranch ratio in insular situations may well parallel that of THORSON: continental offshore areas and ancient archipelagoes such as the Philippines present vast expanses of silty, sandy ocean bottom, while insular situations lack such expanses, and thus the niches occupied by infaunal bivalves. TAKI (1953) has postulated a similar explanation for the paucity of bivalves at Hachijo-jima compared with the over-all picture in Japan, and the hypothesis gains some support from the observations that, in the Hawaiian Islands at least, those bivalves which are present are predominantly epifaunal. Three of the eight families with the highest

* Omit "a" before "higher."

* Omit "observed that" before "Hedley."

proportions of species in the Islands, the Arcidae, Pectinidae, and Erycinidae, are those families which have exploited an epifaunal rather than an infaunal habitat.

It should be pointed out that infaunal bivalves are not entirely absent from the Hawaiian Islands. In shallow water there are large beds of *Tapes philippinarum*, an introduced species, which has taken over areas such as Kaneohe Bay, Oahu; in deep water massive beds of *Pinna* perhaps replace the familiar *Macoma* and *Tellina* communities of temperate waters.

The Archaeogastropod : Neogastropod Proportion

Still another feature of the Hawaiian marine molluscan fauna may also be characteristic of insular marine molluscan faunas in general: the archaeogastropods comprise a proportionately smaller number of species and the neogastropods a correspondingly higher number of species than on continental areas in the Pacific coast or in the Philippines (Text-fig. 2). As in the case of the gastropod-lamellibranch ratio, the figure for Okinawa is intermediate between those of the Hawaiian Islands and the continental areas, while the Seychelles, French Oceania, and Micronesia exhibit approximately the same proportion as do the Hawaiian Islands. In all cases the mesogastropods represent between 42 per cent and 46 per cent of the prosobranchs.

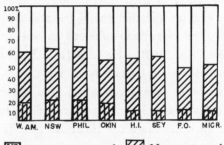

Text-fig. 2. Percentage composition of Gastropoda. W.AM—coast of Western America; NSW—coast of New South Wales; PHIL—Philippine Islands; OKIN—Okinawa; H.I.—Hawaiian Islands; SEY—Seychelles; F.O.—French Oceania; MICR—Micronesia.

This is not quite so easily explained as the gastropod-lamellibranch ratio, although one might speculate that it is external fertilization in archaeogastropods which contributes to their low representation in insular situations. It is intriguing that among the insects in the Hawaiian Islands also the most ancient orders are the most poorly represented while the orders most extensively developed are geologically the youngest (ZIMMERMAN, 1948).

Some Features of the Opisthobranchs

Compared with other molluscan faunas in the Indo-West-Pacific the Hawaiian Islands appear to have a higher proportion of opisthobranchs than occurs elsewhere, although the figure of 22 per cent : 78 per cent opisthobranch : prosobranch is comparable with that for the coasts of Europe (THORSON, 1965). In New South Wales the figure is 18 per cent : 82 per cent opisthobranchs : prosobranchs. While the high

proportion of opisthobranchs in the Hawaiian Islands may merely reflect greater collecting activity, it is noteworthy that on Okinawa, a well-studied area, the population[*]
is 7.6 per cent opisthobranchs : 92.4 per cent prosobranchs.

The dorid nudibranchs are especially distinctive when compared with the dorids
of other faunas: more than 75 per cent are sponge-feeders (YOUNG, 1966) while in
dorid faunas of temperate waters there is a preponderance of ascidian and bryozoan
feeders. It will be interesting to see if this circumstance merely reflects tropical
latitudes or whether it is a feature of insular faunas.

Size and Habitat

Some mention must be also made of size and habitat. It is well known that
animals on the periphery of their ranges often exhibit larger size than they do toward
the center of their distribution; it is not often recognized that some mollusks may
be smaller and that there are also changes in habitat at range limits.

The large size of some cowries in the Hawaiian Islands is well reported (CATE,
1961; KAY, 1961a; KAY, 1961b). For example, the mean length of *Cypraea tigris* in
the Hawaiian Islands is 117 mm; in other areas of the Pacific it is 77 mm. At least
five other species of cowry and several members on the families Cerithiidae and
Conidae also exhibit larger size in the Islands than they do elsewhere in their ranges.
In all these cases the Hawaiian Islands form the north-eastern boundary of the range
in the Pacific.

On the other hand, some mollusks tend to be smaller in the Hawaiian Islands,
and perhaps in all insular faunas, than they are along continental coast-lines. ELIOT
(1906) suggests that the dorid nudibranchs of oceanic islands seem to be smaller than
their continental counterparts. It has not been possible to confirm Eliot's impression
because of the general lack of information on nudibranchs in the Pacific, but it is
noticeable that aeolids are smaller and far less conspicuous in Hawaii than they are
along continental coastlines in temperate waters. Again, however, as in the case of
the sponge-feeding dorids, this may be associated with latitude rather than insular
habitats.

Many of the prosobranchs which are widely distributed in the Indo-West-Pacific
live in deeper water in the Hawaiian Islands than they do elsewhere. *Cypraea tigris,*
C. schilderorum, Distorsio anus, and *Bursa bufonia* are all familiar reef or shallow water
species in various locales in the Pacific and Indian Oceans but in the Hawaiian Islands
all occur at depths of more than 3 m. Approximately 30 per cent of the terebrid
and mitrid species which occur both in Fiji and the Hawaiian Islands occur in shallow
water, at a depth of less than 3 m in Fiji, but at depths of more than 10 m in the
Hawaiian Islands. Similar observations have been made for the fish in the Islands
(GOSLINE, personal communication).

[*] The word "population" should read "proportion."

Endemicity and Derivation

There remain to be discussed the questions of endemicity and derivation. Bio-geographers have long recognized that insular faunas exhibit a higher proportion of endemics than do continental faunas, and EKMAN (1953) finds the "high proportion of endemicity among marine organisms in the Hawaiian Islands" unusual in his study of marine zoogeography. It is perhaps worth mentioning that the words "high pro-portion" do not mean the same thing to the terrestrial biogeographer as they mean to the marine worker: the native terrestrial biota of the Hawaiian Islands exhibits an endemicity of 95 per cent (ZIMMERMAN, 1948) whereas an endemicity of 30–45 per cent is considered high for marine faunas (BRIGGS, 1966).

The figures now available for the Hawaiian marine mollusks show an overall endemicity of about 20 per cent; as we become more knowledgeable about the dis-tribution of marine mollusks in the Indo-West-Pacific, however, that figure may be even lower.

The over-all figure is not in itself particularly usefuly since endemicity varies among groups of mollusks. Those mollusks with long-lived pelagic larvae such as the Cymatiidae and Tonnidae show little regional differentiation in the Indo-West-Pacific. Among other mollusks which live subtidally in the Hawaiian Islands it is difficult to find a pattern: 20 per cent of the Cypraeidae and 60 per cent of the Tur-rinae are endemic but none of the Conidae is restricted to Hawaiian waters. On the other hand, one notes that those forms which live highest along the shoreline appear to have consistently high percentages of endemicity: all four species of Patellidae, 50 per cent of the marine Neritidae, and one out of four species of the Littorinidae are endemic.

While we can find no pattern of endemicity among the Hawaiian marine mollusks comparable to the species swarms of the terrestrial biota, analysis of the endemics does suggest the phylogenetic relationships of the fauna. If well-studied groups such as *Cypraea*, *Strombus*, *Pinna*, and the Turrinae are divided into three elements, those species which occur throughout the Indo-West-Pacific, those which are restricted in their distribution to the Pacific basin, and an endemic element, a very suggestive pattern emerges (Text-fig. 3). The proportion of Indo-West-Pacific species falls and the proportion of Pacific species rises, the further east is the island group in the Pacific, except for the Hawaiian Islands. Here, the proportion of Pacific species is lower than it is for islands at the same longitude (e.g. the Line Islands), and, in ad-dition, an endemic element is present.

The endemic element appears to be more closely related to the Indo-West-Pacific faunal element than to the Pacific species group. In *Strombus*, *S. helli* is apparently an offshoot of *S. haemastoma* which occurs in the Marshall Islands but not in the Line Islands; *S. vomer hawaiiensis* is related to *S. vomer vomer* from Okinawa, and

S. mutabilis ostergaardi is related to *S. mutabilis* which occurs to the west but not to the soutn in the Line Islands (ABBOTT, 1960). Among the Turrinae the Hawaiian subspecies of *Turris crispa* and three species of *Xenoturris* have their nearest relatives either in the Marshall Islands or in Okinawa (POWELL, 1964). All four species of *Cellana* are related to Japanese or Okinawan species, and the endemic species of *Littorina* appears to be related to a form in the northwest Pacific.

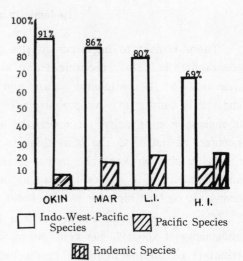

Text-fig. 3. Species of *Cypraea, Strombus, Pinna,* and the Turrinae with an Indo-West-Pacific, distribution, a Pacific distribution, and those endemic to the Hawaiian Islands. OKIN—Okinawa; MAR—Marshall Is.; L.I.—Line Islands; H.I.—Hawaiian Islands.

This evidence is not out of line with what has previously been suggested concerning the relationships of the Hawaiian marine fauna. CLARK'S (1949) studies on ophiuroids, for example, indicate immigration by way of the Caroline and Marshall Islands. The evidence is reinforced by the oceanographers' views on circulation in the North Pacific and the geologists' ideas of the history of the Pacific basin. The oceanographers have recently pointed out that the Hawaiian Islands, at least in the winter months, lie in the waters of the Kuroshio extension of the North Pacific equatorial current. And, finally, MENARD'S (1964) picture of the geological history of the Pacific basin suggests that the first island elements were the now-submerged sea mounts forming the Marcus-Necker ridge which lies immediately to the west of the Hawaiian Islands. These conceivably formed the stepping stones by means of which the Hawaiian fauna was derived from the rich Indo-West-Pacific fauna to the west and north-west.

Summary

Analysis of the composition of the Hawaiian marine mollusks indicates a number of features which appear to be characteristic of insular marine molluscan faunas in general and others which may be peculiar to the Hawaiian Islands. Those features which the Hawaiian marine mollusks share with other insular molluscan faunas are the attentuate character of the fauna which comprises about 1000 species; a high gastropod: low bivalve ratio; and a high neogastropod: low archaeogastropod ratio. A feature of the Hawaiian marine mollusks which may be peculiar is the high proportion of opisthobranchs in the fauna. The isolated position of the Islands which form the north-eastern periphery of the range of a number of Indo-West-Pacific species has stamped the fauna with unique characters: both large and small size, changes in habitat, and endemicity.

The Hawaiian endemics appear to be more closely related to those species which range through the Indo-West-Pacific than to those which are restricted to the Pacific basin.

References Cited

ABBOTT, R.T. 1960: The genus *Strombus* in the Indo-Pacific. *Indo-Pacific Mollusca* 1(2): 33–146, 117 pls.

BERRY, S.S. 1914: The Cephalopoda of the Hawaiian Islands. *Bull. Bur. Fisheries* 32: 255–362, 11 pls.

BRIGGS, J.C. 1966: Oceanic Islands, Endemism, and Marine Palaeotemperatures. *Syst. Zool.* 15: 153–168.

CATE, C. 1961: Description of a new Hawaiian subspecies of *Cypraea tigris* (Linnaeus, 1758). *The Veliger* 3: 107–108.

CLARK, A.H. 1949. Ophiuroidea of the Hawaiian Islands. *B.P. Bishop Mus. Bull.* 195.

DAUTZENBERG, P. and J.L. BOUGE, 1933. Les mollusques testacès marins ètablissements Français de l'Oceanie. *J. Conchyliol.* 77: 41–108; 145–326; 351–469.

DEMOND, J. 1957: Micronesian Reef Gastropods. *Pacif. Sci.* 11: 226–275.

EKMAN, S. 1953: *Zoogeography of the Sea.* Sidgwick and Jackson, London.

ELIOT, C.N. 1906. Report upon a collection of Nudibranchiata from the Cape Verde Islands with notes by C. Crossland. *Proc. Malac. Soc. London* 7: 131–135.

FAUSTINO, L.A. 1928: Summary of Philippine marine and freshwater mollusks. *Monogr. Philipp. Bur. Sci.* 25: 1–384.

HEDLEY, C. 1899: The Mollusca of Funafuti. *Mem. Austr. Mus.* 3: 397–408; 491–535; 549–565.

IREDALE, T. 1910: On Marine Molluscs from the Kermadec Islands and on the sinusigera apex. *Proc. Malac. Soc. London* 9: 68–79.

————— and D.F. McMICHAEL. 1961: A reference list of the marine Mollusca of New South Wales. *Mem. Austr. Mus.* 11: 109 pp.

KAY, E.A. 1961a: A zoogeographical analysis of species of *Cypraea* in the Hawaiian Islands. *Proc. Malac. Soc. London* 34: 185–198.

—————. 1961b: On *Cypraea tigris schilderiana* Cate. *The Veliger* 4: 36–40.

KEEN, A.M. 1958: *Sea shells of tropical west America.* Stanford University Press.

KURODA, T. 1960: *A catalogue of molluscan fauna of the Okinawa Islands.* Tokyo. 106 pp.

MELVILL, J.C. and R. STANDEN. 1895: Notes on a collection of shells from Lifu and Uvea, Loyalty Islands, formed by the Reverend James and Mrs. Hadfield, with a list of species. *J. Conch.* 8: 84–132.

MENARD, H.W. 1964: *Marine geology of the Pacific.* McGraw Hill, New York.

OLIVER, W.R.B. 1915: The Mollusca of the Kermadec Islands. *Trans. Proc. N.Z. Inst.* 47: 509–568.

POWELL, W.A.B. 1964: The family Turridae in the Indo-Pacific. *Indo-Pacific Mollusca* 1(5): 227–346.

TAKI, I. 1953: Molluscan fauna of Hachijo-Jima. Preliminary Report. *Records of Oceanographic Works in Japan.* N.S. 1(1): 124–125.

THORSON, G. 1957: Bottom communities (Sublittoral or shallow shelf). In Treatise on Marine Ecology and Paleoecology, Vol. 1 *Geol. Soc. Am. Mem.* 67.

—————. 1965: The distribution of benthic marine Mollusca along the N.E. Atlantic shelf from Gibralter to Murmansk. *Proc. First European Malac. Congr.*: 5–23.

YOUNG, D.K. 1966: Systematics, food and functional morphology of the feeding apparatus of some dorid nudibranchs. Ph. D. Thesis, University of Hawaii.

ZIMMERMAN, E.C. 1948. *Insects of Hawaii.* Vol. I. University of Hawaii Press, Honolulu.

The Inshore Fish Fauna of Johnston Island, a Central Pacific Atoll[1]

WILLIAM A. GOSLINE[2]

INTRODUCTION

THIS PAPER is primarily concerned with Central Pacific zoogeography. Its main purpose is to trace in so far as possible the derivation and the immigration and emigration routes of the Johnston Island inshore fish fauna. The importance of Johnston for a study of this sort lies in its position between the areas inhabited by the great tropical Pacific fauna to the south and the strongly endemic Hawaiian fauna to the north (Fig. 1).

The first section of this paper records the fishes known from Johnston and presents the taxonomic interpretations upon which the zoogeographic treatment of the second section is based.

Of the collections dealt with, the most important for this paper are those taken by V. E. Brock, Y. Yamaguchi, and the author at Johnston in February 1951. These collections were made possible through the kindness of Colonel Cronau, then commanding officer of the island, and were greatly facilitated by Lt. Col. Eaton and other members of the airforce who were there at the time. In addition, three small collections from the same island were turned over to me by Brock, Schaefer, and Francis respectively. Finally, a reexamination of certain fishes from Johnston recorded by Fowler and Ball (1925) was made possible through the courtesy of the staff of the Bernice P. Bishop Museum.

SECTION 1. FISHES RECORDED FROM JOHNSTON ISLAND

Except for Schultz's (1950: 548) reference to *Cirrhitus alternatus*, the following four works include or cite all of the published records on Johnston fishes.

Smith and Swain (1882) recorded 27 species from the island, 5 of which they described as new.

Fowler and Ball (1925) listed 72 species from Johnston collected by the "Tanager" Expedition of 1923. One of these was described as new.

Schultz and collaborators (1953) in the first volume of their report on "Fishes of the Marshall and Marianas Islands" recorded specimens of about 9 Johnston species. Most of these were referred to only in passing, e.g., in tables; three, however, were described as new.

Halstead and Bunker (1954), in a report on fish poisoning at Johnston Island, listed 60 species investigated.

One hundred and eighteen species of Johnston fishes have been seen by the present author. Species recorded from the island that have not been seen are marked in the species accounts with an asterisk; some of these almost certainly represent misidentifications and others equally certainly do not, but any attempt to decide which are which would only lead to further misidentifications.

It is easy to criticize others for recording species without also providing sufficient descriptive material to determine whether the record has been correctly identified. It is more

[1] Contribution No. 73, Hawaii Marine Laboratory. Manuscript received March 18, 1955.
[2] Department of Zoology and Entomology, University of Hawaii.

Reprinted from *Pacific Science* 9:442–480 (1955), by permission of the author and The University Press of Hawaii.

difficult to write a paper that does not commit the same error and is still sufficiently brief to be publishable. The present account attempts a compromise between these two pitfalls. Species which are sufficiently distinct to be readily recognizable, about which there are at present no zoological or nomenclatorial questions, and whose presence at Johnston there is no zoogeographic reason to doubt, have been recorded by name only. For the others an attempt has been made to give the diagnostic characters of the Johnston specimens on the basis of which the species identification was made. It is clearly recognized that this method only alleviates, and by no means eliminates, the faults of recording species by name only.

This section contains notes on the classification of certain species of *Uropterygius*, *Belone*, *Pseudamiops*, *Scarus*, and *Scorpaena* as well as the records of Johnston fishes. Families are listed in "phylogenetic sequence"; genera and species within the family are taken up alphabetically. Identifications and nomenclature follow Schultz, *et al.* (*op. cit.*) where possible, and various authors for the remaining species. All lengths given in millimeters are standard lengths; total lengths are expressed in inches.

MYLIOBATIDAE

*Aetobatus narinari (Euphrasen)
Fowler and Ball, 1925, 1 spec.; Halstead and Bunker, 1954, 1 spec.

SYNODONTIDAE

Saurida gracilis (Quoy and Gaimard)
5 specs., 69–110 mm., 1951; 1 spec., Brock, 1948.
A double band of teeth on each side of the palate; inner rays of pelvic fins contained about 1.2 times in the length of the outermost rays.

Synodus binotatus Schultz
3 specs., 46–77 mm., 1951.
A single row of teeth on each side of palate; three and a half scale rows between the lateral line and the dorsal origin; peritoneum pale; no black spot on opercle but a dark mark on tip of snout and three dark rings on the back behind the dorsal fin; 9 anal rays; tips of first dorsal rays not reaching tips of succeeding rays when the fin is depressed; dorsal origin equidistant from tip of snout and origin of adipose; tips of central caudal rays not black (cf., Schultz, *et al.*, 1953: 30, 31).

CONGRIDAE

Conger noordziekii Bleeker
1 spec., 255 mm., 1951.
Origin of dorsal over anterior third of the depressed pectorals; a dark longitudinal line extending below and behind eye.

OPHICHTHIDAE

Brachysomophis sauropsis Schultz
1 spec., 362 mm., 1951.
As compared with a 1070 mm. specimen of *Brachysomophis henshawi* from Hawaii, the Johnston specimen differs in having the distance from the tip of snout to the posterior border of the eye contained 9 times in the head length to gill openings instead of 7.2 times, in having the dorsal and anal fins low (the anal does not even extend above the groove that encloses it) and light in coloration instead of well-developed and with the dorsal black-based; in having the pores of the head and body not enclosed in dark areas; and in having no dark bands either along the mid-dorsal line or along the lateral line area of the sides. The Johnston specimen agrees in every way with Schultz's original description of *Brachysomophis sauropsis*.

Leiuranus semicinctus (Lay and Bennett)
6 specs., 133–227 mm., 1951. Fowler and Ball, 1925, 3 specs.
Ovate black saddles about equal in maximum width to the interspaces between them.

Leptenchelys labialis (Seale)
2 specs., 121–134 mm., 1951.

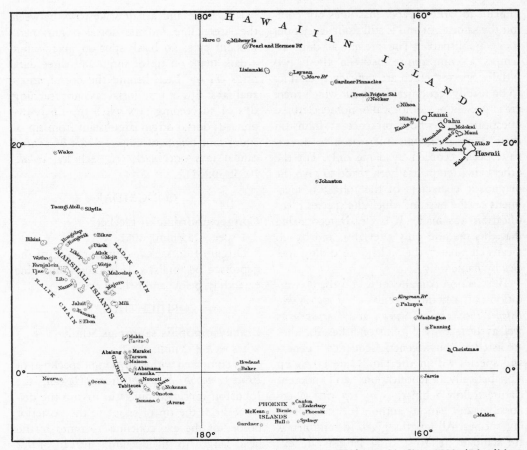

FIG. 1. Chart of the region surrounding Johnston Island. From U. S. Hydrographic Chart 1500, 47th edition.

Ventral surface of snout with a median groove that contains teeth; caudal fin well developed; dorsal origin a little over a head length behind head (cf., Schultz, *et al.*, 1953: 71).

I have dealt elsewhere (1950: 312–314; 1952: 300–306) at some length with the reasons why *Leptenchelys*, *Muraenichthys*, and *Schultzidia* should be placed in the Ophichthidae.

Muraenichthys cookei Fowler

12 specs., 103–173 mm., 1951.

Posterior rim of orbit about over rictus; dorsal origin from 2 to 5 eye diameters ahead of anus; vomerine teeth uniserial (cf., Schultz, *et al.*, 1953: 71, 72).

These specimens are discussed in section 2.

Muraenichthys gymnotus Bleeker

3 specs., 52–118 mm., 1951.

Dorsal fin originating about half a head length behind the anus; rear margin of eye slightly ahead of rictus; teeth on front of maxillary and dentary at least double-rowed; snout sharp, the distance from its tip to the rictus contained about 3.7 times in the head length (cf., Schultz, *et al.*, 1953: 71–73).

Muraenichthys schultzei Bleeker

3 specs., 106–117 mm., 1951. Fowler and Ball, 1925, 12 specs.

Dorsal origin about two-thirds of a head length behind anus; snout bluntly rounded; vomerine teeth two-rowed (cf., Schultz, *et al.*, 1953: 71–73).

Myrichthys bleekeri Gosline

1 spec., 365 mm., 1951. As *Myrichthys colubrinus*, Fowler and Ball, 1925, 12 specs.

Width of black band over gill opening contained two times in the white interspace behind it; only the last two bands completely encircling the body.

Myrichthys maculosus (Cuvier)

5 specs., 275–865 mm., 1951. Fowler and Ball, 1925, 1 spec. As *Myrichthys stypurus* Smith and Swain, 1882, 1 spec.

Round black spots on a greenish background.

Schultzidia johnstonensis (Schultz and Woods)

2 specs., 101–167 mm., 1951. Schultz, *et al.*, 1953, 1 spec.

Maxillary teeth small, in several rows, facing inward; vomerine teeth minute in the small specimen, apparently absent in the larger; no median papilla on upper lip between nostrils (cf., Schultz, *et al.*, 1953: 71).

MORINGUIDAE

Moringua macrochir Bleeker

5 specs., 128–262 mm., 1951.

Lower jaw projecting; lateral line pores 98–110.

The name used for this species follows Gosline and Strasburg (In press).

MURAENIDAE

Anarchias allardicei Jordan and Starks

5 specs., 121–135 mm., 1951.

Pore near posterior nostril lying somewhat ahead of nostril; body color plain brown, the brownish color provided by microscopic brown speckling on a light background (cf., Schultz, *et al.*, 1953: 139).

Anarchias cantonensis (Schultz)

3 specs., 142–163 mm., 1951.

Pore near posterior nostril lying somewhat ahead of nostril; body with a reticulate pattern of dark on light; chin barred (cf., Schultz, *et al.*, 1953: 139).

Anarchias leucurus (Snyder)

35 specs., 103–176 mm., 1951.

Pore near posterior nostril lying slightly behind nostril; body with a reticulate pattern; chin barred (cf., Schultz, *et al.*, 1953: 139).

Echidna leucotaenia Schultz

5 specs., 150–240 mm., 1951.

Body plain brown; fins black-based and white-edged; lower jaw light except for a brown patch below each eye (cf., Schultz, *et al.*, 1953: 100).

Echidna polyzona (Richardson)

1 spec., 63 mm., 1951.

Pebble-like teeth on vomer; about 27 dark bands on body (cf., Schultz, *et al.*, 1953: 100).

Echidna zebra (Shaw)

1 spec., 850 mm., 1951.

Anus well behind middle of body length; black and white stripes on body (cf., Schultz, *et al.*, 1953: 100).

***Gymnothorax buroensis** Bleeker

Halstead and Bunker, 1954, 5 specs. It seems most likely that Halstead and Bunker's record refers to *Gymnothorax eurostus*, the Hawaiian form of *G. buroensis*. Indeed, since none of the Hawaiian "endemic" species are recorded by Halstead and Bunker, such of this element in the Johnston fauna as was taken by these authors must have been misidentified.

Gymnothorax eurostus (Abbott)

20 specs., 158–500 mm., 1951.

Premaxillary teeth divisible into 5 series, these somewhat difficult to distinguish in large specimens; no black blotch surrounding gill opening; body mottled (cf., Schultz, *et al.*, 1953: 109).

These specimens are dealt with in section 2.

Gymnothorax gracilicaudus Jenkins

3 specs., 106–140 mm., 1951.

Teeth not serrate, in three series on premaxillary, those of the median row notably enlarged. Body light with irregular dark vertical bands; no black blotch around gill opening; a prominent white band down the midline of the snout; median fins with broad, plain, light borders; dark pigment forming an irregular band extending from behind eye across rictus; chin and abdomen light; a dark saddle running across top of head and down at least to the level of the eye on either side.

*Gymnothorax javanicus (Bleeker)

Halstead and Bunker, 1954, 2 specs.

Gymnothorax meleagris (Shaw)

3 specs., 230–670 mm., 1951. Fowler and Ball, 1925, 2 specs.; Halstead and Bunker, 1954, 2 specs.

Five rows of teeth on premaxillary; gill opening in a black area; small, round, white spots on a dark ground.

Gymnothorax moluccensis (Bleeker)

1 spec., 257 mm., 1951.

Larger, lateral teeth in both jaws serrate. Body plain brown (cf., Schultz, *et al.*, 1953: 109).

Gymnothorax pictus (Ahl)

As *Lycodontis picta*, Fowler and Ball, 1925, 2 specs., one of these reexamined.

Gymnothorax undulatus (Lacépède)

2 specs., 250 and 850 mm., 1951.

Premaxillary teeth in three series, the central teeth fang-like. Body dark, with narrow white reticulations forming irregular vertical lines; no white streak on snout (cf., Schultz, *et al.*, 1953: 109–113).

Rabula fuscomaculata Schultz

19 specs., 116–149 mm., 1951. Schultz, *et al.*, 1953, 16 specs.

Dorsal fin commencing somewhat less than a head length ahead of anus; dark spots and reticulations on a light ground (cf., Schultz, *et al.*, 1953: 139).

Uropterygius dentatus Schultz

1 spec., 366 mm., 1951. Schultz, *et al.*, 1953, 373 mm., holotype.

Mottled with dark spots, those posteriorly

more or less united into irregular vertical bars; vomerine teeth either absent or made up of a short posterior continuation of the median premaxillary row; both anterior and posterior nostrils pigmented though less so than the rest of the head; gill opening high on the sides.

This specimen seems to be more or less intermediate between *U. dentatus* and *U. supraforatus*. Indeed the distinctions between these two species as given by Schultz (in Schultz, *et al.*, 1953: 141) do not seem to be very clear-cut. Nevertheless, it seems best to follow Schultz in recognizing the Johnston form as *U. dentatus*, at least until such time as specimens of *U. supraforatus* become available for comparison.

For the relationships between *U. dentatus* and *U. fuscoguttatus*, see the account of the latter species.

Uropterygius fuscoguttatus Schultz

3 specs., 129–152 mm., 1951. Schultz, *et al.*, 1953, 1 spec.

At the present time there seem to be three recognized Central Pacific species in the *Uropterygius* group with the gill openings high on the sides and multiserial teeth in both jaws: *U. supraforatus* Regan, *U. dentatus* Schultz, and *U. fuscoguttatus* Schultz. Unfortunately, Schultz has placed his two species, both of which according to specimens and his own figures (in Schultz, *et al.*, 1953: figs. 32, 33) have the gill opening about equally high on the sides, on opposite sides of a major break in his key based on the level of the gill openings. Actually *U. fuscoguttatus* is rather difficult to distinguish from *U. supraforatus* and *U. dentatus*. As compared with these, *U. fuscoguttatus*, judging from Hawaii and Johnston material, is a relatively small species, not attaining a length of over 285 mm. A female 185 mm. is ripe. From *U. dentatus* it can best be distinguished by coloration: *U. dentatus* is an eel with dark spotting and mottling everywhere; *U. fuscoguttatus*, by contrast, is spotted and mottled posteriorly, but the head and forepart of body are plain brown, the brownish color made up of minute, regularly spaced punctulations. In addition *U. fuscoguttatus* has a somewhat longer snout; the distance between the posterior margin of the eye and the most posterior maxillary tooth is considerably less than the distance from the tip of the snout to the posterior nostril (in *U. dentatus* these two distances are about equal). In *U. dentatus* the two jaws are about equal, and the distance from the tip of chin to the most posterior mandibular tooth is contained about 2.4 times in the head length; in *U. fuscoguttatus* the lower jaw is very slightly inferior, and the distance from the tip of the chin to the last mandibular tooth is contained about 2.7 times in the head length. There are also many more teeth in *U. dentatus* than in *U. fuscoguttatus* but since the teeth are multiserial in both species, this difference is difficult to quantify. The features listed above would be adequate for distinguishing the two species if they were the same size. Unfortunately they are not. The largest known specimen of *U. fuscoguttatus* is one from Hawaii measuring 285 mm.; the smallest of the three known specimens of *U. dentatus* is 363 mm.

Uropterygius polyspilus Regan

2 specs., 150 and 180 mm., 1951.

Anus very slightly behind middle of the total length; prominent, roundish dark spots on a light brown background; tip of snout white in alcohol, yellow in life.

Uropterygius tigrinus (Lesson)

2 specs., 670 and 680 mm., 1951. As *Gymnomuraena tigrina*, Smith and Swain, 1882, 1 spec.

Anus far behind middle of total length; prominent, roundish dark spots on a light brown background; snout of the same color as the rest of the body but speckled rather than spotted.

BELONIDAE

Belone platyura Bennett

1 spec., 295 mm., 1951. Halstead and Bunker, 1954, 1 spec. As *Belone persimilis*, Schultz, *et al.*, 1953, 4 specs.

The relationship between *Belone platyura* and *B. persimilis* needs clarification. *B. persimilis* was first differentiated from *B. platyura* by Günther (1909: 340, text fig.) on the basis of the smaller eye. In order to demonstrate this, Günther compared the eye size with the interorbital and with the postorbital head length in the two species (Table 1). In 1943 Schultz (p. 54) placed *B. persimilis* in the synonymy of *B. platyura*, stating: "After measuring a large series of specimens of the large-eyed form *B. platyura* and many of the small-eyed form named by Günther *B. persimilis*, I am of the opinion that when small this species has a small eye and when larger the eye is much larger in proportion." In 1953 Schultz (p. 160) reseparated the two nominal species on the basis of eye size and the relatively shorter postorbital head length of *B. persimilis*. He compared these two characters with one another and each of them with the distance between the pelvic insertion and the anal origin in the two species (Table 1). Whereas Günther believed the two species occurred together over a wide area, Schultz (1953, *loc. cit.*) considered all of his Marshallese material to represent *B. platyura* and all of the Johnston (and by inference Hawaiian) specimens to be *B. persimilis*.

Counts and measurements of the six specimens available to me are given in Table 1. Aside from the characters listed, an attempt was made to find others which might be used for differentiating two species. For example, the length of the anal base was compared with the postanal length, but it was found that this comparison merely demonstrated the difference in the number of anal rays. Again, the Johnston and the larger Hawaiian specimen at present lack cheek scales whereas the other four have such scales, but this may be an artifact of preservation. At first it was thought possible to separate a long, narrow-headed species from one with a relatively short and broad head (the smaller Hawaiian and the

TABLE 1

CERTAIN COUNTS, MEASUREMENTS, AND DIFFERENCES BETWEEN *Belone persimilis?* AND *Belone platyura*
Measurements, except the first, are given in thousandths of the body length as defined

	Belone persimilis?			*Belone platyura*		
	Oahu	Oahu	Johnston	Gilberts	Gilberts	Bikini
Body length, from front of eye to tip of fleshy projection on middle caudal rays.	255 mm.	272 mm.	299 mm.	230 mm.	278 mm.	297 mm.
Distance from front of nasal bones to anterior nostril....................	35.3	34.5	36.8	33.3	38.1	36.4
Horizontal orbit diameter.............	45.2	45.0	44.2	46.1	47.8	50.2
Postorbital head length................	76.2	76.8	73.4	81.3	82.8	77.7
Width of skull in front of eye.........	51.1	50.9	51.2	46.5	56.8	57.2
Width of bony interorbital............	36.5	37.0	34.5	39.1	43.8	43.1
Maximum width of skull across pterotics..	52.5	53.7	53.2	45.9	62.2	62.3
Distance from pelvic insertion to anal origin...........................	184	182	181	189	192	174
Dorsal rays...........................	14	14	14	13	14	14
Anal rays.............................	18	19	19	17	18	18
Pectoral rays.........................	12	12	12	12	12	12
Orbit into bony interorbital:						
Present data......................	0.81 to 1.1			0.85 to 0.92		
According to Günther (1909)........	less than (soft?) interorbital			equals (soft?) interorbital		
Orbit into postorbital head:						
Present data......................	1.67 to 1.70..			1.55 to 1.75		
According to Günther (1909)........	1.6 to 2			1.5 to 1.67		
According to Schultz (1953)..........	1.8 to 2.1			1.5 to 1.8		
Orbit into pelvic-anal distance						
Present data......................	4.1 to 4.2			3.5 to 4.1		
According to Schultz (1953)..........	4.0 to 5.1			3.1 to 3.6		
Postorbital head length into pelvic-anal distance:						
Present data......................	2.3 to 2.5			2.2 to 2.3		
According to Schultz (1953)..........	2.3 to 2.5			2.0 to 2.2		

smaller Gilbertese specimen would constitute the narrow-headed form) but this idea was discarded. In the final analysis it appears that if any separation of two species among the tabulated specimens is made, it should be based on the size of the eye. However, the difference in eye size between the specimens in Table 1 labelled *B. persimilis?* and those labelled *B. platyura* is very slight, and from the Table it is obvious that to state this difference in relation to the interorbital width, the postorbital head length, and only to a lesser extent the pelvic-anal distance obscures rather than clarifies the segregation of two forms. In short, of the characters used by Günther and by Schultz (1953), only two of them will serve to separate the specimens at

hand, and even in these there may prove to be more of a continuous distribution than a separation. Under the circumstances it seems that a convincing means of differentiating *B. persimilis* from *B. platyura*, if both species are valid, remains to be demonstrated; meanwhile there is little practical use in recognizing them. Finally, if the two prove valid, then the nomenclatorial question will arise as to whether the second should be called *B. persimilis*, *B. carinata* (described from the Hawaiian Islands by Cuvier and Valenciennes in 1846), or perhaps by some other early name.

HEMIRAMPHIDAE

Hyporhamphus acutus (Günther)
2 specs., 80 and 163 mm., 1951.

Upper jaw scaled; greatest diameter of the nasal fossa about one third the diameter of the orbit; posterolateral border of fossa with a prominent bony rim; sensory pore on preorbital apparently branched above with a pore in front of eye and another near nasal fossa; inner pelvic ray not elongate. Dorsal base very slightly shorter than base of anal; dorsal with 14 rays, anal with 18 in larger specimen.

The identification of these specimens seems certain, except that the small diameter of the nasal fossa throws them into the genus *Hemiramphus* according to Schultz and Woods' generic key (in Schultz, *et al.*, 1953: 166). Measurement of other available specimens of the same species including Bikini duplicates indicates that the key character referred to will not serve for this species.

EXOCOETIDAE

*Cypselurus poecilopterus (Valenciennes)
Fowler and Ball, 1925, 2 specs.

*Cypselurus simus (Valenciennes)
Fowler and Ball, 1925, 1 spec.

AULOSTOMIDAE

*Aulostomus chinensis (Linnaeus)
Smith and Swain, 1882, 1 spec.; Halstead and Bunker, 1954, 5 specs.

FISTULARIIDAE

Fistularia petimba Lacepède
1 spec., 900 mm., 1951. Fowler and Ball, 1925, 1 spec.

HOLOCENTRIDAE

Holocentrus lacteoguttatus Cuvier
10 specs., 54–109 mm., 1951; 2 specs., 97 and 101 mm., Brock, 1948. Fowler and Ball, 1925, 5 specs.; Halstead and Bunker, 1954, 2 specs.

The two opercular spines subequal in size; body speckled with sooty marks.

Holocentrus microstomus Günther
Fowler and Ball, 1925, 2 specs., one of these reexamined.

Dorsal XI–12; perforated scales in lateral line 48; longest anal spine reaching beyond caudal base.

Holocentrus sammara (Forskål)
3 specs., 117–157 mm., 1951. Halstead and Bunker, 1954, 1 spec.

Brown spotting on a bronze to silvery background; a large dark blotch on the spinous dorsal.

Holocentrus spinifer (Forskål)
4 specs., 151–300 mm., 1951; 1 spec., 261 mm., Schaefer, 1948. Fowler and Ball, 1925, 6 specs.; Halstead and Bunker, 1954, 7 specs. As *Holocentrus leo*, Smith and Swain, 1882, 2 specs.

Holocentrus tiere Cuvier and Valenciennes
8 specs., 121–226 mm., 1951. Halstead and Bunker, 1954, 3 specs. As *Holocentrus erythraeus*, Smith and Swain, 1882, 2 specs.

Perforated scales in the lateral line 50; maxillary longer than eye; dorsal XI–14.

Holotrachys lima (Valenciennes)
1 spec., 115 mm., 1951.

Myripristis argyromus Jordan and Evermann
31 specs., 45–210 mm., 1951; 1 spec., 121 mm., Brock, 1948. Halstead and Bunker, 1954, 3 specs. As *Myripristis murdjan*, Fowler and Ball, 1925, 1 spec., this specimen reexamined.

Perforated scales in the lateral line 34; anal IV, 13; gill rakers $12 + 1 + 25 = 38$; interorbital width contained about 3.7 times in the head length.

*Myripristis berndti Jordan and Evermann
Halstead and Bunker, 1954, 1 spec.

APOGONIDAE

Apogon erythrinus Snyder
15 specs., 30–42 mm., 1951.

Dorsal VI–I, 9; anterior margin of preopercle smooth; anal II, 8; lateral line complete; second spine of first dorsal much longer than third (cf., Lachner, *in* Schultz, *et al.*, 1953: 435).

Apogon menesemus Jenkins

13 specs., 67–128 mm., 1951; 1 spec., 86 mm., Brock, 1948.

Dorsal VII–I, 9; both margins of preopercle serrate; palatine teeth absent; gill rakers (including rudiments) 4 + 1 + 17 = 22; black pigmentation on caudal forming a complete arc.

Apogon snyderi Jordan and Evermann

31 specs., 32–100 mm., 1951; 2 specs., 40 and 97 mm., Brock, 1948. As *Apogon frenatus*, at least in part, Fowler and Ball, 1925, 6 specs.

Dorsal VII–I, 9; both margins of preopercle serrate; palatine teeth present; gill rakers (including rudiments) 4 + 1 + 13 = 18; no circular spot at midbase of caudal fin in specimens over 55 mm. but instead a dark bar that covers the whole fin base; in specimens 50–55 mm. a more or less well-delimited, round dark spot that lies above but touches the lateral line; stripe on sides not well-marked, absent in large specimens; serrations on anterior margin of preopercle reaching a larger size than those on posterior margin; suborbital serrations few in small specimens, numerous in large, but almost always more than 3 (cf., Lachner, in Schultz, *et al.*, 1953: 436, 437).

Apogon waikiki (Jordan and Evermann)

3 specs., 21–36 mm., 1951.

Dorsal VII–I, 9; no serrations on preopercle; palate toothless; lateral line complete; dorsal fin without ocellus; dorsal rounded, dusky at base, the tips of the outer rays white.

Pseudamiops gracilicauda (Lachner)

1 spec., 23 mm., 1951.

Recently Smith (1954) has described the new genus *Pseudamiops* for the single new species *P. pellucidus*. In the same article (p. 794) he erects the "provisional" genus *Lachneria* for the species *Gymnapogon gracilicauda* Lachner. The difference between the two genera according to the descriptions is that *Pseudamiops* is scaled and the specimens on

which *Gymnapogon gracilicauda* was based were naked. Smith suspected that the scales of *G. gracilicauda* had been rubbed off; hence the provisional nature of his genus *Lachneria*. The specimen from Johnston plus two Hawaiian specimens agree well with Lachner's description of *Gymnapogon gracilicauda* except that they are more or less scaled. However, as with *Pseudamiops pellucidus*, the scales are apparently highly deciduous, for none of the three specimens are now completely scaled.

The chief points, aside from squamation, in which the Johnston and Hawaii specimens differ from Lachner's description and figure (in Schultz, *et al.*, 1953: 497, 498, fig. 84) are the following. The present specimens have a very pinched-in abdominal region as though the fishes had been starving; the specimen figured by Lachner does not have this feature, nor does that of *Pseudamiops* figured by Smith. The longest spine of the anal and that of the second dorsal are about half the length of the succeeding soft ray, instead of about four fifths the length of these rays as shown in Lachner's figure. The middle pectoral rays terminate in elongate, soft, fragile filaments. There seem to be at most 6 or 7 teeth on the vomer instead of about 20 according to Lachner (the vomerine teeth of *Pseudamiops* are reduced to one or two). There are no weak spines on the operculum; two are said to be present in *Gymnapogon gracilicauda*. Finally, only one of the three specimens has the system of papillae on the head well developed; however, as Smith has noted the prominence of this character probably varies with the nature of preservation.

From *Pseudamiops pellucidus* the Hawaiian and Johnston specimens differ in having one fewer soft anal ray and in lacking the pigment spots on the head.

It may prove to be that the Hawaiian and Johnston material is a separate species from both Lachner's Marshallese form and Smith's from Africa. However, as Lachner's material was in poor condition it will apparently require comparison with better Marshallese material to determine whether the Hawaiian form is conspecific with it or not.

No such doubt seems possible regarding the necessity of placing the genus *Lachneria* in the synonymy of *Pseudamiops*.

KUHLIIDAE

Kuhlia marginata (Cuvier and Valenciennes)

9 specs., 61–221 mm., 1951. As *Kuhlia taeniura*, Smith and Swain, 1882, 2 specs.

These specimens will be dealt with in section 2.

PSEUDOCHROMIDAE

Pseudogramma polyacantha (Bleeker)

11 specs., 39–74 mm., 1951; 4 specs., 35–51 mm., Brock, 1948.

Dorsal spines VII; no enlarged pores between the eyes.

PRIACANTHIDAE

Priacanthus cruentatus (Lacepède)

2 specs., 127 and 140 mm., 1951; 4 specs., 89–93 mm., Francis, 1948. Halstead and Bunker, 1954, 2 specs.

Soft dorsal rays 13; soft anal rays 14; no dark spots on pelvic fins; caudal fin truncate.

SERRANIDAE

*Pristipomoides sieboldii

Fowler and Ball, 1925, 1 spec.

KYPHOSIDAE

*Kyphosus bigibbus Lacepède

Halstead and Bunker, 1954, 1 spec.

Kyphosus vaigiensis (Quoy and Gaimard)

1 spec., 170 mm., 1951.

Longest dorsal spine longer than longest soft dorsal ray; dorsal XI, 13; anal III, 12 or 13; greatest depth 2.3 in standard length.

MULLIDAE

*Mulloidichthys auriflamma (Forskål)

Halstead and Bunker, 1954, 2 specs. As *Upeneus vanicolensis*, Smith and Swain, 1882,

1 spec. As *Mulloides auriflamma* Fowler and Ball, 1925, 4 specs.

Mulloidichthys samoensis (Günther)

5 specs., 162–219 mm., 1951; 6 specs., 92–101 mm., Francis, 1948; 9 specs., 124–143 mm., Schaefer, 1948. Halstead and Bunker, 1954, 7 specs. As *Upeneus preorbitalis* Smith and Swain, 1882, 1 spec.

A black spot on sides below spinous dorsal; a dark area on inside of gill cover ahead of pseudobranch.

Parupeneus barberinus (Lacepède)

As *Upeneus barberinus*, Fowler and Ball, 1925, 1 spec., this reexamined.

Parupeneus bifasciatus (Lacepède)

8 specs., 53–210 mm., 1951. Halstead and Bunker, 1954, 3 specs. As *Parupeneus crassilabris*, Smith and Swain, 1882.

Depth of body greater than the head length; barbels short, failing to reach the pelvic bases by about three and a half scales; body usually with vertical dark bands, one of these with its anterior border about even with a line drawn between the soft dorsal and anal origins.

*Parupeneus chryserydros (Lacepède)

Halstead and Bunker, 1954, 2 specs. As *Upeneus chryserydros*, Fowler and Ball, 1925, 1 spec.

*Parupeneus crassilabris (Valenciennes)

Halstead and Bunker, 1954, 1 spec.

Parupeneus multifasciatus (Quoy and Gaimard)

3 specs., 175–220 mm., 1951. As *Upeneus velifer* Smith and Swain, 1882, 1 spec.

Depth of body less than the head length; barbels long, failing to reach the pelvic origins by 1 scale; body with dark vertical blotches, one of these with its anterior border extending downward and forward from the last ray of the first dorsal.

*Parupeneus trifasciatus (Lacepède)

Halstead and Bunker, 1954, 4 specs.

CIRRHITIDAE

Cirrhitus alternatus Gill

1 spec., 72 mm., 1951; 1 spec., 119 mm., Brock, 1948. As *Cirrhitus maculatus*, Fowler and Ball, 1925, 1 spec.

These specimens are dealt with in section 2.

Paracirrhites bimacula (Jenkins)

13 specs., 28–60 mm., 1951.

CARANGIDAE

Carangoides ferdau jordani Nichols

1 spec., 318 mm., 1951. Halstead and Bunker, 1954, 5 specs.

Teeth in bands in both jaws; breast naked; depth of body about 2.8 in standard length; anal soft rays 25; 20 gill rakers on lower portion of first arch (cf., Woods, in Schultz, et al., 1953: 505).

*Caranx ascensionis (Osbeck)

Fowler and Ball, 1925, 4 specs.

*Caranx dasson Jordan and Snyder

Fowler and Ball, 1925, 1 spec.

*Caranx gymnostethoides (Bleeker)

Smith and Swain, 1882, 1 spec.

*Caranx lugubris Poey

Halstead and Bunker, 1954, 5 specs.

*Caranx melampygus Cuvier

Halstead and Bunker, 1954, 4 specs.

*Scomberoides sancti-petri (Cuvier)

Smith and Swain, 1882, 1 spec.; Fowler and Ball, 1925, 2 specs.

Trachurops crumenophthalmus (Bloch)

1 spec., 286 mm., 1951; 4 specs., 121–128 mm., Francis, 1948; 2 specs., 173 and 177 mm., Schaefer, 1948.

Shoulder girdle deeply furrowed.

POMACENTRIDAE

Abudefduf imparipennis (Vaillant and Sauvage)

20 specs., 33–50 mm., 1951. Fowler and Ball, 1925, 4 specs.

Preopercle smooth; teeth flattened at tips; dorsal XII, 15; color plain yellowish green; upper base of pectoral pale.

Abudefduf phoenixensis Schultz

2 specs., 50–51 mm., 1951. As *Abudefduf albofasciatus*, Fowler and Ball, 1925, 2 specs.

Preopercle smooth; teeth somewhat flattened at tips; dorsal XII, 18; anal II, 13; caudal peduncle encircled by a black band, followed abruptly by white on the remainder of the caudal peduncle and tail; a round black spot on the soft dorsal.

*Abudefduf sordidus (Forskål)

Fowler and Ball, 1925, 8 specs.; Halstead and Bunker, 1954, 7 specs.

Chromis leucurus Gilbert

2 specs., 61 and 65 mm., 1951; 1 spec., 68 mm., Brock, 1948. As *Chromis dimidiatus*, Fowler and Ball, 1925, 1 spec., 64 mm., this specimen reexamined.

This species is described herewith.

After much vacillation, these plain brown-bodied specimens with a black blotch at the pectoral base are here identified as a color

TABLE 2

CERTAIN COUNTS FOR TWO FORMS OF *Chromis leucurus*

FORM	LATERAL LINE SCALES			TOTAL GILL RAKERS					SOFT DORSAL RAYS			SOFT ANAL RAYS			PECTORAL RAYS		
	15	16	17	27	28	29	30	31	12	13	14	12	13	14	16	17	18
Black and white	2	3		1	2	1	1		2	14	2	2	12	4	1	4	
Plain brown	3	2	1	1	2			2		8		1	7		1	2	2

form of the black and white *Chromis leucurus*. Comparison of the same two forms from Hawaiian material provides the following information: (1) the black and white and the brown specimens differ little in morphological features or in counts (Table 2); (2) ripe individuals of both sexes occur in both color forms; and (3), though the two color forms overlap in size ranges, the plain brown form is represented only by specimens 47 to 70 mm. in standard length, whereas black and white specimens range from 17 to 57 mm. In life both forms may be seen over the same coral head. Presumably the brown form represents an ontogenetic color change that occurs after maturity has been attained.

Chromis vanderbilti (Fowler)

1 spec., 35 mm., 1951.

This specimen differs from Hawaiian and Wake Island material in lacking the black on the lower caudal lobe. There appear to be no other differences. Dorsal XII, 11; anal II, 11, the anterior two-thirds black, becoming abruptly light posteriorly.

Dascyllus albisella Gill

12 specs. 43–88 mm., 1951; 2 specs., 69–75 mm., Brock, 1948.

Though no specimens of *Dascyllus trimaculatus* are readily available, the Hawaiian form seems to differ, among other features, in having more dorsal and anal soft rays. The present (1951) specimens agree with the Hawaiian form in having 15 dorsal soft rays in two specimens and 16 in ten, 14 soft rays in the anal of one specimen, and 15 in the anal of eleven.

*Dascyllus marginatus (Rüppell)

Halstead and Bunker, 1954, 4 specs.

Plectroglyphidodon johnstonianus
Fowler

8 specs., 27–80 mm., 1951. Fowler and Ball, 1925, 1 spec. As *Abudefduf johnstonianus*, Halstead and Bunker, 1954, 1 spec.

Lips plicate; dorsal XII, 18; anal II, 16 or 17.

LABRIDAE

*Bodianus bilunulatus (Lacepède)

As *Harpe bilunulata*, Smith and Swain, 1882, 1 spec.

Cheilinus rhodochrous Günther

3 specs., 146–205 mm., 1951. Halstead and Bunker, 1954, 5 specs. As *Cheilinus digramma*, Smith and Swain, 1882, 3 specs., and Fowler and Ball, 1925, 1 spec.

The 1951 specimens have the elongate head, white band on the caudal peduncle, and IX dorsal spines that seem to characterize this species. No black lines radiating downward from eye.

Epibulus insidiator (Pallas)

9 specs., 73–255 mm., 1951. Fowler and Ball, 1925, 2 specs.; Halstead and Bunker, 1954, 4 specs.

Lower jaw extending backward to isthmus.

*Gomphosus tricolor Quoy and Gaimard

Fowler and Ball, 1925, 2 specs.

Gomphosus varius Lacepède

16 specs., 27–106 mm., 1951; 4 specs., 27–89 mm., Brock, 1948.

A dark stripe through eye; vertical fins dark.

Halichoeres ornatissimus (Garrett)

1 spec., 58 mm., 1951. Fowler and Ball, 1925, 2 specs., these reexamined.

These specimens all have the characteristic dark mark just behind the eye.

Novaculichthys taeniourus (Lacepède)

1 spec., 119 mm., 1951.

Only four lines radiating out from the eye.

Pseudocheilinus sp.

12 specs., 30–55 mm., 2 specs., 40–46 mm., Brock, 1948.

First dorsal rays usually produced into elongate filaments; two longitudinal scale rows on cheek below eye; three or four black longitudinal lines along upper sides; background color of body bluish; 16 rays in the pectoral counting the splint above; no black dot on the caudal peduncle above.

This species will be described elsewhere by Dr. L. P. Schultz.

*Pseudocheilinus hexataenia (Bleeker)

Fowler and Ball, 1925, 6 specs. This record undoubtedly refers to either *Pseudocheilinus* sp. or *P. octotaenia*.

Pseudocheilinus octotaenia (Jenkins)

2 specs., 73 and 85 mm., 1951; 1 spec., 76 mm., Brock, 1948.

First dorsal rays not longer than those of the middle of the fin; three longitudinal rows of scales on cheek below eye; six to eight black longitudinal lines on sides, the lowermost well below the middle of the body; 14 rays in the pectoral fin counting the splint-like ray above.

Stethojulis axillaris (Quoy and Gaimard)

17 specs., 30–71 mm., 1951; 1 spec., 82 mm., Brock, 1948.

One or more black dots along the middle of the caudal peduncle.

Thalassoma ballieui (Vaillant and Sauvage)

Fowler and Ball, 1925, 1 spec. As *Julis verticalis* Smith and Swain, 1882, 1 spec.

Fowler and Ball's specimen has been reexamined. Though in poor condition, it does show the concentration of vertical markings on the scales on the caudal peduncle.

Thalassoma duperrey (Quoy and Gaimard)

16 specs., 55–162 mm., 1951; 1 spec., 146 mm., Brock, 1948. Halstead and Bunker, 1954, 1 spec. As *Julis clepsydralis* Smith and Swain, 1882, 1 spec.

A distinct light brown cross band through shoulder region in life, the fish becoming plain dark in preservative without marks except often for a dark mark on the upper edge of the pectoral base.

Thalassoma lutescens (Lay and Bennett)

5 specs., 53–116 mm., 1951. As *Thalassoma aneitense*, Fowler and Ball, 1925, 1 spec.

This species, of greenish yellow coloration in life, agrees well with Jordan and Evermann's plate (1905, pl. 41, as *T. aneitense*) except that each scale has an indistinct vertical stripe. However, there seems to be no way besides color by which to distinguish these specimens from *T. duperrey*, and it might prove difficult to refute the view that they simply represent a color variant of *T. duperrey* (similar to the yellow phase of *Epibulus insidiator*). The absence of canine teeth given by Jordan and Evermann (*op. cit.*) is valueless. Johnston specimens of *T. lutescens* have canine teeth exactly as in *T. duperrey*.

Thalassoma purpureum (Forskål)

Fowler and Ball, 1925, 1 spec.

This specimen has been reexamined. It has the broad band, branching below, extending

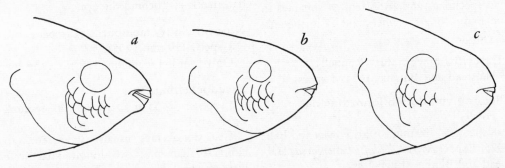

FIG. 2. Heads of species of *Scarus. a, Scarus dubius*, from a specimen 4¼ inches in total length with the mouth slightly open and the lips somewhat retracted; *b, Scarus sordidus*, from a 5¾-inch specimen; *c, Scarus perspicillatus*, from a 5½-inch specimen.

down and back from the eye typical of the species.

Thalassoma quinquevittata (Lay and Bennett)

10 specs., 48–110 mm., 1951; 1 spec., 62 mm., Brock, 1948.

Distance from tip of snout to origin of dorsal less than distance from tip of snout to origin of pelvics; a dark band around chin in adults; several dark marks along dorsal base in young.

SCARIDAE

Calotomus sandvicensis (Cuvier and Valenciennes)

7 specs., 90–235 mm., 1951.

The species of *Calotomus*, like those of *Scarus* (see below), are badly confused, and this must be considered a tentative identification.

Genus SCARUS

The present classification of the species of central Pacific parrot fishes is a mess. However, the group is in the process of being monographed (Schultz, ms.). In view of this the aims of the present account are quite limited. They comprise an attempt to separate what seem to be the three commonest species of the genus *Scarus* in Hawaiian waters (which happen to be the three species taken at Johnston) and to see to what extent the green and brown color phases of these species are correlated with sexual differentiation and maturity.

KEY TO THE SPECIES OF *Scarus* COLLECTED AT JOHNSTON ISLAND

1a. Lower (horizontal) limb of preopercular border relatively little developed (Fig. 2b, c), the length of its free edge (measured to the point at which the border runs vertically) less than the distance from its most anterior point to the midventral line; upper tooth plate never completely covered by the upper lip; pectoral rays usually 14 (not counting

the small splint at the top); outline of the border of pelvic fins usually rounded; outer caudal rays never prolonged; canine teeth at the corners of the upper tooth plate, if present, low and knob like...2

1b. Lower limb of preopercular border relatively well developed (Fig. 2a), its length equal to or greater than the distance from its most anterior point to the midventral line; upper tooth plate, when retracted, completely covered by the upper lip; pectoral rays 13 (14 in one out of 14 specimens); pelvic outlines usually pointed between the 1st and 2nd soft rays; caudal truncate in specimens up to 5 inches in total length (Fig. 3a, b), lunate in larger specimens (Fig. 3c) and usually with the outer rays prolonged in fishes between 8.5 inches and the maximum size attained (which is about 12 inches); adults usually with 1 to 3 conspicuous, conical, pointed canines at either side of the upper tooth plate. Two complete scale rows on cheek with sometimes a third incomplete row below (Fig. 2a); head of moderate size, less than the greatest depth of body in specimens over 6 inches long................**dubius**

2a. Lower of the two scale rows on cheek, if present, incomplete, consisting of 1 to 3 scales; head relatively smaller, its length considerably less than the greatest body depth; attains at least 2 feet in length................**perspicillatus**

2b. Lower of the two scale rows on cheek about as long as the upper, consisting of 5 to 7 scales; head relatively large and bullet shaped, its length about equal to the greatest depth of body; apparently does not reach a length of over 1 foot ....**sordidus**

Scarus dubius (Bennett)

13 specs., 39–162 mm., 1951 (brown form). As *Scarus brunneus*, Halstead and Bunker, 1954, 1 spec.

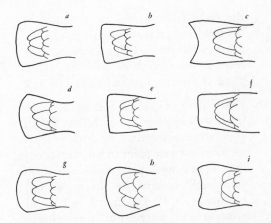

FIG. 3. Caudal fin outlines of *Scarus*. *a–c*, *Scarus dubius*, *a*, 2¾ inches in total length, *b*, 4¼ inches, *c*, 7¾ inches; *d–f*, *Scarus sordidus*, *d*, 3½ inches, *e*, 5¾ inches, *f*, 7 inches; *g–i*, *Scarus perspicillatus*, *g*, 2¾ inches, *h*, 5½ inches, *i*, 12¾ inches.

The rather extensive forward projection of the free preopercular border (Fig. 2*a*) is perhaps the most reliable way of distinguishing the species here tentatively identified as *S. dubius* from the other two species of *Scarus* dealt with here. The following distinguishing features, though helpful, appear to be less reliable. The pectoral rays are usually 13 instead of 14. When the jaws are retracted and the lips are in normal position, the upper lip extends down as a flap over the whole of the upper tooth plate; however, if the jaws are incompletely retracted (even though they may be partially closed as in Fig. 2*a*) or if the lips have been pushed back, the upper tooth plate may protrude. In the other two species the lips never cover the tooth plates except in very small specimens (less than 3 inches in total length). The two, more or less complete scale rows on the cheek will separate *S. dubius* from *S. perspicillatus* but not from *S. sordidus*. Certain features that change with growth are useful in separating *S. dubius* from the other two species if specimens of the same size are compared. Thus *S. dubius* develops a lunate caudal at a length of 7 inches in total length, whereas *S. perspicillatus* does not have a lunate caudal at sizes below 12 inches and *S. sordidus*

apparently never does have a lunate caudal. Again, *S. dubius* at a length of perhaps 7 inches usually develops one or two outwardly projecting canines at each corner of the upper jaw, but the other two species apparently never develop these beyond the stage of small, rounded tubercles.

Among the Hawaiian species of *Scarus* for which accounts are given by Jordan and Evermann (1905) the brown form here called *S. dubius* appears to have been included three times: as *Callyodon brunneus* (p. 349), *C. dubius* (p. 350), and as *C. bennetti* (p. 352). These, except for *C. brunneus*, differ in certain details from the form at hand. The major differences judging from Jordan and Evermann's accounts, are as follows: *Callyodon dubius* is said to have 14 pectoral rays; the pectoral count of the present specimens is usually 13. *C. bennetti* is figured with a rounded caudal (but this may be due to the small size of the specimen), the lips are said not to cover the upper jaw, and there are white lines along the scale rows of the lower sides (I have yet to see such markings). Though it is quite possible that more than one species is represented in the above group, a reexamination of Jordan and Evermann's material would be necessary to determine this. Of the three names, *S. dubius* (Bennett) is the oldest. Bennett's original description (1828: 828; type locality Oahu) is very sketchy. However, Günther has redescribed the type, along with other specimens, in two places (1862: 229; 1909: 313). In both of these redescriptions Günther mentions the presence of two scales in a row below the other two cheek rows. The species here dealt with is the only unspotted, brown Hawaiian *Scarus* known to me in which this third row ever occurs.

Scarus dubius apparently does not reach a large size. The largest brown specimen from Johnston is about 8 inches in total length. The largest specimen mentioned in Jordan and Evermann's accounts of *Callyodon brunneus*, *dubius*, and *bennetti* is 9.5 inches.

Of the five individuals more than 6 inches long from Johnston two, 6.4 and 8 inches long, are mature or maturing females. The ovaries are elongate, paired organs without sharp edges and contain small elongate eggs. The three other specimens, 7 to 7.4 inches in total length, contain in the ovarian position and behind the liver, flat, sharp-edged organs. The extent to which these structures are developed in the three individuals varies greatly. At one extreme they are small and leaf like. At the other they are somewhat larger than the largest ovary in the females mentioned above, rather thick, and overlap the intestines at the sides, above, and behind. These large structures must, I think, be identified as ripe testes.

The brown *Scarus dubius*, like the other two species to be dealt with, seems to have a green counterpart. Before discussing this, it seems advisable to say something about green parrot fishes in general based on experience with the scarids in Hawaii and elsewhere. Young parrot fishes, up to about 2 inches in length, are frequently, perhaps always, a plain light green color. These gradually become brownish with growth and I have never seen a green scarid between 3 inches and about 7 inches long. Green parrot fishes (more than 7 inches long) invariably have adult characteristics. In all the three species dealt with here, the size of the green counterpart is comparable to or somewhat larger than the mature brown form. Thus the green counterparts of small brown forms, e.g., *S. dubius* and *S. sordidus*, are always relatively small while those of large brown forms, e.g., *S. ahula* (=*perspicillatus*), are always relatively large. I have never seen a female green scarid, though, as just noted, some brown specimens appear to be adult males. Finally, green parrot fishes seem to be relatively rare as compared with brown individuals, though the distinctiveness in the color markings of the green as contrasted with brown forms has led to the description of numerous green species.

The green counterpart of *S. dubius* is rep-resented in the University of Hawaii collections by four specimens 170 to 190 mm. in total length that died in the Honolulu Aquarium and by one taken at Kailua, Kona, Hawaii. The aquarium specimens are so badly damaged that an exact correspondence in many morphological characters between them and the brown *S. dubius* could not be checked. They do agree in having two scale rows on the cheek, a relatively long horizontal limb to the free preopercular border, 13 pectoral rays, pointed ventrals, and a rather small head. In only two of the four could gonads be found. In these there were relatively small, elongate, sharp edged organs without eggs that must be considered testes.

The 12 inch Kailua specimen is in better condition and hence of greater interest. It is an unripe male; I can only find a testis on the left side. The description of the morphological characters given for the adult brown *S. dubius* fits this specimen completely. The mouth is closed and the upper lip projects forward as a flap over the whole upper tooth plate. The pectoral rays are 13 on each side and there are two complete rows of scales on the cheek. There is a single outwardly-projecting canine on each side of the upper jaw. The caudal is lunate and the outermost soft pelvic ray extends well beyond the others.

Jordan and Evermann (*op. cit.*) recognize six green species of *Scarus* from the Hawaiian islands: "*Callyodon*" *perspicillatus* (p. 347), *C. jenkinsi* (p. 353), *C. gilberti* (p. 354), *C. formosus* (p. 355), *C. lauia* (p. 355), and *C. bataviensis* (p. 356). Of these *Scarus perspicillatus* has the lower row of cheek scales incomplete, and Brock and Yamaguchi (1954: 154) have already demonstrated that it is the adult male of "*S. ahula.*" The color description and plate given by Jordan and Evermann for *Scarus lauia* is decidedly dissimilar to that of the specimen at hand and seems to represent an entirely different species. As for the remaining forms: *S. jenkinsi*, *S. gilberti*, *S. formosus*, and *S. bataviensis*, there is nothing in Jordan and Evermann to indicate that any or all of them are not the species represented by the Kailua specimen. I can see nothing to indicate that this in turn is not an old male of the brown form represented by *S. dubius*. Since *S. dubius* is the oldest name to be applied in either the brown or the green complex dealt with, it may be, at least provisionally, used for this species.

Scarus sordidus Forskål

78 specs., 57–222 mm., 1951 (75 brown, 3 green); 5 specs., 115–175 mm., Brock, 1948. Fowler and Ball, 1925, 2 specs.

This species does not seem to be among those described by Jordan and Evermann and the identification for it was kindly provided by Dr. L. P. Schultz of the U. S. National Museum. It has a characteristic bullet-shaped head and usually has the tooth plates protruding well beyond the lips. These tooth plates are of a dirty, greenish tinge in alcohol. The caudal of this species is rounded in small specimens but truncate in fishes 5.5 inches in total length and larger. It is the most elongate of the three species, and the eye is smaller than in the other two species at the same size. The anal rays are somewhat shorter than in *S. perspicillatus* (longest anal ray contained 1.85–2.34 in anal base of *S. sordidus*, 1.44–1.98 in *S. perspicillatus*). This form often has a white band on the caudal peduncle and there is frequently a black spot in the middle of the band.

It seems to be the commonest scarid at Johnston and not at all infrequent around Oahu. The largest specimen of this brown form taken is about 9 inches long. Most of the specimens more than 5 inches long are mature females with eggs. The ovaries are similar to those of *S. dubius* and are paired in the single specimen checked. Again certain specimens contain the asymetrical, liver-like structure found in the brown form of *S. dubius*. Of a dozen brown specimens checked, one 4.5 inches long was an immature. The rest are larger, the largest being 8.3 inches in total length. Of these, 8 are mature females, and 3

have a large, flattish liver-like organ in the ovarian position. The size of this flattish organ, when present is, in 2 out of the 3 specimens, larger than the largest ovary. This seems peculiar if it is a testis, but repeated attempts to find eggs in it have failed. The facts that the liver is also present in these specimens, that there are no other gonad-like structures along with it, and that it contains no eggs seems to leave little alternative to identifying the structure as a testis despite its size.

Three green specimens, 10.2 to 10.5 inches in total length, were taken with the brown form from Johnston described above. These all duplicate the brown form of *S. sordidus* in morphological characters, e.g., the long head with greatly protruding, greenish tooth plates, the two complete scale rows on the cheek, rounded pelvics, etc. Though the outer caudal rays extend somewhat beyond the inner ones they are not produced as in the green form of *S. dubius*. There are from 0 to 3 small knobs at the sides of the upper jaw; these do not project outward to nearly the extent that they do in adult *S. dubius*. In all of these there is a flat organ on the right side, but in one of the three it does not seem to occur on the left. In this one the organ on the right side is quite small, in the other two of moderate size, considerably smaller than the same organ at its maximum development in the smaller brown form. I think two of the three green specimens may be considered ripe or ripening males and the third an unripe male. In color, these specimens, though faded, differ considerably from the green form of *S. dubius*. The pelvic and caudal coloration is quite plain and that on the head seems to have consisted of broad, indefinite dark bars around the mouth and behind the eye.

Scarus perspicillatus (Steindachner)

5 specs., 72–290 mm., 1951 (4 brown, 1 green). Smith and Swain, 1882, 1 spec.; Halstead and Bunker, 1954, 12 specs. As *Callyodon perspicillatus* Fowler and Ball, 1925, 4

specs. As *Callyodon ahula* Fowler and Ball, 1925, 2 specs.

Since Brock and Yamaguchi have already demonstrated (1954) that the green *S. perspicillatus* is the adult male of the brown *S. ahula*, and since my material adds little to this information, the account of this species may be cut short. Only five specimens of this species were taken at Johnston, four brown and one green. The green specimen, 14 inches in total length, is a ripe male with very large, paired testes. Of the brown form, specimens 4.5 to 9.5 inches in total length are immatures; the other, 14 inches long, is a ripe or ripening female. The large female differs from the ripe male (and from brown specimens of a similar size from Hawaii) in the considerably greater depth of body, but I can see no other characters on which to separate them.

Additional species of *Scarus* recorded from Johnston are:

***Scarus cyanogrammus** (Jordan and Seale) Halstead and Bunker, 1954, 1 spec.

***Scarus duperrey** (Quoy and Gaimard) Halstead and Bunker, 1954, 1 spec.

***Scarus erythrodon** Cuvier and Valenciennes
As *Callyodon erythrodon*, Fowler and Ball, 1925, 4 specs.

***Scarus forsteri** Valenciennes
Halstead and Bunker, 1954, 1 spec.

CHAETODONTIDAE

Centropyge flammeus Woods and Schultz
4 specs., 70–81 mm., 1951. Woods and Schultz, in Schultz, *et al.*, 1953, 6 specs. As *Holacanthus loriculus*, Fowler and Ball, 1925, 1 spec.

***Centropyge nigriocellus** Woods and Schultz
Woods and Schultz, in Schultz, *et al.*, 1953, 1 spec.

Chaetodon auriga Forskål
14 specs., 112–145 mm., 1951; 1 spec., 117

mm., Schaefer, 1948. Halstead and Bunker, 1954, 7 specs. As *Chaetodon setifer*, Smith and Swain, 1882, 1 spec. and Fowler and Ball, 1925, 5 specs.

Chaetodon citrinellus Cuvier
5 specs., 92–100 mm., 1951. Halstead and Bunker, 1954, 1 spec.

Chaetodon ephippium Cuvier
2 specs., 124 and 158 mm., 1951. Fowler and Ball, 1925, 1 spec.; Halstead and Bunker, 1954, 2 specs.

Chaetodon multicinctus (Garrett)
3 specs., 86–89 mm., 1951. As *Chaetodon punctatofasciatus*, Fowler and Ball, 1925, 3 specs. and Halstead and Bunker, 1954, 2 specs.
This species is dealt with briefly in section 2.

Chaetodon ornatissimus Solander
4 specs., 110–147 mm., 1951. Fowler and Ball, 1925, 3 specs.; Halstead and Bunker, 1954, 4 specs.

Chaetodon quadrimaculatus Gray
2 specs., 108 and 108 mm., 1951. Fowler and Ball, 1925, 3 specs.

Chaetodon trifasciatus Mungo Park
Fowler and Ball, 1925, 5 specs. Determination checked.

Chaetodon unimaculatus Bloch
3 specs., 82–88 mm., 1951; 1 spec., 41 mm., Brock, 1948. Fowler and Ball, 1925, 6 specs.

***Megaprotodon strigangulus** (Gmelin)
Halstead and Bunker, 1954, 1 spec.

ZANCLIDAE

Zanclus cornutus Cuvier
1 spec., 98 mm., 1951. Halstead and Bunker, 1954, 1 spec. As *Zanclus canescens*, Fowler and Ball, 1925, 2 specs.

ACANTHURIDAE

Acanthurus achilles Shaw
18 specs., 114–210 mm., 1951. Halstead

and Bunker, 1954, 4 specs. As *Hepatus achilles*, Fowler and Ball, 1925, 3 specs.

Acanthurus elongatus (Lacepède)
54 specs., 80–126 mm., 1951. Halstead and Bunker, 1954, 13 specs. As *Hepatus lineolatus*, Fowler and Ball, 1925, 5 specs.
A small dark spot at the base of the last dorsal and anal rays.

Acanthurus olivaceus Schneider
1 spec., 200 mm., 1951. Halstead and Bunker, 1954, 6 specs. As *Hepatus olivaceus*, Fowler and Ball, 1925, 1 spec.
Fowler and Ball record 3 specimens of *Hepatus nigricans* from Johnston; one of these is in the Bishop Museum and is *Acanthurus olivaceus*.

Acanthurus sandvicensis Streets
21 specs., 63–127 mm., 1951. As *Acanthurus triostegus*, Smith and Swain, 1882, 2 specs. and Halstead and Bunker, 1954, 5 specs.; as *Hepatus sandvicensis*, Fowler and Ball, 1925, 7 specs.
This species will be treated in section 2.

*Ctenochaetus striatus (Quoy and Gaimard)
Halstead and Bunker, 1954, 7 specs.

Ctenochaetus strigosus (Bennett)
11 specs., 72–106 mm., 1951; 1 spec., 80 mm., Brock, 1948. Fowler and Ball, 1925, 1 spec.
These specimens are included in Randall's report on the genus which is in press.

Naso lituratus (Schneider)
5 specs., 152–210 mm., 1951. Halstead and Bunker, 1954, 7 specs. As *Naseus lituratus*, Smith and Swain, 1882, 2 specs.; as *Acanthurus lituratus*, Fowler and Ball, 1925, 4 specs.

Zebrasoma flavescens (Bennett)
1 spec., 54 mm., 1951. Fowler and Ball, 1925, 3 specs.; Halstead and Bunker, 1954, 1 spec.
Plain yellow in color.

ELEOTRIDAE

Eviota viridis (Waite)
Fowler and Ball, 1925, 3 specs.
These specimens have been reexamined, but are in too poor condition to provide a definite identification.

GOBIIDAE

*Bathygobius fuscus Rüppell
Fowler and Ball, 1925, 4 specs.
There seems no reason to doubt the original determination.

Gnatholepis anjerensis (Bleeker)
5 specs., 19–34 mm., 1951.
Tongue strongly bilobed; anal with 11 soft rays in all 5 specimens.

Zonogobius farcimen (Jordan and Evermann)
5 specs., 16–22 mm., 1951..
These specimens agree well with the description and figure of this species by Jordan and Evermann (1905).

BLENNIIDAE

Cirripectus variolosus (Valenciennes)
52 specs., 24–63 mm., 1951; 2 specs., 55 and 59 mm., Brock, 1948. As *Rupiscartes variolosus*, Fowler and Ball, 1925, 22 specs.
Body plain; nuchal cirri totaling 36 in one specimen; first dorsal rays elongate.

Exallias brevis (Kner)
1 spec., 46 mm., Brock, 1948.
A broad fleshy flap on either side of the chin; scattered reddish spots on the head, body, and fins.

Salarias gibbifrons (Quoy and Gaimard)
17 specs., 23–73 mm., 1951. As *Rupiscartes gibbifrons*, Fowler and Ball, 1925, 1 spec.
Long, simple, slender cirri over eye; middle of eye about over front of upper jaw; a spot between the first two dorsal spines.

BROTULIDAE

Brotula townsendi Fowler
1 spec., 127 mm., 1951.

This specimen has been reported on previously (Gosline, 1953).

MUGILIDAE

Neomyxus chaptalii (Eydoux and Souleyet)
1 spec., 286 mm., 1951. Fowler and Ball, 1925, 5 specs.

Forty-four scales in a longitudinal series.

SPHYRAENIDAE

*__Sphyraena japonica__ (Cuvier)
Fowler and Ball, 1925, 3 specs.

POLYNEMIDAE

*__Polydactylus sexfilis__ (Cuvier and
Valenciennes)
As *Polynemus kuru*, Smith and Swain, 1882, 1 spec.

SCORPAENIDAE

Scorpaenids seem to be rare around Johnston, and the only two species taken are the two that are perhaps commonest around Hawaii. They are not difficult to separate but they have been badly confused. Nomenclatorially the difficulty starts at the generic level. Jordan and Evermann (1905) have placed the two in *Sebastapistes*. Schultz (1943), for reasons which are not clear, divides the members of *Sebastapistes* between *Scorpaenopsis* and *Scorpaena*. Matsubara (1943), who will be followed here, places all of *Sebastapistes* back under *Scorpaena*.

At the specific level a nomenclatorial problem also arises. The oldest name for any Hawaiian species is *Scorpaena asperella* Bennett (1828). The description of this species, based on a single specimen 2 inches long, gives almost no morphological characters of any value, and the coloration does not agree very well with anything subsequently found in the Hawaiian Islands. The type, according to Günther (1873: 80), has been lost. The name *Scorpaena asperella* has been applied in various ways. Günther (1860: 107) considered the species unrecognizable. Jordan and Ever-

mann (1905) thought that the description applied to some Hawaiian species that they did not have. This seems rather unlikely, for of the 11 Hawaiian species described by Bennett 9 of the names have subsequently been identified among the most common of small inshore fishes and the other 2 have never been identified very satisfactorily with anything. One suspects that the difficulty with these 2 lies not in the rarity of the species described but in the nature of Bennett's descriptions. In 1943 Schultz (p. 172) applied the name to a species from Samoa.

I have repeatedly compared Bennett's description with small scorpaenids from Hawaii and can only conclude that it checks about as well (or as badly) with one as with another. Under the circumstances it seems best to follow Günther's usage in considering the name unrecognizable.

The following tabulation of characteristics will serve to distinguish the two species of *Scorpaena* collected at Johnston:

Eight spines on the top of the head above and behind the orbital rim, the front four in a transverse row; pectoral base without scaly sheath; cheek and opercle naked; pectoral with 4 branched rays; suborbital with a single blunt, backwardly projecting knob; no distinct, small dark spots; a black blotch usually present on the posterior part of the spinous dorsal in specimens more than 3 inches long; last dorsal ray attached for most of its length to the caudal peduncle by means of a membrane........
..........................**S. ballieui**

Six spines on the top of the head above and behind the orbital rim; pectoral with a scaly sheath at base that extends well out onto the pectoral fin; cheek and opercle scaled; pectoral with 5 branched rays; suborbital with two divergent, backwardly projecting points; small, distinct dark spots on and below the base of the dorsal fin, on the head, and in the pectoral axil; no black

blotch on the posterior part of the spinous dorsal; last dorsal ray attached to the caudal peduncle for less than half its length.....
...................S. coniorta

Five species of *Sebastapistes* from Hawaii are recognized by Jordan and Evermann (1905: 455–460), and a sixth is described from deeper water by Gilbert (1905: 627). Of these *S. asperella*, as noted above, must apparently be considered unidentifiable. Of the others, *S. coniorta* seems to apply to the scaled-cheek species. Judging from Jordan and Evermann's descriptions, *S. balieui*, *S. corallicola*, and probably *S. galactacma* belong with the naked-cheeked species. *S. coloratus* appears to represent a third species.

At present it seems best to designate the two Johnston species as *Scorpaena ballieui* Sauvage and *S. coniorta* (Jenkins). Other related species have been described from elsewhere in the tropical Indo-Pacific, but in the absence of comparative material it is impossible to determine which of these are the same as the two Johnston species and which are different.

Scorpaena ballieui Sauvage
1 spec., 23 mm., 1951.

Scorpaena coniorta (Jenkins)
1 spec., 51 mm., 1951.

BOTHIDAE

Bothus mancus (Broussonet)
1 spec., 160 mm., 1951. Halstead and Bunker, 1954, 2 specs. As *Platophrys mancus*, Smith and Swain, 1882, 1 spec. and Fowler and Ball, 1925, 3 specs.

Dorsal 96; anal 78.

ECHENEIDAE

Remora remora (Linnaeus)
1 spec., 67 mm. from shark taken outside reef.

Pelvic fins with their inner rays attached to the abdomen for most of their length; laminae 17; lower jaw greatly exceeding upper in length.

BALISTIDAE

Melichthys buniva (Lacepède)
9 specs., 155–185 mm., 1951. Fowler and Ball, 1925, 3 specs. As *Balistes buniva*, Smith and Swain, 1882, 3 specs.

Dorsal and anal black with a narrow blue line at base. A very common species, which seemed to be thriving on the garbage periodically dumped into the lagoon at the time we were there.

*Melichthys ringens (Osbeck)
Halstead and Bunker, 1954, 11 specs.

Melichthys vidua (Solander)
1 spec., 150 mm., 1951. Halstead and Bunker, 1954, 2 specs. As *Balistes vidua*, Fowler and Ball, 1925, 2 specs.

Dorsal and anal light except for the narrow dark borders. Fraser-Brunner's placement (1935: 662) of this species in the genus *Melichthys* seems questionable.

Rhinecanthus aculeatus (Linnaeus)
Halstead and Bunker, 1954, 3 specs. As *Balistes aculeatus*, Smith and Swain, 1882, 2 specs. and Fowler and Ball, 1925, 1 spec. (this record checked).

Three longitudinal rows of black spinélets on the caudal peduncle.

MONACANTHIDAE

*Amanses carolae (Jordan and McGregor)
Halstead and Bunker, 1954, 2 specs.

Amanses sandwichiensis (Quoy and Gaimard)
3 specs., 140–270 mm., 1951. Halstead and Bunker, 1954, 1 spec. As *Monacanthus sandwichiensis*, Fowler and Ball, 1925, 1 spec.

The 140 mm. specimen has no spines on the caudal peduncle; the two larger (190 and 270 mm.) have 4 forwardly projecting spines in two rows on each side.

Pervagor melanocephalus (Bleeker)
3 specs., 82–106 mm., 1951. As *Monacanthus melanocephalus*, Fowler and Ball, 1925, 4 specs.

Dorsal rays 32 in one specimen.

OSTRACIONTIDAE

*Kentrocarpus hexagonus (Thunberg)
Halstead and Bunker, 1954, 1 spec.

*Ostracion cubicus Linnaeus
Halstead and Bunker, 1954, 1 spec.

Ostracion lentiginosum Schneider
15 specs., 76–126 mm., 1951. Fowler and
Ball, 1925, 3 specs. As *Ostracion punctatum*,
Smith and Swain, 1882, 1 spec.

*Ostracion meleagris Shaw
Halstead and Bunker, 1954, 9 specs.

Ostracion solorensis Bleeker
Fowler and Ball, 1925, 1 spec.

This specimen has the upper sides with
alternating brown and white stripes, the
brown ones continuous but the white ones
broken up into segments. Below the banded
area the body is abruptly light. A very slight
dorsal ridge just ahead of dorsal fin; ventro-
lateral ridges expanded into laminae. Cara-
pace closed over behind the dorsal and anal
fins to form two horizontal laminae. Supra-
orbital ridges somewhat raised and rough. No
spines anywhere.

TETRAODONTIDAE

Arothron meleagris (Lacepède)
2 specs., 140 and 160 mm., 1951. Halstead
and Bunker, 1954, 1 spec. As *Tetraodon meleagris*, Smith and Swain, 1882, 3 specs., Fowler
and Ball, 1925, 4 specs.

Head, body, and fins with small light spots
on a dark ground. Outer portions of fins,
except caudal, light.

CANTHIGASTERIDAE

Canthigaster jactator (Jenkins)
3 specs., 40–64 mm., 1951; 1 spec., 52 mm.,
Brock, 1948. Halstead and Bunker, 1954,
1 spec.

Round white spots on a dark ground.

DIODONTIDAE

*Diodon hystrix Linnaeus
Smith and Swain, 1882, 1 spec.

SECTION 2. THE NATURE AND RELATIONSHIPS
OF THE JOHNSTON ISLAND FISH FAUNA

Johnston Island is one of the more isolated
of Pacific atolls. It is separated by some 450
miles of deep water from the nearest reef area,
French Frigate Shoals in the Hawaiian chain
to the north (see Fig. 1). To the south and
east the nearest shoal water (Kingman Reef
in the Line Islands) is about 700 miles away,
whereas the closest land to the west is in the
Marshalls perhaps 1300 miles distant.

The position of Johnston Island poses two
principal questions for the zoogeographer:
(1) to what extent does its isolation give rise
to endemism, and (2) to what extent has
Johnston acted as a stepping stone or filter
bridge between the Hawaiian biota and that
of the Line Islands to the south. An attempt
to answer these two questions constitutes the
present section of this paper.

Before proceeding it seems well to define
certain terms that will be used here. "Central
Pacific" will be employed in a zoogeographic
sense to refer to a faunal area whose limits
are unknown but which includes the Line,
Phoenix, Gilbert, and Marshall islands but
not Johnston and the Hawaiian chain. "Hawaiian" used zoogeographically will refer to
the inshore marine fauna of the Hawaiian
chain together with that of Johnston. "Hawaii" used geographically generally refers to
the Hawaiian chain of islands, though the
fact that the largest island in this chain is also
called Hawaii is admittedly confusing.

The question of endemism among Johnston
fishes is easily dealt with and dismissed. Only
two species of Johnston fishes have not been
taken elsewhere—*Centropyge nigriocellus* and *C.
flammeus*. Neither of these is abundant at
Johnston (the former is known only from one
specimen), and it may well be that they merely

remain uncollected elsewhere. In a few other fishes the Johnston specimens seem somewhat aberrant but probably do not deserve recognition as separate species. The principal significance of this low degree of endemism at Johnston lies in the demonstration that for Pacific island fishes 450 miles of open water without strong current systems has not resulted in much differentiation.

The problem of evaluating Johnston as a filter bridge is far more complex. The present attack on it is divided into two facets. The first approaches the problem in terms of the relative strengths of the various components of the Johnston shallow-water fish fauna. The objective here is to obtain a general picture of the relationships of the fish fauna of Johnston Island. The second deals in greater detail with certain Johnston fishes that are represented by different geographic forms south of the island than occur to the north. Its objective is to trace, in so far as possible, individual migration routes.

Components of the Johnston Fish Fauna

For purposes of the faunal analysis that follows, certain families of fishes have been excluded for one reason or another. First, those fishes that are pelagic or semipelagic as adults are omitted. For these, Johnston may have no significance whatever as a way point, and to include them would only obscure the data. Groups excluded from consideration for this reason are the sharks and rays, the needle fishes, half-beaks, flying fishes, carangids, barracudas, tunas, remoras, and all fishes taken from over 100 feet of water. Second, the parrot fishes and scorpaenids have also been excluded, but for the reason that at the present time they are so confused taxonomically as to make species records worthless zoogeographically. Finally, the species recorded from Johnston by Halstead and Bunker (1954) only will not be considered as I have not been able to check their records. Fowler and Ball's (1925) species have, on the other hand, been included because, as already

mentioned, material upon which their more questionable identifications were based have been reexamined. Following is the reduced list of Johnston species, upon which the following analysis is based.

SPECIES CONSIDERED IN THE ANALYSIS OF THE
IOHNSTON FISH FAUNA

Central Pacific Species Reaching Johnston but
Not Hawaii (Group B of Fig. 4)
Leptenchelys labialis
Muraenichthys gymnotus
Muraenichthys schultzei
Brachysomophis sauropsis
Myrichthys bleekeri
Echidna leucotaenia
Uropterygius polyspilus
Kuhlia marginata
Parupeneus barberinus
Abudefduf phoenixensis
Epibulus insidiator
Thalassoma quinquevittata
Pervagor melanocephalus
Ostracion solorensis

Species Endemic to Johnston (Group G of Fig. 4)
Centropyge flammeus
Centropyge nigriocellus

Hawaiian Species Reaching South to Johnston but
Not Beyond (Group E of Fig. 4)
Muraenichthys cookei
Gymnothorax eurostus
Uropterygius dentatus
Apogon menesemus
Apogon waikiki
Parupeneus multifasciatus
Cirrhitus alternatus
Chromis leucurus
Chromis vanderbilti
Dascyllus albisella
Halichoeres ornatissimus
Thalassoma ballieui
Thalassoma duperrey
Chaetodon multicinctus
Acanthurus sandvicensis
Zonogobius farcimen

Johnston Species Found Both in Hawaii and in the
Central Pacific (Group C of Fig. 4)
Saurida gracilis
Synodus binotatus
Conger noordziekii
Leiuranus semicinctus
Myrichthys maculosus
Schultzidia johnstonensis
Moringua macrochir
Anarchias allardicei
Anarchias cantonensis
Anarchias leucurus
Echidna polyzona
Echidna zebra

Gymnothorax gracilicauda
Gymnothorax meleagris
Gymnothorax moluccensis
Gymnothorax pictus
Gymnothorax undulatus
Rabula fuscomaculata
Uropterygius fuscoguttatus
Uropterygius tigrinus
Aulostomus chinensis
Fistularia petimba
Holocentrus tiere
Holocentrus microstomus
Holocentrus lacteoguttatus
Holocentrus sammara
Holocentrus spinifer
Holotrachys lima
Myripristis argyromus
Apogon erythrinus
Apogon snyderi
Pseudamiops gracilicauda
Pseudogramma polyacanthus
Priacanthus cruentatus
Kyphosus vaigiensis
Mulloidichthys auriflamma
Mulloidichthys samoensis
Parupeneus bifasciatus
Parupeneus chryserydros
Parupeneus pleurostigma
Paracirrhites bimacula
Abudefduf imparipennis
Abudefduf sordidus
Plectroglyphidodon johnstonianus
Bodianus bilunulatus
Cheilinus diagrammus
Cheilinus rhodochrous
Gomphosus tricolor
Gomphosus varius
Novaculichthys taeniourus
Pseudocheilinus sp.
Pseudocheilinus octotaenia
Stethojulis axillaris
Thalassoma lutescens
Thalassoma purpureum
Chaetodon auriga
Chaetodon citrinellus
Chaetodon ephippium
Chaetodon ornatissimus
Chaetodon quadrimaculatus
Chaetodon trifasciatus
Chaetodon unimaculatus
Zanclus cornutus
Acanthurus achilles
Acanthurus elongatus
Acanthurus olivaceus
Ctenochaetus strigosus
Naso lituratus
Zebrasoma flavescens
Bathygobius fuscus
Gnatholepis anjerensis
Exallias brevis
Cirripectus variolosus
Salarias gibbifrons
Brotula townsendi

Neomyxus chaptalii
Polydactylus sexfilis
Bothus mancus
Rhinecanthus aculeatus
Melichthys buniva
Melichthys vidua
Amanses sandwichiensis
Ostracion lentiginosum
Arothron meleagris
Canthigaster jactator
Diodon hystrix

For purposes of assessing the importance of Johnston as a filter bridge for species coming up from the south the following groupings have been made (see Fig. 4): (A) those fishes that never reached Johnston, (B) those that got to Johnston but no farther, (C) those that apparently passed through Johnston on the way from the Line Islands to Hawaii or vice versa, and (D) those that apparently bypassed Johnston. Similarly, the Hawaiian species may be divided into (F) those that never reached Johnston, (E) reached Johnston and stopped, (C) passed through Johnston, and (D) by-passed Johnston.

The stringency of the Johnstonian filtering effect on northbound and on southbound fishes will be shown by the relative strengths of each of the above categories (except D). An attempt to quantify each of these relative to one another is therefore made in Figure 4 by means of the widths of the columns. Widths of columns B, C, E, and G are based directly on the relative number of Johnston species in each of these categories in the list Column D is given no width, because it is impossible to know how much of column D is represented but as yet uncollected at Johnston. Widths for A and F were estimated in a very simple and admittedly imperfect fashion, and indicate only rough magnitudes. Two shallow-water poison stations run at Palmyra, the nearest island to the south of Johnston, by Mr. J. E. King, *et al.*, in approximately the same way as those made at Johnston yielded (among the same fish groups used here) 62 species of which 29 are not known from Johnston or Hawaii. Thus, the number of species in these two collections (and presumably in the Palmyra inshore fish fauna as a whole) that does not get north is calculated as 29/33 of the number that does. Consequently column A is assigned a width slightly less than the combined widths of B and C, which had been calculated previously. Similarly, the width of F is based on an inshore Oahu rotenone station from which 69 species in the same groups were collected. Of these, 17 do not get as far south as Johnston. Hence F is assigned a width about one third (actually 17/52) of the combined widths of C and E.

The fact that there are 16 Hawaiian species found at Johnston but not, apparently, farther south and 14 Central Pacific species that get to Johnston but not farther north indicates that at the present time Johnston is acting as a filter bridge for fishes passing in both directions. The nature of the filtering effect on northbound and on southbound species must now be considered.

Starting at the south, a very large component of the two poison stations run at Palmyra (29 of 52 species) is not known in Johnston or Hawaii. Two very striking members of this component are the genera *Lutjanus* and (except for a single species) *Epinephelus*. One immediately wonders if these fishes never got to the northern islands or whether they got there but have been unable to survive there because of unsuitable ecological conditions. If the latter were correct, one would suspect the colder water temperatures in the north to be either the direct or indirect cause of the unsuitability. There are certain indications that distance rather than water temperature has been the primary cause in preventing Central Pacific species from reaching Johnston and Hawaii. One of these is provided by the fishes of Japan. The southern Japanese Islands are separated by no such deep-water distances from tropical Pacific islands as Johnston is from Palmyra, but surface water temperatures in southern Japan are at least as cold as those of the Hawaiian Islands (Sverdrup, Johnson, and Fleming, 1946: charts II and III, and fig.

32B). Nevertheless, 15 species of *Epinephelus* (Tanaka, 1931: 26) and 14 species of *Lutjanus* (Kamohara, 1954: 114) are recorded from Japan. This suggests that the Hawaiian water temperatures would not be unsuitable for at least some species of *Lutjanus* and *Epinephelus*. An attempt to find an area separated from the tropical Pacific by a deep-water barrier as great as that isolating the Hawaiian Islands and Johnston leads to an examination of the tropical American data. Snodgrass and Heller (1905: 338) list some 13 species of inshore tropical Pacific species as occurring in the islands of the west coast of the Americas. Of these, none belong to the genera *Lutjanus* or *Epinephelus* or to any of the other species that are not represented at Johnston and Hawaii. To state this last matter positively, all 13 have representatives in the Hawaiian Islands today. These two straws in the wind indicate that the great diminution in species between Palmyra and Johnston is caused primarily by (deep-water) distance rather than by temperature. Such a distance effect could, of course, be either primary or secondary. If primary, the fishes themselves have been unable to get to Johnston; if secondary, the fishes may have been able to get there but the organisms they depend upon for a livelihood have not. Though there is no way of determining which of these two possibilities has been realized, it seems improbable that such unspecialized carnivorous genera as *Lutjanus* and *Epinephelus* would have found the food supply inadequate, had they arrived there.

Of those tropical fishes that have reached Johnston, the great majority seem to have passed on through to Hawaii. There are, however, 14 species that are not known north of Johnston. Some of these, e.g., *Epibulus insidiator*, are quite striking members of the tropical Pacific fauna, and it seems improbable that they should go unrecorded in the Hawaiian fauna if they exist there. One suspects that the reason they have not crossed the minor water gap between Johnston and

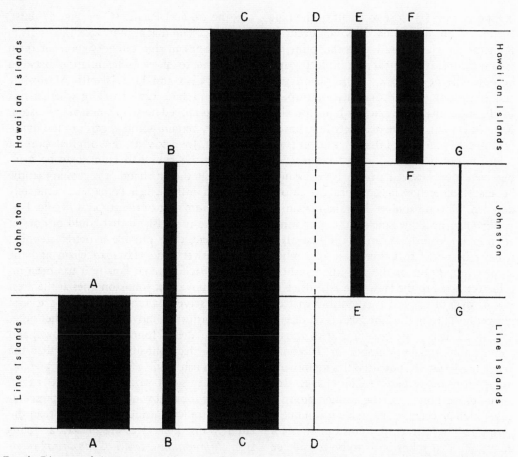

FIG. 4. Diagram of the zoogeographic components making up the inshore fish fauna of Johnston Island and the island chains nearest to Johnston. A, that portion of the Line Island fauna that does not reach Johnston or the Hawaiian Islands; B, that portion of the Line Island fauna that reaches to Johnston but not to the Hawaiian Islands; C, the component that is held in common by the Line Islands, Johnston, and the Hawaiian Islands; D, the component that is common to the Line and Hawaiian Islands but has not, up to now, been recorded from Johnston; E, that portion of the Hawaiian fauna that has reached Johnston but not farther south; F, the portion of the Hawaiian fauna that is restricted to the Hawaiian chain; and G, the component restricted to Johnston Island. Widths of the bars, except D, represent the relative strengths of the various components; for the way in which these widths were calculated, see text.

Hawaii after hurdling the major one between Palmyra and Johnston is that the ecological conditions in Hawaii are not suitable to them. This is of course merely a guess, but it may be noted that the Johnston coral reefs, made up as they are to a considerable extent of *Acropora*, would seem to form a quite different environment from the Hawaiian reefs, where *Acropora*, amongst other elements, is lacking. To bulwark this point further it may be noted that certain rather prominent components of the tropical Pacific fauna that do reach Hawaii are rare there and apparently do not find the environment particularly suitable. In this category belong such species as *Gymnothorax pictus*, *Holocentrus microstomus*, *Thalassoma lutescens*, *Chaetodon citrinellus*, *Chaetodon ephippium*, *Pomacanthus imperator*, and *Acanthurus aliala*.

Summing up for the "northbound" fishes

it appears that: (1) close to a half of the Line Island inshore fish fauna does not occur in Johnston or Hawaii and that the principal reason for this is the great area of deep water between the northernmost Line Island reef and Johnston; (2) the majority of tropical Pacific fishes that have reached Johnston also occur in Hawaii; (3) the relatively few species of tropical Pacific fishes that are known from Johnston but not Hawaii may have reached but have not survived in the latter islands because of differences in ecological conditions between Johnston and the Hawaiian chain.

What may be termed the southbound fishes are now up for discussion. In the first place it must be noted that there is a very much smaller proportion of the Hawaiian inshore fishes restricted to the Hawaiian Islands (F of Fig. 4) than of tropical Pacific fishes that do not get north from the Line Islands (A of Fig. 4). Indeed, it is quite certain that there is a considerably smaller number of Hawaiian "endemics" with the potentialities for moving south than of tropical Pacific fishes that might move north. Of the former group a rather high percentage (though a low number of species) have reached Johnston. It is for this reason that Johnston is to be considered primarily as an outlier of the Hawaiian faunal region rather than as a part of the tropical Central Pacific fauna. The example drawn from the Palmyra and Hawaiian poison stations will bring out this point. In the Hawaiian rotenone station of 69 species, only 17 are restricted to Hawaii, but another 4 are restricted to Hawaii and Johnston. In the Palmyra poison stations of 62 species, 29 are not known north of Palmyra but only 1 is known from Palmyra and Johnston but not Hawaii. On the basis of these figures (fishes found both in Hawaii and Palmyra being excluded) the Johnston inshore fauna is 4/17 Hawaiian and 1/29 tropical Pacific. To what extent other Hawaiian endemics will turn up at Johnston remains to be seen.

Finally, it is necessary to say something of those fishes found today in Hawaii, Johnston,

and the tropical Pacific (C of Fig. 4). First, it seems certain that as more attention is given to the fishes in this category more of them will prove to show differentiation between the Hawaiian and Line Islands. Meanwhile there is no sure way of telling whether this group has moved north or south via Johnston. However, certain points regarding the hypothesis of Johnston as the original port of entry for the Hawaiian fauna may be mentioned. On the one hand, it is certain that the Hawaiian inshore fish fauna was ultimately derived from that of the tropical Pacific. Further, there is no island that could or does at the present time provide a better stepping stone between the Hawaiian chain and the tropical Pacific fauna. Finally it has been indicated above that Johnston does at the present time serve as a terminal point for at least some northward movement. On the other hand, the age of Johnston is unknown, and it may be that Johnston is younger than the Hawaiian fish fauna as we know it at present. If this were so, it would be far easier to explain why the following Hawaiian representatives of tropical Pacific forms rather than the latter forms themselves are present at Johnston: *Muraenichthys cookei*, *Gymnothorax eurostus*, *Cirrhitus alternatus*, *Chromis leucurus*, *Chaetodon multicinctus*, and *Acanthurus sandvicensis*. Because of these features it seems best not to make categorical statements as to whether (or how much of) the Hawaiian fish fauna did or did not originally enter via Johnston. It can, however, be stated that a more plausible port of entry has yet to be found.

Analysis of Individual Species

The individual species investigated here are Johnston fishes represented by different geographic variants in the Central Pacific and in the Hawaiian chain. They do not include all fishes in this category but only those for which sufficient information is available to be worth discussing. The following species complexes will be dealt with (in each pair the Hawaiian form is mentioned first): *Murae-*

nichthys cookei–laticaudata, Gymnothorax eurostus–buroensis, Kuhlia sandvicensis–marginata, Cirrhitus alternatus–pinnulatus, Chaetodon multicinctus–punctato-fasciatus, and *Acanthurus sandvicensis–triostegus.* A uniform treatment for all six species would be desirable in order to enable comparison of all six area by area. Unfortunately the availability of specimens makes this impossible.

Before these species are dealt with, it seems advisable to provide certain background information. The Johnston collections were originally made to check whether the endemic Hawaiian fishes were really species or merely subspecies. It was felt that intergradation between the Hawaiian endemics and their Central Pacific counterparts would occur at Johnston if anywhere. It does not occur there (or elsewhere) among any of the fishes here investigated, and on the basis of absence of intergradation (the term is here used in contrast with introgression) the Hawaiian endemics must be considered full species. But would the Hawaiian endemics interbreed with their Central Pacific counterparts if both were present? There is no way of determining this at Johnston, because the two never occur together there (or elsewhere). When a Central Pacific fish is represented by a variant in Hawaii, either the Central Pacific form (e.g., *Kuhlia marginata*) or the Hawaiian form (e.g., *Muraenichthys cookei, Gymnothorax eurostus, Cirrhitus alternatus, Chaetodon multicinctus,* and *Acanthurus sandvicensis*), or neither, but not both, occurs at Johnston. That this proves nothing regarding the interbreeding potentialities of the two geographic forms has been discussed in an earlier paper (Gosline, In press). The failure to be able to determine whether interbreeding between the Hawaiian endemics and their Central Pacific counterparts would or does occur makes it impossible to prove whether the Hawaiain forms are full species or merely subspecies. This matter has also been discussed elsewhere (Gosline, *op. cit.*). The point here is that the failure to settle the matter has led to considerable zoogeo-

graphic misunderstanding concerning endemism in the Hawaiian inshore fish fauna. For example, Jordan and Evermann (1905: 32) conclude that about 50 per cent of the species of Hawaiian shallow water fishes are endemic; Fowler's (1928) treatment of the same fishes would give a far lower percentage of endemism, perhaps 15 per cent. This appears to be a disagreement concerning the number of endemic Hawaiian fishes, but in reality it is a difference in viewpoint regarding how many Hawaiian endemics should be treated as full species. That one viewpoint is correct and the other incorrect will probably never be proved. About all that can be said is that in general the Hawaiian offshoots of Indo-Pacific species are more distinctive than those that occur anywhere else. Since I believe that Jordan and Evermann's interpretation of Hawaiian endemism in fishes brings out this point more clearly than Fowler's and since no real intergradation can be demonstrated between Hawaiian and Central Pacific forms, it seems preferable to side with Jordan and Evermann.

Muraenichthys cookei–laticaudata

The Hawaiian form, *Muraenichthys cookei*, was described by Fowler (1928: 41, fig. 9). In 1943 Schultz (p. 53) synonymized Fowler's species with *Muraenichthys laticaudata* (Ogilby) described from Fiji. In 1949 Schultz and Woods (p. 172) recognized both species, differentiating them on the basis of the more anterior position of the dorsal origin in relation to the anus in *M. cookei*. The same basis of differentiation is used by Schultz (in Schultz, et al., 1953: 72–73). No other differences between the two species are known. The relationship between the dorsal origin and the anus in specimens of the *M. cookei–laticaudata* complex from several localities is shown in Table 3. (In the table total lengths have not been given since there is no evidence of a change in the dorsal–anus relationship with growth.) Several points can only be suggested by this table since the within-sample variabil-

TABLE 3

THE RELATIONSHIP BETWEEN THE DORSAL ORIGIN AND THE POSITION OF THE ANUS IN SPECIMENS
OF THE *Muraenichthys cookei–laticaudata* COMPLEX

Distances are expressed in thousandths of the standard length. Plus values indicate distances of the dorsal origin
in front of the anus; minus values, distances behind the anus

SPECIES AND LOCALITY	NUMBER OF SPECIMENS	DISTANCE FROM ANUS	
		Average	Range
Muraenichthys laticaudata			
Marshalls	3	—26	—80 to + 11
Muraenichthys cookei			
Hawaiian Islands			
Midway	7	12	0 to + 23
Oahu	7	20	+ 3 to + 39
Johnston	12	50	+15 to +116

ity is high and the available specimens from any one locality few. First, the two "species" cannot always be separated on the basis of the dorsal origin, for the ranges of the Marshallese and Midway specimens overlap. Second, the Marshallese *M. laticaudata* is most like the Midway form of *M. cookei*, which becomes progressively more distinct at Oahu and Johnston. One would like to know the nature of the populations of this species complex at Wake, a northern outlier of the Marshalls and somewhat between the rest of the group and Midway, but it has never been taken there. One would also like to know about the Line Island populations, but again the species complex is unrecorded from there. In the absence of evidence from these rather crucial localities, one can only speculate that the complex moved into Hawaii from the west, becoming further and further differentiated as it moved down the chain and thence to Johnston. Whatever the derivation, the fact remains that in the habitat (Johnston) that most resembles that of the presumably ancestral *M. laticaudata* the differentiation is the greatest and in the habitat that least resembles the Central Pacific (Midway) the differentiation has been least. Thus the character by which *M. cookei* is distinguished from *M. laticaudata* cannot be explained as an adaptation to a cold-water

environment; it would seem rather to be an instance in which differentiation has proceeded independently of the environment.

Gymnothorax eurostus–buroensis

The Hawaiian *Gymnothorax eurostus* is very similar to the Central Pacific species which has been called in recent years *G. buroensis*. Schultz (in Schultz, *et al.*, 1953: 120) has separated the two on the basis of minor color differences. The most important of these is the mottling of the lower jaw in *G. eurostus* as contrasted with the plain throat and lower jaw of *G. buroensis*. Unfortunately, *G. eurostus* at least is very variable in coloration, and almost any color character breaks down in some individuals. The color differentiation of the two species can, however, be supplemented by a number of morphological characters, but for each of these there are, again, individual exceptions. At any given size over perhaps 7 inches, *G. buroensis* is a chunkier fish, and the head especially is higher and blunter, but both species become more heavy-bodied with age. (This and other proportional characters do not seem worth stating quantitatively because of the difficulty of obtaining reliable measurements on morays.) The mouth of *G. buroenis* closes completely; that of *G. eurostus* does not, leaving a gap between the lips just ahead of the eye when the jaw tips are tightly closed. The length of the snout is usually less than the distance from the eye to the rictus in *G. buroensis*, greater in *G. eurostus*. The fifth pore from the front on the chin is usually behind the most posterior pore on the upper lip and behind the eye in *G. buroensis*, under or in front of the last pore of the upper lip and under the eye in *G. eurostus*. There are fewer teeth in the jaws of *G. buroensis* than of *G. eurostus*, but since adult morays usually lose teeth this character again does not seem to merit quantitative analysis. Finally, *G. buroensis* is definitely the smaller of the two species: the largest of several hundred specimens of *G. buroensis* taken by Schultz in the Marshalls (Schultz, *et al.*, 1953: 118) was about 13 inches; the largest of 20 specimens of *G. eurostus* taken by me in Johnston is 20 inches long. In sum then, the two species are rather easy to separate for anyone familiar with them, even though there is no single character on the basis of which it would be possible to correctly identify all specimens.

Due to the nature of the differences between the two species it can only be stated without adequate demonstration that all specimens of this complex from Johnston are typical *G. eurostus*. Specimens from Christmas, in the Line Islands to the south of Johnston, seem to be typical *G. buroensis*. All of the hundreds of specimens from the Hawaiian Islands seen by me, with one exception, are *G. eurostus*. The exception consists of specimens taken by Mr. Tinker of the Honolulu Aquarium from among the heavy fouling on the bottom of a barge that was put in drydock at Pearl Harbor (see Chapman and Schultz, 1952: 528, Edmondson, 1951: 212). The eel that dropped out of this fouling is a typical specimen of *G. buroensis*. Inasmuch as several other fishes, crustacea, and mollusks taken from this fouling have never been recorded elsewhere in Hawaiian waters, and inasmuch as the barge had been towed in from Guam, it seems logical to presume, despite Chapman and Schultz, that these alien forms came in

with the barge from somewhere in the Central Pacific.

Kuhlia sandvicensis-marginata

Despite previous accounts (e.g., Fowler, 1949: 83) there seems to be only one species of *Kuhlia*, namely *K. sandvicensis*, represented in the Hawaiian chain. This species is closely related to *K. marginata* from the Central Pacific, with which it will here be compared. Before doing so it seems well to mention that from published accounts (e.g., Ikeda, 1939: 131–158) *K. boninensis* from the Bonin and Riu Kiu Islands also seems to be near *K. sandvicensis*.

According to Schultz (in Schultz, *et al.*, 1953: 325) *K. marginata* differs from *K. sandvicensis* in having somewhat higher average pectoral and dorsal counts. However, the two species also differ in the number of gill rakers, and it is these that will be emphasized in this analysis.

In the number of dorsal rays, my counts of *K. sandvicensis* agree more closely with Schultz's counts of *K. marginata* than with his data for *K. sandvicensis* (Table 4). Under the circumstances there seems no point in following the analysis of this character further.

The total pectoral ray counts in certain samples of the *K. sandvicensis-marginata* complex are summarized in Table 5. Several aspects of this table warrant discussion. In the

TABLE 4

DORSAL SOFT RAY COUNTS IN THE *Kuhlia sandvicensis-marginata* COMPLEX

SPECIES AND LOCALITY	NUMBER OF SPECIMENS	AVERAGE COUNT
K. sandvicensis		
Hawaiian Islands		
Midway..........	25	11.08
French Frigate.....	5	11.00
Kauai............	25	11.08
Oahu............	25	11.04
Oahu (Schultz)....	9	11.55
K. marginata		
Johnston (Schultz)...	2	11.00
Marshalls (Schultz) ..	10	11.00

first place the several small samples available from Midway vary considerably in average count. What this means is not clear, but it has prevented me from placing too much faith in the results of single larger samples from elsewhere. If one were to exclude the samples from the low Hawaiian Islands (Midway, Lisianski, and French Frigate) one would obtain a correlation between increase in pectoral count and decrease in water temperature for the species complex. On the other hand, if one considered the samples of *Kuhlia sandvicensis* alone, one would obtain a correlation in the reverse direction. An attempt to explain these contradictory trends will be made after consideration of the gill-raker data. Meanwhile, it may be noted that the Johnston fishes appear to be of almost pure Central Pacific stock.

Before proceeding with the gill-raker information, three features should be noted. In the first place, as Schultz (1943: 99) has observed, the young of *Kuhlia* have fewer gill rakers than the adult. By plotting the number of gill rakers against standard length in certain large Hawaiian samples, it was determined that *K. sandvicensis* obtains approximately its full gill-raker complement by about 40 millimeters in standard length. Consequently no fish smaller than 40 millimeters were used in the data which follow. The second point regards the method of making counts. In *Kuhlia* the most anterior one of two rakers frequently taper to almost nothing, and it seems preferable to count only the developed gill rakers. Here, then, only the pectinate rakers are counted; the shorter, nob-topped rakers are omitted. Even this restriction leaves some specimens in which the count remains somewhat questionable. To check the consistency in my own counting, the gill rakers in a sample of 37 fish were recounted at the end of a year. The original count gave an average of 24.41, the later count, 24.57. These and all other counts used here are only those below the angle (excluding the raker at the angle).

TABLE 5

TOTAL PECTORAL RAY COUNTS IN SPECIMENS OF THE *Kuhlia sandvicensis–marginata* COMPLEX

SPECIES AND LOCALITY	NUMBER OF SPECIMENS	AVERAGE COUNT
K. sandvicensis		
Hawaiian Islands		
Midway (Mar., 1949)....	7	14.57
Midway (July, 1949).....	12	14.91
Midway (June, 1950).....	6	14.33
Midway (May, 1951).....	3	15.00
Midway (all specimens)..	28	14.72
Lisianski..........	3	14.33
French Frigate.....	5	14.60
Kauai............	10	14.80
Oahu............	25	14.76
Oahu (Schultz)....	17	15.00
Hawaii...........	22	15.00
K. marginata		
Johnston..........	9	14.00
Line Is.: Palmyra	2	14.00
Wake.............	20	14.00
Marshalls (Schultz) ..	10	13.71

Pectinate gill rakers on the lower limb of the first arch range from 22 to 28 in my samples of *K. sandvicensis*, from 24 to 29 in the smaller numbers of *K. marginata* examined. It seems well to discuss the *K. sandvicensis* samples first, as these are both the largest and the most numerous. In the first place it seems as if those samples containing small fish have somewhat lower average counts than the samples with large fish (Table 6). Perhaps the gill raker number does continue to increase above 40 mm.

With this in mind, the pairs of samples from the same island may be compared. The two Oahu samples were taken in different years from exactly the same tide pool. The difference between the means of these two samples is 0.41. The two samples from Hawaii are of an entirely different sort. One was taken from fresh water, the other from the sea. The difference between the means of these samples is 1.50 gill rakers, though part of this difference may be attributable to the different sized specimens in the sample. At any rate, it seems from the above data that (presumably) environmental differences within areas may play a considerable role in the differentiation of gill raker counts, and this must be kept in mind in assessing the biological significance of the difference between samples.

Even allowing for this variability within areas, the gill raker counts for *K. sandvicensis* at Midway seem to be considerably higher than for other areas. The increase in Midway counts over those of Pearl and Hermes reef some 90 miles away is especially curious.

Among the samples of *K. marginata* about all that can be said is that the counts for the Johnston and Wake specimens seem to be particularly high. On the other hand the few counts from Penrhyn, about as far south of the equator as Johnston and Wake are north, are low. Any attempt to correlate gill-raker

counts with water temperatures in this species complex on the basis of the present material seems fatuous.

Summing up the data for the *Kuhlia sandvicensis–marginata* complex, it may be said that the Johnston and Wake samples show absolutely no indication of introgression from the Hawaiian species so far as gill-raker counts are concerned. Conversely, the samples from the high Hawaiian islands show no sign of intermixing from *K. marginata*. However, the low Hawaiian island samples, particularly those from Midway, show a trend toward the southern form. Since Midway has the water temperatures and total environment least like those of the areas in which *K. marginata* lives, the similarity of the Midway *K. sandvicensis* to *K. marginata* can best be explained by introgression from the latter species. Whether such introgression is brought about through specimens of *K. marginata* coming in from Johnston, Wake, Marcus or elsewhere remains unknown.

TABLE 6

THE NUMBER OF PECTINATE GILL RAKERS ON THE LOWER LIMB OF THE FIRST GILL ARCH IN SAMPLES OF THE *Kuhlia sandvicensis–marginata* COMPLEX

SPECIES AND LOCALITY	NUMBER OF SPECIMENS	AVERAGE COUNT	STANDARD DEVIATION	AVERAGE STANDARD LENGTH IN MM.
K. sandvicensis				
Hawaiian Islands				
Midway (July, 1949).........	25	25.40	1.24	61.0
Midway (June, 1950).........	29	25.28	0.80	over 100*
Pearl and Hermes............	22	24.18	0.73	over 100*
Lisianski...................	39	24.41	0.75	over 100*
French Frigate..............	5	24.20		61.8
Kauai......................	25	24.64	1.25	135.6
Oahu (Waimea, 1948).........	37	24.41	0.75	69.6
Oahu (Waimea, 1949).........	33	24.82	0.73	62.6
Hawaii (Puna Coast).........	22	24.77	0.87	47.0
K. marginata				
Johnston....................	9	27.33	0.50	180.0
Line Is.: Palmyra...........	5	26.40		156.6
Phoenix Is.: Canton.........	3	26.00		198.3
Cook Is.: Penrhyn..........	6	25.67		71.8
Wake.......................	18	27.20	1.24	121.0
Marcus.....................	5	26.00		84.8

* Large specimens discarded in field.

In view of what has been said above, a hypothetical explanation can be given for the relationship between pectoral counts and sea temperatures. The basic assumption is that pectoral counts in this species complex increase with decreasing temperatures. In partial isolation the Hawaiian island populations would then have developed distinctly higher pectoral counts. These would be higher at Midway at the northern end of the chain than at Hawaii at the southern. However, recent introgression from *K. marginata* at Midway could have upset this trend within the Hawaiian chain, giving rise to the reversed picture for pectoral counts within the Hawaiian Islands shown in Table 5.

The fact remains that there is more difference between the *Kuhlia* populations in Johnston and Hawaii, which are almost similar in latitude, than between those of Johnston and Midway, which are very different. The conclusion seems inescapable that if members of the Johnston populations have entered the Hawaiian Islands at all, they have come in via the low northern islands. Why the Central Pacific form of *Kuhlia* rather than the endemic Hawaiian form should be present at Johnston remains a mystery. It does, however, bear out the point, previously established, that some elements of the Johnston biota have entered from the south.

Cirrhitus alternatus–pinnulatus

The two forms in this complex have recently been differentiated by Schultz (1950: 548), but entirely on the basis of coloration, the Hawaiian *C. alternatus* lacking the brown spotting of the Central Pacific species. A check of the usual meristic characters in specimens from Hawaii, Johnston, and Christmas (in the Line Islands) shows no significant differentiation. As Schultz has already pointed out (*loc. cit.*), the Johnston specimens agree completely with the Hawaiian form.

Chaetodon multicinctus–punctato-fasciatus

This species pair has been separated by Woods (in Schultz, *et al.*, 1953: 571, 575,

595) on the basis of coloration and certain counts. The color differences lie chiefly in the nature of the vertical dark bars on the nape and caudal peduncle. The fin ray differences are shown in Table 7. Woods (*loc. cit.*) has also used scale counts, but I have not been able to make sufficiently accurate scale counts in this species to be worth recording.

The Johnston specimens agree with the Hawaiian form in both color and counts.

Acanthurus sandvicensis–triostegus

The *Acanthurus triostegus* complex lends itself admirably to geographic analysis for two reasons. First, its forms are abundant and ubiquitous throughout much of the tropical Indo-Pacific, and, second, they differ in characteristics that are easily seen and calibrated. A preliminary analysis of geographic variation in this complex has recently appeared (Schultz and Woods, 1948: 248–251). According to these authors two species are represented: *Acanthurus sandvicensis* in the Hawaiian Islands and at Johnston, and *A. triostegus* throughout the rest of the area. The differences between these two lie primarily in the shape and extent of the mark below and at base of the pectoral, secondarily in the higher average fin counts of the Hawaiian species.

The Johnston Island population, judging from 21 specimens taken in three Johnston localities, differs in no way that I can determine from the Hawaiian form. If there is any admixture of *A. triostegus* genes in these Johnston specimens, it is not apparent. If, however, populations of the *A. triostegus* complex from the next island groups to the south of Johnston are examined an occasional specimen turns up with more or less strong traces of the Hawaiian pectoral base marking. For a study of possible intergradation between the Hawaiian *A. sandvicensis* and the Indo-Pacific *A. triostegus* it seems advisable therefore to focus attention not on Johnston but on the Line and Phoenix Islands to the south of Johnston.

TABLE 7

FIN COUNTS IN SPECIMENS OF THE *Chaetodon multicinctus–punctato-fasciatus* COMPLEX

SPECIES AND LOCALITY	DORSAL SOFT RAYS					ANAL SOFT RAYS			PECTORAL*		
	22	23	24	25	26	17	18	19	13	14	15
C. multicinctus											
Hawaiian Islands (Woods)			1	7			3	6		5	4
Honolulu.............			1	4	1		3	3		3	
Johnston..............			1	1	1		1	2		3	
C. punctato-fasciatus											
Marshalls (Woods).......	1	2	6	1		4	6		2	6	

* Splint at top of pectoral fin not included.

In color pattern three rather distinctive types have been distinguished in the Central Pacific. (1) In the Marshalls (according to Schultz and Woods, *op. cit.*, p. 250, table 1) specimens of *A. triostegus* almost always have a single spot at the upper end of the pectoral fin base. In addition (Schultz and Woods, in Schultz, *et al.*, 1953: 625) the black marking on the caudal peduncle is "represented by a spot on dorsal and ventral sides, or a saddle, sometimes absent except for a small spot on dorsal surface only, never completely across side of caudal peduncle." (2) *Acanthurus sandvicensis* consistently has a dark bar across the pectoral base, which is continued downward and somewhat backward on the body. On the caudal peduncle there is a black saddle which extends one third to one half way down the side of the peduncle; there is no spotting below this saddle. (3) In the Marquesas (according to Schultz and Woods, 1948, *loc. cit.*) *A. triostegus* consistently has two spots at each pectoral base, one at the upper part of the base as in the Marshallese form, and another on the body just below the base. These two spots are connected in the young. The caudal saddle in the Marquesan specimens is usually as in the Marshallese form but, in 6 out of 18 specimens, "extending down sides of caudal peduncle and joining with spot on lower sides" on at least one side of the body (Schultz and Woods, 1948, *loc. cit.*). All of the three color types cited above may be found in specimens from Line and

Phoenix Island samples in addition to variants not apparently found elsewhere. Quite frequently markings characteristic of two different races occur on the two sides of the same Phoenix or Line Island fish.

If a stripe running down on to the body below the base of the pectoral fin is designated as A, a single spot on the upper part of the pectoral fin base as B, two spots, one on and one below the fin base as C, and a bar across, and limited to, the fin base as D, Table 8 may be prepared. (The A, B, C, and D types are essentially those similarly designated in Schultz and Woods (1948: 249 and in Schultz, *et al.*, 1953: 625). Actually the four types are not sharply distinct in Phoenix and Line Island fishes. In these areas the A type band extends only slightly below the pectoral base (about as in type E of Schultz and Woods and not well below as in *Acanthurus sandvicensis*) and thus can only be distinguished by definition from D. Furthermore in a few specimens the lower part of the stripe of A tends to become separate and thus grades into C. Finally an elongate spot (B) grades into a bar (D).)

From this table it may be seen that between these two samples all combinations of the different types of pectoral marking may and do occur on opposite sides of the same fish. Indeed, 16 out of 60 specimens have different types of pectoral markings on the two sides of the body. The instability in these populations of the types of pectoral markings that are elsewhere nearly constant is excessive.

If one considers B to be the pure Marshall-ese form, C to be the Marquesan, and A and D a tendency toward the Hawaiian species, then the table may be recalculated as is done in Table 9.

Table 9 demonstrates the unity in pectoral markings of the two samples from the northern Line Islands (Christmas) and the southern Phoenix Islands (Hull). These two islands are, incidentally, some 800 air miles from one another. Also, if types B and D really are a tendency towards *A. sandvicensis*, some indication of intergradation with the Hawaiian species seems present in both samples.

Summarizing the data on pectoral markings in the Phoenix–Line populations, it may be said that these contain to some degree all the marking types to be found in the more constant races to the west (Marshallese), north (Hawaiian), and southeast (Marquesan).

In regard to caudal peduncle markings, a similar concentration of variability in the Phoenix and Line Island samples could probably be demonstrated. However, an analysis of the caudal markings suffers from the two facts that the Marshallese and Marquesan races are not particularly constant in this feature and that the Hawaiian marking is to some extent intermediate between the Marquesan and Marshallese pattern. Suffice it, then, to say here that the same bilateral asymmetry in the coloration on the caudal peduncle takes place as occurs in the pectoral marking, that there does not seem to be any correlation between the shape of the marks on the caudal peduncle and those at the pectoral bases, and finally that there are again all gradations between the various types of caudal markings.

The other feature used by Schultz and Woods (*op. cit.*) in separating the forms of the *Acanthurus triostegus* complex is the dorsal, anal, and pectoral fin counts. The Hawaiian species was found to have higher average sample values for each of these fins than samples from elsewhere. Schultz and Woods

go on to note that the somewhat lower water temperatures of the Hawaiian area may be responsible for this.

Dorsal, anal, and pectoral counts of certain samples from the Hawaiian, Line, and Phoenix Islands, along with the average annual water temperatures (as calculated from Charts II and III at the back of Sverdrup, Johnston, and Fleming, 1946) are shown in Table 10. Several points about this table need discussion. The first regards variation within areas. Thus, two samples from the single island of Oahu have an average difference of nearly 0.2 of a dorsal ray. Indeed, one suspects that different populations from the same area might differ by perhaps 0.3 dorsal ray, 0.2 anal ray, and 0.1 pectoral ray, though available data is insufficient to prove this. At least nothing less than such amounts should be considered geographically significant. Second, the various island groups investigated seem to have rather different average counts, as summarized in Table 10. The Phoenix (Hull Island) sample, well to the south of the Line Islands and still farther away from Hawaii seems to be intermediate between the Line and Hawaiian Island samples. Another Phoenix Island lot counted by Schultz and Woods (1948: table I) indicates the same thing. Certainly, no genetic intermixing between the Hawaiian and Line Island samples is indicated. If one attempts to explain the change in average count by temperature effect, the Line Island samples create the same stumbling block as for introgression, for temperatures in the Phoenix Islands seem to be higher (and should therefore give lower, not higher, average counts than for the Line Island lots).

Summarizing for the *Acanthurus sandvicensis–triostegus* complex, the following points may be made. There is no sign of intergradation between *A. sandvicensis* and *A. triostegus* at Johnston; the pure Hawaiian form is represented there. In the Line and Phoenix Island samples there is some indication of the *A. sandvicensis* pectoral marking in some speci-

TABLE 8

Types of Markings at Pectoral Base in Phoenix and Line Island Samples of *Acanthurus triostegus*

For explanation of lettering, see text

LOCALITY	AA	AB	AC	AD	BB	BC	BD	CC	CD	DD
Line Is.: Christmas...............	1	0	1	1	15	1	4	3	0	1
Phoenix Is.: Hull................	4	2	0	1	17	2	3	2	1	1

TABLE 9

Types of Markings at Pectoral Base in Phoenix and Line Island Samples of *Acanthurus triostegus*

LOCALITY	"MARSHALLESE"	"MARQUESAN"	"HAWAIIAN"
Line Is.: Christmas..................	35 (65%)	8 (15%)	11 (20%)
Phoenix Is.: Hull...................	41 (52%)	7 (11%)	18 (27%)

mens. That introgression of *A. sandvicensis* genes into these populations has occured via passage of Hawaiian individuals through the Line Islands is contra-indicated by the average fin counts of Line Island samples.

Results of the Species Analyses

Though the nature of the available material precludes very extensive cross comparisons between species, a certain amount of integration between the results of the various species can be made.

The first point regards the nature of the morphological distinctions of the Hawaiian endemic forms. In an earlier paper (Gosline, In press) it was stated: "In morphological features the Hawaiian endemic fishes show no pattern of divergence from their Central Pacific relatives." However, in view of Strasburg's recent paper (1955) demonstrating that in the *Istiblennius edentulus* complex there is a rather close correlation between fin ray count and water temperature, it seems well to reinvestigate this statement. Among the six species pairs dealt with here, four differ in coloration, three in meristic counts, one in the position of the dorsal origin, and one in the shape of the head. Of those differing in color, *Gymnothorax eurostus* is separable primarily on the basis of the mottling of the

throat, *Cirrhitus alternatus* in the absence of brown spots on the body, *Chaetodon multicinctus* in the presence of more prominent barring on the nape and caudal peduncle, and *Acanthurus sandvicensis* in the long curved streak below the pectoral base. There seems to be no pattern of differentiation here. However, a pattern does emerge from the meristic data. Of those species pairs differing in meristic characters, two of the Hawaiian endemics have more pectoral rays (*Kuhlia sandvicensis* and *Chaetodon multicinctus*), two have more dorsal and anal soft rays (*Chaetodon multicinctus* and *Acanthurus sandvicensis*), and one has *fewer* gill rakers (*Kuhlia sandvicensis*). Thus for fin rays, if not for gill rakers, there does seem to be a trend toward higher meristic counts in these Hawaiian endemics. Other species showing the same trend that are not dealt with here are *Istiblennius zebra* (see Strasburg, *op. cit.*) and *Dascyllus albisella*. However, what has just been said should not obscure the fact that there are many species in which the Hawaiian form shows no increase in counts and at least a few in which a decrease occurs. Thus the Hawaiian trichonotid *Crystallodytes cookei* differs from its Phoenix Island counterpart only, so far as known, in having *fewer* dorsal and anal rays (Schultz, 1943: 266), and the Hawaiian gobioid *Kraemeria bryani* differs

TABLE 10

FIN COUNTS FOR CERTAIN SAMPLES OF THE *Acanthurus sandvicensis–triostegus* COMPLEX
For the counts averages are given above and standard deviations below in parentheses. No standard deviations
were calculated for the counts drawn from Schultz and Woods (1948: table 1)
as these appear to represent combined samples

LOCALITY	AVERAGE ANNUAL SURFACE WATER TEMPERATURE	NUMBER OF SPECIMENS	SOFT DORSAL RAYS	SOFT ANAL RAYS	TOTAL PECTORAL RAYS
Hawaii: Midway....................	22.0° C	18	23.33 (±.57)	20.67 (±.57)	15.89 (±.33)
Hawaii: Oahu (tide pool on exposed NW coast)......................	24.5	20	23.45 (±.55)	20.75 (±.58)	15.85 (±.36)
Hawaii: Oahu (reef-enclosed bay).....	24.5	46	23.28 (±.62)	20.67 (±.47)	15.83 (±.38)
Hawaii and Johnston (from Schultz and Woods)....................		32	23.59	20.84	15.84
Johnston..........................	26.0	21	23.47 (±.60)	20.67 (±.80)	15.81 (±.40)
Line: Palmyra.....................	26.8	36	22.78 (±.59)	19.58 (±.92)	15.50 (±.50)
Line: Christmas....................	26.1	26	22.46 (±.51)	19.46 (±.58)	15.46 (±.51)
Phoenix: Hull.....................	27.3	33	23.03 (±.52)	20.00 (±.49)	15.45 (±.50)
Phoenix (from Schultz and Woods)...		11	23.09	20.36	15.37*
Guam, Marshalls (from Schultz and Woods)........................		21	22.81	20.14	15.19

* Based on 16 specimens.

from its tropical relative *K. samoensis* most significantly in the *lower* number of pectoral rays (Schultz, 1943: 262).

Zoogeographically there are few definite conclusions that can be drawn from the species analysis, though there are several indications. One of the species, *Kuhlia marginata*, has obviously come to Johnston from the south; the other five have come down from the north. The southern *Kuhlia* shows distinct signs of having introgressed into the northwestern Hawaiian Island populations of *K. sandvicensis*, though whether this has been due to immigration from Johnston or elsewhere remains unknown. Since, however, the prevailing current system around Johnston is from east to west, and even northwest, it seems probable that any migration from Johnston would reach the western leeward

Hawaiian Islands rather than the eastern windward islands. Because of this same current system, any Hawaiian fishes arriving at Johnston would probably have come in from the eastern rather than the western islands, and this is what appears to have happened with *Muraenichthys cookei*, judging from the data presented on that species. That Hawaiian endemics, such as *M. cookei*, have gotten from the Hawaiian Islands to Johnston seems certain. That Johnston fishes actually ever got to Hawaii remains unproven.

ZOOGEOGRAPHIC CONCLUSIONS

Although it may be repetitious, it seems well to draw together the results of the second half of this paper for the sake of those who got lost among the pectoral markings of *Acanthurus* or elsewhere.

The Johnston fish fauna is made up of four components (Fig. 4): endemics; fishes that have made Johnston a stopping point on their migrations from the south; fishes that have found Johnston as a way point in their southward travels; and pelagic fishes to whom Johnston is of little or no significance. The last category, which undoubtedly merges into the second and third, has been excluded from consideration in the present paper. The first is made up of only two species which may simply have been as yet unrecorded elsewhere; in any case, there is very little endemism at Johnston. Species that must have come in from the south, since they are as yet unrecorded in Hawaii and those known to have come in from the north, the "Hawaiian endemics," are represented in Johnston in about equal number. In terms of percentages, however, the proportion of the Hawaiian endemic fauna that reached Johnston is far higher than the proportion of the Central Pacific fauna that reached Johnston but not Hawaii. For this reason it is preferable to consider Johnston as an outlier of the Hawaiian faunal area rather than as a peripheral component of the Central Pacific faunal area.

There is no known intergradation between Hawaiian endemics and their Central Pacific counterparts at Johnston. If the Central Pacific form is represented at Johnston it is there in its pure form and the Hawaiian counterpart is absent, and vice versa.

Since many "Hawaiian endemics" are present at Johnston, it is certain that some species at least have traveled from Hawaii to Johnston. It is, however, not proven that any Johnston fishes ever got to Hawaii; nor is it proven that they did not. Consequently, the role that Johnston may have played in the development of the Hawaiian fish fauna remains in doubt. If, however, one rejects Johnston as the stepping stone by means of which the Hawaiian fishes arrived, then one is driven back on immigration routes that, at the present time, are at least equally implausible and unproven.

REFERENCES

AOYAGI, H. 1941. The damsel fishes found in the waters of Japan. *Biogeog.* [*Biogeog. Soc. Japan, Trans.*], 4: 157–279, 49 figs., 13 pls.

BENNETT, E. T. 1828. Observations on the fishes contained in the collection of the Zoological Society. On some fishes from the Sandwich Islands. *Zool. Jour.* 4: 31–43.

BROCK, V. E., and Y. YAMAGUCHI. 1954. The identity of the parrotfish *Scarus ahula*, the female of *Scarus perspicillatus*. *Copeia* 1954: 154–155.

CHAPMAN, W. M., and L. P. SCHULTZ. 1952. Review of the fishes of the blennioid genus Ecsenius, with descriptions of five new species. *U. S. Natl. Mus., Proc.* 102: 507–528, figs. 90–96.

EDMONDSON, C. H. 1951. Some Central Pacific crustaceans. *Bernice P. Bishop Mus., Occas. Papers* 22: 183–243, 38 figs.

FOWLER, H. W. 1928. The fishes of Oceania. *Bernice P. Bishop Mus., Mem.* 10: iii + 540, 80 figs., 49 pls.

——— 1949. The fishes of Oceania—Supplement 3. *Bernice P. Bishop Mus., Mem.* 12: 37–186.

FOWLER, H. W., and S. C. BALL. 1925. Fishes of Hawaii, Johnston Island, and Wake Island. *Bernice P. Bishop Mus., Bul.* 26: 1–31.

FRASER-BRUNNER, A. 1935. Notes on the plectognath fishes.—1. A synopsis of the genera of the family Balistidae. *Ann. and Mag. Nat. Hist.* X, 15: 658–663.

GILBERT, C. H. 1905. The aquatic resources of the Hawaiian Islands. Part II. Section II.—The deep-sea fishes. *U. S. Fish Commis., Bul.* 23: xi + 577–713, figs. 230–276, pls. 66–101.

GOSLINE, W. A. 1950. The osteology and relationships of the echelid eel, *Kaupichthys diodontus*. *Pacific Sci.* 4: 309–314, 7 figs.

——— 1952. The osteology and classification of the ophichthid eels of the Hawaiian Islands. *Pacific Sci.* 5: 298–320, 18 figs.

—— 1953. Hawaiian shallow-water fishes of the family Brotulidae, with the description of a new genus and notes on brotulid anatomy. *Copeia* 1953: 215–225, 5 figs.

—— In press. The nature and evolution of the Hawaiian inshore fish fauna. *Eighth Pacific Sci. Congress, Proc.*

GOSLINE, W. A., and D. W. STRASBURG. (In press). The Hawaiian fishes of the family Moringuidae: another eel problem. *Copeia* 1956.

GÜNTHER, A. C. L. G. 1860. *Catalogue of the acanthopterygian fishes in the collection of the British Museum.* Volume second. xxi + 548 pp. Taylor and Francis, London.

—— 1873–1909. Andrew Garrett's Fische der Südsee. *Mus. Godeffroy, Jour.*, various volumes: 1–515, 180 pls. [separately paged].

HALSTEAD, B. W., and N. C. BUNKER. 1954. A survey of the poisonous fishes of Johnston Island. *Zoologica* 39: 67–81, 1 fig.

IKEDA, H. 1939. Notes on the fishes of the Riu-Kiu Islands. III. A biometric study on the species of Kuhliidae in the Riu-Kiu Islands. *Biogeog.* [*Biogeog. Soc. Japan, Trans.*] 3: 131–158.

JORDAN, D. S., and B. W. EVERMANN. 1905. The aquatic resources of the Hawaiian Islands. Part I.—The Shore Fishes. *U. S. Fish Commis., Bul.* 23 (1): i–xxvii + 1–574, 229 figs., 73 col. pls., 65 black and white pls.

KAMOHARA, T. 1954. On the fishes of the genus *Lutianus* (Lutianidae) from the province of Tosa, Japan. *Jap. Jour. Ichthyol.* 3: 107–115, 2 figs. [In Japanese, with English summary.]

MATSUBARA, K. 1943. Studies on the scorpaenoid fishes of Japan (II). *Sigenkagaku Kenyusyo, Trans.* 2: 171–486, 4 pls., textfigs. 67–156.

SCHULTZ, L. P. 1943. Fishes of the Phoenix and Samoan Islands collected in 1939 during the expedition of the U.S.S. "Bushnell." *U. S. Natl. Mus. Bul.* 180: x + 316, 9 pls., 27 text figs.

—— 1950. Three new species of fishes of the genus *Cirrhitus* (Family Cirrhitidae) from the Indo-Pacific. *U. S. Natl. Mus., Proc.* 100: 547–552, pl. 13.

SCHULTZ, L. P., and L. P. WOODS. 1948. *Acanthurus triostegus marquesensis,* a new subspecies of surgeonfish, family Acanthuridae, with notes on related forms. *Wash. Acad. Sci., Jour.* 38: 248–251, 1 fig.

—— and —— 1949. Keys to the genera of echelid eels and the species of *Muraenichthys* of the Pacific, with two new species. *Wash. Acad. Sci., Jour.* 39: 170–174, 2 figs.

SCHULTZ, L. P., *et al.* 1953. Fishes of the Marshall and Marianas Islands. Vol. 1. *U. S. Natl. Mus., Bul.* 202: i–xxxii + 1–685, 90 figs., 73 pls.

SMITH, J. L. B. 1954. Apogonid fishes of the subfamily Pseudamiinae from South-East Africa. *Ann. and Mag. Nat. Hist.* XII, 7: 775–795, 3 figs., 1 pl.

SMITH, R. M., and J. SWAIN. 1882. Notes on a collection of fishes from Johnston's Island, including descriptions of five new species. *U. S. Natl. Mus., Proc.* 5: 119–143.

SNODGRASS, R. E., and E. HELLER. 1905. Shore fishes of the Revillagigedo, Clipperton, Cocos and Galapagos Islands. *Wash. Acad. Sci., Proc.* 6: 333–427.

STRASBURG, D. W. 1955. North-south differentiation of blenniid fishes found in the Central Pacific. *Pacific Sci.* 9 (3): 297–303.

SVERDRUP, H. U., M. W. JOHNSON, and R. H. FLEMING. 1946. *The oceans.* x + 1087 pp. Prentice-Hall, Inc., New York.

TANAKA, S. 1931. On the distribution of fishes in Japanese waters. *Tokyo Imp. Univ. Faculty Sci., Jour.*, Sect. IV Zool. 2: 1–90, 3 pls.

Section 5

Insular Evolution: Hawaiian Style

INTRODUCTION

Born was the coral polyp, born was the coral,
        came forth
Born was the grub that digs and heaps up the
        earth, came forth
Born was his [child] an earthworm came forth
Born was the starfish, his child the small
        starfish came forth
Born was the sea cucumber, his child the small
        sea cucumber came forth . . .

   From the Kumulipo or Hawaiian Creation Chant,
   M. Beckwith translation

"These Achatinellinae never came from Noah's
        ark."

                                J. T. Gulick, 1858

The more isolated islands are, the more distinctive
are their biotas. The Hawaiian Islands are a land of
great isolation, and their flora and fauna are among
the most distinctive in the world. Endemism is very
high, especially among terrestrial organisms.

   As the ancestral immigrants established themselves
in the Islands, most of them found an ecological vacuum
or near-vacuum. There was little opposition -- few or
no predators, parasites, or disease. They could develop
to their fullest biotic potentials. As each new species
became established, ecological conditions changed,
resulting in more and more diversification. The result
in the Hawaiian Islands: genera developing 50 to 100
or more species in a short period of geological time,
as in the great species complexes of *Drosophila* among
the insects and *Achatinella* among the mollusks. Some
species radiated or diverged far from the ancestral
type (for example, a dragonfly whose larvae develop
among leaves far from water); herbaceous plants became
arborescent; insects developed flightless forms.

The patterns of evolutionary development and the processes involved in that development are the subjects of this section. The papers of Gosline and Briggs discuss these subjects in general, those of St. John on *Gunnera* and Zimmerman on adaptive radiation in Hawaiian insects deal with patterns of evolution, while those of Gillett on hybridization in *Scaevola* and Carson on chromosomes in *Drosophila* treat evolutionary processes.

Considerations Regarding the Evolution of Hawaiian Animals

INTEREST IN THE BIOTAS of oceanic islands is of long standing. There are several reasons for the continuing interest. One is the possibility that insular evolution may in some respects represent a small-scale model of what has occurred on continents. Another is that, despite all the work on the subject, the "hows" and the "whys" of insular evolution remain inadequately answered. Finally, there is the realization that, with the rapid decimation of native insular habitats, it will soon be impossible to study many aspects of the subject (Hubbell, 1967).

The general field of evolution in oceanic animals has been reviewed many times, most recently by Miller (1966) and Carlquist (1965). Zimmerman's summary (1948) for the Hawaiian terrestrial forms is classic. Here, I shall deal with only certain facets of the subject, and I shall cite only those references from the tremendous literature most pertinent to the matter at hand. This selective method of presentation has serious faults, but any attempt to be comprehensive would seem only to obscure the threads of thought that it is the purpose of the paper to present.

Recently, in writing of land plants, Carlquist (1966:433) has spoken of an "insular syndrome of interrelated evolutionary phenomena." Insofar as Hawaiian animals are concerned, what is more striking to me is the diversity of evolutionary results. Such variations occur not only between groups but within some groups as well. For example the evolution of the Hawaiian drepaniid finches has been very different from that of the sea birds.

This diversity of evolutionary results could be exemplified from various animals groups, most notably insects. However, I shall not deal with Hawaiian insects at any length, primarily because of unfamiliarity with them but also

because at the present time they are the subject of an intensive continuing investigation (Zimmerman, et al., 1948—; Spieth, 1966:246). Rather, I shall emphasize the evolutionary problems of three Hawaiian animal groups: the inshore fishes, the achatinellid land snails, and the drepaniid finches. As an introduction to the problems involved the evolutionary status of these three groups in Hawaii is summarized briefly.

The Hawaiian inshore fishes (Gosline, 1958; Gosline and Brock, 1960) form part of a marine biota that is essentially similar to, but somewhat impoverished, as compared with that of the Central Pacific islands to the south and west. There are few conspicuous gaps in the Hawaiian marine biota, and, of those that do occur, at least one—the coral genus *Acropora*—was present in Hawaiian waters in the past (Menard, Allison and Durham, 1962). There seems to be a more or less constant infiltration of non-resident species into the Hawaiian marine biota today, some of which have become established (Doty, 1961), while some have not (Brock, 1948). Intentional introductions of purely marine forms into Hawaiian waters have been mostly unsuccessful. (By contrast, a number of introductions into areas of reduced salinity, e.g., Kaneohe Bay on Oahu, have done quite well.) One of the few that has succeeded, the "Marquesan sardine," has spread throughout the waters of the high Hawaiian Islands in a matter of a few years (Murphy, 1960). Endemism above the species level among Hawaiian fishes is dubious. However, about one third of the inshore species are represented by endemic forms. These can usually be distinguished from Central Pacific counterparts in 100% of the individuals (for some exceptions, see Gosline, 1955). Aside from a few expected correlations between morphological traits and the relatively cool Hawaiian water temperatures (see, for example, Strasburg, 1955), the morphological characters by which the Hawaiian endemics differ from their Cen-

[1] Department of Zoology, University of Hawaii, Honolulu, Hawaii 96822. Manuscript received June 13, 1967.

tral Pacific counterparts appear to be of a random nature. Within any family of fishes represented in Hawaii, the endemic forms are often the most abundant.

In striking contrast with the Hawaiian marine biota, the native terrestrial biota is highly disharmonic or unbalanced. Great groups of animals, e.g., the amphibians, were completely unrepresented, whereas others, e.g., the land snails and drepaniids, proliferated greatly. Not only new Hawaiian species, but also new genera and families evolved. Among the achatinellid land snails, the genus *Achatinella* is restricted to the island of Oahu, but some 100 allopatric forms have been described. No relationship between the peculiarities of these forms and the environment they inhabit has ever been demonstrated. The drepaniid finches seem to have evolved in quite a different way. They inhabited all of the major islands of the Hawaiian chain and some of the smaller islands as well. The most notable differentiation within the group is in beak shape, which is associated with feeding habits (Baldwin, 1953). Several different drepaniids were often sympatric.

One of the main differences between the terrestrial and marine environments in Hawaii is in the amount of change caused by man. The terrestrial environment has been largely transformed, in part directly by man via agriculture, etc., but perhaps more by the indirect effect of animals and plants which man has introduced, intentionally or unintentionally. Many of these introductions have now replaced or are replacing the native biota and are directly or indirectly responsible for the restriction or extinction of native forms.

With this brief background, the question of evolutionary processes will be discussed.

Basic to the evolution (or lack of it) that will occur on any island is the matter of which organisms are there and which are not. To exist, an organism must first arrive, and it then must find an environment in which it can survive and reproduce. Both of these aspects depend in part on the isolation of the island— not isolation in terms of geographical-physical barriers alone, but in terms of these in relation to the ability of the organism to cross them.

The day when isolation could be considered

a causal factor has long since passed. However, that it is a powerful controlling factor is generally recognized. This control acts in two related ways. First, it determines which organisms will get to an island and which will not. The selectivity of this filtering factor will increase with increasing isolation and hence will determine in part the extent to which the island biota resembles its parental biota. The greater the difference between these two biotas, the greater will be the change in biological selection pressures on any organism arriving on the island. This point will be discussed later.

Second, any species that establishes itself on an island should, at least for a while, be preserved from contamination by gene flow from the parental population. If the recent introduction to Hawaii of numerous species (e.g., the Marquesan sardine, the African snail, the garden spider, etc.) is any criterion, the initial immigrants can build up a population of millions of individuals in a few years. Beyond this point contamination from gene flow from a few subsequent immigrants will probably have little effect (Gosline, 1958). There are, however, certain important exceptions to this statement. If, in the process of building up a population from initial immigrants, the population becomes debilitated in some way or loses its ability to cope with diseases or parasites which later immigrants may bring with them, then subsequent immigration may matter a great deal.

Of factors actually causing insular evolution only two will be considered. One is natural selection, and the other the series of features associated with small population size.

It is generally agreed that differentiation proceeds more rapidly in animal populations on small islands than on large ones. The question is: to what extent is this caused by differences in the selective forces on small islands, and to what extent to factors associated directly with small population sizes. A rather large body of data suggests that many of the peculiarities of small-island forms are not *directly* selected by the enviroment. Two examples will suffice. Dowdeswell and Ford (1953 and elsewhere) have shown that on the larger islands of the Scilly group the spotting on the wing of the butterfly *Maniola jurtina* remains about as it is on the adjacent Cornish mainland. On the small islands of the group, however, the number of spots on the wing of the females not only varies from island to island, but increases on some and decreases on others. Second, Mertens (1934:116) has pointed out that the same island may contain a dwarf form of one reptile and a giant form of another. It would be difficult to postulate environmental factors that would select animals in these ways.

If small-population forces are to be postulated for such differences, three possibilities must be considered. The first is the random loss of genes which may occur in small populations by genetic drift (Wright, 1931, etc.). Such a factor would presumably be operative in all small populations. A special case of genetic drift is the phenomenon often called founder effect. This merely expresses the fact that the original immigrants to an island are frequently few in number, and, whether or not they constitute a representative sample, they can bring with them only a small proportion of the alleles present in the parental population (see, for example, Zimmerman, 1948:122, 123). The third possible small-population factor is what Mayr (1954) calls internal selection. In large populations where each gene often has many alleles those which work best as heterozygotes will tend to be selected; on the other hand, in small populations there will be a larger proportion of homozygotes, and alleles which work best in the homozygotic condition will tend to be selected. Thus some shift in internal selection pressure between large and small populations would be expected.

These small-population factors, acting *per se,* should affect insular immigrants during those initial stages when the population is still small (Fig. 1). But there appears to be no known instance in which a change at this stage has been recorded (cf. Mayr, 1954). Furthermore, it is a generally accepted dictum that, other things being equal, the older the island the greater will be the differentiation in its biota; this implies continuous, not just initial, change.

Then how is the differentiation that occurs on islands, and more rapidly on small islands, to be explained? King (1955) conducted selection experiments for DDT resistance on two

cultures of *Drosophila melanogaster.* After a dozen or more generations some degree of DDT resistance began to be built up in both lines. But, as judged from crossbreeding experiments, the resistance had been built up differently in the two lines. King (1955:314) states: "The manner in which a line could respond to selection was to some extent determined by the genetic nature of the sample from which it started, and having started along one certain road, it kept on. The inevitable sampling error which occurs when a line is taken from a larger population is very likely the anlage of the genetic individuality of the line. This is, of course, an example of the principle of genetic drift. . . ." The second example is that reported on by Dobzhansky and Pavlovsky (1957). In this experiment ten cultures from a specially developed laboratory stock of *Drosophila pseudo-obscura* were started with 20 flies each and compared after 17 months with ten other cultures that did not begin with a reduced number of individuals. Those stocks which had started with 20 flies showed more variation than the controls. Again, Dobzhansky and Pavlovsky conclude (1957:316): "Although the trait studied (gene arrangement in the third chromosome) is subject to powerful selection pressure, the outcome of the selection in the experimental populations is conditioned by random genetic drift."

One aspect of these experiments by King and by Dobzhansky and Pavlovsky may well be of importance for insular evolution. In both instances not only were the original samples small, but the selection that was exerted upon them was far different from the selection of the natural environment from which the flies came. It is as though the samples in the experiments were subjected to an intense selection pressure at right angles to the pressures to which the ancestral "wild" forms had presumably adapted themselves. Possibly some of the alleles intensely selected under the laboratory conditions had been of only peripheral significance to the wild stocks and hence variably represented in them. Such alleles would be more subject to sampling error among small founder populations drawn from the parental stock than those previously under intense positive selection pressure.

Insular selection pressures (except, perhaps, for species introduced by and dependent on man) are similarly at an angle to those exerted on the mainland parental form. Insofar as the island biota is different from that whence the immigrants came, it is inevitable that the biological selection pressures on islands will differ. Any immigrant to an island will leave behind at least some of the predators, competitors, diseases, and parasites that the parental mainland stock had to cope with. On the other hand the initial immigrants may well have to adapt to new forms of food, cover, etc. (This will be less true only in degree if a species arrives by a series of island hops.)

There is also evidence that selection pressures on small islands are likely to be more radically different than they are on large islands. Thus, on Manana Island, a small outlier of Oahu without domestic cats, the cat flea (*Ctenocephalides felis felis*) has developed an ectoparasitic existence on rabbits (*Oryctolagus cuniculus*) (Tomich, et al., in press). Again, in the Balearic Islands off Spain, Eisentraut (1949) showed that on the smaller outliers the food of lizards (*Lacerta*) differed considerably from that on the main islands. As the normal insect food became more restricted, these lizards added the normally avoided ants to their diets, and on very small islands ate even flower petals and young plant shoots.

Eisentraut believed that this change in diet had a direct metabolic effect resulting in the melanism frequently found in the small-island populations. To me (cf. Dowdeswell and Ford, 1953) it seems more likely that the morphological changes so frequently found in small poulations are in part the indirect effect of altered selection pressures working with time on the, in part randomly, depleted gene pool of small populations. A gradual reintegration of such a gene pool in response to altered selection pressures would likely involve a change in phenotypic characters that are not themselves selected. Such an interpretation (cf. Mayr, 1954; Dobzhansky and Pavlovsky, 1957) seems to me to provide the best available explanation for the often rather heterogeneous differentiating characteristics of insular endemics, e.g., Hawaiian inshore fishes.

The main reason why the peculiarities of

Hawaiian endemic fishes cannot, apparently, be attributed to small-population losses alone is that in many instances the Hawaiian endemics are not characterized by a simple increase in variability (as in Dobzhansky and Pavlovsky's flies) but rather by new and fairly constant characters entirely outside the range of variability of the ancestral populations (as in King's results). Presumably such characters must have arisen through a reintegration and/or evolution from the ancestral genetic system via direct or indirect selection. The same reasoning would seem to apply to at least some of Eisentraut's melanic lizard populations.

Judging by personal observation and common knowledge concerning recent successful terrestrial introductions of animals to the Hawaiian islands (see also Mead, 1961:180–182; Tomich, et al., in press), there is often (presumably following a longer or shorter period of small numbers) a tremendous initial build-up and "overshoot" in population number (Fig. 1). During my 18 years in Hawaii this has hap-

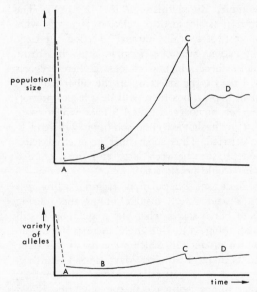

Fig. 1. Theoretical population size (*above*) and allele variety (*below*) plotted against time in a terrestrial animal that successfully immigrates into the Hawaiian Islands for the first time. *A*, Date of arrival; *B*, time when population becomes sufficiently large that small-population genetic factors will *per se* cause no further loss of alleles; *C*, initial peak of abundance; and *D*, subsequent equilibrium. For discussion, see text.

pened with a garden spider (*Argiope appensa*) and the giant African snail (*Achatina fulica*), among the more conspicuous unintentionally introduced forms. If it can be assumed that this cycle happened in the past with our "native" biota, then certain postulates concerning selection pressures would seem to follow.

First, during the period of initial buildup of an introduced form, selection pressure must be very low. (Apparently the other members of the biota are not initially able to cope with or defend themselves from the new introduction.) However, at some point in the buildup, the population becomes excessive, after which it falls drastically to a new fluctuating equilibrium well below the previous maximum. The nature of the factor that sooner or later kills back the initial overshoot is unknown in any particular instance. There is no reason to believe it is the same in all cases, or that it may not be a combination of factors. What is important to the present argument is that after a period of relaxed selection during the population buildup a very severe selection pressure of some sort appears. Some of the various possibilities are as follows.

First, the animal may eat out the available food supply and then die of starvation. This apparently happened to the rabbits introduced to Lisianski Island (Bryan, 1942:192, 193), and almost but, perhaps significantly, not quite with the rabbits on Laysan (Warner, 1963:6, 7; cf. also Tomich, et al., in press).

On a larger island with a more varied biota a second possible situation might occur after the immigrant population had overeaten its original food supply. Assume that an immigrant adapts itself to an insular food supply as close as possible to that of its parental stock. Assume that, having adapted itself to this insular food source, the immigrant builds up a tremendous population under greatly relaxed selection pressure. At some point it will overshoot its new food supply and a severe competition for food will take place. This selection may preserve the best adapted individuals of the original immigrant type, if enough of the food supply is left. It may also preserve those individuals that have differentiated farthest in the direction of adapting to a new food source (Fig. 2). This theoretical possibility has been set up with the evolution of the Hawaiian

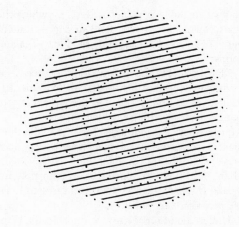

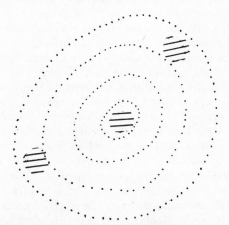

FIG. 2. On a background (*dotted contours*) representing Sewall Wright's adaptive peak concept are shown (*hatched areas*): *above*, a theoretical population just before reaching the initial maximum (*C* in Fig. 1), and, *below*, the same population after an equilibrium size had been reached (*D* in Fig. 1). For discussion, see text.

drepaniid finches, with their various beak types, in mind.

Another possibility is that, following the initial population explosion, some factor other than food supply develops to keep subsequent numbers low. This could be disease or parasitism, some change in other environmental features, or some other factor which would lower the reproductive rate. That the reproductive rate may be diminished has been stressed by Lack (1954). Lack deals especially with changes in egg number in birds. But there is another method, in plants at least, by which the replacement rate may be held in check. Rattenbury (1962:354) has said of New Zealand forms:

"Furthermore, the germination of seeds of many native species is a matter of extreme difficulty, as is evidenced by the sporadic appearance of seedlings which often seem to require special conditions for their development. Competent nurserymen have experienced great difficulty in germinating native seeds, often resorting to powerful treatments for breaking the dormancy. In many cases the viable period is very short."

Under conditions of severe interspecific competition, a reduction in the reproduction rate, however accomplished, would seem to be feasible only to the extent that it enables the species to raise a greater number of offspring (Lack, 1954). To drop below that rate would invite replacement by competitors (including possible subsequent immigrants of the same species). If, however, there is very slight interspecific competition, the reproductive rate might theoretically fall to and somewhat below the maximum possible replacement rate without immediate harm. In my opinion, this is what seems to have occurred in many forms among the native terrestrial Hawaiian biota.

If this is true, a species that experienced essentially no natural selection from infra- and interspecific competition during the initial increase might again avoid natural selection after an equilibrium had been reached. In the process, however, the species would of course lose its aggressiveness, especially as compared with subsequently introduced rapidly breeding forms.

Possible examples of a loss in fertility, apparently before any overpopulation has taken place, are provided by the Hawaiian hawk (*Buteo solitarius*) and the Hawaiian crow (*Corvus tropicus*), both of which are, and so far as known always have been, confined to relatively small areas of the single island of Hawaii. In view of the general adaptability of related mainland forms this geographic restriction is most difficult to explain. Possibly here we have a "depauperization of biotype" (Hultén, 1937) arising from small population effects. Such a "depauperization" of course could and prob-

ably often does result in a lowering of reproductive capacity.

Returning finally to the achatinellid snails of Oahu, it seems obvious from the isolation of many of the colonies of *Achatinella* (even before their extensive extermination by the introduced carnivorous snails *Euglandina* and *Gonaxis;* see Krauss, 1964) that they were not spreading. Presumably they can only have been developed from some more "aggressive" ancestral form (and/or a less dissected topography than exists today). But given the more recent isolation in separate colonies there seems to be no reason why, in the absence of further gene flow, each colony should not evolve in its own way as do so many other small populations, particularly land snails. A basically similar provisional hypothesis has been advanced by Carson (1966:405) to explain the formation of Hawaiian species of Drosophilidae.

ACKNOWLEDGMENTS

My acquaintance with this subject has been gained over the years through the kind help of colleagues too numerous to mention. For specific suggestions and comments on the manuscript I wish sincerely to thank Dr. A. H. Banner, Dr. E. A. Kay, and Dr. C. H. Lamoureux of the University of Hawaii, and Dr. Y. Kondo of the Bishop Museum, all of whom have been residents of Hawaii and interested in the Hawaiian biota for much or most of their lives.

REFERENCES

BALDWIN, P. H. 1953. Annual cycle, environment and evolution in the Hawaiian honeycreepers (Aves: Drepaniidae). Univ. Calif. Publ. Zool. 52:285–398, pls. 8–11, 12 figs.

BROCK, V. E. 1948. An addition to the fish fauna of the Hawaiian Islands. Pacific Sci. 2:298.

BRYAN, E. H., JR. 1942. American Polynesia and the Hawaiian Chain. Tongg Publishing Co., Honolulu. 253 pp., illus.

CARLQUIST, S. 1965. Island Life. The Natural History Press, Garden City, New York. viii + 451 pp., 7 col. pls., text figs.

——— 1966. The biota of long-distance dispersal. IV. Genetic systems in the floras of oceanic islands. Evolution 20:433–455, 2 figs.

CARSON, H. L. 1966. Chromosomal Races of *Drosophila crucigera* from the Islands of Oahu and Kauai, State of Hawaii. Univ. Texas Publ. No. 6615, pp. 405–412, 2 figs.

DOBZHANSKY, T., and O. PAVLOVSKY. 1957. An experimental study of interaction between genetic drift and natural selection. Evolution 11:311–319, 2 figs.

DOTY, M. S. 1961. *Acanthophora,* a possible invader of the marine flora of Hawaii. Pacific Sci. 15:547–552.

DOWDESWELL, W. H., and E. B. FORD. 1953. The influence of isolation on variability in the butterfly *Maniola jurtina* L. Symp. Soc. Exptl. Biol. 7:254–273, 2 maps.

EISENTRAUT, M. 1949. Die Eidechsen der spanischen Mittelmeer Inseln. Mitt. Zool. Mus. Berlin 26:1–225, 10 col. pls., 46 text figs.

GOSLINE, W. A. 1955. The inshore fish fauna of Johnston Island, a Central Pacific atoll. Pacific Sci. 9:442–480, 4 figs.

——— 1958. The nature and evolution of the Hawaiian inshore fish fauna. Proceedings of the Eighth Pacific Science Congress, Vol. 3, pp. 347–357, 1 fig.

——— and V. E. BROCK. 1960. Handbook of Hawaiian Fishes. University of Hawaii Press, Honolulu. ix + 372 pp., 277 figs.

HUBBELL, T. H. 1967. Systematics and the International Biological Program. Systematic Zoology 16:97–99.

HULTÉN, E. 1937. Outline of the History of Arctic and Boreal Biota during the Quaternary Period. Stockholm. 168 pp.

KING, J. C. 1955. Evidence for the integration of the gene pool from studies of DDT resistance in Drosophila. Cold Spring Harbor Symposia on Quantitative Biology. Vol. 20, pp. 311–317.

KRAUSS, N. L. H. 1964. Investigations on biological control of Giant African (*Achatina fulica*) and other land snails. Nautilus 78: 21–27.

LACK, D. 1954. The evolution of reproduction rates. In: Huxley, Hardy and Ford, eds., Evolution as a Process, pp. 143–156. Collier, N.Y.

MAYR, E. 1954. Change of genetic environment and evolution. In: Huxley, Hardy and Ford, eds., Evolution as a Process, pp. 157–180, 3 figs. Collier, N.Y.

MEAD, A. R. 1961. The Giant African Snail. University of Chicago Press, Chicago. xvi + 257 pp., 15 figs.

MENARD, H. W., E. C. ALLISON, and J. W. DURHAM. 1962. A drowned Miocene terrace on the Hawaiian Islands. Science 138: 896–897.

MERTENS, R. 1934. Die Insel-Reptilien, ihre Ausbreitung, Variation und Artbildung. Zoologica (Stuttgart) 32:1–209.

MILLER, A. H. 1966. Animal Evolution on Islands. In: R. I. Bowman, ed., The Galapagos, pp. 10–17. University of California Press.

MURPHY, G. I. 1960. Introduction of the Marquesan sardine, *Harengula vittata* (Cuvier and Valenciennes), to Hawaiian waters. Pacific Sci. 14:185–187.

RATTENBURY, J. A. 1962. Cyclic hybridization as a survival mechanism in the New Zealand forest flora. Evolution 16:348–363, 5 figs.

SPIETH, H. T. 1966. Courtship Behavior of Endemic Hawaiian *Drosophila.* Univ. Texas Publ. No. 6615, pp. 245–314.

STRASBURG, D. W. 1955. North-south differentiation of blenniid fishes in the Central Pacific. Pacific Sci. 9:297–303.

TOMICH, F. Q., C. H. LAMOUREUX, and N. WILSON. In press. Ecological factors on Manana Island, Hawaii. Pacific Sci.

WARNER, R. E. 1963. Recent history and ecology of the Laysan Duck. Condor 65:3–23, 8 figs.

WRIGHT, S. 1931. Evolution in Mendelian populations. Genetics 16:97–159.

ZIMMERMAN, E. C. 1948. Insects of Hawaii. Vol. 1. Introduction. University of Hawaii Press, Honolulu. xvii + 206 pp., 52 figs.

——— et al. 1948—. Insects of Hawaii. Eleven volumes published so far. University of Hawaii Press, Honolulu.

Oceanic Islands, Endemism, and Marine Paleotemperatures[1]

JOHN C. BRIGGS

Abstract

Available data on the marine shore faunas of the old (apparently Pliocene or earlier) and well isolated oceanic islands (300 miles or more from nearest land) reveal a very interesting pattern of endemism. The endemic rate is very low in the north and middle Atlantic, markedly greater in the south Atlantic and Pacific, and exceedingly high in the Sub-Antarctic waters.

It is suggested that this peculiar pattern of endemism may be correlated with the extent of the drop in sea surface temperature that occurred during the Pleistocene glaciations. Contrary to most of the literature on the subject, it seems that the effect of the ice ages on ocean temperature may have been quite different in various parts of the world. The islands that demonstrate the least amount of endemism were probably exposed to the greatest decline in surface temperature.

In the days of Charles Darwin and Alfred Russel Wallace, the oceanic islands and archipelagoes were considered to be fascinating places, and, indeed, it was Darwin's visit to the Galápagos Islands in 1835 that provided him with information essential to his evolutionary theory. Nowadays, the evolutionary biologist tends to focus on short-term problems in his laboratory, not recognizing that, on such islands, he can examine the results of experiments in natural selection, competition, and distribution that have been carried on by nature for thousands of years. For the marine biologist, oceanic islands hold fully as much promise as they do for the investigator of the terrestrial biology, perhaps even more, since in many cases the marine shore fauna is the richer.

Once an island is established, and by means of fortuitous accumulation picks up its founder species, the various populations can be expected to embark immediately on their own lines of evolutionary change. Since relatively small populations are usually involved and because many aspects of the ecology are apt to be different, it may be expected that such change would occur rapidly in comparison to a mainland situation. As a result, oceanic islands that are relatively old should possess faunas that show a high degree of evolutionary divergence. The best indication of the extent of such divergence is probably the rate of endemism.

Although our knowledge of the shore faunas of most oceanic islands and archipelagoes is still quite scanty, enough work has been done on certain groups, particularly the fishes, so that it is often possible to obtain a reasonably good indication of the extent of endemism. Considering only those islands that are so well isolated (300 miles or more from the mainland or nearest island group) that there is not likely to be a sustained gene input, and are apparently also old enough (Pliocene or earlier) to demonstrate marked evolutionary changes, the essential data can be summarized as follows:

Atlantic Ocean[2]

1. Azores—a group of nine islands (36° '50' to 39°44' N, 25° to 31°16' W)

[1] Research for this paper was supported by National Science Foundation grant GB 2836.

[2] Trindade Island off the Coast of Brazil is not included because its fauna is so poorly known. Ascension Island is not considered because it is apparently of quite recent (Pleistocene) origin (Wilson, 1963:536).

Reprinted from *Systematic Zoology* 15:153–163 (1966), by permission of the author and of the editor of *Systematic Zoology*.

about 900 statute miles off the coast of Portugal. The shore fishes are quite well known (Collins, 1954; Albuquerque, 1954–56) but there are *no* endemic species. Age is probably Miocene (Wilson, 1963: 536).

2. Madeira—two islands (32°3′ to 33°7′ N, 16°13′ to 16°38′ W about 500 miles from the coast of Morocco. Invertebrates seem to be poorly known, but the shore fishes have received more attention (Maul, 1948; Albuquerque, 1954–56). The rate of endemism in the latter group is about 3%. Age is probably Miocene but possibly older (Wilson, 1963).

3. Cape Verde Islands—ten main islands (14°47′ to 17°13′ N, 22°52′ to 25°22′ W) about 320 miles west of Cape Verde, Sénégal. The fishes are the best known marine group (Cadenat, 1951, 1961) and demonstrate an endemic level of about 4%. Age is Lower Cretaceous (Wilson, 1963).

4. Bermuda—about 360 small islands (32°14′ to 32°25′ N, 64°38′ to 64°52′ W) about 900 miles from the North Carolina coast. The fishes are known best (Collette, 1962) and endemism is about 5%. Age is probably Eocene or Oligocene (Wilson, 1963).

5. Saint Helena—one volcanic island (15°57′ S, 5°42′ W) about 1200 miles from the west coast of Africa. Endemism in echinoderms is about 50% (Mortensen, 1933) and in shore fishes about 27% (Cadenat and Marchal, 1963; Briggs, 1966). Age is possibly Miocene (Wilson, 1963).

6. Tristan-Gough Islands—three small volcanic islands, Tristan da Cunha, Nightingale, and Inaccessible, are situated close together (about 39° S, 13° W), but Gough Island is well separated, lying about 200 miles to the south (40°20′ S, 9°56′ W). Summary of data for all marine shore species indicated about 23% to be endemic (Holdgate, 1960). Age is probably Miocene (Wilson, 1963).

Pacific Ocean[3]

1. Galápagos Islands—an archipelago consisting of 13 large and many smaller islands (lat. 1° N to 1°30′ S, about 89° to 92° W) about 700 miles off the coast of Ecuador. Endemism in shore fishes is about 27% (Walker and Rosenblatt, 1961:470) and in the brachyuran crabs about 15% (Garth, 1946). Age is possibly Lower Pliocene (Banfield, Behre, and St. Claire, 1956).

2. Hawaiian Islands—a group of 20 islands (18°55′ to 23° N, 154°40′ to 162° W) about 450 miles from Johnston Island (which has a close faunal relationship) and 900 miles from the rest of Polynesia. About 34% of the shore fishes are endemic (Gosline and Brock, 1960). Age is estimated at late Miocene or earlier (Menard, Allison, and Durham, 1962).

3. Juan Fernández Islands—two main islands (33°36′ to 33°48′ S, 78°45′ to 80°47′ W) about 400 miles west of the central Chilean coast. Endemism in shore fishes is 50% or more (Rendahl, 1921; Mann, 1954); average for invertebrates probably about the same (Madsen, 1956; Leloup, 1956; Garth, 1957). Age Upper Cretaceous to Eocene (Mann, 1954).

4. Easter Island—a volcanic island (27° 3′ to 27°12′ S, 109°14′ to 109°28′ W) about 300 miles from Sala y Gómez to the east and 900 miles from Ducie Island to the west. There seems to be about 29% endemism in the shore fishes (Rendahl, 1921) but this result

---

[3] In the eastern Pacific, Guadalupe, Revillagigedos, and Malpelo Islands are all less than 300 miles offshore; Cocos Island is probably of Pleistocene origin (Vinton, 1951:373) and the fauna of Clipperton, San Ambrosio, and San Félix is too poorly known. In the western Pacific, the faunas of Marcus, Wake, and Sala y Gómez Islands are very poorly known. In the Indian Ocean, Cocos-Keeling is probably of Pleistocene origin (Wallace, 1892: 285), and so is St. Paul-Amsterdam (Wilson, 1963).

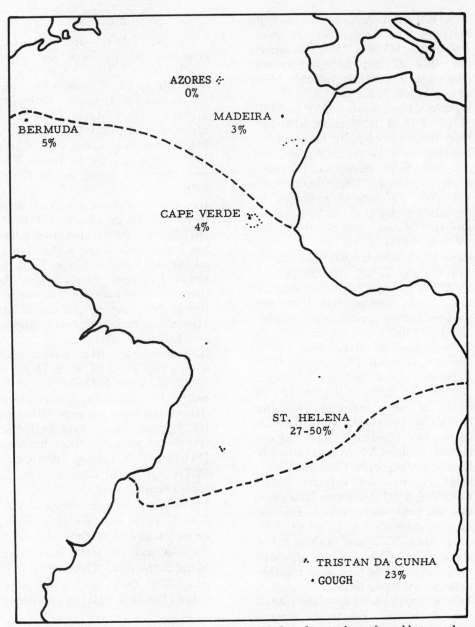

FIG. 1. Atlantic Ocean. Dashed lines represent 20°C surface isotherm for coldest month.

was not based on a large collection. Age unknown.

5. Lord Howe-Norfolk Province—four oceanic localities in the Tasman Sea that apparently share a common fauna. These are: Lord Howe Island, about 300 miles off the east coast of Aus-

tralia, the Middleton and Elizabeth Reefs, a little over 100 miles to the north of Lord Howe Island, and Norfolk Island, about 400 miles northwest of New Zealand. Shore fish endemism appears to be about 22% (Whitley, 1937; Waite, 1916). Age of Lord

Howe Island possibly Pliocene (Etheridge, 1889:124).

6. Kermadec Islands—a volcanic group (30°30′ S, 178°30′ W) about 500 miles northeast of Auckland, New Zealand. Of the mollusks 34% are endemic (Dell, 1958:500) and of the echinoderms 39% (Pawson, 1961:9). Age unknown.

7. Chatham Islands—two main islands (44° S, 176°30′ W) about 400 miles from the southern tip of North Island, New Zealand. Mollusks are known best and demonstrate 15% endemism (Dell, 1960). Other groups may have fewer endemics because of direct currents coming from New Zealand. Age probably Miocene (Fleming, 1962).

8. Antipodes Province—consists of four island groups located to the south and east of the South Island of New Zealand: Auckland Islands 190 miles, Antipodes Islands 490 miles, Campbell Islands 320 miles, and Bounty Islands 490 miles. About 50% of the mollusks are endemic (Powell, 1962) and about 22% of the echinoderms (Knox, 1963). Auckland and Campbell Islands probably were built up largely in the Pliocene (Fleming, 1962).

Sub-Antarctic Seas[4]

1. Kerguelen Islands—comprises over 300 small islands (48°40′ to 49°49′ S, about 70° E) approximately 1,300 miles north of the Antarctic continent. Endemism in shore fishes is about 71% (Nybelin, 1951). Age is probably Miocene (Wilson, 1963).

2. Macquarie Island—a volcanic island (54°30′ S, 158°40′ E) about 400 miles southwest of the Aukland Islands and about 600 miles from the New Zealand mainland. About 64% of the mollusks are endemic (Dell, 1964).

[4] Adequate faunal data are not available for the McDonald, Heard, Marion, Prince Edward, and Crozet Islands. Bouvet Island probably originated in the Pleistocene (Wilson, 1963).

Other groups are not as well known. Age unknown.

3. South Georgia—one large island (54° 30′ S, 37° W) about 300 miles west of the South Sandwich Islands and 800 miles east of the Falkland Islands. The fishes are quite well known, with 57% endemic (Norman, 1938; Nybelin, 1947); 58% of the mollusks are apparently endemic (Powell, 1951). Age unknown.

Pattern of Endemism

When the figures for endemism (representing the degree of evolutionary change) are plotted on a map, an interesting pattern emerges (Fig. 1). Beginning with the locality farthest north in the Atlantic (the Azores), there is no endemism at all. Moving southward, there is about 3% at Madeira, 5% at Bermuda, and 4% at the Cape Verde Islands. But, in the south Atlantic the situation is markedly changed, the endemism at St. Helena apparently about 27% (50% in echinoderms) and that of Tristan-Gough about 23%.

In the Pacific (Figs. 2, 3), the pattern is quite different from that of the Atlantic. The Hawaiin chain reaches as far as 23° N latitude, yet the extent of endemism is relatively large—about 34%. The oceanic islands in the rest of the Pacific, for which data are available, have endemic rates that range from about 15 to 50 per cent, with the average being about 28%. However, it is in the Sub-Antarctic waters of the southern hemisphere (Fig. 4) that the highly peculiar island faunas occur. None of the others have rates that can match those of Kerguelen (71%), Macquarie (64%), or South Georgia (57–58%).

How can this pattern be explained? There seems to be no good correlation with the ages of the islands (insofar as they are known), the extent of spatial isolation (beyond 300 miles), or such present environmental factors as temperature, salinity, and ocean currents.

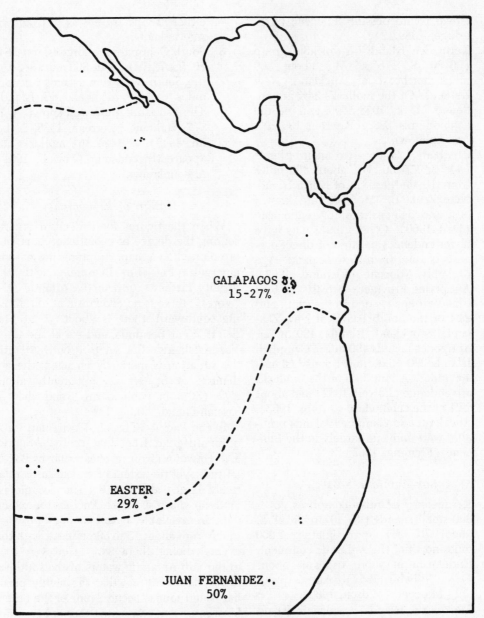

FIG. 2. Eastern Pacific Ocean. Dashed lines represent 20°C surface isotherm for coldest month.

Probable Cause

Of the environmental factors that might be responsible for this anomalous pattern of endemism, temperature is the one that should be given primary consideration. In general, it can be said that the distribution of marine animals is governed very closely by the temperature regime of the surrounding water. Since contemporary temperature records give no clue, it may be worthwhile to examine available estimates for the Pleistocene.

Along most mainland shorelines, marine animals are able to cope with gradual climatic change by slow migration, moving toward the equator in cold periods and toward the poles during warmer periods. However, the shore species found about the various oceanic islands cannot migrate because the surrounding depths do not provide a suitable habitat. If a climatic change in the sea-surface temperature is severe, it is possible that an island fauna would be decimated or even eliminated.

According to the founder principle (Mayr, 1963:529) in evolutionary genetics, oceanic island populations carry such a small reservoir of genetic diversity that they are highly vulnerable to the dangers of inbreeding. Also, the uniformity of the insular environment is said to result in a one-sided type of selection. Consequently, island populations are liable to become extinct under adverse conditions. It may well be that such populations are even more sensitive to temperature change than their mainland relatives.

Paleotemperature Measurements

The oxygen isotope (O^{18}/O^{16}) method, developed by H. C. Urey in 1947, and the information provided by the change in coiling direction of certain species of Foraminifera (Ericson and Wollin, 1954; Ericson, 1959; Ericson, Ewing and Wollin, 1964) have made possible numerous estimates of Pleistocene marine temperatures. A survey of this information gives the impression that sea-surface temperatures in general underwent comparatively extensive fluctuations. In a major work on the Pleistocene (Flint, 1957:439) it was noted that "surface sea-water temperatures in the tropics have fluctuated within a range of 6°C throughout much of Pleistocene time." Another important work (Charlesworth, 1957:696) mentioned that the approach of glacial conditions was widely felt in the world's seas, with cold water animals displacing the warm water species; and a third work (Schwarzbach, 1963:199) stated that "the surface temperatures of the oceans fluctuated by some 6°C; as many as seven cycles

have been demonstrated in the Caribbean and 15 in the Pacific."

The primary source of the data which led to the foregoing conclusions was a paper by Emiliani (1955), giving the results of using the oxygen isotope method to determine paleotemperatures from tropical Atlantic and Pacific deep-sea cores. But, the evidence from a Pacific core (Swedish deep-sea core 58 from the eastern equatorial Pacific) showed temperature oscillations of only about 2°–3°C during the Pleistocene, while the Atlantic material gave evidence of 6° to 7°C changes. This discrepancy was explained later (Emiliani, 1964) on the basis that the Pacific material did not provide a clear temperature record due to a local vertical circulation of surface water and that only foraminiferan species of deeper habitats were available for analysis. In this most recent paper, Emiliani also suggested that the Pleistocene fluctuations for the eastern equatorial Pacific were about 4°–6°C and that those of the tropical Atlantic and Caribbean amounted to about 9°C. A popular magazine article on the same subject (Emiliani, 1958) described a sharp Pleistocene drop in "the oceans' surface temperature."

The only clearly stated exception to the general picture of widespread, relatively high-amplitude fluctuations of ocean surface temperature was published recently (Ericson and Wollin, 1964:255). Here, the authors expressed the opinion that, during the ice ages, a cooling of the Pacific similar to that of the Atlantic did not occur because the Bering Strait was closed, preventing an outflow of ice into the Bering Sea. They also noted that, in Pacific cores examined so far, it has been difficult to discern any climatic zonation at all, and the faint traces that were present seemed to be in opposite phase to zonation of the Atlantic.

If all the islands considered were exposed to about the same degree of temperature fluctuation, as is suggested by most of the current literature, then the problem still remains. However, it is important to realize

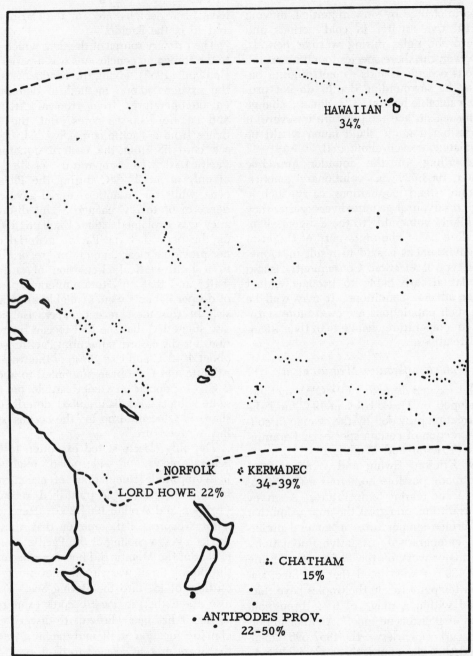

FIG. 3. Western Pacific Ocean. Dashed lines represent 20°C surface isotherm for coldest month.

that, so far, the new methods for the determination of paleotemperatures have been used very little and that perhaps it is risky to attempt broad generalizations of the type quoted above. We should note particularly that those deep-sea cores indicating 6° to

9°C oscillations, as the result of oxygen isotope analysis, have come *only* from the northern part of the tropical Atlantic and Caribbean.

Evidence From Certain Islands

The geographical location of certain of the oceanic islands has an important bearing on the matter. From evidence provided by correlating worldwide distribution patterns with the surface temperature regime (Briggs, 1966), it can be said that a tropical fauna would not be able to survive if the average temperature for the coldest month dropped much below 20°C. Bermuda, St. Helena, the Hawaiian, Galápagos, Cape Verde, and Easter Islands possess tropical shore faunas and are located quite close to the 20°C winter isotherm (Figs. 1, 2, and 3).

In the northern tropical Atlantic, the faunas of Bermuda and the Cape Verde Islands were almost certainly decimated by the severe (6° to 9°C) drop in surface temperature. The approximately 11,000 years that have passed since the last glaciation have allowed the accumulation of a fairly rich fauna, but this time has apparently not been sufficient for much evolutionary change. Therefore, despite their relatively great age and isolation, these islands exhibit very low rates of endemism (4–5%).

In the South Atlantic, St. Helena displays a relatively high degree of endemism despite its proximity to the edge of the tropics. The same can be said for the Hawaiian, Galápagos, and Easter Islands in the Pacific. This evidence suggests that these faunas could not have been subjected to temperature changes of the same magnitude as those that occurred in the North Atlantic. Otherwise, these areas also would have had to be essentially repopulated since the last ice age and, consequently, would now demonstrate but little endemism. It does not seem possible that an ice age temperature drop of more than 3°C could have taken place in the tropical South Atlantic or the tropical Pacific oceans.

Probable Pleistocene Temperature Distribution

Judging from the extent of the various Pleistocene glaciations and their probable effects on climate, the response of sea-surface temperature is likely to have been as follows: (1) The lowest ice age temperature (and thus the greatest fluctuation) probably occurred in the North Atlantic since it is a relatively small ocean area with large land masses on either side and since the land was covered with ice as far south as the southern British Isles on the east and New Jersey on the west; (2) the middle Atlantic was somewhat less affected since the water area is relatively larger and there was little direct contact with the glaciers; (3) the South Atlantic was considerably less affected since the oceanic area is still larger and the glaciation in the southern hemisphere was relatively slight (Charlesworth, 1957).

The same kind of reasoning can be followed for the Pacific and Sub-Antarctic oceans: (1) The North Pacific occupies a relatively large area, and there was, during the ice ages, apparently relatively little contact with the glaciers (Charlesworth, 1957); also, perhaps not much floating ice was present since a good portion may have been held back by the Bering Land Bridge (Ericson and Wollin, 1964), so the temperature drop probably was not very large; (2) the middle and southern Pacific is a huge oceanic area with a correspondingly large heat budget, so the temperature change was also probably quite small; (3) the Sub-Antarctic seas are now influenced by their contact with the Antarctic ice pack and its zone of floating ice; this state of affairs also prevailed during the ice ages (although the ice pack was somewhat larger), so temperatures in that area have probably remained steady.

Conclusion

Since marine animals in general are highly sensitive to temperature change, it is suggested that Pleistocene temperature fluctuations were responsible for the present anomalous pattern of endemism found

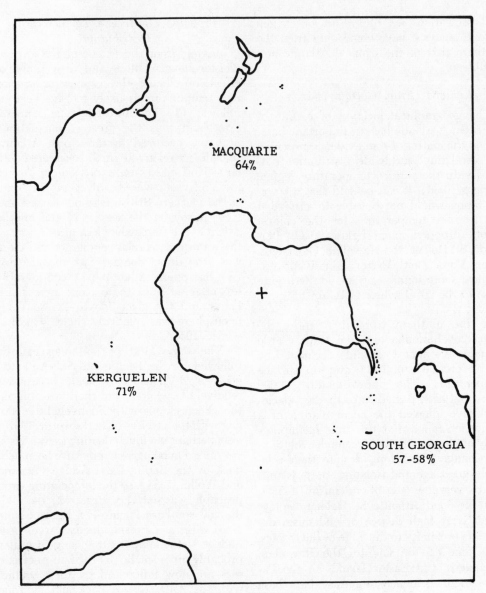

Fig. 4.   Antarctic continent and surrounding seas. South pole represented by a cross.

in the shore faunas of the old, well-isolated, oceanic islands. The pattern of endemism seems to indicate that the effects of Pleistocene glaciation on sea-surface temperatures were quite different in various parts of the world. The major temperature drop apparently took place in the northern and middle Atlantic, the change in the South Atlantic and Pacific was relatively small, and in the Sub-Antarctic seas there was probably very little difference.

It is predicted that, when paleotemperature determinations are made from cores taken over a wide geographic area, a differential pattern of the foregoing type will be found rather than one indicating a similar Pleistocene temperature history for all the oceans.

REFERENCES

ALBUQUERQUE, R. M. 1954–56. Peixes de Portugal e ilhas adjacentes chaves para a sua determinacão. Portug. Acta Biol. (B) 5:i–xvi + 1–1164, 445 figs.

BANFIELD, A. F., C. H. BEHRE, and D. ST. CLAIR. 1956. Geology of Isabela (Albemarle) Island, Archipiélago de Colon (Galápagos). Bull. Geol. Soc. Am. 67:215–234, 4 figs., 4 pls.

BRIGGS, JOHN C. 1966. Marine zoogeography. (Manuscript in progress. To be published by McGraw-Hill.)

CADENAT, J. 1951. Lista provisoria dos peixes observados nas ilhas de Cabo Verde, de 1 de Maio a 24 de Junho de 1950. "Cabo Verde," April 19.
1961. Notes d'ichtyologie ouest-africaine. XXXIV. Liste complémentaire des espéces de poissons de mer (provenant des côtes de l'Afrique occidentale), etc. Bull. Inst. Française Afr. Noire, Sér. A, 23:231–245.

CADENAT, J. and E. MARCHAL. 1963. Résultats des compagnes océanographiques de la Reine-Pokou aux îles Sainte-Héléne et Ascension. Poissons. Bull. Inst. Française Afr. Noire, Sér. A, 25:1235–1315, 48 figs.

CHARLESWORTH, J. K. 1957. The Quaternary era. Vol. 2:595–1700, figs. 113–326, pls. 25–32. Edward Arnold, London.

COLETTE, B. B. 1962. Hemiramphus bermudensis, a new halfbeak from Bermuda, with a survey of endemism in Bermudian shore fishes. Bull. Mar. Sci. Gulf and Caribb. 12:432–449, 1 fig.

COLLINS, B. L. 1954. Lista de Peixes dos Mares dos Açores. Açoreana, 5(2):102–142.

DELL, R. K. 1958. The marine mollusca of the Kermadec Islands in relation to the molluscan faunas in the south west Pacific. Proc. Eighth Pacific Sci. Congr. 3:499–503, map.
1960. Chatham Island marine Mollusca based upon the collections of the Chatham Islands expedition, 1954. Bull. New Zealand Dept. Sci. Indust. Res. 139:141–157, 1 fig.
1964. Marine Mollusca from Macquarie and Heard Islands. Rec. Dominion Mus., Wellington, 4:267–301, 36 figs.

EMILIANI, C. 1955. Pleistocene temperatures. Journ. Geol., 63:538–578.
1958. Ancient temperatures. Scientific American for Feb. (reprint by W. H. Freeman Co.) p. 1–11, 11 figs.
1964. Paleotemperature analysis of the Caribbean cores A 254-BR-C and CP-28. Bull. Geol. Soc. Am. 75:129–144, 7 figs.

ERICSON, D. B. 1959. Coiling direction of Globigerina pachyderma as a climatic index. Science 130(3369):219–220.

ERICSON, D. B. and G. WOLLIN. 1954. Coiling direction of Globorotalia truncatulinoides in deep-sea cores. Deep-Sea Res. 2:152–158.

1964. The deep and the past. Alfred Knopf, New York. xiv + 292 + ix, 29 figs.

ERICSON, D. B., M. EWING, and G. WOLLIN. 1964. The Pleistocene Epoch in deep-sea sediments. Science 146(3645):723–732, 5 figs.

ETHERIDGE, R., JR. 1889. The physical and geological structure of Lord Howe Island. In Lord Howe Island, etc. Mem. Australian Mus., Sydney, no. 2:100–126.

FLINT, R. F. 1957. Glacial and Pleistocene geology. John Wiley, New York. xiii + 553 p., 5 pls.

FLEMING, C. A. 1962. New Zealand biogeography. A paleontologist's approach. Tuatara 10:53–108, 15 figs.

GARTH, J. S. 1946. Distributional studies of Galápagos Brachyura. Allan Hancock Pacific Exped. 5:603–648, 10 charts.
1957. The Crustacea Decapoda Brachyura of Chile. Rept. Lund Univ. Chile Exped. 1948–49. Lunds Univ. Årsskrift, N. F. Avd. 2, 53(7):1–130, 11 figs., 4 pls.

GOSLINE, W. A. and V. E. BROCK. 1960. Handbook of Hawaiian fishes. Univ. Hawaii Press, Honolulu. ix + 1–372 pp., 277 figs., 2 pls.

HOLDGATE, M. W. 1960. The fauna of the mid-Atlantic islands. Proc. Roy. Soc. London, Ser. B, 152:550–567, 5 figs.

KNOX, G. A. 1963. The biogeography and intertidal ecology of the Australasian coast. Oceanog. Mar. Biol. Ann. Rev. 1:341–404, 5 figs.

LELOUP, E. Polyplacophora. Rept. Lund Univ. Chile Exped. 1948–49. Lunds Univ. Årsskrift. N. F. Avd. 2, 52(15):1–94, 53 figs.

MADSEN, F. J. 1956. Asteroidea. Rept. Lund Univ. Chile Exped. 1948–49. Lunds Univ. Årsskrift, N. F. Avd. 2, 52(2):1–53, 1 fig. 6 pls.

MANN, G. 1954. La vida de los peces en aguas Chilenas. Ministerio de Agricultura y Universidad de Chile, Santiago. 342 p., illus.

MAUL, G. E. 1948. Peixes. In Noronha e Sarmento, Vertebrados da Madeira, vol. 2, p. 1–181. Junta Geral, Distrito Autónoma do Funchal.

MAYR, ERNST. 1963. Animal species and Evolution. Harvard Univ. Press, Cambridge. xiv + 1–797 p., 201 figs.

MENARD, H. W., E. C. ALLISON, and J. W. DURHAM. 1962. A drowned Miocene terrace in the Hawaiian Islands. Science 138(3543):896–897.

MORTENSEN, T. 1933. The echinoderms of St. Helena (other than crinoids). Vidensk. Medd. naturh. Foren. 93:401 (not seen)

NORMAN, J. R. 1938. Coast fishes. Part III. The Antarctic zone. Discovery Rept. 18:1–104, 62 figs., 1 pl.

NYBELIN, O. 1947. Antarctic fishes. Scientific results of the Norwegian Antarctic Expeditions 1927–1928 et Seq., No. 26, Det. Norske Videnskaps-Akademi i Oslo. 76 p., 6 pls.

1951. Subantarctic and Antarctic fishes. Scientific Results of the "Brategg" Expedition 1947–48 No. 2, Kommandor Chr. Christensens Hvalfangstmuseum i Sandefjord Pub. Nr. 18, 32 p., 3 figs.

PAWSON, D. L. 1961. Distribution patterns of New Zealand echinoderms. Tuatara, 9:9–18.

POWELL, A. W. B. 1951. Antarctic and subantarctic Mollusca: Pelecypoda and Gastropoda. Discovery Rept. 26:47–196, 14 figs., 6 pls.
1962. Shells of New Zealand. Fourth ed. Whitcomb and Tombs, Christchurch. 203 p., 36 pls.

RENDAHL, H. 1921. The fishes of the Juan Fernandez and Easter Islands. In Carl Skottsberg, The Natural History of Juan Fernandez and Easter Islands, vol. 3, p. 49–68. Almquist and Wiksells, Uppsala.

SCHWARZBACH, M. 1963. Climates of the past. Van Nostrand, London. xii + 328 p., 134 figs.

VINTON, K. W. 1951. Origin of life on the Galápagos Islands. Am. Jour. Sci. 249:356–376, 2 figs., 2 pls.

WAITE, EDGAR R. 1916. A list of the fishes of Norfolk Island, and indication of their range to Lord Howe Island, Kermadec Island, Australia, and New Zealand. Trans. Roy. Soc. S. Australia 40:452–458, 3 pls.

WALKER, B. W. and R. H. ROSENBLATT. 1961. The marine fishes of the Galápagos Islands. Abstracts of symposium papers, Tenth Pacific Sci. Congr., Honolulu, Hawaii: 470–471.

WALLACE, A. R. 1892. Island life. Second ed. Macmillan and Co., London. xx + 563 p., 26 figs.

WHITLEY, G. P. 1937. The Middleton and Elizabeth Reefs, South Pacific Ocean. Austr. Zool. 8:199–273, 1 fig., 5 pls.

WILSON, J. T. 1963. Evidence from islands on the spreading of ocean floors. Nature 197:536–538, 4 figs.

JOHN C. BRIGGS is Professor of Zoology and Chairman of the Department of Zoology and Oceanography at the University of South Florida, Tampa, Florida 33620.

ENDEMISM IN THE HAWAIIAN FLORA, AND A REVISION OF THE HAWAIIAN SPECIES OF GUNNERA (HALORAGIDACEAE) HAWAIIAN PLANT STUDIES 11[1]

BY

HAROLD ST. JOHN
Professor of Botany, University of Hawaii

ENDEMISM IN THE HAWAIIAN FLORA

ENDEMISM in its flora has long made the plants of the Hawaiian Islands famous. Of the islands or floristic regions of the world having a flora of more than a few species, they are said to have the world's largest percentage of endemics.

Prof. A. Guillaumin (Proc. 3rd. Pan. Pacif. Sci. Congr. Tokyo 1: 930, 1926) in his review of the Pacific island floras calculates that endemism for the Hawaiian Phanerogams is 66 per cent. He does not state how he arrived at this figure but his totals of the species are evidently those of Wm. Hillebrand. This early botanist, Hillebrand (Fl. Hawaiian Ids. p. XVII, 1888), calculated that of the native Phanerogams, 574 were endemic, while 246 only were indigenous, and 24 of early aboriginal introduction, and the total of native Phanerogams and Vascular Cryptogams was 860. It is apparent that Guillaumin used this total of 860 indigenous Vascular Plants and Hillebrand's figure of 574 indigenous Phanerogams in computing the percentage of en-

---

[1] This is the eleventh of a series of papers designed to present descriptions, revisions, and records of Hawaiian plants. The preceding papers have been published as Occasional Papers Bishop Museum 10(4), 1933; 10(12), 1934; 11(14), 1935; 12(8), 1936; 14(8), 1938; 15(1), 1939; 15(2), 1939; 15(22), 1940; 15(28), 1940; 17(12), 1943; Lloydia 7:265–274, 1944; Bull. Torrey Bot. Club 72:22–30, 1945.

Reprinted, in abridged form, from *Proceedings of the California Academy of Sciences,* ser. 4, 25(16): 377–419 (1946), by permission of the author and the California Academy of Sciences.

demism, which he calculated as 66 per cent. Had he used 705 native species
and 574 endemics, which are Hillebrand's truly comparable figures for the
Phanerograms, the endemism would figure out as 81 per cent, which was the
estimate of Hillebrand, previous to his death in 1886. All species published
since that date or unknown to Hillebrand, Guillaumin seems to reject by his
phrase that the area presents an extraordinary number of varieties which are
sometimes considered as species of narrow geographic localization ("présente
un nombre extraordinaire de variétés, considérées parfois des comme espèces et
étroitement localisées."). D. H. Campbell used the same figures from Hillebrand, but he correctly calculated the endemism of Phanerograms as 81.42 per
cent (The Derivation of the Flora of Hawaii, Univ. Ser. Stanford Univ., Publ.
15, 1919). Also R. Kanehira apparently used the same figures as he lists the
Hawaiian endemism as 81 per cent (Proc. 6th Pacif. Sci. Congr. 4:610, 1940).
Guillaumin concludes (pp. 921, 931) that in the Hawaiian flora the Australian,
New Zealand, and even Polynesian elements are almost completely lacking,
that the flora has strong relationships with the American flora and should be
considered a part of the Mexican floristic region. The present writer disputes
all of these conclusions of Guillaumin.

The interpretations of C. Skottsberg seem more truly in accord with the
facts. He divided the Hawaiian species of Phanerograms (Bull. Bishop Mus.
16:6, 1925) as 32.3 per cent Old-Pacific; 29 per cent Australian-Polynesian;
26.5 per cent Indo-Malayan; 7.5 per cent American; 3.3 per cent widespread;
1.2 per cent Subantarctic; and 0.2 per cent Boreal. The widespread or Pantropic and the Subantarctic may well have immigrated by the same route as
the other groups from Oceania. If these, then, are all added, the total is 92.3
per cent for the plants with a probable southwestern origin that came or whose
ancestors came as a stream of plant immigrants through Polynesia. Later
Skottsberg discusses the genera (Proc. Linn. Soc. 151:182–186, 1939), their
relationship, and probable route of immigration. Of more than 200 genera,
18 are Pantropic, 15 Paleotropic, 49 Malesian, 12 littoral are widespread, 57
Austral, 22 Boreal, 9 aquatics apparently Boreal, and 13 Neotropical. This
review of the Hawaiian genera gives the same picture as with the species: a
large majority Indo-Malayan or Polynesian, small minorities Boreal and
American.

The same early source, Hillebrand, was used by J. C. Willis (Proc. Linn.
Soc. London 148:86–91, 1936) in his contemporary discussion of regional
endemism. Hillebrand's figures should not be discounted. They were based
on his excellent flora and were correct for his time, that is 58 years ago. Still, to
discuss the endemism of the Hawaiian flora today and to use only Hillebrand's
figures is not the modern scientific method, which should use all available
evidence. Since 1886 in Hawaii there has been a great deal of arduous exploration of the rain forests and the precipitous mountains. Here and elsewhere
a large amount of floristic and monographic work has been published. To overlook and reject all the work of C. B. Clarke, Heller, Rock, C. N. Forbes,

Beccari, Léveillé, Skottsberg, Christensen, Degener, St. John, Sherff, Yuncker, Christophersen, Caum, Hitchcock, Hochreutiner, Pilger, von Poellnitz, Radlkofer, Oliver, Danser, Heimerl, Keck, Krajina, Whitney, Hosaka, Fosberg, Egler, Lam, Croizat, Sleumer, and others, is not the way to arrive at a modern estimate of the known Hawaiian flora. Skottsberg used the more sound method of including subsequent publications (Bull. Bishop Mus. 16:5, 1925) when he gave a tentative estimate of the indigenous Hawaiian Phanerogams as about 900 species. Later he revised this figure to between 1,000 and 1,100 (Proc. 6th Pacif. Sci. Congr. Berkeley 4:685, 1940). The writer keeps a check list of the Hawaiian flora. There are quite a number of the recently proposed segregate species which he has not included, awaiting time to verify their status, but many will doubtless be accepted. When eventually added in, they will increase rather than diminish the percentage of endemism. At present the writer's figures for endemism of Hawaiian Phanerogams is 90 per cent, based on totals of 1795 indigenous, and 1614 endemic species and their subdivisions. Estimates by some others exclude all subdivisions of species, but here each is included as a unit.

Some Hawaiian genera contain species that are homogeneous and widespread, occurring unmodified on all or nearly all of the large islands. Examples are given in the two following lists.

I. HOMOGENEOUS WIDESPREAD SPECIES IN GENERA MONOTYPIC IN THE HAWAIIAN ISLANDS

Freycinetia arborea Gaud.
Joinvillea Gaudichaudiana Brogn. and Gris
Dianella sandwicensis H. and A.[2]
Anoectochilus sandwicensis Lindl.
Liparis hawaiiensis Mann
Habenaria holochila Hbd.
Pilea peploides H. and A.
Argemone alba Lestib. var. *glauca* Prain
Osteomeles anthyllidifolia Lindl.
Erythrina sandwicensis Degener
Strongylodon lucidus Seem.
Plumbago zeylanica L.
Osmanthus sandwicensis (Gray) B. and H.
Nertera depressa Banks and Soland.

II. HOMOGENEOUS WIDESPREAD SPECIES IN GENERA WITH SEVERAL HAWAIIAN SPECIES

Smilax sandwicensis Kunth
Chenopodium oahuense (Meyen) Aellen[3]
Peperomia leptostachya H. and A.

There are other Hawaiian species widespread among the larger islands, but which are not homogeneous, having a tendency to vary. These variations are in part recognized as described varieties but in large part are unrecognized,

[2] The recently described *Dianella lavarum* Degener and *D. multipedicellata* Degener are considered exact synonyms.

[3] *Chenopodium sandwicheum* Moq. forma *macrospermum* Aellen and forma *microspermum* Aellen are not separable, as the larger and smaller seeds occur on a single plant.

forming a part of the heterogeneous population now included in the species. Such ones are listed below.

III. POLYMORPHIC WIDESPREAD SPECIES

Rumex giganteus Ait.
Charpentiera obovata Gaud.
Charpentiera ovata Gaud.
Broussaisia arguta Gaud.
Acacia Koa Gray
Ilex anomala H. and A.
Cheirodendron Gaudichaudii (DC.) Seem.
Vaccinium calycinum Sm.
Vaccinium dentatum Sm.
Styphelia Tameiameiae (Cham.) F. Muell.
Myrsine Lessertiana A.DC.
Gouldia terminalis (H. and A.) Hbd.

Other genera, usually with many species, show a conspicuous segregation into species, usually each species being restricted to a single island or even to a single mountain range or valley on the particular island. Such genera are the following:

IV. GENERA WITH NUMEROUS SPECIES THAT ARE NARROW ENDEMICS

Astelia, Schiedea, Pelea, Fagara, Hibiscus, Viola, Labordia, Haplostachys, Phyllostegia, Stenogyne, Cyrtandra, Coprosma, Hedyotis, Clermontia, Cyanea, Delissea, Lobelia, Bidens, Dubautia, and *Lipochaeta.*

The Hawaiian plants here listed illustrate a progressive series: 1, genera monotypic in Hawaii occurring as invariable wides on all the principal islands; 2, species that are invariable wides, belonging to genera with several Hawaiian species; 3, species that are wides, but showing variability on the various islands; and 4, general with many Hawaiian species, typically with different, distinct species on each island. These species represent degrees of increasing differentiation and presumably of decreasing age. They show evidences of speciation. The results of this species formation can be seen in the percentages of endemism here presented and discussed.

REVISION OF THE HAWAIIAN SPECIES OF GUNNERA

One of the most famous of the genera occurring in the Hawaiian Islands is *Gunnera,* called by the natives "apeape." It is a giant herb with a stem 12 to 15 cm. or more in diameter, fleshy, 2 to 6 meters tall, the base decumbent and prostrate. The paired stipules are large, pale, and conspicuous. From near the summit are produced several alternate leaves on fleshy petioles 6 to 13 dm. long. The blades are rounded, shallowly lobed, like great parasols 4 to 20 dm. in diameter. Axillary panicles 8 to 10 dm. long bear numerous minute green flowers and later tiny yellow, orange, red, or purplish drupes. The plant itself is so bizarre as to hold the attention and interest of all observers, whether scientific or not. Thus its occurrence is shown even on the tourist maps.

The habitat of the "apeape" is also noteworthy. It occurs on precipitous slopes with the soil saturated from the run-off of the boggy mountain summits.

It is usually on the face or the foot of a precipice ("pali" in Hawaiian) and is often difficult of access. It forms a definite vegetational belt between the Middle Forest and the Upper Forest, at anywhere from 2,500 to 5,000 feet altitude. Because of the distinctive, giant leaves, this belt of "apeape," though narrow, is often so conspicuous that it can be seen from a distance of two or three miles.

The "apeape" was discovered in 1819 by Charles Gaudichaud, who published it in 1830 as *Gunnera petaloïdea*. Subsequent collections have revealed that *Gunnera* occurs on Kauai, Oahu, Molokai, Maui, and Hawaii. Hillebrand interpreted these as different locality records for the single species. This has been the generally accepted view, that the same species occurred on all of the islands.

The taxonomic history since the original publication by Gaudichaud has been brief. Alphonse De Candolle described a specimen collected on Kaui [= Kauai] by the United States Exploring Expedition as *G. petaloidea* Gaud. *β Kauensis* A.DC. (De Candolle, Prodr. Reg. Veg. 16(2):597, 1868). His four word description included only two characters, almost glabrous, the bracts shorter. We now find no differences in the Kauai plants in pubescence, and the bracts appear to be alike. This plant was treated later as an unnamed variety, *G. petaloidea* Gaud. *β* (Hillebrand, Fl. Haw. Ids. 124, 1888). In 1930 it was again distinguished by two botanists in almost simultaneous publications. *Gunnera kauaiensis* Rock in Caum (Occ. Pap. B. P. Bishop Mus. 9(5):3–4, pl. I, 1930, Sept.). Rock described it from a new type specimen, Rock, 5,053 from Mt. Waialeale. The second author, Krajina, redescribed it as *G. Dominii* Krajina (Acta Bot. Bohemica 9:50, ill. p. 51, 1930, without precise date), citing as synonyms the varieties of De Candolle and of Hillebrand, but listing only his own collection from "montis Waialeale." It is apparent from the characters given below that this Kauai plant with peltate blades and red to purplish drupes is a distinct species. Several attempts to learn from Prague the exact month and day of publication of Krajina's paper have failed. A new search is being made for the date. In the meantime, the name given by Rock is accepted as it is dated to the month.

Krajina also described and illustrated from his own collections *G. petaloidea*. He published as two new varieties: var. *kaalensis* (p. 50) from his collection on Puu Kaala, Oahu; and var. *mauiensis* from his collection by Waikamoi Stream, east Maui. Krajina apparently did not examine Gaudichaud's type specimen, nor did he indicate whether or not either of his two varieties was to be considered var. *typica* though with a different name. Duplicates of Krajina's collections have not yet reached the Bishop Museum, nor has the writer seen them in other herbaria. Still, there is no difficulty in matching them. Dr. V. Krajina was a fellow at the Bishop Museum in 1929–30, a keen, energetic botanist who soon became my good friend and I took him on many field trips. His type of var. *kaalensis* was collected on my class trip to Puu Kaala at the well-known locality above the fire-brick* trail from Schofield

---

*For "fire-brick" read "fire-break."

Barracks. My collection, St. John 10,072, was made at the same spot and time as Krajina's and there are numerous other collections from this locality. His type of var. *mauiensis* was collected at another often visited spot where the Olinda Pipe Line Trail crosses Waikamoi gulch. There are several other collections from the same spot.

That recounts the known taxonomic history of this genus in Hawaii. The plant is known to all collectors and there are several standard, fairly easily accessible localities. The writer has collected it on Kauai, Oahu, Maui, and Hawaii, but any new locality is always noteworthy. On Oahu it has been repeatedly collected on the wet, windward side of Mt. Kaala in the Waianae Mountains. There are two or three collections from the drier, leeward side of the same mountain. Also, Miss Marie Neal of the Bishop Museum tells the writer that she has observed *Gunnera* in the same mountain range on the adjacent peak, Puu Kalena, on its northeast or windward side.

The preferred habitat is steep, water-soaked slopes on the windward side of a mountain range. It has long puzzled the writer that the "apeape" was abundant in the Waianae Mts. and not in the Koolau Range, the more easterly mountain chain on Oahu. The Waianae Mts. are rather arid, lying in the lee of the Koolau Range which gets the impact of the moist northeast trade winds and receives most of their moisture, while but little of it reaches the Waianae Mts. Only the highest peak, Mt. Kaala (called Puu Kaala on the earlier, 1917, official topographic map) gets a considerable rainfall. It is just far enough to the north to receive the impact of the northeast trade winds which sweep over or past the descending, low, north end of the Koolau Range. This is only about 1,000 feet high at this point, not high enough to cause the precipitation of all the moisture. Hence, Mt. Kaala with its large flat summit at 4,025 feet altitude and its upper ridges get enough rainfall to support a luxuriant rain forest. The summit has a swampy forest except for some boggy openings near its center. The average annual rainfall is now known to be 91 inches (Feldwisch, W. E., First Progress Rept., Hawaii Territorial Planning Board 121, 1939).

The Koolau Range, Oahu, running from southeast to northwest, forms the backbone of the eastern side of the island. It rises abruptly close to the shore, and the section above 1,500 feet in height extends for about 25 miles, making a barrier almost exactly at right angles to the prevailing northeast trades. There are numerous sharp peaks that rise from the range, the highest being Puu Konahuanui with twin peaks 3,105 and 3,150 feet high. The several rain gauging stations show a high rainfall, as this mountain range catches much of the moisture from the clouds. The rainfall is more than 100 inches annually for most of this ridge and at the wettest station is 311 inches. There are miles of wind-swept precipices ("pali") and steep slopes with much water seepage from the higher peaks, just the kind of habitat that usually supports *Gunnera*. The writer had botanized these brinks and declivities at many localities along the Koolau Range, and had never found the "apeape." Yet, this *Gunnera* is a plant that one cannot easily overlook. With its bizarre leaves like huge umbrellas, it is always the biggest and most conspicuous plant in its area. There were no specimens from the Koolau Range in the Bishop Museum, yet the plant has been reported from there. Prof. Vaughan MacCaughey listed it as rare in the rain forests of Manoa Valley (Am. Journ. Bot. 4 : 600, 1917). In the same year in a short article about *Gunnera petaloidea* (Am. Journ. Bot. 4 : 38, 1917, the reprints incorrectly printed vol. 1) he stated that among its typical habitats were "Ka-ala and Kona-hua-nui summit ridges on Oahu (2,500–4,000 ft.)." The 4,000 foot record is certainly that for the often visited station of Mt. Kaala in the Waianae Mts. Hence, we infer that his station on the 3,150 foot peak Puu Konahuanui was at about 2,500 feet altitude. Mac-Caughey did exploring and original research in Manoa Valley which heads on the slope of Puu Konahuanui. The plant is unmistakable, so there would seem no reason to question this record, yet corroborating specimens were much to be desired.

Some years ago the writer had an enterprising young man as a student, John R. Coleman. He was enlisted in the United States Marine Corps and was stationed in Honolulu with a company doing guard duty at the docks. At his request he was given continuous and regular night guard duty. This left his day time free and enabled him to attend the University of Hawaii. It was not obvious when he slept, but he did not sleep in class. He completed the course on elementary botany and on week ends he often joined advanced classes on collecting trips to the mountains. One Sunday he induced two other marines to join him, and from Nuuanu Pali they started to climb the knife-edged ridge that culminates in Puu Konahuanui. As he led the way and scrambled up one precipitous slope, the bushes, soil, and all caved away. He managed to make headway over the landslide and surmounted the ledge. All the footholds were destroyed, so his companions could not follow, and turned back. Coleman went on, climbed to the summit, and descended by a more southerly route. The next day he brought me a 10 cm. tip from a fruiting inflorescence with half ripe drupes, of a specimen that seemed to be *Gunnera*. He reported collecting it near the summit on Oct. 19, 1930. This specimen gave partial proof of the occurrence in the Koolau Range, but it was incomplete. At last, in June 1942 the proof was furnished by two students, L. Eubank and A. D. Conger, who, on a wet day amid swirling clouds and rain, ascended Puu Konahuanui. They observed and collected abundant and complete material. They reported the three small colonies to be on the Manoa or leeward slope. A second visit on Sept. 13, 1942 by A. D. Conger, H. St. John, and R. P. St. John was also in the clouds and intermittent rain, but thrice the clouds lifted to reveal the slopes, valleys and the shore line. All three patches proved to be on the windward or Kailua side. Any mountaineer will understand how in following forking, intricate ridges in dense clouds, one can lose track of the directions. One locality was a single plant some 250 feet below the lower or south peak which is mapped and triangulated as Puu Konahuanui. The two others were on the east face of a northeast ridge of the north or higher peak. There were numerous plants in a steep, brushy, hanging valley at 2,950 feet altitude. Though both Miss Eubank and Mr. Conger previously slid down the cloud-blanketed slope to the plants, then scrambled up again, on the second trip no one wanted to try it again. It was very dangerous, and when clear of clouds it was obvious that an uncontrolled slip on the steep, slippery clay would give one a flying start over the 1,000 foot precipice. Later a fourth colony was located. On May 9, 1943 the writer conducted a student party of nine from Tantalus to the summit of Puu Konahuanui. Clouds blanketed the precipices on the east slope hiding the single plant on the South Peak. From the North Peak a descent was made down the secondary ridge towards Kailua. The middle and inaccessible colony of *Gunnera* was again seen far below in the cloud. Neither the writer nor his son Robert could locate the third colony, though this time a rope was at hand for a descent to it. The clouds hid it completely. Climbing up again, the descent was made along the main divide to the road at Nuuanu Pali. On this divide a new colony was found, also on the east face, in a moist, precipitous, hanging valley at 2,300 feet altitude. By the use of a rope the colony was visited and specimens collected. There were more than 12 plants, up to 4 meters tall, some exposed, others half hidden by the thicket of *Pipturus albidus* and *Cyrtandra paludosa*. The specimens collected have been deposited in the Bishop Museum. These plants from the Koolau Range were critically compared with those from the east side of Mt. Kaala in the Waianae Mts. and were found to be identical in structure and quite inseparable, though the blades are smaller, the length along the midrib not exceeding 4 dm.

While investigating this material the writer took occasion to assemble all available specimens and to evaluate the species and varieties described from the other Hawaiian Islands by Rock and by Krajina. Its massive fleshy stems, giant fruit clusters, and rounded leaves, 1 to 2 meters in diameter, cannot well be compressed upon a standard herbarium sheet, so that the collector is forced to take sample fragments which are inevitably incomplete, and the leaves selected are often the smaller ones. Hence, all taxonomists revising the group and writing descriptions from the available herbarium material present measurements which are true as far as they go, but minimize the size of the giant stems, leaves, and inflorescences. Several of the writer's whole numbers including many unmounted duplicates are available, but still there are gaps. From east Maui there are no mature stipules, and from west Maui there are no petals, and mature drupes and stones are needed from Molokai and from Makaha Valley, Oahu. Still the collections are numerous and have proven sufficient. At a glance they all look alike, but on close study differences are noted in the floral and fruiting morphology. It is curious that most of the characters are minute, a difference in shape to be seen with a lens or in size measured in fractions of a millimeter. Seedlings are often collected. Since they produce smaller stipules and blades that are much smaller and more reniform, they have not been included in our descriptions. The only large parts furnishing characters are the stipules and the leaves as to lobing and toothing and pubescence. When contrasted throughout, several correlated characters mostly of floral and fruiting anatomy are found. When separated on these characters, the segregates are found to agree in leaf and stipule characters and to have good geographic correlations. Each island has one local kind, except Maui and Oahu which have two each. When evaluated, the number and sort of characters would indicate that these segregates are properly considered species.

The original species was *Gunnera petaloïdea* Gaudichaud (Voy. "Uranie," Bot. 512, 1830). The plant was not illustrated and the 16 word description includes only the major features, but none of the ones now found serviceable in distinguishing the local species. Neither Rock nor Krajina gave any discussion as to the nature of *G. petaloïdea* Gaud. or its type locality. That published by Gaudichaud was "In insulis Sandwicensibus (Alt. 450–500 hex.)." No island is specified, and the statement of altitude in fathoms is unusual, but was perhaps natural after months at sea on a sailing vessel! Search has been made for any detailed itinerary of Gaudichaud. He published none, and the narrative by the commander, Capt. Louis de Freycinet, and those by other members of the expeditions give much on the physique and social habits of the native inhabitants, but nothing on the route of the collecting botanist. On the "Uranie" voyage they spent 20 days in the Hawaiian Islands and Gaudichaud was on shore 7 days. The writer has long marveled at the large number of the endemic species and genera that he collected and described on this first voyage. Starting from the harbor, with no good roads, no cut mountain trails, to get up into the dense, native forests and through them to the cloud zone was a herculean task. Then, over half of his collections were lost when the homeward bound ship was wrecked on the Falkland Islands. All were soaked in sea water, but he rescued many by drying them before a bonfire on the beach. These experiences are mentioned in a few brief words, but what stark tragedy they describe! What a grand naturalist he must have been, yet no portrait of him is known! He did not specify where his shore trips were made, but the ship made landings on Aug. 8, 1819 at Kayakoua [Kailua, Hawaii]; Aug. 12 at Bay of Kohaïhaï [Kawaihae, Hawaii]; Aug. 17–25 at Raheina [Lahaina, Maui]; Aug. 26–30 at d'Onorourou [Honolulu, Oahu]. So the seven days on shore were divided among these localities, but just how is not known. In one day from the arid regions near Kailua and Kawaihae, it would not have been possible to ascend to the habitat of *Gunnera* on the far side of the Kohala Mts. Hence, the island of Hawaii can be eliminated. Back of Lahaina, Maui, the mountains rise abruptly from near the shore, and on the steep upper slopes of the valleys *Gunnera* is abundant. From Honolulu it would have been possible to find *Gunnera* in either mountain range. However, the east cliffs of Mt. Kaala were distant and difficult of access. It is unlikely that he could have gotten there. Puu Konahuanui is only 6 miles in an air line from the harbor of Honolulu. It is known that he climbed to the cloud zone at the crest of the Koolau Range, because he collected *Lobelia Gaudichaudii* which is restricted to that area. Hence, it can be deduced that Gaudichaud probably collected the

Gunnera in the mountains of west Maui or in the Koolau Range near Honolulu, Oahu. In 1935 the writer photographed in Paris Gaudichaud's type specimen of *G. petaloïdea,* reproduced here as Pl. 38. The data on the sheet read
"90. Uranie, Ins. Sandwich. C. Gaudichaud." Stipules are lacking and the
pieces of the inflorescence do not permit one to detect the minute floral differences from the photograph. However, the margin of the leaf is well shown.
The distinct, rounded lobes and the low, rounded teeth or crenations of the
leaf margin match exactly those of the species of west Maui, so that it is to
be taken as the type locality.

The Hawaiian species all belong to the subgenus *Panke* (Molina) Schindler
(Engler, Pflanzenreich IV, fam. 225 : 117, 1905). This subgenus has a remarkable distribution, occurring also in the Cordilleras from Mexico to Chili,
and on Juan Fernandez (Skottsberg, C., Proc. 6th Pacif. Sci. Congr. Berkeley
4 : 696, map 14, 1940).

In the ensuing systematic treatment are given key, diagnoses, and descriptions of the species as at present understood.

All the specimens examined and cited and the new types are in the B. P.
Bishop Museum, Honolulu, except the Gaudichaud type of *G. petaloïdea*
which is in the Museum d'Histoire Naturelle, Paris.

KEY TO THE HAWAIIAN SPECIES OF GUNNERA

Blades peltate; drupes red to purplish . . . . .7. *G. kauaiensis* Rock
Blades basifixed; drupes yellow, orange (or reddish in *G. mauiensis*)
    Stipules scurfy on back or finally glabrate,
        Petals entire, obtuse, glabrous; sepals 0.6–0.8 mm long, rounded, lacerate; anthers
            1.2–1.3 mm. long; peduncle bractless except at base; blade margin lack-
            ing mucros . . . . .5. *G. kaalaensis* (Krajina) St. John.
        Petals lacerate-fimbriate, often acuminate; sepals 1–1.2 mm. long, broadly deltoid,
            deeply lacerate; anthers 1.6–2.2 mm. long; peduncle bracted; (stipules
            apparently scurfy); teeth of blade margin with revolute mucros
                                      6. *G. makahaensis* St. John.
    Stipules not scurfy on the back,
        Stipules glabrous,
            Sepals 1.5–2 mm. long, ovate, deeply lacerate, the lacerations fimbriate; petals
                entire . . . . .1. *G. petaloïdea* Gaud.
            Sepals 0.6–0.8 mm. long, broadly deltoid to rounded, lacerate; petals minutely
                lacerate . . . . .2. *G. molokaiensis* St. John.
    Stipules pubescent,
        Petals 1.5 mm. long, entire or somewhat erose; sepals 0.4–0.6 mm. long, semi-
            oval, the obtuse tip minutely ciliate; anthers 1.9–2 mm. long, elliptic
            oblong . . . . .3. *G. mauiensis* (Krajina) St. John.
        Petals 0.8–1 mm. long, sparsely lacerate; sepals 1–1.2 mm long, oblong lan-
            ceolate, the tip lacerate; anthers 1.5–1.7 mm. long, oval
                                      4. *G. Eastwoodae* St. John.

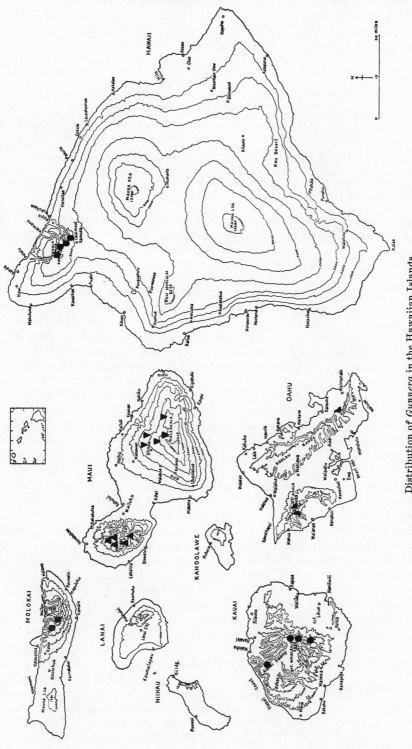

Distribution of *Gunnera* in the Hawaiian Islands.
Square: *Gunnera molokaiensis*; Erect Triangle: *G. petaloïdea*;
Inverted Triangle: *G. mauiensis*; Shield: *G. Eastwoodae*; Circle: *G. kauaiensis*; J: *G. makahaensis*; L: *G. kaalaensis*.

Adaptive Radiation in Hawaii with Special Reference to Insects[1,2]

Elwood C. Zimmerman

B. P. Bishop Museum, Honolulu, Hawaii 96818 U.S.A.

ABSTRACT

The Hawaiian biota originated from ancestors which arrived accidentally from various directions across open sea. These plants and animals became established in a favorable environment on a young, rapidly changing geological substrate where environmental pressures were limited. Processes of adaptive radiation were thus given much freedom for operation in a sort of "biological vacuum." This condition resulted in an astonishing proliferation of species, species diversification, adaptive morphology, and habitat utilization. The many empty ecological niches have been filled by plants and animals delicately adapted to them and resulting in the development of remarkable differences from their nearest relatives in other areas. This flourishing adaptive radiation would continue today, but its variety and rapidity have been slowed to a disturbing degree by the vastly increased activities of man. The new unfavorable conditions introduced by man have doomed a large fraction of the biota to extermination, and it is doubtful if such an unique biological flowering will ever again be duplicated on earth.

WHEN A ZOOLOGIST thinks of adaptive radiation in Hawaiian organisms, I presume that the example that may first come to mind is the classic model exemplified by the truly wonderful radiation evolved in the drepaniid birds. The botanist will think of lobelias and composites. There are, however, many equally exciting examples to be witnessed in the remainder of the biota, although many of them may not be so obvious at first sight, and few persons are so fortunate to see such wondrous things as Professor Carson's male *Drosophila* which has evolved huge scent-dispersing brushes at the end of his tail which he curls over his head and shakes at his ladylove to overwhelm her with a shower of aphrodisiac perfume. The more one studies the Hawaiian biota the more one becomes astonished at the adaptive flexibility of organisms and what may develop given time and opportunity. Many organisms have strong adaptive potential and require only time and opportunity to release it. A better place for such release can hardly be imagined than Hawaii.

The Hawaiian Islands constitute a wonderful natural laboratory where we may observe many evolutionary phenomena in active process in the early stages of operation and often in simplified and clearly defined form uncluttered by many of the masking effects that may be present in continental environments. The endemic terrestrial biota is strongly disharmonic, or unbalanced. There are no endemic mammals, with the exception of a geologically recently arrived American bat, no endemic

amphibians, no endemic reptiles, and no true freshwater fishes. About 60 species of perching birds are known, and these represent only six families, and more than two-thirds of these belong to the endemic Drepaniidae.[*] The endemic flora of about 2000 species of higher plants is a rich one, but it, too, is disharmonic and represents only about 275 ancestral immigrant stocks. The endemic Hawaiian flora contains no gymnosperms, no oaks, no elms, willows, or maples, no figs, no mangroves, only one genus of palms, only a few inconspicuous orchids, and it lacks many of the characteristic genera commonly found in the south and western Pacific.

The endemic insects probably number about 6500 species, but these represent only a few of the world's insect families in only about one-third of the orders of insects. They have descended from only about 250 ancestral immigrants. Perhaps only one plant or insect founder gained successful access to Hawaii in each 25,000 to 100,000 years of the subaerial history of the archipelago.

The Hawaiian Islands are truly oceanic and have all been born sterile from great depths of the sea. Hence, the endemic terrestrial biota arrived by chance dispersal across open ocean. Upon becoming established, the colonizers mostly found large areas of land uninhabited by similar or competing organisms and open for unimpeded colonization on mountains that rise from sea level to nearly 4300 m (14,000 ft), from hot lowland deserts to cool upland rain forests to mountain bogs where the annual precipitation is as great as 16 m (52 ft), to cold high-altitude deserts where frost and snow are common. The biota was confronted by all forms of land from the extremes of bare new lava flows and barren ash fields to deep, matured, old soils—from flatlands to

[1] Prepared during the tenure of a grant from the National Science Foundation.

[2] Paper presented as a contribution to the Symposium on Adaptive Aspects of Insular Evolution sponsored by The Association for Tropical Biology and held at the Mayagüez Campus of the University of Puerto Rico, June 15–19, 1969.

Reprinted from *Biotropica* 2(1):32–38 (1970), by permission of the author, the Association for Tropical Biology, Inc., and Washington State University Press.

[*] For "Drepaniidae" read "Drepanididae."

subvertical walls of deeply eroded valley systems and faulted mountains—from scattered dryland vegetation through dense forests to dwarfed subalpine vegetation—from deep, dark, dank, calm canyons to wind-blasted exposed terrain. And all of this land was and is subject to rapid geological change. New land open to colonization is conducive to adaptive radiation and speciation.

As the successful ancestral immigrants established themselves in Hawaii, many found ecological vacuums or near-vacuums. Most of them met with little or no opposition or competition, there were few or no predators, parasites, or diseases, and many of them multiplied and spread rapidly and often explosively soon after colonization. Others found conditions less favorable or unfavorable, most failed to become established and others proved poor colonizers. The initial outburst of population increase and dispersal evidently was usually followed by population fragmentation and isolation of small units.

Recently, for example, a Californian *Anacamptodes* moth became established in Hawaii, and it spread rapidly and became ubiquitous over most of the lowlands of the main islands. Its population soon reached extraordinary size, and the ensuing damage to its host plants was severe. Then predators and parasites began adapting to it, and as their pressures increased the moth population decreased in a remarkable way. Soon it was nearly impossible to discover an individual of the moth in areas where previously they had been seen in thousands. In some areas they became so rare that the best way of ascertaining their presence was to search for their larvae in the mud nests of an immigrant eumenid wasp that preyed upon them. The wasp could find them when the entomologist could not.

If a land bird colonizer arrived with a parasitic infection that required an intermediate host to sustain it, the parasite would perish because no intermediate host was available. If Polynesian man arrived infested with filarial worms, filariasis could not become established because there were no mosquitoes in Hawaii to transmit it. Adult insect colonizers most frequently would arrive without parasites and predators of their eggs, larvae, pupae, or themselves. Plants became established free from the pests and diseases that plagued their forebears. Most organisms were free to develop to the fullest of their biotic potentials once they overcame the formidable obstacles of colonization, and many derived species became very narrowly or delicately adapted in the generally favorable environment. As each new species became established, the ecological conditions changed. The changes probably often were more rapid than would occur in closed and balanced continental ecosystems; some changes may have been catastrophic while others were highly favorable. When new plants became established, they often not only changed the character of the forest and the interrelation of plant and plant, but they provided new and more diversified food for the herbivores, which in turn were given renewed opportunity for development and diversification. Over and over again, at long and irregular intervals of time, an "ecological boiling" occurred as new form after new form became established and each exerted its influence on the previously established forms, and new equilibria after new equilibria were struggled for. The interplay of all of these events, conditions, and opportunities made possible an extraordinary speciation and adaptive radiation that can only be considered as explosive. Thus, in comparatively short geological time, many genera in Hawaii developed from more than 100 to 300 or even more than 500 autochthonous species. Some genera developed more species in Hawaii, or at least they have now more living species in Hawaii than in other parts of the world where they have existed for much longer periods of time than in Hawaii. There appear to be more living species of *Drosophila* in Hawaii than in America north of the tropics—possibly 600 or 700 or more species—and *Drosophila* has been in North America for more than 30 million years. Some groups such as the primitive *Proterhinus* weevils found a haven and flourished in Hawaii where they occur today in vast numbers, whereas their group is represented elsewhere by only a few relict forms in such widely separated places as the Canary Islands, New Zealand, Australia,* New Caledonia, and the south central Pacific.

Hawaii is an area of comparatively few genera, but most of the genera contain large numbers of closely allied species displaying narrow geographical and ecological endemism, and within the groups are displayed some highly instructive forms of evolutionary radiation. Some species or groups of species have radiated and diverged far from ancestral type or habit. Thus, we find such unusual things as a terrestrial damselfly larva that lives in vegetable litter on the ground far from water. Some plants that are herb-like in their ancestral homes have become radically changed in Hawaii: violets became Hawaiian shrubs; lobelias became arborescent; derivatives of simple American tarweeds have become remarkable forms bearing little resemblance to ancestral type. Some insects and birds that became flightless could never have survived under the rigors of continental competition. Many species have become narrowly specialized and so delicately adjusted to their ecosystems that they succumb easily to competition by newly

* Omit "Australia."

introduced continental forms or environmental change. Hawaiian forests retreat and disappear rapidly before the onslaught of introduced goats, cattle, sheep, horses, swine, deer, and rats, and then most of the multitudes of organisms that have developed over thousands or millions of years of intimate association with the forests disappear forever. All of the several species of flightless rails of the main Hawaiian Islands, and evidently some that were never preserved as samples in any museum, have been exterminated by introduced cats, rats, swine, and mongoose. Some extraordinary endemic plants have been brought to the brink of extinction or have been exterminated because they could not withstand new pressure brought upon them by introduced rats which eat their fruit and seeds. The endemic insect faunas of the lowlands of all of the islands mostly have been exterminated throughout the range of the voracious introduced predatory ant *Pheidole megacephala* (Fabricius) which now swarms by millions over vast areas of lowlands below about 700 meters elevation and which penetrates to higher altitudes in areas disturbed by man. The endemic Hawaiian fauna contains no ants, and, of course, most endemic insects adapted to a fauna where no ants exist cannot withstand the pressures exerted by such aggressive ants as *Pheidole* when they are introduced.

About 70 years ago, a remarkable English naturalist, R. C. L. Perkins, collected an astonishing flightless fly on the forest floor of a well-known mountain at the edge of Honolulu. He saw it there by the hundreds, and with it was a complex of many other endemic insects in extraordinary abundance. That fly was never found again, because the *Pheidole* ant extended its range into the area where the fly had become narrowly adapted, and the ant exterminated it. Moreover, the area is today a mostly unexciting place to visit because its native fauna has been decimated. Entomologists have found the very trees beneath which the type specimens of the fly were collected, and they have searched over most of the surrounding area of the small mountain in fruitless search for the flightless fly. It is evidently gone forever.

The absence of continental predators such as ants and various parasites resulted in the development of a delicately balanced insect fauna that has suffered terribly since the accidental or intentional introduction by man of such predators and parasites. The introduction of several species of parasitic wasps decimated the endemic moth populations and changed the character of the moth fauna in only a few years. It is now common to obtain nothing but foreign parasites when one attemps to rear wild-caught moth eggs or larvae. Insect diseases, too, have had enormous effect on the endemic insects. Where many insects of various kinds swarmed in vast numbers at the beginning of this century, they are today rare or absent. Their delicately adapted systems are unable to withstand continental-type pressures. Because of the lack of continental-type competition, parasitism, and predation, there is a notable absence of extreme forms of adaptive protective devices in the Hawaiian insect fauna. One does not see there unusual morphologically bizarre protected forms or species with bright warning colors or patterns. Adaptation is opportunistic, and in Hawaii it appears mostly directed toward the simple filling of ecological voids and taking advantage of the available supplies of food. Much of the protective adaptation in Hawaii is simply a continuation of ancestral types such as caterpillars that blend with their food plants and moths that are cryptically colored to resemble the backgrounds on which they rest, and, in general, not much novelty is displayed because of the lack of strong predator pressure. One interesting feature is that small moths of several genera in different families have developed closely similar bold black and white color patterns.

Most of us are familiar with crane-flies or daddy-long-leg flies, the Tipulidae. This is a very large family of flies, and Professor Charles Alexander alone has described more than 10,000 species. The larvae of most known species are dwellers in the soil, and some live in damp, rotting vegetation and some are aquatic. In Hawaii, a most unusual divergent adaptation has occurred, and there a species [*Limonia foliocuniculator* (Swezey)] independently has developed the extraordinary larval habit of becoming a miner in the living leaves of *Cyrtandra* (Gesneriaceae). This is the only recorded occurrence of such a habit amongst the many thousands of species of the family in the world. We know nothing of why this divergent habit should have developed. The available normal niches for the family in Hawaii remain unfilled, the family is not extensively developed in Hawaii, and surely this leaf-mining fly was not forced into its strange leaf-mining habit by competition. Has it occupied this new niche simply because it was open and available and nothing prevented it from occupying that niche?

The beetle genus *Proterhinus* has perhaps more than 250 species in Hawaii. The larvae of most of the species are typical wood-boring weevil larvae. However, several species independently have developed leaf-mining larvae. One of these mines the leaves of *Astelia,* a monocot, and two mine the leaves of the saxifrage *Broussaisia,* a dicot. Another species has become a borer in the living stems of *Broussaisia.* *Proterhinus* has radiated in its food adaptations so widely that we expect to find species in every endemic woody plant as well as in most of the larger ferns in Hawaii. The genus, probably a Cretaceous relict, found in Hawaii a perfect haven with a vast array of open food niches, and *Proterhinus* has proceeded to fill them as if drawn into them by vacuums, and almost every acceptable food source in the forests has been invaded by them. In Hawaii they are among the most common of all native insects. In contrast to this condition, in the South Pacific they are few in species, and they are mostly individually scarce or rare. There they are confronted by a competing genus of weevils (*Miocalles*) with similar habits, and wherever the two genera occur together, *Miocalles* is abundant in species and individuals and *Proterhinus* is scarce.

There are more than 200 species of delphacid leafhoppers in Hawaii. The species of one endemic genus is confined to poisonous *Euphorbia* plants, and they are unique amongst the Delphacidae of the world in having their heads drawn out into extraordinary horn-like processes. All of the other species of the family in Hawaii have flat or nearly flat faces, but this genus, *Dictyophorodelphax,* has the face prolonged to form a process that may be longer than the entire body. One wonders why such a strange horn should originate *de novo* in a Hawaiian complex of species that otherwise is conservative and what possible function it could have. Upon dissection, we find that an extraordinary diverticulum of the gut extends out into the horn. Knowing that the leafhoppers are confined to a diet of the poisonous sap of *Euphorbia,* we might infer that the horn is an adaptation for the utilization of the poisonous food. This theory sounds plausible, and it may be true, but there is another Hawaiian leafhopper in a closely allied genus that is found on one of the same species of *Euphorbia* in the same mountain range as one of the species of *Dictyophorodelphax,* and it has a normal form and lacks any indication of modification for utilizing the poisonous *Euphorbia.* It would appear that we know nothing about the reasons for the development of the astounding cephalic horns of these species.

Another species of the same family of leafhoppers has nymphs that have become adapted to live between the close-fitting leaf bases of *Freycinetia.* The nymphs have become flattened so that they can insinuate themselves between the leaf bases where they feed on tender tissue. No other nymphs are known to have such adaptations.

Two other allied leafhoppers live on an endemic *Acacia,* and both species may be found on the same tree at the same time. These two leafhoppers are remarkably narrowly adapted to live on different parts of the same plant. The so-called leaves of the *Acacia* are not complete leaves but are only modified flattened petioles called phyllodes. The true leaves are compound, paler in color, and are produced only on young plants or from adventitious shoots. One of the pair of leafhoppers is confined to the phyllodes, and the other attacks only the true leaves. The phyllode species has a modified ovipositor and inserts its eggs in the edges of the phyllodes. The other species lays its eggs in tender young shoots. The species on the phyllodes is darker greenish brown, and the species on the true leaves is pale green to match the paler color of the true leaves.

True bugs of the family Saldidae are found in most temperate and tropical regions. They are characteristically a terrestrial group, and most of them live at the edges of streams, lakes, or seashore. In Hawaii, however, species have become adapted to live in trees. It is surprising to one familiar with collecting these bugs in most regions of the world to go to Hawaii and there to find them on shrubs and trees in the forests far from water.

The wasp genus *Odynerus* is found in many parts of the world, but in Hawaii it has speciated to form the greatest concentration of species of any known comparable area. There are more than 100 Hawaiian species. Most of the species of the world build their nests in the ground or utilize existing holes such as crevices in rocks, old insect borings, and pith cavities. In Hawaii, however, some species have developed independently the habit of making free mud pots for their nests. No other endemic Hawaiian insects make mud pots, but the habit is not uncommon on the continents. Why should such a habit be developed independently in Hawaii and what is its adaptive significance? Before man caused such alteration and devastation in the Hawaiian biota, *Odynerus* wasps swarmed in countless millions. What conditions might have existed then that we cannot see today? Now the populations of *Odynerus* are decimated, why, we do not know, although I surmise that foreign diseases may be involved. Many species have been brought to the brink of extinction or have been exterminated in the face of ample food supplies. A person may now search for many months without being able to find the species of which I spoke that makes the mud pots. We cannot always tell from an examination of the present situation what the conditions were when various forms of adaptation evolved.

The Hawaiian *Odynerus* wasps represent a double invasion with a long interval of time between the invasions. The older of the two groups is much more sensitive to the changing conditions of today, and it is the representatives of the older, more narrowly adapted species that have suffered the greatest decimation. Several of the more recent, less narrowly adapted forms even today maintain themselves in the lowlands where most of the older species have been made scarce or have been exterminated.

Thanks to the National Science Foundation, I have in process a study of an Hawaiian genus of small moths known as *Hyposmocoma*. I have already examined about 350 species in this one genus, and it is possible that there are more than 500 species in Hawaii. Compared with this, a recent monograph of the entire family to which it belongs lists only 67 species for North America. One is immediately confronted with the question: Why is it that on little and young Hawaii probably more than 500 species have evolved in this genus, whereas in gigantic and ancient North America there are only 67 species known in the entire family?

The radiation in form and habit is so astonishing in *Hyposmocoma* that the species are presently separated into 14 supposed genera, but after detailed study I have found that only one genus is involved. The group has long been in a state of explosive speciation and radiation and is diverging in many directions. Its extremes may at first sight appear to represent distinct genera, but the links that tie the extremes together remain, and the blends from one extreme to another can be demonstrated.

We really know very little about this astonishing *Hyposmocoma* group, and a proper study of the genus is worthy of a full lifetime of work. The progenitors of this enormous, tightly knit cluster of closely allied forms found in Hawaii extraordinary favorable conditions, and the descendants have exploited the environment to the fullest by astonishing adaptive radiation. Species are found from the seashore through the dry lowland forests to the rain forests and to the high mountains, and from seemingly barren lava flows to dense jungle. Although our knowledge is fragmentary, we know that the habits of the larvae are remarkably diverse. Many larvae live in portable cases, but many do not make cases. Many are found on nearly bare rocks where they evidently feed upon lichens or fungi. Some are found in barren areas of comparatively new lava flows far from forests and where there is little other insect life. Some of them glean their food from the surfaces of the bark of various living trees, and others bore in or under dead bark. Some live in dead stems, in limbs, or in dead logs. Some form silken tunnels in moss. Some bore in living wood, stems, or pith; some feed upon the lower surfaces of fern fronds and others bore in living ferns. Some species feed amongst vegetable trash on the ground

and some feed on the wooly tomentum near the bases of palm fronds.

The known food of the larvae of *Hyposmocoma* ranges from fungi, lichens, mosses, and ferns all the way up through most of the families of higher plants, and I suspect that all suitable higher plants in Hawaii serve or have served as food for species of *Hyposmocoma*. It is, however, significant that no species has yet been found to eat a sedge or a grass, and, strangely, none has yet been found to be a leaf miner. Why?

In contrast to the wonderful adaptive success of the *Hyposmocoma* moths in Hawaii, it will be of interest to compare one of the many genera that have not been so adaptable and appear to be at "dead ends" in their ability for adaptive radiation. As an example, one may mention the strange weevil genus *Nesotocus*. *Nesotocus* appears to be an ancient relict in Hawaii. There is no doubt that *Nesotocus* is one of the oldest genera of beetles in the Hawaiian fauna. It is so peculiar that no living relative outside of Hawaii is known, and there are even questions as to what subfamily it belongs. In contrast to the huge endemic proliferations of other genera in Hawaii, only four closely similar species of *Nesotocus* are known. The larvae are confined to three genera of araliaceous trees and mostly to the single genus *Cheirodendron*. The weevils are rarely found, but on occasion host plants are seen riddled by many larval tunnels. I have seen such trees, but, although I am a weevil specialist, I never collected *Nesotocus* on its host plant during my many years in Hawaii. What a contrast there is between *Nesotocus* and such successful and adaptable genera as *Drosophila* and *Hyposmocoma!*

It is of interest also to mention here that, surprisingly, there are only two endemic butterflies in Hawaii. Each of the butterflies is widely spread over the main islands. Although they are highly distinctive species well separated from all allied species elsewhere, and thus they appear to have entered Hawaii a rather long time ago, they do not appear to show any tendency to speciate, and each species is able to develop on several different host plants, although the principal host of one is the urticaceous *Pipturus* and the principal host of the other is the legume *Acacia*.

Only one genus of bees [*Hylaeus* (=*Nesoprosopis*) of the Colletidae (=Hylaeidae)] is represented in the endemic Hawaiian fauna. There are more than 50 known Hawaiian species, and these evidently have sprung from a single ancestral immigrant. This endemic complex has developed species and species groups that have radiated from the stem form to such a degree that some workers might consider some of them to represent different genera were it not for the known intermediate forms. The most remarkable Hawaiian development is the production of a cluster of five or more species which have in Hawaii independently adapted themselves to be cleptoparasites. The females of the normal species have the forelegs adapted for gathering pollen. The cleptoparasites have lost their pollen-collecting apparatus, and they gather no pollen or nectar and make no nests. Instead, they lay their eggs in the fully provisioned nests of the industrious species, and they are thus a kind of cuckoo bee. The industrious species choose two principal kinds of sites for building their nests. Some species build their nests in burrows in the ground, and some nest in hollow stems or in old beetle tunnels in wood. Strangely, the cleptoparasites are known to attack only the nests of those species that burrow in the ground. Another astonishing thing is that, in contrast to the black coloration of their hosts, most of the cleptoparasites independently have developed a reddish color simulating that of cleptoparasitic bees of other genera on the continents. Why such a development should arise independently in Hawaii where there is only the one genus of bees, I do not know.

Continental bees generally are more numerous in the drier, more open areas and are scarce in dense, damp forests. Various Hawaiian bees have been able to penetrate a variety of ecological situations, and a few species even have become adapted to dense, damp jungles. These forest-dwellers nest mostly in burrows in standing trees in contrast to the coastal and dry zone species which nest in the ground.

One of the most remarkable of all forms of adaptive radiation in Hawaii is that exhibited by the damselflies or Odonata. Typically, the larvae of damselflies are truly aquatic organisms that live on the bottoms of ponds and streams and obtain their oxygen through the mechanism of extensively tracheated, delicate anal gills. One such ancestral immigrant damselfly found its way to Hawaii ages ago, and from it have sprung more than 25 endemic forms. Some of these have retained the typical ancestral aquatic larval forms, but the group has been evolving in an astonishing way to become adapted to live on land. Thus, the larvae of some species are able to leave the streams or ponds in search for food amongst damp vegetation at the edges of the water, others are able to live on oozing wet banks or at the edges of waterfalls, and several species have made a drastic change and have become adapted to live in the axils of the leaves of certain forest plants where debris collects in small amounts of water, and these larvae have become adapted to survive dry periods when the water in the leaf axils is lost.

These arboreal larvae seem almost to dislike being flooded with water and may at times after rains be seen to have crawled away from the water accumulated in the leaf axils. Thus, there are examples of species adapted to various niches from river bottom to arboreal. However, the most remarkable of all is an astonishing species whose larvae have become truly terrestrial. The larvae of this species have become adapted to live in leaf litter on the ground beneath dense masses of vegetation far from water. The species has thus departed greatly from the ancestral type, and it has taken an enormous step toward the development of an entirely new group of terrestrial carnivores. It would appear that it is from such extraordinary adaptive radiation that new major taxa might be produced, and the phenomenon is here demonstrated most lucidly before our eyes.

This change from aquatic to semi-aquatic to arboreal to terrestrial habit has demanded considerable morphological and physiological change in the gills, and there is a beautiful transition series displayed by the gills of the various species from the long, thin, delicate, highly tracheated gills of the aquatic forms to the short, thick, opaque, densely hairy gills of the terrestrial species. There must also be changes in the function of the spiracles.

It may now be appropriate to cite an example of competition between species which attempt to fill the same niche. The Mediterranean fruitfly [Ceratitis capitata (Wiedemann)] has been in Hawaii a long time and is widely distributed there. About 1945, the Oriental fruitfly (Dacus dorsalis Hendel) was accidentally introduced to Hawaii. The Oriental fruitfly is larger and more aggressive than the Mediterranean fruitfly, and it attacked the same fruits as well as additional kinds. The Oriental fruitfly would not tolerate the Mediterranean fruitfly in its vicinity, and whenever the two species met the Oriental fruitfly would chase away the Mediterranean fruitfly. Thus, if a Mediterranean fruitfly attempted to oviposit on a fruit where there was an Oriental fruitfly, the Oriental fruitfly would attack it viciously and drive it away and thus frustrate its attempt to oviposit. A dramatic reduction in the populations of the Mediterranean fruitfly soon followed, and in areas where the Mediterranean fruitfly had been common, it virtually disappeared. In areas that had long been known to average several Mediterranean fruitflies per host fruit, the average dropped to as low as one larva per 100 fruits. The Oriental fruitfly thus essentially replaced the Mediterranean fruitfly over vast areas of the warmer parts of Hawaii. However, it is less adapted to the cooler uplands, and there the Mediterranean fruitfly was able to maintain itself.

Bananas were introduced to Hawaii by Polynesian man about 1000 years ago. There are no endemic bananas or banana relatives in Hawaii or on any nearby archipelagos. There are, however, several species of *Hedylepta* moths that evidently have developed new Hawaiian species on the banana in various areas of the Islands. These moths are narrowly adapted to banana. Long study has produced no evidence that these species reproduce on any host other than banana. We assume, therefore, that these banana-eating moths originated in Hawaii after the banana was introduced. Hence, they are species that appear to have developed in less than 1000 years after a new source of food became available to them.

In conclusion, we may say that Hawaii has a relatively simple, disharmonic biota whose ancestors crossed the open sea by accident and became established in a favorable environment upon rapidly changing substrata where environmental pressures were mostly reduced or minimal. Great momentum has been given to the processes of adaptive radiation and speciation by the peculiar circumstances and opportunities of the island ecosystems. The result has been an unusual proliferation of species and much radiation, diversification, and narrow adaptation. It is as if great vacuums existed and species have rushed in to attempt to fill almost every available unoccupied ecological niche. There is even the tendency for species to enter environmental categories foreign to their genera, families, or even their orders. New habits have arisen independently in the islands: nonparasitic bees have developed cleptoparasites; aquatic damselflies have produced arboreal and terrestrial species; delicately winged Neuroptera have given rise to flightless "monsters" encased in coriaceous, armor-like, nonfunctional forewings; the drepaniid birds have rushed in to fill gaps and developed into sickle-billed nectar-suckers, grosbeak-like seed-crackers, heavy-billed fruit-eaters, sharp-billed insect-catchers, some almost woodpecker-like and others almost parrot-like in habit. This extraordinary Hawaiian biota would have continued its remarkable adaptive radiation at a rapid rate had man not caused its recent decimation. Now a drastic new set of unfavorable conditions faces the delicately adapted biota, and a large fraction of it is doomed to extermination. What the future holds for it we cannot predict, and we shall not know anything like it again. Many of its glorious products, the fruit of ages, have already vanished, and its very mountains are being washed back into the sea whence they came.

HYBRIDIZATION AND ITS TAXONOMIC IMPLICATIONS IN THE *SCAEVOLA GAUDICHAUDIANA* COMPLEX OF THE HAWAIIAN ISLANDS

GEORGE W. GILLETT

University of Hawaii, Honolulu

Accepted April 5, 1966

The family Goodeniaceae embraces a total of about 14 genera and 320 herbaceous and shrubby species, of which nine genera and about 250 species are restricted to Australia (Krause, 1912; Engler and Melchior, 1964). The genus *Scaevola* includes perhaps 90 species of which about 65, nearly all herbaceous, are confined to Australia. Of the approximately 25 scaevolas that occur outside of Australia, about 20 comprise the exclusively woody section *Sarcocarpaea*. This section portrays an evolutionary line that has been highly successful in crossing ocean barriers, for it extends from Australia to the Marquesas, Hawaii, Formosa, Java, and to the shores of the Indian Ocean, South Atlantic Ocean, and the Caribbean Sea. Dispersal has been accomplished through the evolution either of buoyant fruits conveyed by ocean currents, or of edible, fleshy drupaceous fruits carried by birds (Guppy, 1906; Carlquist, 1965).

It is likely that the ingress of representatives of the genus *Scaevola*, section *Sarcocarpea*, to the Hawaiian Islands involved at least three dispersal events. Of the seven indigenous Hawaiian species, only the beach species, *Scaevola sericea*, is ocean dispersed and it very probably arrived through a separate introduction. The six upland species all have conspicuous, nonfloating drupaceous fruits associated with bird dispersal. Of the latter it would seem less speculative to credit the highly distinctive montane *S. glabra* (*Camphusia glabra*) to a separate introduction. The remaining five indigenous, bird-dispersed upland species may have evolved from a single introduction. Two of the latter species, *S. gaudichaudiana* Chamisso and *S. mollis* Hook. & Arn., along with numerous related popula-

tions, constitute the *S. gaudichaudiana* complex.

This complex occurs on the older, western group of the Hawaiian Islands including Molokai, Lanai, Oahu, and Kauai. The two species are distinguished by five character differences that are presented below:

	S. gaudichaudiana	*S. mollis*
Corolla color:	White	Violet
Vesture:	Glabrous	Sericeous
Diameter of fruit:	3–4 mm.	8–9 mm.
Length of peduncle:	40–60 mm.	3–15 mm.
Hydathodes on leaf (1 side of mid-vein):	0–15	25–40

Morphological features of *Scaevola gaudichaudiana* are portrayed in Fig. 1; those of *S. mollis* in Fig. 2; and those of intermediates in Figs. 3 and 4. The two species are separated by eco-geographic differences, for populations of *S. gaudichaudiana* occur between 300 and 800 meters on Molokai, Lanai, Oahu, and Kauai, while those of *S. mollis* occur only on Oahu, and at generally higher elevations. *Scaevola mollis* is restricted to the high ridges of the Koolau Range, eastern Oahu, and to isolated summits of the Waianae Range, western Oahu. Its habitats are characterized by high rainfall and exposure to the northeast trade winds.

Populations of *Scaevola gaudichaudiana* are relatively common, for this is one of the very few indigenous species that is able to hold its ground in the mesic to dry, weed-infested lowlands. Graphically expressed, the morphology of *S. gaudichaudiana* individuals would be characterized on the scatter diagrams of Fig. 6 as rayless circles falling in the lower right-hand corner.

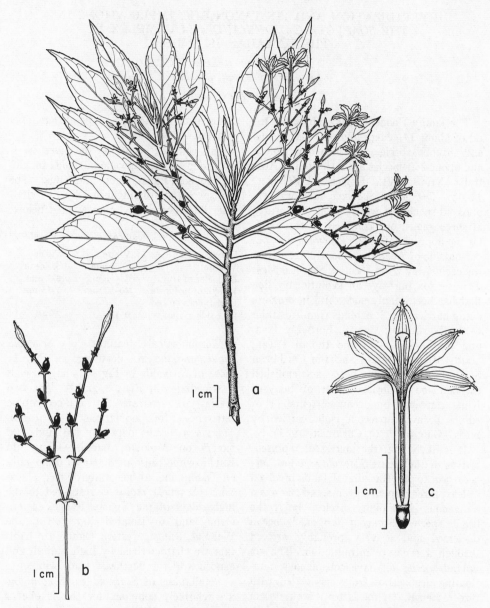

Fig. 1. Representative specimen of *Scaevola gaudichaudiana*: (a) flowering branch; (b) mature inflorescence; and, (c) flower at anthesis. Drawn from *Gillett 1417*, Wiliwilinui Ridge, Oahu.

Populations of *S. mollis* are often encountered on the higher ground of the Koolau Range and are amply documented in the herbarium. These populations would be portrayed in the upper left-hand corner of the scatter diagram as circles with long rays.

Intermediate populations occur in certain areas, but are not common. These populations are usually highly variable and portray a mixture of expressions of each cited character. Their presence suggested the occurrence of hybridization or some other noteworthy evolutionary mechanism. It

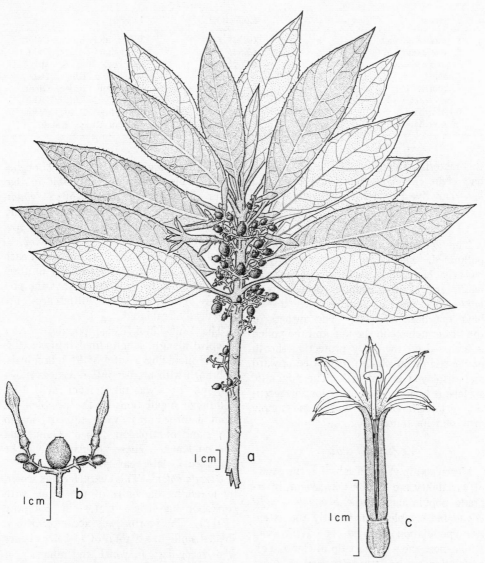

FIG. 2. Representative specimen of *Scaevola mollis*: (a) flowering branch; (b) mature inflorescence; and, (c) flower at anthesis. Drawn from *Gillett 1407*, Wiliwilinui Ridge, Oahu.

therefore is appropriate that they be given particular emphasis in this study.

Chromosomes

Chromosome counts have been obtained from microsporocytes by the acetocarmine squash technique, and these are listed beyond. Voucher specimens are deposited in the University of Hawaii Herbarium.

The chromosome complement was char-acterized by normal pairing with no univalents and no evidence of chromosome aberrations. The pollen mother cells consistently exhibited normal meiotic behavior. A close cytological relationship between the two species is indicated by the high incidence of closed bivalents in the chromosome complement of one plant of obvious hybrid origin (*Gillett 1581*, Fig. 3). In

Specimen	*n*	Collector	Locality
S. gaudichaudiana	8	*Gillett 1450*	Wiliwilinui Ridge, Oahu.
S. gaudichaudiana	8	*Gillett 1404*	Wiliwilinui Ridge, Oahu.
S. gaudichaudiana	8	*Gillett 1628*	Wahiawa Bog, Kauai.
S. mollis	8	*Gillett 1406*	Wiliwilinui Ridge, Oahu.
S. mollis	8	*Gillett 1421*	Wiliwilinui Ridge, Ohau.
Intermediate	8	*Gillett 1580*	Wiliwilinui Ridge, Oahu.
Intermediate	8	*Gillett 1581*	Wiliwilinui Ridge, Oahu.
Intermediate	8	*Gillett 1549*	Kalalau Ridge, Kauai.

this material, 13 out of 29 microsporocytes had eight closed bivalents and none had less than five closed bivalents.

Pollination

The flowers in this complex are insect pollinated. The exotic honey bee (*Apis*) has been seen pollinating flowers of *Scaevola mollis* and of intermediates similar to *S. mollis*, but indigenous pollinating insects have not been observed. The anthers of the flower dehisce in the bud and the pollen is amassed on the hairy protective sheath of the stigma on which it is carried upward and displayed at anthesis. The stigmatic surface is later fully exposed for the reception of foreign pollen, so that there is ample provision for outcrossing.

Variation Studies

Nearly optimal conditions for the study of variability are manifest in several intergrade populations of the *Scaevola gaudichaudiana* complex, particularly the extensive population studied on Wiliwilinui Ridge, near the southeast tip of Oahu. This population occurs at an elevation of about 600 meters over an area approximately 250 meters long and 15 meters wide. The habitat has been subjected to man-caused disturbances over the past 25 years, for a power line and trail run along the crest of the ridge bisecting the area longitudinally. The vegetation of this area is largely indigenous, the associated genera including *Metrosideros* (Myrtaceae), *Pelea* (Rutaceae), *Bobea* and *Straussia* (Rubiaceae), *Myrsine*, *Pittosporum*, *Wikstroemia* (Thymelaeaceae), *Antidesma* (Euphorbia-

ceae), *Clermontia* and *Cyanea* (Lobeliaceae). This population is notable in that quite distinct plants both of *S. gaudichaudiana* and of *S. mollis* are present. Here one can observe plants of both species and putative hybrids (Figs. 1, 2, 3, and 4) growing within a few meters of each other. The habitat is so essentially uniform that there can be little doubt that the previously cited character differences are genetically regulated.

The Wiliwilinui Ridge population was sampled along a longitudinal transect, this sample including a total of 81 individuals. A branch with mature inflorescences, flowers, and fruits was taken from each. Five additional populations of the complex, all from disturbed areas, were studied: one on the island of Molokai, two on Oahu, and two on Kauai. These populations will be discussed in later paragraphs.

Corolla color.—This character was scored by matching the bases of the petals with corresponding color plates in Ridgway (1912). The scoring was accomplished in shaded sunlight. A total of 11 color classes were recognized in which the intensity of pigmentation increases progressively from white to anthracene violet:

Color	Scoring Value
White	0
Pallid Blue-Violet	1
Pale Hortense Violet	2
Pale Blue-Violet	3
Pale Lavender Violet	4
Pale Mauve–Light Mauve	5
Light Lavender-Violet	6
Lavender-Violet	7
Pleroma Violet	8
Haematoxylin Violet	9
Anthracene Violet	10

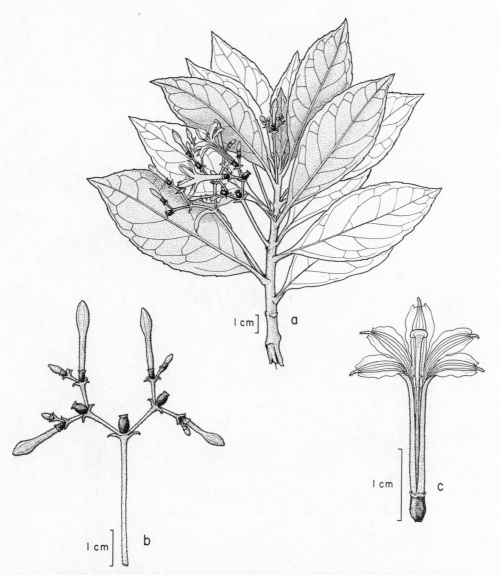

Fig. 3. Putative hybrid of *Scaevola gaudichaudiana* × *S. mollis*: (a) flowering branch; (b) mature inflorescence; and, (c) flower at anthesis. Drawn from *Gillett 1581*, Wiliwilinui Ridge, Oahu.

All of the above color classes are represented in the first population. They portray clearly a quantitative, clinal pattern of variability, indicating that corolla color is probably regulated by a polygenic system.

Pubescence.—The mature fruit was chosen as an objective and easily referable site for scoring this character, and a total of six pubescence classes were recognized. These were determined by arranging a large number of randomly selected fruits in a linear order with the glabrous condition on one end progressing to the densely pubescent fruits on the other. Representative fruits of six classes were secured to a sheet of paper and used as standards for scoring the population sample. The standards were

Fig. 4. Putative hybrid of *Scaevola gaudichaudiana* × *S. mollis*: (a) flowering branch; (b) mature inflorescence; and, (c) flower at anthesis. Drawn from *Gillett 1582*, Wiliwilinui Ridge, Oahu.

drawn accurately in the fresh condition (Fig. 5) and the drawing was subsequently used in scoring additional populations. The six classes do not portray completely the number of intergradations between the glabrous and strongly pubescent extremes of this character, but seem to constitute the practical number of categories that can be accurately and readily employed in scoring a polygenic character of this type.

Fruit diameter.—Diameters of the mature fruits were measured to the nearest millimeter. The six size classes, each class one millimeter in breadth, ranged from a minimum of three millimeters through a maximum of nine millimeters, with a clinal, polygenic variability clearly portrayed.

Length of peduncle.—The peduncle, or stem, of the inflorescence was measured to the nearest millimeter. This character

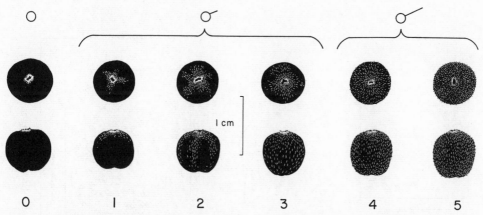

Fɪɢ. 5. Mature fruits utilized for scoring pubescence in the *Scaevola gaudichaudiana* complex. Scatter diagram symbols are shown above.

showed a very great range of expression, with some inflorescences nearly sessile and a continuous intergradation from this condition to peduncles as long as 55 mm. In the Wiliwilinui population a total of 19 classes were rather evenly distributed between these extremes and no class had more than seven of the 81 individuals measured. A very obvious polygenic control is indicated for this character. It was selected as the abscissa of the scatter diagrams.

Number of leaf cusps.—The leaf margins in plants of this complex are characterized by a greater or lesser number of serrations, the tips of which are called cusps, or hydathodes. The number of hydathodes on the leaf margins of *Scaevola mollis* is uniformly high and is undoubtedly related to the consistent occurrence of this species in wet habitats. On the other hand, *S. gaudichaudiana*, which occurs on less humid habitats, has leaves with very few hydathodes, in some cases none. The hydathodes were counted along one margin of the lamina between the tip and the base. Counts were made from five mature leaves and the median value was taken as the expression of central tendency for a given plant. The median values of the Wiliwilinui Ridge population produced a continuous series of classes from a low of six to a high of 22, and three isolated classes from 24 to 36. The distribution appeared to be slightly

skewed to the lower end of the series, but definitely has the metrical expression of a polygenic character. The number of hydathodes was chosen as the ordinate of the scatter diagram.

Scatter diagram.—Variation in all of the character differences outlined for the Wiliwilinui Ridge material is summarized graphically in the scatter diagram of that population in Fig. 6. In this the characters represented by the "ray" symbols (fruit diameter, flower color, pubescence) are necessarily portrayed with only three classes of expression instead of the much larger number that we know exists. The recombinations on the diagrams are therefore many fewer than the actual number. Even in this relatively simplified expression the variability of the Wiliwilinui Ridge population is impressive. The diversity in the five additional populations on Molokai, Oahu, and Kauai, when combined with that of the Wiliwilinui Ridge material would perhaps approximate the magnitude of diversity in this complex. The graphical summary of the intermediate recombinations corresponds reasonably well to the variability to be expected in experimental F_2 and back-cross hybrids (Gillett, 1955).

DISCUSSION

Each of the scatter diagrams of Fig. 6 portrays the variability in a relatively small

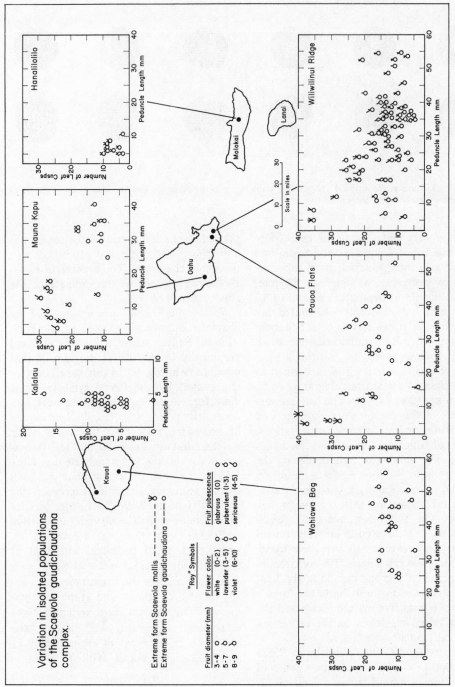

FIG. 6. Variability in isolated populations of the *Scaevola gaudichaudiana* complex in the Hawaiian Islands.

sample of a given population. A broader expression of variability would be obtained from larger samples, and the inclusion of additional populations would increase considerably the number of known recombinations.

While the Kalalau (Kauai) sample appears to be relatively uniform it is only a small facet of the extensive variability on Kauai, another expression of which is portrayed in the Wahiawa Bog material. The Kalalau population has strong similarities to the Hanalilolilo (Molokai) population which in turn falls within the facies of the Wiliwilinui Ridge population. These data suggest that the populations on all the islands are products of a common gene pool. Ample verification of this point has been provided by the examination of extensive herbarium collections and by field observations on Molokai, Oahu, and Kauai.

It is clear that the diversity in this complex is continuous, or clinal, and that it is indicative of introgressive hybridization (Anderson, 1953), characterized by reciprocal gene flow into each of the parent species. This gene flow has been sufficient to produce a very large number of recombinations yet has not obscured the parental lines. The intermediate populations of the complex comprise a diverse assemblage that is highly refractory to conventional systematic treatments.

The Hawaiian flora contains many genera in which polymorphism is so extensive as to mark them as extremely difficult taxonomic subjects (Fosberg, 1948). It would be premature to ascribe hybridization as the basis for all such problems, but hybrids have been observed within and between several "difficult" genera including *Dubautia* × *Raillardia* (Sherff, 1935; Keck, 1936), *Bidens* (Sherff, 1937), *Gouldia* (Fosberg, 1937), *Pipturus* (Skottsberg, 1934), *Viola* (Skottsberg, 1939), and *Vaccinium* (Skottsberg, 1927). Hillebrand (1888) emphasizes the extraordinary polymorphism in Hawaiian *Cyrtandra* by the statement: "The variations affect nearly every part of the plant, and branch out and

intercross each other in manifold ways to such an extent that it is next to impossible to define exact limits of species." This amply describes the results of hybridization even though the term is not employed. Polymorphy is so extensive in Hawaiian genera that in routine identifications it is invariably necessary, using recent monographs and revisions, to extrapolate metrical, "key" characters or to rely heavily on locality information. Some of the "problem" genera in the Hawaiian flora are undoubtedly related to evolutionary dynamics other than hybridization, but hybridization is sufficiently important to merit a more thorough study comparable to those of Cockayne and Allen (1934), and Rattenbury (1962) in the New Zealand flora.

Hybridization is widespread in the New Zealand forest flora, occurring in at least 45 families, 92 genera, and involving 478 species of vascular plants (Cockayne and Allen, *op. cit.*). Some of the New Zealand genera in which hybridization occurs, including *Coprosma* (Rubiaceae), *Metrosideros* (Myrtaceae), *Plantago*, *Pittosporum*, and *Astelia* (Liliaceae), also contribute highly polymorphic elements in the Hawaiian flora. Introgressive hybridization has recently been reported in New Zealand *Metrosideros* (Cooper, 1954, 1958), a notoriously polymorphic genus in Hawaii. In addition to possessing common floristic elements, New Zealand and Hawaii are islands remote from source areas. It is appropriate, therefore, to review the evolutionary dynamics proposed by Rattenbury (*op. cit.*) for the New Zealand forest flora. This significant essay advances the hypothesis of cyclic hybridization as a mechanism for survival in the New Zealand forest flora, particularly in those genera with outbreeding systems and diaspores sufficiently vagile to form isolated, small populations. It is proposed that the cycles of hybridization are correlated with climatic fluctuations in the Pliocene and Pleistocene.

The dynamics of recurrent hybridization are conspicuous in Hawaii. The Hawaiian flora is generally characterized by outbreeding systems, and there is a conspicuous trend toward the dioecious condition. The genera of the Rubiaceae have a pronounced flower dimorphism including heterostyly (Skottsberg, 1944). Heterostyly also occurs in *Wikstroemia* of the Thymelaeaceae (Hillebrand, 1888). Many genera are characterized by the dioecious condition, the examples too numerous to mention here. This subject has recently been reviewed (Carlquist, 1966a). The production of edible fruits well equipped for dispersal and subsequent establishment of isolated populations is a notable attribute of the Hawaiian flora (Carlquist, 1966b). The conspicuous, edible portion may be provided by the sepals (*Alsinodendron*, Caryophyllacea; *Neraudia, Pipturus, Touchardia*, Urticaceae), or mature ovary (*Scaevola; Coprosma*, Rubiaceae; *Vaccinium*, Ericaceae; *Ilex*, Aquifoliaceae; *Broussaisia*, Saxifragaceae; *Phyllostegia*, Labiatae; and many others).

Because of the subtropical character of the climate in Hawaii it might be assumed that the climatic fluctuations of the Pleistocene were very mild, providing little stimulus for cyclic hybridization. However, Selling (1948) reports that these changes, at least in Late Quarternary, have imposed conspicuous fluctuations in the floras of West Maui and Kauai. The recent discovery of a lignite stratum 600 feet below the arid plain west of Pearl Harbor, Oahu (Stearns and Chamberlain, 1966), is an indication of very extensive climatic changes. Lastly, the limited expression of Pleistocene glaciation on Mauna Kea, Hawaii, does not in itself imply limited climatic changes. Areas with no glacial activity might well have had climatic changes quite sufficient in magnitude to threaten or eliminate many subtropical species.

The area of Oahu is only 600 square miles, while that of North Island is over 44,000 square miles. The Hawaiian flora is thus confined to extremely small areas from which it has virtually no latitudinal escape from the extinction threat imposed by volcanic activity and climatic change. The very restricted area of this archipelago would therefore cause a far more conspicuous expression of cyclic hybridization as a survival mechanism than has been noted by Rattenbury for New Zealand. Escape from extinction would accrue only to those evolutionary lines with genetic resources sufficient to generate extreme recombination types. Phyletic groups capable of replenishing their gene pools through hybridization would thus have an advantage in the insular situation. After the dispersal of such recombinations and the establishment of isolated, small populations, further climatic fluctuations would bring on a repetition of the process.

TAXONOMIC IMPLICATIONS

The clinal diversity in the *Scaevola gaudichaudiana* complex poses an extremely difficult taxonomic problem. It may well be argued that the entire complex constitutes a biological species (Grant, 1957), and that the two extreme expressions of the complex, *S. gaudichaudiana* and *S. mollis*, are really interbreeding subspecies. However, the retention of these taxa at the species level appears to be equally useful and is compatible with the species concept of most workers.

The very large number of recombinations graphically portrayed in Fig. 6 adequately emphasize the hopeless proliferation of names that would result if different hybrid populations were given formal names. To date, 19 formal taxonomic descriptions have been accorded hybrid populations, including six species, seven varieties, and six forms, an imposing burden, indeed. A reasonable alternative to the current, and future, plethora of names would be the use of the formula, *S. gaudichaudiana* × *S. mollis*, to designate hybrid populations.

SUMMARY

The Hawaiian endemics, *Scaevola gaudichaudiana* and *S. mollis*, are diploids (n = 8) which comprise, with a broad range of intermediates, an interspecific complex with populations occurring on the islands of Molokai, Lanai, Oahu, and Kauai. Populations of *S. mollis* occur only on Oahu, but those of *S. gaudichaudiana* and of intermediates are found on all four islands. On Wiliwilinui Ridge, Oahu, the two species are sympatric, the plants of each species occurring within a few meters of each other, accompanied by a hybrid swarm. Some recombination types are comparable to those of isolated populations on Molokai and Kauai, as well as Oahu, suggesting that these and other similarly isolated populations originated through natural hybridization and subsequent dispersal, probably by birds, of the conspicuous drupaceous fruits. The evolutionary dynamics appear comparable to those operative in cyclic hybridization as proposed by Rattenbury for the New Zealand flora.

ACKNOWLEDGMENTS

Appreciation is extended to Setijati Notoatmodjo, Thelma de Ausen, and Pualani Sakimura, who scored material for the scatter diagrams, and to Elvera Lim who assisted in the chromosome studies. The assistance of the Research Committee, University of Hawaii, and of the National Science Foundation (Grant GB 3336) is gratefully acknowledged.

LITERATURE CITED

ANDERSON, E. 1953. Introgressive hybridization. Biol. Rev., **28**: 280–307.

CARLQUIST, S. 1965. Island life. A natural history of the islands of the world. Natural History Press, New York.

——. 1966a. The biota of long-distance dispersal. IV. Genetic systems in the floras of oceanic islands. Evolution, **20**: 433–455.

——. 1966b. The biota of long-distance dispersal. I. Principles of dispersal and evolution. Quart. Rev. Biol., in press.

COCKAYNE, L., AND H. H. ALLEN. 1934. An annotated list of groups of wild hybrids in the New Zealand flora. Ann. Bot., **48**: 1–55.

COOPER, R. C. 1954. Pohutukawa × Rata. Variation in *Metrosideros* (Myrtaceae) on Rangitoto Island, New Zealand. Rec. Auckland Inst. Mus., **4**: 205–212.

——. 1958. Pohutukawa × Rata No. 2. Variation in *Metrosideros* (Myrtaceae) in New Zealand. Rec. Auckland Inst. Mus., **5**: 13–40.

ENGLER, A., AND H. MELCHIOR. 1964. Syllabus der Pflanzenfamilien. Band II. Gebruder Borntraeger, Berlin-Nikolasse.

FOSBERG, F. R. 1937. The genus *Gouldia*. Bull. Bishop Mus., **147**: 1–82.

FOSBERG, F. R. 1948. Derivation of the flora of the Hawaiian Islands. Pp. 107–109, *in* Insects of Hawaii, vol. 1, Univ. Hawaii Press, Honolulu.

GILLETT, G. W. 1955. Variation and genetic relationships in the Whitlavia and Gymnobythus phacelias. Univ. California Publ. Bot., **28**: 19–78.

GRANT, V. 1957. The plant species in theory and practice. Pp. 39–80, *in* The species problem, A.A.A.S., Washington, D. C.

GUPPY, H. B. 1906. Observations of a naturalist in the Pacific between 1896 and 1899. II. Plant dispersal. Macmillan, London.

HILLEBRAND, W. 1888. Flora of the Hawaiian Islands. Heidelberg.

KECK, D. D. 1936. The Hawaiian silverswords. Occas. Papers Bishop Mus., **11**: 1–38.

KRAUSE, K. 1912. Goodeniaceae und Brunoniaceae. *In* Das Pflanzenreich. Heft 54. Engelmann. (J. Cramer), Weinheim.

RATTENBURY, J. A. 1962. Cyclic hybridization as a survival mechanism in the New Zealand forest flora. Evolution, **16**: 348–363.

RIDGWAY, R. 1912. Color standards and color nomenclature. Published by the author. Washington, D. C.

SELLING, O. H. 1948. Studies in Hawaiian pollen statistics. Part III. On the Late Quaternary history of the Hawaiian vegetation. Bishop Mus. Spec. Publ., **39**: 1–154.

SHERFF, E. E. 1935. Revision of *Tetramolopium, Lipochaeta, Dubautia,* and *Raillardia*. Bull. Bishop Mus., **135**: 1–135.

——. 1937. The genus *Bidens*. Field Mus. Nat. Hist., Bot. Ser., **16**: 1–709.

SKOTTSBERG, C. 1927. *Artemisia, Scaevola, Santalum,* and *Vaccinium* of Hawaii. Bull. Bishop Mus., **43**: 1–89.

——. 1934. *Astelia* and *Pipturus* of Hawaii. Bull. Bishop Mus., **117**: 1–77.

——. 1939. A hybrid violet from the Hawaiian Islands. Bot. Not., pp. 805–812.

——. 1944. On the flower dimorphism in Hawaiian Rubiaceae. Arkiv för Botanik. Band **31A** (4), 1–28.

STEARNS, H. T., AND T. CHAMBERLAIN. 1966. Deep cores on Oahu, Hawaii, and their bearing on the geological history of the Central Pacific basin. Pacific Science, in press.

Chromosome Tracers
of the Origin of Species

Some Hawaiian *Drosophila* species have arisen from
single founder individuals in less than a million years.

Hampton L. Carson

The most spectacular aspect of organic evolution is the origin of adaptations (*1*). These arise primarily as the
result of genetic changes which are incorporated into populations through the
action of natural selection on a variable
and freely recombining pool of genes.
The population genetics of such evolutionary change has been well understood since the theoretical work of the
1930's (*2*). The origin of certain adaptations on the microevolutionary level
(for example, protectively colored moths
in industrially blackened areas) has been
closely analyzed (*3*).

Adaptive evolution is basically a phyletic process—that is, it occurs during
succeeding generations within naturally
interbreeding populations of a single
biological species. To put it another
way, this kind of evolutionary change
can occur without any multiplication of
reproductively isolated population units,
or species. Both phyletic change and
speciation are evolutionary processes—
that is, both involve descent with
change. Whereas phyletic evolution has
yielded to elegant mathematical and
experimental analysis, the speciation
process has been generally refractory
to studies of comparable precision. In
this sense, the origin of species is a
major unsolved problem of evolutionary
biology. The present article provides a
new approach which may help in its
solution.

Speciation is almost exclusively a
geographical process (*4*). Populations of
existing species are entities distributed
in space and time; somehow, such
a species population becomes split into
subpopulations (subspecies). In time,
one or more of these latter may emerge
as species.

The difficulties of studying the dynamics of geographic speciation are
manifold. In the first place, it is a slow
process by human standards. The formation of a species in the usual continental situation probably takes thousands or hundreds of thousands of years
or more, even in organisms which have
a relatively rapid generation time. Furthermore, the geographical relationships
of most organisms are extraordinarily
complex. Species populations which
are in the crucial initial stages of evolutionary divergence may be very difficult
to recognize. Many species have world-
wide or at least continental distributions; this makes it difficult to decide
which portion of the species, if any,
deserves study from the point of view
of the speciation process. Then again,
continental or widespread species often
have enormous populations, through
which gene flow may be active. Such
flow may inhibit the very speciation
processes the evolutionist wishes to concentrate on. If endemic continental
species with small, semi-isolated populations are selected for study, it is often

Reprinted from *Science* 168:1414–1418 (19 June 1970), by permission of the author and *Science*. Copyright 1970 by the American Association for the Advancement of Science. The author is at present professor of genetics at the University of Hawaii.

difficult or impossible to tell whether this represents an incipient species or whether it is an ancient isolation with secondary intergradation. Continents and their biotas are thus frequently too complex geographically, histori- cally, and ecologically to permit accu- rate inferences concerning the process of the origin of species. Islands, espe- cially oceanic islands, have simpler conditions.

An oceanic island is one that is thrown up in the vastness of one of the earth's great oceans. The volcanic action which is frequently responsible pro- duces at first a fiery, sterile mass. When cooling occurs, life starts to move in. Mostly it comes by chance, through long-distance dispersal, especially if the islands concerned—like the Hawaiian Islands, for example—are thousands of miles from any other land mass. Those lucky few propagules that may reach a new volcanic island and establish col- onies set in motion forces which pro- vide a new evolutionary beginning for the group concerned. Even though the propagule that arrives may already have millions of years of evolution behind it, the isolation from its ancestral relatives and contemporaries, coupled with the new, raw, and often difficult ecolog- ical conditions it faces, provides a re- newed evolutionary opportunity. The results often strike the continental bi- ologist as bizarre, "explosive," or other- wise extraordinary when measured against experience with life on the continents.

Contemplating the fauna of the oce- anic Galápagos Islands, Darwin wrote, with characteristic understatement, "the inhabitants of these islands are emi- nently curious." As everyone knows, his observations of the simplified conditions existing there led him to a train of thought which catapulted evolutionary thinking into the center of biological attention, a position which it still holds today.

The Hawaiian Islands are in many ways uniquely suited for the study of the process of speciation. They are by far the most isolated oceanic islands in the world. The archipelago is 2000 miles (3200 kilometers) from any con- tinent and lies in the warm tropical region of the Pacific Ocean. The vast volcanoes, of which the islands are the emergent tops, rise to great heights; the summit of Mauna Kea is more than 4200 meters above sea level and acquires a snow mantle each winter. The slopes of the islands erode rapidly under the heavy tropical rains. The older volcanic domes are dissected into deep valleys, separated by sharp ridges. Most of the rain falls on the windward slopes, leaving the lee sides desert-like. These features combine to produce extraordinarily diverse habitats: there are windswept alpine meadows, rain forests, and blisteringly hot southwest- ern lowland slopes.

Terrestrial life came to Hawaii by chance from all directions; descendants of these few ancestors have populated the islands with a unique biota. Chance, it appears, not only affected what orga- nisms reached the older islands 5 mil- lion or more years ago but also played a role in the spread of life within the archipelago from the older islands to the younger. Although this evolution has produced some remarkable bio- logical innovations and adaptations, the paramount feature is the enormous number of species of flowering plants, ferns, terrestrial invertebrates, and, especially, insects (5).

The genus *Drosophila* as it exists on the continents includes hundreds of species of small flies most of which are adapted to humid environments where they breed on decaying or fermenting vegetation. They are easy to handle in the laboratory, and certain species have become prime objects for the study of evolutionary and population genetics (6). From the Hawaiian Islands, con- siderably smaller in area than the state of Massachusetts, more than 250 spe- cies of the genus *Drosophila* have been described (7). All but about 12 have

evolved in Hawaii and are found nowhere else. This number is approximately one-fourth of the species of the
genus known in the entire world. It is
probable, furthermore, that many
Drosophila species in Hawaii are yet to
be described. The islands also have a
large number of species of Drosophilidae belonging to genera closely related
to *Drosophila* (for example, *Scapto-
myza*). Clearly, Hawaii has one of the
greatest concentrations of this family of
flies in the world.

The Hawaiian Islands appear to be
geologically very recent (8). Thus, potassium-argon measurements (9) indicate
that the oldest lava flows, on the northernmost island, Kauai (Fig. 1), are approximately 5.6 million years old, an
age that places them in the late Pliocene. On the other hand, the island of
Hawaii appears to have been formed
very recently indeed. Thus, lava flows
on the Kohala volcano yield both potassium-argon and paleomagnetic data
which indicate that the mountain is
no older than 700,000 years (late
Pleistocene). The four southernmost
volcanoes, two of which are currently
active, are even younger than this. The

adjacent island of Maui, separated
from Hawaii by a 30-mile-wide channel
(Fig. 1), is also of Pleistocene age; its
lava flows give ages from 1.3 to 1.5
million years. Thus, Maui is considerably older than Hawaii. The channel
between the two islands (Alenuihaha
Channel) is 1950 meters deep, and it
appears that Maui was never connected
to Hawaii by a land bridge. On the
other hand, there is strong evidence
that Pleistocene land bridges once
linked the present islands of Maui,
Molokai, and Lanai (Fig. 1).

In short, it is clear that the island
of Hawaii is the youngest in the archipelago. In this article I focus attention
on the origin of certain of the *Drosophila* species endemic to this island.
Chromosomal data make it possible to
trace the precise ancestry of a number
of these species from certain Maui
populations.

Chromosomes of Hawaiian Drosophila

Extensive accounts of the evolutionary biology of Hawaiian *Drosophila*
have been recently published (*10–12*).

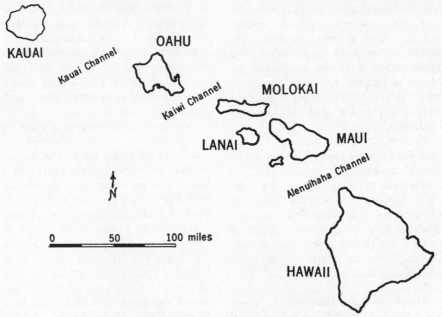

Fig. 1. The six major islands of the Hawaiian Archipelago.

Among these are descriptions of nearly a hundred species of large flies forming a clear subgroup belonging to the genus *Drosophila*. Because they are characterized by patterns of dark spots on the wings, these species have been informally referred to as the "picture-winged" flies (see cover). All so far examined have a metaphase chromosome group of $2n = 12$ (*13*). The five major polytene chromosomes of 69 of these species have been mapped in terms of a set of arbitrary Standard band sequences—namely, those found in the species *D. grimshawi* from Auwahi, Maui. Banding comparisons of unknowns with the Standard have been facilitated by the use of a binocular drawing tube (*14*). This device permits comparison of the sequence of a chromosome of unknown banding order under the microscope directly at table level with a photographic cutout of a known Standard sequence (Fig. 2).

Except for one case of an apparent deletion, all microscopically observable polytene chromosome mutations in these species are due to changes in gene order (paracentric inversions). One hundred and fifteen inversions have been fixed among the 69 species of picture-winged flies (*10*). Each inversion has been designated by a separate lower-case letter after the chromosome number; the alphabet has been used several times with numerical superscripts—for example, a^2, b^2, and so on. By means of the method of Wasserman (*15*), a chromosomal phylogeny based on inversion-sharing has been prepared. Such phylogenies contain no intrinsic information about the direction of evolution. That is, it is possible to start at any point and derive all the other sequences in a stepwise fashion. The designation of a starting point, which converts such a relationship diagram into a phylogeny showing direction of evolution, must come from information outside the data on chromosomal sequences.

Relevant outside geographical and geological information exists in this case. First, it seems clear that the *Drosophila* fauna of the Hawaiian Islands is derived from the mainland, rather than vice versa. In this connection, one of the picture-winged subgroups (the *D. primaeva* subgroup, known so far only from Kauai) shows a sequence in the relatively conservative chromosome 5, which is the closest arrangement among any of the island flies to the homologous chromosome in certain Palearctic-Nearctic mainland species of the subgenus *Drosophila* (*16*). This fact places the *D. primaeva* subgroup at the base of the Hawaiian chromosome phylogeny. Further evidence on the direction of evolution comes from facts pertaining to the increasing geological youth of the Hawaiian islands as one proceeds southeastward from the northernmost major island, Kauai. These facts all serve to

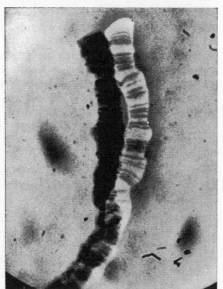

Fig. 2. Photomicrograph of a chromosome end (left, darker object) viewed simultaneously with a cutout of a photograph (right, lighter object) of a portion of the homologous chromosome of the Standard, *Drosophila grimshawi*. The image of the chromosome end is juxtaposed to the cutout at table level by a binocular drawing tube. This facilitates matching of the banding orders.

Table 1. Comparison of chromosomal formulas between certain *Drosophila* species from the island of Hawaii and their Maui counterparts. Lowercase letters refer to specific fixed inversions.

Island	Species	Chromosomal formula				
		Set No. 1				
Hawaii	D. silvestris	Xijkopqrst	2	3d	4b	5
	D. heteroneura	Xijkopqrst	2	3d	4b	5
Maui	D. planitibia	Xijkopqrst	2	3d	4b	5
		Set No. 2				
Hawaii	D. ciliaticrus	Xg	2	3o	4	5
	D. engyochracea	Xg	2	3	4l	5
	D. murphyi	Xg	2	3/3o	4	5
Maui	D. orphnopeza	X	2	3/3o	4	5
	D. balioptera	Xg	2	3	4	5
	D. orthofascia	Xg	2	3n	4	5
		Set No. 3				
Hawaii	D. setosimentum	Xikouvwxym^2	2cdl	3fjkl	4bopqb^{2}c^{2}d^{2}e^{2}f^{2}n^{2}o^2	5f
	D. ochrobasis	Xikouvwxym^2	2cdk	3fjk	4bopqb^2	5f
Maui	D. adiastola	Xikouvwxy	2cd	3fjk	4bopq	5f

focus on, and to underscore, the newness—indeed, the present terminal nature in space and time—of the fauna of the island of Hawaii itself.

Origin of Species on
the Island of Hawaii

Of approximately 21 species of picture-winged flies in collections from the island of Hawaii (Fig. 1), 17 have been analyzed for polytene chromosome sequences. All 17 are highly distinctive species. They are endemic to this island, being found nowhere else in the world, not even on the island of Maui, only 30 miles away. Although much smaller in size than Hawaii, the Maui complex is richer in species of this group. Of approximately 41 species known in collections, 30 have been analyzed chromosomally.

So far, all of the species from the island of Hawaii tested by hybridization techniques appear to be reproductively isolated from all other species. Thus, in studies with laboratory strains, no fertile hybrids have been obtained between any of the Hawaii species or between these species and their Maui relatives. The data, however, are not extensive (*17*).

Seven of the 17 species from Hawaii are of particular interest. The chromo-

somal formulas for these species relative to the Standard (X 2 3 4 5) are given in Table 1. The method of notation may be illustrated by the formula for *Drosophila ciliaticrus*, which differs from the Standard by one inversion in the X chromosome (Xg) and one in chromosome 3 (3o). Illustrations showing the breakpoints of these inversions have been published (*10*). Chromosomes 2, 4, and 5 of this species have the Standard gene order.

The seven Hawaii species listed in Table 1 fall into three sets; each set is related to one or more species known from Maui. The first set of two species, *Drosophila silvestris* and *D. heteroneura*, are homosequential—that is, they have identical arrays of fixed inversion sequences relative to the Standard. In addition, the two species are homosequential with respect to a third species, *D. planitibia* from Maui (Table 1).

Homosequential species are a striking feature of Hawaiian *Drosophila*. Their homosequentiality not only underscores their very great basic similarity but also makes clear the fact that much evolutionary chromosome change occurs at the submicroscopic or molecular level (*18*). In addition to *D. planitibia* and its two Hawaii relatives, 11 more such homosequential sets have so far been recognized from all the islands, involving 36 species in all (*12*). Members of a homosequential set often vary so much that studies of morphology, genitalia, and behavior sometimes fail to suggest that they should be grouped together.

In the present case, however, the significant fact is that, of the 13 species which fall into the *Drosophila planitibia* subgroup of the picture-winged flies (*10*), only *D. planitibia, D. silvestris,* and *D. heteroneura* have the key inversion Xr. This is one of the nine inversions by which the X chromosome of these species differs from Standard. Thus, of all the possible candidates for an ancestor of the two Hawaii members, only *D. planitibia* of Maui fulfills the requirements chromosomally.

Accordingly, it is concluded not only that the ancestor of the Hawaii species was derived from Maui but also that it may be specifically traced chromosomally to a population ancestral to the present-day *Drosophila planitibia.* A founder which crossed the Alenuihaha Channel following the raising of the island of Hawaii above sea level is inferred (Fig. 3) The chromosomal formula for this putative ancestor is given across the arrow in Fig. 3.

A founder for the *Drosophila murphyi* complex of three species (Table 1, set No. 2) can also be inferred; it has some special properties of interest. All three species from Hawaii show the inversion Xg. *Drosophila ciliaticrus* has, in addition, the fixed condition 3o, but *D. murphyi* populations are polymorphic, carrying both the Standard 3 and 3o. All expected karyotypes (the homozygotes 3/3 and 3o/3o as well as the heterozygote 3/3o) have been found within present-day populations of this latter species. *Drosophila engyochracea* does not have 3o but has a new fixed inversion (4 1) which it does not share with any other known species.

No single Maui species is known which combines both the fixed Xg and the polymorphic 3/3o karyotypes. On the other hand, two species collectively fulfill these conditions. Thus, *Droso-*

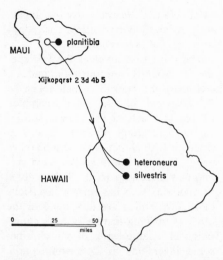

Fig. 3. A postulated interisland species founder going from Maui to Hawaii during the late Pleistocene. The open circle represents a population ancestral to the three present-day species *Drosophila planitibia, D. heteroneura,* and *D. silvestris* (solid circles). The inferred chromosomal formula of the interisland founder is superimposed on the arrow.

phila balioptera has Xg only, whereas *D. orphnopeza* populations, like those of *D. murphyi,* are polymorphic for 3/3o. This species, however, has the Standard X chromosome. Accordingly, it is inferred that an ancestral population once existed on Maui which was polymorphic for both X/Xg and 3/3o. A migrant from this population, carrying Xg in the fixed state and the heterozygous condition 3/3o, reached the island of Hawaii as the founder which subsequently gave rise to the *D. murphyi* cluster of species. Present-day *D. murphyi* appears to have the chromosomal formula closest to that of this putative ancestor (Table 1 and Fig. 4). In the process of descent, it appears that *D. ciliaticrus* has fixed 3o, whereas *D. engyochracea* has refixed Standard 3. As in the case of the *D. planitibia* subgroup, the key inversions which serve as tracers are unknown in species other than those listed and, most significantly, are not found among any of the many species known from Oahu or Kauai. They appear to be specific

"Maui-Hawaii" markers, having apparently arisen by mutation in a past population on the Maui complex.

The third case involves the two species *Drosophila setosimentum* and *D. ochrobasis* of Hawaii, which relate to *D. adiastola* of the Maui complex (Table 1). Each of the Hawaii species has a basic group of 18 inversions in common with *D. adiastola*. On the other hand, the two Hawaii species have certain new inversions (Xm^2, 3l, and $4b^2$). In addition, each has certain inversions of its own which are not found in the other. A striking feature is the accumulation of a large series of 4th chromosome inversions in *D. setosimentum*. This process appears to be continuing, as *D. setosimentum* shows extensive intraspecific 4th chromosome polymorphism in addition to the fixed inversions shown in Table 1 (*10*).

As in the other two cases of Table 1, it is concluded that the two modern Hawaii species of this complex are descended from a founder stemming from a population directly ancestral to present-day *Drosophila adiastola* and homosequential with it (Fig. 4).

Of the five members of the *Drosophila adiastola* subgroup of flies of the Maui complex, two others are homosequential with *D. adiastola* and appear to mark equally well the ancestral lineage of the two Hawaii species. One of these, *D. cilifera*, is endemic to Molokai, and the other, *D. peniculipedis* of Maui, has a peculiar constriction in chromosome 4 which is not found in the Hawaii species. In any event, the founder is likely to have been derived from a population ancestral to these three homosequential species, rather than from any one modern species.

The three cited founder events are not isolated cases; there are at least three other known instances of one or more Hawaii species that has its closest chromosomal relative on Maui (*10*). They are less diagrammatic than the cases discussed above, however, because, in these other instances, similar homosequential species occur on Oahu

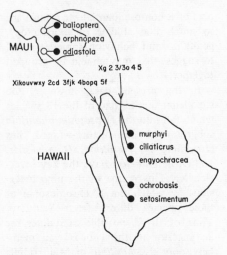

Fig. 4. Two additional interisland species founders going from Maui to Hawaii (see legend to Fig. 3, and text).

or Kauai, thus founders could have come to the island of Hawaii directly from one of those islands, bypassing Maui.

The Founder Event and Speciation

The island of Hawaii, which is the youngest in the archipelago, has apparently received much of its picture-winged *Drosophila* fauna from the adjacent island of Maui. In three especially clear instances the founders may be traced chromosomally to Maui only, and their precise inversion formulas may be inferred. The species of the island of Hawaii are endemic to that island, and, since the island appears to be no more than 700,000 years old, the evolutionary events which produced the species must have consumed less time than that. Thus, these species must have evolved less than three-quarters of a million years ago on the island of Hawaii. Such precise statements can rarely be made about evolutionary events.

There is no evidence of repeated simple colonizations of the island of Hawaii. No subspecies of species from Maui or any other island have as yet been found there, at least in the group under discussion. This suggests that the founder event is an exceedingly rare one, and that the break between the donor population and the new colony on the invaded island is a deep one biologically.

One of the most striking features of this situation is the fact that speciation invariably has followed the founder event. This suggests further that the founder event may be accomplished by a single propagule, probably a single fertilized female.

In Figs. 3 and 4, three founder events have been postulated as being responsible for the origin of seven species. In each case the law of parsimony has been invoked and it has been assumed that, for instance, only a single founder was ancestral to the clusters of two (or, in one case, three) species which occur on the island of Hawaii. On the other hand, the "one founder, one new species" view might be defended. It appears, however, that if such double colonizations from a chromosomally identical stock did occur, the likely result would be subspecies of some Maui species, not new unique species, such as are observed.

As was proposed above, evolution seems very often to display two major processes: an adaptation (fitness for a specific function in a specific environment) appears to be made by intraspecific phyletic change, whereas species result from a multiplicative process whereby populations become divided and isolated. The situation on oceanic islands, as revealed in the data given here, suggests a clarifying separation, in time and in process, of these two aspects of evolution. Thus, the hypothesis may be made that a speciation phase precedes an adaptive phase. The speciation episode appears to be characterized by the successful colonization of a relatively open ecological habitat by a single founder female. This event would be expected to have several important genetic consequences. First, a maximization of the phenomenon of

random genetic drift would be accomplished as the new colony is formed. Second, early success of the new colony in a locally permissive habitat might result in a population flush. Certain new genetic recombinants might be multiplied and preserved by chance in the demes which survive the inevitable population crash.

The resulting interdeme selection and related processes, it is argued, might well lead to the appearance of a genetic gap between the new colony and its progenitor. This gap might be recognized as the equivalent of speciation (19). In my view, this might be accomplished in a relatively small number of generations. If this is the case, then the synthesis of species under controlled conditions might indeed be accomplished in the laboratory or field plot more easily than has been previously thought. Indeed, a striking report of a suggestive case has appeared recently (20).

When the gene pool of a population is being rigorously shaken up by chance events of the kind discussed above, speciation is not likely to be accompanied by adaptive evolution. It is suggested that, where species founders play a role, as in these terrestrial populations of oceanic islands, the adaptive evolutionary phase is likely to occur only after the chance events leading to speciation are essentially complete. Thus, the gene pool of the new species undergoes new phyletic evolution in isolation from its ancestors and contemporaries. Since genetic drift and the founder effect undoubtedly provide a genetic revolution (21), the species is faced with the alternatives of extinction or the welding of a somewhat discordant gene pool into something ecologically workable. The result is seen in the somewhat bizarre yet generally well-adapted products of insular speciation.

The separation of phyletic evolution from speciation, as called for in the foregoing hypothesis, would not, of course, be expected to apply to all patterns of speciation. For example, where a widespread continental species becomes broken up into subspecies, the result is frequently a gradual population change involving both adaptation and speciation. Thus, in these cases, it is probable that speciation and adaptation are synchronic population processes. Only where the founder effect is prominent may the features of the two processes be clearly seen as essentially separate evolutionary phases, one with and one without a large element of chance.

Summary

Organic evolution produces species and adaptations. Data from terrestrial populations existing on oceanic islands suggest that the processes whereby species and adaptations arise are different and are sometimes separated in time. Thus, in *Drosophila* from the island of Hawaii, speciation appears to follow the establishment of a new island population from a single founder individual from a nearby island. In these cases, it is hypothesized, speciation is characterized by isolation, random genetic drift, and the abrupt, nonadaptive changes in the gene pool which would be expected to immediately follow the founder event. The process is aided by interdeme selection. Adaptations, which follow in time, are forged genetically by the well-known intrademic processes of mutation, recombination, and selection.

References and Notes

1. V. Grant, *The Origin of Adaptations* (Columbia Univ. Press, New York, 1963); B. Wallace and A. M. Srb, *Adaptation* (Prentice-Hall, Englewood Cliffs, N.J., 1964).
2. R. A. Fisher, *The Genetical Theory of Natural Selection* (Clarendon, Oxford, 1930); J. B. S. Haldane, *The Causes of Evolution* (Longmans, Green, London, 1932); S. Wright, *Genetics* 16, 97 (1931).
3. H. B. D. Kettlewell, *Annu. Rev. Entomol.* 6, 245 (1961).
4. E. Mayr, *Animal Species and Evolution* (Harvard Univ. Press, Cambridge, Mass., 1966).
5. E. C. Zimmerman, *Insects of Hawaii* (Univ. of Hawaii Press, Honolulu, 1948), vol. 1.
6. J. T. Patterson and W. S. Stone, *Evolution in the Genus Drosophila* (Macmillan, New York, 1952).
7. D. E. Hardy, *Insects of Hawaii* (Univ. of Hawaii Press, Honolulu, 1965), vol. 12.
8. H. T. Stearns, *Geology of the State of Hawaii* (Pacific Books, Palo Alto, Calif., 1966).
9. I. McDougall, *Bull. Geol. Soc. Amer.* 75, 107 (1964); *ibid.* 80, 2597 (1969).
10. H. L. Carson and H. D. Stalker, *Univ. Tex. Publ. No. 6818* (1968), p. 355.
11. W. B. Heed, *ibid.*, p. 387; H. T. Spieth, *Evol. Biol.* 2, 157 (1968).
12. H. L. Carson, D. E. Hardy, H. T. Spieth, W. S. Stone, in *The Evolutionary Biology of the Hawaiian Drosophilidae, Essays in Evolution and Genetics in Honor of Theodosius Dobzhansky*, M. K. Hecht and W. C. Steere, Eds. (Appleton-Century-Crofts, New York, 1970), p. 437.
13. F. E. Clayton, *Univ. Tex. Publ. No. 6818* (1968), p. 263; *Univ. Tex. Publ. No. 6918* (1969), p. 96.
14. The binocular drawing tube was obtained from Wild Heerbrugg Instruments Company.
15. M. Wasserman, *Amer. Natur.* 97, 333 (1963).
16. H. D. Stalker, *Proc. Int. Congr. Genet. 12th* (1968), vol. 1, p. 194; H. L. Carson and H. D. Stalker, *Univ. Tex. Publ. No. 6918* (1969), p. 85.
17. H. Yang and M. R. Wheeler, *Univ. Tex. Publ. No. 6918* (1969), p. 133.
18. H. L. Carson, F. E. Clayton, H. D. Stalker, *Proc. Nat. Acad. Sci. U.S.* 57, 1280 (1967).
19. H. L. Carson, in *Population Biology and Evolution*, R. C. Lewontin, Ed. (Syracuse Univ. Press, Syracuse, N.Y., 1968), p. 123.
20. Th. Dobzhansky and O. Pavlovsky, *Proc. Nat. Acad. Sci. U.S.* 55, 727 (1966).
21. E. Mayr, in *Evolution as a Process*, J. Huxley, Ed. (Allen and Unwin, London, 1954), p. 157.
22. Support for this work came from NIH grant GM10640 to the University of Hawaii and from NSF grants GB3147 and 7754 to Washington University and GB711 to the University of Texas. I thank Geraldine Oda and Marion L. Stalker for preparing the figures. A list of the many contributors to this work has been published [see Carson *et al.* (12)].

Section 6

Hawaiian Natural History: Past and Present

INTRODUCTION

Soon the waves scudded along from distant regions
a stray cocoanut, a hard-shelled bean or pandanus
seed; the winds carried over the almost microscopical spores of cryptogamous plants and seeds
endowed with wings of parachutes . . . birds
dropped a small amylaceous or grass seed, entangled in their feathers elsewhere; and last of
all came man, bringing with him the means of
sustenance -- probably the banana and breadfruit.
But man, after having been deposited here, was
cut off from his anterior home, and therefore
with, or soon after his arrival, his agency
ceased. Only with the appearance of the white
man another era dawned; he at once bound this
isolated group to the five continents, and established a highway on which what lived or
breathed in distant regions might wend its way
hither.

William Hillebrand, 1856

One of the most peculiar characteristics of an island
ecosystem is its extreme vulnerability, its tendency
toward great instability when its isolation is broken
down and toward rapid increase in entropy when change
has set in. Before the advent of man, most old island
ecosystems reached relative stability and changes were
slow. The arrival of the Polynesian in Hawaii nearly
1,000 years ago increased to some extent the degree
of instability of the systems; with the advent of
Western man this increase has often assumed catastrophic
proportions, with losses in biotic diversity, soil
development, and the capacity of soils for water retention, and with the disruption of biotic communities.

The effects of Western man on the Hawaiian ecosystem are detailed in the papers of Hubbell on the
biology of islands and of Berger on birds, both in
Section 4, and in Zimmerman's account, in Section 5,
of adaptive radiation in insects. In this section, the
Hawaiian ecosystem as it was affected by the Polynesian

557

settlers is discussed by Newman. The final paper is a
summary by Kay of the development of our knowledge of
Hawaiian natural history from the discovery of the
Islands in 1778 by Captain Cook to the twentieth century.

MAN IN THE PREHISTORIC HAWAIIAN ECOSYSTEM

T. Stell Newman[1]

Man is a supreme egotist. We often consider ourselves to be separate from the rest of nature, and, in fact, superior to it. This point of view is changing as it becomes clearer that a close relationship exists between mankind and the rest of the world--witness the present concern with population growth and pollution. Overpopulation and pollution affect both man and the rest of nature, illustrating that man is an active ingredient in nature. People generally have yet to realize, however, the extent to which the rest of nature affects man.

This article applies the "ecosystem concept" to the study of prehistoric Hawaiians and prehistoric Hawaii, as an illustration that man as a part of nature affects, and is affected by, the whole. Odum has defined the ecosystem as

> any area of nature that includes living organisms and nonliving substances interacting to produce an exchange of materials between the living and non-living parts. . . . The ecosystem is the basic functional unit in ecology, since it includes both organisms (biotic communities) and abiotic environment, each influencing the properties of the other. . . . [1959:10-11]

This paper describes a portion of the Hawaiian ecosystem during the period when Hawaii was occupied

---

[1]Archeologist, Division of State Parks, Department of Land and Natural Resources, State of Hawaii.

solely by Polynesians. The focus is on the relationships
between man and the rest of the ecosystem that may be
seen through a study of Hawaiian fishing and farming.
Fishing and farming formed the primary subsistence
base for the Hawaiians and show most clearly that the
Hawaiians were a part of the general Hawaiian ecosystem.

CULTURE

Although there is always an interplay between the
biological nature of man and the ecosystem of which he
is a part, the Hawaiians inhabited the Hawaiian ecosystem for such a relatively short time that probably
little genetic change occurred. On the other hand, the
Hawaiian way of life, or culture, both influenced and
was influenced by the Hawaiian ecosystem.

Man's culture allows him, as an intelligent animal,
to pass knowledge, attitudes, and behavior patterns from
one generation to the next, enabling knowledge to accumulate over time. Culture is essentially an ecological
adaptation that provides the means for extracting from
an ecosystem almost all that is required for the adequate support of human life. It must be remembered
that culture is more than technology; it includes also
patterns of behavior, social groupings, and mental
attitudes. All these are part of man's cultural adaptation to nature. Two factors act in concert to shape
the particular culture that will be held by any group
of men: (1) the specific cultural heritage of the
accumulated knowledge, mental attitudes, and patterns
of behavior, and (2) the specific nature of the ecosystem of which that culture is a part.

A study of the interaction between Hawaiians and
the remainder of the Hawaiian ecosystem is most readily
accomplished through an understanding of the ancestral
culture brought to Hawaii, the ways in which that culture was adaptive in the Hawaiian ecosystem, the

qualities of the ecosystem that constrained and channeled Hawaiian culture, and the effects of Hawaiian
culture on the ecosystem.

THE CULTURE BROUGHT BY THE POLYNESIAN SETTLERS

The initial settlers of the Hawaiian Islands were
Polynesians who seem to have come from the Marquesas
Islands of Central Polynesia in the fifth to seventh
centuries A.D. These migrants did not arrive in Hawaii
with mental vacuums; they brought an Oceanic culture
that had developed during several thousand years of
migration from Southeast Asia.

The migration to Hawaii and to Polynesia was possible only because the ancestors of both were seafaring
people who passed down their knowledge from generation
to generation. During the movement across the Pacific
from Asia, knowledge of boats, the sea, navigation,
and fishing was continually developed and refined, to
be woven into the fabric from which Polynesian culture
emerged when the islands of Eastern Oceania were reached.

The ancestors of the Polynesians brought from their
homeland an extensive inventory of useful plants: food
plants such as taro, yams, and breadfruit; fiber plants
such as the paper mulberry; and medicinal plants of
many varieties. The food plants were the basis of a
well-developed agricultural economy, although the primary farming implement was a simple digging stick. The
people using these digging sticks, however, developed
a vast knowledge about farming techniques, engineering,
plant adaptations, and environmental factors affecting
their crops. This cultural knowledge accumulated over
many generations and enabled the Polynesians to have a
highly effective agriculture.

Domesticated land animals were also part of the
economy of the ancestral stock from which the Polynesians
derived. The pig and the dog were probably brought from

the Southeast Asian mainland, while the jungle cock, or
chicken, may have come from there or from Southeast
Asian islands and Melanesia. The pig, dog, and chicken
were the only domesticated animals of these people and
of their Polynesian and Hawaiian descendants. However,
these animals provided valuable supplementary food and
they were carefully bred and raised.

Besides these plants and animals, techniques for exploitation of land and sea, and other facets of Oceanic
economy, the early voyagers crossing the Pacific to Polynesia brought with them a body of accumulated knowledge,
a heritage of particular ways of thinking and patterns
of behavior, as well as attitudes toward one another
and toward nature. These cultural factors worked in
concert to produce Polynesian culture--and this was the
culture brought by the first settlers to Hawaii. Their
culture emphasized fishing and farming, with some dependence upon domesticated animals. Virtually all other
aspects of Polynesian culture, such as social organization, religions, and politics, were related to these
basic adaptations to island ecosystems.

The first settlers in Hawaii brought a culture
already well adapted to island living and based on the
exploitation of the sea and the land. It is not known,
nor is it knowable, if the first settlers in Hawaii
brought with them all the useful plants and animals
carried across the Pacific by their ancestors. It is
known, however, that all (plus the sweet potato from
South America) were present in Hawaii by the time
Captain Cook arrived in A.D. 1778.

PRE-POLYNESIAN HAWAIIAN ECOSYSTEM

It would have been very difficult for the first
Hawaiians to survive in Hawaii had they been totally
dependent upon land resources, for little land food
was available in Hawaii at the time of their arrival.

Scholars such as Zimmerman (1965) indicate that none of
the major plants or land animals used for food by the
Polynesians were present in Hawaii when the settlers
arrived. *Pandanus (hala)* and edible ferns were about
the only plant foods available, while birds and the
bat were practically the only land animals suitable
for food.

Unlike the foodless land, the sea abounded in food
for the settlers. Furthermore, the settlers with their
Polynesian culture knew how to exploit efficiently the
marine resources of the sea. Thus, the first settlers
in Hawaii must have depended almost entirely upon the
sea and its products for their subsistence. This would
have been the case even had the initial settlers brought
food plants and domesticated animals with them, for it
would have been necessary to hoard and tend the plants
and animals carefully for a number of years before they
could be used as food. This almost total dependence
upon the sea would have lasted until crops were growing
well and the domesticated animals were reproducing in
sufficient numbers. Only then could the land be exploited for Hawaiian subsistence needs.

The food crops eventually became well enough developed, however, and the Hawaiians then shifted from a
sea-oriented to a land-oriented economy. By the time
of Captain Cook's arrival, the main emphasis of Hawaiian
subsistence was upon land foods, although the sea continued to produce a substantial portion of their diet.

HAWAIIAN SEA EXPLOITATION

Although little specific information exists on
prehistoric Hawaiian sea exploitation practices, there
is no reason to expect them to have been substantially
different from practices described for the time of
contact in 1778 (Newman 1970). A reconstruction of
marine exploitation practices at the time of European

contact would include: (1) hand collection, (2) poisoning, (3) snaring, (4) spearing, (5) basket traps, (6)
nets, (7) fishhooks and line, (8) fishponds.

Hand Collection

Hand collection was practiced in shallow water, both
on the surface and by diving. Some types of fish were
caught by hand in shallow pools as well as by divers
in underwater caves. Other food items collected by hand
included crabs, lobsters, eels, sea urchins, sea cucum-
bers, shellfish, octopi, shrimp, and seaweed. Much of
this type of exploitation was practiced at night, particularly for mobile fauna.

Poisoning

Poisonous plants used were *ahuhu (Tephrosia purpu-
rea)* or *'ākia (Wikstroemia sandwicensis)*. The plants
were collected and brought to the area to be fished.
There they were placed on a suitable rock surface and
pounded thoroughly just before use. Divers stuffed the
pounded fibers into an underwater cave which had been
sealed earlier to trap the fish inside. After a few
minutes, the dead fish were retrieved from the cave;
the poison did not affect the fish as human food if
the fish were properly cleaned.

Snaring

Eels and lobsters were often caught by snaring.
A noose on a pole was placed in front of an eel hole
and bait was placed outside; when the eel stuck its
head outside the hole and through the noose to get the
bait, the noose was drawn tight and the eel brought to
the surface with the pole. To snare lobster, a noose
attached to a long pole with a forked end was lowered
near bait, and the line was slipped under the tail of
the lobster.

Spearing

Fish spears were about 6 feet long (2 meters), made
of a hard wood, and used underwater by a diver who positioned himself on the bottom and impaled fish on the
spear as they came close. It was possible to spear more
than one fish per dive by allowing the fish to slip down
the spear after they were pierced. Use of spears above
the surface of the water was restricted to spearing
turtles, octopi, and fish mesmerized by torchlight at
night in shallow water.

Basket Traps

Relatively few basket traps were made, and most
were used by women to catch shrimp and fish in shallow
water. The traps were woven from fresh vines or flexible branches into box-shaped designs. In one common
technique, a simple basket was lowered to the bottom
in shallow water, often with a bait of pounded shrimp
inside; when fish entered the trap, a woman watching
nearby would dive to bring the trap to the surface. A
more sophisticated version had a conical woven entry
protruding into the interior where it terminated in an
opening only large enough for a fish to squeeze through.
The trap, baited with seaweed, ripe breadfruit, or
cooked sweet potatoes, was lowered to the bottom, and
when fish entered by the conical entry they were unable
to find their way back out again.

Nets

Gill Nets

Gill nets were designed to entangle the fish in a
net with a fairly large mesh instead of merely trapping
them within an encircling small-mesh net wall, as was
done with seines and bag nets. Gill nets were made in
different sizes according to the type of fish to be
caught and the inshore habitat to be exploited. Three

basic techniques were used in gill netting: (1) letting
the net remain stationary and allowing the fish to entangle themselves in the mesh; (2) driving the fish into
a stationary net; or (3) moving the gill net to encircle
the fish and then scaring them into the entangling mesh.

Seine Nets

A Hawaiian seine was a net deployed in shallow water
and moved horizontally, trapping fish by impounding them
within a complete circle formed by the net, or between
the net and the shoreline. The fish were not normally
entangled in the mesh as with a gill net, but rather
were kept within a small circle by the net wall where
they could be scooped out with small bag nets or dragged
bodily onshore, net and all. A bag net was often used
in conjunction with a seine; this combination will be
discussed later.

Bag Nets

Bag nets were made into enclosed purses with only
one open end, usually held open by flexible sticks; or
alternately they were flat pieces of netting that were
closed into self-contained bags by manipulating attached
flexible sticks in a particular manner to seal them.
Bag nets were extensively used in conjunction with
seines, as well as by themselves in specialized techniques. Bag nets used alone were more important than
either gill nets or seines used alone and were either
hand-held or manipulated by attached ropes.

Baits were often used to attract fish into the
bag nets. Common baits were cooked sweet potatoes;
kukui and coconut meat; raw mashed bananas, breadfruit,
or taro; pounded up fish, sea urchins, shrimp, or eels;
whole small fish; or a special mixture called *palu* which
was the cooked ink bag of the octopus pounded into a
paste with ingredients added, such as the juices of
various plants. These different baits were often mixed

with sand to make the bait sink, and then placed in the
water near the bag net, as well as inside it, to attract
fish. When the fish were inside the bag, it was lifted
to the surface by the attached ropes.

Seine/Bag Net Combinations

When bag nets were used with seines, the bag was
laced in the center between two seine net sections, so
that each seine net formed a long wing on each side of
the bag and served to channel or direct the fish into
the bag. Long ropes with dried ti or convolvulus leaves
lashed to them by their stems were often tied to the
ends of the seine nets. These bushy ropes, called *lau*,
served to drive the fish ahead when the leaves swirled
and waved in the water, creating threatening shadows
that frightened the fish. *Lau* ropes were also used with
seine nets without bags and with bag nets without seines
for the same purpose.

The *lau* ropes were then drawn in such a way as to
force the fish between the seine wings and toward the
bag. When the encircling *lau* was drawn toward the bag
tightly enough, the fish were driven into it by fishermen who beat the water; the bag was then drawn up and
the fish removed.

Fishhooks and Line

Fishing with hook and line was done in two basic
ways: (1) surface trolling with a lure, and (2) subsurface angling with bait or lure.

Surface Trolling with Lure

Surface trolling was carried out in offshore
waters with a special pearl-shell lure attached by a
12-foot (4-meter) line to a bamboo pole and manipulated
by a fisherman in a canoe. A school of offshore carnivorous surface-feeding fish, usually tuna, was first

located, and the canoe was carefully positioned ahead of
the school in the direction the fish were feeding. Sometimes small, live bait fish were taken from a special
baitbox lashed to the canoe and thrown overboard to
attract the fish. When the school of tuna neared the
canoe, the paddlers kept the canoe in, or quite near,
the school while the fisherman stood erect in the stern
and slapped the lure smartly on the water behind the
canoe and then skittered it across the surface to imi-
tate the small fish upon which the tuna were feeding.
When a fish struck the lure, the fisherman would jerk
the pole to set the lure hook and lift the fish out of
the water, catching it momentarily under his arm to
extract the lure before dropping the fish into the
canoe and casting again. This type of fishing had to
be done swiftly for the school soon moved away.

Subsurface Angling with Bait

Subsurface angling was done with a pole and line
in shallow water, and with hand lines for deep-water
bottom fishing. The baits used were the same as those
listed under bag net baits. Some were attached directly
to the hook, while the *palu* bait was merely rubbed on
the hook; often a bag of bait was lowered near the
baited hooks and released underwater.

Deep-water bottom fishing: Deep-water bottom fishing used a rig of multiple incurved hooks attached by
short leaders to the main 3/8-inch (1.7-centimeter) fish
line at intervals close to the bottom. Each short line
with the hook attached was supported by a section of
coconut midrib lashed perpendicular to the main fish
line which served to keep the multiple hooks separated
from one another and from the main line. Figure 1
illustrates this technique. These rigs were used to
tap the benthic habitat at depths of up to 1,200 feet
(350 meters), catching deep-water fish such as snappers.

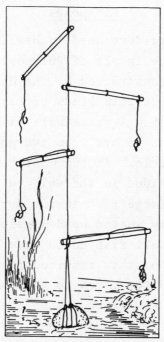

Fig. 1. Deep-water bottom fishing rig.

Pole, line, and hook techniques: Poles were used
in catching tuna with a pearl-shell lure but not in
exploiting deep-water or benthic areas, where hand lines
were used. Evidently much inshore subsurface fishing
was also practiced with hook, line, and pole, using
baits of crushed sea urchins, crabs, shrimp, or *palu* to
catch shallow-water fish.

Subsurface angling with a lure for octopus: A
special octopus lure was made by opposing a specially
prepared cowry shell with a shaped stone weight; the
two were lashed to a short, wooden shank which had a
bone hook tied to its distal end, covered with a skirt
of ti leaves. The lure was lowered to the bottom and
jiggled up and down to attract an octopus; when the
octopus wrapped his tentacles around the cowry shell,
the line was hauled up to bring the octopus to the
surface where it was killed with a club.

Fishponds

Fishponds were developed in Hawaii, where they
appear to be unique in all of Polynesia. These salt-
water ponds were constructed by the Hawaiians to act as
holding areas for certain kinds of fish, principally
mullet and milkfish. A stone wall was constructed in
shallow-water areas to arc from two points on the shore
in a large semicircle. In the most common type several
openings were provided in the wall to allow for water
changes, and the large fish inside were prevented from
escaping by closely spaced wooden poles within these
wall openings. Small fish could move freely through
these barriers; when they remained inside too long,
however, they grew too large to get out again. Ample
food for the fish was grown inside the ponds, or else
the fish were fed by the Hawaiians. When fish were
required, nets were used to catch them.

This technique is in fact a form of marine farming
or aquaculture. Other styles of fishponds served more
as fish traps, in that the fish were not continually
raised or stored inside, but rather were trapped and
used immediately when they had wandered inside the
structure.

Summary

The techniques used by the Hawaiians to exploit
the sea included fishing with hook and line by both
surface trolling and subsurface angling, netting, spearing, hand catching, poisoning, snaring, and the use of
basket traps. These are essentially pursuit techniques,
whereby the Hawaiian actively sought to catch and immediately use the sea creatures. On the other hand,
most fishponds involved raising crops of fish which
were essentially stored until needed by the Hawaiians
for food.

Those parts of the Hawaiian marine ecosystem that were affected by the use of these cultural techniques are described below.

THE HAWAIIAN MARINE ECOSYSTEM

The Hawaiian marine ecosystem may be described in many ways, but this discussion is limited to those aspects which regulated Hawaiian exploitation practices. Only the southeastern one-third of the entire island chain is considered, since the northwestern portion was uninhabited except for marginal settlements at Necker and Nihoa islands. This limits the geographical coverage to the major islands--Niihau, Kauai, Oahu, Molokai, Lanai, Maui, Kahoolawe, and Hawaii.

Topography

A geographical parameter of major import comprises the volcanic processes by which these islands were built up from the ocean bottom. Underwater volcanic lava flows consolidated to form relatively steep-sided bases for all of the Hawaiian islands, bases built up through some 15,000 feet (4,600 meters) of water. These island bases are less than about 150 miles (250 kilometers) in width at the bottom, yielding an average underwater slope of about 2,000 feet per mile (400 meters per kilometer). The steep underwater gradient creates a very narrow band of shallow water surrounding each island, a factor of major importance in Hawaiian fishing.

Data have been presented to show that the maximum depth to which the Hawaiians were able to fish was about 1,200 feet (350 meters) below the surface; the water area of the Hawaiian Islands of depths less than this figure is extremely limited.

Basic Marine Habitats

The effect of this limited shallow-water area on
the marine biota is seen in the division of the waters
surrounding the Hawaiian Islands into three basic habitat types--the pelagic, benthic, and inshore areas--
each with its characteristic fauna. The pelagic habitat,
quite uniform in temperature and salinity, ranges from
the surface to perhaps 600 feet (200 meters) in depth
and is located in the open sea offshore from the islands
(Gosline and Brock 1965:6). Comparatively few species
of fish are found in the pelagic habitat, and those
exploited by the Hawaiians were surface-feeding carnivores such as tuna, albacore, and barracuda. There is
also an inshore pelagic (neritic) zone, defined by
Gosline and Brock (1965:7) as the upper water layers
where the total depth is less than about 600 feet (200
meters). In this subzone are often found the usual
pelagic species as well as others restricted to this
zone.

The benthic, or bottom, habitat, is the sea floor
at depths from about 180 to 900 feet (60 to 300 meters)
in which the fish fauna is only poorly known (Gosline
and Brock 1965:7).

The inshore or reef habitat extends from the above-
surface splash and surge pools to a depth of about 180
feet (55 meters) (Gosline and Brock 1965:5). As noted
above, this area is quite limited in extent in the
Hawaiian Islands because of the steepness of the underwater base. Only in embayed areas, such as Kaneohe
Bay on Oahu, does the horizontal extent of the zone
exceed one-half mile (0.8 kilometers). The largest
marine biomass (weight of all living creatures) is
found in this inshore habitat, and it was the habitat
most extensively exploited by Hawaiians.

Reefs

A second factor of great importance is that reef-
protected areas are not common in Hawaiian waters.
Shallow-water areas where coral is dominant were found
in only about one-third of the areas surveyed by the
Hawaiian Fish and Game Division during submarine fish
transects (Gosline and Brock 1965:8). The only barrier
reef found in the Hawaiian Islands is a small one in
Kaneohe Bay, Oahu; the other reefs are of a discontinuous fringing type, varying in presence, size, and depth
by geographic position (Moberly and Chamberlain 1964:
10-11). Yet reefs were areas of major maritime exploitation. Since the distribution and physical characteristics of reefs largely control the types of marine
fauna in an area, the Hawaiian exploitation practices
were closely linked to the type and location of reefs.

Wave Action and Habitats

Another major environmental factor affecting
Hawaiian exploitation practices was wave action, a
primary habitat parameter for much of the Hawaiian
marine biota (Gosline and Brock 1965:10-13; Gosline
1965). Four vertical habitats may be delimited in the
inshore area on the basis of wave action: the supra-
surge zone, the surge zone, the reef-protected zone,
and the subsurge zone (Gosline and Brock 1965:10-15).

The supra-surge zone lies above mean water level
and consists of pools filled by spray or intermittent
wave action. Few fish exploited by the Hawaiians live
in the supra-surge zone, although it was probably a
major shellfish exploitation zone. The surge zone
itself is an area with much horizontal water movement
through wave action. The surge zone extends from the
surface to some 10 to 25 feet (3 to 8 meters) in depth
in protected areas, and down to over 65 feet (20 meters)

in exposed areas. The calm subsurge zone has the
largest fish population; the distinction between the
surge zone and the top of the subsurge zone is quite
marked on a populational basis. The reef-protected
zone is likewise a calm-water area of great fish biomass, distinct from the subsurge zone primarily in
depth.

Swell Systems

The inshore vertical habitats described above vary
in size and distribution on the basis of the swell system involved, for the swell systems striking the islands
differ in azimuth, intensity, and periodicity.

Swells in Hawaii consist of four broad types: (1)
the northeast trade waves, (2) the southern swell, (3)
the North Pacific swell, and (4) the Kona storm waves
(Moberly, Baver, and Morrison 1965:590). These wave
systems are caused primarily by surface-wind patterns
which, in turn, are controlled on a seasonal basis by
meteorological pressure cycles. Various combinations
of these wave systems may be present at any one time,
but generally the dominant system during the months of
April to November is the northeast trade swell. This
system is present from 90 to 95 percent of the time
from April to November and from 55 to 65 percent of
the time from December to March (Chamberlain 1968:181).
It impinges on the northeast or windward coastline,
producing strong and consistent wave action resulting
in a windward enlargement of the supra-surge and surge
biotic zones. For example, the *'opihi* (Patellidae)
is a shellfish particularly adapted to the supra-surge
zone (cf. Kay 1969); it is noticeably more prevalent
along rocky windward coastlines.

The southern swell is felt in Hawaii about 53
percent of the time from April through October, striking
exposed southern and southwestern coasts. Kona storm
waves are short-term waves generated by low-pressure

storm systems near Hawaii; they roll in from the south
and southwest some 9 percent of the year, usually during
the winter months. The North Pacific swell is produced
by storms in the northern Pacific and is responsible,
often, for the largest waves to reach Hawaii. These
waves occur primarily from October to May along northeast to northwest exposures (Chamberlain 1968:181-182).
These last three wave systems are not as constant as
the northeast trade-wind swell system and have less
effect in producing large and consistent supra-surge
and surge habitats. They are important because they
transform inshore bottom habitats by a periodic movement of sand deposits (Chamberlain 1968).

These different swell systems cause a horizontal
zonation around the islands on the basis of swell
action. The largest, most consistent, and generally
highest-energy-packed waves flow against the windward
(eastern) coastline while swell action is much less
pronounced along leeward (western) shores.

Upwelling

Wind action over the leeward shore probably also
results in the production of minor upwelling, generating
vertical currents by surface friction, bringing up the
colder and nutrient-laden lower waters. Although this
phenomenon is most pronounced along the leeward coasts
of continental land masses (Ryther 1969:73), it quite
likely occurs along the leeward coast of the Hawaiian
Islands as a "micro-upwelling" condition and makes a
horizontal differential in available nutrients between
the leeward and windward areas.

Biomass Differential between Leeward and Windward Sides

There is a distinct possibility that a biomass
differential exists between the windward and leeward
sides of the islands which may be explained in part by

upwelling. Direct support for this thesis, moreover,
comes from the observation of Gosline (1965:829) that
relatively few carnivores are to be found in areas
affected by wave or surge action; rather they are found
in the deeper, unaffected waters where they presumably
have a larger trophic-level biomass upon which to feed.
Since more of the relatively short, shallow-water slope
of the island base is taken up with supra-surge and
surge zones on the windward sides, it would seem reasonable to assume that a larger subsurge zone exists
on the leeward side, and hence more carnivores. Obviously, where more predators are present there must be
a larger supporting lower trophic-level biomass upon
which they feed.

Second, the total number of species present is
greater in the subsurge zone than in the surge zone,
and although this is not a direct measure of biomass,
it is indicative. The long-term pounding of the trade-
wind swell system against the windward coast results in
a further reduction of the windward total shallow-water
zone, causing a lower marine biomass to windward.

Finally, the leeward waters of Molokai, Maui,
Lanai, and Kahoolawe are remnants of a once-contiguous
island mass, since submerged, leaving relatively shallow
water saddles between these islands. This shallow area
is windward of Lanai and Kahoolawe, but these islands
are relatively well sheltered from trade-wind effects
by the mountains of Molokai and Maui.

Historical studies also show that most fishing
tended to take place along the leeward coastlines,
although this may have been due also, in part, to the
difficulties of fishing in the rough waters of the
windward shore. For example, little fishing was described by Ellis (1963) for the windward coastline of
Hawaii Island in 1823, while it was a very important
activity in leeward areas.

Bottom Conditions

Other biotic marine zonation occurs in Hawaii on the basis of underwater topography and bottom conditions. Each type of bottom, such as sandy, muddy, silty, coralline, or rocky, supports a distinctive assemblage of both fish and invertebrates. This is most pronounced with shellfish, of which gastropods are generally found under clear, unsilted conditions while lamellibranchs (bivalves or pelecypods) are primarily adapted to silty and more polluted conditions (Doty 1968:15).

Summary

Distributions of marine biota and the corresponding Hawaiian sea exploitive techniques appear to have been regulated by a combination of water depth, bottom morphology, and wave action generated by surface wind patterns.

With these data of the Hawaiian marine ecosystem, it is now possible to note the ways in which that ecosystem acted to channel and restrict Hawaiian exploitive techniques.

EFFECTS OF THE HAWAIIAN MARINE ECOSYSTEM ON HAWAIIAN EXPLOITIVE TECHNIQUES

Inshore Exploitation

An analysis of the marine zones in which marine organisms normally are found shows a pronounced correlation between habitat and exploitive technique. The inshore habitat was exploited by subsurface angling with pole, line, and fishhooks for fish within the surge and portions of the subsurge zones, while octopus was taken by hand line and cowry-shell lure from the subsurge zone. Only gill nets primarily tapped the surge

and reef-protected zones; seine/bag combinations were
able to exploit the subsurge zone to a depth of about
50 feet (15 meters) through the use of *lau* ropes to
drive the fish into the shallower surge and reef-
protected zones where the fish could be surrounded by
the seine and forced into the central bag. The surge
zone and upper portions of the subsurge zone were
exploited by divers hand-collecting fish, crustacea,
molluscs, and echinoderms, and sometimes using spears,
hand-held small bag nets, or poison. Basket traps and
snares were used in the surge and reef-protected zones,
and in portions of the subsurge zone. Molluscs, crustacea, fish, echinoderms, and seaweed were collected
by hand from the tidal pools, supra-surge zone, and
shallow-water surge zones from above the surface. Spears
and hand-held bag nets were similarly used in shallow-
water areas, particularly at night, to collect fish and
octopi.

The inshore area has the largest biomass; the greatest number of different exploitation techniques were
used within it; and it was the primary maritime exploitation zone of the Hawaiians.

Bottom Fishing

The lower limits of the subsurge zone of the inshore
area and the beginning of the benthic zone are poorly
defined by marine biologists and also in the exploitation
practices of the Hawaiians. At a depth of about 15 feet
(5 meters) hand-line fishing with baited hooks replaced
pole and line fishing.

Benthic Exploitation

Bottom exploitation by hand lines continued from
a depth of about 15 feet (5 meters) throughout the inshore area and into the benthic habitat to a maximum
depth of about 1,200 feet (350 meters). There was no

apparent exploitation of the middle portion of the
benthic and pelagic zones, between about 25 feet (8
meters) below the surface to 25 feet (8 meters) above
the bottom. The fish caught in the benthic zone were
primarily various types of large snappers and groupers;
it may well be that a reasonably large biomass exists
in this habitat.

Pelagic Exploitation

The transition between the inshore area and the
pelagic zone is similarly indistinct, for some generally
pelagic fish are found quite close to the shore at times.
Gosline and Brock (1965) recognized this problem from a
zoological standpoint and defined the surface waters
inshore of about the 600-foot (200 meter) depth as the
inshore pelagic zone. This distinction is immaterial
to this paper, for the true pelagic zone generally
occurs within one-half mile (0.8 kilometers) of the shore
in Hawaii, and although it is reasonable to expect some
use of trolling gear in the more inshore area, it must
undoubtedly have been the predominant technique for
exploiting the pelagic zone. Other techniques were
variations of surface fish-drives into bag nets. In
any case, only the upper 25 feet (8 meters) of the
pelagic zone were exploited by the Hawaiians. Furthermore, although the pelagic zone extends indefinitely
across the ocean as its upper water area, it is unlikely
that the Hawaiians ventured far offshore in their pelagic fishing.

Horizontal Limits to Pelagic Fishing

Bait fish are quite delicate and tend to die rather
quickly in the bait tanks of modern tuna boats, and
much the same problem would probably have occurred with
the Hawaiian bait box. It would be expected that every
effort was made to fish as close to the source of the

bait supply as possible, not only because of the short
bait life, but also because of the need to replenish
the supply.

Also, although schools of pelagic fish are to be
found scattered over the ocean, the signs by which these
schools can be located are seen more commonly near shore.
For instance, flocks of birds circling over feeding tuna
schools signaled the presence of the schools to the
Hawaiian fishermen. Drifting flotsam and jetsam attract
pelagic fish (Gooding and Magnuson 1967), and it would
be expected that such floating materials would be more
common close to the islands and would have served as
signals for fish concentrations. Finally, the size of
the canoes would have limited the amount of bait that
could be carried and also the amount of fish that could
be brought home.

In essence, what is suggested is that although the
pelagic zone is practically boundless, the Hawaiians
most likely exploited only the zone fairly near the
islands, probably to a distance of no more than 5 or
10 miles (8 to 16 kilometers) offshore.

Hawaiian Emphasis on Pelagic Fishing

The role of pelagic fishing in Hawaiian subsistence
patterns has been emphasized by many authors, but it
would appear from this study that pelagic fishing was
of tertiary importance--behind the exploitation of
both benthic and inshore areas. This spectacular technique seems to have caught the attention of the early
observers, who described it as a major fishing technique. In terms of consistent food supply, however,
it is a reasonable conclusion that inshore was the
primary area, followed by the benthic. Although the
yield would be high for successful fishing trips in
the pelagic area, the yield would be completely unpredictable for several reasons:

1.   Tuna, the primary fish taken, occur in schools which move continually (tuna must move to respire, and so they never stop); hence the precise location of a school could not be predicted.

2.   Only those schools associated with drifting objects or birds could normally be located from a distance, which eliminated all schools unassociated with these signs except for chance sightings.

3.   Even when a school was located, it might not have been possible for a canoe to reach it, for tuna swim at a speed of 0.6 to 13.9 miles per hour (0.3 to 6.9 meters per second) (Manar 1966:8); and even if fishing began in a school, this same speed might have caused the canoe to lose the school before many fish were caught.

4.   When a school was overtaken and fishing began, often only about 50 percent of the schools would bite (Uchida 1966:148).

5.   Schools are composed of fish of the same size (Nakamura 1967:3), and a school of small tuna will yield a lower biomass than a school of big tuna because the time required to land a large tuna is about the same as for a small one, and the fishermen had perhaps 10 to 15 minutes in which to work before the school outdistanced the canoe. It is suggested that, as a means of obtaining food, fishing for tuna or other pelagic fish was only supplementary to inshore and benthic habitat exploitation or to use of land foods. There is a possibility that it was limited to those who could afford to take the chance of not catching any-thing--either the higher socioeconomic levels of Hawaiian society whose food was obtained through the efforts of lower-ranking people, or those with adequate food supplies from other sources.

This argument is an extension of what ecologists term "Liebig's Law," which simply states that a population is limited by whatever necessary component occurs in minimal quantity (Liebig 1965:12-14). Obviously a population cannot exceed its food supply for long without a population reduction, and hence not only is quantity of food important, but its predictability or consistency of availability is critically important. If food supplies oscillate widely over a long period of time, the population will tend to reach stability at the largest number that can be supported with the minimal level of food during the period. Thus, although large catches of tuna might occur, it would never be a major source of food to maintain a population because of the unpredictability of the catch. Not only is tuna unpredictable in fishing, it is also a seasonal resource, for the tuna migration arrives primarily during the summer months in Hawaii.

Hawaiian Maritime Econiches

These marine zones are not human habitats, for habitat literally means the place of residence, or where an organism is found (Odum 1959:27). Man's habitat must have air, and this eliminates the sea for the Hawaiians; but the sea is a human econiche. The econiche is an ecological concept that carries the association of both location and behavior; thus, although man does not live in the sea, the Hawaiians did exploit various portions of it, and these may be termed human econiches. Figure 2 illustrates the Hawaiian maritime econiches for A.D. 1800 that were derived from this study.

Summary

In summary, the Hawaiians depended primarily on relatively stable inshore resources which yielded a high and consistent biomass through the use of diverse exploitive techniques. Practically every available culturally acceptable and sufficiently nutritive marine

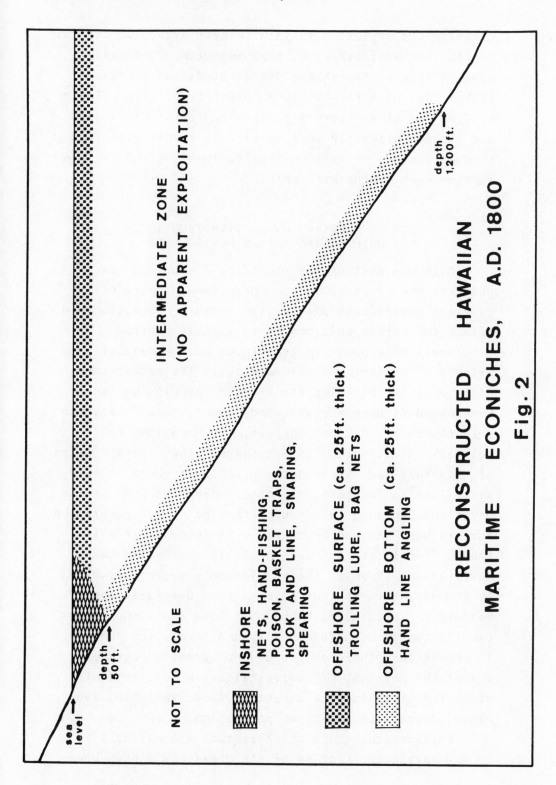

sea level

depth 50 ft.

depth 1,200 ft.

INTERMEDIATE ZONE
(NO APPARENT EXPLOITATION)

NOT TO SCALE

INSHORE
NETS, HAND-FISHING,
POISON, BASKET TRAPS,
HOOK AND LINE, SNARING,
SPEARING

OFFSHORE SURFACE (ca. 25 ft. thick)
TROLLING LURE, BAG NETS

OFFSHORE BOTTOM (ca. 25 ft. thick)
HAND LINE ANGLING

RECONSTRUCTED HAWAIIAN
MARITIME ECONICHES, A.D. 1800

Fig. 2

organism was exploited in this inshore area. The benthic
habitat was most likely of next importance and was exploited solely through the use of hand-line angling
techniques, primarily to take larger fish. The pelagic
habitat was of tertiary significance to the Hawaiians
and yielded primarily surface-feeding carnivorous fish
through the use of surface-trolled lures, although some
species were caught with nets.

EFFECT OF HAWAIIAN EXPLOITIVE TECHNIQUES
ON THE HAWAIIAN MARINE ENVIRONMENT

Although most of the preceding discussion has emphasized the constraining or channeling effects of the
Hawaiian environment on Hawaiian culture, Hawaiians did
affect the marine environment to a small degree.

Hawaiian exploitive techniques were essentially
methods of capturing marine creatures for rather immediate use. Maintaining the Hawaiian population level
was dependent upon a stable food supply, and, where the
sole source of food was the sea, the Hawaiians could
not fish out a section of the sea or otherwise sterilize
it. If they did, their own population numbers necessarily had to decrease. In other words, as long as the
Hawaiians depended solely upon the sea, their population
numbers were limited by the food resources available
there. The first Hawaiians probably reached an uneasy
equilibrium, wherein the population supported itself
by the marine foods available without degrading those
resources. Naturally, there must have been some minor
oscillation in both food supply and population numbers.
The Hawaiians, therefore, could not greatly degrade
either the physical or biological marine environment
without diminishing the amount of food available, and,
hence, decreasing their own population.

Furthermore, it is unlikely that all marine life
in any particular section of the coast could have been

completely eliminated by the Hawaiians--at least not
for long. Most marine creatures exploited are mobile
at least during some stages in their life history, and
they tend rapidly to reenter an area where a population
has been eliminated.

Nor did the cultural techniques of the Hawaiians
include any that could cause significant changes in
the marine ecosystem. The early Hawaiians had no chemicals with which to greatly pollute the waters, no
earth-moving equipment to alter the coastline, and
neither the need nor the technology to blast new harbors
or create marinas.

The only major way in which the Hawaiians affected
the marine ecosystem was through the construction of
fishponds in shallow-water areas. These ponds acted
as settling basins where materials from the land formed
muddy or silty bottom areas.

HAWAIIAN LAND EXPLOITATION

By contrast, the effect of the Hawaiian on the
land was very important, for significant biological
and abiotic changes occurred because of Hawaiian farming practices.

Hawaiian agriculture was based on root and tree
crops, primarily taro, sweet potatoes, and breadfruit.
Additional food was obtained from other domesticated
plants, such as arrowroot, sugarcane, pandanus, and
yams. The primary farming implement was the digging
stick, a type of tool most often associated elsewhere
with extensive instead of intensive land exploitation
(Boserup 1965). In Hawaii, however, this simple tool
was part of a sophisticated farming technology efficiently using natural resources such as surface water
for irrigation, soil and/or rocks for banking both
flooded and unflooded fields, dead vegetable matter
for fertilizer, and field-boundary vegetation for wind

protection and water retention (Newman 1970). Hawaiian farming practices involved both irrigated and unirrigated fields, or what could be called wet and dry farming.

Irrigated Farming

Taro was the only irrigated crop grown in pre-European Hawaii, but not all taro was grown in this manner. Irrigated taro was raised in rectangular fields, usually about 30 by 60 feet (10 by 20 meters) in size, with earthen embankments surrounding all sides to retain the water. These fields had to be located near running surface water and usually had small drainage channels connecting the fields to the water source.

Hawaiian irrigated taro fields resembled Asian rice paddies in general form and in many of the techniques of their use. Taro was planted and periodically flooded during its growing period. Sometimes a slow but continual water flow was maintained through the fields, keeping the taro flooded at all times. *Hau (Hibiscus tiliaceus)* limbs were occasionally thrown into the fields to act as organic fertilizer.

Irrigated field systems were often extensive and elaborate, often stepped down valley bottoms and even down sloping valley sides. The amount of manpower necessary to establish these fields was enormous, as was the labor necessary to maintain them. However, irrigated taro was the most productive of all Hawaiian crops in terms of yield per field area.

Unirrigated Farming

Many crops, such as dry-land taro, sweet potatoes, yams, and breadfruit trees, were not irrigated at all. Some, such as sweet potatoes and taro, were grown within rectangular fields on sloping tablelands. Garden farming was practiced in rocky areas where the plants were scattered asymmetrically throughout. Many plants

were simply grown in forest clearings in an appropriate
area.

Whereas irrigated fields were farmed continuously,
unirrigated fields and growing areas occasionally had
to be allowed to go fallow. This was necessary because
continuous farming of unirrigated lands resulted in the
gradual removal of plant nutrients, which had to be
replenished by allowing the land to rest for perhaps
5 to 10 years. In some areas this simply meant abandon-
ing a growing area when it showed a poor crop return
and clearing a new one, often by fire, from the surrounding forest. In other areas the fields were formal-
ized into field systems, with some fields used while
others lay fallow before being replanted and used again.

Summary

Although the Hawaiian used merely a simple digging
stick to till the soil, he had not only an extensive
knowledge of crop characteristics and the effect of the
Hawaiian environment on their successful growth, but
also the necessary engineering skills to master the
Hawaiian environment to increase crop yields. Different
crops were grown in different areas to take advantage
of favorable environmental conditions. These environmental conditions established limitations on where and
how the Hawaiian food plants could be economically
grown.

THE HAWAIIAN LAND ECOSYSTEM

Geology

Topography

A number of the abiotic factors influencing marine
biota and Hawaiian exploitation patterns were also important environmental parameters of the land ecosystem.

In particular, the nature of island genesis and the
resulting steep underwater slope of the island bases
were major factors in the land ecosystem, for the slope
of the general terrain is also steep. Over 50 percent
of the land in the Hawaiian Islands lies at elevations
in excess of about 2,000 feet (600 meters) above mean
sea level (Blumenstock and Price, this vol.) This single
factor made about half the land area in Hawaii unsuitable for Hawaiian farming techniques because about
2,500 feet (750 meters) was, in general, the upper
elevation limit for Hawaiian agriculture.

Landscape Age

The age of the landscape was another major factor
limiting Hawaiian farming. Irrigated taro cultivation
is dependent upon an adequate and predictable source
of surface water, normally from streams and rivers;
such surface streams are commonly restricted to the
heavily eroded valleys along high rainfall coasts.
There are leeward (western) valleys with surface water,
and broad windward (eastern) valleys only on the older
islands--Kauai, Oahu, and West Maui. On Hawaii, the
youngest island, and newer portions of older islands,
such as East Maui, valleys tend to have been formed
only along the heavy rainfall areas of the windward
coasts. On the very young islands, or on young portions of old islands, if there were irrigated agricultural systems at all they were along the windward
coasts. Thus, irrigated agriculture was found along
the windward coast of Haleakala, Maui, but not on its
leeward side, and in the valleys of windward Kohala,
Hawaii Island, but not on the leeward side. The lower
windward flanks of Mauna Kea, Mauna Loa, and Haleakala
have only small valleys (an indicator of geologic
youthfulness) and probably had some irrigated areas,
but the small size of the valleys alone would prevent
any major population carrying capacity for irrigated crops.

Similarly, the soils of very young land areas are usually quite porous, and virtually no surface water is present except in areas above the 100-inch rainfall line. Thus, although rainfall is quite heavy just to the leeward of the summit in the high regions of Kohala, the surface waters percolate into the soil long before they reach the agricultural areas. Young terrain, therefore, can support only dry-land agriculture along slope or plateau lands.

Climate

Topography and landscape age are important in limiting the nature of Hawaiian land exploitation, but climate is of at least equal importance. The geological processes have provided the raw materials upon which Hawaiian agriculture is based, but it is the climatic factors described by Blumenstock and Price (in this volume) that have molded and changed these raw volcanic materials into soil and have provided adequate moisture, proper temperatures, and suitable sunlight levels to support plant life. These various factors work in concert to determine the nature of the vegetation that can flourish in Hawaii.

Wind Action and Rainfall

Wave action caused by surface wind was of major importance in establishing biotic habitats in the sea. Surface wind patterns also greatly influenced Hawaiian agriculture by delimiting suitable crop habitats through regulating the amount, duration, periodicity, and type of moisture available to specific land areas.

The dominant wind pattern is that of the northeast trade wind which flows over Hawaii during the greater part of the year. This trade wind is usually less than about 10,000 feet (3,000 meters) in thickness, resulting in a sheet of wind moving across the

ocean, while relatively calm air lies above. The trade
wind strikes the coastal areas along the northeastern
shores at a direct azimuth, and the northeast and southeast to south coasts somewhat obliquely. This moisture-
laden air flows onto these coastlines, but the land mass
shelters the opposite leeward coastline from the moist
air. It is the interaction of wind and topography which
induces most of the rain to fall on the windward areas.

Orographic Flow

After flowing onto the land masses along their
windward sides, the trade-wind sheet is lifted by oro-
graphic action to higher altitudes where the wind mass
either moves over the top of the land terrain--in the
case of low-altitude land masses--or splits and flows
around the flanks of the higher masses, such as Mauna
Kea and Mauna Loa on Hawaii Island and Haleakala on
Maui. This action varies with the velocity and thickness of the trade-wind sheet, which sometimes splits
around the lower masses or may even go over the tops
of Mauna Kea, Mauna Loa, and Haleakala.

As the moist air is lifted and its temperature
decreases, the relatively humidity increases to the
point of saturation and rainfall results. If the trade
wind normally flows up and over the high terrain, rainfall is deposited along the entire slope up to the
summit and then for a distance to leeward, this latter
usually in the form of wind-blown showers. If the
trade wind splits to flow around the high mountain
masses, the rainfall increases rapidly with elevation
to approximately 4,000 to 6,000 feet (1,200 to 1,800
meters) and then begins to decrease, leaving extremely
arid conditions in the area above the major trade-wind
flow. This latter phenomenon is restricted to Mauna
Kea, Mauna Loa, and Haleakala, for everywhere else in
the Islands the trade wind generally flows over the
summits of the land masses.

There is great variation in amount, nature, peri-
dicity, and duration of rainfall depending on geographical location in relation to the trade wind and elevation. Hawaiian agriculture was in turn limited by these
factors of moisture.

Rainfall and Soil

The type of soil was evidently not a very important limiting factor in Hawaiian agriculture, for
historical records show crops to have been grown on
every type, from lava to the finest of alluvial soils.
The limiting nature of the soil seems to have been
associated with its nutrient levels, and these are
directly correlated with rainfall. Continuous rains
in windward areas produce leached soils, poor in plant
nutrients. In exceptional cases windward soils are
not poor, for example where alluvial deposits are
constantly added, or where flowing surface streams
were used to irrigate taro paddy soils. Both of these
conditions continually replace plant nutrients, allowing intensive agriculture.

Summary

In summary, the land parameters affecting Hawaiian agriculture were landscape age, topography,
geographical position of the Islands in the Pacific,
geographical position in relation to the trade winds,
and of most importance, the amount, periodicity, and
type of moisture. These factors apply to the Hawaiian Islands in general and Hawaii Island in particular.

EFFECT OF THE HAWAIIAN LAND ECOSYSTEM
ON HAWAIIAN FARMING

The preceding section on the land ecosystem
illustrated many ways in which Hawaiian farming practices were channeled or restricted. These limitations

may be made more specific by focusing on a single
island instead of on all the major islands at once.
This is because the diversity of the land environments
in Hawaii was reflected in regional diversity of Hawaiian farming practices. Not only did agriculture vary
from island to island, but it also varied from section
to section of the same island. The following discussion is limited to Hawaii Island, but much of the
information is applicable to the other islands as well.

Environmental Parameters of Hawaii Island Farming

A study of early journals disclosed a wealth of
information on Hawaii Island farming, including both
practices and crop distributions. These data were
meshed with modern descriptions of the farming areas
to produce a list of major environmental variables
restricting Hawaiian farming (Newman 1970). It was
found that farming areas on Hawaii Island generally
fell within the following parameters:

Clime: Virtually always humid or subhumid;
generally subhumid.

Mean annual rainfall: 20 to 150 inches (0.5 to
4 meters); generally 40 to 80 inches (1 to 2 meters).

Elevation: Sea level to 2,500 feet (750 meters);
windward zones (eastern) vary generally from 200 to
1,000 feet (60 to 300 meters); leeward zones (western)
generally vary from 1,000 to 2,500 feet (300 to 750
meters).

Slope: 0 to 35 percent; usually from 0 to 20
percent.

Drainage: Almost all lands are well drained.

Soil parent material: Almost always volcanic ash.

Soil type: Generally alluvial, reddish brown,
humic latosol or hydrol humic latosol, although reddish
prairie and lithosol may have been included.

These agricultural lands lie as a band around the

lowland sections of the island. The interior sections
and much of the lowland nonagricultural areas are
expanses of barren lava, completely unsuited for agriculture. Although Hawaii Island is the largest of the
Hawaiian Islands, it had little land that was well
suited for aboriginal agriculture.

These agricultural lands encompass a variety of
different subtypes. Differences in agricultural lands
and the accompanying cultural practices appear to be
closely correlated with differences in the type, duration, amount, and periodicity of moisture. These
aspects of moisture are, in turn, controlled by three
broad sets of variables: elevation, topography, and
geographical location in relation to the prevailing
northeastern trade wind (or lowland-upland, valley-
tableland, and windward-leeward). Virtually all other
ecological factors, such as flora, climatology, soils,
and topography, are functions of these three sets of
variables; hence Hawaii Island agriculture was primarily limited by considerations of moisture.

Hawaii Island Agricultural Zones

These broad variables, the environmental characteristics of each agricultural area, and cultural
information derived from historical sources were synthesized into a tentative classification system for
the native Hawaiian agricultural zones on Hawaii Island
(see Fig. 3). The division is made first geographically between valleys and tableland areas, and then culturally between irrigated and dry land farming.

Irrigation (valleys)

Location: Eastern Kohala in Waipio, Waimanu,
Honokane, and Pololu valleys (and possibly small areas
in the little valleys along the Hamakua coast from
Waipio to Hilo).

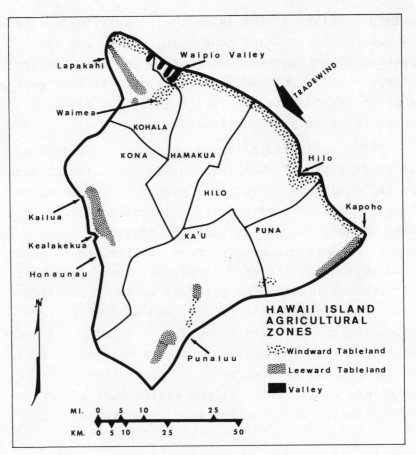

Fig. 3

Demography: Greater population density than occurs in other areas, but a rather low total population in a clustered settlement pattern.

Crops: Irrigated taro, bananas, sugarcane.

Distinctive agricultural practice: Irrigation of taro.

Physical setting: Valley topography, windward location, near 0-degree slope, alluvial soils, 0- to 100-foot (0- to 30-meter) elevation.

Dryland Farming (tableland)

Location: Tableland areas along the lower slopes of Hawaii Island.

Demography: Lower population density than in
valleys or in major coastal fishing villages; settlement pattern was apparently a generally dispersed
arrangement of single-family dwelling areas; there was
little or no clustering into concentrated villages in
the agricultural areas themselves, although such clustering did occur with associated coastal fishing
villages.

Crops: Unirrigated taro, sweet potatoes, bananas,
yams, breadfruit, *olonā* (a fiber plant), sugarcane,
and the paper mulberry.

Distinctive agricultural practices: Sweet potato
and unirrigated taro cropping.

Physical setting: Tableland topography, 100- to
about 2,500-foot (30- to 750-meter) elevation.

Tableland dry farming areas may be further divided
into areas of scattered and somewhat isolated farms
(primarily in the windward regions) and areas of patterned and contiguous fields making up cohesive systems
(generally to leeward).

Scattered Fields

Location: Northeast Kohala, Hamakua coast from
Waipio to Hilo, the Puna coastal strip from Hilo to
Kapoho, sections north of Punaluu, and inland on the
Ka'u-Puna district boundary.

Demography: Less concentration of population in
the agricultural areas than in areas of field systems,
and with few fishing villages on the coast (except
possibly for parts of the Puna area). The settlement
pattern was characterized by scattered fields or
gardens with isolated small villages or family habitations.

Crops: Same as the general dry land farming type.

Distinctive agricultural practices: Scattered
fields, gardens and habitations; generally less

intensive cultivation of available land. No major
field systems.

Physical setting: Tableland topography, generally
windward location, 100- to 2,500-foot (30- to 750-
meter) elevation.

Field Systems

Location: West Kohala, an area to the west of
Waimea, the Kona coast from Kailua to Honaunau, the
Ka'u area to the west and another to the north of
Punaluu, and possibly portions of the Puna coast south-
west of Kapoho.

Demography: Fairly dense population along the
coast, particularly in fishing villages associated with
inland agricultural field systems. The density was
greater in both the coastal villages and the inland
agricultural areas than occurred in the scattered farm
area (generally to windward), but probably less dense
than in the valleys where irrigated agriculture was
practiced.

Crops: Same as the general dry land farming
category.

Distinctive agricultural practices: Massive field
systems in contradistinction to the scattered fields
generally found to windward. The Kohala system, for
example, measures about 2 by 13 miles (3 by 21 kilometers), and the Kona system measures about 3 by 18
miles (5 by 30 kilometers).

Physical setting: Tableland topography, generally
leeward location, 1,000- to 2,500-foot (300- to 750-
meter) elevation.

Conclusions

This section provides an outline of the environmental factors characteristic of native Hawaiian
agricultural zones. Certain other conclusions of a

more general nature may also be drawn from these data:

1. In areas of field systems, the agricultural zones seem to have been larger and contributed to a greater population.

2. The particular crops grown in an area were most dependent upon the moisture available, its quantity, and periodicity. These factors, in turn, were dependent upon the geographical location of the area in terms of three pairs of variables: windward-leeward location, lowland-upland elevation, and table-land-valley topography.

3. The geographical areas most intensively cultivated by the Hawaiians are not those most intensively cultivated today. Leeward areas with massive field systems were the largest native agricultural areas, but today the West Kohala and Ka'u areas are pasture lands, while the Kona system is only partially under coffee cultivation. On the other hand, the most extensive sugarcane cultivation in the entire State today lies between Waipio Valley and Hilo, where only scattered fields were under Hawaiian culture. The controlling factor seems to be the ability of modern farming to use machinery and provide the necessary fertilizers to supplement the water-rich but leached windward soils. The Kona system lies in an area that is difficult to cultivate with modern mechanized methods because of sloping, uneven terrain, and has been agriculturally abandoned except for coffee, a non-machine crop.

4. The impression is given in the general literature on Hawaiian farming that large-scale irrigation systems existed throughout the Islands and that the primary dependence was on irrigated taro. Very few sources even mention nonirrigated farming. However, the most important native agricultural areas of Hawaii Island were not those that were irrigated, but rather

the leeward field systems. Irrigation may have been
dominant on the other islands, but Hawaii Island must
be exempted from this generalization.

Summary

The Hawaiian land ecosystem is clearly seen to
have placed restrictions on Hawaiian farming practices.
On Hawaii Island these environmental parameters limited
the production of native crops by Hawaiian agricultural
practices to only certain land areas.

EFFECT OF HAWAIIAN FARMING PRACTICES
ON THE HAWAIIAN LAND ENVIRONMENT

Unlike the minimal effect of sea exploitation
practices on the Hawaiian marine ecosystem, the Hawaiian
farming practices wrought dramatic and far-reaching
changes in the land ecosystem.

The general botanical information available seems
to indicate that forests were much more extensive before
the Hawaiians arrived. In many areas these forests
would originally have extended well down into the areas
developed by the Hawaiians for agriculture during their
occupation of these islands. If this is indeed the
case, then these forests were extensively cleared to
prepare the land for planting the Hawaiian crops. Such
deforestation would have resulted in certain predictable changes in the land.

Effects of Deforestation

The most obvious change which occurs with deforestation, or forest reduction, is a shift in plant
community constitution as new floral successions begin.
A reduction of forest cover increases the amount of
solar radiation reaching the soil; soil moisture is
lowered (Thornthwaite 1956:578; Albrecht 1956:651);
soil chemistry is altered (Raikes 1967:77; Bartlett

1956:697); soil structure collapses (Blaut 1960:194);
soil permeability is reduced, resulting in less retention of surface water, faster run-off, and a lower water
table (Sears 1956:478-479; Raikes 1967:68). Topsoil is
then carried off by sheet or gully erosion (Leopold
1956:639; Strahler 1956:623). This topsoil loss results
in lowered nutritive levels of the soil and reduces the
carrying capacity for the land (Albrecht 1956:672).

Microclimatic Changes

Changes in microclimatic conditions are also caused
by deforestation, which increases wind velocity by
removing surface friction and the superstructure that
kept the winds aloft. Increased wind velocities decrease soil and atmospheric moisture, especially when
coupled with increased surface temperatures resulting
from greater solar penetration. The elimination of
trees decreases the amount of moisture returned to the
atmosphere through plant respiration--often a very
substantial amount of water (Mangenot 1963:119). The
direct interception of atmospheric moisture by trees
is well documented in Hawaii (Ekern 1964), and this
water source would be lost by deforestation. The role
of Hawaiian vegetation and microclimatic conditions
is discussed by Egler as follows:

> Hosaka . . . writes that he has often ob-
> served the rain clouds sweep over the
> Koolau range at Waipio, disappearing at
> the native forest edge, except where they
> continue in a mile-long tongue out over
> the Eucalyptus plantations. In conclu-
> sion, it may be said that no meteorologic
> data exist in Hawaii to indicate any in-
> fluence of the vegetation on climate. In
> the opinion of the writer, however, and
> as indicated by Hosaka's observations, the
> influence of the vegetation on the absorp-
> tion and retention of radiant energy,
> together with the influence of transpira-
> tion on the moisture content and tempera-
> ture combine to determine whether or not

> oncoming currents of air will or will not
> lose the moisture which they bear . . . .
> Historic evidence of springs and of Hawai-
> ian villages in areas now arid imply
> strongly that desiccation has occurred in
> the past . . . .[1947:402]

Once the forests were cleared for farming still
other changes would have occurred. Fields were prepared
by reshaping the face of the land with digging sticks--
perhaps as much as 100 square miles of the Hawaii Island
sloping tablelands were totally churned up as field
systems were developed. Surface streams were diverted
and channeled through irrigated taro fields. Native
plants were prevented from re-entering the fields by
the Hawaiians, who ensured that only their crops would
grow there. Continual production of crops on the same
land areas resulted in the gradual depletion of plant
nutrients and eventually necessitated the cessation of
farming on these lands. These fallowed lands tended
initially to support a growth of grasses. Thus, grass-
lands in Hawaii extended in concert with this fallowing
practice, resulting in their great extent as noted by
the early explorers in Hawaii.

CONCLUSION

This paper has shown the many ways in which Hawaiian cultural patterns and the Hawaiian ecosystem affected one another before the arrival of the Europeans. The
introduction of Hawaiian culture into this island ecosystem merely added another ingredient to that ecosystem. The Hawaiian and his culture were not separate
from nature in Hawaii but were part of it. Each part
influenced, and was influenced by, the rest of the
Hawaiian ecosystem.

REFERENCES

Albrecht, William A. 1956. Physical, chemical, and biochemical changes in the soil community. In William L. Thomas, Jr., ed., Man's role in changing the face of the earth, p. 648-676. University of Chicago Press.

Bartlett, H. H. 1956. Fire, primitive agriculture, and grazing in the tropics. In William L. Thomas, Jr., ed., Man's role in changing the face of the earth, p. 692-720. University of Chicago Press.

Blaut, J. M. 1960. The nature and effects of shifting agriculture. In Symposium on the impact of man on humid tropics vegetation, p. 185-202. UNESCO Science Co-operation Office of Southeast Asia, Djakarta.

Blumenstock, David I., and Saul Price. 1967. Climates of the states: Hawaii. Environmental Science Data Service, Climatology of the United States No. 60-51. (Revised version included in this volume.)

Boserup, Ester. 1965. The conditions of agricultural growth. Aldine Publishing Co., Chicago.

Chamberlain, Theodore. 1968. The littoral sand budget, Hawaiian Islands. Pacif. Sci. 22(2):161-183.

Cobb, John N. 1902. Commercial fisheries of the Hawaiian Islands. Report of Commissioner of Fish and Fisheries, p. 381-499.

Doty, Maxwell S., ed. 1968. Biological and physical features of Kealakekua Bay, Hawaii. Hawaii Botanical Science Paper No. 8. University of Hawaii, Honolulu.

Egler, Frank E. 1947. Arid southeast Oahu vegetation, Hawaii. Ecol. Monogr. 17(4):383-435.

Ekern, Paul G. 1964. Direct interception of cloud water on Lanaihale, Hawaii. Proc. Soil Sci. Soc. 28(8):419-421.

Ellis, William. 1963. Journal of William Ellis. Advertiser Publishing Co., Honolulu. (Reprint of the 1827 London edition.)

Gooding, Reginald M., and John J. Magnuson. 1967. Ecological significance of a drifting object to pelagic fishes. Pacif. Sci. 21(4):486-497.

Gosline, William A. 1965. Vertical zonation of in-
    shore fishes in the upper water layers of the
    Hawaiian Islands. Ecology 46(6):823-831. (Reprint-
    ed in this volume.)

Gosline, William A., and Vernon E. Brock. 1965. Hand-
    book of Hawaiian fishes. University of Hawaii
    Press, Honolulu.

Kay, E. Alison. 1969. Tales of the opihi. Hawaiian
    Shell News, n.s. 112, 18(4):1-2.

Leopold, Luna B. 1956. Land use and sediment yield.
    In William L. Thomas, Jr., ed., Man's role in
    changing the face of the earth, p. 639-647. Uni-
    versity of Chicago Press.

Liebig, Justus. 1965. Organic chemistry in its appli-
    cation to vegetable physiology and agriculture.
    In Edward J. Kormandy, ed., Readings in ecology,
    p. 12-14. Prentice-Hall, Englewood Cliffs.
    (Reprint of the 1840 article.)

Manar, Thomas A. 1966. Progress in 1964-65 at the
    Bureau of Commerical Fisheries Biological Labora-
    tory, Honolulu. United States Department of the
    Interior Circular 243.

Mangenot, G. 1963. The effect of man on the plant
    world. In F. R. Fosberg, ed., Man's place in the
    island ecosystem: a symposium, p. 117-132. Bishop
    Museum Press, Honolulu.

Moberly, Ralph Jr., and Theodore Chamberlain. 1964.
    Hawaiian beach systems: final report. Hawaii
    Institute of Geophysics, University of Hawaii.

Moberly, Ralph Jr., L. David Baver, Jr., and Anne
    Morrison. 1965. Source and variation of Hawai-
    ian littoral sand. J. Sediment. Petrol. 35(3):
    589-598.

Nakamura, E. L. 1967. A review of field observations
    on tuna behavior. Food and Agriculture Organiza-
    tion of the United Nations, Bergen, Norway.

Newman, T. Stell. 1970. Fishing and farming on the
    island of Hawaii in A.D. 1778. Division of State
    Parks, Honolulu.

Odum, Eugene P. 1959. Fundamentals of ecology.
    W. B. Saunders Co., Philadelphia.

Raikes, Robert. 1967. Water, weather and prehistory.
    John Baker, London.

Ryther, John H. 1969.   Photosynthesis and fish pro-
    duction in the sea. Science 166:72-76.

Sears, Paul B. 1956.   The processes of environmental
    change by man. In William L. Thomas, Jr., ed.,
    Man's role in changing the face of the earth,
    p. 471-486. University of Chicago Press.

Strahler, Arthur N. 1956.   The nature of induced
    erosion and aggradation. In William L. Thomas,
    Jr., ed., Man's role in changing the face of the
    earth, p. 621-638. University of Chicago Press.

Thornthwaite, C. W. 1956.   Modification of rural
    microclimates. In William L. Thomas, Jr., ed.,
    Man's role in changing the face of the earth,
    p. 567-583. University of Chicago Press.

Uchida, Richard N. 1966.   The skipjack tuna fishery
    in Hawaii. In Thomas A. Manar, ed., Proceedings
    of the Governor's conference on central Pacific
    fishery resources. State of Hawaii, Honolulu.

Zimmerman, Elwood C. 1965.   Nature of the land biota.
    In F. R. Fosberg, ed., Man's place in the island
    ecosystem. Bishop Museum Press, Honolulu.

HAWAIIAN NATURAL HISTORY: 1778-1900

E. Alison Kay[1]

Describing "this groupe of Isles which Captain Cook
has denominated *Sandwich Isles* in honour of his lordship
. . . ," Captain Clerke, second in command of the third
voyage to the Pacific undertaken by Captain James Cook,
commented that "from their situation on the Globe we
should suppose them to abound in many good things but
their abundance is such as we never before had any idea
of" (Clerke, in Beaglehole 1967). If the term "abundance" may be taken as referring to richness in natural
history, Clerke's words were prophetic, for in the
nearly two hundred years since their discovery the
Hawaiian Islands have become scientifically renowned for
their volcanoes and coral reefs, and for a biota even
richer and more intriguing to the evolutionist than that
of the Galápagos.

The purpose of this study is to provide a summary
of development of our knowledge of Hawaiian natural
history from the time of Captain Cook's discovery of the
Islands in 1778 to the beginning of the twentieth
century. I have found it convenient to divide the
story into three phases: one, from 1778 to 1850, which
was dominated by the explorer-naturalists; a second,
beginning in 1820 and lasting until about 1900, when
residents in the Islands, as well as visitors, contributed to the knowledge of Hawaiian natural history; and
a third, from the turn of the century to the present,
which constitutes the modern period. Reflected in each
of the periods is the broad background of the history
of science: those years immediately subsequent to the

---

[1]General Science Department, University of Hawaii,
Honolulu, Hawaii.

Linnaean revolution in taxonomy when the sciences were
primarily descriptive and when exploration played an
important role in the accumulation of data, those years
of the great Darwinian synthesis which are concomitant
with the popularization of science in both Europe and
the United States, and those in which science has become
a dominant cultural and professional force in our lives.

In constructing the story, I have drawn freely on
the accounts of voyages, journals, and biographies of
the naturalists involved. The chapters in the history
of Hawaiian botany by McCaughey (1917, 1918-1919) and
Bryan (1921), ichthyology by Jordan and Evermann (1905),
ornithology by Rothschild (1893), and volcanology by
Jaggar (1913) and Hitchcock (1911), as well as the
bibliographies of Illingworth (1923), Macdonald (1947),
Merrill (1937), and Stearns (1935), have also provided
many insights into a literature which is encompassed by
the term "natural history": botany, zoology, vulcanol-
ogy, geology, and mineralogy.

THE EXPLORER-NATURALISTS

Captain Cook and the Discovery of the Sandwich Islands

The Hawaiian Islands were discovered on a voyage
sponsored not only for national aims but also for
scientific purposes. The secret instructions given to
Captain Cook at the beginning of his third voyage into
the Pacific enjoined him both to attempt to find "a
North East, or North West Passage, from the Pacific
Ocean into the Atlantic Ocean" and "carefully to observe
the nature of the Soil & the Produce thereof; the
Animals & Fowls that inhabit or frequent it . . . .
And, if you find any Metals, Minerals or valuable
Stones, or any extraneous Fossils, you are to bring
home Specimens of each, as also of the Seeds of such
Trees, Shrubs, Plants, Fruits, and Grains, peculiar to
those Places, as you may be able to collect" (Secret
Instructions, in Beaglehole 1967).

Captain Cook's first voyage to the Pacific, to
observe the transit of Venus across the face of the sun
and to find the much-discussed southern continent, was
the first large maritime expedition to be sponsored by
the two most important British scientific organizations
of the day, the Royal Society and the Board of Longitude.
Cook's second voyage also reflected the interest of
these organizations. On the first two voyages the ships
were staffed with naturalists and artists, such as
Joseph Banks and his associates Daniel Solander and
Sydney Parkinson on the first, and Reinhold and
Georg Forster and William Hodges on the second.

The naturalists of the third voyage are less well
known, for they were selected primarily by Cook himself,
with little influence from the Royal Society: William
Anderson, surgeon on the *Resolution* "who became in fact
if not in name" the expedition naturalist (Smith 1960);
William Ellis, surgeon's mate on the *Discovery* whose
bird paintings contributed to the science of the voyage;
John Webber, the artist commissioned by the Admiralty to
make "drawings of the most memorable scenes of our
transactions" (Beaglehole 1967); and David Nelson,
botanist at Kew Gardens, included at the behest of
Joseph Banks. To that list of naturalists may be added
the names of William Bayley, astronomer; William Bligh,
of subsequent *Bounty* fame, who was responsible for charting harbors and anchorages; and John Ledyard, an
American, whose vivid descriptions of countryside and
native customs are valuable documentation of conditions
in the Hawaiian Islands when the Cook ships arrived.

Anderson's observations of terrain and biota form
the basis for the account of natural history in the
official versions of the voyage, but Anderson became ill
in Tahiti, and although he saw something of the Islands
when the *Resolution* touched at Kauai in February 1778,
he died in August of that year en route to Alaska.
Captain King, who took command of the *Discovery* after

Cook's death, notes that the natural history observations
subsequent to Anderson's death are less complete than
they would otherwise have been, and that the observations
in the Hawaiian Islands were also limited by the short
time that the ships' companies were ashore, for of the
three and one-half months the *Resolution* and *Discovery*
were in Hawaiian waters "not more than a fifth part of
the above time was spent ashore" (King, in Beaglehole
1967).

Despite these shortcomings, the topography, biota,
people, and customs of the Hawaiian Islands were described in astonishing detail. Landing at Kauai and Niihau
in 1778, Cook's men sighted Oahu from offshore. In 1779
the ships anchored in Kealakekua Bay, Hawaii, sailed
past Maui and Molokai, touched briefly at Oahu, and
landed again at Kauai and Niihau. The natural history
specimens procured were obtained only from the islands
of Hawaii, Kauai, and Niihau.

The volcanic nature of the Islands was made clear
in the descriptions of Kauai and Hawaii. The southern
shore of Kauai rose "in a gentle slope from the sea shore
to the foot of the Mountions that are in the middle of
the island, except in one place, near the east end where
they rise directly from the sea; here they seemed to be
formed of nothing but stone which lay in horizontal
stratas . . ." (*Journals*, in Beaglehole 1967). On
Hawaii, Ka'u was "as barren waste looking a country as
can be conceived to exist in the Neighbourhood of a fine
one, & this owing to the ravages of a Volcano, which we
suppose to have formerly existed on [Mauna Loa], since
we could discern black Streaks coming from the Mountain
even down to the Seaside" (*Journals*, in Beaglehole 1967).

The members of the ships' companies produced charts
of anchorages, discussed tides, and enumerated a table
of lunar and tidal observations in Hawaiian waters.
Bligh's charts of Waimea Bay, Kauai, and Kealakekua Bay,
Hawaii, the latter approximately four minutes in error,

placing it further west than it actually is, remained
(with those made during Vancouver's voyage in 1794) the
basis for charts of the islands until 1848 (Healy 1960).
The tides were described as "so inconsiderable that with
the great surf which broke against the shore, it was
hardly possible to tell any time whether it was high or
low water or that the water was ebbing or flowing"
(*Journals*, in Beaglehole 1967). A current "setting to
the westward of N. westward" on the south side of Kauai
was also noted.

The vegetation on Kauai, Niihau, and Hawaii was
described in various passages, a list of 15 birds and
one of 30 plants were compiled (Clerke, in Beaglehole
1967), and the relationships of the animals and plants
were discussed. On Kauai, Cook wrote, "we saw no wood
but what was up in the interior part of the island and
a few trees about the villages; we observed several
plantations of Plantains and sugar canes, and places that
seemed to be planted with roots." On Niihau, "The
ground over which I walked was covered with shrubs and
plants, some of which sent forth the most fragrant smell
I had anywhere met with in this sea" (*Journals*, in
Beaglehole 1967). The only account of the forested
interior of Hawaii is that of John Ledyard who described
it during a frustrated attempt to climb Mauna Loa:
"After leaving the bread-fruit-forests we continued up
the ascent to the distance of a mile and an half further,
and found the land thick covered with wild fern . . . .
We found the country here as well as at the sea shore
universally overspread with lava, and also saw several
subterranean excavations that had every appearance of
past eruption and fire. . . . we had also shot a number
of fine birds of the liveliest and most variagated plumage
that any of us had ever met with, but we heard no melody
among them. . . . the woods here are very thick and
luxuriant, the largest trees are nearly thirty feet in
the girt" (Ledyard 1963). The biota was compared with

that of other Polynesian islands the ships had visited:
"Kauai . . . produceth all the sorts of fruits and
roots that are found at Otaheite or any other place of
the South Sea Islands, but nothing seemed to be in great
plenty, but Potatoes, which are the largest I ever
saw. . . . The tame animals are hogs, dogs, and fowls,
all of the same kind as at Otaheite and equally as
good. We saw no other wild animals than rats, small
lizards, and birds" (*Journals*, in Beaglehole 1967).

In addition to the narrative, collections of
natural history curiosities and paintings of birds
resulted from the voyage of discovery. Webber and
Ellis each painted several watercolors and between them
illustrated 12 species of Hawaiian birds. These
paintings, together with the skins obtained during the
voyage, served as the basis for the descriptions of
Hawaiian birds in Latham's (1785-1853) *General Synopsis
of Birds* (see Lysaght 1959). A single fish went into
the Banks museum; with another specimen of the same
species from Tahiti, it was described by Brussonet
in 1792 (Jordan and Evermann 1905). Two shells
(*Hydatina physis* and *Nerita polita*), taken to England
unofficially by crew members who had been bribed by
London dealers to supply the curiosity cabinets of
wealthy Londoners, were illustrated in *The Universal
Conchologist* (Martyn 1784). And a variety of
curiosities, such as shells and birds from the
Sandwich Islands, were displayed with objects of
ethnographic interest in the Sandwich Room of the
Leverian Museum in London from 1780 until the Museum's
dispersal in 1792 (Donovan 1806).

Voyages up to 1850

The success of the Cook voyages stimulated a
series of Pacific expeditions sponsored between 1792
and 1850 not only by England but also by Russia, France,
Prussia, Denmark, and the United States. Many of these
voyages of exploration touched at the Hawaiian Islands.

At least six English voyages contributed to the
knowledge of Hawaiian natural history begun by the Cook
voyage. The first of the now famous Hawaiian land
shells was described in an appendix on natural history
in Captain George Dixon's (1789) account of the second
group of British voyagers to touch at the Hawaiian
Islands. The shell *Helix apexfulva* [=*Achatinella
apexfulva*] was figured from a specimen taken from a lei,
and it had a hole in the spire. Dixon also recorded
and illustrated a crab (*Cancer raninus = Ranina ranina*
Linnaeus) and "the yellow-tufted bee-eater" (*Moho
apicalis* Gould, 1861) from the Hawaiian Islands.
Captain George Vancouver, whose ships visited the
Islands three times between 1792 and 1794, was the first
to mention active volcanoes: ". . . we had a most
excellent view of Mowna Roa's snowy summit, and the
range of lower hills that extend towards the east end
of Owyhee. From the tops of these . . . several columns
of smoke were seen to descend which Tameameah and the
rest of our friends said were occasioned by the
subterranean fires that frequently broke out in violent
eruptions. . ." (Vancouver 1798). The botanist on
Vancouver's voyage, Archibald Menzies, not only made
extensive collections of Hawaiian plants but successfully ascended both Hualalai and Mauna Loa, estimating
their heights, recording temperatures at different
elevations, and describing the vegetation (Menzies
1920). The voyage of the *Blonde* under the command of
Captain Lord Byron in 1825, with James Macrae as
botanist and Andrew Bloxam as naturalist, supplied
the English conchologist William Swainson with five
species of land shells for which Swainson (1828) erected
the genus *Achatinella*. Macrae, climbing Mauna Kea, was
the first botanist to describe the silversword[2] (Macrae
1922). The ship's company also visited Kilauea, which

---

[2]The silversword was given its scientific name by
W. J. Hooker from specimens collected by David Douglas.

was sketched by Robert Dampier, and the crater of Kilauea
was mapped by Lieutenant Charles Malden. The voyages of
Captain Frederick W. Beechey in the *Blossom* in 1826-1827
with the botanists George T. Lay and Alexander Collie,
of Captain Edward Belcher in the *Sulphur* in 1837 with
the surgeon-naturalist Richard Brinsley Hinds (1968),
and those of Captain Kellett and Lieutenant Wood in the
Herald and *Pandora* in 1847 with the botanist Berthold
Seeman all provided plants, fish, and shells
for herbaria and museums in Britain and on the
Continent.

Two Russian voyages, both under the command of
Lieutenant Otto von Kotzebue, one in 1815 in the brig
Rurick and the second in 1823 in the sloop *Predpriatie,*
produced much of scientific interest from the Hawaiian
Islands. The scientists on these voyages included the
surgeon F. E. Eschscholtz and the naturalist-poet
Adelbert Chamisso. Eschscholtz' (1821) description of
the endemic butterfly *Vanessa tameameah* is the first
description of an Hawaiian insect. Chamisso, whose name
is perpetuated in the scientific epithets of such
familiar Hawaiian plants as the naupaka (*Scaevola
chamissoniana*) and hapu'u fern (*Cibotium chamissoi*),
collected and described many plants.

Of the French expeditions which visited the Islands,
that of the *Uranie* under Captain Louis de Freycinet in
1819 and that of the *Bonite* under M. Vaillant in
1836-1837 are the most significant from the standpoint
of contributions to Hawaiian natural history. The
botanist Charles Gaudichaud Beaupré accompanied both
voyages and collected a large number of endemic species.
The medico-naturalists Jean René Constant Quoy and
Joseph Paul Gaimard, the zoologists on the *Uranie,* made
the first actual collection of fishes in the Islands.
J. F. T. Eydoux and L. F. A. Souleyet, who contributed
to the zoology of the voyage of the *Bonite,* described
12 marine mollusks.

Among the last of the great exploring expeditions
to visit the Hawaiian Islands prior to 1850 was that
sponsored by the United States. The United States
Exploring Expedition, commanded by Charles Wilkes,
differed from the earlier voyages in that a corps of
professional scientists accompanied the ships:
James Dwight Dana, mineralogist; Joseph Brackenridge
and Charles Pickering, botanists; Horatio Hale,
philologist; Joseph Cuthuoy, conchologist; Titian Peale,
naturalist, among others. The scientists spent six
months in 1840-1841 exploring and collecting on Kauai,
Oahu, and Maui, and making detailed observations of the
volcanoes on Hawaii. The United States Exploring
Expedition reports fill 24 volumes and atlases which
contain many references to Hawaiian natural history,
including descriptions of plants (Gray 1854-1857;
Brackenridge 1854-1855), crustacea (Dana 1852-1853),
corals (Dana 1846-1849), and shells (Gould 1852).

One of the most noteworthy results of the expedition
from the standpoint of Hawaiian natural history was the
work of James Dwight Dana. For Dana, the voyage with
Wilkes was what the voyage of the *Beagle* had been for
Charles Darwin only a few years before. Dana not only
collected an enormous amount of data and hundreds of
specimens, but began immediately on his return to the
United States to synthesize his results, supervising the
publication of three volumns of the expedition reports.
The influence of the Hawaiian Islands is seen in his
history of the volcanic activity of Kilauea (Dana 1850b),
in *Corals and Coral Islands* (Dana 1853) which includes
a lengthy description of Hawaiian coral reefs, and in
Volcanoes and Volcanic Characteristics (Dana 1890),
published fifty years after his first visit to the
Islands.[3]

---

[3]Dana visited the Islands a second time in 1887
when he was 74 years old.

Independent Travelers

Besides government expeditions, in the early years
of the nineteenth century, innumerable private commercial
voyages ventured into the Pacific. Independent travelers who were interested in natural history visited the
Islands on these ships.

David Douglas, whose name is commemorated in that
of the Douglas fir, is perhaps the best known of these
early scientists. While visiting the Islands for about
10 days in August and September 1832, Douglas was so
intrigued with the vegetation that he returned the
following year (December 1833) for more extensive exploration. He not only managed to send many plants from Oahu
and Hawaii to Sir Joseph Dalton Hooker at Kew Gardens,
but he also dispatched a pair of nene geese which arrived
alive in England, where they were bred (Bennett 1840;
and see Vigors 1834). Carrying barometer, thermometer,
and chronometer, Douglas climbed both Mauna Loa and
Mauna Kea, estimating their heights and describing their
craters. Douglas' death in a cattle pit on Mauna Kea
in July 1834, remains an intriguing mystery: did he
accidentally fall in, or was he murdered?

In 1833, a few months prior to Douglas' second
visit, Meredith Gairdner, a young Edinburgh-trained
surgeon, visited Honolulu briefly, while en route to
employment in the Pacific Northwest with the Hudson's
Bay Company. Gairdner undertook a 10-day exploration
of Oahu on foot (Gairdner 1834), summarizing his observations in a "Physico-Geognostic Sketch of Oahu"
(Gairdner 1835), the first account of the topography and
geology of any one of the Islands. Gairdner returned
to the Islands in 1836 and, ill with consumption, died
in Honolulu the following year.

Six months after Douglas' death, in January 1835,
Thomas Nuttall and John K. Townsend arrived in Honolulu.
Nuttall, who had resigned as botanist of the Botanic

Garden at Harvard, and Townsend, ornithologist with the
Academy of Natural Sciences of Philadelphia, were explor-
ing the continental United States under the auspices
of the Wyeth Expedition when they decided to visit the
Islands. They toured Oahu and Kauai, collecting plants
(Nuttall, 1838, 1843), crustacea (see Randall 1839),
shells (see Conrad 1837), and fish (see Abbott 1860).
The impressions of the naturalists were recorded in
Townsend's (1839) *Narrative of a Journey* . . . , and
Nuttall's memories of Hawaii were lyrically described in
his introduction to *The North American Sylva* (Nuttall
1852): ". . . the beauties of a tropical vegetation;
a season that knows no change; but that of perpetual
spring and summer: an elysian land, where Nature offers
spontaneous food to man." On a second visit to the
Islands in 1836, Townsend joined the Prussian naturalist
Ferdinand Deppe, who was collecting specimens for the
Berlin Museum, in trips on both Oahu and Hawaii. On
that tour Deppe collected two species of birds for
which the genus *Hemignathus* was erected (Newton 1892).

Summary of the Explorer-Naturalist Phase

By 1850 there were scattered in the narratives and
atlases of the exploring expeditions, and in brief notes
in contemporary scientific journals (for example,
Menzies 1828-1829; Bennett 1828; Douglas 1834a), a
variety of reports on topography, volcanic activity, and
coral reefs of the Hawaiian Islands, and descriptions
and records of several hundred animals and plants
resulting from the collecting activities of the explorer-
naturalists.   Except for the brief lists, compiled
from various sources, of birds (Hartlaub 1854) and plants
(Endlicher 1836; and see St. John 1940), and Dana's
reports of Hawaiian volcanoes (1850a, 1850b), no synthetic accounts of Hawaiian natural history resulted from the
visits of the explorer-naturalists. It was Charles Darwin who called for such a reckoning. Writing to Joseph
Dalton Hooker in 1850, Darwin pleaded: "How I wish you

would work out the Pacific floras. . . . But of all
places in the world I should like to see a good flora
of the Sandwich Islands. I would subscribe 50 pounds to
any collector to go there and work at these islands"
(Darwin, in Darwin 1903).

It is not difficult to find reasons for the lack of
synthetic accounts of Hawaiian natural history in the
work of the explorer-naturalists. The naturalists came
from a variety of backgrounds and each served a science
based on observation and classification rather than
one of synthesis and theory. They were subject to the
exigencies of the ships on which they traveled, and to
a variety of hazards. Perhaps most important of all,
they were strangers in a strange land.

For the most part, the explorer-naturalists were
not scientists as we should recognize them today.
Indeed, the description of Menzies by the Hawaiians as
"the red faced man who gathered grass and cut the legs
off men" (Douglas 1834b), would serve, with few modifications, to describe many of the naturalists who visited
the Islands prior to 1850: surgeons, pharmacists, ships'
captains, and draughtsmen who were scientists because
they were intrigued with the curiosities of nature.

Even the most experienced naturalists among those
nineteenth-century explorers were faced with a baffling
array of difficulties in the pursuit of their directives
and of their individual interests. The ships on which
they traveled could not remain indefinitely in any one
port while the scientists made their observations:
Cook's ships were in port about 20 days; Vancouver's men
spent no more than 30 days ashore; and of the 20 days
the *Uranie* spent in the Islands, Gaudichaud was ashore
only 7 days. Recognizing the limitations imposed by
short visits, Langsdorff (1813-1814) wrote, "How many
unknown plants might here be discovered, and what contributions might be collected towards the geography and
natural history of plants. It were much to be wished

that some zealous naturalist would remain at least a
year upon this island [Oahu] to study these subjects."
Nor was travel to the interior of the islands easy. It
took Menzies, by canoe and on foot, 10 days to travel
from the anchorage at Kealakekua Bay to the top of Mauna
Loa, and Douglas' journey to the summit of Mauna Kea
required 14 days.

A variety of hazards were reflected in the fate of
the collections. Douglas' complaint that the "vile cock-
roaches ate up all of the Paper" on which his astronomical observations were recorded was perhaps not unexpected
in the tropics. Other events were not anticipated: many
of the collections of the United States Exploring Expedition were lost in the wreck of the *Peacock*,[4] as were 18
cases of collections of the *Uranie* when she was wrecked
near Cape Horn. Several collections were mixed during
the course of long voyages that touched at many ports, or
in the workrooms of the closet naturalists who described
the specimens. Three molluscan species collected on the
west coast of America during the voyage of the *Herald*
were erroneously attributed to the Hawaiian Islands
(Forbes 1852), while one species collected by Nuttall
which actually occurs in the Islands bears the specific
epithet *californiensis* because the shells were erroneously labeled (see Conrad 1837 for *Perna* [=*Isognomon*]
californiensis).

One of the most challenging difficulties was that
of recognizing strange plants in an unfamiliar land.
Chamisso (1821) vividly described the dilemma: "Once in
my wanderings through the fertile valley back of Hanaruru
[Honolulu] I found upon the banks of an irrigated patch,
in which taro was being pulled, a beautiful grass which
I could not remember having previously seen, and of which
I forthwith picked some samples. As I was thus occupied,
an Owaihan met me and seized me and berated me, and whom

---

[4]The United States Exploring Expedition suffered
another setback when nearly all the copies of the
reports on birds and mammals were destroyed by fire.

I could only pacify with much trouble. I related the incident to Marini [Don Francisco de Paula y Marin, a
Spaniard resident in the Islands], and showed him the
grass. The man was his tenant, the grass was rice,
which, after many earlier trials had at last germinated
in the Islands. Let botanists laugh at me, the same
thing might have happened to any one of them. In the
herbarium I had not mistaken Oryza sativa."

Despite their varied backgrounds, the difficulties
they encountered, and the empirical focus of their observations, the explorer-naturalists hinted at a number of
interesting aspects of Hawaiian natural history. Cook's
scientists had noted the similarity between Hawaiian
plants and animals and those of Polynesia; Kotzebue
(1821) stressed the fact that the flora of the Islands
had nothing in common with that of California; Douglas
(1834b) saw great opportunities in the profuse vegetation:
"In Ferns alone, I think there must be five hundred
species"; and Seeman (1853) mused on the origin of a
flora which had its relationships in a direction opposite
to that of the trade winds. Meyen (1835) was the first
to recognize the land shells as more than just species to
be described: "It is very remarkable how nature, in
creating certain species of the animal and vegetable
kingdoms, is held so closely to certain localities. . . .
The woods of Brazil are filled with horrible amphibians
and numberless insects, and it is seldom that one touches
a branch or tree or a leaf of a plant without feeling a
beetle or some other insect; but here on the island of
Oahu, there is instead a great scarcity of insects. If
you look on the lower surface of the leaves or if you
shake the trees, instead of insects falling off, there
are prettily shaped, and often brightly colored, snails.
. . . It is the numberless land-shells that here on the
Sandwich Islands have been awarded the leaves of trees
by nature, instead of the insects."

The explorer-naturalists not only described
Hawaiian natural history and collected specimens for

herbaria and museums in Europe, but they also contributed
to it. Captain Cook left on Niihau a "Ram goat and two
Ewes, a Boar and Sow pig of the English breed, and the
seeds of Millons, Pumpkins and onions" (*Journals*, in
Beaglehole 1967). It was the Vancouver voyage, however,
which unknowingly upset the future of Hawaiian botany.
The "young bull calf nearly full grown, two fine cows,
and two very fine bull calves, all in high condition"
which Vancouver left on Hawaii were to multiply so
rapidly within the next thirty years that Ellis (1827b)
wrote of "immense herds of them." Interestingly,
Kotzebue (1821), noting the progress of the introductions, suggested that "the art of using the productions
already existing, is a more urgent want than the
introduction of new ones."

RESIDENT NATURALISTS

Within 40 years of their discovery, the Hawaiian
Islands were established as an essential port of call in
the vast network of commerce generated throughout the
Pacific by the voyages of exploration. The missionaries,
businessmen, physicians, ministers, surveyors, and all
the others who settled in the Islands not only were a
force in a changing governmental structure and growing
economy but also contributed another dimension to the
development of knowledge of their natural history.

The Missionaries

On April 4, 1820, The American brig *Thaddeus*, 164
days out of Boston, anchored at Kailua, Hawaii. Aboard
were seven men and their wives in the service of the
American Board of Commissioners of Foreign Missions, the
first of twelve missionary companies to settle in the
Hawaiian Islands between 1820 and 1844. The missionaries, like the explorer-naturalists, arrived in a land of
strange plants and animals, where "I do not recollect
ever seeing a single plant which is indigenous to these

islands, nor a shrub or tree, growing in the U. States.
While in America I attended to botany considerably--but
here I have not know [sic] the scientific names of 4/5
of the plants growing about my own door" (Baldwin, in
Alexander 1953). In their unfamiliar surroundings the
missionaries began painstakingly to record their observations on "volcanic phenomena," "Taro--its nature and
means of cultivation," "the salt lake," "the Dracaena or
ti plant," and so forth, in letters and journals (see,
for example, the chapter headings in Ellis 1827b;
Stewart 1830), and often they thoughtfully shipped
parcels of lava, shells, corals, and plants to relatives
and friends 5,000 miles away.

The missionaries' abilities as natural historians
were first brought to the attention of American and
British scientists in 1826 by Benjamin Silliman, editor
of the *American Journal of Science*, the leading
scientific journal of the time in the United States.
Silliman (see Ellis 1826a) printed an extensive excerpt
from William Ellis' *Narrative of a Tour Through Hawaii*
which had appeared in 1825 in Boston, and this excerpt,
as well as others from Ellis' *Narrative*, was reprinted in
Britain in the *Philosophical Magazine* (Ellis 1826b,
1826c) and the *Edinburgh Journal of Science* (Ellis
1827a).

The Reverend William Ellis, a visiting member of the
London Missionary Society, and three of the resident
American missionaries (Asa Thurston, Joseph Goodrich,
and Artemas Bishop) had undertaken a walking tour around
the island of Hawaii between June and August 1823 to
survey the island for potential stations for mission
work. The *Narrative* summarized the missionaries'
accomplishments from the standpoint of future mission
work, and, in addition, reported "considerable information on a variety of subjects. . . such as the natural
scenery, productions, geology, and curiosities; the
traditionary legends, superstitions, manners, customs,

etc." (Ellis 1827b). It was some of that "considerable information" which Silliman printed in the *American Journal of Science*, recognizing its scientific worth in a preface: "It is with great pleasure that we add our warm commendation of the late effort of the missionaries. Situated in a remote island in the vast expanse of the Pacific . . . remote from the lights of science . . . we certainly owe them many thanks for the great amount of valuable information which they have, *incidentally*, contributed to the subject of natural history of one of the most remarkable volcanic regions in the world" (in Ellis 1826a).

By far the greatest curiosity in the Islands was the volcano. Vancouver had seen columns of smoke issuing from the mountain, but it was Ellis and his party who first described Hawaiian lavas, and Kilauea in eruption. The next account of the volcano was also that of a missionary, the Reverend C. S. Stewart (1826), who visited Kilauea in July 1825, with Captain Lord Byron and some members of the company of the *Blonde*. Subsequent to these descriptions, missionaries reported on volcanic activity in scores of letters and notes published. in the *American Journal of Science, Proceedings of the Boston Society of Natural History, Science*, and other journals, between 1826 and 1900. The authors of these reports represent a remarkably large part of the roster of missionary families that settled in Hawaii: Alexander (1886), Baldwin (1852), Bishop (1887), Coan (1851), Emerson (1887), Goodrich (1826), Gulick (1864), Kinney (1852), Lyman (1849), and Whitney (1868). Their zeal as volcano observers is no better described than by the Reverend Joseph Goodrich (1829) in a note accompanying lava specimens sent to Professor Silliman at Yale, commenting that "all were taken either hot or warm from the bottom of the crater."

The Reverend Titus Coan was the most prolific reporter of those early missionary volcano observers,

describing the activity and appearance of Kilauea and
Mauna Loa in more than 30 letters and notes appearing in
the *American Journal of Science* between 1850 and 1882.
Coan was familiarly known as "the bishop of Kilauea,"
and it was said that he "cared for it as he did for all
his parishioners" (Brigham 1909). Sarah Joiner Lyman
(Mrs. David B. Lyman) was another faithful chronicler of
the volcano. In her "Earthquake Book" she recorded
accounts of earthquakes felt in Hilo between 1833 and
1885. An extract from the notebook was published in the
American Journal of Science (Lyman 1859),[5] and the notebook was also recognized for its useful information by
Wilkes (1845)[5] and Hitchcock (1911).

The contributions of the first generation of missionaries to knowledge of the biota took a different
form from their volcano reports. Only two publications
on the biota were provided by members of the pioneering
mission companies: Edward Bailey's (1882) list of ferns
which was privately printed and C. H. Wetmore's (1890)
list of fishes in the *Hawaiian Annual*. Instead, the missionaries collected shells and plants, sending their
material abroad for identification. The Reverend C. S.
Steward provided Professor J. C. Green (1827) of
Philadelphia with the first specimens of *Achatinella* to
be described in the United States. The Reverend Edward
Johnson sent shells to Jesse Wedgewood Mighels (1845) in
Maine. Henry Dimond wrote G. B. Sowerby (first of the
name), in London, describing his collection (Matheson
1961), and was in correspondence with the American
conchologist C. B. Adams (1857), who described
Achatinella dimondi, among other species, from Dimond's
collection. The botanists of the United States Exploring

---

[5]A misprint in the *American Journal of Science*
attributed Mrs. Lyman's journal extract to S. C. Lyman,
and this was misinterpreted in Macdonald's (1947)
bibliography as C. S. Lyman. Wilkes (1845) attributed
the notebook to D. B. Lyman, Mrs. Lyman's husband.

Expedition were assisted in their explorations by the
Reverend John Diell, who also corresponded with Asa Gray
at Harvard to whom he sent Hawaiian plants (Dupree 1953;
Gray 1893).

The Missionary Sons

The missionary fathers' interest in natural history
was transmitted to their sons, from whose pens came a
myriad of reports between 1858 and the turn of the
century. These papers differ from the earlier work in
that they span a variety of aspects of Hawaiian natural
history: birds, shells, plants, geology, mineralogy,
and astronomy.

Of the missionary sons who were interested in the
biota, the names Dole, Gulick, and Baldwin are perhaps
best known. John T. Gulick, who spent a lifetime in
mission work in China and Japan, was interested in land
shells. As a student at Punahou School Gulick speculated
on the origin of the Hawaiian land shells (Gulick 1932),
and he utilized his collections and observations in constructing his argument for natural selection, summarized
in one of the great classics of Darwinism, *Evolution:
Racial and Habitudinal* (Gulick 1905). Sanford Ballard
Dole, jurist and president of the short-lived Republic
of Hawaii, published a checklist of birds while a student
at Williams College (Dole 1869). The list was favorably
noted by two ornithologists, P. L. Sclater (1871) and
A. H. Newton (1892), the latter commending it as a
"serviceable piece for future work." David Dwight
Baldwin, who became a leading educator in the Islands,
was also interested in land shells, publishing "the most
important expression of the work of this period" (Pilsbry
and Cooke 1911) in a series of papers (Baldwin 1893,
1895, 1903). Baldwin also compiled a list of mosses
(Baldwin 1876) and a list of indigenous trees (Baldwin
and Auld 1891).

Several missionary sons were also proficient in the
physical sciences. One, Titus M. Coan, followed in his

father's footsteps and wrote about volcanoes (Coan
1889, 1910). The works of Sereno E. Bishop include
papers on climate (Bishop 1881), volcanic activity
(Bishop 1887), and currents (Bishop 1904). Bishop was
awarded the third Warner Essay Prize, in competition with
world-renowned astronomers, for his theory explaining
red sunset glows and other atmospheric phenomena as due
to the eruption of Krakatoa (Bishop 1886), and, because
he was the first observer of one of these phenomena, it
received the name "Bishop's Ring." The mapping of the
Hawaiian Islands was undertaken by William D. Alexander,
who, having achieved recognition as an educator in the
Islands, became surveyor general of the Hawaiian Kingdom
in 1870 and initiated the task of surveying and mapping
all the islands and publishing geodetic tables (Alexander
1871). One of Alexander's assistants in the Survey,
Curtis J. Lyons, became government meteorologist and is
called "the father of the Hawaiian weather bureau."
A. B. Lyons, whose college education prepared him for
work in pharmaceutical chemistry and who was for a time
consulting chemist with Parke Davis and Company, returned
to the Islands to teach natural history and published a
paper on the chemistry of Hawaiian soils (Lyons 1896),
as well as papers on other subjects.

The Missionary Background

Fully one-quarter of the approximately 80 missionary
names associated with the Hawaiian Islands are in one way
or another connected with the development of knowledge
of the Islands' natural history. It is worth exploring
the background of their contributions.

For the most part, the missionary fathers had been
educated in New England institutions during those early
years of the nineteenth century when science was just
beginning to emerge as an academic discipline in the
universities. One of the most successful of the early
nineteenth-century scientists was Benjamin Silliman, who

initiated Yale University's lead in the sciences, a
pre-eminence maintained by such figures as C. S. Lyman,
professor of physics and astronomy, and J. D. Dana,
professor of geology. The missionary tie with Yale was
a strong one. Dr. Baldwin and the Reverend Joseph Goodrich were students at Yale under Silliman; the latter
was described by Silliman (in Ellis 1826a) as having
"applied himself with diligence to the study of mineralogy and geology." The Reverend C. S. Lyman visited the
Islands as a missionary, establishing his ties with the
mission families in 1846. And James D. Dana and the
Reverend Titus Coan met during the visit of the United
States Exploring Expedition in 1840-1841, forming a
friendship which was to last a lifetime, the two corresponding until Coan's death in 1882. Silliman, Lyman,
and Dana not only encouraged the mission fathers'
interest in natural history, especially with respect to
volcanic activity, but sponsored the publication of their
reports in the *American Journal of Science*.

Interested in natural history themselves, the
missionary fathers fostered their sons' interests.
Dr. Baldwin recorded his son David Dwight's tenth birthday with the note, "Our little boy . . . is extremely
fond of botany, is collecting for himself, and can preserve some plants for you" (Baldwin, in Alexander 1953).
Five years later Dr. Baldwin forwarded a box of corals
gathered by his son to Professor Silliman, who "answered
in careful detail the missionaries' questions about them
and thanked him for the 'very beautiful' corals, some of
which Professor Dana was 'examining with reference to
his great work on corals'" (Alexander 1953).

Another stimulating contact with the scientific
world for the mission families was with the explorer-
naturalists. David Douglas was a guest of the Goodrich
family in Hilo. Thomas Nuttall and John K. Townsend
stayed with the Gulicks on Kauai (Townsend 1839). And
Dr. Baldwin told of the excitement of the visit of the

scientists of the United States Exploring Expedition.
"We had the pleasure of having all the scientific corps
. . . with us for some time," wrote Baldwin. "They
lodged at our houses & lived at our tables. Two of them
were accomplished botanists, & afforded me more assistance as to the vegetable productions of this part of the
world than all I have had from other sources since I
have been in the Islands" (Baldwin, in Alexander 1953).

At Punahou School, founded in 1841 for the education
of the mission children, natural history pursuits were
one of the few forms of entertainment available. "The
rarest days of all were those we spent hunting for tree
shells, the famous *Achatinellidae*. . . . I still feel the
exhilaration of those excursions, the zest of coming
upon a hidden surprise of nature, some fine specimen of
those beautiful shells, each ridge, each valley revealing
its peculiar variety" reminisced one Punahou boy (Oliver
Emerson, in Alexander and Dodge 1941). Indeed, land
shells so intrigued the mission sons that three of the
missionaries wrote independently of the boys' "concho-
logical fever" (Alexander, in Alexander 1934; Baldwin,
in Alexander 1953; and Wilcox, in Damon 1950).

When the mission children embarked for college in
New England, they took with them their natural history
collections: skulls, shells, birds, and plants. "That
box of skulls was a lucky thing for me," wrote Sanford
Ballard Dole to his father, "especially in introducing
me among the scientific men of Boston" (Dole, in Damon
1957). The "scientific men" included Dana, Asa Gray,
and Louis Agassiz. At Yale (where three of the mission
sons won the Astronomical Prize for their scientific
prowess), Williams, and Amherst, the college students
nurtured their interests joining college natural history
societies and such organizations as the Lyceum of
Natural History in New York (Gulick 1932) and the Boston
Society of Natural History (Dole, in Damon 1957). On
their return to the Islands to become educators, lawyers,

and business men, they continued to write, collect, and
encourage studies on Hawaiian natural history.

As remarkable as the interest and productivity of
the missionary resident naturalists is the reflection
in their work and reminiscences of the changing philosophy of science in the nineteenth century. In the 1820s,
as S. E. Bishop (1916) described it, "Of geology we never
heard. The globe had been created in six ordinary days,
and there was no mystery about it. Six thousand years
was the limit of past earthly chronology." Within 30
years, John T. Gulick was writing, "These Achatinellinae
never came from Noah's ark" (Gulick 1932), and Bishop
himself had become one of the earliest supporters of
Darwinism.

Other Resident Naturalists

Others in the growing community of Americans and
Europeans in the Hawaiian Islands after 1850 were also
interested in natural history.

The most distinguished figure among the resident
naturalists was William Hillebrand, who for 20 years
(1851-1871) practiced medicine in the Islands, serving as
the first director and head physician of the Queens'
Hospital, as president of the Board of Health, and as a
member of the Privy Council in the Hawaiian Kingdom.
Hillebrand's avocation was botany: ". . . he prosecuted
unremittingly the study of the Hawaiian flora, visiting
all the larger islands, penetrating the inmost recesses
of their deepest and darkest ravines and climbing to the
summits of their loftiest mountains. He gradually formed
about his home an extensive garden, crowded with the
greatest variety of shrubs and trees gathered from all
parts of the world at great expense. The cultivation of
this garden [now called Foster Gardens] was his greatest
delight" (W. F. Hillebrand, in Hillebrand 1888).
Dr. Hillebrand's knowledge of Hawaiian botany was summarized in what is still the great classic of Hawaiian
botany, *Flora of the Hawaiian Islands*, published

posthumously in Germany in 1888.

The first book with colored illustrations of
Hawaiian flowers appeared three years prior to Hillebrand's *Flora*. This was *Indigenous Flowers of the
Hawaiian Islands* by Mrs. Francis (Isabella) Sinclair, Jr.
(1885). Mrs. Sinclair collected and painted flowers
during a long residence on Kauai and Niihau. She sent
her specimens for identification to Sir Joseph Dalton
Hooker of Kew Gardens, and the book consists of her
paintings, notes on the habits of the plants, and
Hooker's identifications.

Two of the resident naturalists were especially
interested in mollusks. Wesley Newcomb, a physician, was
intrigued with land shells. During his five-year residence (1850-1855), he accumulated a collection of
Achatinellidae which nearly 40 years later was still
regarded as "the finest in existence" (Stearns 1892).
Newcomb described 97 species of *Achatinella* (see, for
example, Newcomb 1854, 1858). William Harper Pease, a
surveyor who arrived in Honolulu from the United States
in 1850, spent the rest of his life in the Islands
collecting and writing on Hawaiian and Pacific mollusks.
During his 18-year residence he published 66 papers on
the Pacific biota, 17 of which dealt with Hawaiian
animals, and he described 273 species of Hawaiian
mollusks (see, for example, Pease 1860, 1861, 1862).

Insects, which had largely been ignored by the
explorer-naturalists, were the hobby of the Reverend
Thomas Blackburn, chaplain of the Episcopal Church.
Blackburn has been called "the father of Hawaiian
entomology"; during his six-year residence (1877-1883)
he managed, between parish duties, to collect insects
"sufficient to keep almost a dozen specialists (principally in the British Museum) busy describing his material
in addition to all the descriptions that he himself prepared for the press" (Illingworth 1923). Blackburn's
special interest was the Coleoptera, and he was the
first to recognize the high percentage of endemism in

the insect fauna.

A businessman and sometime member of the Privy
Council of the Hawaiian Kingdom, William Lowthian Green
was interested in volcanoes. His most ambitious work,
Vestiges of the Molten Globe (Green 1875, 1887), stimulated work on the theory of volcanic action (Hitchcock
1911).

There was one full-time naturalist among the
resident naturalists, Andrew Garrett, who arrived in the
Islands in 1849. Garrett earned his living collecting
natural history specimens both in the Islands and elsewhere in the Pacific for J. G. Anthony, Louis Agassiz,
and the House of Godeffroy. Garrett's work on the
Hawaiian biota includes descriptions of shells (Garrett
1857) and fish (Garrett 1863, 1864).

Several resident naturalists also contributed to the
growing body of information on Hawaiian natural history
through their activities as collectors. The names of
two Frenchmen appear on the labels attached to many
specimens from the Islands in the museums of Paris.
Jules Rémy spent four years in botanical and ethnological
research in Hawaii, from 1851 to 1855; and Theo. Ballieu,
French Commissioner to the Hawaiian Kingdom, sent fish
(described by Vaillant and Sauvage 1875), birds, invertebrates, and plants to Paris. Two men who were long-time
residents of Kauai contributed collections to the
Smithsonian Insitution in Washington, D. C., and the
Bernice Pauahi Bishop Museum in Honolulu. Valdemar Knud-
sen, rancher and agriculturalist, arrived on Kauai in
1853 and during his 40-year residence collected birds,
reptiles, fish, and plants which he sent to Washington
(see, for example, Stejneger 1887). As a schoolboy,
John M. Lydgate accompanied Dr. Hillebrand on many of
his botanical expeditions among the Islands, and compiled
a list of ferns as a young man (Lydgate 1873). Lydgate
was for many years a minister on Kauai; his botanical
collections are now in the Bishop Museum, and he wrote on

various aspects of his collecting activities for the
Hawaiian Annual (Lydgate 1881, 1910).

Scientific Societies, Publications, and Museums

The interests of resident naturalists in the Hawaiian
Islands reflected the preoccupation with natural
history which permeated the culture of the eastern seaboard of the United States during the first half of the
nineteenth century. It was only natural that they should
transfer one of the traditions associated with the
natural history movement in New England to the Islands,
that of the lyceum or society.

The first scientific organization in Hawaii, the
Sandwich Islands Institute, founded in 1837, was a
replica of the scientific societies which flourished in
Massachusetts, Connecticut, New Hampshire, Pennsylvania,
and New York. Thirty-one residents and eleven honorary
members, calling themselves "an Association of Gentlemen,"
organized the Institute "for the intellectual and moral
improvement of its members," and particularly to gather
scientific information about Polynesia. Institute
meetings, at which papers were read every alternate
Tuesday evening, were held in the Seamen's Bethel. The
members of the Institute also sponsored the publication
of the *Hawaiian Spectator*, two volumes of which appeared
in 1838 and 1839. The journal, "devoted to making
Hawaiian science known to the world," contains, among
others, articles on tides, climate, volcanic activity,
and a reprint of Gairdner's (1835) paper on the geology
of Oahu.

A successor to the Sandwich Islands Institute did
not appear until 1850 when the Royal Hawaiian Agricultural Society was founded "to foster the interests of
Agriculture in all its various branches." At six annual
meetings Hillebrand, Newcomb, Pease, and other residents
discussed soils, indigenous plants, and introductions, as
well as the cultivation of rice, coffee, and sugarcane,
in reports published in the *Transactions of the Royal*

Hawaiian Agricultural Society issued between 1850 and
1856. The Planters' Labor and Supply Company replaced
the Royal Hawaiian Agricultural Society in 1864, and it,
in turn, evolved in 1895 into the still vigorous Hawaiian
Sugar Planters' Association.

The Natural History and Microscopical Society,
founded in 1876 "at the request of His majesty the King
. . . to create a taste for scientific subjects, and to
assist in acquiring and diffusing knowledge of Natural
History amongst us" (Prospectus, in Bushnell 1969) was
almost as short-lived as was the Royal Hawaiian Agricultural Society. William L. Green and Curtis J. Lyons
were vice-president and recording secretary, respectively.
A binocular microscope from Messrs. Beck and Company of
London, journals--among them the *American Journal of
Science, Journal of Applied Chemistry, Scientific American*
--and books were ordered but the organization disbanded
April 14, 1884, when its members donated "their interests
in and to the effects of said Society to the Honolulu
Library and Reading Room Building Fund" (in Bushnell
1969).

In addition to the publications of the Sandwich
Islands Institute and Royal Hawaiian Agricultural Society,
there were other publications in which the resident
naturalists reported on Hawaiian natural history.
Indeed, in most of the local periodicals appearing in
the Islands from 1830 to 1900--*The Polynesian, The
Friend, The Pacific Commercial Advertiser, The Maile
Quarterly*--can be found articles, lists, and comments on
Hawaiian natural history. Two noted that "scientific
researches" were of particular interest. Among the
"Geological Notices" of the *Sandwich Islands Monthly
Magazine*, in 1856, are excerpts from Dana's (1850a)
report on geology and an article by W. L. Green on
volcanoes. In the *Islander*, in 1875, there is a list of
Hawaiian cryptogams compiled by Bailey. The most
versatile forum, however, was the *Hawaiian Almanack and*

Annual founded by Thos. Thrum in 1875, described as "A
Handbook of valuable and statistical information relating to the Hawaiian Islands." In issues appearing
through the turn of the century there are not only
meteorological and tide tables, but compilations on
natural history solicited by Thrum from the resident
naturalists--for example, Dole (1878) updated his list
of birds; Blackburn (1882) summarized his knowledge of
insects; Bishop (1881) discussed the Hawaiian climate;
Baldwin (1886) analyzed the land shells; A. B. Lyons
(1891) described some Hawaiian fossils.

The birth of the museum idea in Hawaii was revealed
in the *Hawaiian Spectator* in 1838, which noted that a
museum was a desirable objective of the Sandwich Islands
Institute. A room in the Seamen's Bethel was set aside
for the purpose, and here were displayed, according to
Richard Brinsley Hinds (1968) who was in Honolulu at the
time, "a few shells & minerals, a large black bear, a
very few native weapons, poor Douglas' snowshoes, etc."
Subsequent to that first attempt, the possibility of a
more extensive museum was discussed by some of the
missionary sons at college in New England in 1854 (Gulick
1932), but the idea did not take more substantial form
until 1872 when legislation was adopted and a small
appropriation made for "a national museum, representing
archeology, literature, geology and national history of
our kingdom" (in Kent 1965). The new National Museum
occupied rooms in Aliiolani Hale (now the Judiciary
Building) in Honolulu from 1875 until about 1890. It
was replaced by the Bernice Pauahi Bishop Museum, the
gift of Charles Reed Bishop, in 1890. Intended originally to house Princess Bernice Pauahi Bishop's collection
of Hawaiian and Polynesian antiquities, the Bishop Museum
within a few years of its founding also incorporated
collections of birds, shells, plants, etc., and remains
a leading scientific institution in the Islands today.

Visitors from 1850 to 1900

Although the period from 1820 to 1900 was dominated by the activities of the resident naturalists, visitors also played a role in the development of knowledge of Hawaii's natural history during those years.

With few exceptions the great voyages of exploration ceased after 1850. Among the last were those of the Swedish vessel *Eugenie*, commanded by Captain Virgin, which visited the Islands in 1852; that of the *Donau*, of the Austrian East Asiatic Exploring Expedition, in 1870; and that of the first modern oceanographic expedition, the *Challenger* in 1876. The visit of the *Eugenie* is chiefly notable for the insect collections made by its naturalists (see, for example, Stal 1859), and that of the *Donau* for the botanical work of Heinrich Wawra (1872-1873). In the 50 volumes of the *Challenger* reports there are various references to, and descriptions of Hawaii's marine fauna, including fish (Gunther 1880) and mollusks (Smith 1885; Watson 1886). There were also brief visits by ships of the United States government in connection with various surveys in the Pacific, such as that of the *Portsmouth* in 1873-1874 (see Streets 1877 for descriptions of fish). Honolulu was one of the three stations selected by the British to observe the transit of Venus in 1874, and a party of astronomers under Captain George Tupman spent several months in the islands during that year (Airy 1881).

As the voyages of exploration became less frequent the number of visiting naturalists increased. These visitors differed from the earlier explorers in that they were professionaly trained scientists or collectors, and they came for specific reasons. The visit of Horace Mann, Jr., and William T. Brigham from May 1864 to May 1865 was the first example of this type of trip. Mann, a student in botany, and Brigham, an instructor in geology, were sent by Professor Asa Gray "for the purpose

of studying especially the Botany of the Group." Mann
(1866-1871) reported extensively on his botanical
findings; Brigham (1868) wrote also on volcanoes.

During the latter part of 1870 and in the 1880s
there were at least six visitors who came with specific
questions in mind. Oscar Finsch, the ornithologist,
visited briefly in 1879 on his quest for information on
Pacific birds (Finsch 1880). In 1882 Captain C. E. Dutton
of the United States Ordnance Corps arrived to study
the volcanoes of Maui and Hawaii (Dutton 1884). Alexander
Agassiz was in the Islands in 1885 to study coral reefs
(Agassiz 1889). James D. Dana returned to Hawaii in
1887 to fill in some of the gaps in his information on
the volcanoes. "In the belief that I would be able to
throw some light on the Geographical Distribution of the
species which constitute the very peculiar Avifauna of
this Archipelago" the energetic young Englishman, Scott
Wilson, collected birds in the Islands in 1887 and 1888
(Wilson and Evans 1890-1899). E. D. Preston was engaged
in astronomical observations on Oahu in 1887 and returned
in 1891-1892 to make measurements of the force of gravity
and variations in latitude (Preston 1888, 1895). And
during the summer of 1889, O. P. Jenkins, then professor
of biology at De Pauw University, made the most extensive
collection of fish gathered in Island waters up to that
time (Jenkins 1903).

In the 1890s several distinguished scientists
visited briefly, among them G. D. Sollas who had super-
vised the borings through the reef at Funafuti, T. D. A.
Cockerell who collected some coccid insects (Cockerell
1898), and H. B. Guppy. Guppy, ever aware of methods of
distribution in plants and animals, noted numbers of insects on the summit of Mauna Kea and commented that
their occurrence at such an elevation was "very suggestive, and shows how readily insects (even the parasitical
bug) may find their way into the upper air-currents"
(Guppy 1897). The flora and fauna of Laysan were

studied by Dr. Schauinsland of the Berlin Museum who
spent three months on the island (Schauinsland 1899).
Intrigued with Wilson's bird collections, the English
ornithologist Walter Rothschild commissioned Henry Palmer
to make another collection in the Islands between
December 1890 and August 1893 (Rothschild 1893-1900).
Midway during Palmer's visit, R. C. L. Perkins was
appointed by a committee of the Royal Society and the
British Association for the Advancement of Science "to
report on the present state of our knowledge of the
Sandwich Islands and to take steps to investigate
ascertained differences in the fauna" (Sharp 1899-1913,
vol. 3). Perkins arrived in March 1892 and remained
until the end of the summer of 1894; he returned again in
March 1895 and stayed until 1897. The three-volume
Fauna Hawaiiensis (Sharp 1899-1913), which resulted
from Perkins' work, is a momumental tribute to the work
of the naturalists of the late nineteenth century.

Contributions of the Resident Naturalists

For the most part, the resident naturalists, like
the explorer-naturalists, were amateurs rather than
professional scientists. As collectors of plants, shells,
fish, birds, and geological specimens, they contributed
to the collections of Hawaiian natural history in the
herbaria and museums of Europe and the United States,
as had the explorer-naturalists. As describers of the
biota, they supplemented the records begun by the
explorers. But here the similarities end, for others of
their contributions are in marked contrast to those of
the explorers in both object and scope. The records of
the explorers are sparse and scattered; those of the
residents include both compilations and summaries of
biota and geological phenomena in American scientific
journals and publications in the Islands. The explorers
hinted at some of the peculiarities of the Hawaiian
biota; the residents showed percipient recognition of
endemism and variation within a single species, and they

saw with remarkable discernment the changes in the biota
wrought by the activities of the haole.

The reasons for the contrast are not difficult to
find. The explorers traveled "the earth with the speed
of a cannon ball [and were] expected to have investigated
the whole of it" (Chamisso 1821); the residents were
provincial in their interests and leisurely in their
explorations. Edward Bailey's (1882) comment on fern
collections describes the difference: "A long residence
at the Islands enables [the resident] to study our ferns
in their localities and seasons, which vary, with different species through the entire year. It is only thus
that they can be seen in perfection and properly studied.
He has this advantage over the transient collector and
the student of dried specimens."

Another reason for the difference lies in the
periods of time in which the explorers and the residents
worked. The explorers visited the Islands when observation and classification were dominant themes in
science; the era of the resident naturalists spans not
only the period of classification, but that in which
Darwinian and geological theory revolutionized scientific
thinking, and in which, in the United States at least,
the practical importance of scientific studies was recognized.

With time at their disposal and with the keen eyes
of observers, the residents' records of volcanic activity
established the foundation on which the history of the
eruptions of Kilauea and Mauna Loa between 1820 and 1900
is now largely based. Their achievements as recorders
have been acknowledged by Dana (1890), Hitchcock (1911),
and Jaggar (1913).

The residents produced not only "the good flora of
the Sandwich Islands" for which Darwin had called, but
"serviceable" lists of birds and shells. The recognition
of endemism in the insect fauna by Blackburn, and of
variation in single species of land shells as well as

the apparent isolation of species from ridge to ridge
and valley to valley by Gulick added another dimension
to the understanding of the Hawaiian biota. These lists
and the speculations of Blackburn and Gulick brought the
peculiarities of the Hawaiian biota into focus for those
scientists abroad who were sensitive to the implications
of Darwinian evolution--geographical distribution,
isolation, inheritance from a common ancestor. Sclater
(1870), Newton (1892), and Rothschild (1893-1900),
familiar with the work of the residents, echoed Darwin's
plea for a flora with a call for studies of the fauna of
the Hawaiian archipelago.

These scientists were spurred to action by still
another factor brought to their attention by the residents: that of the rapid changes occurring in the native
biota. In 1856, in the *Sandwich Islands Monthly
Magazine*, one of the residents writing on land shells
noted "the numerous herds of wild cattle rushing with
their extended horns through the forests, in all directions have under our observations, nearly extinguished
many fine species that we had formerly found in abundance
in the same localities" (Frick 1856); and another writer
noted that the plateau of Waimea, Hawaii, had been de-
spoiled entirely of its original forest by wild cattle.
The same year, at the annual meeting of the Royal
Hawaiian Agricultural Society, Hillebrand asked, "Where
are the forests of sandal trees?" But it was Mrs.
Sinclair (1885) who described the problem most eloquent-
ly:

> The Hawaiian flora seems (like the native human
> inhabitant) to grow in an easy, careless way,
> which, though pleasingly artistic, and well
> adapted to what may be termed the natural state
> of the islands, will not long survive the
> invasions of foreign plants and changed condi-
> tions. Forest fires, animals and agriculture,
> have so changed the islands, within the last
> fifty or sixty years, that one can now travel
> for miles, in some districts, without finding a
> single indigenous plant; the ground being
> wholly taken possession of by weeds, shrubs,

and grasses, imported from various countries.
It is remarkable that plants from both tropical and temperate regions seem to thrive
equally well on these islands, many of them
spreading as if by magic, and rapidly extermin-
ating much of the native flora.

Thus Scott Wilson was brought to the Islands not
only by his desire to study the geographical distribution
of birds, but also "by the opinion expressed by many
competent judges that several of the native species of
birds were in process of extirpation, through the
destruction of the forest and the introduction of foreign
arrivals" (in Wilson and Evans 1890). And R. C. L. Perkins initiated his studies on the Hawaiian fauna because
of the urgings of A. H. Newton and P. L. Sclater that the
Royal Society and the British Association for the Advancement of Science should sponsor research in the
Islands where "there is strong evidence that the fauna
is rapidly disappearing" (Flower 1891).

The resident naturalists of the last decades of
the nineteenth century were also instrumental in guiding
the course of scientific activity in the Islands from
amateur status to that of professional. Scientific
amateurs themselves, in the sense that they had been
educated "when the prevailing theory in collegiate train-
ing was that of a bird's eye view of human knowledge"
(Anon. 1913), the residents both influenced the course of
science because of their positions as leaders in education, business, and government, and participated in the
change in status.

The growth of agriculture, on which Hawaii was
entirely dependent for its economy during the latter part
of the nineteenth century, made it necessary to solve a
variety of increasingly complex problems. What varieties
of cane produced the best yields? How does one soil type
differ from another? What fertilizers should be used?
How are armyworms and cutworms controlled? The Planters'
Labor and Supply Company and the Hawaiian Sugar Planters'
Association, successors to the Royal Hawaiian

Agricultural Society, not only brought together men with
agricultural interests, but as potent groups influenced
the government of the Hawaiian Kingdom to recognize the
scientific implications, as well as the economic aspects
of sugar production.   Sanford Ballard Dole was a key
figure in many projects undertaken jointly by the
planters and the government. When Punahou School's first
chemistry teacher was appointed in 1885, the Hawaiian
government and the Planters' Labor and Supply Company
provided part of the money for his salary to make his
services available to the planters for soil analyses.
And it was in part through the influence of the planters
that an 1890 act of the legislature was passed to prevent
the further introduction of plant diseases, blight, and
insects injurious to vegetation.   Concomitantly with that
act, Professor Albert Koebele, distinguished entomologist
from California, was hired as government entomologist to
inaugurate a program for the control of insect pests.
In 1892 the planters also influenced passage of legislation establishing the Bureau of Agriculture and Forest-
ry, which has since evolved into the presently con-
stituted Department of Land and Natural Resources of the
State of Hawaii.

     Practicality and science also merged in the
activities of the Government Survey, which, under the
leadership of W. D. Alexander as surveyor general, was
inaugurated for the purely practical purpose of informing
the government how much land there was, where it was,
and where the boundaries of various parcels were located.
To establish the foundations for the survey, Alexander
embarked on a complex series of triangulations in 1871.
Accurate triangulations depended, however, on accurate
determinations of longitude and latitude, neither of
which was available, and determination of these parameters, in turn, necessitated astronomical, hydrographic,
and meteorological investigations. Working closely with
the U. S. Coast and Geodetic Survey, Alexander arranged

for the services of E. P. Dutton for the astronomical and
magnetic work, and borrowed a tide gauge from the U. S.
Coast and Geodetic Survey in 1880. In the 1880s the
Government Survey also took charge of Government time,
establishing standard time in the Islands in 1896. The
Survey entered into hydrographic work in 1881 when
Captain Jackson, a retired officer in the British Navy,
surveyed some of the harbors; this work was expanded by
the U. S. Coast and Geodetic Survey and the U. S. Fish
Commission after 1898 when the Hawaiian Islands were
annexed to the United States. C. J. Lyons, who assisted
in the early triangulations on Maui and Hawaii, became
increasingly involved with meteorological problems,
initiating a Meteorological Service, and, in 1900,
regular rainfall reports (Lyons 1903).

        In guiding the work of the Government Survey, in
seeing the opportunities offered in the different fields
of investigation, and in being able to expand the office
to encompass not only surveying and mapping, but meteor-
ology and hydrology, Alexander established a pattern
which was little changed when the functions of the Survey
were taken over by the United States government through
such offices as the U. S. Coast and Geodetic Survey, in
1898. As practical as was the work of the government
Survey, Dana (1890) pointed out that the maps produced
by Alexander and the members of his Survey team were
also a "contribution to science of the highest value
and interest."

THE MODERN PERIOD

        With the turn of the century there is discernible a
third phase in the history of Hawaiian natural history,
for in the Islands, as elsewhere, scientific professionalism had come of age. The period of the scientific
leadership of the amateur natural historian in Hawaii
came to an end, perhaps 50 years after it had terminated
on the eastern seaboard of the United States. Coan,

Hillebrand, and Pease had died in the last decades of
the nineteenth century; Alexander, Bishop, and Gulick
wore their years lightly during the first decades of the
twentieth century, but their leadership in Hawaiian
science was gradually transferred to professionally
trained men who came to live in the Islands.

Coan and the other resident chroniclers of the
volcanoes were replaced by a staff of professional
volcanologists at the Volcano Observatory, established in
1913. The surveying and meteorological activities of
Alexander, Bishop, and Lyons were undertaken by scientists assigned to local and federal agencies. The land
shells were studied by a Yale-trained zoologist, C. M.
Cooke, Jr.,[6] at the Bishop Museum, where botanists,
ornithologists, and icthyologists were also working. In
place of the lone Episcopal chaplain who had collected
insects in the 1870s and 1880s, there were in Hawaii in
1905 sufficient entomologists to found an Entomological
Society. And replacing the Sandwich Islands Institute,
with its grand aspirations, came a host of organizations
where professional scientists met to discuss their
common interests: the Hawaiian Chemists' Association
in 1922, the Hawaiian Botanical Society in 1924, and
the Hawaiian Academy of Science in 1925.

To chronicle more than 70 years of the development
of science in the Islands in the twentieth century is beyond the scope of this paper. William T. Brigham's
vision of the direction science should take, elaborated
in 1906, was a viable prophesy for the general outline
which was to be realized, however. Brigham (in Porteus
1962) proposed a college for the study of ethnology and
general biology, one division of which would be a marine
biological station modeled on that at Naples; a second
division would be a zoological garden and aviary for

---

[6]C. M. Cooke, Jr., was himself a missionary scion,
grandson of Amos Starr Cooke of the Eighth Company; as
a schoolboy at Punahou he spent his spare time and
holidays in search of land shells. He received his doc-
toral degree in zoology for work done under A. E. Verrill.

studies of tropical fauna, with the Leeward Islands perhaps serving as a refuge; a botanical garden came third;
and the fourth division, for ethnological study, would
use the Bishop Museum as a nucleus for research.
Brigham's proposal has essentially materialized. The
University of Hawaii, with its departments of anthropol-
ogy, botany, and zoology, was founded in 1907. A marine
biological station associated with the University of
Hawaii was founded in 1920 and has since evolved into the
Hawaii Institute of Marine Biology. The Leeward Islands
were added to the National Wildlife Refuge System in 1909
by executive order of President Theodore Roosevelt.
Three botanical gardens flourish in Hawaii today--the
city-owned Foster Gardens, the Lyon Arboretum which is a
part of the University of Hawaii, and the Pacific
Botanical Gardens chartered in 1970. And the Bishop
Museum continues to lead the way in ethnological studies
not only in the Islands, but throughout the Pacific.

SUMMARY

The history of Hawaiian natural history, from the
time of the discovery of the Islands in 1778 by Captain
Cook to 1900, is discussed in terms of three periods. In
the first, from 1820 to 1850, the explorer naturalists
of the great voyages of exploration and independent
travelers, such as David Douglas, dominated the picture,
producing a variety of reports on topography, volcanic
activity, and coral reefs, and descriptions and records
of several hundred animals and plants. Except for brief
lists of birds and plants, and Dana's descriptions of
Hawaiian volcanoes, no synthetic accounts of Hawaiian
natural history resulted from the visits of the explorer-
naturalists. During the second phase, extending from
1820 to 1900, resident naturalists, missionaries, physicians, surveyors and housewives, contributed to the
development by chronicling daily the activity of the
volcano, producing summary accounts of the biota, and
recognizing peculiarities in the biota, such as endemism

and variation within a single species. As educators and
government leaders the resident naturalists during the
last two decades of the nineteenth century established
the foundation for twentieth-century science. In the
third phase, which began with the turn of the century,
scientific professionalism came of age in Hawaii.

REFERENCES

Abbott, C. C. 1860. Descriptions of new species of apodal fishes in the museum of the Academy of Natural Sciences of Philadelphia. Proc. Acad. Nat. Sci. Philad. 12:475-479.

Adams, C. B. 1857. Descriptions of new species of *Partula* and *Achatinella*. Ann. Lyceum Nat. Hist. N. Y. 5:41-44.

Agassiz, A. 1889. The coral reefs of the Hawaiian Islands. Bull. Mus. Comp. Zool. Harv. 17:121-170.

Airy, G. B. 1881. Account of observations of the transit of Venus 1874 . . . . H.M. Stationery Office, London.

Alexander, J. M. 1886. The craters of Mokuaweoweo, on Mauna Loa. Nature 34:232-234.

Alexander, M. C. 1953. Dr. Baldwin of Lahaina. Berkeley [privately printed].

_____ 1934. William Patterson Alexander in Kentucky, the Marquesas, Hawaii. Honolulu [privately printed].

Alexander, M. C., and C. P. Dodge. 1941. Punahou 1841-1941. Univ. California Press, Berkeley.

Alexander, W. D. 1871. Geodetic tables prepared for the Hawaiian Government Survey. Government Printing Office, Honolulu.

Anon. 1913. A fragrant life [obituary of W. D. Alexander]. The Friend 15:56-57.

Bailey, E. 1882. Hawaiian ferns, a synopsis. T. G. Thrum, Honolulu.

Baldwin, D. D. 1852. Eruption of Mauna Loa. Amer. J. Sci., ser. 2, 13:299.

_____ 1876. List of Hawaiian mosses and Hepaticae. Hawaiian Annual, p. 40-42.

_____ 1886. The land shells of the Hawaiian Islands. Hawaiian Annual, p. 55-63.

_____ 1893. Catalogue of land and freshwater shells of the Hawaiian Islands. Press Publishing Co., Honolulu.

_____ 1895. Descriptions of new species of Achatinellidae from the Hawaiian Islands. Proc. Acad. Nat. Sci. Philad. 47:214-236.

_____ 1903. Descriptions of new Achatinellidae.
Nautilus 17:34-36.

Baldwin, D. D., and W. Auld. 1891. List of indigenous
Hawaiian woods, trees, and large shrubs. Hawaiian
Annual, p. 87-91.

Beaglehole, J. D., ed. 1967. The journals of Captain
James Cook. Vol. 3. The voyage of the *Resolution*
and *Discovery* 1776-1778. The University Press,
Cambridge.

Bennett, E. T. 1828. On some fishes from the Sandwich
Islands. Zool. J. 4:31-32.

Bennett, F. D. 1840. Narrative of a whaling voyage
round the globe . . . 1833 to 1836 . . . . 2 vols.
R. Bentley, London.

Bishop, S. E. 1881. Causes of the peculiarity of
Hawaiian climate. Hawaiian Annual, p. 44-49.

_____ 1886. The origin of the red glows. Hawaiian
Gazette Publishing Co., Honolulu.

_____ 1887. The recent eruption of Mauna Loa.
Science 9:205-207.

_____ 1904. The cold current system in the Pacific.
Science 20:338-340.

_____ 1916. Reminiscences of old Hawaii. Hawaiian
Gazette Publishing Co., Honolulu.

Blackburn, T. 1882. Hawaiian entomology. Hawaiian
Annual, p. 58-61.

Brackenridge, W. E. 1854-55. Botany, Cryptogamia.
Filices including Lycopodiaceae and Hydropterides.
U. S. Exploring Expedition Reports, vol. 16, 357 p.
Atlas, 1855.

Brigham, W. T. 1868. Notes on the eruption of the
Hawaiian volcanoes. Mem. Boston Soc. Nat. Hist.
1:564-587.

_____ 1909. The volcanoes of Kilauea and Mauna Loa.
Mem. Bishop Mus. 2 (4):1-222.

Bryan, E. H., Jr. 1921. The background of Hawaiian
botany. Mid-Pacif. Mag. 37:33-40.

Bushnell, O. A. 1969. Much ado about little things:
microscopes and microscopists. Hawaiian J. Hist.
3:101-109.

Byron, G. A. 1826. Voyage of H.M.S. *Blonde* to the Sandwich Islands in the years 1824-25. J. Murray, London.

Chamisso, A. von. 1821. Reise um die Welt mit der Romanzoffischen Entdeckungs Expedition in den Jahren 1815-1818. [English translation by M. and H. Hormann, Sinclair Library, University of Hawaii.]

Coan, T. 1851. On the eruption of Mauna Loa in 1851. Amer. J. Sci., ser. 2, 13:395-397.

Coan, T. M. 1889. The Hawaiian Islands, their geography, their volcanoes, and their people. Bull. Amer. Geogr. Soc. 21:149-166.

_____ 1910. Eruptions of Kilauea. Science 32:716-718.

Cockerell, T. D. A. 1898. The Coccidae of the Hawaiian Islands. Entomologist 31:239-240.

Conrad, T. 1837. Descriptions of new marine shells from Upper California, collected by Thomas Nuttall, Esq. J. Acad. Nat. Sci. Philad. 7:227-268.

Damon, E. M. 1950. Letters from the life of Abner and Lucy Wilcox. Honolulu [privately printed].

_____ 1957. Sanford Ballard Dole and his Hawaii. Pacific Books, Palo Alto.

Dana, J. D. 1846-49. Zoophytes. U. S. Exploring Expedition Reports, vol. 7, 740 p.

_____ 1850a. Geology. U. S. Exploring Expedition Reports, vol. 10, 756 p.

_____ 1850b. Historical account of the eruptions on Hawaii. Amer. J. Sci., ser. 2, 9:347-364.

_____ 1852-53. Crustacea. U. S. Exploring Expedition Reports, vols. 13 and 14, 1592 p.

_____ 1853. Corals and coral islands. Dodd & Mead, New York.

_____ 1890. Characteristics of volcanoes, with contributions of facts and principles from the Hawaiian Islands . . . . Dodd & Mead, New York.

Darwin, F., ed. 1903. More letters of Charles Darwin. 2 vols. J. F. Murray, London.

Dixon, G. 1789. A voyage around the world, . . . 1785-1788 . . . . 2nd ed. G. Golding, London.

Dole, S. B. 1869. A synopsis of the birds hitherto
    described from the Hawaiian Islands. With notes.
    Proc. Boston Soc. Nat. Hist. 12:294-309.

——— 1878. List of birds of the Hawaiian Islands.
    Hawaiian Annual, p. 41-58.

[Donovan, E.] 1806. Catalogue of the Leverian Museum.
    London.

Douglas, D. 1834a. Volcanoes in the Sandwich Islands.
    J. Roy. Geogr. Soc. 4:333-343.

——— 1834b. [Letters to W. J. Hooker]. Published in
    W. F. Wilson, ed., David Douglas, botanist at
    Hawaii. Honolulu (1919).

Dupree, A. H. 1953. Asa Gray. 1810-1888. Belknap
    Press, Cambridge, Mass.

Dutton, E. E. 1884. Hawaiian volcanoes. U. S. Geolog-
    ical Survey, Fourth Annual Report, p. 75-219.

Ellis, W. 1826a. Volcano of Kiraurea. Amer. J. Sci.
    ser. 1, 11:362-376.

——— 1826b. Volcano in Owhyee. Phil. Mag. 67:229-
    231.

——— 1826c. Notice of the volcanic character of the
    island of Owhyee . . . . Phil. Mag. 68:187-205;
    252-267.

——— 1827a. Description of the volcano of Kiraurea,
    in Owhyee, one of the Sandwich Islands. Edinburgh
    J. Sci. 6:151-153.

——— 1827b. Narrative of a tour through Hawaii.
    2nd ed. H. Fisher, Son and P. Jackson, London.
    Reprint.

Emerson, J. S. 1887. Kilauea after the eruption of
    March, 1886. Amer. J. Sci., ser. 3, 33:87-95.

Endlicher, S. 1836. Bemerkungen über die Flora der
    Sudseeinseln. Ann. Wiener Mus. Nat. 1:131-190.

Eschscholtz, J. F. von. 1821. *In* O. von Kotzebue,
    A voyage of discovery into the South Sea and
    Bering's Straits. Longman, Hurst, Rees, Orme, and
    Brown, London. Reprint. Da Capo Press, New York,
    1967.

Finsch, O. 1880. Ornithological letters from the
    Pacific. No. 1. Ibis, ser. 4, 4:75-81.

Flower, D. 1891. Report of the Committee . . . appointed to report on the present state of our knowledge of the zoology of the Sandwich Islands, p. 357. British Association for the Advancement of Science.

Forbes, E. 1852. On the marine Mollusca discovered during the voyages of the *Herald* and *Pandora*, by Capt. Kellett, R. N. and Lieut. Wood, R. N. Proc. Zool. Soc. London [for 1850], p. 270-274.

Frick, D. 1856. Notes on Hawaiian terrestrial conchology. Sandwich Islands Month. Mag. 1:137-140.

Gairdner, M. 1834. Observations during a voyage from England to Fort Vancouver, on the north-west coast of America. Edinburgh New Phil. J. 16:290-302.

_____ 1835. Physico-geognostic sketch of the island of Oahu, one of the Sandwich group. Edinburgh New Phil. J. 19:1-14. Reprinted in the Hawaiian Spectator 1:1-18 (1838).

Garrett, A. 1857. New species of marine shells of the Sandwich Islands. Proc. Calif. Acad. Sci. 1:102-103.

_____ 1863. Descriptions of new species of fishes. Proc. Calif. Acad. Sci. 3:63-66.

_____ 1864. Descriptions of new species of fishes. Proc. Calif. Acad. Sci. 3:103-107.

Goodrich, J. 1826. Notice of the volcanic character of the island of Hawaii. Amer. J. Sci., ser. 1, 11:2-7.

_____ 1829. [On Kilauea and Mauna Loa]. Amer. J. Sci., ser. 1, 16:345-347.

Gould, A. A. 1852. Mollusca and shells. U.S. Exploring Expedition Reports, vol. 12, 510 p.

Gray, A. 1854-57. Phanerogamia. U. S. Exploring Expedition Reports, vol. 15, 777 p.

Gray, J. L., ed. 1893. Letters of Asa Gray. 2 vols. Houghton, Mifflin, Boston.

Green, J. C. 1827. Description of two new species of Achatina from the Sandwich Islands -- with some remarks on the ti, the plant on which these shells are commonly found. Maclurian Lyceum Contributions 1:47-50.

Green, W. L. 1856. Extinct coast craters of Oahu. Sandwich Islands Month. Mag. 1:1-3.

        1875-87. Vestiges of the molten globe. Part 1
————[1875], E. Stanford, London. Part 2 [1887],
Hawaiian Gazette, Honolulu.

Gulick, A. 1932. Evolutionist and missionary John
    Thomas Gulick. University of Chicago Press.

Gulick, J. T. 1905. Evolution: racial and habitudinal.
    Carnegie Institute, Washington.

Gulick, O. H. 1864. [On Kilauea caldera in 1863].
    Amer. J. Sci., ser. 2, 37:417.

Gunther, A. 1880. Report on the shore fishes procured
    during the voyage of H.M.S. *Challenger* in the years
    1873-1876. Challenger Reports, Zoology, vol. 1,
    82 p.

Guppy, H. B. 1897. On the summit of Mauna Kea. Nature
    57:20-21.

Hartlaub, G. 1854. Zur Ornithologie Oceanien's. J.
    Orn., Lpz. 2:160-171.

Healy, J. R. 1960. The mapping of the Hawaiian Islands,
    1778-1848. Master's thesis, University of Hawaii.

Hillebrand, W. 1888. Flora of the Hawaiian Islands.
    C. Winter, Heidelberg.

Hinds, R. B. 1968. The Sandwich Islands. From Richard
    Brinsley Hinds, Journal of the voyage of the
    Sulphur (1836-1842). Edited by E. A. Kay. Hawaii-
    an J. Hist. 2:102-135.

Hitchcock, C. H. 1911. Hawaii and its volcanoes. 2nd
    ed. Hawaiian Gazette, Honolulu.

Illingworth, J. F. 1923. Early references to Hawaiian
    entomology. B. P. Bishop Museum Bull. 2, 63 p.

Jaggar, T. 1913. Scientific work on Hawaiian volcanoes.
    Hawaiian Volcano Observatory, Special Bulletin, 15 p.
    Hawaiian Gazette, Honolulu.

Jenkins, O. P. 1903. Report on collections of fishes
    made in the Hawaiian Islands, with descriptions of
    new species. Bull. U.S. Fish Comm. 22:417-511.

Jordan, D. S., and B. W. Evermann. 1905. The aquatic
    resources of the Hawaiian Islands, Part I. The
    shore fishes. Bull. U. S. Fish Comm. 23:1-574.

Kent, H. 1965. Charles Reed Bishop, man of Hawaii.
    Pacific Books, Palo Alto.

Kinney, H. 1852. [Letter]   Amer. J. Sci., ser. 2,
    14:257-258.

Kotzebue, O. von. 1821. A voyage of discovery into the
    South Seas and Bering's Straits. Longman, Hurst,
    Rees, Orme, and Brown, London. Reprint. Da Capo
    Press, New York, 1967.

Langsdorff, G. H. von. 1813-14. Voyages and travels in
    various parts of the world, during the years 1803-
    1807. 2 vols. H. Colburn, London.

Ledyard, J. 1963. John Ledyard's journal of Captain
    Cook's last voyage. Edited by J. K. Munford.
    Oregon State University Press, Corvallis.

Lydgate, J. M. 1873. A short synopsis of Hawaiian
    ferns. Honolulu.

_____ 1881. Indigenous ornamental plants. Hawaiian
    Annual, p. 25-28.

_____ 1910. The endemic character of the Hawaiian
    flora. Hawaiian Annual, p. 53-58.

Lyman, C. S. 1849. Observations on the "old crater"
    adjoining Kilauea [Hawaii] on the east. Amer. J.
    Sci., ser. 2, 7:287.

Lyman, S. C. [error for S. J.] 1859. A record of the
    earthquakes, kept at Hilo, Hawaii. Amer. J. Sci.,
    ser. 2, 7:264-266.

Lyons, A. B. 1891. Fossils at Hawaii Nei. Hawaiian
    Annual, p. 100-104.

_____ 1896. Chemical composition of Hawaiian soils
    and of the rocks from which they have been derived.
    Amer. J. Sci., ser. 4, 2:421-429.

Lyons, C. J. 1903. A history of the Hawaiian Government
    Survey with notes on land matters in Hawaii.
    Appendixes 3 and 4 of the Surveyor's Report for
    1902. Honolulu.

Lysaght, A. 1959. Some eighteenth century bird paint-
    ings in the library of Sir Joseph Banks (1743-1820).
    Bull. Brit. Mus. Nat. Hist. (Historical Series)
    1:251-371.

McCaughey, V. 1917. American explorers of Hawaii.
    Mid-Pacif. Mag. 14:281-285.

_____ 1918-1919. History of botanical exploration in
    Hawaii. Hawaiian For. Agric. 15 (1918):388-396, 417-429,
    508-510; 16 (1919):25-28, 49-54.

Macdonald, G. A. 1947. Bibliography of the geology and
    ground-water resources of the island of Hawaii,
    annotated and indexed. Hawaii Division of Hydrog-
    raphy Bull. 10, 191 p.

Macrae, J. 1922. With Lord Byron at the Sandwich Islands
    in 1825. Being extracts from the Ms diary of James
    Macrae, Scottish botanist. Edited by W. F. Wilson.
    Honolulu.

Mann, H., Jr. 1866-1871. Flora of the Hawaiian Islands.
    Proc. Essex Inst. 5:113-144 (1866), 161-176 (1867),
    233-248 (1868); 6:105-112 (1871).

_____   1871. Enumeration of Hawaiian plants. Proc.
    Amer. Acad. Arts Sci. 7:143-235.

Martyn, T. 1784. The universal conchologist. Vol. 1.
    London.

Matheson, C. 1961. G. B. Sowerby the first and his
    correspondents. Part II. J. Soc. Bibl. Nat. Hist.
    4:253-266.

Menzies, A. 1828-29. Some account of an ascent and
    barometrical measurement of Wha-ra-rai, a mountain
    in the Island of Owhyee; extracts from the Ms
    journal of Archibald Menzies, Esq. Magazine
    of Natural History 1:201-208(1828); 2:435-442
    (1829).

_____   1920.   Hawaii Nei 128 years ago.   Edited by
    W. F. Wilson. Honolulu.

Merrill, E. D. 1937. Polynesian botanical bibliography.
    B. P. Bishop Museum Bull. 144, 194 p.

Meyen, F. J. F. 1835. Reise um die Erde ausgefuhrt auf
    dem Kongiglich Preussischen Seehandlungs-Schiffe
    Prinzess Louise commandirt von Capitain W. Wendt in
    den Jahren 1830, 1831, und 1832. 2 vols.
    Sander'sche buchhandlung, Berlin. [W. D. Alexander
    translation in the B. P. Bishop Museum, Honolulu].

Mighels, J. W. 1845. Descriptions of shells from the
    Sandwich Islands and other localities. Proc.
    Boston Soc. Nat. Hist. 2:18-25.

Newcomb, W. 1854. Descriptions of seventy-nine new
    species of Achatinella (Swains.), a genus of pul-
    moniferous mollusks, in the collection of Hugh
    Cuming, Esq. Proc. Zool. Soc. London:1-31.

Newton, A. H. 1858. Synopsis of the genus Achatinella.
    Ann. Lyceum Nat. Hist. N. Y. 6:303-336.

_____ 1892. Ornithology of the Hawaiian Islands.
Nature 45:465-469.

Nuttall, T. 1838. On a new species of Tacca. Amer. J.
Pharm. 9:305-306.

_____ 1843. Description and notices of new or rare
plants in the natural orders Lobeliaceae. Compa-
nulaceae, Vacciniaceae, Ericaceae, collected in a
journey over the continent of North America and
during a visit to the Sandwich Islands and upper
California. Transactions of the American Philosophical Society, II, 8:251-272.

_____ 1852. The North American sylva. Vol. 1.
Philadelphia.

Pease, W. H. 1860. Descriptions of new species of
Mollusca from the Sandwich Islands. Parts I, II.
Proc. Zool. Soc. London:18-36; 141-148.

_____ 1861. Descriptions of forty-seven new species
of shells from the Sandwich Islands, in the collection of Hugh Cuming, Esq. Proc. Zool. Soc. London:
431-438.

_____ 1862. Catalogue des espèces de Rissoina
des îles Sandwich et description d'une espèce
nouvelle. J. Conch. 10:381-383.

Pilsbry, H. A., and C. M. Cooke. 1911. Manual of
conchology. Ser. 2, vol. 21. Philadelphia.

Porteus, S. D. 1962. A century of social thinking in
Hawaii. Pacific Books, Palo Alto, Calif.

Preston, E. D. 1888. On the deflection of the plumb-
line and variations of gravity in the Hawaiian
Islands. Amer. J. Sci., ser. 3, 36:305-317.

_____ 1895. Determinations of latitude, gravity and
the magnetic elements at stations in the Hawaiian
Islands . . . 1891, 1892. U. S. Coast and Geodetic
Survey Report of the Superintendent, year ending June
30, 1895. Appendix No. 12, p. 509-639.

Randall, J. W. 1839. Catalogue of Crustacea brought by
Thomas Nuttall and J. K. Townsend . . . . J. Acad.
Nat. Sci. Philad. 8:106-147.

Rothschild, W. 1893-1900. The avifauna of Laysan and
the Hawaiian possessions. R. H. Porter, London.

St. John, H. 1940. Hawaiian plants named by Endlicher
in 1836. Hawaiian plant studies 8. B. P. Bishop
Mus. Occ. Pap. 15:229-238.

Schauinsland, H. 1899. Drei Monate auf einer Korallenin-
    seln, Laysan. Bremen.

Sclater, P. L. 1870. The transit of Venus in 1874 and
    1882. Nature 1:527.

_____ 1871. Remarks on the avifauna of the Sandwich
    Islands. Ibis, ser. 3, 1:356-362.

Seeman, B. 1853. Narrative of the voyage of H. M. S.
    Herald . . . 1845-51 . . . . 2 vols. Reeve and
    Co., London.

Sharp. D. ed. 1899-1913. Fauna Hawaiiensis; being the
    land fauna of the Hawaiian Islands . . . . 3 vols.
    The University Press, Cambridge.

Sinclair, Mrs. F., Jr. 1885. Indigenous flowers of the
    Hawaiian Islands. Samson, Low, Marston, Searle,
    and Rivington, London.

Smith, B. 1960. European vision and the South Pacific
    1768-1850. University Press, Oxford.

Smith, E. A. 1885. Report on the Lamellibranchiata
    collected by H. M. S. "Challenger" during the years
    1873-1876. Challenger Reports, Zoology, vol. 13,
    331 p.

Stal, C. 1859. Hemiptera. *In* C. A. Virgin, Voyage
    autour du monde sur la Frégate Suédoise l'Eugenie
    . . . 1851-1853. Zoologie. P. A. Norstedt et Fils,
    Stockholm.

Stearns, N. D. 1935. Annotated bibliography and index
    of the geology and water supply of the island of
    Oahu, Hawaii. Hawaii Division of Hydrography,
    Bull. 3, 74 p.

Stearns, R. E. C. 1892. In memoriam--Dr. Wesley New-
    comb. Nautilus 5:121-124.

Stejneger, L. 1887. Birds of Kauai Island, Hawaiian
    archipelago, collected by Mr. Valdemar Knudsen,
    with descriptions of new species. Proc. U. S.
    Nat. Mus. 10:75-96, 97-102.

Stewart, C. S. 1826. Volcano of Kiraurea. Amer. J.
    Sci., ser. 1, 11:362-376. Reprinted, Edinburgh
    New Phil. J. 3:45-60 (1827).

_____ 1830. Journal of a residence in the Sandwich
    Islands, during the years 1823, 1824, and 1825.
    2nd ed. Reprint. University of Hawaii Press,
    Honolulu, 1970.

Streets, T. H. 1877. Contributions to the natural
    history of the Hawaiian and Fanning islands and
    Lower California. U.S. Nat. Mus. Bull. no. 7,
    p. 7-172.

Swainson, W. 1828. The characters of *Achatinella*,
    a new group of terrestrial shells, with
    descriptions of six species. Quart. J. Sci. Lit.
    Arts 1:81-86.

Townsend, J. K. 1839. Narrative of a journey across
    the Rocky Mountains to the Columbia River, and a
    visit to the Sandwich Islands, Chili, etc. With
    a scientific appendix. H. Perkins, Philadelphia.

Vaillant, L., and H. E. Sauvage. 1875. Note sur
    quelques espèces nouvelles de poissons des Iles
    Sandwich. Rev. Mag. Zool. pure appl., ser. 3,
    p. 278-287. [Not seen]

Vancouver, G. 1798. Voyage of discovery to the North
    Pacific Ocean 1790-1795. 3 vols. G. G. and J.
    Robinson, London.

Vigors, N. A. 1833. On a new species of barnacle goose
    (*Bernicla Sandvicensis*) presented by Lady Glengall.
    Proc. Zool. Soc. London:65.

Watson, R. B. 1886. Report on the Scaphopoda and
    Gastropoda collected by H.M.S. Challenger . . .
    1873-76. Zoology. Challenger Reports, vol. 15,
    756 p.

Wawra, H. 1872-1873. Skizzen von der Erdumseglung
    S. M. Fregatte "Donau" (die Hawaiischen Inseln).
    Oesterreichischer botanische Zeitschrift 22:
    222-227, 259-265, 297-302, 332-335, 362-368,
    397-405 (1872); 23:23-29, 60-64, 94-99 (1873).

Wetmore, C. H. 1890. Concerning Hawaiian fishes.
    Hawaiian Annual, p. 90-97.

Whitney, H. M. 1868. [On the 1868 eruption of Mauna
    Loa]. Amer. J. Sci., ser. 2, 46:112-115.

Wilkes, C. 1845. Narrative of the United States Explor-
    ing Expedition. U. S. Exploring Expedition Reports,
    vol. 4.

Wilson, S. B., and A. H. Evans. 1890-1899. Aves
    Hawaiiensis. R. H. Porter, London.